Early Ceramic Population Lifeways and Adaptive Strategies in the Caribbean

edited by
Peter E. Siegel

BAR International Series 506
1989

B.A.R.

5, Centremead, Osney Mead, Oxford OX2 0DQ, England.

GENERAL EDITORS

A.R. Hands, B.Sc., M.A., D.Phil.
D.R. Walker, M.A.

BAR -S506, 1989: 'Early Ceramic Population Lifeways and Adaptive Strategies in the Caribbean'

© The Individual Authors, 1989

The authors' moral rights under the 1988 UK Copyright, Designs and Patents Act are hereby expressly asserted.

All rights reserved. No part of this work may be copied, reproduced, stored, sold, distributed, scanned, saved in any form of digital format or transmitted in any form digitally, without the written permission of the Publisher.

ISBN 9780860546474 paperback
ISBN 9781407347974 e-book
DOI https://doi.org/10.30861/9780860546474
A catalogue record for this book is available from the British Library
This book is available at www.barpublishing.com

CENTRO DE INVESTIGACIONES INDIGENAS DE PUERTO RICO

The Centro de Investigaciones Indígenas de Puerto Rico (CIIPR) is a nonprofit anthropological research center founded and supported by Gaspar Roca. It is dedicated to the study of the Amerindian heritage in the Caribbean Basin. Archaeological and ethnographic research is conducted to realize the goals of the CIIPR. Chartered in April 1985, it has thusfar sponsored two major projects: (1) Ethnographic and ethnoarchaeological expeditions to two villages of the Waiwai Indians, one in southern Guyana on the Essequibo River and the other in northern Brazil on the Jatapuzim River. In addition to important demographic, social organizational, and cosmological data this project resulted in a large and diverse collection of material culture of the Waiwai, Wapishiana, Trio and other groups of the region. (2) A large-scale multidisciplinary archaeological project centered on the early Ceramic age site of Maisabel, which is located on the north coast of Puerto Rico. As part of this project, the CIIPR has supported investigations in zooarchaeology, archaeobotany, and human osteology. Several of the papers in this book discuss Maisabel from various perspectives. The on-going Maisabel Project currently is in the fourth year of continuous work. Project staff are now cataloging, tabulating, and analyzing the artifacts and features recovered in the 14 month excavation. These data will be published as a separate CIIPR monograph.

The South Amerindian ethnographic and the Maisabel archaeological specimens represent the nucleus of a collection planned to be used in a museum devoted to Amerindian lifeways, cultures, and adaptive strategies in the Caribbean. This museum will have both teaching and display goals, focusing especially on how interpretive conclusions are derived by researchers from diverse perspectives. In this regard it will show how anthropology is a *dynamic* and *didactic* enterprise rather than the dismal display of static "culture facts" that so often characterizes anthropology museums.

Over the last four years the CIIPR has been building an extensive research library devoted to Caribbean archaeology, ethnography, and ethnohistory as well as to general anthropological/archaeological method and theory. Currently the institution subscribes to 48 journals and has more than a thousand books in its holdings, and is continuously adding new books, back issues and complete runs of selected journals. Along with maps, photographs, and video/sound documentation this library is already an important archive for Caribbean research.

The CIIPR supports graduate-level instruction and seminars in archaeological method and theory by visiting scholars at the Centro de Estudios Avanzados de Puerto Rico y el Caribe and has disseminated its own findings by sending CIIPR staff to present papers at local, national and international conferences of archaeology and anthropology.

Finally, as this book attests, the CIIPR is committed to the support of scholarly interactions related to Caribbean Amerindian studies. Part of the developmental program is to initiate its own publication series serving as an outlet for high-quality work by regional researchers. With the combined museum and publication programs the Centro de Investigaciones Indígenas de Puerto Rico is striving to make an important contribution to the furtherance and dissemination of knowledge about the heritage of the Caribbean peoples to both the scientific and lay communities.

FORWARD

Research into the early Ceramic age of the Caribbean recently has become the center of relatively intensive investigations. Caribbean archaeologists are shifting the emphasis of research from purely time-space systematics to include processes of culture change, adaptation, site formation and behavioral organization. The unifying element that brings together this seemingly disparate collection of papers into a coherent package is the common concern for understanding the mechanisms and processes of population dispersal into the insular environment and for the dynamics of culture change, interaction, and adjustment to this setting. As a result of shifting theoretical perspectives different approaches are being taken to the examination of regions, the excavation of sites and the ways assemblages are being analyzed. Of course, the problem orientation of each investigator determines the specific approach taken.

The papers in this volume may be divided generally into four thematic parts. These themes are not mutually exclusive and the implications of one study often are relevant for a study in a different theme. Furthermore, authors do not necessarily agree on results of analyses, theoretical frameworks, or analytical methods. This is an indication that Caribbean archaeology is on a healthy developmental track. We are talking *to* each other, rather than past one another.

Theme 1 is concerned with regional settlement patterns and subsistence adaptations. The papers by Jay Haviser, Birgit Morse, Alick Jones, Susan deFrance, Peter Drewett, William Keegan, and David Watters and Irving Rouse deal with this problem. Haviser is concerned with documenting changing adaptive strategies on Curaçao by monitoring site locations and settlement types through time. Similarly, Morse examines the distribution of Saladoid settlements on St. Croix, but since she deals with a comparatively narrow range of time her study is synchronically based.

Jones and deFrance conduct zooarchaeological analyses of Ceramic age deposits from the Indian Creek (Antigua) and Maisabel (Puerto Rico) sites, respectively. It is interesting to compare and contrast the results of these two studies, given the analytical and methodological frameworks. Further, the two sites are both early Saladoid, thus providing us with a useful perspective on adaptive variation related to microenvironmental differences. Drewett's Barbados study is similar to Haviser's in that he summarizes all known site locations through time. Keegan presents a set of theoretical expectations for adaptive shifts by the Ceramic age groups in the Caribbean. This study is useful in that it represents a base-line model, against which new data may be evaluated. Finally, Watters and Rouse present an overview paper on the effects of environmental diversity on settlement locations and subsistence strategies in the Caribbean.

One of the major conclusions that may be drawn from the papers in Theme 1 is that broad generalizations regarding subsistence adaptations in the Caribbean are likely to mask much of the local variation in specific contexts. For instance, deFrance, Drewett, and Watters and Rouse clearly demonstrate the importance of specifying the details of particular assemblages and their contexts prior to offering generalizations concerning the adaptive strategies. Only with such fine-grained studies will we begin to unravel the complexities of insular adaptations and to understand changes under various conditions.

A second theme consists of one paper by Louis Allaire. Volcanism recently has become an important issue for archaeologists. The Lesser Antilles are volcanic islands and the effects of volcanic processes are likely to have been of great importance to the prehistoric occupants. Allaire reviews the volcanic activities on Martinique and offers some ideas concerning human adjustment to these catastrophic events during the Saladoid period.

The third theme addressed in this volume relates to site structure and community organization. In order to adequately address this problem large horizontal areas need to be excavated in addition to testing for site boundaries. The papers by Aad Versteeg (Golden Rock, St. Eustatius), and Peter Siegel (Maisabel, Puerto Rico) are case studies.

Finally, in theme 4, Miguel Rodríguez, Peter Roe, and Irving Rouse deal with stylistic development and change in the Saladoid assemblages to discuss population movement and cultural interactions. Rodríguez is concerned primarily with the distribution of the controversial zoned incised crosshatched ceramic ware and how it relates to the cultural groupings in the northeastern portion of the Caribbean. Rouse deals with cultural affinities between the various Saladoid complexes of the Lesser Antilles, as well as the processes involved in the prehistoric migrations from South America. Further, he is interested in the interactions that occurred between the cultures on either side of the final Saladoid frontier. Roe's paper deals with a great many topics and is, perhaps, the most provocative one of the volume. The grammatical analysis of surface decorative designs and vessel forms is relatively novel for Caribbean archaeology, but represents a logical outgrowth from Rouse's pioneer studies in modal analysis. If nothing else, Roe has made a major contribution by noting the relationship between societal complexity and the locus or emphasis of art.

In the last section of the book Anna Roosevelt discusses the relative strengths and weaknesses of the papers. She offers insights into the variety of subjects raised, often challenging us, constructively, to consider alternative ideas and to develop better our middle-range theory and test implications.

This collection of papers represents a wide range of current perspectives on Ceramic age archaeology in the Caribbean. Of course, it is only a sampling of some of the research being conducted. To the extent that any of the studies presented here elicit alternative proposals, additional research, or substantive reactions then the volume will have been successful.

Most of the papers in this book were prepared originally for a symposium held on April 29, 1988 at the 53rd Annual Meeting of the Society for American Archaeology in Phoenix, Arizona. The papers by Jones, Drewett, Watters and Rouse, and Rodríguez were solicited later to round out the volume. Karl Hutterer and Anna Roosevelt were the discussants for the symposium. Roosevelt retained her position as discussant for this book.

The Centro de Investigaciones Indígenas de Puerto Rico (CIIPR) provided a grant covering the travel expenses for the symposium participants and discussants who came from Europe, the Caribbean, and North America, and for a post-symposium banquet. In addition, the CIIPR provided valuable support in the form of secretarial assistance, photocopying services, long-distance phone calls, regular and express mail, and computer hardware and software purchases. On behalf of the volume contributors, I would like to express my sincere gratitude and appreciation to the CIIPR Director, Gaspar Roca, for his steady support, encouragement, and foresight in this project. The Fundación Puertorriqueña de Conservación provided us with the use of their laser printer for the initial formatting of the book. Evelyn Estrada always performed admirably, and amazingly was able to remain cheerful in the face of numerous tedious chores associated with the production of this volume. Likewise, Rosa García, the Maisabel Lab Director, spent many long hours "after work" assisting in the proof-reading of the manuscripts. I would like to thank the B.A.R. General Editors, Anthony Hands and David Walker, for their invaluable assistance and advice during all stages of the volume preparation. Finally, my thanks go to all of the volume participants for their timely contributions and for putting up with my numerous nudging letters, phone calls, and editorial comments. They, like the Saladoid colonists, are pioneers.

Peter E. Siegel
San Juan, Puerto Rico
May 1989

CONTENTS

CENTRO DE INVESTIGACIONES INDIGENAS DE PUERTO RICO	iii
FORWARD	v
CONTRIBUTORS	ix

PART 1: REGIONAL SETTLEMENT PATTERNS AND SUBSISTENCE ADAPTATIONS ... 1

A COMPARISON OF AMERINDIAN INSULAR ADAPTIVE STRATEGIES ON CURAÇAO
Jay B. Haviser ... 3

SALADOID SETTLEMENT PATTERNS ON ST. CROIX
Birgit Faber Morse ... 29

THE DATING OF EXCAVATION LEVELS USING ANIMAL REMAINS:
A PROPOSED SCHEME FOR INDIAN CREEK, ANTIGUA
Alick R. Jones ... 43

SALADOID AND OSTIONOID SUBSISTENCE ADAPTATIONS:
ZOOARCHAEOLOGICAL DATA FROM A COASTAL OCCUPATION ON PUERTO RICO
Susan D. deFrance ... 57

PREHISTORIC CERAMIC POPULATION LIFEWAYS AND ADAPTIVE STRATEGIES
ON BARBADOS, LESSER ANTILLES
Peter L. Drewett ... 79

TRANSITION FROM A TERRESTRIAL TO A MARITIME ECONOMY:
A NEW VIEW OF THE CRAB/SHELL DICHOTOMY
William F. Keegan ... 119

ENVIRONMENTAL DIVERSITY AND MARITIME ADAPTATIONS
IN THE CARIBBEAN AREA
David R. Watters and Irving Rouse ... 129

PART 2: VOLCANISM AND ARCHAEOLOGY ... 145

VOLCANIC CHRONOLOGY AND THE EARLY SALADOID OCCUPATION
OF MARTINIQUE
Louis Allaire ... 147

PART 3: SITE STRUCTURE AND COMMUNITY ORGANIZATION ... 169

THE INTERNAL ORGANIZATION OF A PIONEER SETTLEMENT IN THE
LESSER ANTILLES: THE SALADOID GOLDEN ROCK SITE ON ST. EUSTATIUS,
NETHERLANDS ANTILLES
Aad H. Versteeg ... 171

SITE STRUCTURE, DEMOGRAPHY, AND SOCIAL COMPLEXITY
IN THE EARLY CERAMIC AGE OF THE CARIBBEAN
Peter E. Siegel ... 193

PART 4: CERAMIC STYLE, POPULATION MOVEMENT, AND INTERACTION — 247

THE ZONED INCISED CROSSHATCH (ZIC) WARE OF EARLY
PRECOLUMBIAN CERAMIC AGE SITES IN PUERTO RICO AND VIEQUES ISLAND
Miguel Rodríguez — 249

A GRAMMATICAL ANALYSIS OF CEDROSAN SALADOID VESSEL FORM
CATEGORIES AND SURFACE DECORATION: AESTHETIC AND TECHNICAL STYLES
IN EARLY ANTILLEAN CERAMICS
Peter G. Roe — 267

PEOPLES AND CULTURES OF THE SALADOID FRONTIER
IN THE GREATER ANTILLES
Irving Rouse — 383

PART 5: COMMENTARY — 405

DISCUSSION OF EARLY CERAMIC POPULATION LIFEWAYS
AND ADAPTIVE STRATEGIES IN THE CARIBBEAN
Anna C. Roosevelt — 407

CONTRIBUTORS

Louis Allaire is Associate Professor of Anthropology at the University of Manitoba in Winnipeg, Canada. His principal interests include the later post-Saladoid archaeology and ethnohistory of the Lesser Antilles, especially the Suazoid series and the Island Caribs. His field work has focussed on the island of Martinique and his research has involved prehistoric technology, ceramic functions, subsistence and settlement patterns, as well as art and mythology.

Susan D. deFrance is a doctoral student in Anthropology at the University of Florida, Gainesville. Her primary research interests include prehistoric and historic zooarchaeology. The article in this volume is a product of Master's research conducted at the University of Florida and sponsored by the Centro de Investigaciones Indígenas de Puerto Rico. deFrance is currently involved in historical zooarchaeological research of Spanish colonial sites in Peru.

Peter L. Drewett is Senior Lecturer in Prehistory at the Institute of Archaeology, University College London. He holds a Ph.D. from London University and is currently directing the Barbados Archaeological Survey, a joint project between the University of London and the Barbados Museum and Historical Society.

Jay B. Haviser has been an archaeologist for the Netherlands Antilles Central Government since 1982, with archaeological field work in other areas of the Caribbean since 1975. He holds a doctorate from the Rijksuniversiteit te Leiden, Netherlands (1987), with research interests in the Caribbean Basin, cultural ecology and applied archaeology.

Alick Jones (Ph.D. Bristol 1963, Postdoc University of California, Los Angeles 1964) is presently Head of the Department of Pure & Applied Zoology at the University of Reading, United Kingdom where his work is mainly concerned with protozoan physiology and stress assessment in domesticated animals. From 1975-1978 he was Professor of Biology at the University of the West Indies, Barbados. During that time he was introduced to Archaeology by Desmond Nicholson in Antigua who persuaded him to undertake an analysis of the faunal remains from the Indian Creek site.

William F. Keegan, Assistant Curator of Caribbean Prehistory in the Florida Museum of Natural History, and Adjunct Assistant Professor of Anthropology in the University of Florida. His main research interest is the colonization of islands by humans.

Birgit Faber Morse was born in Denmark and received her undergraduate training at the University of Copenhagen and an M.A. degree in Archaeology from Yale University. She is currently working with Virgin Islands artifact collections at the Yale Peabody Museum and the Danish National Museum where she is a Research Affiliate.

Miguel Rodríguez obtained his M.A. in Puerto Rican and Caribbean Studies/Archaeology from the Centro de Estudios Avanzados de Puerto Rico y el Caribe in 1983. Currently, he is the Director of the University of Turabo Museum and an Instructor at the University. His interests lie in the early Ceramic age populations of the Caribbean, insular human adaptations and regional reconnaissance studies. He is President of the Puerto Rican Association of Anthropologists and Archaeologists and Vice-President of the International Association for Caribbean Archaeology.

Peter G. Roe has worked in the Peruvian montaña on Late Prehistoric archaeology (Cumancaya Tradition) and Shipibo Indian ethnography (verbal and visual art) since 1969. He received his Ph.D. from the University of Illinois at Urbana-Champaign in 1972, and has taught at the University of Delaware since 1974 where he is now an Associate Professor of Anthropology. Since 1978 he has also worked in Caribbean archaeology (Puerto Rico,

Saladoid Series) and is currently Consulting Curator for the Centro de Investigaciones Indígenas de Puerto Rico.

Anna C. Roosevelt is a Research Associate in the Department of Anthropology, American Museum of Natural History in New York and an Adjunct Professor and Visiting Curator in Anthropology at the University of Florida, Gainesville. She was Curator of South and Central American Archaeology at the Museum of the American Indian and an Adjunct Professor in the Anthropology Department at New York University. Her research has focused on the prehistory of the tropical lowlands of South America. She surveyed and excavated sites in the Middle Orinoco in the 1970s and has been working in the Lower Amazon in the 1980s.

Irving Rouse is Charles J. MacCurdy Professor Emeritus of Anthropology at Yale University and Curator Emeritus in its Peabody Museum of Natural History. He specializes in Caribbean prehistory and has also been concerned with problems of classification, analysis, and interpretation of archaeological materials.

Peter E. Siegel, Ph.D. Candidate in Anthropology, State University of New York, Binghamton and Research Associate, Centro de Investigaciones Indígenas de Puerto Rico. His research includes stone tool technological/functional analysis, evolution of complex society, and the prehistoric use of space.

Aad H. Versteeg is a Research Fellow of the Institute of Prehistory, Leiden State University, Holland. He received his Ph.D. from this university, focusing on a study of prehistoric coastal cultures in western Suriname. Since 1984, he has been directing the St. Eustatius Archaeological Project. Recently, his research program has expanded to include the examination of archaeological sites on Aruba.

David R. Watters is an Associate Curator of Anthropology at the Carnegie Museum of Natural History, Pittsburgh. He received his Ph.D. from the University of Pittsburgh in 1980. His research interests include maritime adaptations and ties between oceanography and prehistory, especially in the northern Lesser Antilles.

PART 1:

REGIONAL SETTLEMENT PATTERNS

AND

SUBSISTENCE ADAPTATIONS

A COMPARISON OF AMERINDIAN

INSULAR ADAPTIVE STRATEGIES ON CURAÇAO

Jay B. Haviser

ABSTRACT

This paper presents an overview of general human adaptation and culture specific adaptive responses to the same insular, semi-desert environment by different Amerindian societies who inhabited Curaçao. Data were collected from site catchment analyses, archaeological excavations, anthropological insights, and concepts of contagious vs. symbiotic settlement patterns, to allow for suggestions about socioeconomic subsystems during the prehistory of Curaçao.

INTRODUCTION

The objective of this paper is to distinguish variable adaptive strategies of Amerindians during the prehistoric and early historic occupations on Curaçao, in order to gain knowledge about different socio-economic subsystems. This was accomplished by quantifying geographic characteristics of the primary archaeological settlements on the island. The theoretical principles which form a basis for much of this study are related to the Fritz and Plog "Principle of Least-Cost" model (1970), Higgs and Vita-Finzi "Site Catchment Analysis" model (1972), and the Flannery and Coe "Contagious vs. Symbiotic" settlement distribution model (1968). However, Hodder and Orton (1976) have criticized an exclusive emphasis on the economic factors of settlement patterns, and thus this study is also oriented towards aspects of individual cultural perspectives and rationality. Following Jochim (1976), this study is looking for the preference order of culturally defined goals and value systems, which exhibit the rationalities of a given society. This paper is a summary of the author's doctoral dissertation (Haviser 1987) and thus most of the figures used here are from that previous publication.

PHYSICAL SETTING AND THE ARCHAEOLOGICAL SITES

Curaçao, with 444 km^2, is the second largest among the small islands and atolls roughly parallel to the Venezuelan coast west of Paria (Figure 1). It is primarily a semi-desert island with xerophytic vegetation, similar to the adjacent areas of Goajira, northwestern Venezuela, and the coastal islands from Aruba to Margarita. Based on archaeological and palynological evidence from Venezuela (Mangelsdorf and Sanoja 1965:108) and Columbia (Schreve-Brinkman 1978:94) we can suggest that these semi-desert conditions have been relatively stable for the last 3,000 years, with a period of slightly increased precipitation from about 3,000 to 5,000 years ago. This climatic zone is called the Southern Caribbean Region.

The data for this study are 97 Amerindian sites located on Curaçao, of which 49 (50.5%) are of the Ceramic/Historic age, 27 (27.8%) are of the Archaic age, 13 (13.4%) are rock-drawing sites and 8 (8.3%) are sites unidentified as to cultural affiliation (Figures 2 and 3). These sites have been classified by the postulated degree of occupational intensity and site function. The degree of occupational intensity was calculated using the vertical and horizontal dimensions of the artifact deposits at each site (Figure 4). The individual site functions are suggested by identification of the number and variety of tool types compared with the composition of other deposits at each site (Figure 5). The Ceramic age sites consist of seven permanent sedentary communities and 42 resource extraction camps with varying degrees of limited occupational intensity. The Archaic age sites consist of one primary base settlement, ten intensive resource extraction camps and 16 limited occupation camps.

Three archaeological excavations were conducted for this study at sites representing the Archaic (St. Michielsberg C-013), Ceramic (De Savaan C-021), and Historic (San Hironimo C-060) ages respectively. This allowed for the identification of distinct artifact assemblages for each age, which were associated with 21 radiocarbon dates from various archaeological contexts on Curaçao (Figure 6). The Archaic age on Curaçao was identified from about 2540 to 1840 B.C., whereas evidence for the Ceramic age first appears at about A.D. 450 and continues up into the Historic age, with the most recent dates of an Amerindian settlement on Curaçao at about A.D. 1625.

The distinctive excavated artifact assemblages are related to the locational characteristics of settlements for each age. Shellfish remains from the St. Michielsberg Archaic deposits indicate that a wide range of species were procured, with a heavy reliance on bivalves and the land snail *Cerion uva* (Figure 7). During the Ceramic age, shellfish exploitation becomes more specialized with a focus on the *Strombus gigas*, *Cittarium pica* and *Pinctada radiata*. The Historic age Amerindian shellfish use is also specialized, with an emphasis on chitons (*Tectarius muricatus*) and two varieties of oysters (*Ostrea equestris* and *Isognomon alatus*).

Other faunal data also indicate dietary shifts through time by the Amerindians (Figure 8). The use of vertebrate animals is relatively unchanging for all three ages, except that no mammals were noted for the Archaic and there was a heavy reliance on the sea turtle (*Chelonia mydas*) during the Ceramic age. However, the combined evidence of vertebrate and invertebrate remains (specificly crab), indicate a clear preference for crabs, and most prominently the land crab (*Cardisoma* sp.) during the Archaic age.

Another important distinction between artifact assemblages of these ages on Curaçao is in the raw materials used for stone tool production. There is a preference for limestone and shale during the Archaic age, whereas chert and basalt are the preferred raw materials for tool manufacture during the Ceramic and Historic ages (Figure 9). A wide variety of lithic raw materials were employed during the post-contact period, including such imports as serpentine, nephrite and tar, which occur less frequently during the prehistoric period.

CHRONOLOGICAL FRAMEWORK FOR THE CERAMIC AGE

IN THE SOUTHERN CARIBBEAN REGION

As to regional correlations, the Amerindian ceramic decoration and construction techniques found on Curaçao are related to the Dabajuroid Series of northwestern Venezuela (Rouse and Cruxent 1963) and to the De Savaan Style of Curaçao and Bonaire (Haviser 1987). Figure 10 is a chronological chart for most of the Southern Caribbean Region, including Guajira (Cruxent and Rouse 1961), Maracaibo/Coro (Rouse and Cruxent 1963, with re-identifications by Gallagher 1976), Curaçao (Haviser 1987), Bonaire (from radiocarbon dates and excavation results as yet unpublished by Haviser), and Los Roques, Tucacus, Puerto Cabello, Barcelona and Margarita (Rouse and Allaire 1978).

The early Colombian/Venezuelan Andean complexes influence the Guajira/Maracaibo areas, as evidenced by similarities in the Kusu phase early incised ceramics with pottery from Barlovento, Colombia (Reichel-Dolmatoff 1955). This was followed by the First Painted Horizon then Second Painted Horizon in Guajira and an apparent hybrid of the First Painted Horizon and Tocuyanoid Series in the Maracaibo area, becoming more Tocuyanoid with time.

The Dabajuroid Series has its heartland in the Coro/eastern Maracaibo area with a strong subsequent presence on Curaçao and Bonaire (and Aruba), then with later expansion east along the Venezuelan coast to Puerto Cabello, Barcelona and Margarita. There is no evidence of a westward coastal expansion of the Dabajuroid Series. On Margarita, these Dabajuroid influences occur after the Saladoid peoples had reached that island during their migrations out of the Orinoco Basin.

The coastal Venezuelan area has some rather complex associations, as seen by an early Barrancoid presence in the Puerto Cabello area, which later is segmented by numerous localized or imported developments, such as with the Tierroid, Ocumaroid, Dabajuroid and a continuation of the Barrancoid Series. Such a late period diversity fits well with the suggestion by this author (Haviser 1987:146), that Puerto Cabello has the geographic characteristics to be a major trading center, at the convergence of different environmental zones. Furthermore, work by Zucchi and Tarble (1984) is leading towards important new discoveries concerning the origins of the Barrancoid Series in the middle and upper Orinoco regions. The evidence from Tucacus and Los Roques islands indicates the localized Valencioid Series on the mainland and into the adjacent islands of that area. For the purpose of the present paper, evidence of the Dabajuroid Series over most of the Southern Caribbean Region is the significant aspect of Figure 10.

AMERINDIAN SETTLEMENT PATTERNS ON CURAÇAO

After identifying discrete artifact assemblages, site types, and temporal separation of the Amerindian settlements on Curaçao, the geographic dispersion of the sites themselves was studied. All major settlements, including the base settlement and the four largest resource extraction camps of the Archaic age, and the seven Ceramic/Historic age sedentary communities, were submitted to a point pattern technique of site catchment analysis. The primary purpose of this proceedure is to quantify geographic characteristics of the Amerindian settlement locations for all ages. Differences in preferred location were used to interpret adaptive responses during these ages.

Shown in Figures 11 and 12 are the locations on Curaçao of the studied catchment areas for the primary Amerindian settlements of the Archaic and Ceramic ages. Each site catchment was examined within a 3 km radius, that was sub-divided into 1 km rings. For each catchment the following environmental characteristics were measured: topography, geomorphology, geological features, potable water sources, major drainage basins, soils suitable for maize and/or manioc cultivation, mangroves, tidal salt areas, clay sources and other archaeological sites. A point pattern technique was used to quantify the proportional ratios of each characteristic (Figure 13). The relative value of each geographic characteristic in a sample area was calculated by the percentage of points representing those characteristics at radii of 1 km, 2 km, and 3 km from the settlement. In Figures 14 to 18 are presented some examples of actual site catchment maps from the Archaic and Ceramic age primary settlements, using the same legend as indicated in Figure 13. Note the position of the Ceramic age settlements, each being situated in a similar environmental setting and surrounded by similar environmental resources. The dispersion of settlements in this manner is suggestive of Flannery and Coe's (1968) "contagious" distribution pattern, whereby all settlements are in the same type of environmental setting and all utilize the surrounding environments in a similar way. This is contrary to Flannery and Coe's "symbiotic" distribution pattern, whereby settlements are spread over different environments with trade and interaction among them. One important aspect of these Ceramic age settlement patterns is that from the earliest Ceramic age occupation of the island, to the Historic age, this distribution pattern is consistent. With the ancestors of these Ceramic age peoples also being from a semi-desert environment in northwestern Venezuela, it is suggested here that only minor adaptive shifts were required in their move to Curaçao. This was not the case with the Ceramic age in the northern Lesser Antilles, such as the island of St. Martin. On St. Martin, it was found that the artifact assemblages, dietary habits, and settlement patterns of the early Ceramic age are quite different from those of the late Ceramic age (Haviser 1988). With the origin of these early Ceramic age peoples from the tropical riverine environments of the Orinoco Basin and Guianas, new aspects of adaptation were required for them to survive in the insular tropical conditions of the Lesser Antilles. Thus, the environmental setting of the homeland for the early Ceramic age peoples was a critical factor in the degree of adaptation required for them to establish themselves on different islands in the Caribbean.

The last catchment area example (Figure 19) shows the only excavated Historic age Amerindian settlement location as being anomalous, compared to the Ceramic age environmental settings, and possibly the result of intended hinterland concealment from the Spanish. Similar cases of post-contact Amerindian settlement isolation in the interior have been noted on Trinidad (Boomert 1984) and Panama (Steward 1979).

The identification of a contagious settlement pattern for the Curaçao Ceramic age is suggestive of relatively self-sufficient local communities. Considered with archaeological evidence and ethnographic data this can be indicative of a Sedentary Horticultural level of social organization (Steward 1960). This pattern is in contrast to a symbiotic distribution pattern, which is usually associated with more complex social organization, as in chiefdoms, as noted with the Caquetio of northwestern Venezuela (Hernandez de Alba 1963). Rouse (1987) has clearly noted the importance of distinguishing between chiefdoms (which are political units) and interaction spheres (which are social units), by noting the Greater Antilles example of interaction among the Classic Tainos, Sub-Tainos, and Guanahatabeys, without the presence of an overall political organization. Such a social interaction sphere is most probable during the pre- and proto-historic period between the island Curaçao and the Caquetio Chiefdom of northwestern Venezuela, as suggested by a contagious rather than symbiotic settlement distribution pattern on Curaçao.

The individual point pattern results at 1 km radii were compiled for each of the major settlements on Curaçao. Then, five Archaic age and seven Ceramic/Historic age catchment results were grouped, producing Archaic age totals and Ceramic/Historic age totals. As a standard for comparison, the entire island of Curaçao was measured for the area totals of each environmental characteristic used in the point pattern study. A characteristic was considered important when its combined age results showed a percentage ratio greater than the calculated total island ratio for that characteristic (Figure 20).

SUMMARY OF THE POINT PATTERN STUDY

The objective of this paper is to quantify geographic characteristics and to make comparisons of these data, which can be related to the Archaic and Ceramic ages on Curaçao, in order to gain knowledge about the insular adaptations and economic subsystems of those different cultural groups. What follows is a brief summary and interpretation of the study, which is discussed in greater detail elsewhere (Haviser 1987).

To synthesize the data we should formulate a perspective of the island from various levels of interdependent cultural and environmental relationships. First, we will identify the general aspects of basic human-land interaction within the overall environmental zone. Second, the more subtle technological and cultural prescriptions as exhibited by the specific adaptations will be identified.

The entire semi-desert Southern Caribbean Region can be seen as one environmental zone, with a specific array of plants and animals and characterized by particular climatic, topographic and general geographic conditions. The island of Curaçao is but one small part of this semi-desert environmental zone. There are several environmental constraints that affect all human populations on Curaçao. The most obvious of these are the scarcity of fresh water sources, intense sun with rapid evaporation and a sparsity of naturally available terrestrial floral and faunal food resources. Curaçao, as a example of this semi-desert climatic zone, provides data useful for observing general adaptive responses of the human populations.

The data show that primary settlements are within a maximum of 2 km distance from a potential fresh water source and most are within 1 km distance. Present archaeological and historical evidence indicates that the Ceramic age and Contact Period peoples would dig for fresh water, whereas the Archaic age peoples were apparently without the knowledge to dig for water, and located their primary settlements within 5 km of permanent natural springs.

Due to the sparsity of naturally available terrestrial floral and faunal food sources on Curaçao, the marine resources become very significant for human survival in this semi-desert environment. This reliance on marine resources is again seen as a general adaptive response. All but one of the major settlements on Curaçao are within 2 km distance from either the open sea or inland saltwater bays, and again the majority of settlements are within 1 km of marine resources. The one anomalous case was probably a response to the Spanish conquerors as opposed to a subsistence oriented site selection. The majority of primary settlements are within 1 km of inland bays, thus indicating a preference for the calmer waters and easily available food sources at the inland bays.

As we observe the more subtle aspects of technological capabilities and cultural perspectives, we are able to identify specific adaptations to a complex of relationships, limited by the climatic zone yet dependent upon a specific range of resources, which each society decides to utilize as its individual ecological setting. The previously identified general adaptive responses of settlement near fresh water sources and marine resources can be considered as general human adaptation to this climatic zone, and therefore are basic to cultural or technological potentials of human habitation on Curaçao, be it prehistoric or early historic. As we begin to observe the particular adaptive responses within this environmental zone by different technological and cultural groups, the uniqueness of those adaptive responses becomes more evident.

Specific Adaptation #1: Avoidance of the Sun

As an initial example we can see that there is a basic human need to avoid the intense sun and rapid evaporation which occurs within this environmental zone. The Archaic age peoples on Curaçao dealt with this problem by inhabiting the rock shelters and caves on the island, along with the possible construction of some forms of temporary brush windbreaks on open sites. This adaptation, together with a lack of evidence for agriculture, is suggestive of a hunter-gatherer level of social organization (Haviser 1987:138). In contrast, during the Ceramic age, sedentism allowed for the accumulation of more material culture, which included the construction of more permanent pole construction huts for protection from the elements, and which were close to their agricultural fields (Haviser 1987:66). From these two basically different subsistence systems and lifeways we may further suggest that the Archaic age peoples were more directly bound to environmental constraints, and thus their perspective of a suitable ecological setting including shelter was limited to a specific complex of availabilities within the general environmental zone. However, the Ceramic age people were able to exceed the bounds of environmental contraints, with the creation of permanent artificial shelter situated where they chose to position it. This ability to create artificial shelter allowed the Ceramic age peoples to focus on a different complex of environmental resources.

Specific Adaptation #2: Relative Position to Coast

There is a slightly greater coastal orientation of the Archaic settlements than the Ceramic age settlements (Figure 20), with a single site (C-001) specifically accounting for the Ceramic age association directly with the open sea. The Archaic age settlements are clearly more directly situated on the inland bay shorelines, whereas the Ceramic age settlements tend to be slightly more inland away from the bay shore. The open plain/rolling hills areas are more associated with the Ceramic age settlements. Although the Archaic age settlements approach a normal ratio, compared to the island standard for association with hilly lands, the primary settlements are more frequently in direct association with rock shelter locations than are Ceramic age settlements. The highest hilltops of the western half of the island are associated with Ceramic age sites, while the karst topography of the limestone coasts are associated with the Archaic age sites.

Specific Adaptation #3: Relative Position to Lithic Sources

The position of settlements in relation to the different geological formations clearly demonstrates the different lithic resource areas exploited by these two cultures. For the Archaic age it can be seen that the limestone producing Seru Domi Formation, and the shale producing Midden Curaçao Formation are both above normal ratios for association. These formations are also the primary location of rock shelters and the major dwelling area of the *Cerion uva* land snail. This is quite distinctive when one observes that the Ceramic age settlements have minimal or no association with these formations, and yet focus on the chert producing Knip Group with more than twice the normal ratio for that formation, and an above normal ratio for the basalt producing Curaçao Lava Formation.

Specific Adaptation #4: Proximity to Fresh Water

The presence of potential water sources is evident at all of the primary settlements within 1 km radius, except for one Archaic age and one Ceramic age settlement, both of which do have sources within 2 km. As stated earlier, the primary core of Archaic age settlements is also located within 5 km of the natural springs at the Rooi Rincon Archaic age site. Referring to the radiocarbon dates for the Rooi Rincon and St. Michielsberg sites, we see that the earliest settlement locus for the Archaic age was directly associated with the natural spring of Rooi Rincon roughly 4,000-4,500 years ago. Subsequently, a relocation of the settlement core followed to the more mangrove/inland bay associated site of St. Michielsberg about 3,800 years ago. This sequence of settlement locations suggests an initial perception of the permanent water source locus as "a priori" by the Archaic age peoples. They later modified their rational priorities to allow for increasing resettlement adjacent to the mangrove/inland bay resources, which were in closest proximity to the permanent water source.

Many potential water sources are located near the outlets of the major drainage basins on Curaçao, and can relate to the presence of major drainage basins at all of the Ceramic age settlements and some of the Archaic age settlements. However, upon closer observation of the catchment maps, one clearly sees a stronger association between the Ceramic age settlements and major drainage basins than exists in the Archaic age.

Specific Adaptation #5: Agriculture

The Ceramic age association with the major drainage basins, also relates to the very important above normal ratios of the soils suitable for maize and manioc with the Ceramic age settlements. Although there is an apparent above normal ratio of Archaic age settlements and soils for maize, this is not the case with those soils for manioc. It could even be postulated that some particularly valuable naturally available plant occurred at these maize suitable soils during the Archaic age.

The emphasis on agricultural activities during the Ceramic age may be a partial explanation for specialized shellfish exploitation of the largest meat producing species. Furthermore, the concentration on rocky coast shellfish species during the Historic age may relate to an avoidance of Europeans at the bay areas, and/or a decline in necessity for shell material at the settlement due to the introduction of iron tools.

Specific Adaptation #6: Mangrove Resources

Present and postulated ancient mangrove stands are the characteristic most significantly above the normal ratio for any of the Archaic age sample results, with almost ten times the postulated mangrove ratio for the island. Postulation of ancient mangrove stands was based on early historical maps prior to modern development, and to the required living conditions for mangroves matched with inland bay areas on Curaçao. The St. Michielsberg catchment map (Figure 14) shows minimal mangroves in 1962, yet historical data and the habitat conditions of the inland bay adjacent to this site suggest that extensive mangroves were at this bay. The mangroves are also the primary habitat for all of the bivalve shellfish used during the Archaic age, as well as the primary dwelling area for the land crab (*Cardisoma* sp.). Ceramic age results show only a slightly above normal ratio for mangroves, which exaggerates the different cultural preferences for this geographic characteristic.

Specific Adaptation #7: Tidal Salt Areas/Clay Sources

Both the Archaic and Ceramic age sample results show an above normal ratio for tidal salt areas, which most probably can be ascribed to the association with inland bays during both of these ages. The minor presence of clay sources during both the Archaic and Ceramic ages indicates that clay was not an important factor in settlement placement for the prehistoric peoples during either age.

By applying the data presented for general human adaptation to the environmental zone, we see that there is a tendency towards a *Bay Complex with water sources* territoriality for the human inhabitation of Curaçao. Furthermore, as we observe the data in more detail, we can identify a different ecological emphasis for each distinctive cultural group. For the Archaic age there is a *mangrove-rock shelter* emphasis within the Bay Complex, whereas for the Ceramic age there is a *suitable soils-drainage basin* emphasis within the Bay Complex. As an additional comment, we can note that the early Europeans also exhibited a general human adaptation to the Bay Complex, however their settlements show a *deepwater bay* emphasis, obviously for navigation of large sailing ships.

By identifying the changes in the exploitation of specific ecozones within the same Bay Complex of this general environmental zone, from the Archaic to Ceramic to Historic ages, we are able to clearly visualize the changes of human adaptive response via different technological and cultural perspectives. These changing cultural ecological adaptations constitute the creative process which is the essence of human habitation on islands such as Curaçao.

REFERENCES CITED

Boomert, A.
    1984   The Arawak Indians of Trinidad and Coastal Guiana, ca.1500-1650. *Journal of Caribbean History* 19(2):123-188.

Cruxent, José M. and Irving Rouse
    1961   *Arqueologia cronologica de Venezuela*, vol.2. Estudios Monograficos VI, Union Panamericana, Washington, D.C.

Flannery, Kent V. and Michael D. Coe
    1968   Social and Economic Systems in Formative Mesoamerica. In *New Perspectives in Archeology*, edited by Sally R. Binford and Lewis R. Binford, pp. 267-284. Aldine, Chicago.

Fritz, John M. and Fred T. Plog
    1970   The Nature of Archaeological Explanation. *American Antiquity* 35:405-412.

Gallagher, Patrick
    1976   *La Pitía: An Archaeological Series in Northwestern Venezuela*. Yale University Publications in Anthropology No.76. New Haven.

Haviser, Jay B.
    1987   *Amerindian Cultural Geography on Curaçao*. Ph.D. dissertation, Rijksuniversiteit te Leiden. STICUSA, Amsterdam.

    1988   *An Archeological Survey of St.Martin-St.Maarten*. Reports of the Archeological/Anthropological Institute of the Netherlands Antilles No. 7. Willemstad, Curaçao.

Hernández de Alba, Gregorio
    1963   The Tribes of Northwestern Venezuela. In *The Circum-Caribbean Tribes*, edited by Julian H. Steward, pp. 469-474. Handbook of South American Indians, vol.4. Bureau of American Ethnology Bulletin No.143. Smithsonian Institution. Government Printing Office, Washington, D.C.

Higgs, E.S. and C. Vita-Finzi
    1972   Prehistoric Economies: A Territorial Approach. In *Papers in Economic Prehistory*, edited by E.S. Higgs, pp. 27-36. Cambridge University Press, Cambridge.

Hodder, Ian and Clive Orton
    1976   *Spatial Analysis in Archaeology*. Cambridge University Press, Cambridge.

Hummelinck, P. W.
    1940   *Studies on the Fauna of Curaçao, Aruba, Bonaire and the Venezuelan Islands*. Natuurwetenschappelijk Studiekring voor Suriname en de Nederlandse Antillen No. 66. Utrecht.

Jochim, Michael A.
    1976   *Hunter-Gatherer Subsistence and Settlement: A Predictive Model*. Academic Press, New York.

Mangelsdorf, R. and M.O. Sanoja
    1965   *Early Archaeological Maize from Venezuela*. Harvard Botanical Leaflets 21(4).

Cambridge.

Reichel-Dolmatoff, G.
    1955   Excavaciones en los conchales de la costa de Barlovento. *Revista Colombiana de Antropologia* 4:247-271.

Rouse, Irving
    1987   Origin and Development of the Indians Discovered by Columbus. *Proceedings of the San Salvador Conference on Columbus and His World* 1:293-312. Bahamian Field Station, San Salvador, Bahamas.

Rouse, Irving and José M. Cruxent
    1963   *Venezuelan Archaeology.* Yale University Press, New Haven.

Rouse, Irving and Louis Allaire
    1978   Caribbean. In *Chronologies in New World Archaeology,* edited by R.E. Taylor and Clement W. Meighan, pp. 431-481. Academic Press, New York.

Schreve-Brinkman, E.J.
    1978   *A Palynological Study of the Upper Quarternary Sequence in the El Abra Corridor and Rock Shelters (Columbia).* Unpublished Ph.D. dissertation, University of Amsterdam, Amsterdam.

Steward, Julian H.
    1960   Evolutionary Principles and Social Types. In *The Evolution of Man: Mind, Culture and Society,* edited by Sol Tax, vol. 2. University of Chicago Press, Chicago.

    1979   *Theory of Culture Change: The Methodology of Multilinear Evolution.* Reprinted. University of Illinois Press, Urbana. Originally published 1955, Board of Trustees University of Illinois, Urbana.

Zucchi, A. and K. Tarble
    1984   Los Cedeñoides: un nuevo grupo prehispánico del Orinoco medio. *Acta Científica Venezuelana* 35(3-4):293-309.

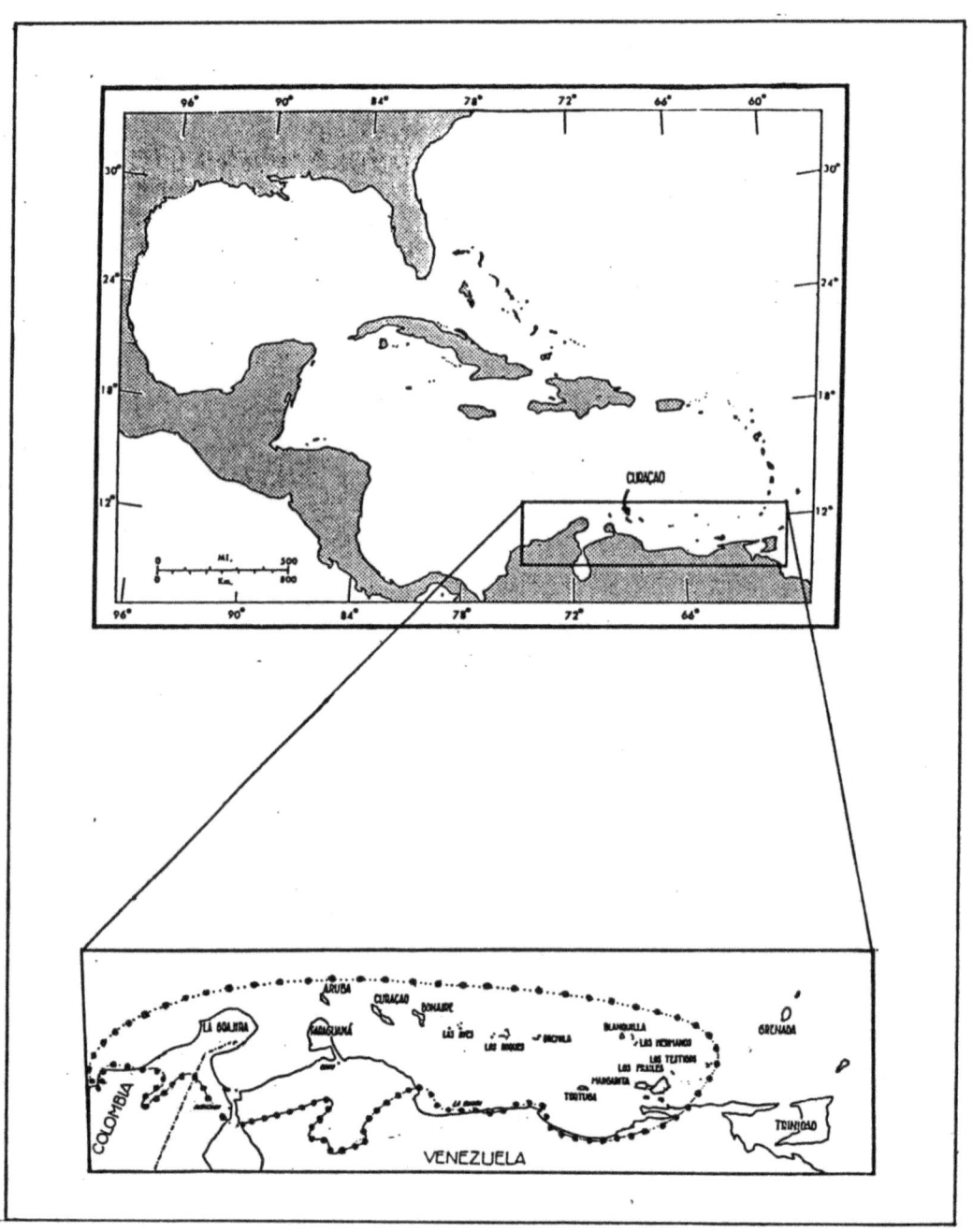

Figure 1. Top: Curaçao in the Caribbean Basin. Bottom: Detail of the Southern Caribbean Region, dotted line indicates dry region with less than 680 mm rainfall per year (from Hummelinck 1940:119).

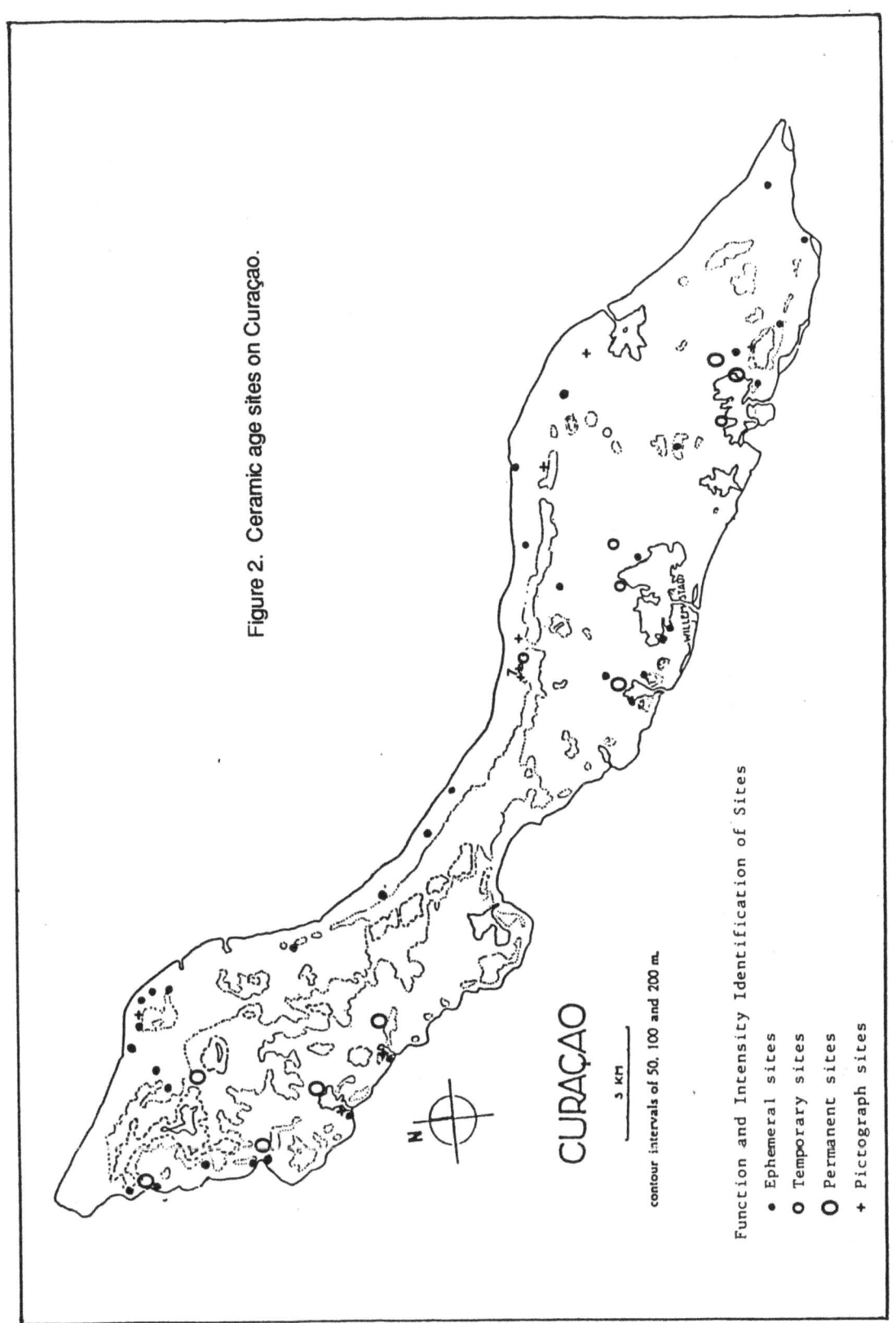

Figure 2. Ceramic age sites on Curaçao.

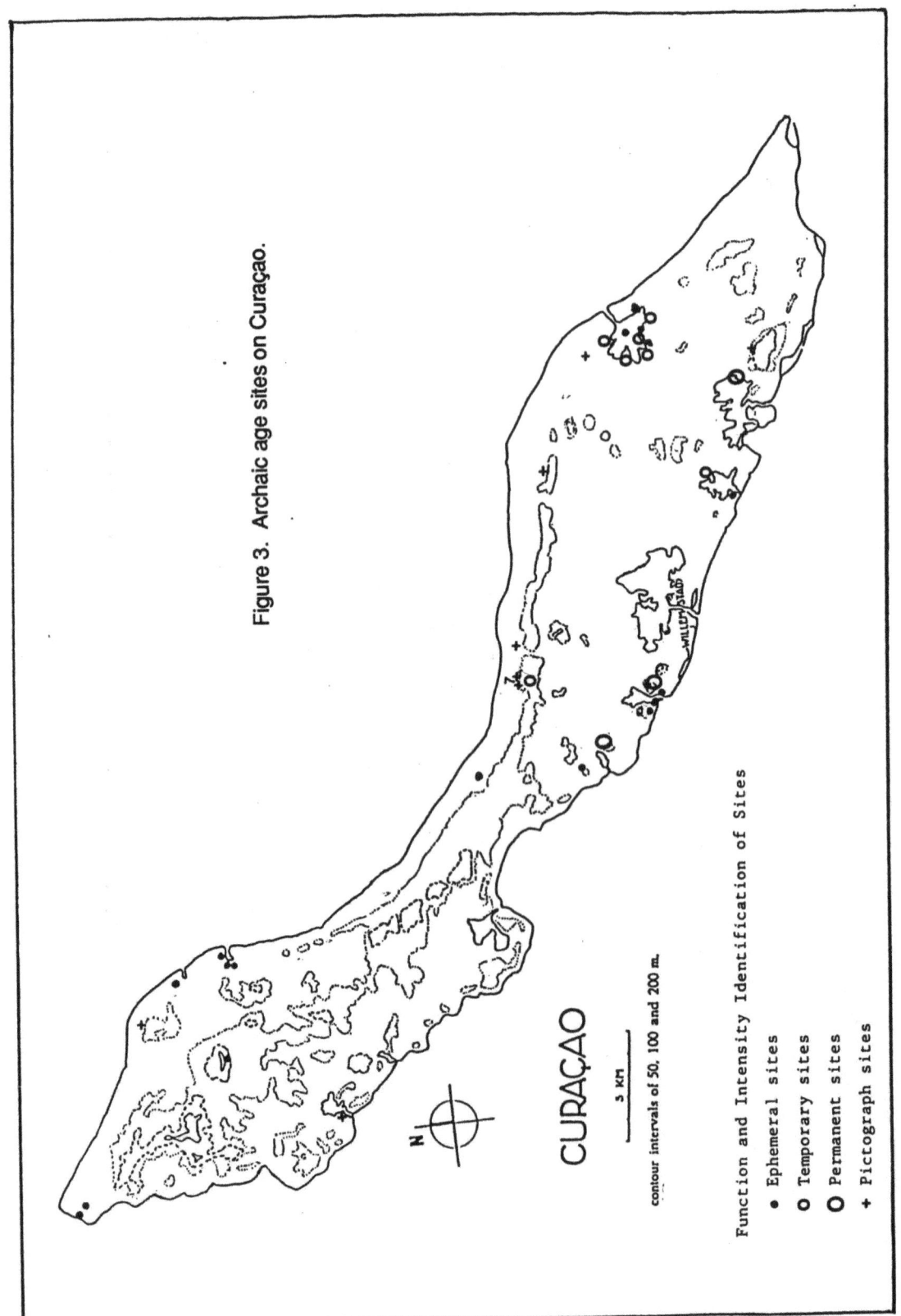

Figure 3. Archaic age sites on Curaçao.

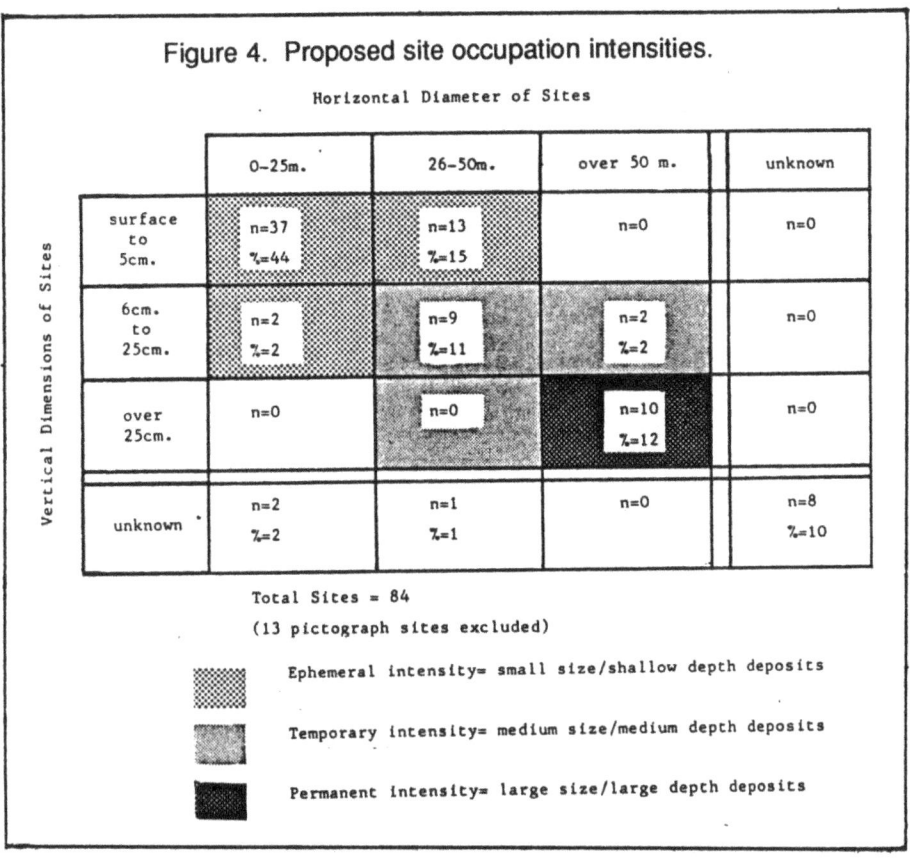

Figure 4. Proposed site occupation intensities.

Horizontal Diameter of Sites

Vertical Dimensions of Sites	0–25m.	26–50m.	over 50 m.	unknown
surface to 5cm.	n=37 %=44	n=13 %=15	n=0	n=0
6cm. to 25cm.	n=2 %=2	n=9 %=11	n=2 %=2	n=0
over 25cm.	n=0	n=0	n=10 %=12	n=0
unknown	n=2 %=2	n=1 %=1	n=0	n=8 %=10

Total Sites = 84

(13 pictograph sites excluded)

Ephemeral intensity= small size/shallow depth deposits

Temporary intensity= medium size/medium depth deposits

Permanent intensity= large size/large depth deposits

Composition of Sites

Presence of Tool Types at Sites	shell only n=3	shell stone only n=29	shell stone ceramic only n=30	shell stone (with or without ceramic) faunal bone only n=12	shell stone (with or without ceramic) faunal bone human bone n=9
no tools	2	19	20	—	—
shell gouge	—	5	3	6	9
shell adze	—	—	—	—	5
shell celt	1	4	6	10	8
shell scoop	—	—	—	2	7
utilized coral	—	1	1	6	9
ground bone	—	—	—	—	3
ground limestone	—	—	—	2	2
ground siltstone	—	—	—	1	6
ground basalt	—	—	1	1	7
chipped basalt	—	4	4	7	9
chipped shale	—	4	—	3	2
chipped chert	—	2	4	8	9
cassava grater	—	—	—	—	7
drill	—	—	—	2	6
core	—	—	—	1	5
hammerstone	—	—	—	4	7
anvil	—	—	—	1	1
matate	—	—	—	—	4
ornamental objects	—	—	—	7	7
imported objects	—	—	—	—	4
	Limited Resource Extraction	Limited Resource Extraction	Limited Resource Extraction	Intensive Resource Extraction	Pase Settlement/ Sedentary Community

Figure 5. Proposed site functions.

sample-laboratory	site	material	unit/level	dates B.P.	dates Christian	
IVIC-247 (Caracas)	Rooi Rincon	charcoal	#28/0-25 cm	4490 ± 60	2540 B.C.	
IVIC-246 (Caracas)	Rooi Rincon	charcoal	#28/25-50 cm	4160 ± 80	2210 B.C.	
IVIC-234 (Caracas)	Rooi Rincon	charcoal	P.H./0-20 cm	4110 ± 65	2160 B.C.	
IVIC-242 (Caracas)	Rooi Rincon	charcoal	P.H./20-30 cm	4070 ± 65	2120 B.C.	Archaic Age
IVIC-240 (Caracas)	Rooi Rincon	charcoal	#5/25-50 cm	3990 ± 50	2040 B.C.	
GrN-9994 (Groningen)	St.Michielsberg	shell	Unit B/60-70 cm	3820 ± 70	1870 B.C.	
AA1NA-102 (Oklahoma)	St.Michielsberg	shell	Unit B/70-80 cm	3820 ± 65	1870 B.C.	
AA1NA-103 (Oklahoma)	St.Michielsberg	shell	Unit B/70-80 cm	3790 ± 50	1840 B.C.	
GrN-12914 (Groningen)	De Savaan	human bone	S-1/0-25 cm	1500 ± 200	A.D. 450	
IVIC-237 (Caracas)	San Juan	charcoal	C.B./25-50 cm	1440 ± 60	A.D. 510	
IVIC-250 (Caracas)	Knip	charcoal	#26/0-25 cm	1230 ± 60	A.D. 720	
IVIC-233 (Caracas)	Knip	charcoal	#9/0-25 cm	910 ± 50	A.D. 1040	Ceramic Age
IVIC-244 (Caracas)	Knip	charcoal	#9/25-50 cm	830 ± 60	A.D. 1120	
GrN-9995 (Groningen)	De Savaan	shell	level 3/35-45cm	740 ± 60	A.D. 1210	
GrN-12979 (Groningen)	De Savaan	human bone	S-2/0-25 cm	660 ± 20	A.D. 1290	
IVIC-249 (Caracas)	Knip	charcoal	#27/0-25 cm	630 ± 60	A.D. 1320	
IVIC-248 (Caracas)	Knip	charcoal	#26/25-50 cm	630 ± 50	A.D. 1320	
GrN-9997 (Groningen)	San Hironimo	charcoal	Unit I/10-15 cm	420 ± 15	A.D. 1530	
GrN-9996 (Groningen)	San Hironimo	shell	Unit I/10-15 cm	350 ± 50	A.D. 1600	Post - Contact
IVIC-241 (Caracas)	Gaito	charcoal	#8/0-25 cm	340 ± 50	A.D. 1610	
GrN-9998 (Groningen)	San Hironimo	charcoal	Unit IV/10-15 cm	325 ± 35	A.D. 1625	

Figure 6. Radiocarbon dates for Curaçao.

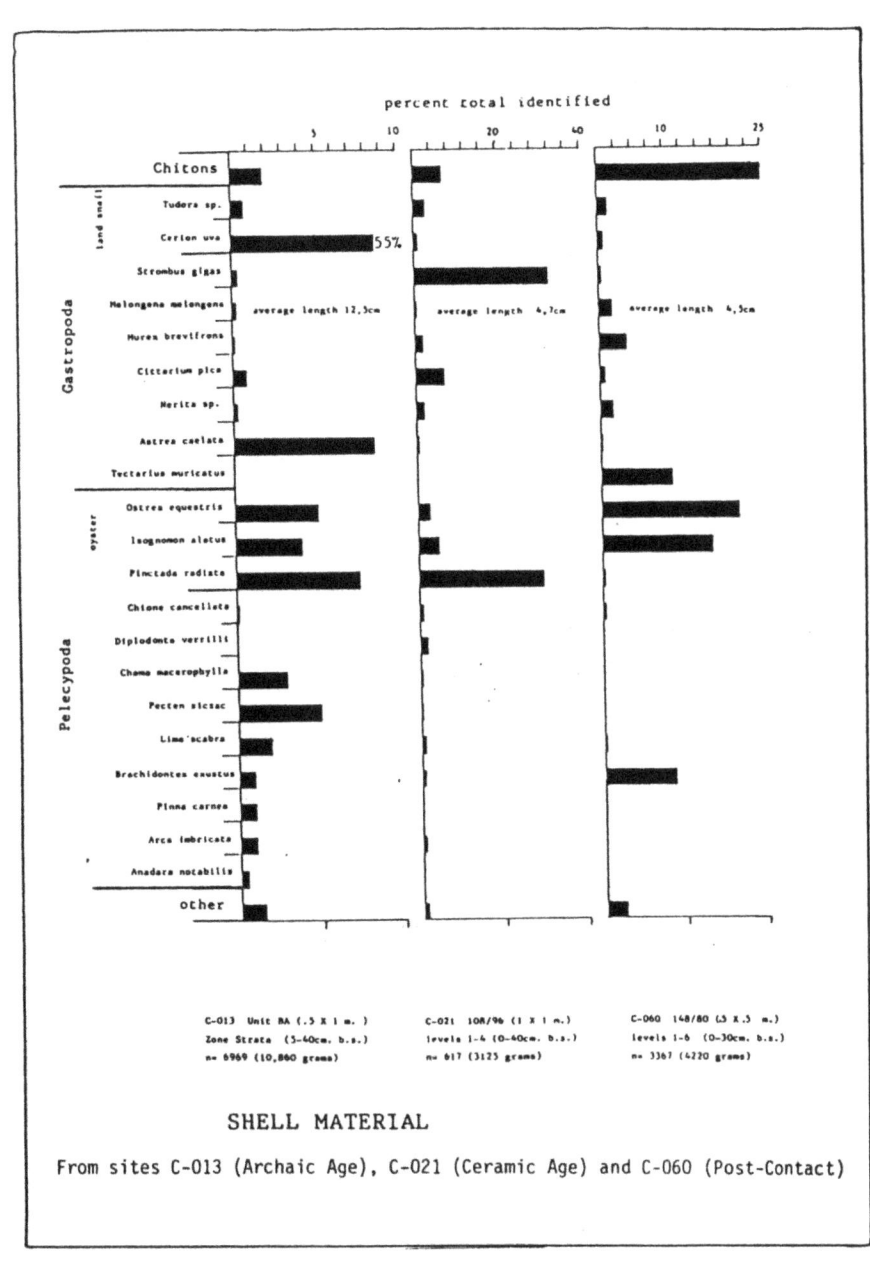

Figure 7. Shell material excavated on Curaçao.

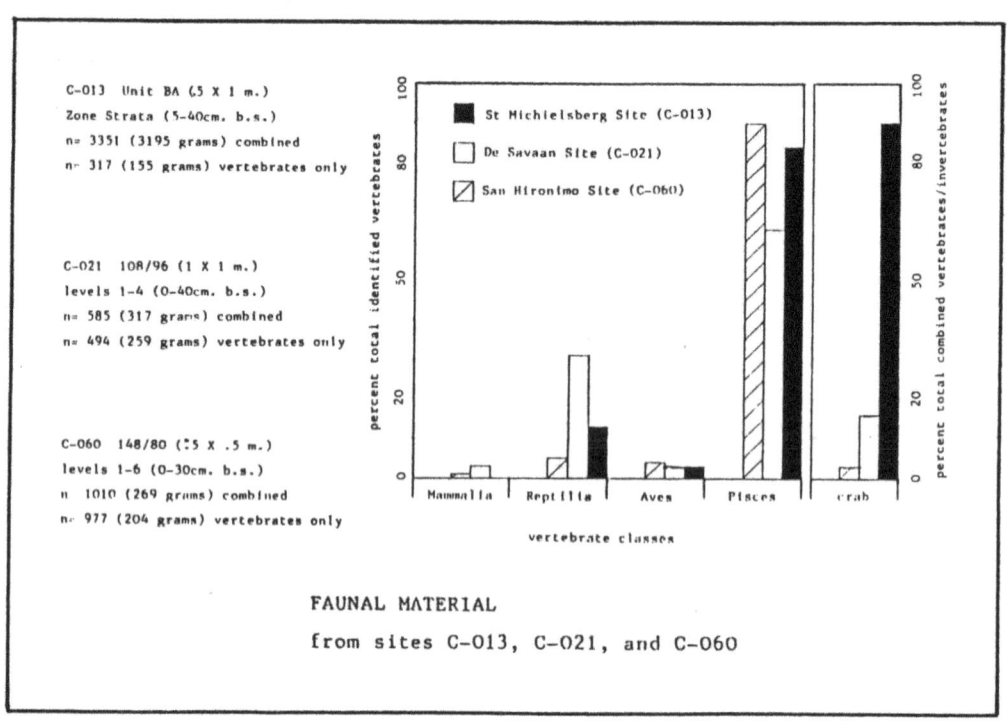

Figure 8. Other faunal material excavated on Curaçao.

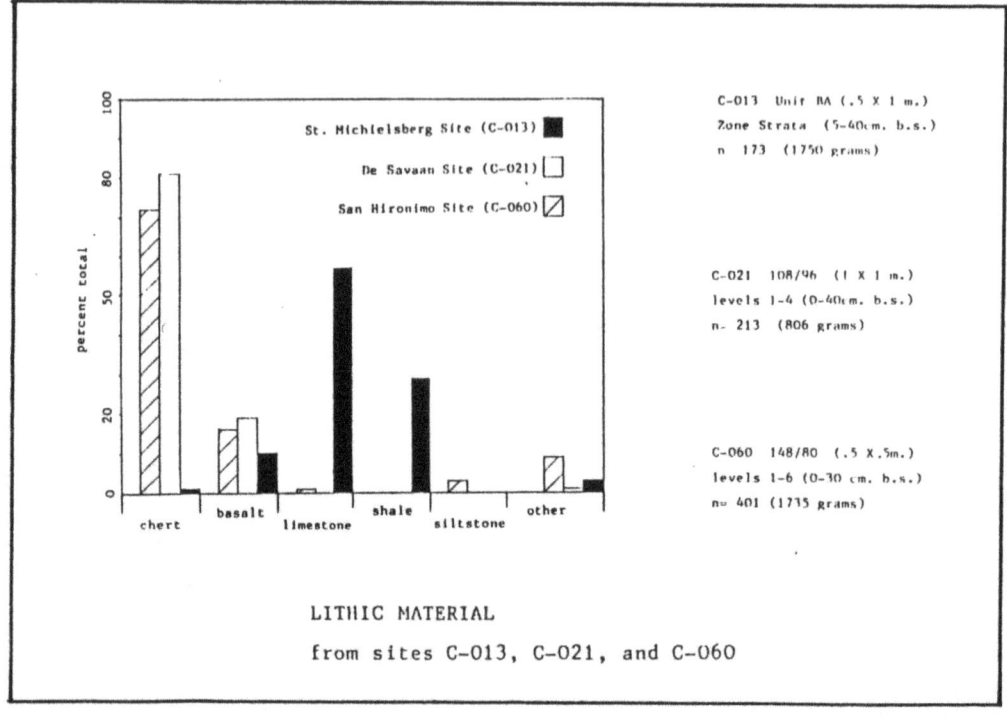

Figure 9. Lithic material excavated on Curaçao.

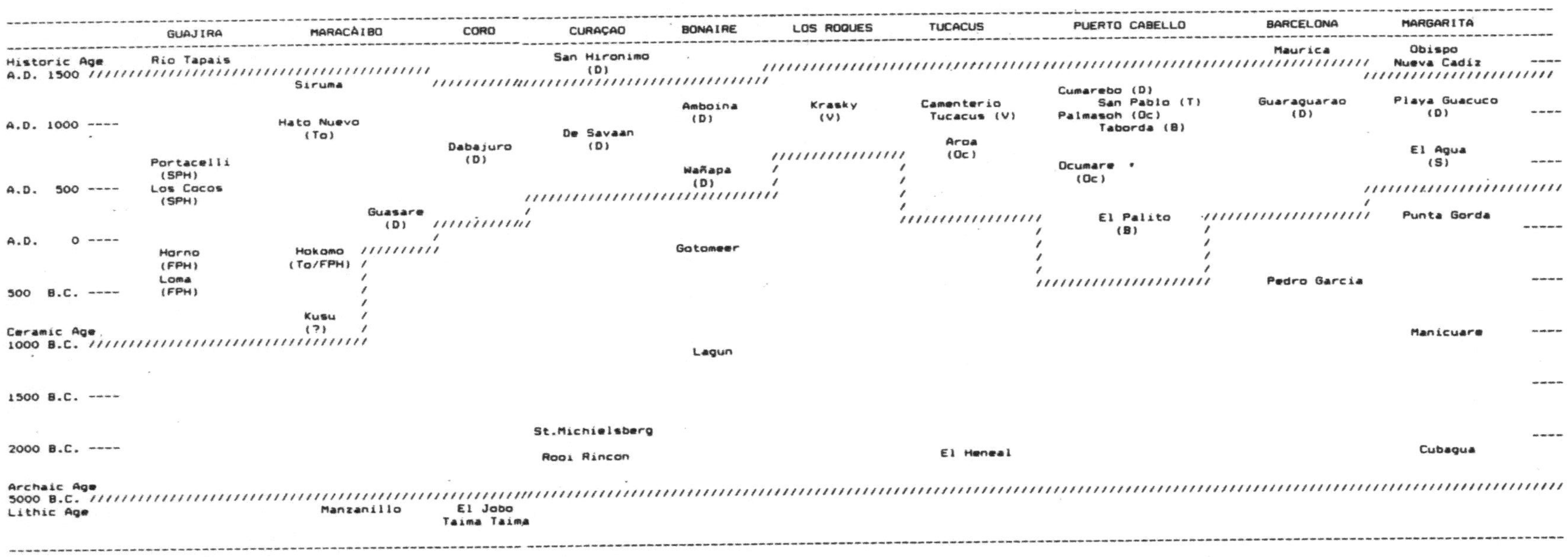

	GUAJIRA	MARACAIBO	CORO	CURAÇAO	BONAIRE	LOS ROQUES	TUCACUS	PUERTO CABELLO	BARCELONA	MARGARITA
Historic Age A.D. 1500	Rio Tapais		Siruma	San Hironimo (D)					Maurica	Obispo Nueva Cadiz
A.D. 1000		Hato Nuevo (To)		De Savaan (D)	Amboina (D)		Cementerio Tucacus (V)	Cumarebo (D) San Pablo (T) Palmasch Oc) Taborda (B)	Guaraguarao (D)	Playa Guacuco (D)
A.D. 500	Portacelli (SPH) Los Cocos (SPH)	Dabajuro (D)			WaRapa (D)	Krasky (V)	Aroa (Oc)	Ocumare * (Oc)		El Agua (S)
A.D. 0	Horno (FPH)	Guasare (D) Hokomo (To/FPH)		Gotomeer				El Palito (B)	Pedro Garcia	Punta Gorda
500 B.C.	Loma (FPH)	Kusu (?)								Manicuare
Ceramic Age 1000 B.C.										
1500 B.C.				Lagun						
2000 B.C.				St.Michielsberg Rooi Rincon			El Heneal			Cubagua
Archaic Age 5000 B.C. Lithic Age		Manzanillo	El Jobo Taima Taima							

Figure 10. Compiled regional prehistoric chronologies.

Venezuelan Series:
(B) =Barrancoid; (D) =Dabajuroid; (Oc) =Ocumaroid; (S) =Saladoid;
(T) =Tierroid; (To) =Tocuyanoid; (V) =Valencioid.

Colombian Horizons:
(FPH) =First Painted Horizon; (SPH) =Second Painted Horizon

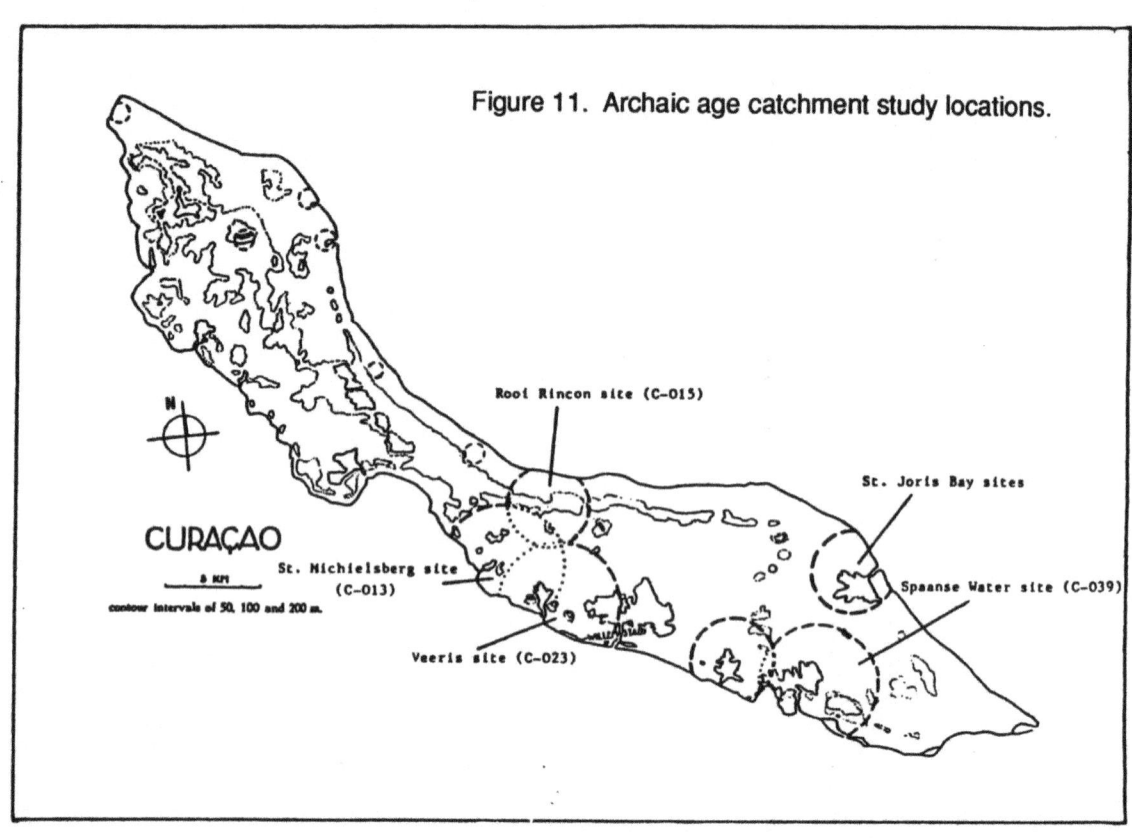

Figure 11. Archaic age catchment study locations.

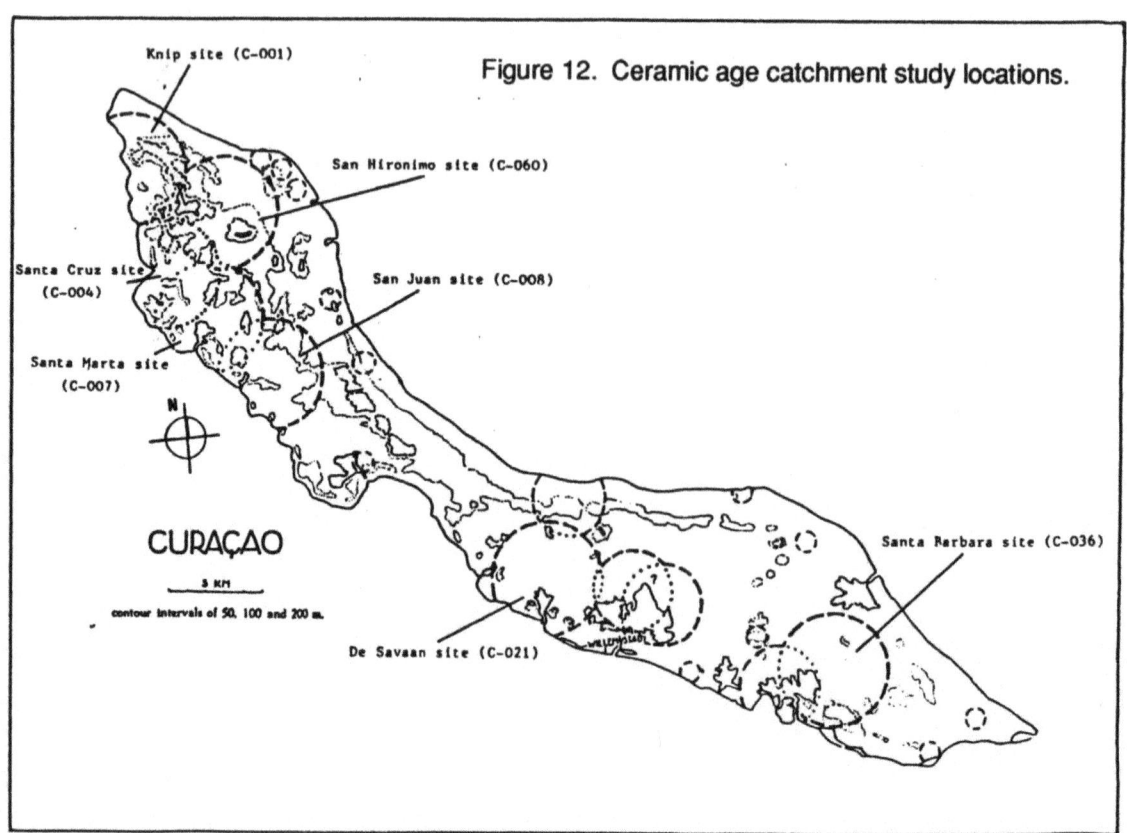

Figure 12. Ceramic age catchment study locations.

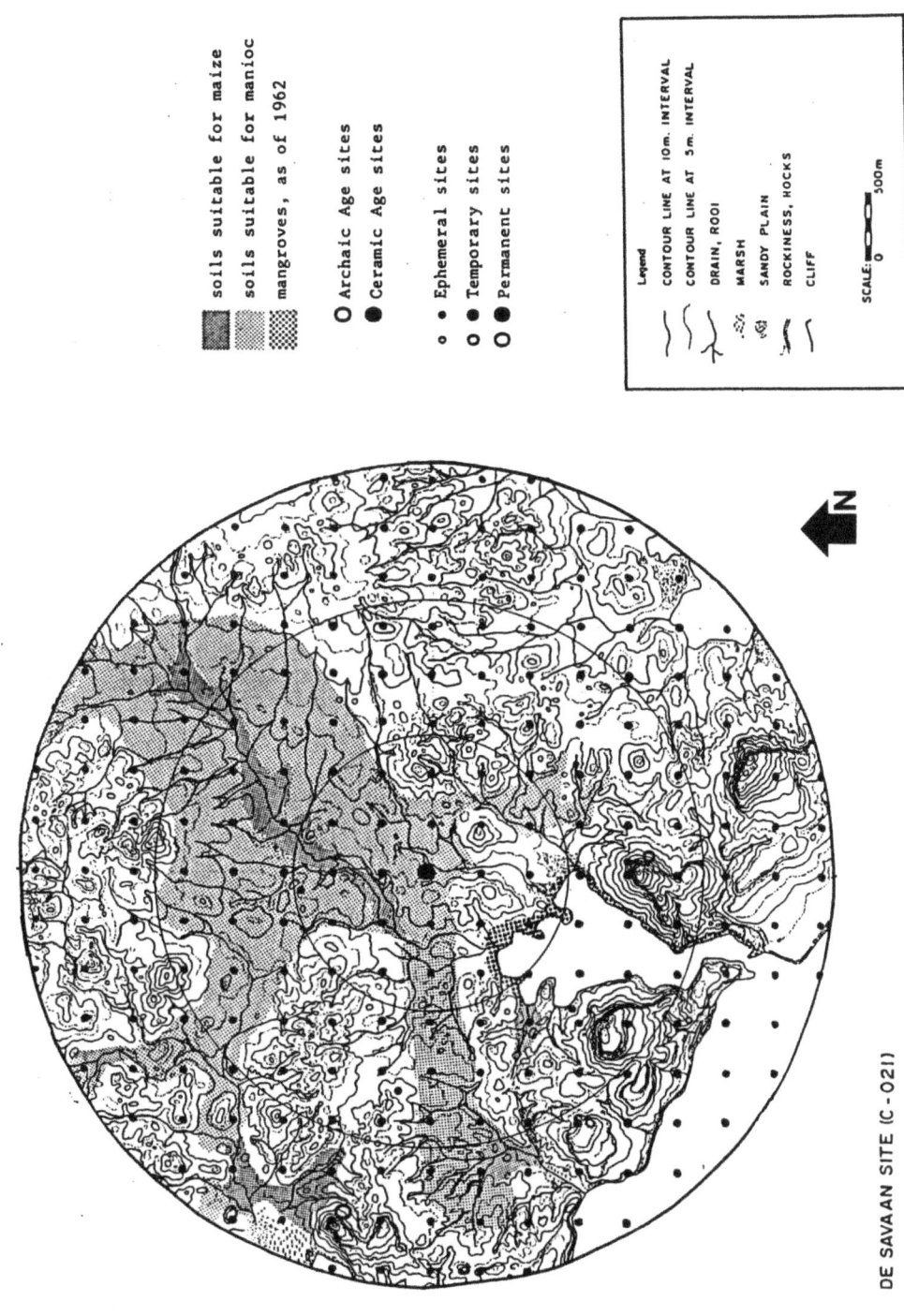

Figure 13. Example of Points Pattern (221 points) used on a sample area of 3 km radius from primary settlement.

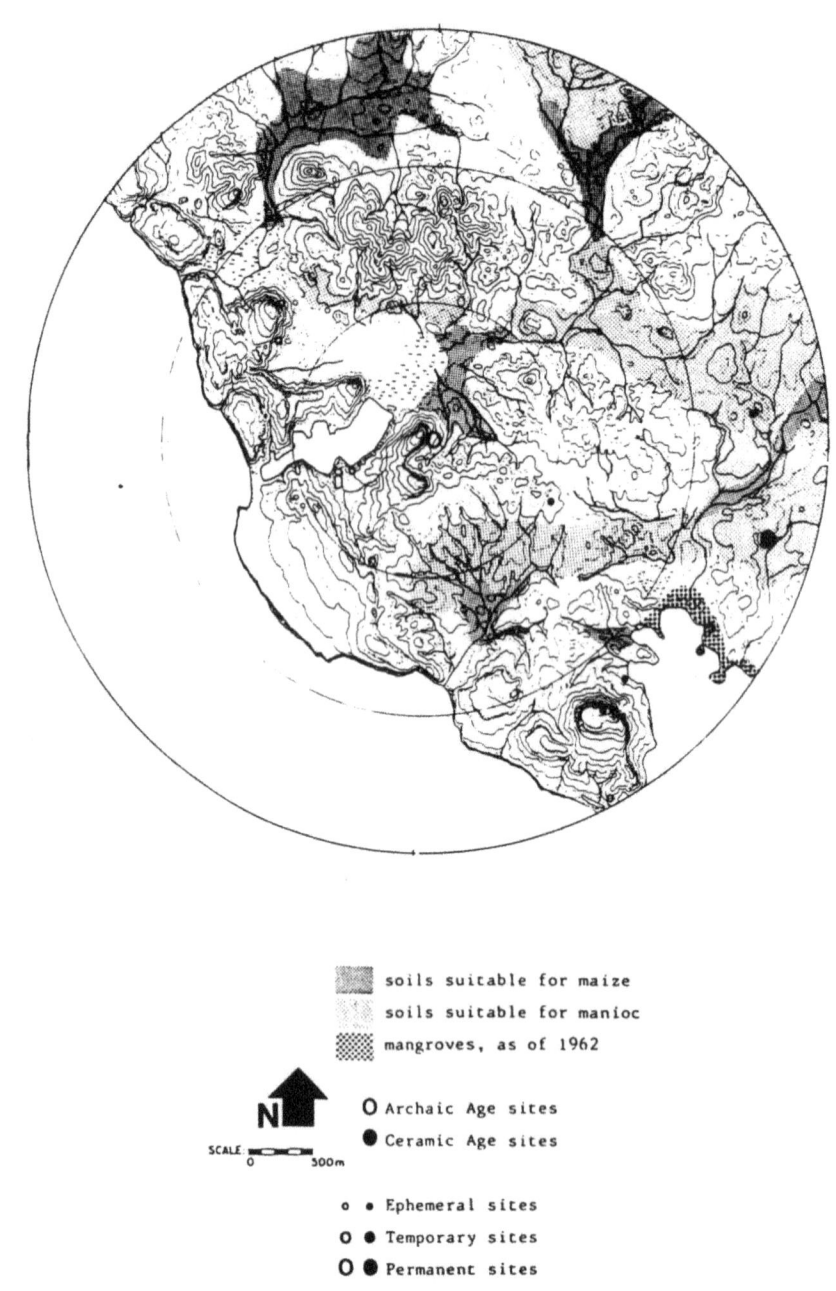

Figure 14. St. Michielsberg (C-013) catchment area.

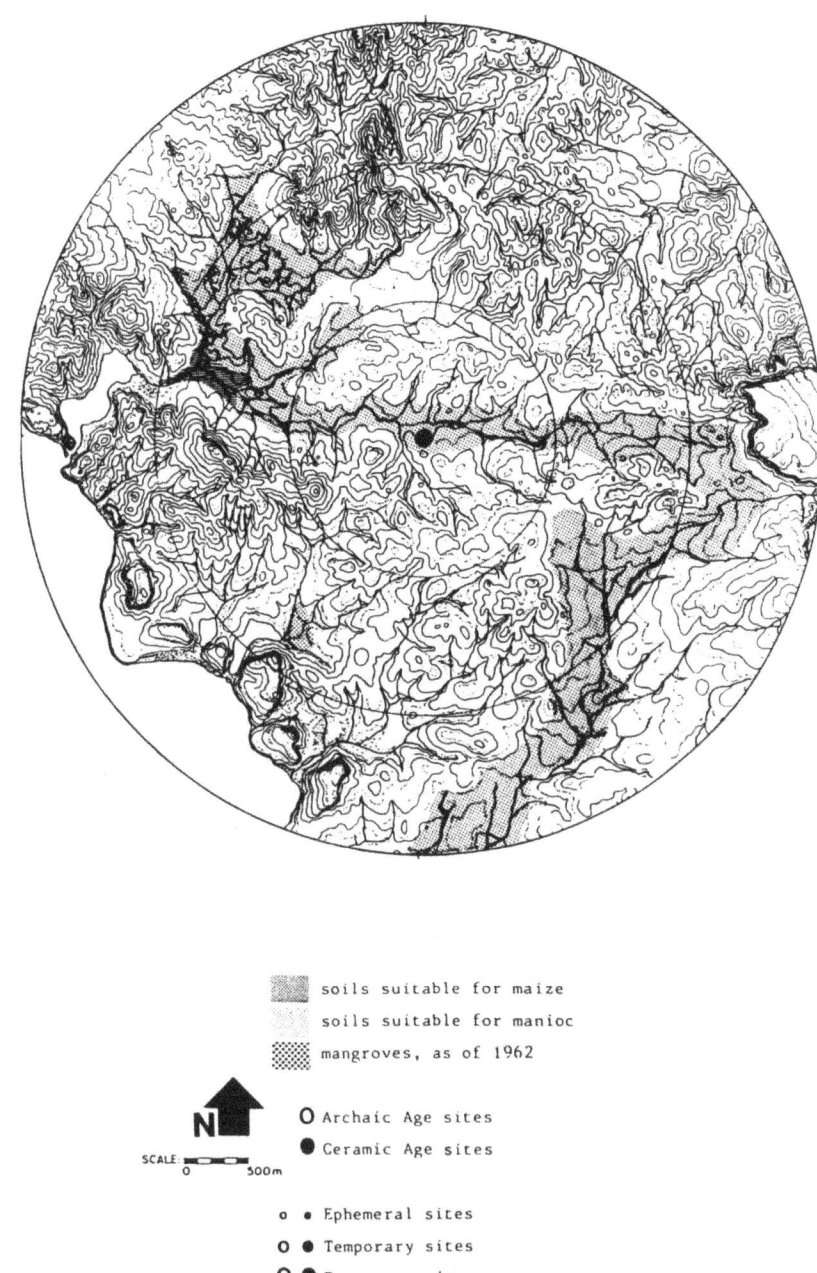

Figure 15. San Juan (C-008) catchment area.

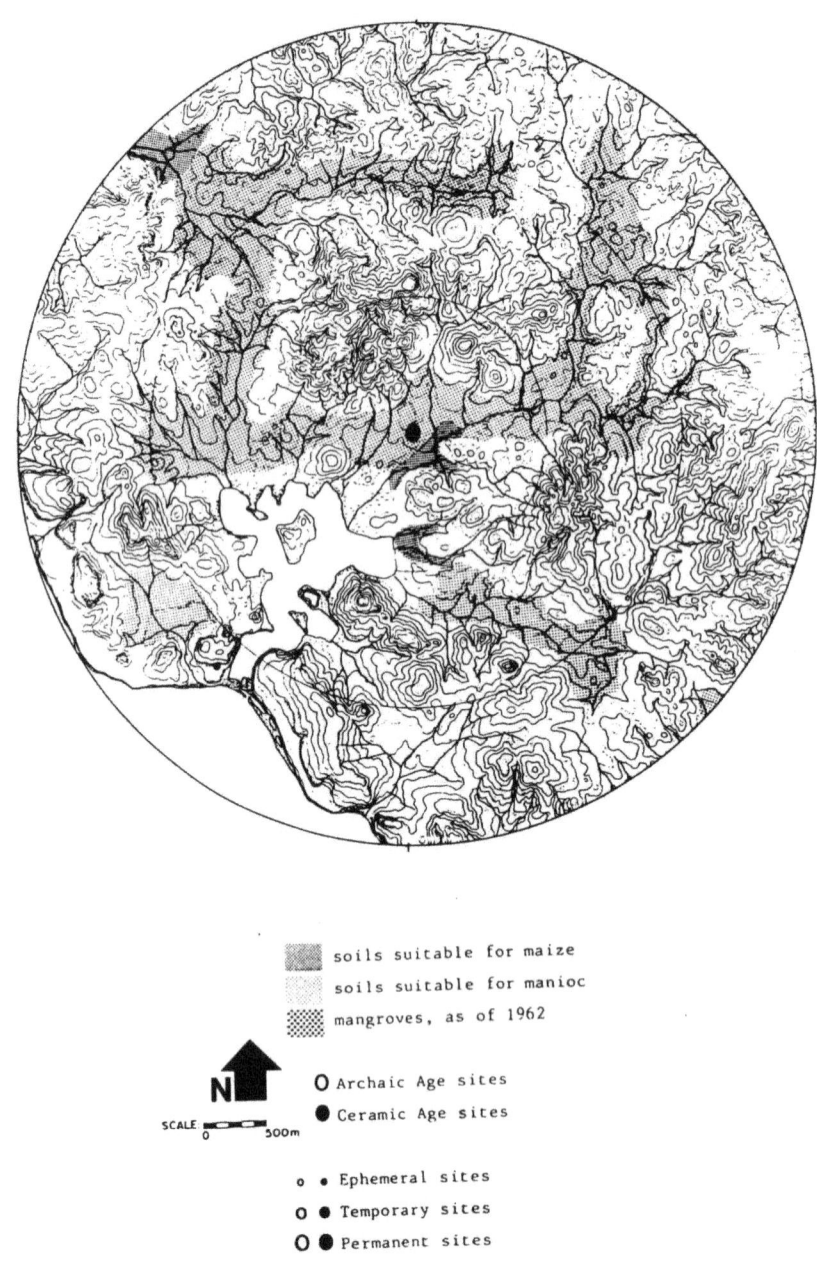

Figure 16. Santa Marta (C-007) catchment area.

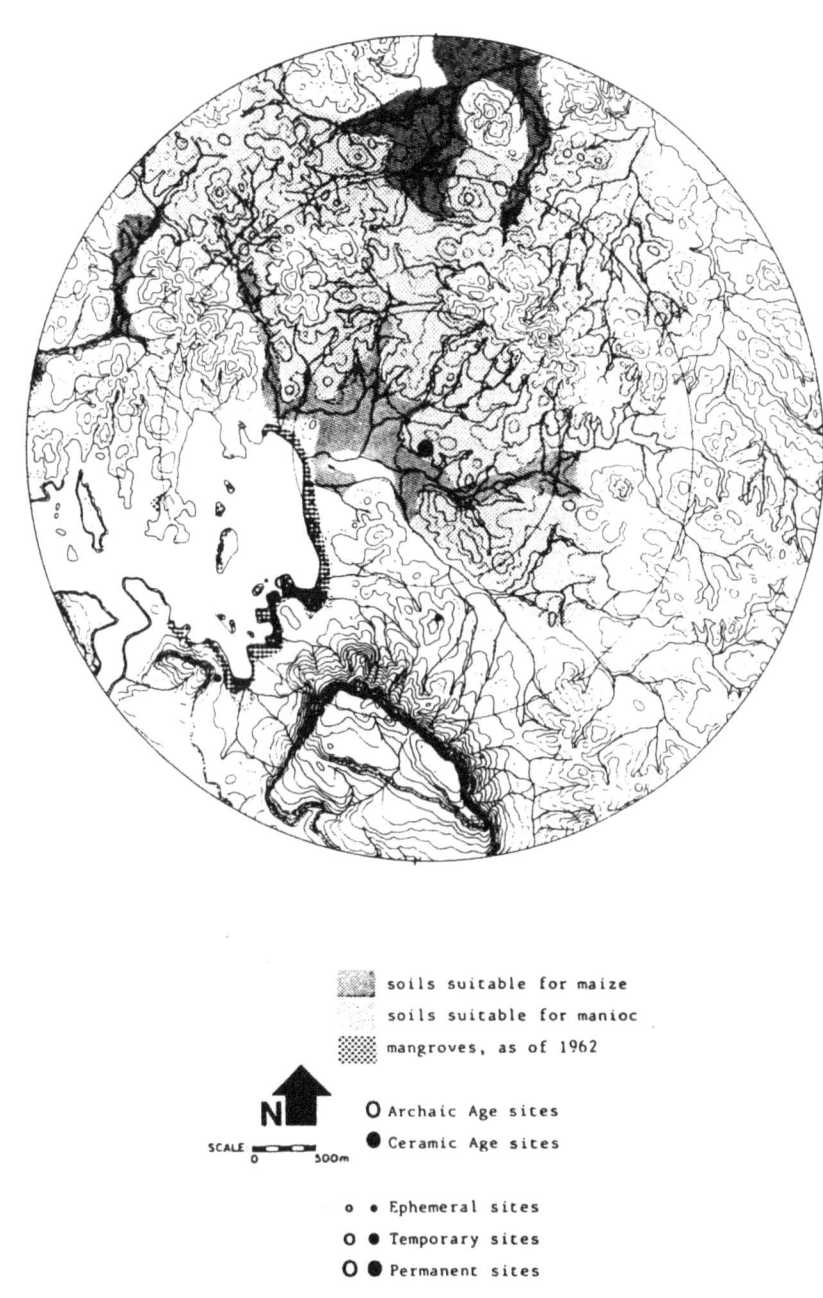

Figure 17. Santa Barbara (C-036) catchment area.

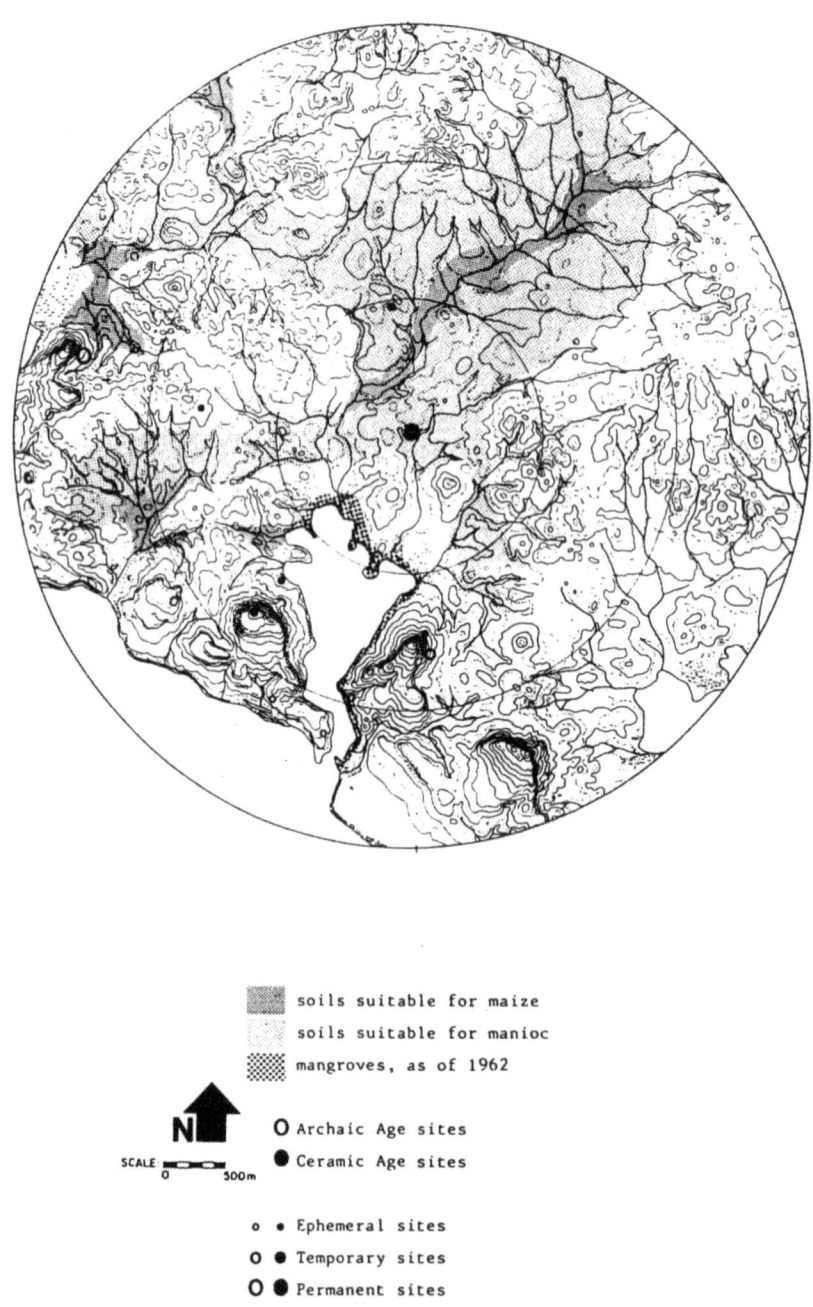

Figure 18. De Savaan (C-021) catchment area.

Figure 19. San Hironimo (C-060) catchment area.

	Combined Areas of Archaic Age 1 km. radius (105 points)		Curaçao Area Totals, approximate percentages	Combined Areas of Ceramic Age 1 km. radius (147 points)	
	n=	%		n=	%
geomorphology:					
coastal	17	16.2	11%	16	11.2
open plain/rolling hills	38	36.2	53%	114	80.3
hilly land	29	27.6	28%	10	7.0
highest hilltops	0	0.	3%	0	0.
open sea			0%		
inland bay	21	20.0	5%	2	1.5
	105	100.0	100%	142	100.0
elevation:					
0 - 49 m.	96	91.4	82 %	111	78.2
50 - 99 m.	9	8.6	15 %	24	16.9
100 - 200 m.	0	0.	2.8%	7	4.9
over 200 m.	0	0.	.2%	0	0.
	105	100.0	100 %	142	100.0
geology: (lithics/vegetation)					
Seru Domi formation	59	56.2	32%	11	7.7
Midden-Curaçao formation	9	8.5	7%	0	0.
Knip group	0	0.	9%	33	23.2
Curaçao Lava formation	37	35.2	52%	98	69.1
	105	100.0	100%	142	100.0
resource areas:					
soils for maize	8	7.6	4.7%	13	9.2
soils for manioc	12	11.4	18.6%	40	28.1
mangroves	10	9.5	1 %	2	1.5
tidal salt areas	10	9.5	1.5%	6	4.2
clay sources	2	1.9	3 %	1	.7
other	63	60.1	71.2%	80	56.3
	105	100.0	100 %	142	100.0
potable water sources	7 (1 spring)		50 potential loci (2 springs)	10	
major drainage rooi	* *		34 major drainage rooi	*******	
sites	Archaic	Ceramic	Archaic=27sites / Ceramic=49sites	Archaic	Ceramic
Ephemeral	5	2	17	38		4
Temporary	3	1	7	4		
Permanent	3		3	7		7

Figure 20. Comparison of combined age results with the calculated overall Curaçao island totals. Archaic sites used: C-013, C-015, C-023, C-035, C-039. Ceramic age sites used: C-001, C-004, C-007, C-008, C-021, C-036, C-060.

SALADOID REMAINS AND ADAPTIVE STRATEGIES

IN ST. CROIX, VIRGIN ISLANDS

Birgit Faber Morse

ABSTRACT

The St. Croix artifact collections from five major institutions have been analyzed and their typology established. At least 10 settlements have produced artifacts belonging to the Saladoid series, dating from Period II. Eight sites were within 1 km of the coast and most were located near rivers, thus providing access to both coastal and terrestrial resources. The other two were 3-4 km inland in river valleys, and one of these was upstream from the Salt River site, the largest coastal settlement and the only one with continuous habitation throughout the Ceramic age. Comparison is made with Saladoid remains and adaptive strategies in Vieques and Puerto Rico.

INTRODUCTION

St. Croix is located in the northeastern corner of the Caribbean Sea and lies about 100 km southeast of Puerto Rico, about 60 km south of St. Thomas and St. John and southeast of Vieques. The closest of the Lesser Antilles is Saba at a distance of 150 km (Figure 1). The island is 35 km long, reaches a width of 10 km and is triangular in shape. It rests upon a submarine platform and constitutes, with its outlying cays and fringing reefs, a rather isolated geographic unit (Meyerhoff 1927).

The earliest known settlers on St. Croix are the Saladoid peoples. No preceramic period has yet been documented. This is in contrast to most of the surrounding islands, where Archaic remains have been found. The aim of this paper is to tentatively reconstruct the Saladoid lifeways and adaptive strategies in St. Croix. This has been done partly by analysis of Cruzan artifact collections from five major institutions and partly by study of site locations and available subsistence data.

HISTORY OF RESEARCH

The first systematic archaeological survey of St. Croix was carried out in 1916-1917 by Theodoor deBooy for the Museum of the American Indian in New York City. It was started at the time of the United States acquisition of the Danish West Indies, which also included St. Thomas and St. John. Slightly earlier, Jesse Walter Fewkes of the Smithsonian Institution had visited St. Croix and collected artifacts from the surface of several sites. He and deBooy did not agree on some of the issues of Virgin Islands prehistory, especially over the connections Fewkes saw between the prehistoric cultures of Puerto Rico and the Virgin Islands (deBooy 1919:20; Fewkes 1922:168).

The Danish anthropologist, Gudmund Hatt, was the first to examine the stratigraphic and seriational ordering of Virgin Islands ceramics and to draw chronological conclusions. He excavated numerous sites on all three islands during 1922-1923 and divided Virgin Islands prehistory into three periods: (1) Krum Bay, which was preceramic, (2) Coral Bay-Longford, characterized by white-on-red painted pottery and (3) Magens Bay-Salt River, which had modeled-incised pottery. Hatt came to the conclusion that the early ceramics originated in the Lesser Antilles to the south and the later ceramics in the Greater Antilles to the west (Hatt 1924:33). In 1952 Irving Rouse refined the sequence and later Gary Vescelius (1979) inserted Prosperity as the initial ceramic phase in the Virgin Islands (Figure 2). This phase includes polychrome painting and complex incised designs, characterized by zoned, fine-line cross-hatching (Rouse 1982:49).

THE COLLECTIONS

During the last two years I have been able to study the St. Croix artifact collections in five major institutions and have worked on establishing their typology. The largest of the Cruzan collections are in the Danish National Museum in Copenhagen. Prehistoric artifacts from Denmark's West Indian colony began to arrive at this museum in the middle of the last century, donated by interested plantation owners and visitors; and the earliest catalogue was started at that time. Around the turn of the century Captain H. U. Ramsing of the Danish Royal Engineers undertook limited excavation in a midden at the Salt River site, which had been known for some time, and presented his findings to the museum. Shortly thereafter a Danish planter, Gustave Nordby, who for many years devoted himself to Cruzan archaeology, began to donate from his considerable collection (Yde 1947). Gudmund Hatt learned about the sites he visited and excavated on St. Croix from Nordby (Hatt 1924:30). Hatt's extensive collection is also housed at the museum. In the mid-1950s Frieda Møller Jørgensen donated artifacts excavated over a period of years from her family's properties adjacent to the Salt River and Richmond sites. The provenience for almost all these collections is good and Hatt's field notes, although not easy to read, are quite helpful in regard to his excavations at the Salt River site. Represented in these accumulated collections are Saladoid assemlages from eight different settlements.

The Virgin Islands collections at the Museum of the American Indian in New York were studied next. The largest part of the Cruzan material came from de Booy's excavation at the Salt River site in 1916-1917. From the same site are also a few stone artifacts collected by Fewkes. During the early 1920s a small collection was donated from the Richmond site (Skinner 1925). In the mid-1930s the museum sponsored an excavation, under the direction of Lewis Korn, at the Aklis site on the Concordia estate, southwest of Frederiksted. The material he recovered is kept at the museum, but nothing has yet been published about it. The provenience for the artifacts is good, and the three sites mentioned here all contain material from the Saladoid period.

The Cruzan collections in the Smithsonian Institution in Washington consist primarily of artifacts from Herbert W. Krieger's excavation there in 1937. Fewkes visited St. Croix in 1912 (Fewkes 1922) and collected a number of artifacts, but the provenience for most of these is not good. Krieger undertook excavations at four major sites on the island (Krieger 1938) and archaeological material from two of these were found to belong to the Saladoid period.

The collection housed in the National Park Service museum at Fort Christianvaern, St. Croix, was made by Folmer Andersen, an avid amateur archaeologist and administrator of the Bethlehem complex of factory and plantations, which owned the St. George estate. Andersen instructed the workmen who cultivated the fields to preserve any artifacts that they discovered. During excavation in the 1920s he acquired most of his collection not only from St. George but also from other Cruzan sites, and made careful descriptions of the ceramics and their provenience. Most of the large collection from St. George dates from the Saladoid period, and four other sites have also yielded material from the same time (Andersen 1931).

The last collection researched is at the Yale Peabody Museum. Gary Vescelius undertook a comprehensive survey of St. Croix during the summer of 1951 under the auspices of the Yale Peabody Museum and the St. Croix Museum Commission. Vescelius and his team surface collected at 35 sites and excavated about a dozen of these. His essay "The Cultural Chronology of St. Croix" was submitted to Yale as a senior thesis (Vescelius 1952). The stratigraphy of the excavations and the detailed provenience of the artifacts make this the best research collection of them all. Archaeological material from nine sites were judged to belong to the Saladoid period.

During the late 1970s when Vescelius was Territorial Archaeologist for the Virgin Islands, he and Linda Robinson excavated at the Prosperity site, St. Croix, but nothing yet has been published about the excavation. Irving Rouse (personal communication 1987) has seen the artifacts and agrees with Vescelius that some of them belong to the initial ceramic phase on the island. Linda Robinson has graciously loaned the author some of her research material from this excavation.

Upon completion of the analysis of these collections, artifact assemblages from at least 10 sites were found to contain material belonging to the Saladoid period. Most sites are represented in more than one collection and two are in all of them.

CULTURAL SEQUENCES

At the present time no preceramic period has been established on St. Croix, in contrast to St. Thomas, where the archaic Krum Bay tradition, Perod I, was discovered by Hatt (1924; Figure 2). Pottery making arrived from South America via the Lesser Antilles at the beginning of Period II. From a ceramic point of view, this epoch is characterized by a single Saladoid subseries, the Cedrosan Saladoid, which can be divided into two periods on the basis of the changes of style within them (Rouse 1986). Period IIa, the Prosperity phase, dates from before the time of Christ to A.D. 400 (as evidenced by a median date of A.D. 180 from a Cedrosan Saladoid site in St. Thomas [Rouse, this volume:Table 1]) and Period IIb, the Coral Bay-Longford phase, from A.D. 400 to 600 (Rouse 1982).

The ceramics from the Prosperity phase are considered the highest technologically on St. Croix. The thinnest sherds tend to be very fine and hard with an average thickness of only 0.5 cm, and with a small amount of fine sand as temper. Vessel forms vary greatly from bowls that can be round, boat-and kidney-shaped (Figure 3a) to bottles and jars with circular to ovoid shapes (Figure 3b). Designs are modeled, incised and/or painted. Modeling is mostly seen on lugs in zoo- and anthropomorphic forms, incision and punctation are often used to accentuate features (Figure 3c).

Diagnostic traits of the Prosperity phase ceramic designs include the use of incision to create cross-hatched zones (Figure 3d,e,f), polychrome painting (Figure 4a) and modeling-incision (Figure 3c). All three features had disappeared by the end of Period IIa. Besides the type site only three other Cruzan settlements, St. George, Richmond and Salt River, have yielded ceramics from this initial Saladoid phase.

White-on-red painted pottery continued through the later Coral Bay-Longford phase (Figure 4b,c) but seems to have died out by A.D. 600, leaving only monochrome painting and plain modeled lugs. All 10 settlements have material belonging to Period IIb, and none of them are known to have been abandoned at the close of this phase. In fact, many new villages were established around the old sites during Period IIIa, suggesting that the older centers generated a number of satellite communities (Vescelius 1952).

Included in both Hatt's and Vescelius's Saladoid collections are a number of other types of artifacts. Both had numerous plain thick sherds of clay griddles used for baking, and stone artifacts for hammering and grinding, as well as rectangular adzes and petaloid celts made from green-grey indigenous rock. Further, the Hatt collection contains several plain three-pointed stones and perforated stone beads from the Richmond and Salt River sites (Figure 4d,e). The Prosperity site yielded several beautiful small frog figures of green-blue and yellowish-brown stones (Hatt 1941; Figure 4f). During Vescelius's excavations there in the late 1970s many complete, fragmentary and unfinished examples of beads and pendants were discovered in semiprecious, imported material, such as amethyst, carnelian, and garnet (Vescelius and Robinson 1979).

ENVIRONMENTAL SETTING

The shoreline of St. Croix has changed over the last 10,000 years, and where earlier a submergence had taken place, it is possible that this was followed by a very slight emergence. Many recent beach deposits have accumulated along the coast, particularly at the island's southwestern point (Figure 5). This is due to erosion on the windward or easterly side and subsequent current transport and deposition of sediment on the leeward side (Cederstrom 1941). Several bays and estuaries have been closed off by sand beach and barrier-reef growth, and the lagoon behind eventually ended up as swamp. Krause Lagoon and Great Pond on the south shore are examples of this evolutionary process (Figure 5).

The Prosperity settlement was located about 0.5 km inland on the west coast on a slightly raised plateau. Part of the land between the site and shore is swampy, and may well have been an estuary two millennia ago that gradually became landlocked. Changes in relative sea level and in the shoreline should therefore be taken into account when archaeologists are looking for early ceramic and preceramic sites on St. Croix, since these could be buried in sand and other sediments.

Within its area of less than 220 km^2 the island is divisible into several geographic zones, whose character must have had a considerable effect upon the early prehistoric settlements. The two major physiographic areas are: (1) the late Cretaceous Oldland, underlain by rock of volcanic origin, and (2) the central Kingshill Plain, based upon tertiary marls and limestones, which divides the Oldland into a northwestern and eastern part. Part of the latter area is covered by alluvium (Cederstrom 1941; Figure 5).

Presently, the climate is subtropical with moderate to limited rainfall and lies within the belt of northeast tradewinds. The daily temperature fluctuations seldom exceed 6-7° C, and the mean varies between 25° C in February to 29° C in September. Many different floral environments, ranging from arid brush through beach and savanna types to tropical rainforest, characterize the different sections of the island (Lassen 1896).

ADAPTIVE STRATEGIES

Prehistoric artifacts and sites have been found in almost every sector of the island. The only exceptions are the eastern Oldland and the central Kingshill Plain. Most of the sites are situated on or near the coast and in the vicinity of sheltered bays, reefs, or small islands (Hatt 1924:30).

Eight of the 10 settlements that have produced artifacts from the Saladoid period are located within 1 km of the present coast. Two of these, Salt River and Richmond, are directly on the north coast of the island. The other six, including Prosperity and Sprat Hall on the west coast and Aklis, Longford, Fairham and Great Pond on the south shore are up to 1 km inland. They are near streams and/or close to lagoons on flat, cultivable land. The final two Saladoid settlements are situated 3-4 km inland in fertile river valleys, one, St. George with easy access to the south, while the other, Glynn, has access to the north coast (Figure 5). Glynn is upstream from the Salt River site, the largest coastal settlement on St. Croix and the only one with continuous habitation throughout the Ceramic and Historic ages.

All 10 sites are situated either on alluvial soil or near river valleys whose deltas were filled with alluvium (Figure 5). Apparently, the early Saladoid people chose locations with access to both coastal and terrestrial resources, thus meeting the requirements for both fishing and horticulture. Probably, they settled in the same kind of microenvironments from which they had come. Therefore, it is important to examine Saladoid remains not only in terms of their artifactual traits but also in terms of their distinctive settlement patterns and subsistence systems, which are evidenced by their site locational and compositional characteristics (Watters and Rouse, this volume).

Most archaeological sites on St. Croix consist of rather shallow middens and many of them have been ploughed or otherwise disturbed. According to Vescelius (1952) a few deeper deposits were stratified and he was able to correlate particular strata with specific cultural periods. Many deposits are dispersed over a large area, resulting in horizontal rather than vertical separation of the different time periods.

During deBooy's excavation on the island in 1917 he collected a certain number of unmodified shells and bones from the midden at Salt River, which later were submitted to specialists for identification. The findings were published in the monograph on his work, but he only made a few remarks as to the amount of certain types of faunal remains at the site and who had identified them (deBooy 1919).

Hatt tried to do some shell sampling during his excavation at Salt River in 1923, which he mentioned in his field notes, but these were not particularly systematic either. In Puerto Rico, Rainey (1940) differentiated between what he called the *Crab* and the *Shell* cultures, associating the first with the early ceramic period, which still holds some validity today.

Vescelius saved the animal remains from certain excavation units at three major sites during his excavations in 1951. One sample comes from the lower stratum of a midden at the Richmond site, which dates from late in Period IIa. Shell accounted for over 96% of the sample by weight, two-thirds of which was the large conch (*Strombus gigas*), while bone was estimated to be only 3% of the total (Vescelius 1952).

In 1976 a small excavation took place at Glynn, the Period IIb inland site, located on a slope upstream from Salt River. An analysis of the mollusk shell assemblage discovered here was carried out by Robinson (1976). Her findings of a maximum of 32 marine genera and 41 species indicate that the prehistoric settlers here were exploiting three types of shallow marine environments: (1) a mangrove swamp with associated mudflats, (2) a grass-covered sand bed and (3) an exposed rocky shore. The closest mangrove area is located at the outlet of Salt River into Sugar Bay (Figure 5), over 2 km from the settlement. This type of environment is a source for over two-thirds of the total mollusk specimens, of which the two most important elements are the West Indian Pointed Venus (*Anomalocardia brasiliana*), a small sturdy shell, and the Caribbean oyster (*Crassostrea rhizophorae*) (Warmke and Abbott 1961). Glynn is nearly 4 km from the closest reef-protected rocky shore at Salt River Point, and about 5 km from an open sandy shore - the other two types of environments that are represented by the rest of the mollusk specimens (Robinson 1976).

On the basis of Vescelius's and Robinson's excavations at the Prosperity site in the late 1970s, it was noted that blue land crabs (*Cardisoma guanhumi*) are abundant in the earlier

Saladoid period and not so common in the later one. Crab remains increased significantly in most excavation units at about 50-65 cm below ground surface, and the claws were larger in the lowest levels. In the more densely packed middens the crab claws often represent up to 85% of the average invertebrate assemblage - by count of minimum number of individuals. Frequently, the rise in crab refuse is accompanied by a reduction in landsnail remains, possibly indicating that a change in vegetation or human activity occurred at this time (Linda Robinson, personal communication 1987). Vescelius (1979) mentions that bivalves comprise less than 5% of the average shell assemblage by count; whereas univalves are much more numerous, representing more than 80 kinds of gastropod - none of which were especially important, except for the ever-present conch and welk (*Cittarium pica*). This diversity is also a feature of the Saladoid shell assemblages from Hacienda Grande in Puerto Rico (Rouse and Alegría 1989) and the Sorcé site on Vieques (Chanlatte Baik and Narganes Storde 1983).

The number of marine mollusk species represented in the Saladoid deposits at Prosperity is very similar to a modern specimen collection, with the exception of the Virgin Neriti (*Neritina virginea*), a lagoonal and brackish water dweller, whose natural habitat disappeared at some point in the past. Vertebrate remains are also present in the assemblage, but in small quantities and for the most part are represented by medium and small fishes and some rodents (Linda Robinson, personal communication 1987).

COMPARISON

No radiocarbon dates are available from the excavations at the Prosperity site or from other Cedrosan Saladoid assemblages on St. Croix, but we have the earlier mentioned date from St. Thomas, 60 km to the north (A.D. 180). Vieques is located at the same distance to the northwest and Puerto Rico slightly farther away (Figure 1), and from both islands many new dates are available relating to the two Saladoid subseries (Rouse and Alegría 1989:Tables 8,9).

Vescelius and Robinson (1979) felt that the deposits from Prosperity quite confidently could be dated on the basis of the pottery they contained and named it the Prosperity style. It is closely related to the Hacienda Grande style of Puerto Rico and the La Hueca style of Vieques and to various other Saladoid styles of the eastern Caribbean.

The Prosperity style pottery is classified into three kinds: (1) plain ware, (2) painted ware, combining up to three color designs and curvilinear incisions and (3) the zoned incised crosshatched (zic) pottery. The three wares are found within the same excavation units at Prosperity (Linda Robinson, personal communication 1987). At Richmond and Salt River the first two wares were found during Vescelius's excavations in 1952. The zic pottery from these sites is represented in the Andersen and Jørgensen collections but its specific location is not mentioned. The St. George settlement extended over a large area and Andersen (1954) undertook excavation in four different fields. All three ceramic wares are present in the collection, but it is not known if they were found together or in separate areas.

The Sorcé and St. George sites are similar in several respects. Both are located inland near small rivers or streams and compete with each other in richness of ceramics and ornaments. At Sorcé, however, the zic ware was discovered without painted ware in the La Hueca component of the settlement (Chanlatte Baik 1983).

Beads and pendants of semi-precious stones were found in the early Saladoid assemblages on both St. Croix and Puerto Rico, and a large deposit was discovered on the island of Montserrat in the Lesser Antilles (Harrington 1924). The exotic material of these ornaments does not seem to be indigenous to the islands and suggests inter-island trade among the early inhabitants from as far away as the coast of South America.

CONCLUDING REMARKS

This research shows that at least 10 Cedrosan Saladoid Cruzan settlements existed during Period II. Only four sites have yielded archaeological material from the initial Prosperity phase, Period IIa, while all 10 were represented during Period IIb (Figure 2).

This study corroborates established findings in the Puerto Rican area in regards to artifacts, site locations and certain subsistence data. There is, however, a great need for further information, particularly radiocarbon dates, in order to link temporally the early Saladoid settlements of St. Croix with those in Puerto Rico and the Lesser Antilles. The Salt River site, the largest coastal settlement on St. Croix, seems to be the one site that still has the most archaeological material available, and it is the only one known to have been inhabited throughout the Ceramic age (Vescelius 1952). A thorough investigation of this settlement undoubedtly will yield important information regarding the time-space systematics of the early Ceramic age in this portion of the Caribbean.

Acknowledgments. I wish to thank the Danish National Museum, the Yale Peabody Museum, the Museum of the American Indian, the Smithsonian Institution and the National Park Service museum in St. Croix and their curatorial staffs for help in facilitating access to their Cruzan artifact collections. I am also grateful to Heidy Fogel for help in drafting and William Sacco for photographic assistance. Linda Robinson was very helpful in providing drawings and unpublished data, for which I am most appreciative. My deepest appreciation goes to Professor Irving Rouse for his constructive advice and encouragement throughout this project.

REFERENCES CITED

Andersen, Folmer
    1931   Catalogue of Archaeological Collection from St. Croix. Ms. on file, St. Croix Museum, Christiansted, St. Croix, Virgin Islands.

    1954   *Notes on St. Croix*. St. Croix Museum Collection. Christiansted, St. Croix, Virgin Islands.

Cederstrom, D.J.
    1941   Notes on Physiography of St. Croix, Virgin Islands. *American Journal of Science* 239:553-576.

Chanlatte Baik, Luis A.
    1983   *Catálogo arqueología de Vieques: exposición del 13 de Marzo al 22 de Abril de 1983*. Museo de Anthropología, Historia y Arte. Universidad de Puerto Rico, Río Piedras.

Chanlatte Baik, Luis A. and Yvonne M. Narganes Storde
    1983   *Vieques-Puerto Rico: asiento de una nueva cultura aborigen Antillana*. Privately printed, Santo Domingo.

deBooy, Theodoor
    1919   *Archaeology of the Virgin Islands*. Indian Notes and Monographs, vol.1(1). Museum of the American Indian Heye Foundation, New York.

Fewkes, Jesse Walter
    1922 *A Prehistoric Island Culture Area of America*. Bureau of American Ethnology Bulletin No. 34. Smithsonian Institution, 1912-1913, pp. 35-281. Government Printing Office, Washington, D.C.

Harrington, Mark R.
    1924 A West Indian Gem Center. *Museum of the American Indian Heye Foundation Indian Notes* 1(4):184-89.

Hatt, Gudmund
    1924 Archaeology of the Virgin Islands. *Proceedings of the International Congress of Americanists* 21(1):29-42.

    1941 Had West Indian Rock Carvings a Religious Significance? *Nationalmuseets Skrifter, Etnografisk Række* 1:165-202.

Krieger, Herbert W.
    1938 Archaeology of the Virgin Islands. *Smithsonian Explorations* 1937:95-102.

Lassen, Holger
    1895-1896 Momenter af Vestindiens Geografi. *Geografisk Tidskrift* 13:60-85.

Meyerhoff, Howard A.
    1927 *The Physiography of the Virgin Islands, Culebra and Vieques*. Scientific Survey of Porto Rico and the Virgin Islands, vol. IV. The New York Academy of Sciences, New York.

Rainey, Froelich G.
    1940 *Porto Rican Archaeology*. Scientific Survey of Porto Rico and the Virgin Islands, vol. XVIII-part 1. The New York Academy of Sciences, New York.

Robinson, Linda S.
    1976 Analysis of a Mollusk Shell Assemblage from Glynn I, St. Croix. Government of the Virgin Islands of the United States. *Office of the Territorial Archaeologist Bulletin* 15:1-9.

Rouse, Irving
    1952 *Porto Rico Prehistory: Introduction; Excavations in the West and North*. Scientific Survey of Porto Rico and the Virgin Islands, vol. XVIII-part 3. The New York Academy of Sciences, New York.

    1982 Ceramic and Religious Development in the Greater Antilles. *Journal of New World Archaeology* 5(2):45-55.

    1986 *Migrations in Prehistory: Inferring Population Movement from Cultural Remains*. Yale University Press, New Haven.

Rouse, Irving and Ricardo E. Alegría
    1989 *Excavations at María de la Cruz Cave and Hacienda Grande, Loiza, Puerto Rico*. Yale University Publications in Anthropology, New Haven, in press.

Skinner, Alanson
    1925 Archaeological Specimen from St. Croix, Virgin Islands. *Museum of the American Indian Heye Foundation Indian Notes* 2:109-115.

Vescelius, Gary S.
    1952 *The Cultural Chronology of St. Croix.* Unpublished senior honor thesis, Department of Anthropology, Yale University, New Haven.

    1979 Archaeology of the Virgin Islands,1: Changing Patterns of Resource Utilization. Ms. on file, Department of Anthropology, Peabody Museum, Yale University, New Haven.

Vescelius, Gary S. and Linda S. Robinson
    1979 Exotic Items in Archaeological Collections from St. Croix: Prehistoric Imports and their Implications. Ms. on file, Department of Anthropology, Peabody Museum, Yale University, New Haven.

Warmke, Germaine L. and Abbott, R. Tucker
    1961 *Caribbean Seashells.* Livingston, Narberth, Pennsylvania.

Yde, Jens
    1947 *En Vaerdiful Gave fra Vestindien.* Nationalmuseets Arbejdsmark, Nordisk Forlag, Copenhagen.

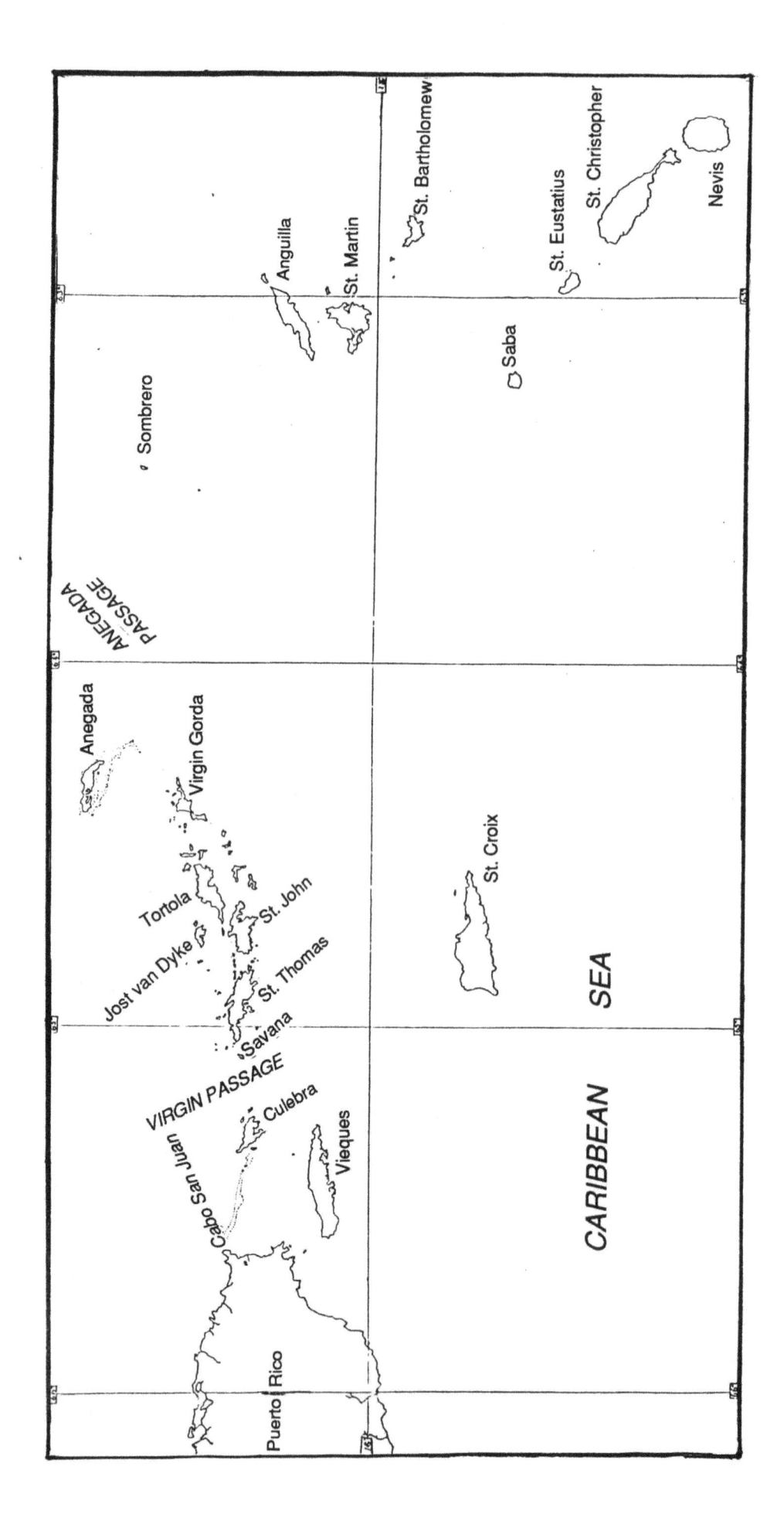

Figure 1. The geographic position of St. Croix in the Caribbean Sea.

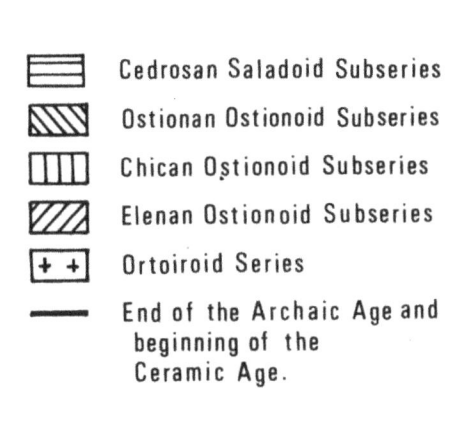

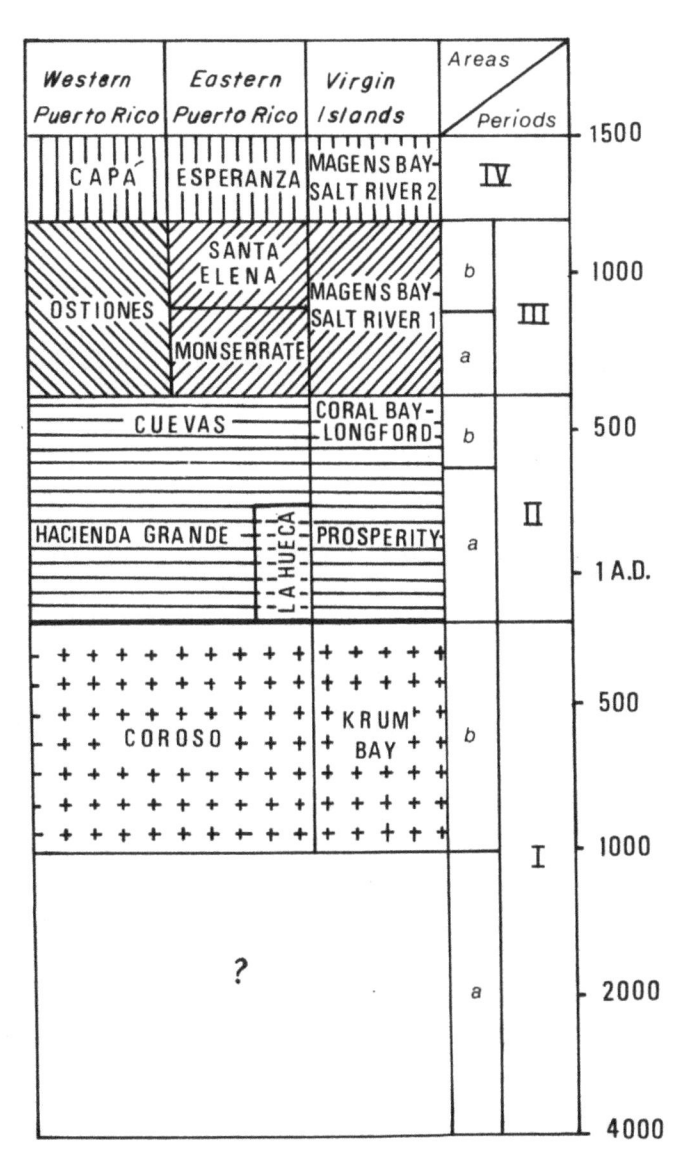

Figure 2. Periods and culture areas in Puerto Rico and the Virgin Islands (from Rouse, this volume:Figure 3).

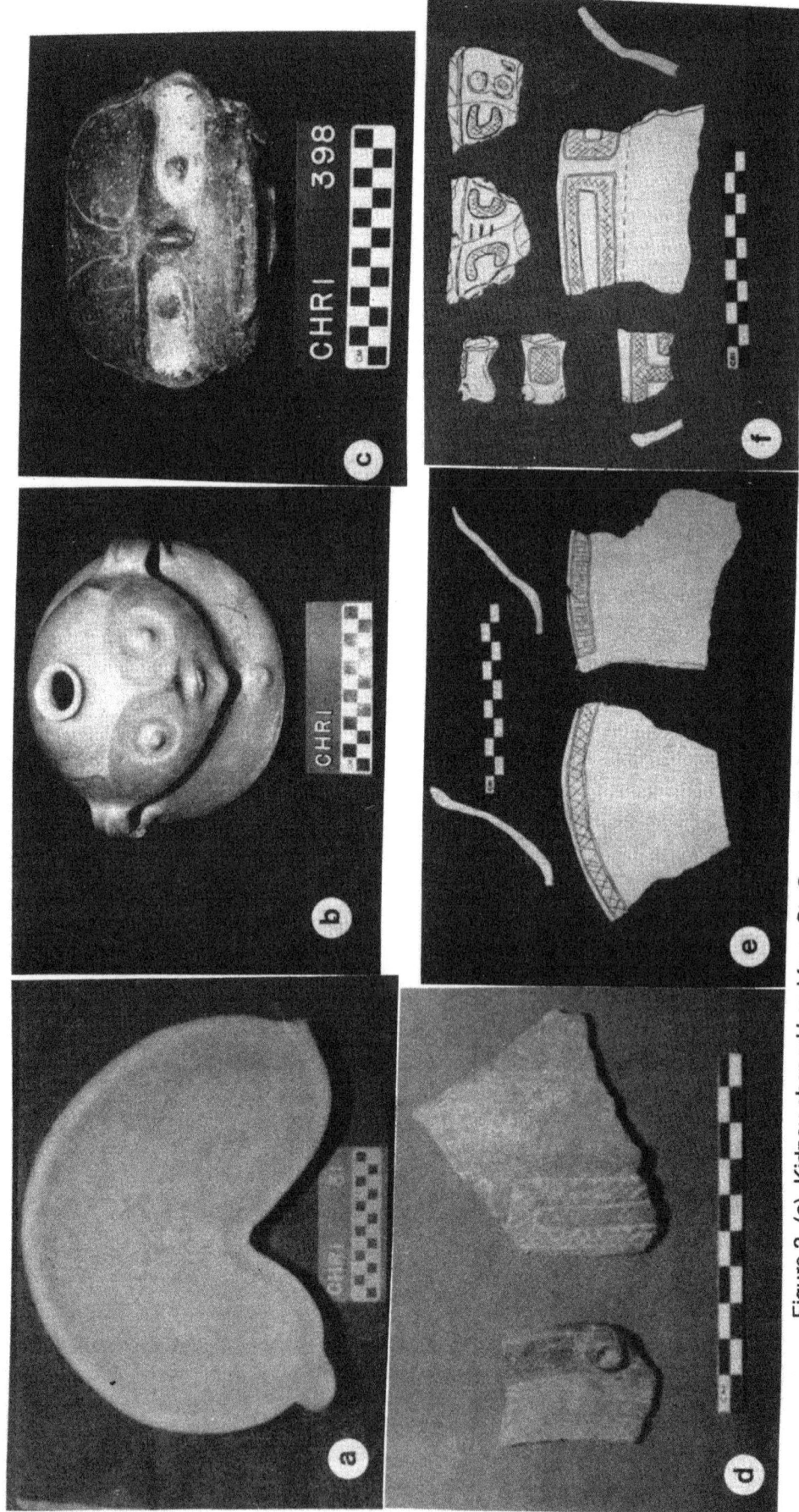

Figure 3. (a) Kidney-shaped bowl from St. George (St. Croix Museum). (b) Jar with circular to ovoid shape from St. George (St. Croix Museum). (c) Partially restored bowl with modeling-incision from Prosperity (St. Croix Museum). (d) Sherds with simple zic incision and coffee bean knob from Richmond and Salt River (Danish National Museum). (e) Sherds with simple zic incision from Prosperity (drawing by Linda Robinson). (f) Sherds with complex zic incision and coffee bean knobs from St. George (drawing by Linda Robinson).

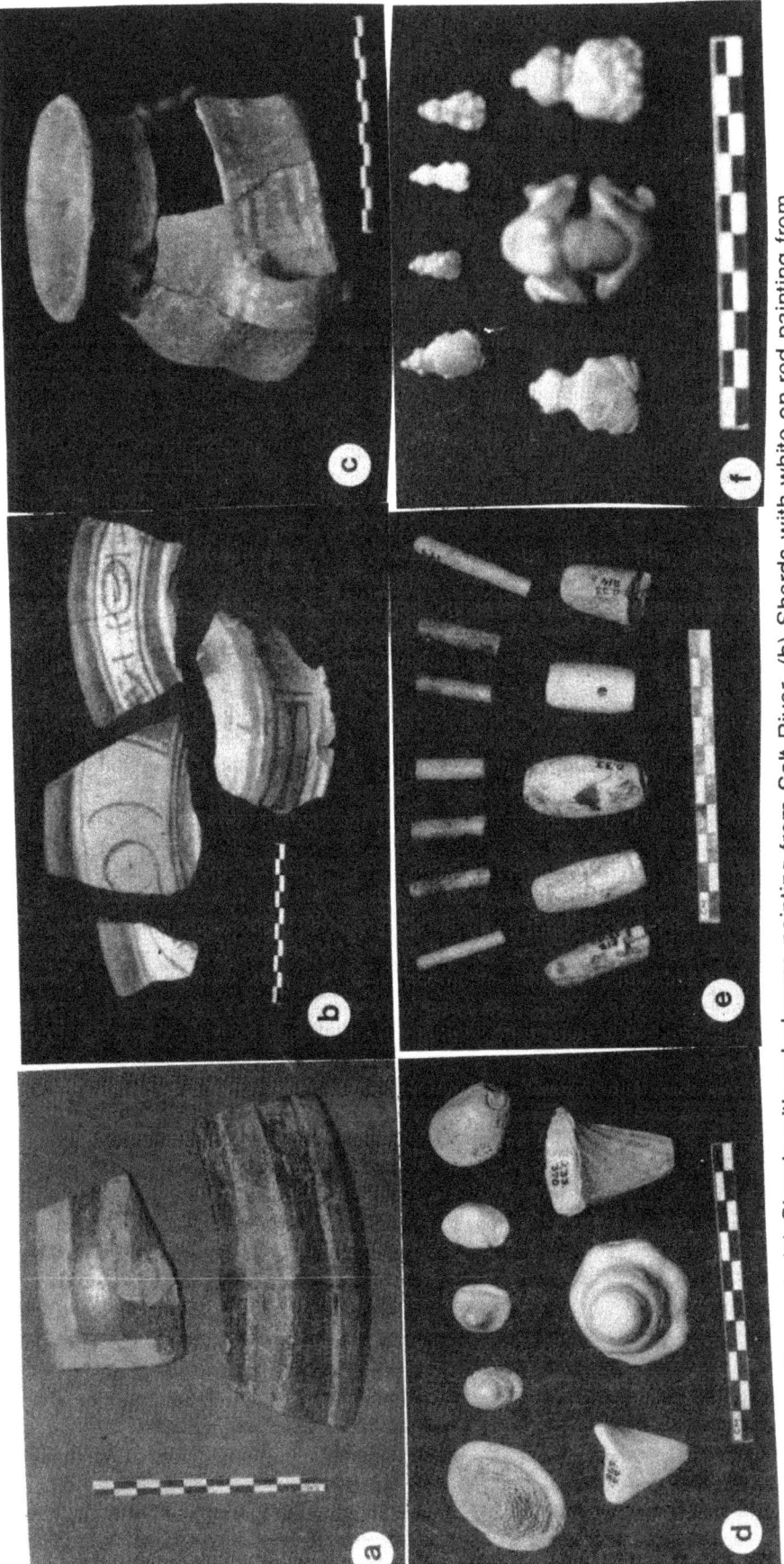

Figure 4. (a) Sherds with polychrome painting from Salt River. (b) Sherds with white-on-red painting from Longford. (c) Partially restored bowl with white-on-red painting from Salt River. (d) Three-pointed zemis of stone, shell and coral from Richmond and Salt River. (e) Perforated stone beads from Richmond and Salt River. (f) Frog figurines of stone from Prosperity. (Danish National Museum)

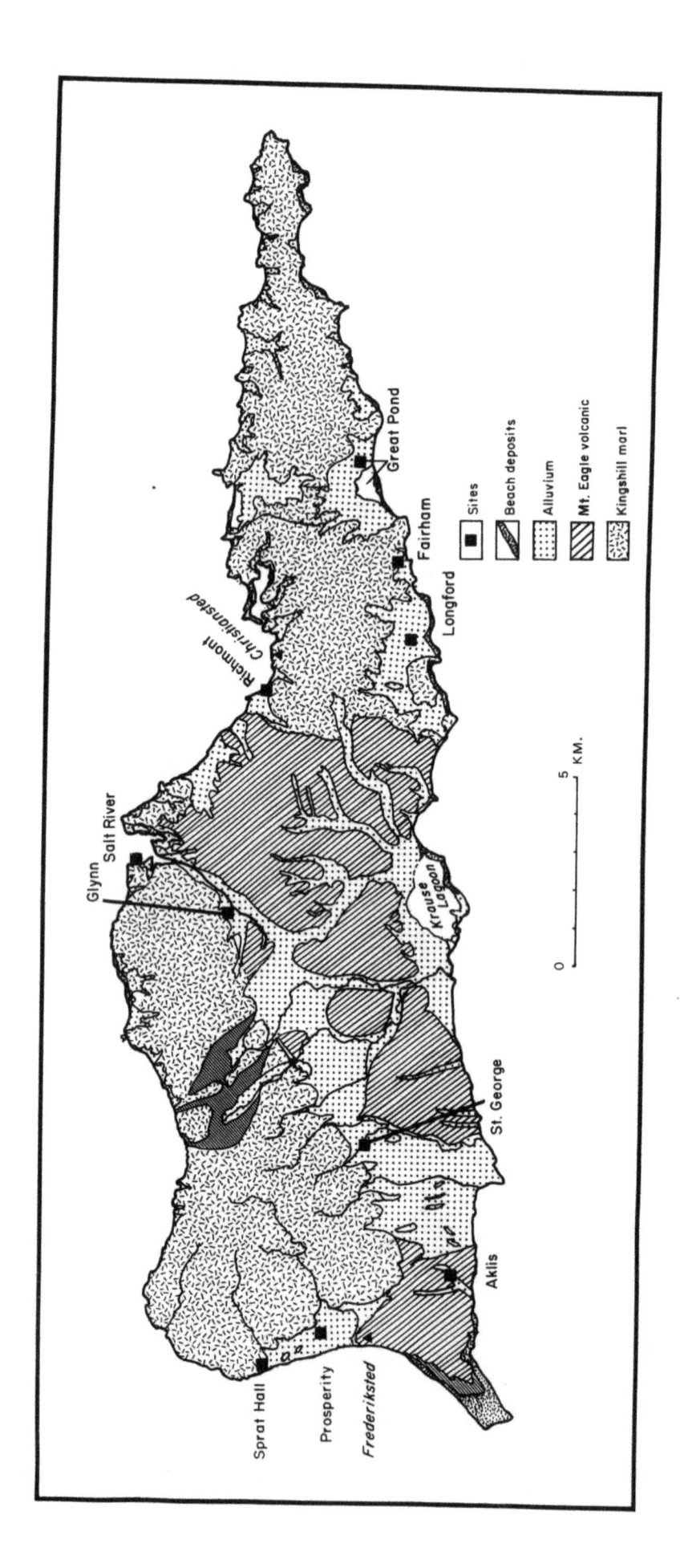

Figure 5. Geological map of St. Croix, Virgin Islands (from Cederstrom 1941). Archaeological sites have been added.

THE DATING OF EXCAVATION LEVELS USING ANIMAL REMAINS:

A PROPOSED SCHEME FOR INDIAN CREEK

Alick R. Jones

ABSTRACT

Detailed analysis of the faunal remains from the Indian Creek site, Antigua, together with published data on pottery styles and radiocarbon dates from the same site, has lead to the identification of at least seven chronological phases (A-G). The existence of these phases suggest that different parts of the midden represent different periods of occupation. Any one section of the midden shows two or three distinct periods of deposition. As a group the seven phases have been provisionally dated between A.D.150-1120, and each contains a characteristic assemblage of faunal remains. Although the scheme will need to be tested against new C-14 dates from future excavation, it should enable investigators of this midden to date relatively small samples to within about a 100 year period. Similar analyses could equally well be applied to other West Indian middens. Such detailed examination of animal remains not only assists with dating and stratigraphy but also reveals useful information on changing patterns of resource exploitation.

INTRODUCTION

Rainey's (1940) classic work on Caribbean middens emphasised their uniformity especially in respect of the crab/shell transition that has so much taken the attention of Antillean archaeologists. Despite the fact that the transition takes place at different times on different islands and that it does not always involve the same species of crab (Goodwin 1980; Jones 1985) study of the transition is a phenomenon that has given us a sense of common purpose. However I suspect that the simplicity of the concept has obscured and distracted us from subtleties hidden in the animal remains of the middens. This paper seeks to do two things: first, to demonstrate that within the crude subdivisions of the faunal record that we already recognise, a greater degree of resolution can be achieved, and second, to put that more detailed account of animal exploitation to use as a means of disentangling, at least to some extent, the stratigraphy and chronology of those parts of the Indian Creek midden that have been excavated.

Harris (1979:xi) has written "The notion that the features of an archaeological site may be found in a stratified state, the one layer or feature upon the other, is of first importance in the investigation of ... our past..." In stratigraphical terms the problems posed by the Indian Creek midden are of course trivial as there seems to have been very little disturbance of the site subsequent to deposition and almost nothing by way of later, infilled pits. The only complication which has arisen in some areas is that of human burials (Desmond Nicholson, personal communication 1977) but these did not occur in the excavations reported in this paper. The problem of Indian Creek, and I suspect many other West Indian middens, is that of a discontinuous record. Worse still, the discontinuities occur at different time points in different parts of the midden. Doubtless, this difficulty could be overcome by detailed radiocarbon dating. However this would be expensive, prohibitively so if a large scale excavation of this large site were to be undertaken. Pottery sherds are plentiful at the site and they too can be used to establish approximate dates. However, the published work on Indian Creek pottery (Rouse 1976) suggests that this approach would only give us approximate dates within broad time bands. Thus, for example, Mill Reef pottery has been associated with radiocarbon dates ranging from A.D. 445 to 1165. No doubt detailed examination of the pottery and other artifacts could narrow the probable date of a given level. Nonetheless this approach would seem to be time-consuming both in the field (to obtain sufficient material) and in the laboratory, whilst in the final analysis it is unlikely to be particularly accurate.

An alternative strategy proposed, and tested, here is that the animal remains vary sufficiently with time to provide relatively fine temporal resolution from fairly small samples (less than 0.01 m^3). For Indian Creek, and I suspect for most other sites, the success of this method depends not on single indicator species but on the analysis of the whole assemblage, even sometimes on the average size of skeletal elements. Just as this method is based on an examination of all of the animal remains, so it must be recognised that these stand in the context of the other materials recovered and the other tests available. The most accurate dating will clearly result from the broadest possible approach.

SITE AND METHODS

The site at Indian Creek, Antigua, and its context have been described by Olsen (1974), Rouse (1976), and Jones (1985). In 1973 Yale University and the Antigua Archeological Society excavated six pits at Indian Creek under the supervision of Dr. Irving Rouse. The excavations, usually 16 m^2 in surface area, followed 25 cm artificial levels and were up to 1.5 m deep. Jones (1980a, 1980b, 1985) carried out two series of much smaller excavations in 1977-1978 and 1979, which were primarily for faunal analysis. These excavations had a surface extent of either 0.0625 m^2 or 0.5 m^2 and utilised arbitrary levels having half the depth of Rouse's, i.e. 12.5 cm. All figures for the faunal remains quoted in this paper are for a volume of 25 x 25 x 12.5 cm (7812 cm^3), which is equivalent to the volume of earth excavated in each level of the 1977-1978 dig. These excavations were dug in the walls of three of Rouse's pits so that a reasonable correspondence can be assumed to exist between Rouse's and Jones's levels. To assist in comparing the two data sets the numbering of levels as used by Rouse has been retained by Jones, except that of course there are two of the latter's for each of the former's leading to Jones's designation of, for example, 3a and 3b for Rouse's 3. The only departure from this scheme is in Jones's pit I where levels 1 and 2 were, as with Rouse, 25 cm deep. Pits I, II and III are respectively pits 5, 6 and 4 of Rouse (1976).

All of the faunal data used in this report derive from the 1977-1978 and 1979 excavations. The methods used for obtaining the material are given in full in Jones (1985) and some of the data presented in that paper are used here. Information on radiocarbon dates and pottery styles is from Rouse (1976).

RESULTS

Figure 1 and Table 1 summarize a hypothesised sequence for those parts of the Indian Creek midden excavated from pits I, II and III of Jones (1985), respectively 5, 6 and 4 of Rouse (1976). What follows is a summary of the evidence in support of this sequence. The divisions of time, here termed "phases," will be treated in the order of the supposed chronology and ordered alphabetically. Each phase also has a roman numeral to identify the pit from which the material came and a number indicating whether it is the first, second or third phase to be identified from that pit (first if earliest). Thus "Phase D [Pit I(2)]" is fourth in the overall sequence, derives from Pit I and is the second oldest phase to be identified from that pit.

Phase A [Pit II(1)]

This is the earliest faunal material excavated as determined by four radiocarbon dates ranging from A.D. 185-280. The animal material is varied and plentiful averaging 594 g per level. In its earliest period it contains very high numbers of crab chelae (ca. 30), rice rat bones (ca. 60) and fish vertebrae (ca. 30 per level) but these numbers decrease so that by the end of this phase they are in the region of one-half to one-third of the initial values. Vertebrate remains constitute (by weight) a large percentage of the total of crab shell, bivalve shell and vertebrate bones (CBV) (Figure 3), and this is the only phase from which bird bones were recovered. All the crab remains come from *Cardisoma* and bivalves are absent. Pottery from similar levels nearby have been classified by Rouse as Late Indian Creek. The material from this phase constitutes a considerable depth totalling about 0.75 m although it would appear from the C-14 dates to span only about 100 years. This suggests that there was considerable localisation of the population to this part of the site (at least for their garbage disposal) around the second and third centuries A.D. None of the other pits on the site yielded C-14 dates for this period. It would seem likely that the earlier settlers at Indian Creek had moved to the locality of this pit from the outlying area excavated by Rouse (1976) and labelled by him pit 1. Charcoal from this shallow section of the midden yielded C-14 dates of A.D. 35 and 95 along with pottery classified as Early Indian Creek. The *subjective* impression of phase A is one of richness and plenty in terms of the quality and quantity of both artifacts and food remains. Things were never again so beautiful nor life so easy at Indian Creek.

Phase B [Pit I(1)]

The earliest C-14 date for this phase is A.D. 445 but that is not from the lowest material, which may be 50 or so years older. Whereas in phase A rice rat bones were about double the number of fish vertebrae at any one level, here fish vertebrae are clearly more plentiful. They are also larger than those found in most of the earlier phase having an average centrum diameter of 9.5 mm. Although there is still little evidence of bivalves (only a few *Donax* and *Codakia*), the vertebrates now constitute a lower proportion of total CBV (Figure 2). The pottery is still regarded as Late Indian Creek. What is assumed to be the upper part of this phase and the bottom of the next one in this pit (level 5a) coincides with two samples of charcoal dated at A.D. 445 and 720; evidence suggestive of an interface representing a time gap in the record. Thus this phase would appear to cover a period from the late fourth to perhaps the early sixth centuries.

Phase C [Pit III(1)]

Pit III is the most difficult to interpret. Its earliest C-14 date is A.D. 685 and the pottery from the lower levels belong to the Mill Reef style. The animal remains are relatively sparse, usually less than 200 g per level. However, what there is from the lower levels is similar in many ways to Phase D, to which the C-14 dates link it. In particular there is a small percentage, usually less than 10% of CBV, of non-oyster bivalves especially *Donax* and *Brachidontes* (Figure 4). Unfortunately time did not permit a second excavation at this part of the site in 1979 so that no data are available on the breakdown of the vertebrate material. In total these seem not to be plentiful in comparison to the other major components. One curious feature of this phase is the large weight of gastropods (other than top-shells) recovered, mostly of *Nerita* spp. In light of two carbon dates from A.D. 685 and 810 and the similarity of the faunal remains to ninth century material from pit 1 (see below) it would seem we can be confident in placing this material in a 150-year period spanning late seventh to early ninth centuries. The general impression of the material from this pit is one that contrasts with the richness of pit 2. Even when there are deposits apparently contemporary with those of other pits (e.g. pit I) the suggestion is that the producers of the material in pit III were either in some way less privileged or that this section of the midden was used in a different, perhaps less regular, way than others.

Phase D [Pit I(2)]

As has been mentioned above, the carbon dates for level 5 of this pit were A.D. 445 and 720 suggesting that this level spans a discontinuity. Material in the level immediately above confirms that supposition with carbon dates of A.D. 850 and 870. The faunal material is of interest in that it seems to be the earliest with a large proportion of bivalve shells; the crab/shell transition has been passed. There is still quite a large percentage of crab remains in the CBV (on average about 20%; Figure 2) supporting the contention (Jones 1985) that, at Indian Creek at least, this "transition" is due to the addition of bivalves to the diet rather than their displacing crabs which in fact never completely disappear from the faunal record. However it is interesting to note that for the first time at Indian Creek some of the crab chelae recovered (about 10%) belong not to *Cardisoma guanhumi* but to the terrestrial hermit-crab *Coenobita clypeatus*. The bivalve shell, whilst containing some oyster species of mangrove origin, is also rich in rock and sandy beach species including *Brachidontes recurvus*, *Donax denticulatus* and *Arca zebra*. The vertebrate remains, although fairly plentiful, contain relatively few rice rat bones (ca. 5 per level) but quite large quantities of medium-sized fish bones. This rather narrow deposition of material at pit I spans only about three 12.5 cm levels which contain only small absolute amounts of animal remains. The soil profile indicates a sharp difference between the sandy, pale layer containing this material and the richer, darker strata above and below.

Phase E [Pit II(2)]

The early material from this pit (Phase A) yielded radiocarbon dates between A.D. 185 and 280 (see above). From level 2 of this pit however we have a radiocarbon date of A.D. 880. This suggests that there was a considerable period of time during which this area of the midden was not used. However, in terms of the percentages of animal remains there is not an abrupt change from crab dominated to shell dominated remains. This is possibly due to physical mixing at the interface between the two strata. However, it is very noticeable that while the bivalves of the slightly earlier phase D contained some oysters mixed with other species, in this level oysters dominate particularly in the latest material. There is some indication that in levels 2a and 2b this domination is less complete than in 1a and 1b. This may be due to the aforementioned mixing with older material or it may indicate a real change taking place during the deposition of this material. Whatever the explanation, the level 1 bivalve material was judged to be at least 75% oyster with only *Analamalocardia* and *Donax* significantly represented in the remaining fraction. Thus we would seem to have evidence here of more than one change of emphasis in bivalve eating. The phenomenon noted in phase D that some crab chelae derive from *Coenobita* is observed in this phase too with hermit-crabs constituting an estimated 5-10% of crab fragments in level 2b but increasing to about 45% in level 1a. These levels are also marked by the considerable presence of the topshell, *Cittarium pica*, but it is apparent that their contribution represents the remains of many smaller shells than is the case elsewhere in the midden. The vertebrate remains also suggest we may be dealing with two separate sets of material in these four levels for whereas in levels 2a and 2b vertebrates represent a relatively high percentage of CBV (over 20%; Figure 3), the values for levels 1a and 1b are much lower (9.1 and 8.3%). The 1979 excavation showed low and declining numbers of rice rat bones and low but fairly steady numbers of fish vertebrae of medium size.

It is unfortunate in view of the possibility that this material represents two separate depositions that we only have the single radiocarbon date (from level 2). However, this author would be prepared to predict that a radiocarbon date for level 1 would be significantly later especially in view of the large quantities of gastropod shells recovered (see phase G below). Until we have more information it seems prudent not to put an end date on this phase.

Phase F [Pit III(2)]

From levels 3a to the surface of pit III the animal remains are dominated by bivalve shells and there is quite a sharp transition between level 3a and the crab-rich 3b just below it. However, this change probably coincides with a temporal gap in the record. We have two C-14 dates from this phase, A.D. 55 (most likely in error) and A.D. 930. Although these dates do not in themselves suggest a gap, the pottery styles, the soil profile and the nature of the faunal remains do. The pottery from these upper levels has been assigned to Marmora Bay, an Elenoid style which is a good deal different from the Saladoid Mill Reef sherds from the levels below. The notes on soil refer to the stone-free, lumpy texture of 3b and below in sharp contrast to the crumbly, fine soil with many small stones of 3a and above. The bivalve assemblage bears a strong resemblance to that in phase E being particularly rich in oyster shells (with the exception of level 3a which contains mostly *Donax*). This contrasts with the bivalve fauna of phase D (assumed to be earlier) which is low in oysters and contains many *Brachidontes*. Another important bivalve in this assemblage is *Phacoides* which, although it is found in small numbers elsewhere on the site, is particularly plentiful here. This phase would seem to start about the mid-ninth century and whilst the end date is not clear the animal remains are fairly homogeneous right up to the surface and suggest a fairly short time-span.

Phase G [Pit I(3)]

Some of Indian Creek's latest radiocarbon dates have been obtained from the upper levels of this pit, namely A.D. 1050 and A.D. 1105 from levels 3 and 2 respectively. The pottery of these levels like that of phase F (above) has been classified as Marmora Bay. Thus, compared with the lower material from this pit which has been assigned to the eighth and ninth centuries what we have here is considerably later and once again there is the likelihood of a temporal discontinuity. The animal material from these levels are characterised by the presence of considerable numbers of gastropod shells. Even excluding *Cittarium*, marine gastropods constituted over 8% of the animal remains recovered from this phase. *Cittarium* shells were plentiful but smaller on average than those found in other phases. The bivalve shells indicate some degree of shift away from the oysters which so dominate slightly earlier material (e.g. phase E). Here they are present in considerable quantities but with a significant admixture of *Donax* and *Arca*. The general impression is one of a move away from the mangrove swamps and towards a more generalised gathering of rock and sand shore molluscs with increasing emphasis on gastropods. This seems to have been the time at which the occupants quit Indian Creek, possibly to settle at the more littorally placed Freeman's Bay site (Rouse 1976).

DISCUSSION AND CONCLUSIONS

Great attention has been paid to the question of the crab/shell transition in Arawak middens (Rainey 1940; Carbone 1980; Goodwin 1980; Jones 1985; Keegan 1985; deFrance, this volume). Those of us excavating such middens recognise the obviousness of this transition in excavation profiles. (I can remember being struck by it on my first 'tourist' visit to Indian Creek as someone totally naive of all archaeology let alone Caribbean archaeology.) The debate surrounding this transition rumbles on with little sign of the emergence of a consensus view. Perhaps for too long we have been preoccupied by these discussions and that the time is now ripe for us to turn our attention to other aspects of the changing patterns of resource exploitation by the Arawaks; time for us to look in more detail at other quantifiable features of the midden and their faunal material.

The results presented above have revealed a number of points worthy, in my view, of further investigation. The first is that at Indian Creek at least some terrestrial resources were exhausted very quickly (e.g., easily caught, mainly ground-nesting birds) after the Arawak's arrival. This is the view also of Wing et al. (1968) for Mill Reef where birds, in particular, rapidly disappear from the faunal record. Secondly, the interpretation of crab to shell as a terrestrial to littoral transition (Goodwin 1980) is too simplistic. Long before there was a decline in crab remains there was a relative shift from rice rats to fish (Phases A to B to C, Table 1). Thirdly, the decline in *Cardisoma* remains coincides with increased use of *Coenobita*. Presumably this reflects a scarcity of *Cardisoma* (relative to demand and for whatever reason) resulting in the use of this other easily available land crab. But why was it not exploited earlier? Once again, we have here an example of the fact that animal resources are not necessarily exploited in proportion to their availability.

At this point bivalves also begin to appear in the record. With these animals too, the picture which emerges is far from simple. At first there are many shells from sandy and rocky shores (*Donax, Brachidontes*) and only later do the oysters (particularly *Crassostrea rhizophorae*) dominate. Later still there are few oyster shells and a marked increase in *Arca*. We have little understanding of the relative roles of these various bivalves or of the significance of the changing patterns of exploitation. Social standing of the consumer may have been influential and seasonal exploitation may have been important as has been shown for other bivalve-eating groups (Claassen 1986; Lightfoot and Cerrato 1988). Ecological changes may also have played their part as Wing et al. (1968) have suggested for the exploitation of fish at Mill Reef. Gastropod molluscs also suggest fluctuating attention by the Indian Creek inhabitants. For example, Phase C included many *Nerita* shells; rocky shore animals which are easily collected but largely absent except in this phase. Even here they only contributed minimally to the diet. Later, in Phase G a much wider range of gastropods are present but especially *Murex* perhaps collected in the mangroves along with oysters. Once again their contribution to the total meat intake must have been trivial. We can only speculate on fluctuating fads in the Indian Creek diet. Some, probably the more important ones, must have been driven by necessity whilst others I suspect were motivated by much more whimsical prejudices. It would seem that there is much scope for such prejudice when calories are unlikely to be limiting because of cassava yields (Carneiro 1973; Erlandson 1988) and when protein sources are many and varied. Optimal foraging theory although often useful and appropriate (Glassow and Wilcoxon 1988) needs to be tempered with choice when time is a resource that is not limiting.

Although no nutritional analysis has yet been carried out for individual levels at Indian Creek, earlier analysis of the total animal remains from individual pits (Jones 1985) has shown the relative importance of vertebrate animals as food over crabs and especially bivalves and gastropods. Of all the *common* food animals, the rice rat is the one most likely to be reduced in numbers by predation. However, even in this case, immigration from outside the hunting area and rapid recovery if predation pressure was reduced, for even a short time, is likely to have prevented a profound reduction in population in the long term. In support of this, rice rat bones are a continuing element in all of the samples. The question of the diminution of crab numbers by over-exploitation has been debated elsewhere (Goodwin 1980; Jones 1985) and there is no new evidence presented here which strongly favours one or other of the various arguments. I still favour the hypothesis that crabs became a diminished proportion of the total diet through a constant yield of crab being utilised by an increased human population necessitating the exploitation of new forms of food, in this case bivalves. There seems little doubt that recruitment of *Cardisoma* with its planktonic larva is unlikely to be affected by the localised depredations of the Arawaks and that the total amount of crab meat available per unit area would vary only slightly from year to year. Of course many other factors (climate, habitat destruction) may have modified this general picture. Fish too are unlikely to be over-exploited given the large reservoir of unexploitable stock capable of immigration into the areas cropped by the Indian Creek residents. Once again, climatic or other ecological factors and techniques of fishing may have affected the number and species caught. Molluscs, especially bivalves, are relatively sedentary and over-exploitation in this case is not to be discounted. A small mangrove swamp could be cleared of its oysters quite quickly and the regeneration of the stocks to animals of worthwhile size could take some years. The overall impression at Indian Creek is of a relatively small population of humans at first surrounded by a plethora of animals on which to feed. However, as this population grew the major food animals could no longer supply sufficient protein; some had become at least locally extinct (shearwater), some had been reduced in numbers to a fairly constant minimum (rice rat, *Cardisoma*), whilst others (fish) could only be exploited in a fixed area of habitat (e.g. reef). At this point the human inhabitants turn increasingly to less preferred animals such as bivalves and gastropods.

The analysis of the Indian Creek material has been hampered by the author's inability to analyse the fish bones. Clearly the range of detailed changes would be extended once that has been rectified. Thorough icthyological studies of this site are a major priority.

The second objective of this investigation was to attempt a definition in temporal terms of the midden usage at least for the three areas excavated both by the author and the Yale/AAS group. Table 1 and Figure 1 review the proposed scheme which can easily be tested by attempting to date new excavations at Indian Creek. Certainly it seems likely to be robust enough for areas close to those already investigated. Whether or not it could be used on other areas of the midden is less certain. There seems no doubt that sufficient time-dependant variability exists in the faunal remains that along with other information (pottery, soil etc.) a date to within 100 years is probably possible without recourse to radiocarbon dating. Perhaps one useful way forward, in view of the small samples needed, is to use multiple coring (Stein 1986). This would give enough material in each core (about 5 cm diameter) to be useful and permit statistically valid numbers of cores to be taken and analysed. However, it must be stressed that the present scheme depends for its absolute (as opposed to relative) dating on the radiocarbon dates of Rouse (1976). There are some anomalous results in these data and some confirmation or modification of these would give greater confidence to a dating scheme based on animal remains. Nonetheless there is an internal consistency between the majority of the radiocarbon dates available and a temporal scheme based on faunal analysis.

An objection to this type of analysis is the possibility that different types of activities took place at different parts of the site and that the differences reported here are not parts of a uniform temporal sequence. There is very likely to be an element of such spatial differentiation and I have already referred to the apparent differences between Pits II and III. There are also some examples of particular remains being found in one pit only. For example the large quantities of small gastropods, most *Nerita*, found in Phase C do not appear anywhere else on the site. Such shells are often bored (Jones 1980b) and are unlikely to be important in the diet; perhaps this is a "recreational" area. However, overall, the evidence suggests a uniformity of general usage across the whole site. The crab/shell transition is found in all pits investigated at a similar date, about A.D. 850 (Jones 1985). In the cases where there seems to be a temporal overlap between pits, the faunal analysis of the material is similar as exemplified by Phases C and D (see description above). No matter which pit the material comes from, there is a logical sequence relating the radiocarbon dates to the faunal material; no one pit stands out from that general conclusion.

REFERENCES CITED

Carbone, Victor A.
   1980   Some Problems in Paleoecology in the Caribbean Area. *Proceedings of the International Congress for the Study of the Pre-Columbian Cultures of the Lesser Antilles* 8:118-126. Tempe.

Carneiro, Robert L.
   1973   Slash-and-Burn Cultivation among the Kuikuru and its Implications for Cultural Development in the Amazon Basin. In *Peoples and Cultures of Native South America*, edited by D.R. Gross, pp. 98-123. Doubleday/Natural History Press, New York.

Claassen, Cheryl
   1986   Shellfishing Seasons in the Prehistoric Southwestern United States. *American Antiquity* 51: 21-37.

Erlandson, Jon M.
   1988   The Role of Shellfish in Prehistoric Economies: a Protein Perspective. *American Antiquity* 53: 102-109.

Glassow, Michael A. and Larry R. Wilcoxon
   1988   Coastal Adaptations Near Point Conception California, with Particular Regard to Shellfish Exploitation. *American Antiquity* 53: 36-51.

Goodwin, R. Christopher
   1980   Demographic Change and the Crab-Shell Dichotomy. *Proceedings of the International Congress for the Study of the Pre-Columbian Cultures of the Lesser Antilles* 8:45-68. Tempe.

Harris, Edward C.
   1979   *Principles of Archaeological Stratigraphy*. Academic Press, London.

Jones, Alick R.
   1980a Animal Food and Human Population at Indian Creek, Antigua. *Proceedings of the International Congress for the Study of the Pre-Columbian Cultures of the Lesser Antilles* 8:264-273. Tempe.

   1980b A Report of Two Types of Modification to Gastropod Mollusc Shells from Indian Creek, Antigua. *Journal of the Virgin Islands Archaeological Society* 9:31-40.

   1985   Dietary Change and Human Population at Indian Creek, Antigua. *American Antiquity* 50: 518-536.

Keegan, William F.
   1985   *Dynamic Horticuluralists: Population Expansion in the Prehistoric Bahamas*. Ph.D. dissertation, University of California, Los Angeles. University Microfilms, Ann Arbor.

Lightfoot, Kent G. and Robert M. Cerrato
   1988   Prehistoric Shellfish Exploitation in Coastal New York. *Journal of Field Archaeology* 15: 141-149.

Olsen, Fred
   1974   *Indian Creek: An Arawak Site on Antigua West Indies*. University of Oklahoma Press, Norman.

Rainey, Froelich G.
    1940   *Porto Rican Prehistory*. Scientific Survey of Porto Rico and the Virgin Islands, vol. XVIII-parts 2 and 3. The New York Academy of Sciences, New York.

Rouse, Irving
    1976   Cultural Development on Antigua, West Indies: a Progress Report. *Actas de XLI Congress Internacional de Americanistas* 3:701-709. Mexico City.

Stein, Julie K.
    1986   Coring Archaeological Sites. *American Antiquity* 51: 505-527.

Wing, Elizabeth S., Charles A. Hoffman and Clayton E. Ray
    1968   Vertebrate Remains from Indian Sites on Antigua, West Indies. *Caribbean Journal of Science* 8:123-139.

TABLE 1 Characteristics of the proposed Phases A-G for the Indian Creek Midden.

Phase	Radio-Carbon dates[1] calendric AD	Pits and levels from 1977-7	Proposed time span calendric AD	Pottery Style[1]	Formal Characteristics	Soil
A	185, 200, 235, 280	II 3a-5b	150-300	Late Indian Creek	1. Relatively large numbers of crab chelae, rice rat bones and fish vertebrae. Rice rat bones out-number fish vertebrae. Bird bones present. Vertebrates >20% of CBV. 2. No bivalves. 3. Crab chelae all *Cardisoma*	Sandy with much crab
B	445, 445, 510	I 5b/6a-7b	380-520	Late Indian Creek/Mill Reef	1. Large fish vertebrae (c.9.5 mm centrium diameter) out-number rice rat bones. 2. Few bivalves, usually *Donax* or *Codakia*.	Sandy with much crab
C	685, 810	III 3b/4a-5b	650-850(?)	Mill Reef	1. Few animal remains (c.200 gm per level). 2. Up to 10% of CBV is bivalve mainly *Donax* and *Brachidontes* 3. Large numbers of small gastropods usually *Nerita* spp. sometimes constituting as much as 10% of all animal remains.	Consolidated with few stores grading into sandy with crab.
D	720, 850, 870	I 4a-5b	700-880	Mill Reef	1. Fish vertebrae very much more plentiful than rice rat bones. 2. Up to 10% of crab remains from *Coenobita*. 3. Bivalves 10-60% of CBV with oysters, *Brachidontes*, *Donax* and *Arca*.	
E	880	II 1a-2b	850-1000+(?)	Mill Reef	1. Few rice rat bones. 2. Crab remains 5-45% *Coenbita*. 3. Bivalves plentiful and dominated by oysters. No *Arca*. 4. Many small *Cittarium*.	Crumbly and fairly dark to sandy.
F	55(?), 930	III 1a-3a/3b	900-1000(?)	Mamora Bay	1. Similar to E but non-oyster bivalves include *Phacoides*.	Crumbly with many small stones
G	1050, 1105	I 1a-3b	1000-1120	Mamora Bay	1. Plentiful bivalves with oysters and very many *Arca*; some *Anadora*. 2. Many gastropods, frequently *Murex* spp. but few *Nerita*.	Soft brown.

1. From Rouse (1976)

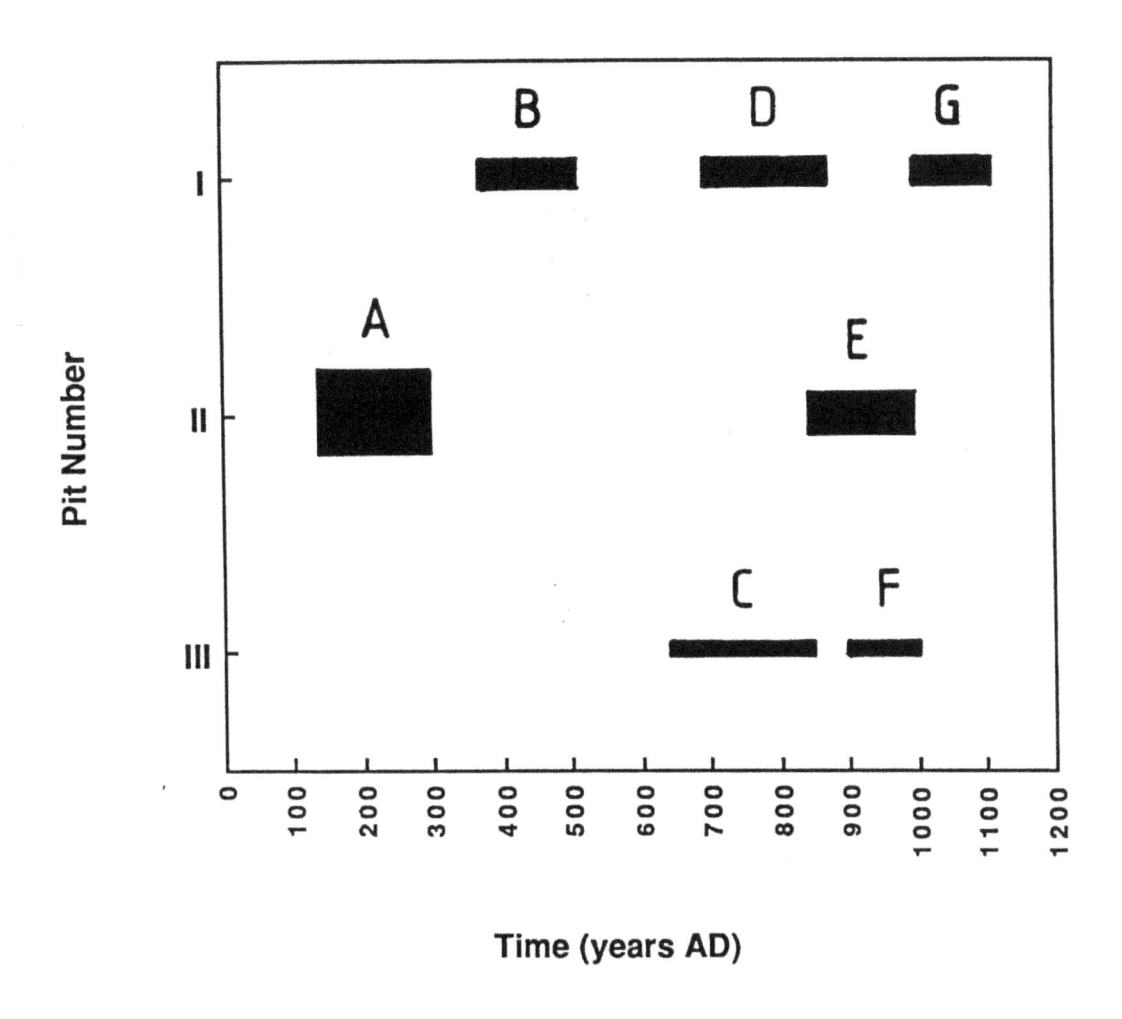

Figure 1. Diagram illustrating the hypotheses put forward in the text in respect of the dating of remains from Pits I, II and III. The bars indicate the period of time over which material was deposited; the thickness of the bars is an approximate indication of the quantity of material deposited. See Table 1 and text for full explanation.

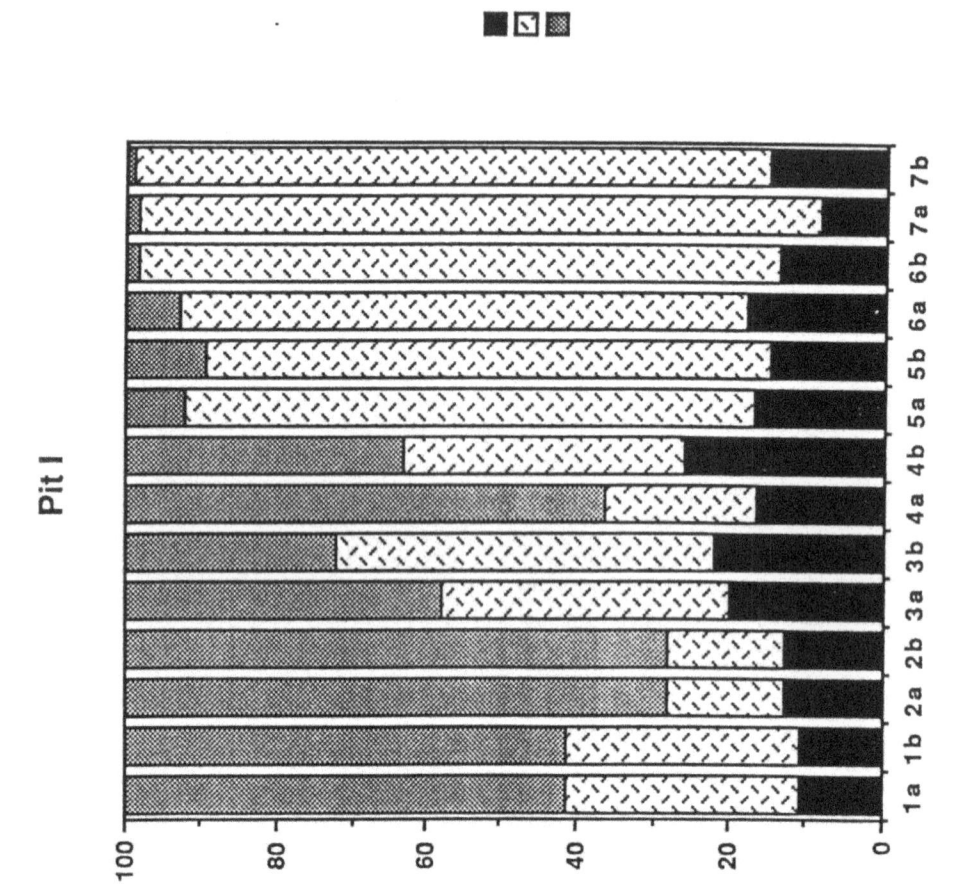

Figure 2. Relative percentage by weight of crab, bivalve and vertebrate remains (CBV) from Pit I.

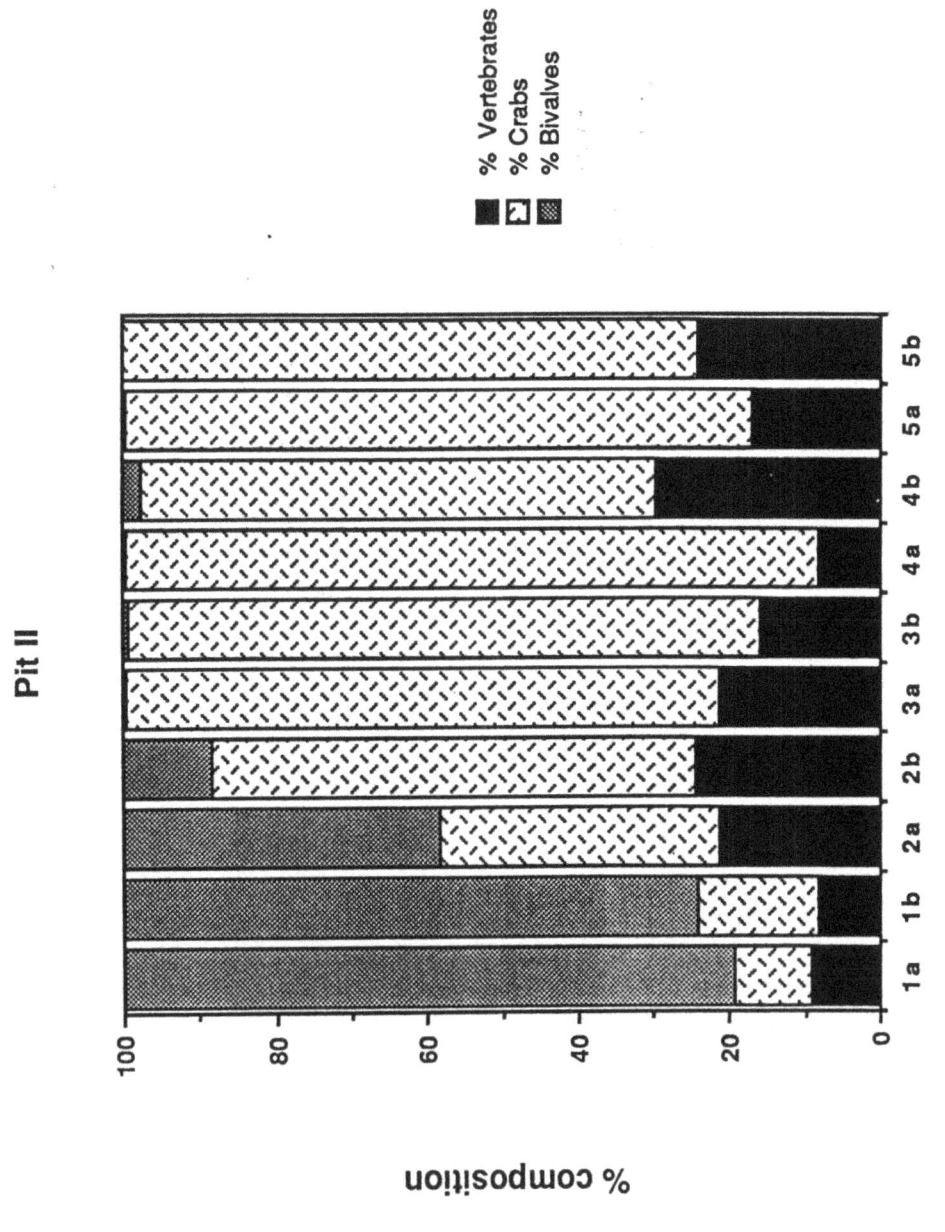

Figure 3. Relative percentage by weight of crab, bivalve and vertebrate remains (CBV) from Pit II.

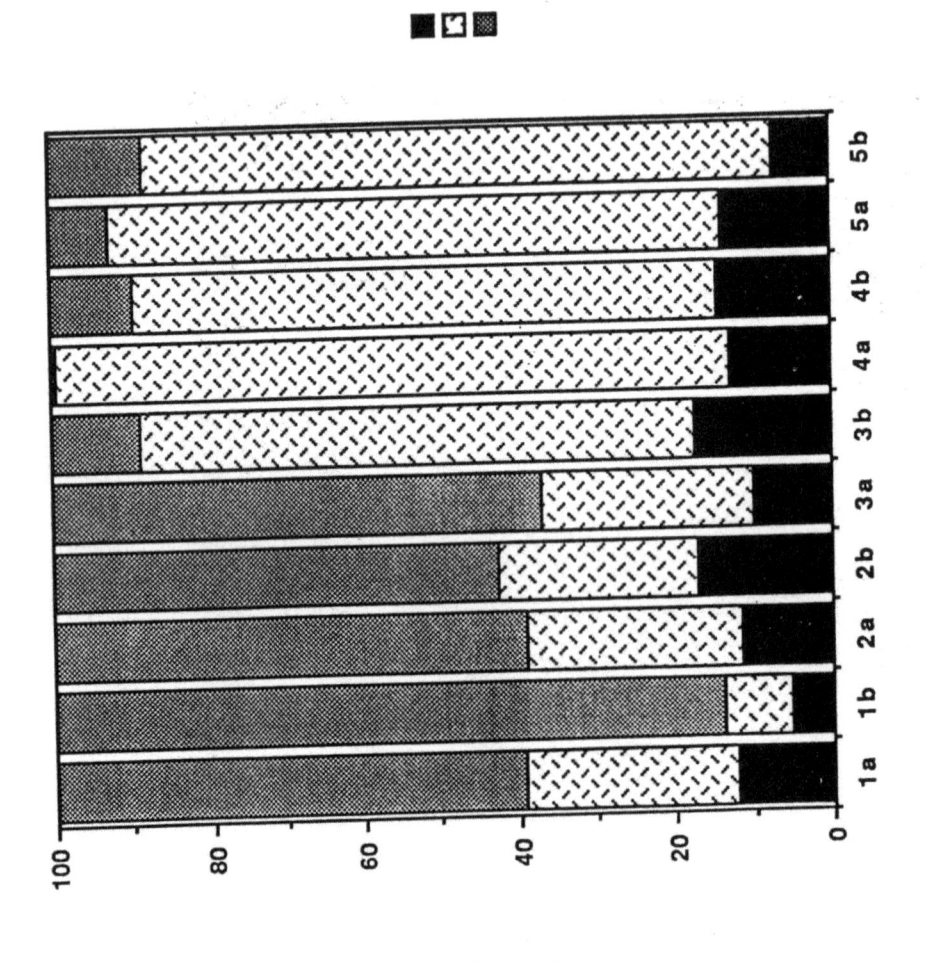

Figure 4. Relative percentage by weight of crab, bivalve and vertebrate remains (CBV) from Pit III.

SALADOID AND OSTIONOID SUBSISTENCE ADAPTATIONS:

ZOOARCHAEOLOGICAL DATA FROM A COASTAL OCCUPATION ON PUERTO RICO

Susan D. deFrance

ABSTRACT

A zooarchaeological analysis of vertebrate and invertebrate remains from the Maisabel site located on the north coast of Puerto Rico allows for the reconstruction of Saladoid and early Ostionoid subsistence adaptations. Results are presented for several research questions concerning the local economy, including evidence for temporal variability in subsistence adaptations, species and habitat exploitation, and probable procurement methods. Subsistence implications for other coastal and non-coastal Saladoid/Ostionoid occupations are discussed.

INTRODUCTION

The colonization and settlement of the Caribbean by Ceramic age populations provide excellent opportunities to study the development of island adaptations and subsistence systems. These inhabitants introduced cultigens to the islands and supplemented their diets with animal proteins. One aspect of early Ceramic age occupation that has received considerable attention concerns shifting patterns of resource utilization; specifically, the transition from a terrestrial based subsistence economy to a maritime orientation -- or the land crab-marine shell dichotomy (Rainey 1940; Carbone 1980; Goodwin 1980; Jones 1985; Keegan 1985).

A variety of models have been proposed to explain this dietary shift. These have included pan-Caribbean models, such as Rainey's (1940) proposal of secondary population migrations or Carbone's (1980) paleoenvironmental dessication theory. Others have attempted to relate this change to island settlement and the need for intensification and diversification as a result of population pressure (Goodwin 1980), diet breadth expansion from reduced cost-benefit ratios (Keegan 1985), or reduced food yields to an increasing population (Jones 1985).

In this paper I will review these models in light of zooarchaeological data collected from a Saladoid and Ostionoid site located on the north central coast of Puerto Rico (Figure 1). Reconstructing the subsistence adaptations of the site's occupants permits a variety of research questions to be addressed. Through the analysis of faunal remains from a range of contexts and time periods, it is possible to examine evidence for a terrestrial to maritime shift in the use of resources. The present study is also concerned with determining the primary sources of animal proteins, the habitats in which these resources were procured, and the probable subsistence technologies used by the inhabitants. This paper summarizes a more detailed faunal study presented elsewhere (deFrance 1988).

MATERIALS AND METHODS

The faunal data were obtained from excavations conducted at the Maisabel site, located approximately 30 km west of San Juan, in Vega Baja, Puerto Rico (Figure 2). The excavations and multidisciplinary analytical phases of the project have been sponsored by the Centro de Investigaciones Indígenas de Puerto Rico (CIIPR [Siegel and Roe 1987]). A program of extensive excavations was conducted at the site under the direction of Peter Siegel. A discussion of the structure and organization of the site is presented by Siegel (this volume), therefore, my discussion will concern only areas from which faunal remains were analyzed.

In selecting contexts for faunal analysis, an effort was made to choose undisturbed deposits representing the temporal and functional range of the site and that also contained quantifiable amounts of faunal material. Based on these criteria, samples were selected from five areas of the site (Figure 3):

(1) From the northern mound, Mound 1, a stratigraphic column (10 cm arbitrary levels) of flotation material was analyzed from a 2x2 m square excavated to a depth of 1.6 m. This mound is composed of a dense land crab and shell matrix and dates to the Hacienda Grande phase of the Saladoid period.

(2) A similar stratigraphic column, 1.2 m deep, was analyzed from an excavation unit on Mound 2, a large oblong mound located to the south of Mound 1. This unit's temporal placement is slightly later than that of Mound 1, dating to the transitional late Hacienda Grande/early Cuevas phases.

(3) To the west of Mound 1 another zone of Saladoid occupation was analyzed (unit N112W88). The material from a 40 cm column was examined, as was the material from a Saladoid pit feature, Feature 104, uncovered deeper in the unit. Both contexts date to the Hacienda Grande phase.

(4) A sample was analyzed from a context dating to the late Saladoid/early Ostionoid time periods (unit N32E32). Two strata from this later period were analyzed. Although this sample is comparatively small, it is one of the few contexts dating to the Ostionoid period.

(5) Faunal remains were also examined from an area of contiguous excavations between the two mounds, referred to as the macroblock. In this area Feature 101 was uncovered: a large linear stain (Figure 4) that is believed to have functioned as a drainage ditch encircling a large oblong structure (Siegel and Bernstein 1987). Zooarchaeological remains from four of the units in which the feature was identified were combined analytically to form a single sample. This feature and the majority of the macroblock contexts date to the subsequent Ostionoid time period (Siegel, this volume).

For all five of these areas the faunal remains studied were taken from flotation samples that had been water-separated using 1/16 in (1.6 mm) mesh screen. The average volume of a flotation sample (before water-separation) was 3 l for Mound 1, and 10 l for the remainder of the site.

In addition to flotation samples, and in order to determine if excavation screen size was resulting in recovery biases or underrepresentation of species abundance/diversity, subsamples were studied. The subsamples were taken from 2 x 2 m units excavated in 10 cm levels, and were dry screened using coarse meshes (1/8 in [3.2 mm] and 1/4 in [6.4 mm]).

These coarse-screened materials were selected from three of the five sampling areas: Mound 1, Mound 2, and the upper strata of N112W88. Within N112W88, one half of the pit

Feature 104 was coarse-screened (1/4 in mesh) and the other half was water-separated. Both halves were analyzed.

The identification of the faunal remains was made possible through the use of the comparative collection housed in the Zooarchaeology Laboratory, Florida Museum of Natural History, University of Florida. The comparative collection was augmented by the availability of over two hundred modern vertebrate and invertebrate specimens collected in Puerto Rico during the summer of 1986 under the sponsorship of the CIIPR. These comparative materials will serve as the nucleus of a collection for future Caribbean zooarchaeologicl research conducted by the CIIPR. Once identification was completed, the faunal remains were quantified using number of individual specimens (NISP), minimum numbers of individuals (MNI), and skeletal and shell mass allometry. Dimensional allometric scaling was conducted on a portion of the fish and crab remains.

When the data from these samples are combined, 25,394 vertebrate and invertebrate specimens representing a minimum of 4,957 individuals were identified (Figure 5). In terms of both NISP and MNI, invertebrates are more common, accounting for 58% of the fragments and 85% of the individuals. However, based on estimates of edible meat weight, vertebrate species were apparently of greater dietary importance because they account for 77% of the total estimated usable meat weight for the site as a whole.

The contexts analyzed indicate that at least 155 species were used (Figure 6). The vertebrate species that can be considered edible include six species of mammals, at least eight species of birds, and six species of reptiles, including two species each of turtle, snakes, and lizards. Both cartilaginous and bony fishes are represented, however, only three species of cartilaginous fishes were identified as compared to 64 species of bony fishes. The invertebrates that can be considered food items include two species of crustacea, 43 of marine gastropods, 20 of bivalves, and chitons (Figure 7). A large number of small terrestrial snails was also identified. However, only one of these can be considered comestible due to the small size of the individuals. The samples selected for analysis and the screen sizes employed resulted in substantial variation in both species composition and abundance. This variability will be discussed within the context of broader interpretations of the prehistoric subsistence patterns.

RESULTS

Previous models of settlement and subsistence for early Ceramic age occupations in the Lesser and Greater Antilles (e.g., Goodwin 1979; Jones 1985; Roe 1985) suggest that the subsistence adaptations of the early Saladoid occupants were based primarily on terrestrial resources, particularly the hutia (*Isolobodon portoricensis*), which is a medium-sized rodent, and land crabs (*Cardisoma* sp. and *Gecarcinus* sp.). According to these models, the later phases of Saladoid occupation and the subsequent Ostionoid components exhibit a reduced reliance on terrestrial fauna and a concomitant increase in utilization of marine resources, particularly invertebrates.

In contrast to the inland riverine settlement patterns of early Saladoid sites in the Lesser Antilles, such as St. Kitts, Maisabel has early Saladoid components and is located directly on the coast. Not suprisingly, Maisabel's settlement location and zooarchaeological data are most similar to early Ceramic age sites on the north coast of Puerto Rico, such as Hacienda Grande (Roe 1985; Wing 1989). Maisabel's location on the north central coastal plain provided the occupants with soils suitable for horticulture and with access to a diversity of aquatic and terrestrial habitats. The faunal data indicate that during the early phases of occupation there existed a well-established maritime economy in combination with terrestrial resource use.

Terrestrial Economy

The terrestrial resources are similar to those identified at other early Ceramic age sites. Allen's hutia (*Isolobodon portoricensis*) is the most common mammal in the samples. Other rodents such as the spiny rat (Echimyidae) are also present. Hutias could have been hunted easily in the vicinity of the site. No other terrestrial mammals that could be considered food items were identified in the analyzed samples. However, a lower leg bone of a dog was observed in the coarse-screened material from an excavation unit on Mound 2.

The most common birds are dove species, which also could have been easily captured near the site with a simple snare net technology or trapping devices. Bird species present in very low quantities include herons, egrets, members of the duck family, and finches. Two reptile species were identified: the iguana and the pygmy boa. Neither is present in great abundance.

Undoubtedly, the most important terrestrial resources in the early Saladoid contexts were the blue land crabs, (*Cardisoma guanhumi*). Crab remains were densest in the areas of the site dating to the Hacienda Grande and early Cuevas phases. No crab remains were recovered from the macroblock samples or from N32E32 (Ostionoid and Late Saladoid/Ostionoid transitional, respectively).

In order to determine if the crab populations were being impacted through time, dimensional measurements were taken of land crab mandibles and dimensional allometric scaling estimates of crab size and weight were made for the various contexts that contained crab remains (Figure 8). A sample of 119 measurable blue land crab mandibles were recovered from the Hacienda Grande phase contexts on Mounds 1 and 2 and from Feature 104 in N112W88. The size and weight estimates of the crabs from a sample of Mound 1 material indicate that specimens ranging from 40 to 100 mm wide and from 35 to 335 g were consumed (Figures 9 and 10). Significantly, a large number of the crab mandibles were recovered only in the fine-screened (1/16 inch) flotation samples. These mandibles indicate that much smaller crabs were captured as compared to the estimates provided by the mandibles in the coarse-samples.

Land crabs would have been available in large quantities to the east of the site in the extensive mangrove swamp associated with the Cibuco River. This is also where land crabs are harvested today. Prehistorically, land crabs could have been hunted in the vicinity of their burrows at night with the aid of torches and large numbers of females could have been captured during their mass spawning migrations to salt or brackish waters in the summer and fall months.

Aquatic Economy

In contrast to the terrestrial resources, the aquatic fauna are more diverse and indicate that a number of habitats were exploited, requiring a greater repertoire of procurement strategies and techniques. The present analysis is unique for Caribbean studies in that fine-screened samples of both vertebrate and invertebrate remains have been analyzed in a comparable fashion. Therefore, the reconstruction of aquatic resource use is unbiased.

Within the vicinity of the site the aquatic areas available for exploitation included the freshwater habitats of the Cibuco River, the estuarine resources at the mouth of the river, the neritic and littoral habitats along the coast (including waters within two protected lunate bays), and the pelagic waters further offshore. The aquatic vertebrates identified in the samples indicate that all of these areas were exploited, but that procurement activities centered on the neritic waters and the estuarine resources near the mouth of the Río Cibuco.

The north central coast of Puerto Rico is not characterized by the development of extensive offshore fringing reefs such as those that occur in other parts of Puerto Rico and the Caribbean

(Kaye 1959:107). However, an extensive trench of submerged limestone, that comprises the littoral and benthic realms of the north coast (Kaye 1959:107), would have provided covering and resources similar to a reef structure. This area would have been inhabited by common reef species, both carnivorous and omnivorous.

The fishes that are most abundant are common tropical marine fishes such as parrotfishes, grunts, wrasses, triggerfishes, and groupers (Table 1). The fine-screened samples indicate that large numbers of sardines and shad or herring had also been used in all of the time periods represented. These samples also include juvenile individuals of fishes such as snappers, mullet, and jacks; as well as adult specimens that attain a small body size-- for example, mojarras, needlefish, gobies, and sleepers. The coarse-screened samples, such as the Saladoid sample from N112W88, dramatically underrepresent the smaller fish forms (Figure 11).

The complex of reef fishes represented in the site are species most easily captured in traps set in areas of submerged limestone or near turtle grass beds within the bays. The small fishes, particularly the schooling species such as the sardines, suggest that fine mesh nets were employed in littoral areas with unobstructed substrates. The mangrove estuary at the interface of the river and the ocean most likely was inhabited by juvenile fishes of several species while further upriver freshwater sleepers were captured.

Other aquatic vertebrate species probably were captured in the pelagic waters further from shore. At least two species of tuna were identified, as were sharks. Either of these two forms may have been captured while they were feeding in shallower waters.

Aquatic non-fish species identified in the samples include sea turtle and manatee, which may have been hunted in pelagic waters; although sea turtles could have been taken while they were nesting on the beaches or feeding on turtle grass in the shallow waters. The remains of freshwater pond or river turtle and at least one species of aquatic snake are represented. Both of these animals would have been common in the Cibuco River.

In terms of marine mollusks (Table 2), gastropods that inhabit the intertidal littoral zone such as nerites, neritina, top-shell, limpets, and chitons are most common in the samples analyzed. Conch, a deeper water littoral species, is also common. The identified bivalves, which include sea scallops, jewel boxes, and pectens, are forms that inhabit grass beds or sandy bottomed areas, such as are found within the protected bays.

DISCUSSION

It is evident that even during the early stages of occupation at Maisabel a maritime component was well established. During the later phases of Saladoid occupation and during the Ostionoid period, there is a reduction in terrestrial faunal refuse, especially land crabs, in the deposits. This dietary change involved the intensification of an already well developed maritime economy.

Maisabel shares with other early Ceramic age Caribbean sites the characteristic decline in land crab use through time. To explain the decline in crab refuse observed at a number of Puerto Rican sites, Rainey (1940) originally proposed that a second migration of mollusc-consuming peoples entered the Caribbean and introduced new ceramic types. It is now generally recognized that the crab/shell stratigraphic break represents a cultural continuum, with a dietary change rather than a demographic one (Rouse 1986).

Subsequently, Carbone (1980) proposed that a pan-Caribbean microclimatic change resulted in desiccation and a reduction in the habitats suitable for the moisture-dependent land crabs. This theory has been refuted based on archaeological evidence that the dietary change occurs at different times on different islands-- generally later in time as one travels northward through the island arc.

Two other proposals have related the dietary change to island colonization and population expansion. Goodwin (1979, 1980) attributes the rise of a maritime economy to population-induced stress that resulted from rapid population increases in an environmentally restricted island setting. The Lotka-Volterra predator-prey model used to analyze the crab remains from Saladoid sites on St. Kitts is said to indicate a population undergoing predation. Unfortunately, the only archaeological evidence of impact is a decline in the number of crab remains through time.

More recently, Keegan (1985) proposed that the exploitation of terrestrial resources following colonization of a new island provided high average returns and involved low risk capture techniques. Based on concepts of optimal foraging theory and microeconomics he suggests that as population size increased, the high yield terrestrial resources were depleted and lower return food groups such as marine fishes and mollusks had to be consumed.

Keegan assumes that many of the prehistoric terrestrial resources were available in the same quantities as modern specimens. The fossil record of hutia in the West Indies suggest that the species common at Maisabel was introduced by human agents from neighboring Hispaniola (Morgan and Woods 1986); therefore, their population densities may have been considerably lower when the site was initially occupied. Also, the Maisabel data do not indicate that terrestrial resources were preferred in the early phases of occupation; only that land crab use declined in later periods.

Based on settlement and faunal data from Indian Creek on Antigua, Alick Jones (1985) argued that Saladoid population densities were too low to have impacted the land crabs. However, Jones also suggested that land clearing and other human activities may have reduced the area suitable for crab habitation or that as human population size increased, the land crabs provided lower food returns. The low estimate of site population density is based on extremely tenuous data. Therefore, it is not a reliable criterion for concluding that humans were not impacting the crab populations.

The analysis of land crabs from the Maisabel samples indicates that the site's occupants were not exclusively selecting adult crabs, but used both juveniles and adults. Although the samples do not indicate that *only* smaller crabs were available in the later periods as would be expected if human exploitation pressure was affecting the crab populations, it is probable that the population structure was being impacted based on the archaeological evidence that both large and small crabs were harvested in the early phases of occupation.

Modern studies of land crabs in the Caribbean indicate that intensive exploitation of large individuals results in an increase in the population density of small crabs over time. This overexploitation eventually will result in a reduction in the average size of the crabs -- however, the crabs recover rather rapidly from exploitation either through the surviving crabs or through recolonization of an area (Alan Pinder, personal communication with Peter Siegel 1986). Interestingly, the crabs represented archaeologically are larger than the modern specimens collected in the same area, thereby indicating that human exploitation can affect the population structure.

The Maisabel data suggest that the crab population was being impacted by predation and therefore as smaller crabs became increasingly common they were excluded from the diet. In the case of Maisabel, the resulting effect on the subsistence system was the intensification of an already existing maritime food base. It is possible that by the time Maisabel was settled the Saladoid peoples had developed a greater knowledge of island resources and procurement strategies and were therefore less dependent on terrestrial resources. Terrestrial resource use and inland settlement in Lesser Antillean sites may not reflect greater returns for lower risk, but rather the exploitation of resources that were more abundant in the vicinity of the dietary staple crops.

CONCLUSIONS

Future research should be directed at refining information on the population structure of the land crabs and human-induced changes in crab population densities. Further studies should also be directed at identifying the full range of marine resources through the recovery of faunal remains with fine-mesh screens. By means of precise subsistence reconstructions it may be possible to document further variations in Saladoid adaptations that can be related to: (1) variability in ecological settings and (2) historical patterns of colonization and adaptation by Ceramic age peoples..

Acknowledgments. The Centro de Investigaciones Indígenas de Puerto Rico sponsored this research. The CIIPR provided the funds enabling me to travel to Puerto Rico in order to build a faunal comparative collection and for the year-long analysis. The monies were administered by the University of Florida Division of Sponsored Research.

REFERENCES CITED

Carbone, Victor A.
    1980 Some Problems in the Cultural Paleoecology in the Caribbean Area. *Proceedings of the International Congress for the Study of the Pre-Columbian Cultures of the Lesser Antilles* 8:98-126. Tempe.

deFrance, Susan D.
    1988 *Zooarchaeological Investigations of Subsistence Strategies at the Maisabel Site, Puerto Rico.* Unpublished Master's paper, Department of Anthropology, University of Florida, Gainesville.

Goodwin, R. Christopher
    1979 *The Prehistoric Cultural Ecology of St.Kitts, West Indies: A Case Study in Island Archaeology.* Ph.D. dissertation, Arizona State University. University Microfilms, Ann Arbor.

    1980 Demographic Change and the Crab-Shell Dichotomy. *Proceedings of the International Congress for the Study of the Pre-Columbian Cultures of the Lesser Antilles* 8:45-68. Tempe.

Jones, Alick R.
    1985 Dietary Change and Human Population at Indian Creek, Antigua. *American Antiquity* 50:518-536.

Kaye, Clifford A.
    1959 Shoreline Features and Quaternary Shoreline Changes, Puerto Rico. *United States Geological Survey Professional Papers* 317-B, 49.

Keegan, William F.
   1985   *Dynamic Horticulturalists: Population Expansion in the Prehistoric Bahamas*. Ph.D. dissertation, University of California, Los Angeles. University Microfilms, Ann Arbor.

Morgan, Gary S. and Charles A. Woods
   1986   Extinction and the Zoogeography of West Indian Land Mammals *Biological Journal of the Linnean Society* 28:167-203.

Rainey, Froelich G.
   1940   *Porto Rican Archaeology*. Scientific Survey of Porto Rico and the Virgin Islands, vol. XVIII-part 1. The New York Academy of Sciences, New York.

Rouse, Irving
   1986   *Migrations in Prehistory: Inferring Population Movement from Cultural Remains*. Yale University Press, New Haven.

Roe, Peter G.
   1985   A Preliminary Report on the 1980 and 1982 Field Seasons at Hacienda Grande (12 PSj7-5): Overview of Site History, Mapping, and Excavations. *Proceedings of the International Congress for the Study of the Pre-Columbian Cultures of the Lesser Antilles* 10:151-180. Montréal.

Siegel, Peter E. and David J. Bernstein
   1987   Sampling for Site Structure and Spatial Organization in the Saladoid: A Case Study. Paper presented at the 12th International Congress of Caribbean Archaeology, Cayenne, French Guiana.

Siegel, Peter E. and Peter G. Roe
   1987   The Maisabel Archaeological Project: A Long Term Multi-Disciplinary Investigation. Paper presented at the 12th International Congress for Caribbean Archaeology, Cayenne, French Guiana.

Wing, Elizabeth S.
   1989   Animal Remains from the Hacienda Grande Site, Puerto Rico. Appendix to *Excavations at María de la Cruz and Hacienda Grande, Loiza, Puerto Rico* by Irving Rouse and Ricardo E. Alegría. Yale University Publications in Anthropology, New Haven, in press.

Wing, Elizabeth S. and Sylvia J. Scudder
   1980   Use of Animals by the Prehistoric Inhabitants on St. Kitts, West Indies. *Proceedings of the International Congress for the Study of the Pre-Columbian Cultures of the Lesser Antilles* 8:237-245. Tempe.

Table 1. Habitats of the Predominant Fish Families.

Family	Habitat
Clupeidae (herrings, sardines)	seasonally in neritic waters
Belonidae (needlefishes)	shallow waters, surface
Holocentridae (squirrelfishes)	shallow reef and inshore water
Centropomidae (snooks)	mangrove sloughs
Serranidae (sea bass)[a]	shallow to deep water reefs
Carangidae (jacks)[a]	shallow to deep water reefs
Lutjanidae (snappers)[a]	shallow to deep water reefs
Gerreidae (mojorras)	neritic waters
Haemulidae (grunts)	shallow reefs, tidal grass flats
Sciaenidae (drum)	mangrove sloughs
Labridae (wrasses)	shallow reefs
Scaridae (parrotfishes)	shallow to deep reefs, tidal flats
Mugilidae (mullet)	mangrove sloughs
Eleotridae (sleepers)	freshwater and mangrove sloughs
Scombridae (tuna, mackeral)	pelagic, inshore for feeding
Balistidae (triggerfishes)	shallow to deep reefs

[a] enter shallow grass flats primarily to feed

Table 2. Preferred Habitats of the Major Gastropod Families and Bivalve Genera.

Family or Genus	Habitat
Fissurellidae (limpets)	intertidal rocky areas
Trochidae (top-shells)	littoral and supralittoral rocks
Turbanidae (turbans)	littoral and supralittoral rocks
Neritidae (nerites)	supra littoral rocky areas
Littorinidae (periwinkles)	supralittoral rocky areas
Strombidae (conches)	turtle grass beds (shallow to deep)
Cypraeidae (cypreas)	intertidal waters
Marginellidae (olive snails)	turtle grass beds, shallow waters
Anadara	offshore and muddy areas
Arca	attached to rocky substrate by byssus
Pecten	semi-infaunal and in grass beds
Lima	common under rocks in shallow
Ostrea	attached to substrate in shallow water
Codakia	shallow water grass beds
Chama	rocky areas in crevices and under stones
Trachycardium	shallow water habitats
Laevicardium	shallow water habitats
Mactrellona	shallow water habitats
Tellina	sandy, shallow waters
Donax	very shallow, sandy habitats
Chione	shallow water habitats

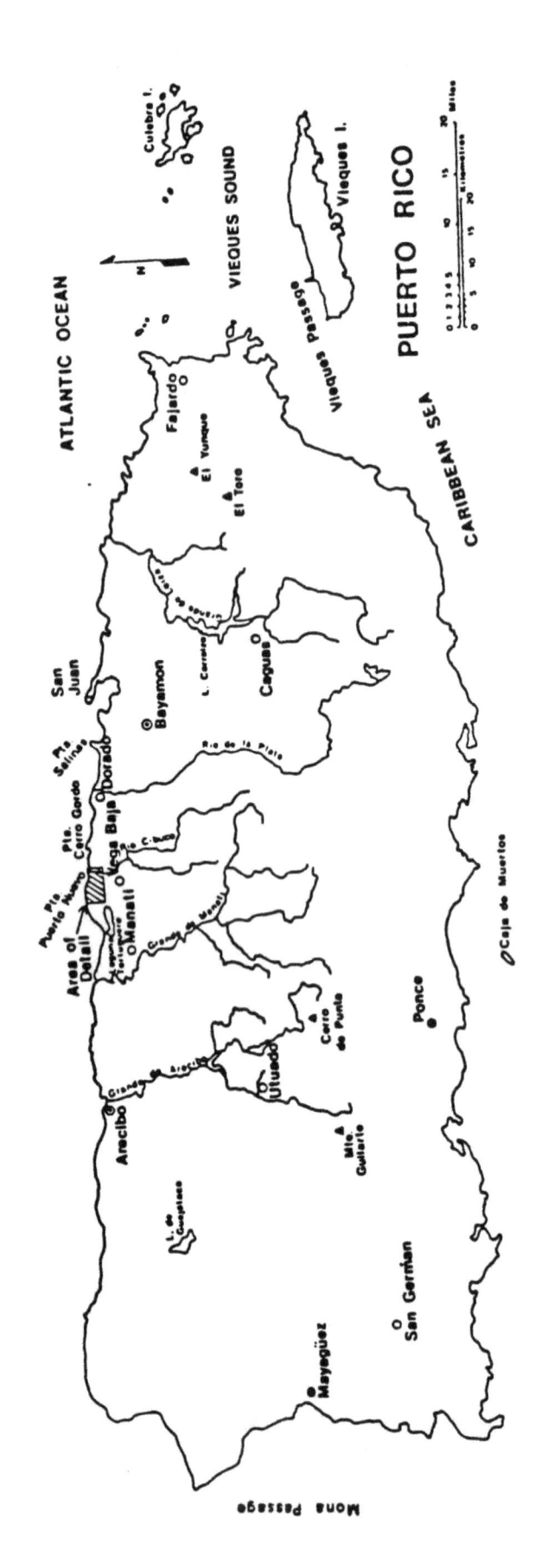

Figure 1. Location of Maisabel site on Puerto Rico.

Figure 2. Location of Maisabel and surrounding environs.

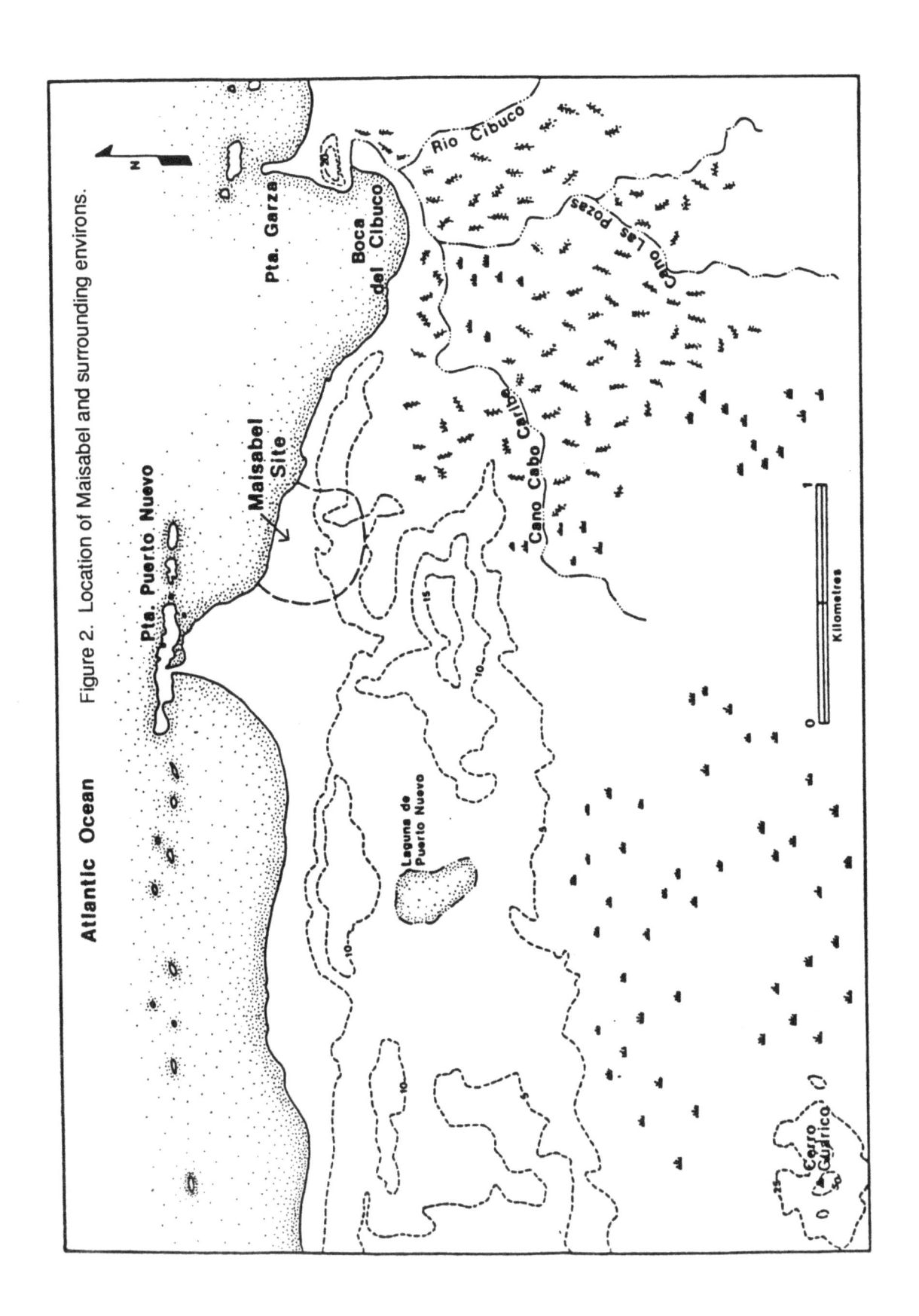

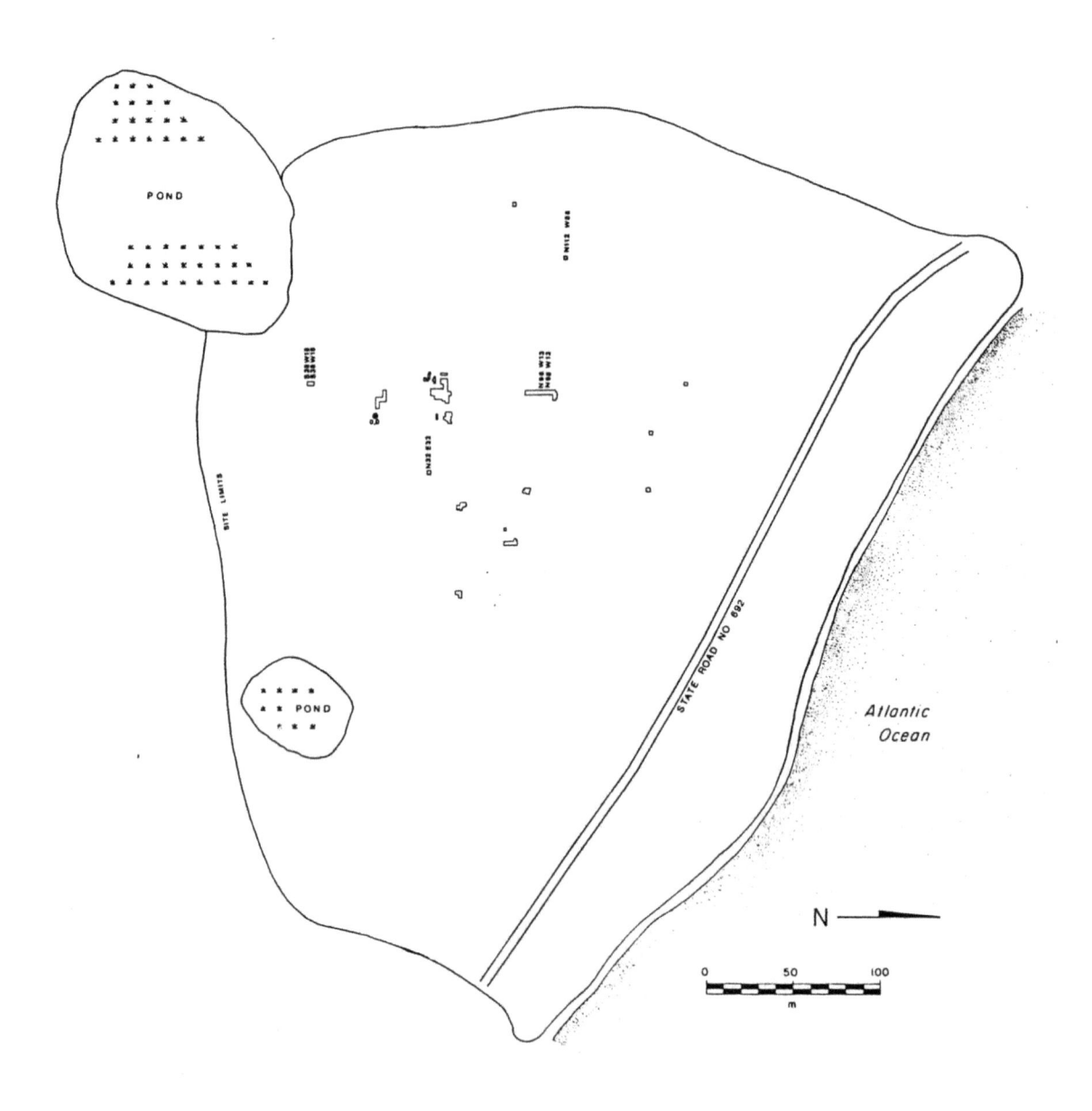

Figure 3. Location of analyzed contexts.

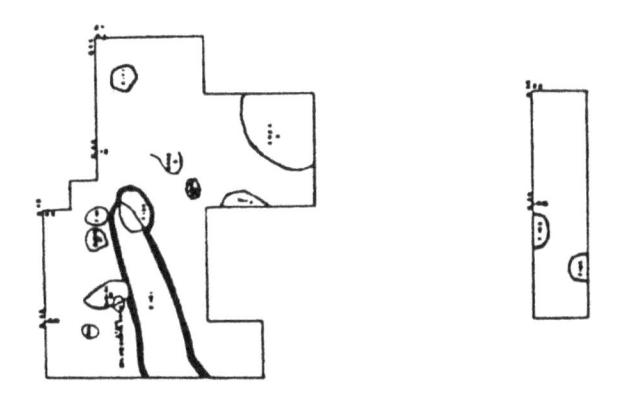

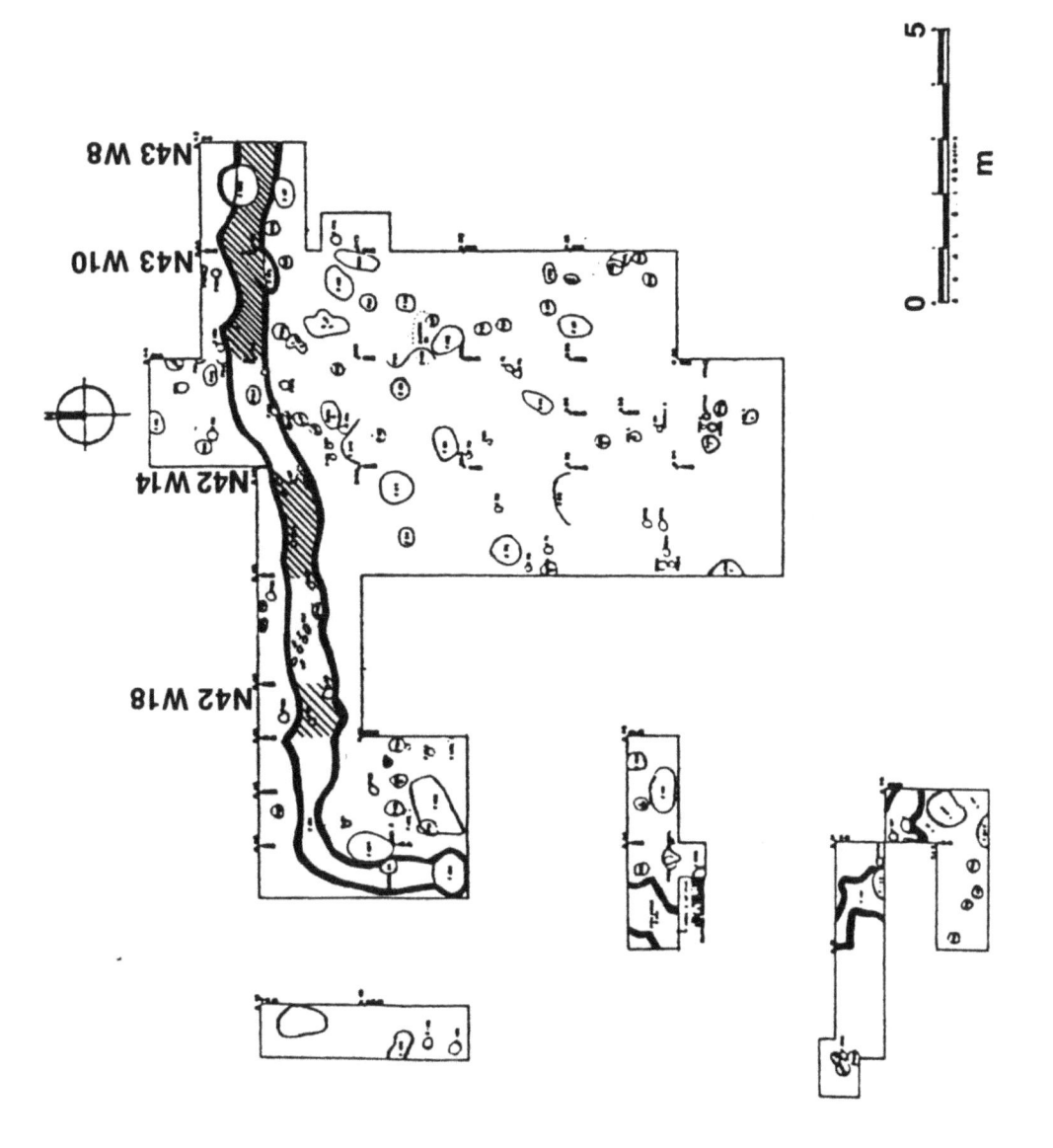

Figure 4. Location of macroblock analyzed contexts.

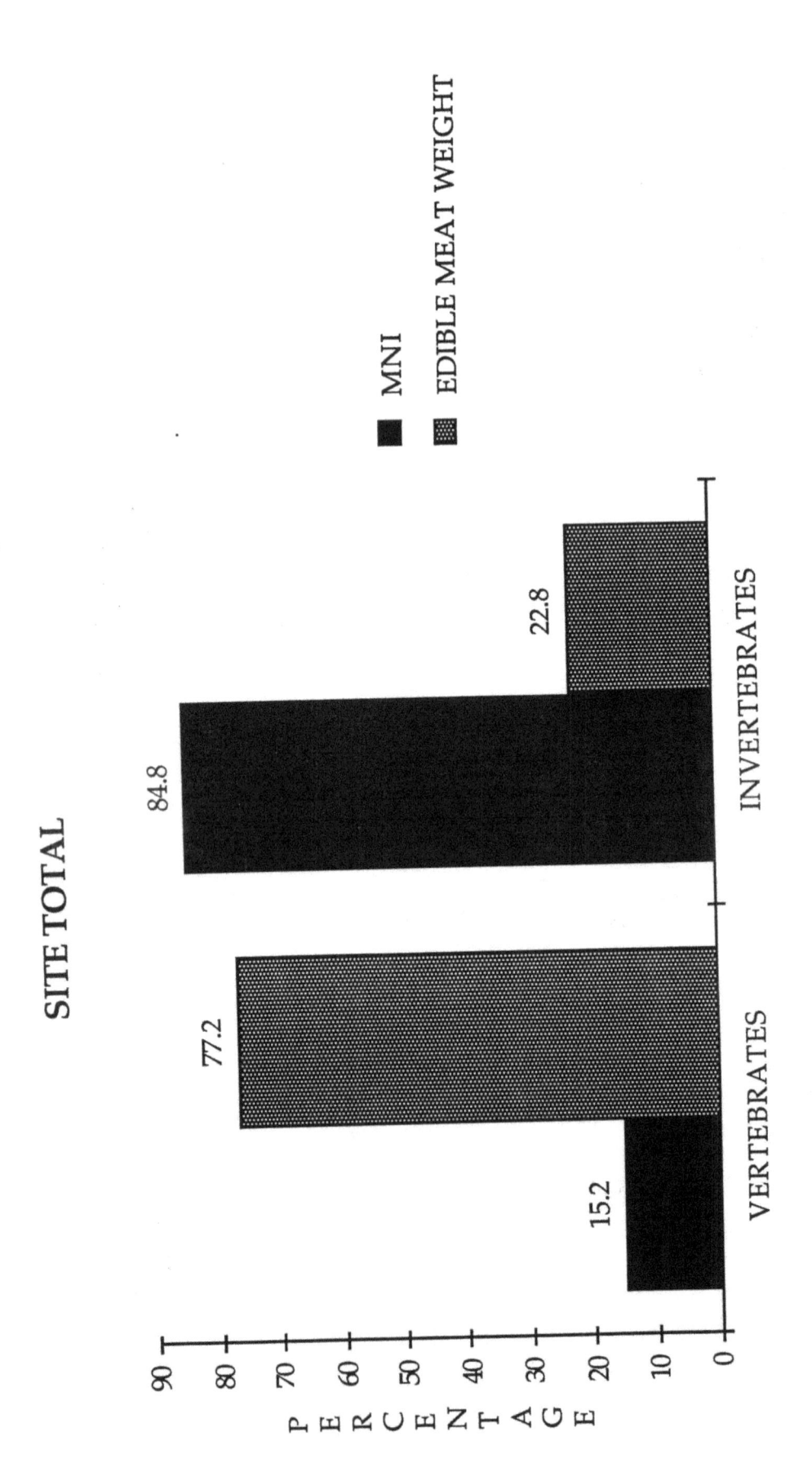

Figure 5. Comparison of vertebrate and invertebrate edible meat weight and minimum number of individuals.

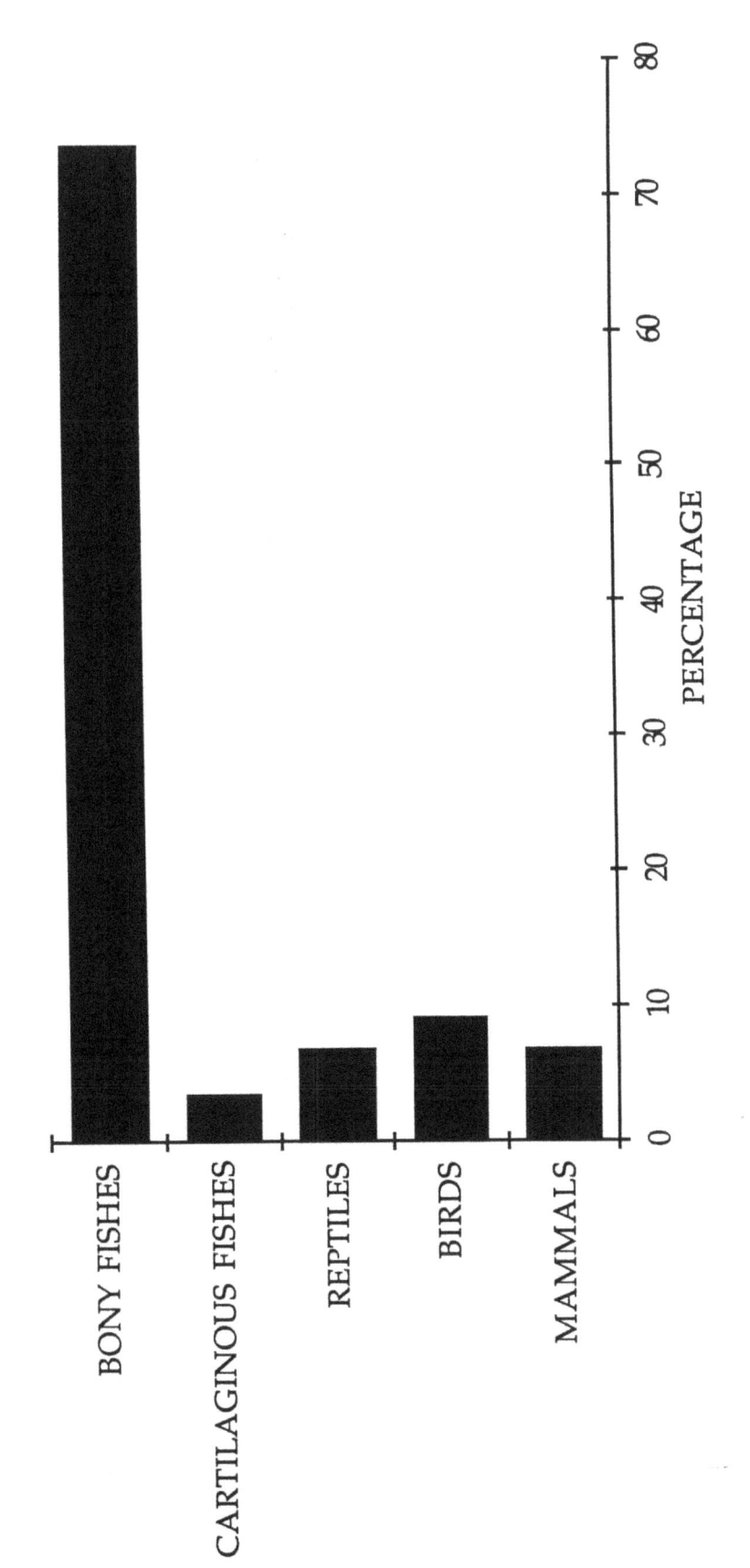

Figure 6. Percentages of identified vertebrate species by class.

IDENTIFIED INVERTEBRATE SPECIES

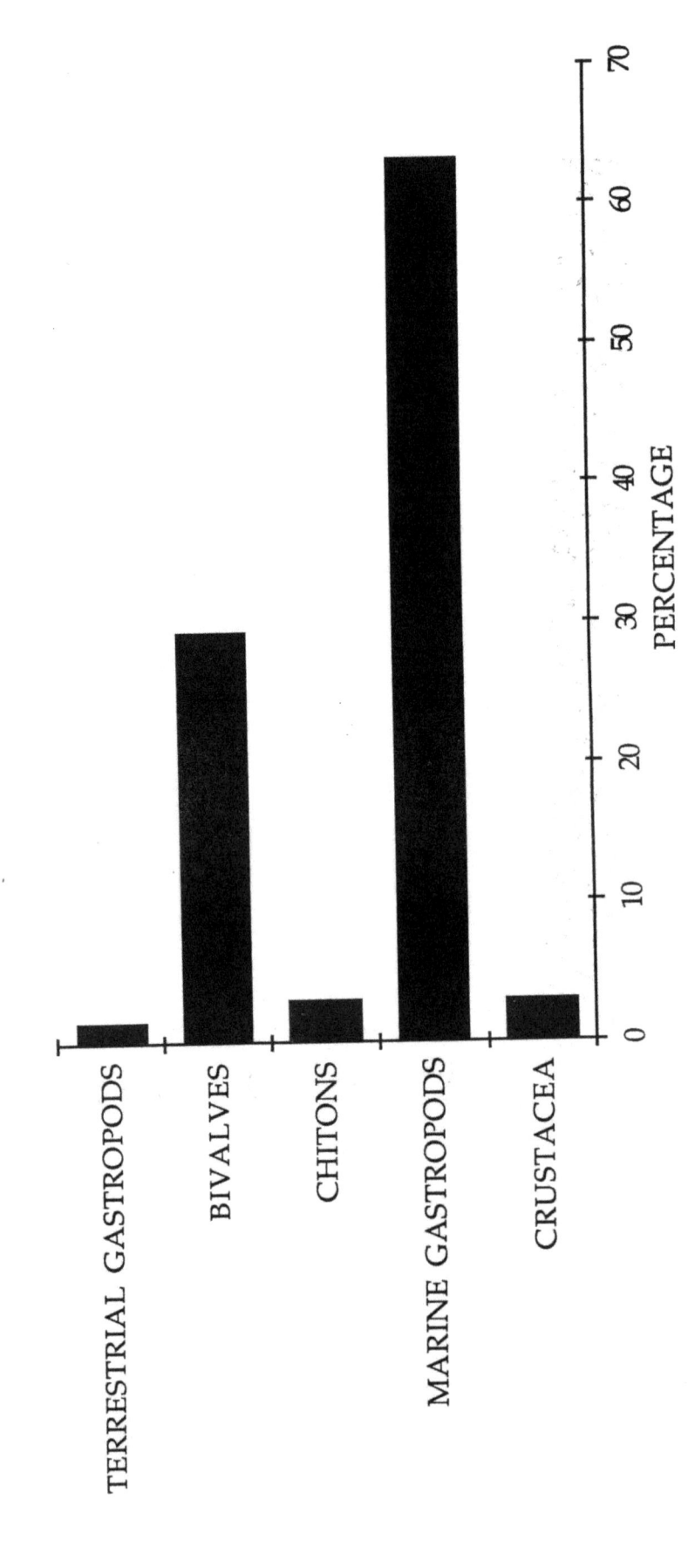

Figure 7. Percentage of identified invertebrate species by class.

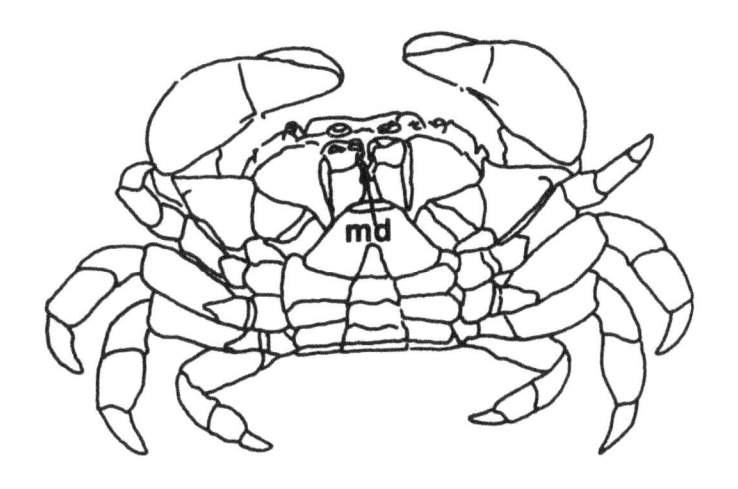

md : mandible

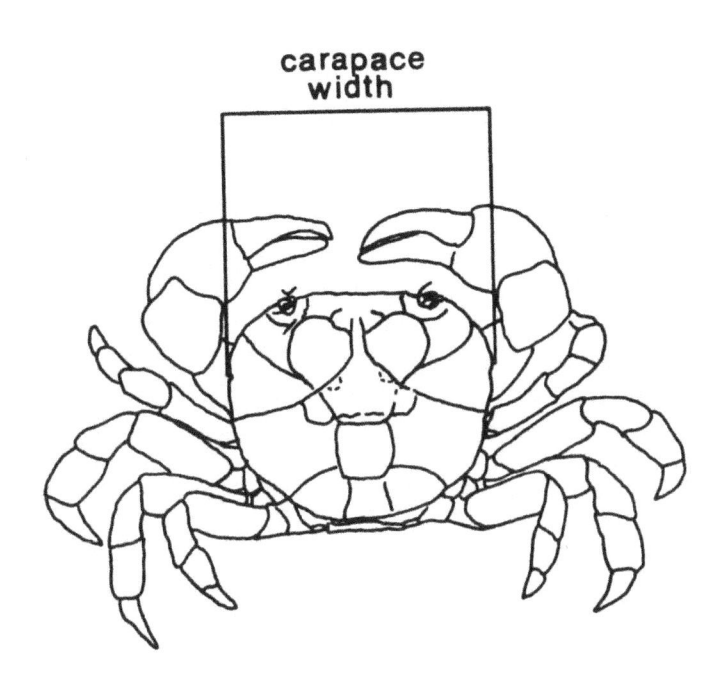

carapace width

Figure 8. Location of land crab mandible and measurement of carapce width.

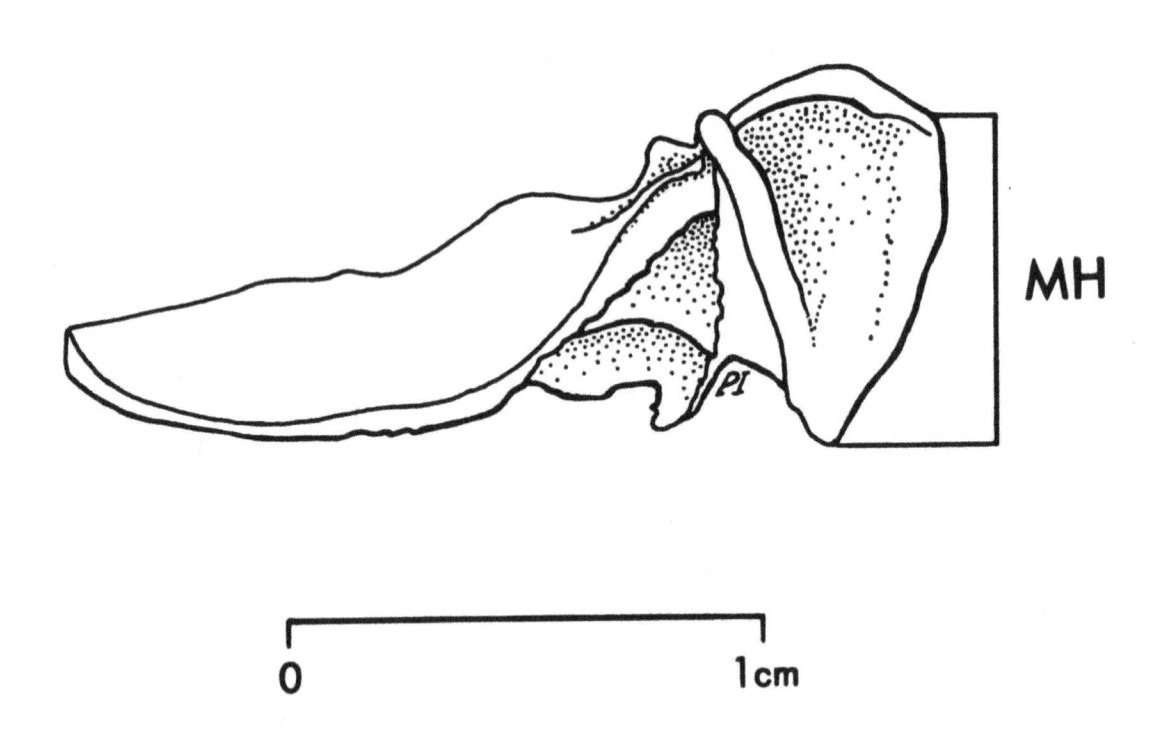

Figure 9. Interior view of left land crab mandible.

N98W13 60-70cm COARSE AND FLOTATION

■ COARSE

▦ FLOTATION

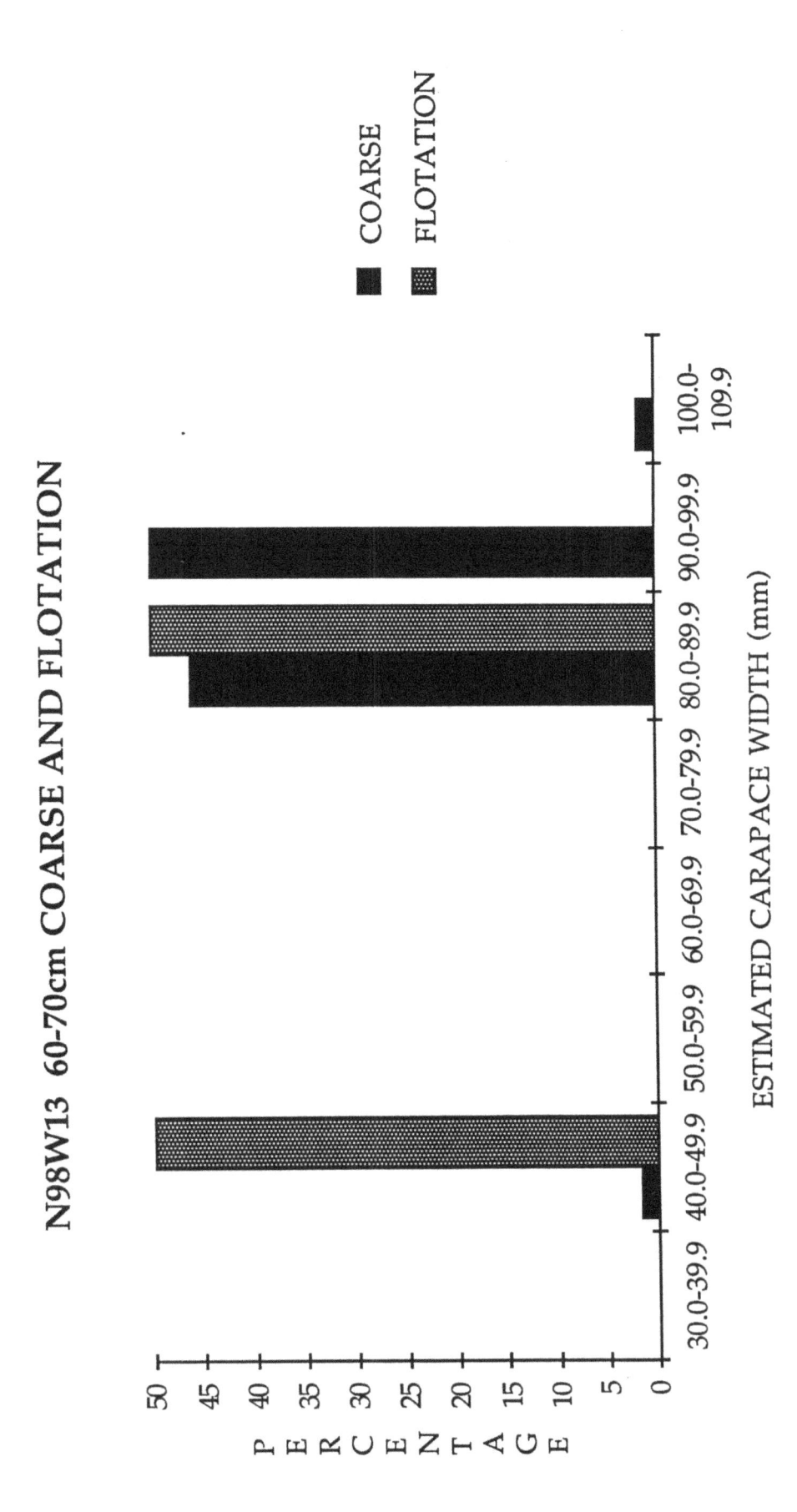

Figure 10. Size ranges of land crabs, N98W13.

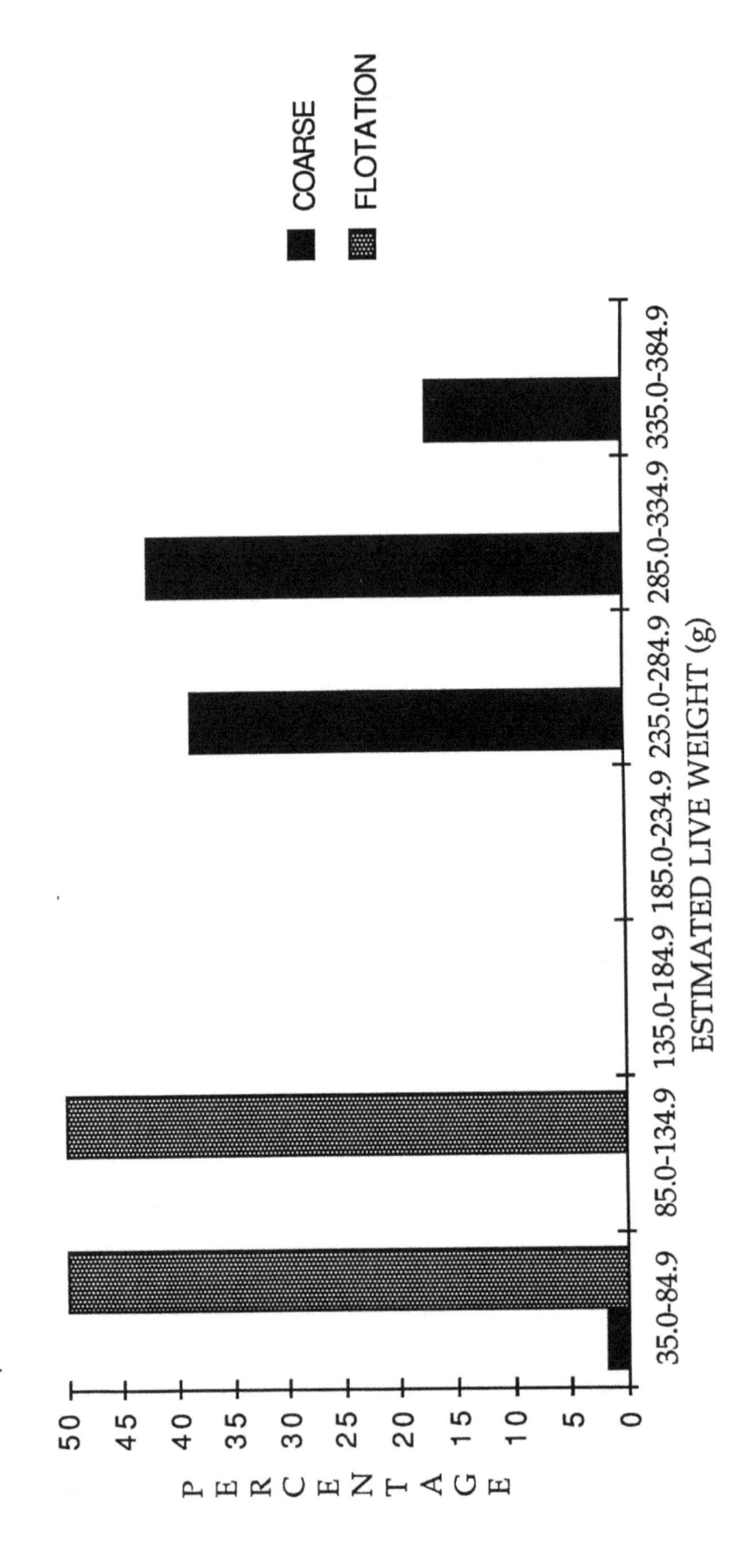

Figure 11. Weight ranges of land crabs, N98W13.

N112W88 FEATURE 104 COARSE AND FLOTATION

■ COARSE
▦ FLOTATION

FISH VERTEBRAL WIDTHS (mm)

PERCENTAGE

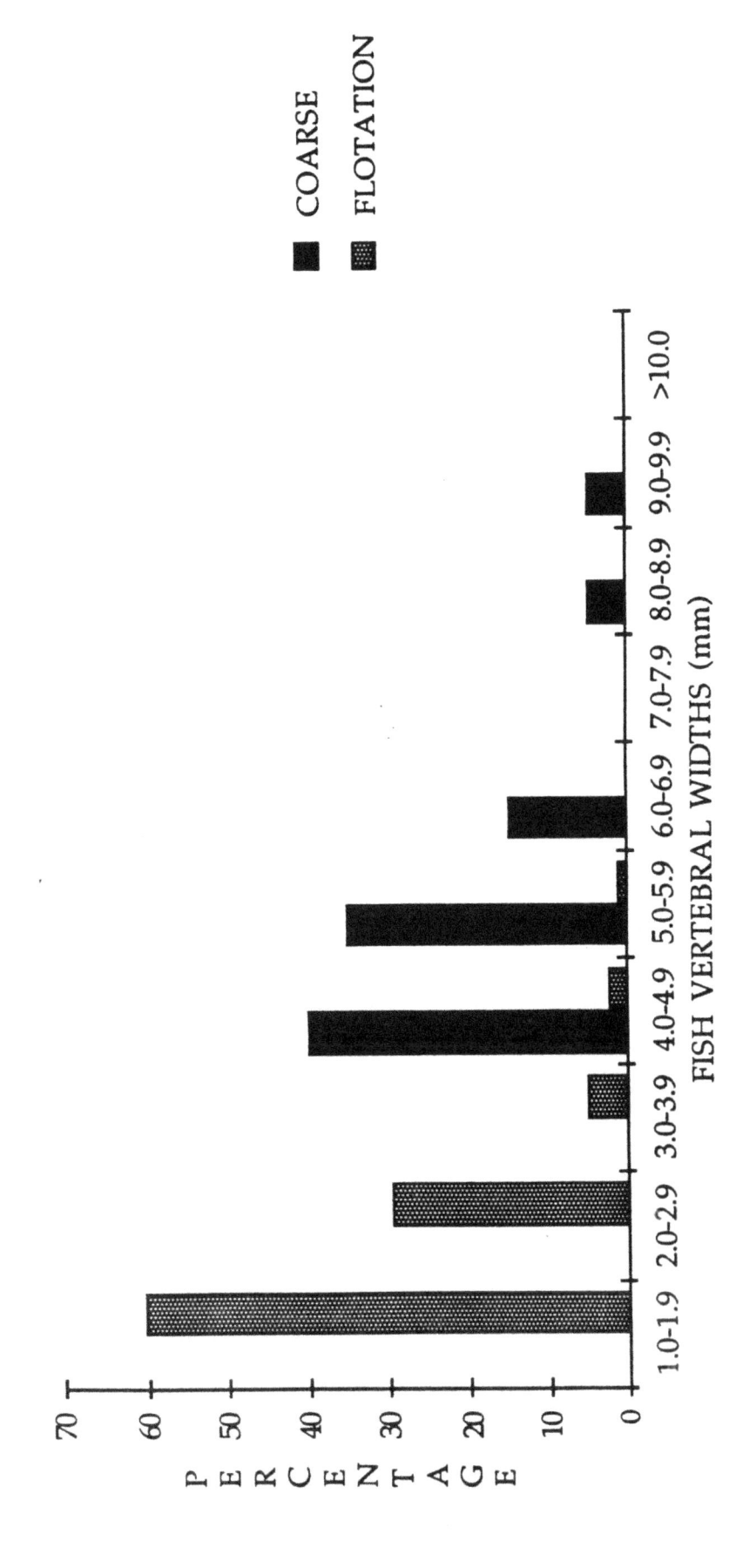

Figure 12. Size ranges of fishes, N112W88, Feature 104.

PREHISTORIC CERAMIC POPULATION LIFEWAYS AND

ADAPTIVE STRATEGIES ON BARBADOS, LESSER ANTILLES

Peter L. Drewett

ABSTRACT

Barbados is a small, largely coral, island to the east of the Lesser Antilles. It was probably settled by Amerindians originating ultimately from the Orinoco Basin of South America, but whose lifeways had become adapted to Island habitats as the result of movement through the Lesser Antilles. Current fieldwork has confirmed settlement from ca. A.D. 350-1500 with evidence of house structures, ceramics, shell technology and some stone working. Subsistence was adapted to the island environment. No land mammals were present on Barbados, so most protein was derived from marine resources with both inshore and deep-water fishing supplementing the extensive use of shellfish. Although somewhat isolated from major developments in the Caribbean, Barbados developed an extremely successful, if somewhat short-lived, prehistoric community.

INTRODUCTION

Barbados is a small, largely coral, island situated to the east of the main string of volcanic islands which comprise the Lesser Antilles (Figure 1). As such it was unlikely ever to have been on major migratory or trade routes through the Caribbean. This may be one reason why archaeologists working in the Caribbean have largely ignored the island. Little systematic fieldwork or excavation had been undertaken on the island until the establishment of the Barbados Archaeological Survey as a joint venture between the Barbados Museum and the Field Archaeology Unit, Institute of Archaeology, University College London, in 1984. Fieldwork, data collection and analysis are still in progress, so this is very much an interim report and should be treated as such. I hope, however, that this paper will underline the fact that Barbados, rather than being a cultural backwater in prehistory (Barton 1979:79) developed its own dynamic cultural traditions within more general pan-Caribbean ones. In many ways the relative isolation of Barbados enhanced the possibilities of indigenous cultural development away from the pressures of developments elsewhere in the Lesser Antilles.

THE NATURAL BACKGROUND

With the exception of small deposits of ash within the Oceanic Group of the Scotland District, Barbados is unique within the Lesser Antilles in that it is entirely composed of sedimentary rocks of non-volcanic origin (Figure 2). These sedimentary deposits contain no hard rocks suitable for utilization by prehistoric humans. The geology of Barbados comprises essentially three elements. The Scotland formation to the northeast of the island consists of Eocene and Miocene sediments. These are surrounded to the south and west by coral rock terraces of Pleistocene date. More recent are coastal deposits of dune and marine beach material, particularly on the west and southern coasts.

The geology of the Tertiary rocks of the Scotland District has been extensively studied by Drs. A. Senn and P. H. Baadsgaard (Senn 1940; Baadsgaard 1960) with more recent studies brought together by Barker and Poole (1982). There is some disagreement over the origin of the Scotland deposits. Barker and Poole (1982) favour a shallow-water estuarine deltaic or lagoonal origin for the sediments while other authorities prefer to see them as deep-water marine turbidities (Senn 1940). Whatever their origin, the Scotland Group appears to contain a continuous succession of some 2,800 m of sandstones and shales of Lower Eocene date.

Above the Scotland Formation are eroded remains of the Oceanic Group deposits. These pale grey, siliceous, radiolarian-rich mudstones and whitish grey, globigerina-rich marls are deep water sediments requiring sea water depths of over 1,000 m for their deposition. Within the Oceanic Group are grey beds of volcanic ash up to 30 cm thick. The whole Oceanic Series is between 350 m and 700 m thick developing from the Middle Eocene to the Lower Middle Miocene.

Lying unconformably on the Oceanic Series are limestones and sandy marls of the Bissex Hill Formation. The final elements of the geology of the Scotland District are the sedimentary intrusive rocks of the Joe's River Beds, which are post-mid Miocene in date. These consist of dark grey to black structureless, squeezed, slickensided, commonly oil-soaked, greasy clays with fragmented sandstones, grits, ironstones and limestones (Poole and Barker 1983). These deposits are thought to have been formed by intense lateral compression of oil- and gas-filled rocks at a considerable depth, which injected them along faults and into domes. This probably happened during the Pliocene (Andean) Orogeny when the Tertiary rocks of Barbados were shear-faulted and intensely folded.

When exactly the island of Barbados arose from the sea is uncertain. It is likely that a great land mass formed at the end of the Late Miocene-Pliocene Andean Orogeny, which subsequently eroded away and submerged in Pliocene times. Towards the end of the Pliocene further uplift probably resulted in the origin of the island as we see it today.

Around the uplifted Eocene and Miocene deposits of the Scotland District developed coral rock deposits. These consist of three main reefs formed and uplifted during the Pleistocene. Radiometric dating has demonstrated that the upper coral rock is up to 700,000 years old and that the lower coral rock is less than 127,000 years old (Broeker et al. 1968). The coral rock deposits consist primarily of robust in situ corals within a matrix of calcareous sand and mud. Channels cutting through the coral include deposits of well-washed and graded fore-reef sands.

Recent deposits include drifts of head and scree resulting from erosion, storm beaches up to 6 m high, and dunes up to 10 m. Most small rivers are flanked by small amounts of alluvium, while the Greenland river valley contains extensive spreads of alluvium and terrace material.

By the first human settlement, Barbados probably was not significantly dissimilar to today in terms of size and shape. Currently it covers approximately 433 km^2 and is roughly triangular in shape, being some 34 km long by 23 km wide. The climate is maritime and tropical, with a sub-humid to humid rainfall regime. The annual average rainfall is 60.24 inches (1530.1 mm), but there is considerable variation both within and between years (Vernon and Carroll 1965). The persistent northeast trade winds blow from east southeast to east northeast across the island. The east coast is severely affected by large quantities of salt spray carried in these winds.

Following uplift during the Pleistocene, soils developed both on the Scotland and coral rock formations. These soils would have reflected closely the parent rocks, but agriculture over the last 359 years has modified them. The soil fertility in prehistoric times undoubtedly was greater than it is today.

The soils (Vernon and Carroll 1965) overlying the coral rock formation are derived largely from the eroded coral itself, but also contain evidence of volcanic ash falls during their development. The soils contain flakes of volcanic glass together with specks of feldspar and pyroxene (Harrison 1920). Other soils closely reflect their parent rock and many are very young soils, particularly resulting from extensive colluviation in valleys.

There is little doubt that the soils held dense forest cover at the time of prehistoric settlement. Certainly early historic settlers refer to dense vegetation having to be cleared for cultivation (Ligon 1970). None of this primary forest survives today, although Turner's Hall Wood in Scotland District and Forster Hall Wood, if not indeed original forest, reflect likely primary forest conditions. Detailed botanical studies by Gooding and others indicate that little of the original flora of Barbados survives (Gooding et al. 1965). Trees present in prehistoric times which survive today, however, probably include the Barbados Evergreen (*Ficus nitidia*), Cabbage Palm (*Roystonea oleracea*), Coconut Palm (*Cocos nucifera*), Cordia (*Cordia sebestena*), Lignum Vitae (*Guaiacum officinale*), Matae (*Pariti tiliaceum*), Manchineel (*Hippomane mancinella*), Pawpaw (*Carica papaya*), Sea Grape (*Coccoloba uvifea*) and Silk Cotton (*Ceiba pentandra*).

There is little evidence for the presence of land mammals on Barbados in the prehistoric period. The only animals mentioned by European settlers were wild hogs left by a Portuguese sailor, Pedro a Campos, in 1536 "to breed there for future wanderers" (Harlow 1926). The island was, however, clearly surrounded by ample supplies of fish, shellfish and crustaceans, considerable evidence for which has been found on all sites excavated.

HISTORY OF RESEARCH

An interest in the prehistoric inhabitants of Barbados began with the publication of shell tools and pottery by Rev. Griffith Hughes in 1750 (Hughes 1750). Serious study of prehistoric artifacts did not, however, begin until the nineteenth century when another clergyman, Rev. Grenville Chester, collected and then presented his collection to the British Museum. His better specimens were published in Britain in the *Archaeological Journal* (Chester 1870) and later in the *Journal of the Anthropological Institute of Great Britain* (Forte 1882). These limited data were used by both Joyce (1916) and Lovén (1935) in more general works on the prehistory of the region. Another nineteenth century collection, made by Sir Thomas G. Bridge, was published by Im Thurn in 1884.

During the early part of this century a series of local collections was made from several coastal sites on the island. Cooksey (1912) and Sinckler (1918) mention collections made by J. Hudson, J. L. K. Pedder, E. G. Sinckler and E. K. Taylor. A particularly significant event for the development of archaeology in Barbados was the brief visit of Jesse Walter Fewkes to the island in 1912. He collected from several sites and published two papers on the prehistory of the island (Fewkes 1915, 1922).

The most extensive collector of prehistoric material on the island was C.N.C. Roach, who collected during the 1930s. Remarkably, he published his findings in a series of no less than 13 articles between 1936 and 1939 (Roach 1936a, 1936b, 1936c, 1937a, 1937b, 1937c, 1937d, 1938a, 1938b, 1938c, 1939a, 1939b, 1939c). These articles, well illustrated with photographs, cover the full range of surviving material culture including pottery, shell and stone tools. Even some evidence of subsistence economy is presented in the careful identification of fish represented in ceramic form (Roach 1939c).

On May 8, 1934, the Barbados Museum was opened to the public following an Act of Incorporation granted on May 31, 1933 (Devenish 1984). The Museum became the focal point for archaeological research on the island with three successive Directors having a strong interest in the prehistory of the island. E. M. Shilstone, N. Connell and R. V. Taylor all collected and excavated on a number of sites including Chancery Lane, Palmetto Bay, Greenland and South Point (Taylor 1986). During this period a general prehistory of the island was written by G. T. Barton (Barton 1979).

During the late 1950s and 1960s visits by two American archaeologists enabled the valuable local work to be put into a wider framework. In 1957 Marshall McKusick visited the island and undertook some surface collections (McKusick 1960). More extensive work, including excavations, was undertaken by Ripley and Adelaide Bullen in 1966 and 1967 at South Point, Chancery Lane, Peak Bay and Sam Lord's Castle. Regrettably, these excavations were never fully published, although accounts appeared in Bullen (1966) and Bullen and Bullen (1968).

Little work on the prehistory of Barbados took place during the 1970s. A small scale excavation of Mapp's Cave was supervised by Robert Riordan between 1971 and 1973, as part of a project studying the Mapp's Sugar Plantation (Lange and Handler 1980), and the Museum continued its policy of collecting achaeological material.

The appointment of Arie Boomert as Senior Research Fellow in Archaeology at the University of the West Indies, and of Mr. David Devenish, followed by Miss Allisandra Cummins, as Directors of the Barbados Museum, led to the development of professional interest in the prehistory of Barbados. Mr. Boomert, although based in Trinidad, visited Barbados on several occasions and published his views on the present state of prehistoric knowledge in 1987 (Boomert 1987). The Museum decided, in 1984, to invite in a team of archaeologists to study the prehistory of the island. This led to the establishment of the Barbados Archaeological Survey in 1984. Each year since then the author has taken a team of archaeologists and students to Barbados to work with, and train, local enthusiasts (Drewett 1985, 1986, 1987, 1988, 1989; Drewett and Harris 1989). During the period of the survey the Museum was also able to employ a United States Peace Corps archaeologist, Steven Hackenberger, who undertook a series of valuable rescue excavations (Hackenberger 1987, 1988). What follows is largely based on primary field research undertaken by the Barbados Archaeological Survey, supplemented by Steven Hackenberger's work and that of some 225 years of collection and study.

DATING AND CULTURAL SEQUENCE

No absolute dating has yet been attempted for material recovered by the Barbados Archaeological Survey. Before the project started, Barbados had only two C-14 dates, one for a shell gouge from Greenland, and the other from charcoal recovered by Bullen from Chancery Lane (Table 1). Two somewhat anomalous dates were obtained from rescue excavations at the Goddard site (Hackenberger 1988) and a thermoluminescence date obtained from pottery from the Shell Oil Site (Hackenberger 1988). A programme of absolute dating is planned as part of the current project, but at present, dating of the cultural sequence on Barbados is based largely on ceramic sequences.

There is clear evidence in Trinidad, Tobago, Martinique, Antigua and St. Kitts of settlement by pre-ceramic communities who hunted, gathered wild food and fished (Boomert 1987). They made stone and shell tools but did not use pottery. To date there is no evidence of such pre-agricultural settlers in Barbados.

During the first centuries B.C. and A.D. the first settlers who made pottery migrated from the mainland of South America into the Lesser Antilles. Figure 1 shows the most likely routes of these migrations, based both on geography and also absolute and relative dates. These earliest settlers used pottery of the Saladoid tradition, for which the type site is Saladero on the Orinoco River in Venezuela (Rouse and Cruxent 1963). Rouse (this volume) considers the Cedrosan Saladoid subseries in the Guianas and Trinidad to be the oldest insular pottery tradition in the Caribbean. This tradition consists of thin, hard, well-finished pottery tempered with fine sand or ground shell. Forms include inverted bell-shaped bowls, bottles, jars and bottomless cylindrical vessels. Some forms are incised and painted with white-on-red. Fine lined incised zoned cross-hatchings and button-shaped applied lugs are typical (Boomert 1987).

It is arguable whether any material of Cedrosan Saladoid type is present in Barbados. Mary Hill Harris, working on the Barbados ceramics for the Barbados Archaeological Survey, suggests that an unprovenanced sherd currently in the Harrison's Cave Collections, being characteristically painted with white-on-red, may be Cedrosan Saladoid. One *adorno* in the Barbados Museum has typical zone incised cross-hatching, while a rim sherd from Level 3 in Bullen's excavations in Chancery Lane has the typical flared concavo-convex shape (Harris in Drewett 1987). There is therefore the slight possibility of activity on Barbados prior to the arrival of Barrancoid influence after A.D. 350. It should be pointed out, however, that the two C-14 dates from the Goddard Site (Hackenberger 1988) are likely to pre-date human activity on the site as the pottery is of Troumassoid type. The probabilistic error limits assigned to these dates do not, however, render them totally unacceptable, although calendar dates towards the end of the error limits would be the most acceptable.

At present it appears most likely that Barbados was first settled by agriculturalists using Saladoid pottery with Barrancoid influence, perhaps soon after A.D. 350. Boomert has suggested that this material should be grouped into the Palo Secan subseries, named after the Palo Seco complex in Trinidad (Boomert 1987).

Material of the Palo Secan subseries type on Barbados spans the period ca. A.D. 350-650. Most sherds are either surface finds, from old collections or colluvial deposits located during excavations. Sherds, for example, came from the deeper deposits excavated by Bullen at Chancery Lane, and from Hillcrest where deep gullies had been filled in by rapid colluviation. This would suggest primary agriculturalists moving into uncleared forest areas and causing massive local erosion as the result of forest clearance that would have upset fragile local ecosystems.

Pottery of the Palo Secan subseries on Barbados has thickened, triangular or flanged rims rather than the flaring one of the Cedrosan Saladoid type. Surfaces are often polished and pinky-buff in colour, with rims often painted red. A groove is frequently cut at the base of the rim. Hollow-backed zoomorphic *adornos* predominate (Harris in Drewett 1987).

Soon after A.D. 650 local pottery styles develop in Barbados, as they do indeed in many parts of the Lesser Antilles. Rouse et al. (1985) suggest these developments took place without external intrusions. Following work by Allaire (1977) and McKusick (1960) Boomert has suggested that the term 'Troumassoid' could be used for the developing ceramic series during the period A.D. 650-1100 in Barbados and the Lesser Antilles (Boomert 1987). This series clearly developed locally out of the Cedrosan Saladoid subseries.

The final ceramic phase in Barbados is represented by Suazoid pottery, which has close similarities with pottery from adjacent islands, particularly St. Lucia. Characteristic utilitarian pottery of Suazoid type is an extremely thick and unevenly finished ware, with rows of fingertip and nail impressions decorating the rim. Tripod, oval bowls are common with round, sometimes shouldered, legs. Anthropomorphic *adornos* dominate, often with gashed, slanting eyes, modelled noses with punctated nostrils and gashed mouths.

The end of prehistoric occupation on Barbados is uncertain. The first English settlers of Barbados in 1627 said the island was uninhabited. This is confirmed by earlier references by a Portuguese slaver in 1536, and by Rodrigo de Figueroa in 1518 (Barton 1979), both of whom referred to the island as uninhabited. The Suazoid phase is therefore likely to have ended on Barbados by about A.D. 1500 at the latest.

SETTLEMENT PATTERN AND MORPHOLOGY

Figure 3 illustrates the distribution of known prehistoric settlements on Barbados. All except four are coastal in location. The greater number of sites in the northeast of the island is almost certainly a result of the ease of location there, and probably does not illustrate great density of population. This area now has no cultivation, little building, and virtually no soil. Artifacts are easily locatable whereas deposition, cultivation and building on the west and south coasts have clearly masked many sites. Likewise inland cultivation, erosion and subsequent colluviation have very obviously caused a similar problem. However, even taking into consideration post-depositional processes, it is evident that the settlement pattern is largely determined by the location of water, and easy access to the sea.

Following an extensive field survey over the winter of 1985-1986 (Drewett 1987) four sites were selected for detailed study. These are the coastal sites at Heywoods on the west coast, Hillcrest on the east coast and two south coast sites at Chancery Lane and Silver Sands. To these may be added that of rescue excavations undertaken by Steven Hackenberger at Goddard on the west coast, and the inland site at Greenlands.

The three sites of Heywoods, Silver Sands and Chancery Lane are all similar in terms of location, although post-occupation processes, particularly at Heywoods, have somewhat masked the similarities. All three sites are on natural marine inlets where the development of dunes and beach material has trapped water to create salt marshes. All sites would therefore have had access to the triple resource areas of sea, land and salt marsh.

The Chancery Lane site is clearly a multi-component site, occupied perhaps throughout the prehistory of Barbados (Figure 4). The popularity and success of this site are probably largely a result of its location. It is situated on low sand dunes towards the middle of Long Bay on the south coast of Barbados. The sand dunes hold back a salt marsh with a degraded cliff line to the northwest. Prehistoric artifacts have been found over the last 50 years in an area some 500 m x 50 m, although later dune and beach development may have masked more of the site. Indeed, it is possible to find sherds over practically the whole area illustrated on Figure 4. Previous excavations include those in the 1930s by Mr. E. M. Shilstone (Taylor 1986), Mr. N. Connell in 1948 (Taylor 1986), Mr. Clarke Holman in the 1950s (personal communication 1987) and Mr. R. Bullen in 1966-1967 (Bullen and Bullen 1968).

Excavations by Shilstone and Connell concentrated on the recovery of artifacts and clearly illustrated extensive use of the site over 1,000 years. Mr. Clarke Holman, having established that burials on the site were often covered with stones, prodded large areas of the loose dunes and dug down to any stones hit. This led him to recover a series of crouched burials particularly towards the northern end of the site.

In 1966 Mr. R. Bullen excavated two trenches at Chancery Lane, and for demonstration purposes, in 1967 he dug a third trench virtually linking the first two. Regrettably, his interim report does not publish a plan (Bullen and Bullen 1968). However, further research in the Bullens' archives in Florida will no doubt confirm that he excavated in the area immediately to the northeast of our 1987 trenches (Figure 4).

Bullen's Trench A was 8 x 20 feet (2.44 x 6.1 m) and revealed four stratigraphic zones. This trench was of considerable depth (for Barbados), being 5 feet (1.52 m) deep at its maximum. Trench B appears to have been dug to the southeast of Trench A. It was a smaller trench, only 4 x 8 feet (1.22 x 2.44 m) and only 30 inches (76.2 cm) deep. Bullen's excavations appeared not to have located any features or burials, but what was simply an activity area and possible midden deposit.

Returning to Chancery Lane in 1987 the Barbados Archaeological Survey excavated four trenches (3 x 4 m) at right angles to the sea, towards the centre of the spread of surface artifacts and southwest of Bullen's excavations (Figure 4). This provided data on the natural development of the site, in addition to its archaeological sequence. The excavations showed that the dune area covered a preserved sand rock bench. The earliest inhabitants probably settled on this bench, with their rubbish eroding into natural hollows. The great depth of Bullen's Trench A is probably one such hollow.

Trench I (Figure 4) consisted of some 40 cm of light grey clayey sand resting on a shelf of natural sand rock. Four burials, three in natural hollows and one in a dug pit, were excavated within Trench I, and will be considered further below (see Human Remains). Trench II was excavated 15 m southeast of Trench I and contained 1.5 m of fine, light grey windblown sand above a sand rock platform. No man-made features were located, but clearly the area had been used to dump domestic rubbish including pottery and shellfish refuse. Trench III, although only 60-80 cm deep, revealed the most complex stratigraphy on the site. The trench is clearly within an area intermittently occupied from Saladoid through to Suazoid times. Two postholes located possibly represent timber uprights from a house. In addition a shallow pit, perhaps dug for storage, was located. Trench IV, excavated 17 m southeast of Trench III, contained entirely natural beach sand with no artifacts, suggesting recent sand dune and beach deposition.

The limited excavations at Chancery Lane indicate a site occupied for about 1,000 years although possibly intermittently. Both during and after occupation the site has been subjected to considerable transformation processes. When first occupied, the site probably consisted of a sand rock bench protecting a marine inlet between it and the degraded cliff line to the northwest. With the development of dunes and storm beach material on the sand rock bench, the marine inlet was probably blocked off from the sea creating a salt marsh which partly survives today. This would have been an ideal resource area for the extensive Suazoid population which inhabited the site. Finally, after the site was deserted, or perhaps causing its desertion (?), sand dunes developed and a storm beach built up on the seaward site.

Little can be said about the morphology of the settlement at Chancery Lane. There were possibly house structures on the sand rock bench, with burials to the northeast and northwest. Activities on the ridge included food preparation involving shellfish, fish and cassava (see Economy and Subsistence, below).

The site at Silver Sands (Figure 5), also on the south coast, is similar to Chancery Lane in terms of location, although evidence to date suggests a shorter-lived site, occupied during the second half of the prehistoric occupation of Barbados. A preliminary study of the topography of the area indicates extensive landscape changes since the prehistoric period. A degraded coral cliff line marks the northern limit of the site. To the south is a sand bar and dunes, which probably developed from the southwest. The dunes have in recent years choked up a small marine inlet. This inlet is known to have been open some 150-200 m inland until recent times. Further inland, in the prehistoric period, the inlet opened into a shallow basin containing a salt marsh (Figure 5 - area around Trenches 1 and 3). Moving dunes and beach sand have gradually filled in the salt marsh and marine inlet, a process almost certainly begun in the prehistoric period.

In advance of development work by the Barbados Ministry of Labour, four trenches were excavated at Silver Sands in 1988. The four trenches were located in an attempt to relate natural features and their evolution to the archaeology of the site. Trench 1 (Figure 5) was excavated in an area where topsoil had already been stripped off by machine. This trench was on the edge of the degraded cliff line which had largely eroded away in this area. Considerable occupation debris including pottery, shell tools and food debris was located. This probably derives from a major occupation area to the north and west. Trench 2 (Figures 5 and 6) was cut through the edge of the marine inlet where surface indications suggested a midden. The trench (Figure 6) cut through a substantial midden which overlay earlier occupation horizons. Cut into the midden, and therefore post-dating it, was a burial pit containing a crouched burial. Trench 3 (Figure 5) was excavated within the area of the infilled salt marsh. It contained some 60 cm of marsh clays and silts, but little occupation debris. Trench 4 (Figure 5) was cut 1.5 m through windblown sand. A prehistoric occupation horizon was located at 70 cm containing pottery, shell tools and food debris.

The limited excavations at Silver Sands suggest activity similar to that at Chancery Lane with settlement around a marine inlet which, on being choked up by dune and beach deposit development, became a salt marsh offering considerable potential as a food source.

Sample excavations at Heywoods on the west coast indicated that originally the site was very similar to Chancery Lane and Silver Sands, although extensively transformed through agricultural activities over the last 250 years. The site at Heywoods covers an area some 300 m along the coast immediately north of the Heywoods Holiday Village, with pottery spreads inland for about 150 m (Figure 7). Two major alterations appear to have taken place since the site was deserted by its prehistoric population. Firstly, the area has been extensively cultivated, perhaps to a depth of some 60 cm, for sugar cane. Secondly, the construction of the coast road resulted in dune material being dumped to the west of the road line. Six trenches, each 2 x 1 m were excavated, two on the sand dunes or beach deposit west of the old coast road, and four at right angles to the sea across the site.

Trenches 1 and 6 were excavated through beach and dune material. Although prehistoric material was found in all levels it is probable that the material is all part of the same assemblage, deposited in accumulating sand which has since been subjected to transformation processes. Trench 2 revealed only 38 prehistoric sherds, but this trench showed evidence of considerable disturbance in the historic period. The section suggests that this area represents the ploughed-down remains of the landward side of sand dunes. Thus the main prehistoric element from this area may have been removed. The number of prehistoric potsherds increased to 179 in Trench 3, but rapidly declined to five in Trench 4 and none in Trench 5. A tentative interpretation of the soil profiles at Heywoods suggests sand dunes and beach material (Trenches 1-3) holding back a salt water lagoon (Trenches 4 and 5) with perhaps intermittently a habitable and cultivable area between (Trench 3).

None of the three 'lagoon' sites of Chancery Lane, Silver Sands or Heywoods have produced good evidence of house structures, although all possibly had such structures. More extensive excavations at Hillcrest on the east coast and Goddard on the west coast have revealed domestic structures, so some greater detail of site morphology can be presented.

The Goddard Site was revealed as the result of a rescue excavation by Steven Hackenberger in 1986. An area some 50 x 70 m was test-trenched with 1 x 1 m test pits on a regular grid (Hackenberger 1987). In doing so, more than half of an oval post-built house plan was discovered (Figure 8). The house consisted of two concentric ovals of earth-fast posts. A fire pit was located in the western part of the house, to the north of a partition wall or windbreak. A single extended burial was found off centre within the southeastern quadrant of the house. A pit containing three bottomless stacked pots to the west of the house may be interpreted as a water hold, as even today it is filled with fresh spring water (Hackenberger 1988). The pottery associated with this house has not yet been studied but appears to be mainly of Troumassoid type, indicating that the C-14 dates (see Table 1) may predate occupation on the site.

Excavations at Hillcrest on the east coast revealed a much smaller post-built structure also associated with Troumassoid pottery. The prehistoric site at Hillcrest is situated on a promontory some 30-35 m above sea level, and so is situated quite differently than the four sites considered so far (Figure 9). Five test trenches were excavated in 1985-1986 and these were followed up by a further 16 (1 x 1 m) trenches and an area excavation in 1987-1988 (Drewett 1987, 1989). The test trenches indicated that the promontory originally consisted of a series of east-west ridges separated by gullies. These gullies were filled with up to 2 m of colluvial deposits, which appear to have accumulated rapidly following the arrival of the Saladoid settlers. Such rapid depositon of colluvium is probably the result of forest clearance for agriculture. Test Trench 18 was the only trench which located any structural features (a posthole), so an area of 60 m^2 was excavated around it. The area excavation was dug in 2 cm spits down to 30 cm, where natural bedrock was located. All artifacts and ecofacts were recorded on overlay plans by spit. This will enable the spatial distribution of artifacts to be directly associated with features excavated into the underlying bedrock.

Two main phases of construction were located, although based on pottery styles both are late in the Troumassoid/Suazoid period (Figure 10). Period I consisted of a line of postholes (Figure 10 [Contexts 15, 13, 45, 8, 37, 48 and 18]) possibly part of a building or fence line, together with a deep burial pit (Context 16). These features were sealed beneath a midden deposit of pottery and shellfish refuse spread around the eastern edge of a small Phase II round house. The edge of this round house is marked by a circle of coral fragments and rubbish some 13 m in diameter. Within this circle is a horse-shoe shaped setting of post holes.

The only inland site examined in recent years was a small-scale rescue project undertaken on the extensive site of Greenland (Hackenberger 1987, 1988). Observation of a new road cutting through the site located Troumassoid pottery, two burials and what was thought to be a house floor, although only revealed in section.

As can be seen, Barbados to date has offered limited evidence of site morphology, although excavations over the last four years have shown the considerable potential available on the island. To date we have evidence for both large (ca. 14 m diameter) and small (ca. 5 m diameter) timber framed round houses. This hints at a possible settlement unit rather like that excavated at Golden Rock, St. Eustatius (Versteeg et al. 1986; Versteeg, this volume). The fact that large round houses were being constructed by Amerindians on Barbados, as at the Goddard Site, would certainly suggest that the Hillcrest structure was either for a very small family group, or ancillary to the main round house. Ancillary structures, fulfilling a variety of functions, are of course common among agricultural communities worldwide (Drewett 1979).

Burial and death rituals were clearly an integral part of life within the prehistoric settlements on Barbados. Burials were found within, or adjacent to, settlement areas at Chancery Lane, Silver Sands, Hillcrest, Goddard and Greenlands (see below).

The disposal of rubbish in middens adjacent to domestic structures and activity areas on Barbados is similar to the midden location at the Golden Rock site, St. Eustatius (Versteeg et al. 1986). Although still at a preliminary stage, fieldwork and data analysis from Barbados indicate that the model of settlement morphology presented by the Golden Rock site may be directly relevant to prehistoric settlement on Barbados.

MATERIAL CULTURE

The surviving material culture utilized by the Amerindians of Barbados consists entirely of pottery, stone and shell. The bulk of material culture must have been made of organic material: wood, feathers, plants and the like, none of which are likely to survive in Barbados unless perhaps carbonized.

The main ceramic assemblages, Palo Secan Saladoid, Troumassoid and Suazoid have been referred to above. The pottey is coil- or slab-made with finishes, decoration and forms varying between periods. Fabric analysis, by Caroline Cartwright and Mary Hill Harris, confirms that there are no major differences in fabric between periods, contrary to other islands. A typical Barbados fabric is non-calcareous with inclusions of small to medium sub-rounded quartz particles, having some iron minerals and some organic voids. Variation appears to be basically on a site-by-site basis, suggesting a domestic potting industry with little movement of its products between sites or islands. Analysis by X-ray fluorescence of a sample of 31 sherds of Barbados pottery led Diksic et al. (1981) to suggest that a sherd of Saladoid Palo Secan pottery may have originated somewhere other than Barbados. Certainly early settlers are likely to have brought some pottery with them, but it should be pointed out that all of the constituents in the sherds analyzed are present in local clays on the island.

Preliminary analysis of the function of prehistoric pottery on Barbados based on all characteristics suggests a fairly simple division into storage vessels, cooking pots, griddles and 'ceremonial' pottery such as those probably used for hallucinogenic drugs.

Stone artifacts used by the prehistoric inhabitants of Barbados may be divided into two groups: those made of local, largely sedimentary materials, and those made of volcanic materials almost certainly imported from other islands. Artifacts made of foreign stone include axes, pestles, hammerstones, beads, pendants and three-pointed stones. A preliminary study of the stone axes by Caroline Cartwright has shown that the majority of the axes studied to date are of pyroxene hornfels. As this usually indicates a contact metamorphism source area, the adjacent islands of St. Lucia or St. Vincent appear to be possible sources. The axes are usually fairly small with an average measurement of 7.2 cm and width of 3.5 cm. They are often trapezoidal or triangular, with oval cross sections (Types A1 and A2 in Boomert 1979). Very few 'eared' axes are known from Barbados, and some that are known may have been brought in as collectors' items in the Historic period. No axes have yet been found in securely dated contexts on Barbados.

Particularly important button- and barrel-shaped beads made of diorite are thought by Boomert to represent trade pieces from Tobago. Beads similar to those from the Roach Collection, now housed in the Harrison's Cave Collection, were shown to have been manufactured in Tobago. Such diorite beads have been found throughout the Lesser Antilles (Boomert 1985). Other odd imported rocks include a piece of pumice carefully carved into a zoomorphic form from Silver Sands on the south coast (Figure 16, No. 2).

Analysis of the non-imported stone objects by Caroline Cartwright suggest five main categories of tool type:

1) Axe forms (Figure 13, Nos. 1 and 2).
2) Medium grained smoothed and rounded 'polishers,' pebbles and grinder/sharpeners (Figure 13, No. 3).
3) Fine-grained smoothed wedge-shaped 'polishers' (Figure 13, No. 5).
4) Knives (Figure 13, No. 4).
5) Projectile points (Figure 13, Nos. 6 and 7).

Types 2-3 are common on all sites and clearly represent an essential part of the material culture of the prehistoric population. The few stone objects found in dated contexts are associated with Troumassoid and Suazoid pottery. The source of many of the rocks is likely to be the Scotland District of Barbados, suggesting local movement of raw materials. Some of the sandstones may, however, derive from the recent sand rock deposits around the south coast.

With the absence of suitable hard stones on the island, shell, particularly the Queen Conch (*Strombus gigas*), was extensively used as a raw material. Conch shell axes and adzes clearly dominate the shell tool assemblage. Caroline Cartwright has suggested that five main types of axes/adzes were manufactured in Barbados:

Type I (Figure 14, No. 1)

> The typical "Barbados adze" with its distinctive 'twist' and scoop-like reverse side. This type commonly measures from 13-17 cm in length, with a maximum width of between 5.2-6.5 cm. Average weight is around 220 g.

Type II (Figure 14, No. 2)

> 'Adze' without the 'twist,' but with rounded top and pointed base, generally finely-ground on both sides. Average dimensions: 8.5-12.5 cm in length and 3-4.5 cm maximum width; around 167 g being the usual weight.

Type III (Figure 14, No. 3)

> This is a variant of Type I, a 'twisted adze' with a diagonal fracture of the top - either deliberate or accidental. This type commonly measures 11 cm in length and has a maximum width of around 4.5 cm. Average weight is 160 g.

Type IV (Figure 14, No. 5)

> This is a variant of Types I and III. A 'twist' may be present, but the significant diagonal top has been ground down rather than fractured, resulting in a wedge shape when viewed in section. Average dimensions: 12.5 cm in length with a maximum width of 6.3 cm; usually around 192 g in weight.

Type V (Figure 14, No. 4)

> This type comprises small (chisel-like) 'adzes' with a wedge-shaped top section. These 'adzes' are often highly polished and decorative, and may be non-utilitarian in function. Generally they measure 5.2-6.5 cm in length with a maximum width of 2.3-2.5 cm and around 20 g in weight.

The utilization of these 'adzes'/'axes' continues to be the subject of much discussion (Cartwright in Drewett 1987). The available literature lists possible uses including tools for the shaping of wooden dugout canoes, hoes, digging sticks, hatchets (sometimes hafted) and so on. Special attention is therefore being paid to a programme of microwear study. The specimens from the Oxford and Cambridge museums have been examined by Roger Grace (Institute of Archaeology, University College London) who summarizes the current positon as follows:

> The microscopic examination of shell axes from Barbados has revealed the presence of polish and striations on the surfaces, with some differentiation between the assumed working edge and the body of the axes. However, it is not possible to determine whether or not these microscopic wear traces are due to use, or produced during the

manufacture of the axes, without experiments being carried out into the manufacture of such axes to produce comparative material for the study of the polishes. In addition to the possibility of isolating microwear traces attributable to use, the manufacturing process can be studied by comparing manufacturing traces produced by different methods of experimental replication with the microwear traces on the archaeological material, so that the precise method of manufacture of these axes may be determined [Roger Grace, personal communication 1987].

As this experimental replication by Caroline Cartwright and Roger Grace proceeds, a corpus of data is being established, but some factors (other than those inherent in microwear trace examination itself) complicate the issue. These include the varying condition of the bulk of 'adze'/'axe' specimens which were generally casually collected and are housed in museum collections, specimens which are worm-drilled, extensively water-worn or eroded, or made from 'fossil' conch and the absence at present of a well-defined chronological framework for the shell tool typology. Clearly, there is a need for freshly-excavated specimens from datable archaeological contexts within the spectrum of a site and its environs. These would represent ideal candidates for future scientific research.

Strombus gigas has also been used whole or fractured for hammerstone or pounder-like tools. Other tool types resembling chisels, awls, gorges, spatulae, scrapers and picks have been recognized in the literature (Figure 15). Hopefully, through the study of microwear we may be in a position to re-define and formalize the use of these functional terms. Conch fragments have also been dressed and carved into discoidal pieces, perforated beads, pendants, plaques, rings and phallic symbols (Figure 15). Some incised pieces have been suggested as the teeth of wooden statues (Devenish 1986). Other, more decorative pieces (e.g., in the Harrison's Cave collection), include carved conch representing birds, sharks, "bound prisoners" and so-called sacred objects. A particularly fine example was excavated from Silver Sands in 1988 (Figure 16, No. 1). Frog and face pendants are also seen (in the Barbados Museum collection). Conch debitage associated with artifact or decorative object manufacture is present to some extent in the museum collections, but obviously collectors have tended to retrieve finished items.

Apart from *Strombus gigas*, other marine molluscs may have been manufactured into tool or decorative object types. The literature suggests that *Chama* sp. valves and split *Cittarium pica* specimens were used for receptacles (Barton 1979), *Mactra* sp. valves for scrapers (Boomert 1987), *Cypraea* sp. fragments for spoons/spatulae (Boomert 1987) and *Cypraea* sp. and *Conus* sp. were perforated or split for decorative objects (Ronald Taylor, personal communication 1987). When considering these suggestions, the role of marine gastropods drilling other molluscs for food and wave action rounding and smoothing mollusc fragments must be accounted for. Birds, animals, and humans may fracture or smash molluscs to retrieve the meat on settlement sites, transitory camps and 'workshop' sites alike. Remnants of food debris must be set aside in the definition of artifactual material.

ECONOMY AND SUBSISTENCE

Barbados is likely to have had few land mammals or rodents other than the rice rat (*Oryzomys* sp.) at the time of its first settlement by man. Prehistoric humans introduced the small Indian dog, bones of which have been found at Chancery Lane and Silver Sands. If land hunting had been a part of the subsistence strategy practised by the arriving Amerindians, they would have had to quickly adapt to an essentially marine source of food protein. Marine resources were, however, considerable and varied. There is clear evidence for fishing, collecting shellfish, catching turtles and eating sea urchins and crabs.

Dr. E. Wing's pioneering work on Bullen's fish remains from Chancery Lane (Wing 1968) is being greatly enhanced by her work on the Barbados Archaeological Survey's current programme of excavations. The analysis of Bullen's fish remains showed that many marine resource areas were utilized. Parrotfishes (*Scarus* sp., *Sparisoma* sp.), triggerfishes (*Balistes* sp., *Melichthy* sp.), porkfishes (*Anisotremus* sp.) and porcupinefishes (Diodontidae) were all caught on the inshore banks and reefs which could be walked or swum to from the settlement at Chancery Lane. Canoes would have been required to fish for snapper (*Lutjanus* sp.) from the offshore banks while shark (Squaliformes), jack (*Caranx* sp.) and sheephead (*Calamus* sp.) were fished from reefs and more open water habitats.

Preliminary analysis of the extensive bone assemblage wet sieved from the Suazoid site at Silver Sands using a 1 mm mesh in 1988 shows a similar range to Chancery Lane. The assemblage appears to be dominated by reef species (parrotfishes, surgeonfishes, triggerfishes, grouper, grunt and jack) as well as pelagic species (flyingfishes, needlefishes and tuna) (Table 2). Rarer fishes include the amberjack (*Seriola*) and the horse-eye trevally (*Caranx latus*) (Elizabeth Wing; personal communication 1988).

The other sites excavated by the Barbados Archaeological Survey have produced fewer fish remains. Heywoods has been studied and included herring (Clupeidae), flyingfishes (Exocoetidae *Hirundichthys* sp.), grouper (Serranidae *Epinephelus* sp.), jack (Carangidae), schoolmaster (Lutjanidae, *Lutjanus apodus*), snapper (*Lutjanus* sp.), parrotfishes (Scaridae, *Scarus* sp. and *Sparisoma* sp.) together with tuna (Elizabeth Wing, personal communication 1988). Hillcrest, which contrasts markedly with the location of Chancery Lane, Silver Sands and Heywoods, produced fewer fish bones and their analysis is awaited.

Turtles appear to have been caught on south coast sites, perhaps as they laid eggs on the gently sloping sandy beaches. Turtle remains have been excavated, both at Chancery Lane and Silver Sands where turtle bones were also carved into pendants (Figure 16, No. 3). Sea urchin remains (*Tripneustes* sp.) have been recovered from all sites including the inland site at Greenlands some 3 km from the sea. Crabs were also probably eaten in small quantities as their remains have been found at Chancery Lane, Silver Sands, Heywoods and Hillcrest. No indication of feasting of crabs of the type located in the northern Caribbean (Rouse, this volume) has been located.

Clearly shellfish were a major source of protein for prehistoric humans on Barbados. All sites excavated have produced considerable quantities of shells. *Strombus gigas* dominate the shell assemblages on the south and west coasts, but were largely absent from the east coast site of Hillcrest and the inland site of Greenlands. This almost certainly reflects shoreline conditions rather than selection. Preliminary evidence suggests all shellfish available locally were collected on a site-by-site basis. The archaeological deposits at Chancery Lane provide a provisional list of species identified. In addition, the back plates of a rock chiton (*Chiton tuberculatus*) are common on all sites, being particularly plentiful at Hillcrest.

It may be assumed that the flora of Barbados was utilized by the prehistoric occupants, but to date the only securely dated carbonized material has come from the 1987 excavations at Chancery Lane. Here charcoal from Suazoid contexts was identified by Caroline Cartwright as coconut shell (*Cocos nucifera*).

Direct evidence for the cultivation of cassava is minimal although food residues on Suazoid pottery from Silver Sands are possibly carbonized cassava flour. Positive identification is, however, awaited. Indirect evidence in the form of griddle plates, possibly used for cooking cassava bread, is however common on all sites. In addition, small sharp stone flakes from Greenland and the Shell Oil Depot Site may have been used in graterboards used to shred cassava (Hackenberger 1988).

In conclusion it may be said that whatever the primary subsistence strategies practised by the earliest inhabitants of Barbados before they settled on the island, once they arrived in Barbados they had to adapt to local resources. Few land animals were available for hunting, so much of the protein intake had to be obtained from the sea. Birds, too, are likely to have formed part of the diet, although as yet the only evidence for the utilization of this resource is from Silver Sands where a ring-necked duck (*Aythya collaris*) has been located (Elizabeth Wing, personal communication 1988). Cassava was certainly grown, but to date the only evidence for the collection of wild fruits is the carbonized coconut from Chancery Lane.

RELIGION, BURIAL PRACTICES AND HUMAN REMAINS

The material culture of Barbados includes a range of objects which may be interpreted as having a socio-religious function within Amerindian society. Triangular ground three-pointed stones have been recovered from a number of sites, and presumably relate to the pan-Caribbean use of similar objects. Likewise small ceramic vessels designed for inhaling drugs are relatively common, particularly in the Roach Collection housed at Harrison's Cave.

Clay body stamps are known from a number of sites. One from the Shell Oil Depot Site appears to have dual male/female sexual representations. Many of the carved shell objects from Barbados may have had specific functions within the socio-religious life of the Amerindians. A number of examples of what appear to be mouth/teeth representations have been recovered and are generally interpreted as being the surviving element of wooden anthromorphic representations (Figure 15, No. 4). It is likely that the discs of shell found at Silver Sands and elsewhere probably represent the eyes of such statues (Figure 15, No. 1). Small anthropomorphic representations in shell are not common from Barbados, but two particularly fine examples have been recovered from recent excavations at the Shell Oil Depot Site (Hackenberger 1987) and Silver Sands (Figure 16, No. 1).

Evidently burial rites were a significant aspect of the religious life of the prehistoric population of Barbados. Prior to 1985 burials had been recorded from Chancery Lane, Greenland, Maxwell and Brandons. None of these burials were adequately recorded and only the bones from Greenland survived. Since 1985 eight sites have produced 16 burials. These burials, all of Troumassoid/Suazoid date, if representative of burial rites on the island, show considerable variety. Two burials were crouched and buried in a sitting position in pits, seven were crouched but lying on their sides (e.g., Figure 17), two burials were extended lying on their backs, two were clearly disarticulated prior to burial, and three were groups of disturbed bones making the original mode of burial uncertain. Although the sample is extremely small, it may be significant that the two crouched burials sitting in pits were both female, while the disarticulated burials were both male. The remaining extended, crouched and disturbed burials were both male and female.

At both Greenland and Hillcrest multiple burial pits were found. At Greenland a deposit of disarticulated bones derived from a mature male was placed on top of the crouched burial of another mature male. At Hillcrest two crouched females, one in a sitting position, were buried with the disarticulated remains of a male in his 30s.

Objects appear rarely to have been buried with bodies in Barbados. A possible exception is the extended burial within the Goddard house, where a clay zoomorphic figure head and a red-slipped clay disc were found by the skull, and a small triangular piece of ground coral was found by the forearm. The other inhumation at Goddard was buried with the forebody of an immature Indian dog.

Detailed studies of the human material from Silver Sands, Hillcrest and Chancery Lane by D. R. Rudling (Rudling in Drewett 1988, 1989) have revealed evidence for deliberate, although mild, flattening in the mid-frontal zone of two of the skulls from Hillcrest. This artificial deformation was probably caused by cradling practices, either by binding or boarding (Brothwell 1972:72). In addition, he has noted some evidence of osteoarthritic lipping.

One of the most serious health problems the population of Barbados faced related to dental abnormalities. Of the nine reasonably preserved skulls no less than six had serious tooth loss. In several cases tooth loss was so great that the mandible had resorbed, concealing all sign of even the tooth sockets. At first a local genetic abnormality resulting in partial or total anodontia was considered, but the presence of abrasive elements in the diet appears to be the most likely cause of tooth abrasion and loss.

ORIGINS, ADAPTIVE STRATEGIES AND DECLINE

OF THE HUMAN POPULATION IN PREHISTORIC BARBADOS

The study of the lifeways of prehistoric man outlined above is proceeding as part of the work of the Barbados Archaeological Survey. Evidence to date would suggest an ultimate South American origin for the prehistoric population of Barbados. Likely routes of migration are from the Orinoco Basin and the Guiana coastal plain, through Trinidad and Tobago and/or through Grenada, the Grenadines, St. Vincent and St. Lucia. Ceramic similarities are greatest with material from St. Lucia (cf. Friesinger 1984) and St. Vincent (cf. Bullen and Bullen 1972), as would be expected given the closeness of these islands.

Dr. Wing has suggested that at first Amerindian migrants would have attempted to duplicate their traditional customs and foodways as closely as possible (Wing 1987). With the absence of a significant land fauna on the islands of the Lesser Antilles they may have introduced animals to provide a meat supply. The agouti (*Dasyprocta*) was certainly introduced to St. Lucia where bones have been recovered from the site currently under excavation at Pointe de Caille (Friesinger 1984). The opossum (*Didelphis*) was also recorded on Grenada and St. Lucia (Wing 1987).

The land mammals appear, however, to have been present on the islands of the Lesser Antilles in very low numbers, so once any Amerindian group left the land mass of South America rapid adaptations would be required. The main change would have been towards recovering the major protein element of their diet from the sea rather than land. This basic adaptation is likely to have taken place prior to arrival in Barbados. The final link with foodways of South America was, however, broken with the settlement of Barbados, for little evidence has yet been found for any introduced land animals other than the Indian dog.

Barbados also required adaptation in the field of material culture as well as foodways. The island being without a source of hard stone, it was impossible to make the fine volcanic axes produced on the other islands of the Lesser Antilles. Instead, shell became the primary raw material used for tool making. This led to the development of an extremely fine shell tool industry, perhaps unmatched anywhere else in the Lesser Antilles.

In terms of density of sites, the population of Barbados peaked during Suazoid times ca. A.D. 1100-1400. A population in the thousands appears not unlikely. What happened between ca. A.D. 1400 and 1518 when Rodrigo de Figueroa described the island as deserted, is uncertain. It is difficult not to see a tragic end to the Amerindian population of Barbados. With little surface water, its over-use and fouling by a large Amerindian population may have been one reason for population decline or an abandonment of the island. Evidence from Hillcrest and Chancery

Lane indicates large scale anthropogenic soil erosion, probably resulting from agriculture. The fragile forest soils of Barbados may have simply been over-utilized and without land animals adding manure, the soils may have become too infertile for agriculture, although of course other forms of manuring may have been practised. Whatever was causing the decline, the extensive tooth loss evident in the population may have added to the population's environmental problems. Alternatively, the population may have been decimated by contact with some other Amerindian group (e.g., those known by Europeans as Caribs) or with some as yet unrecorded group of Europeans, perhaps early Spanish slavers.

The Amerindian population of Barbados adapted to the environmental conditions they found on the island and, as a group, they flourished and developed an indigenous culture - in its own way as unique as any prehistoric culture. Events, environmental or historical, were suddenly and finally too much for this fragile relationship between culture and nature, and within a very short period the Amerindian population of Barbados was gone.

Acknowledgments. I should particularly like to thank the Director of the Barbados Museum, Allisandra Cummins and her Curators Philippa Newton, Steven Hackenberger (U.S. Peace Corps), and Lesley Whatley for their considerable help and support of this project. I should also like to thank all the project members, in particular Caroline Cartwright (stone and shell), Elizabeth Wing (marine resources), David Rudling (human skeletal material), Mary Hill Harris (pottery), Robert Scaife (flora) and Lysbeth Drewett (illustration) for their contributions. Christine Crickmore typed the text, which has benefited considerably from comments by Irving Rouse, Elizabeth Wing, and Peter Siegel.

REFERENCES CITED

Allaire, Louis
    1977 *Later Prehistory in Martinique and the Island Caribs: Problems in Ethnic Identification.* Ph.D. dissertation, Yale University. University Microfilms, Ann Arbor.

Baadsgaard, P.H.
    1960 Barbados, W. I.: Exploration Results 1950-1958. *Proceedings of the International Geological Congress* 21:21-27. Copenhagen.

Barker, L.H. and E.G. Poole
    1982 *The Geology and Mineral Assessment of the Island of Barbados.* Barbados Government Report, Bridgetown.

Barton, G.T.
    1979 *The Prehistory of Barbados.* Reprinted. Originally published 1953, Advocate, Barbados.

Boomert, Aad
    1979 The Prehistoric Stone Axes of the Guianas: A Typological Classification. *Journal of Archaeology and Anthropology* 2:99-124.

    1985 *Preliminary Report on the 1985 Tobago Archaeological Project.* University of the West Indies, Trinidad.

    1987 Note on Barbados Prehistory. *Journal of the Barbados Museum and Historical Society* 38:8-43.

Broeker, W.S., D.L. Thurber, J. Goddard, R.K. Matthews, and K.J. Mesolella
1968 Milankovitch Hypothesis supported by Precise Dating of the Coral Reefs and Deep Sea Sediments. *Science* 159:297-300.

Brothwell, D.R.
1972 *Digging up Bones*. 2nd ed. Britsh Museum of Natural History, London.

Bullen, Ripley P.
1966 Barbados and the Archaeology of the Caribbean. *Journal of the Barbados Museum and Historical Society* 32:16-19.

Bullen, Ripley P. and Adelaide K. Bullen
1968 Barbados Archaeology:1966. *Proceedings of the International Congress for the Study of Pre-Columbian Cultures in the Lesser Antilles* 2:134-144. Barbados.

1972 *Archaeological Investigations on St. Vincent and the Grenadines, West Indies*. American Studies Report No. 8. The William C. Bryant Foundation, Gainesville.

Chester, G.J.
1870 The Shell Implements and other Antiquities of Barbados. *Archaeological Journal* 27:43-52.

Cooksey, C.
1912 The First Barbadians. *Timehri* 3(2):142-144.

Devenish, D.C.
1984 Barbados Museum, Past, Present and Future. Ms. on file, Barbados Museum and Historical Society, Bridgetown.

1986 The Use of Conch Shells in Prehistoric Barbados with Special Reference to Two Figurines. *Journal of the Barbados Museum and Historical Society* 37:365-370.

Diksic, M., J.-L. Galinier, and I. Yaffe
1981 Barbados and the Archaeology of the Caribbean. *Journal of the Barbados Museum and Historical Society* 36:229-235.

Drewett, P.L.
1979 New Evidence for the Structure and Function of Middle Bronze Age Round Houses in Sussex. *Archaeological Journal* 136:3-11.

1985 Barbados: The Prehistory of an Island. Pilot Survey. Ms. on file, Institute of Archaeology, University of London.

1986 A Survey of Prehistoric Barbados. *Caribbean Conservation News* 4(5):16-18.

1987 Archaeological Survey of Barbados. 1st Interim Report. *Journal of the Barbados Museum and Historical Society* 38:44-80.

1988 Archaeological Survey of Barbados. 2nd Interim Report. *Journal of the Barbados Museum and Historical Society* 38:196-204.

1989 Archaeological Survey of Barbados. 3rd Interim Report. *Journal of the Barbados Museum and Historical Society* 38:338-352.

Drewett, P.L. and M. H. Harris
    1989   Archaeological Survey of Barbados 1985-1987. Paper presented at the 12th International Congress for Caribbean Archaeology, Cayenne, French Guiana.

Fewkes, J. W.
    1915   Archaeology of Barbados. *Proceedings of the National Academy of Science, United States* 1(1):47-51.

    1922   *A Prehistoric Island Culture Area of America.* Bureau of American Ethnology Bulletin No. 34. Smithsonian Institution, 1912-1913, pp. 35-281. Government Printing Office, Washington, D.C.

Forte, J.
    1882   Note on Carib Chisels. *Journal of the Anthropological Institute of Great Britain* 40:2-3.

Friesinger, H.
    1984   *Grabungen und Forschungen auf St. Lucia.* Mitteilungen der Prahistorischen Kommission de Osterreichischen Akademiei der Wissenschaften 13. University of Vienna, Austria.

Gooding, E.G.B., A.R. Loveless, and G.R. Proctor
    1965   *Flora of Barbados.* Her Majesty's Stationery Office, London.

Hackenberger, S.
    1987   *Archaeological Investigations, Barbados, West Indies, 1986.* Ms. on file, Barbados Museum and Historical Society, Bridgetown.

    1988   An Abstract of Archaeological Investigations by the Barbados Museum, 1986. *Journal of the Barbados Museum and Historical Society* 38:155-162.

Harlow, V.T.
    1926   *A History of Barbados, 1625-1685.* Oxford University Press, London.

Harrison, J.B.
    1920   The Extraneous Minerals in the Coral Limestones of Barbados. *Quarterly Journal of the Geological Society* 75:158-172.

Hughes, G.
    1750   *Natural History of Barbados.* Privately printed, London.

Im Thurnim, E.F.
    1884   Notes on West Indian Stone Implements; and other Indian Relics. *Timehri* 3:103-137.

Joyce, T.A.
    1916   *Central American and West Indian Archaeology.* G.P. Putnam's Sons, New York.

Lange, Frederick W. and Jerome S. Handler
    1980   The Archaeology of Mapps Cave: A Contribution to the Prehistory of Barbados. *Journal of the Virgin Islands Archaeological Society* 9:3-17.

Ligon, R.
    1970   *A True and Exact History of the Island of Barbados.* Reprinted. Frank Cass, London. Originally published 1647, Privately printed, London.

Lovén, Sven
   1935 *Origins of the Tainan Culture, West Indies.* Elanders Bokfryckeri Äkfiebolag, Göteborg.

McKusick, M.B.
   1960 *The Distribution of Ceramic Styles in the Lesser Antilles, West Indies.* Ph.D. dissertation, Yale University. University Microfilms, Ann Arbor.

Poole, E.G. and L.H. Barker
   1983 *The Geology of Barbados.* Survey No. 1229. Directorate of Overseas Survey, London.

Roach, C.N.C.
   1936a Old Barbados, Ch. 1, Arawak and Carib. *Journal of the Barbados Museum and Historical Society* 3:137-148.

   1936b Old Barbados. Ch. 2, Arawak and Carib. *Journal of the Barbados Museum and Historical Society* 3:211-222.

   1936c Old Barbados, Ch. 2, Arawak and Carib. *Journal of the Barbados Museum and Historical Society* 4:12-21.

   1937a Old Barbados, Ch. 3, Shell Implements. *Journal of the Barbados Museum and Historical Society* 4:53-67.

   1937b Old Barbados Ch. 3, Spear-heads. *Journal of the Barbados Museum and Historical Society* 4:109-122.

   1937c Old Barbados Ch. 3 (continued). *Journal of the Barbados Museum and Historical Society* 4:167-179.

   1937d Old Barbados Ch. 4, Stone Implements. *Journal of the Barbados Museum and Historical Society* 5:3-10.

   1938a Old Barbados Ch. 5, Pottery. *Journal of the Barbados Museum and Historical Society* 5:85-100.

   1938b Old Barbados Ch. 5, Pots. *Journal of the Barbados Museum and Historical Society* 5:130-143.

   1938c Old Barbados Ch. 5, Rare Vessels. *Journal of the Barbados Museum and Historical Society* 4:26-40.

   1939a Old Barbados, Ch. 6, Pottery Handles. *Journal of the Barbados Museum and Historical Society* 6:74-86.

   1939b Old Barbados Ch. 7, Fishing: Canoe Building and Hunting. *Journal of the Barbados Museum and Historical Society* 6:139-151.

   1939c Old Barbados Ch. 7, Fishing and Hunting. *Journal of the Barbados Museum and Historical Society* 6:191-197.

Rouse, Irving, Louis Allaire, and Aad Boomert
    1985   Eastern Venezuela, the Guianas, and the West Indies. Ms. prepared for an unpublished volume, *Chronologies in South American Archaeology*, compiled by Clement W. Meighan, Department of Anthropology, University of California, Los Angeles.

Rouse, Irving, and José M. Cruxent
    1963   *Venezuelan Archaeology*. Yale University Press, New Haven.

Senn, A.
    1940   Palaeogene of Barbados and its Bearing on the History and Structure of the Antillean-Caribbean Region. *Bulletin of the American Association of Geology* 24:1548-1610.

Sinckler, E.G.
    1918   The Indians of Barbados. *Timehri* 3:48-55.

Taylor, R.V.
    1986   Archaeological Events in Barbados. *Journal of the Barbados Museum and Historical Society* 37:337-342.

Vernon, K.C., and D.M. Carroll
    1965   *Soil and Land-Use Surveys*. No. 18. University of the West Indies, Cave Hill, Barbados.

Versteeg, A.H., L. van der Valk, and H.J. Putker
    1986   Archaeological Investigations on St. Eustatius (Netherlands Antilles). Interim Report. Ms. on file, Institute of Prehistory, Leiden State University, Leiden.

Wing, Elizabeth S.
    1968   Aboriginal fishing in the Windward Islands. *Proceedings of the International Congress for the Study of Pre-Columbian Cultures in the Lesser Antilles* 2:103-107. Barbados.

    1987   Human Exploitation of Animal Resources in the Caribbean. Ms. on file, Zooarchaeology Laboratory, Florida Museum of Natural History, University of Florida, Gainesville.

Table 1. Radiometric Dates.

Site	Material	Laboratory	Date (B.P.)[a]	Date (B.C./A.D.)
Carbon 14 Dates				
Greenland	Shell gouge	BM-128	850±150	A.D. 1100
Chancery Lane	Charcoal	I-2486	1570±95	A.D. 380
Goddard	Charcoal	Beta-20723	1950±150	A.D. 0
Goddard	Charcoal	Beta-19969	2253±55	285 B.C.
Thermoluminescence Dates				
Shell Oil	Pottery	Alpha-3185[b]		A.D. 846-1214

[a] The C-14 dates are uncorrected.

[b] From Hackenberger (1988).

Table 2. Faunal Identifications from the Silver Sands Site.

Taxa	Fragment Count	%	Minimum Number of Individuals	%
Oryzomine	29	2	4	4
Canis familiaris	4	0	2	2
Indet. mammal or bird	7	1	0	0
Aythya collaris	1	0	1	1
Laridae	1	0	1	1
Porphyrula martinicus	2	0	1	1
Indet. bird	4	0	0	0
Cheloniidae cf. *Chelonia*	55	4	3	3
Ginglymostoma cirratum	1	0	1	1
Murinidae cf. *Gymnothorax*	2	0	1	1
Hirundichthys affinis	124	9	3	3
Belonidae cf. *Strongylura*	5	0	1	1
Holocentrus sp.	2	0	1	1
Epinephelus sp.	11	1	3	3
Epinephelus cf. *morio*	3	0	1	1
Carangidae	1	0	0	0
Caranx hippos	1	0	1	1
Caranx latus	15	1	3	3
Caranx cf. *lugubris*	1	0	1	1
Caranx ruber	9	1	2	2
Seriola sp.	1	0	1	1
Lutjanus sp.	4	0	2	2
Anisotremus surinamensis	2	0	1	1
Haemulon sp.	22	2	5	5
Labridae	2	0	0	0
Halichoeres sp.	6	0	1	1
Scaridae	4	0	0	0
Scarus sp.	7	1	3	3
Sparisoma sp.	60	5	7	7
Sparisoma cf. *rubripinne*	2	0	1	1
Sparisoma viride	92	7	10	10
Acanthurus sp.	233	17	28	27
Scombridae	39	3	3	3
Auxis sp.	6	0	1	1
cf. *Euthunnus* sp.	10	1	1	1
cf. *Thunnus* sp.	6	0	1	1
Scorpaena sp.	4	0	1	1
Balistidae cf. *Balistes*	18	1	6	6
Diodon sp.	2	0	1	1
Indet. fish	535	40	0	0
TOTAL	1333		103	

Table 3. Marine Mollusc Identifications from the Chancery Lane Site.

Cypraea zebra	*Nassarius* sp.
Cypraea sp.	*Tonna* sp.
Nerita tessellata	*Purpura patula*
Nerita visicolor	*Thais rustica*
Nerita peloronta	*Tectarius muricatus*
Nerita sp.	*Conus* sp.
Neritina relivata	*Tericula imperialis*
Charonia variegata	*Cassis* sp.
Cittarium pica	*Phalium* sp.
Cymatium nicobaricum	*Fissurella nodosa*
Cymatium sp.	*Modulus* sp.
Natica correna	*Astraea* sp.
Melongena melongena	*Fasciolaria* sp.
Cypraecassis testiculus	*Voluta musica*
Strombus gigas	*Arca imbricata*
Lucapina aegis	*Arca* sp.
Calliostoma sarcodum	*Codakia orbicularis*
Daphnella stegeri	*Codakia* sp.
Arene cruentata	*Antigona listeri*
Planaxis sp.	*Phacoides pectinatus*
Cancellaria sp.	*Lima* sp.
Littorina ziczac	*Chama* sp.
Columbella sp.	*Pteria* sp.

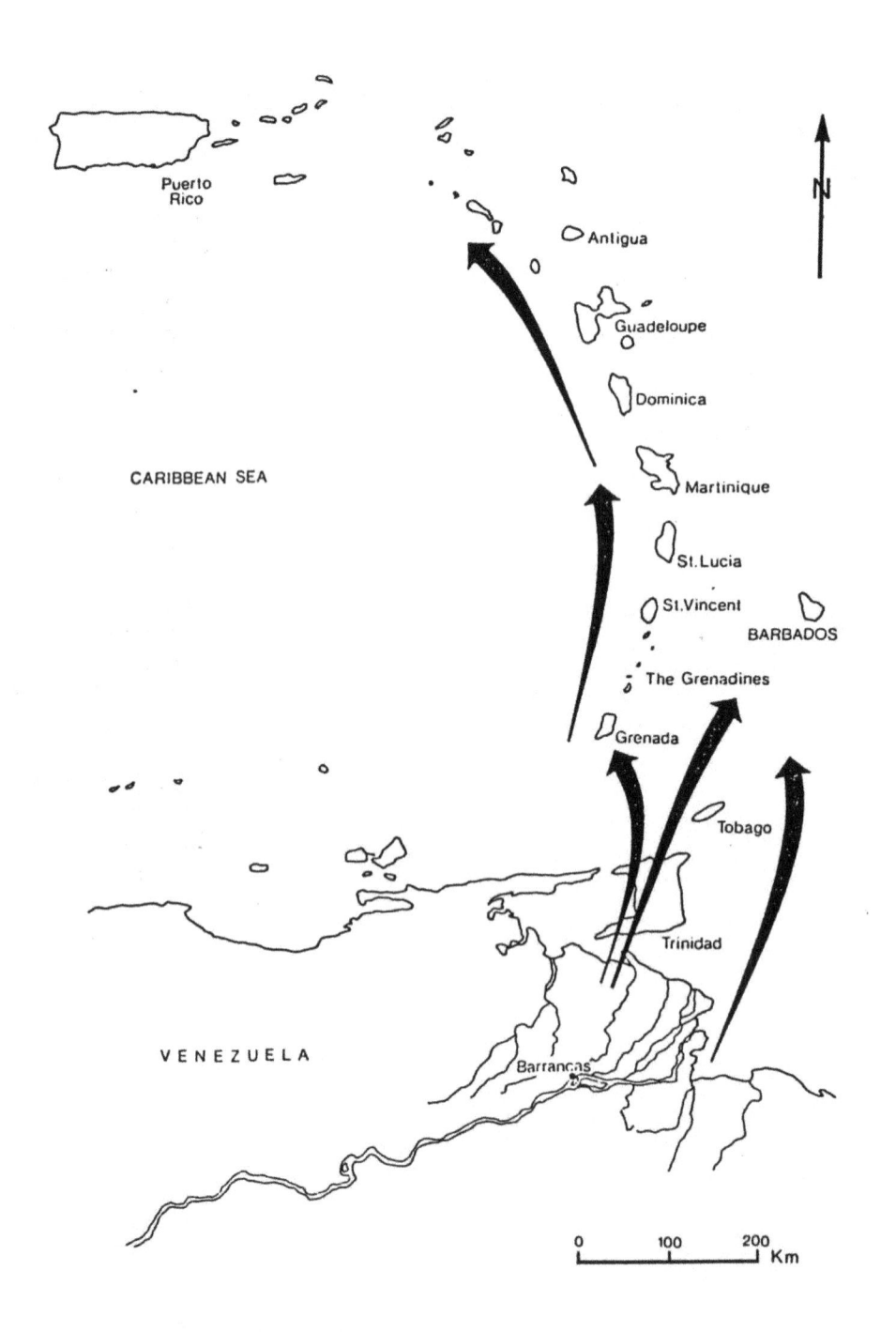

Figure 1. The Lesser Antilles. Location of Barbados and possible migration routes.

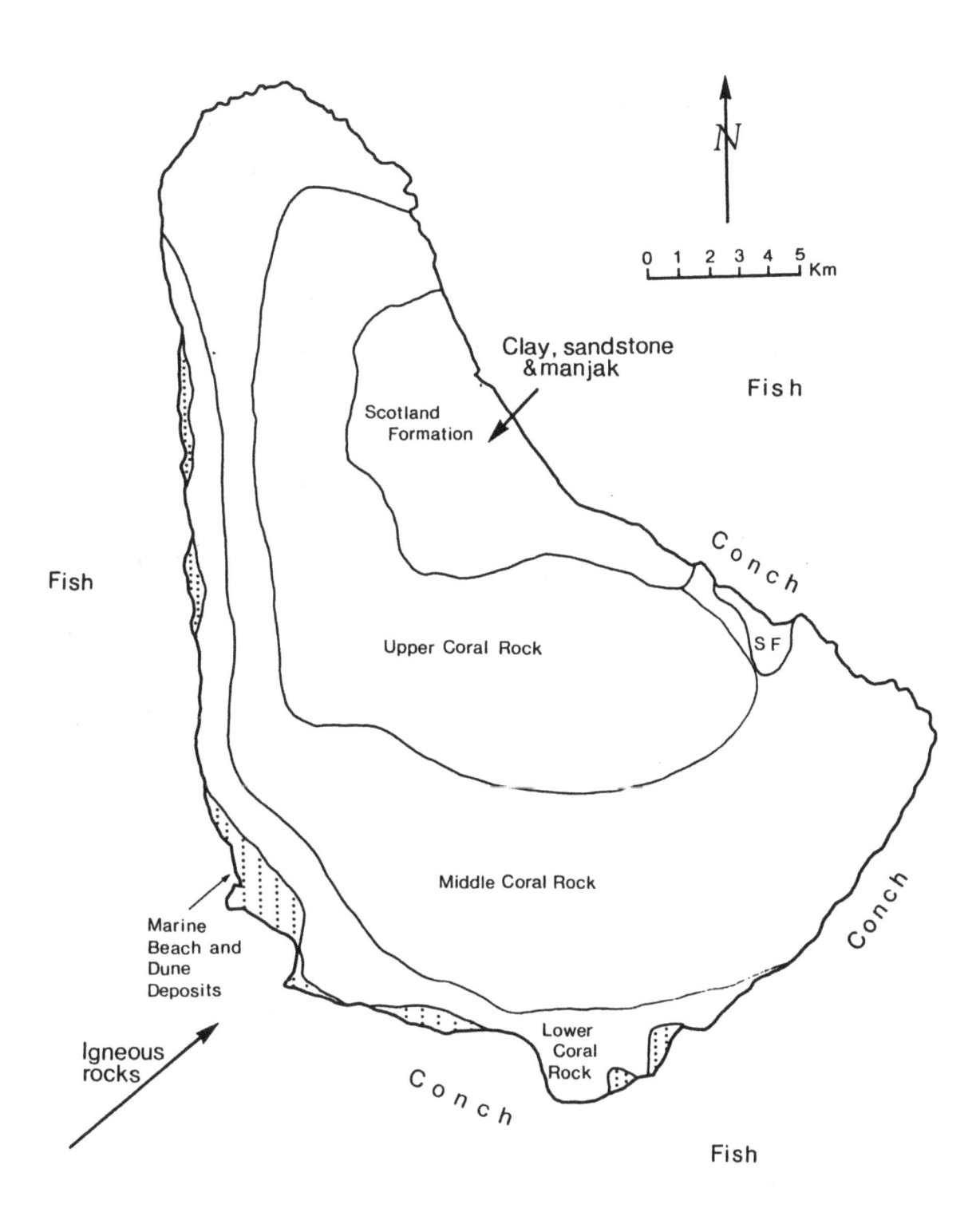

Figure 2. A simplified geological map of Barbados with main offshore resources.

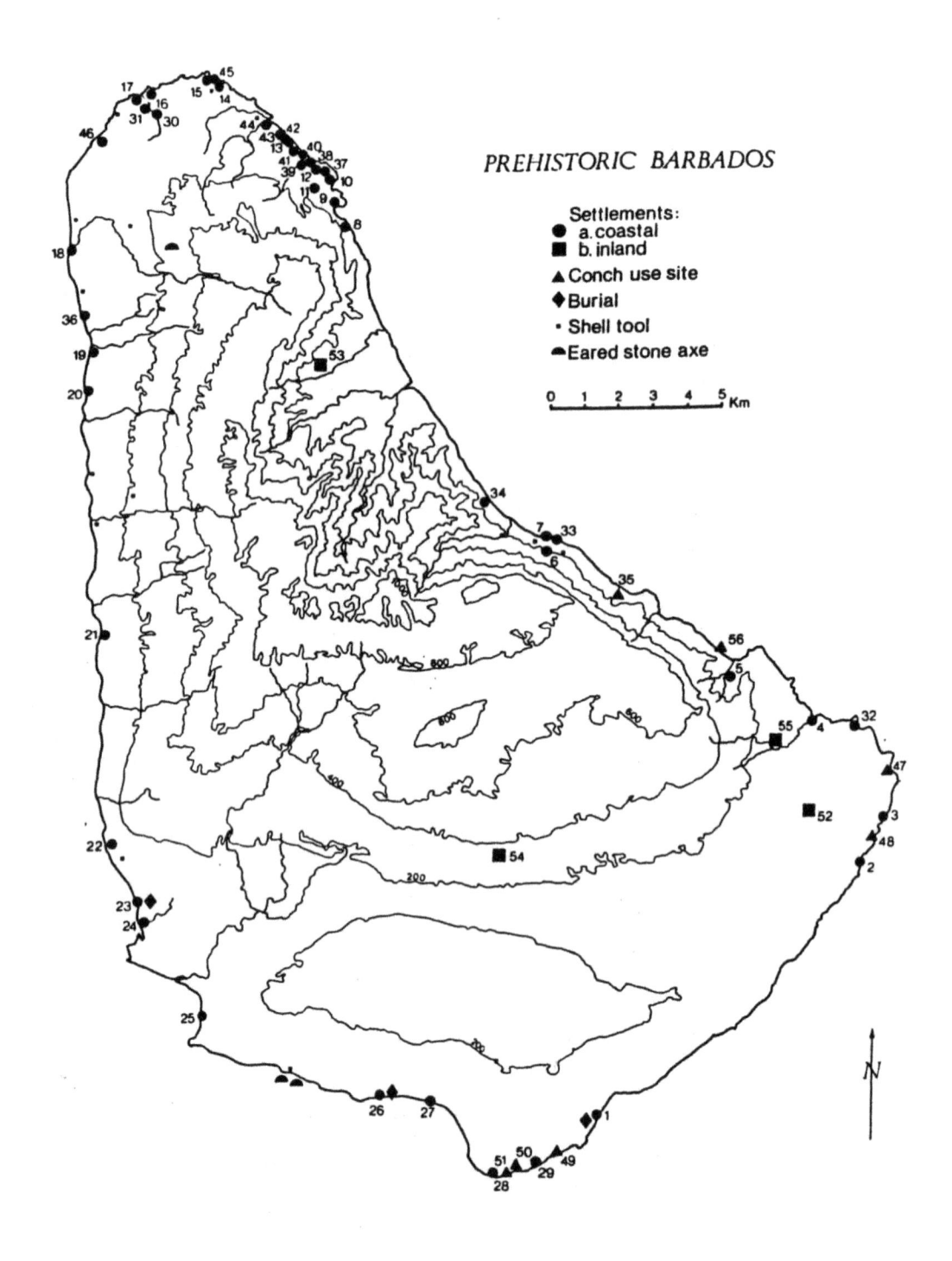

Figure 3. Distribution of prehistoric settlements on Barbados. Sites excavated by the Barbados Archaeological Survey 1985-1988 are: (1) Chancery Lane, (29) Silver Sands, (19) Heywoods, and (33) Hillcrest.

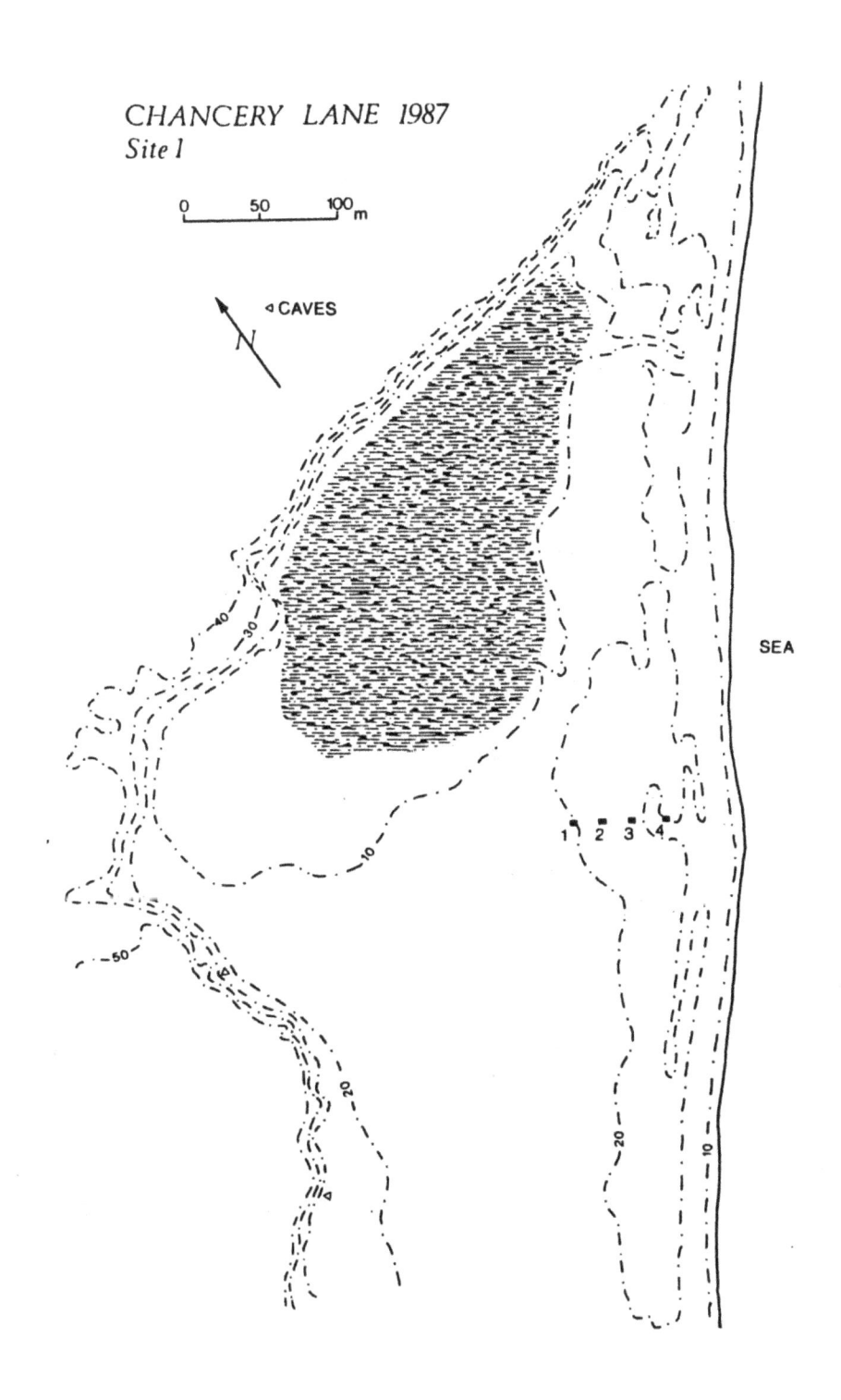

Figure 4. Chancery Lane. General site plan and location of trenches excavated in 1987.

SILVER SANDS 1988

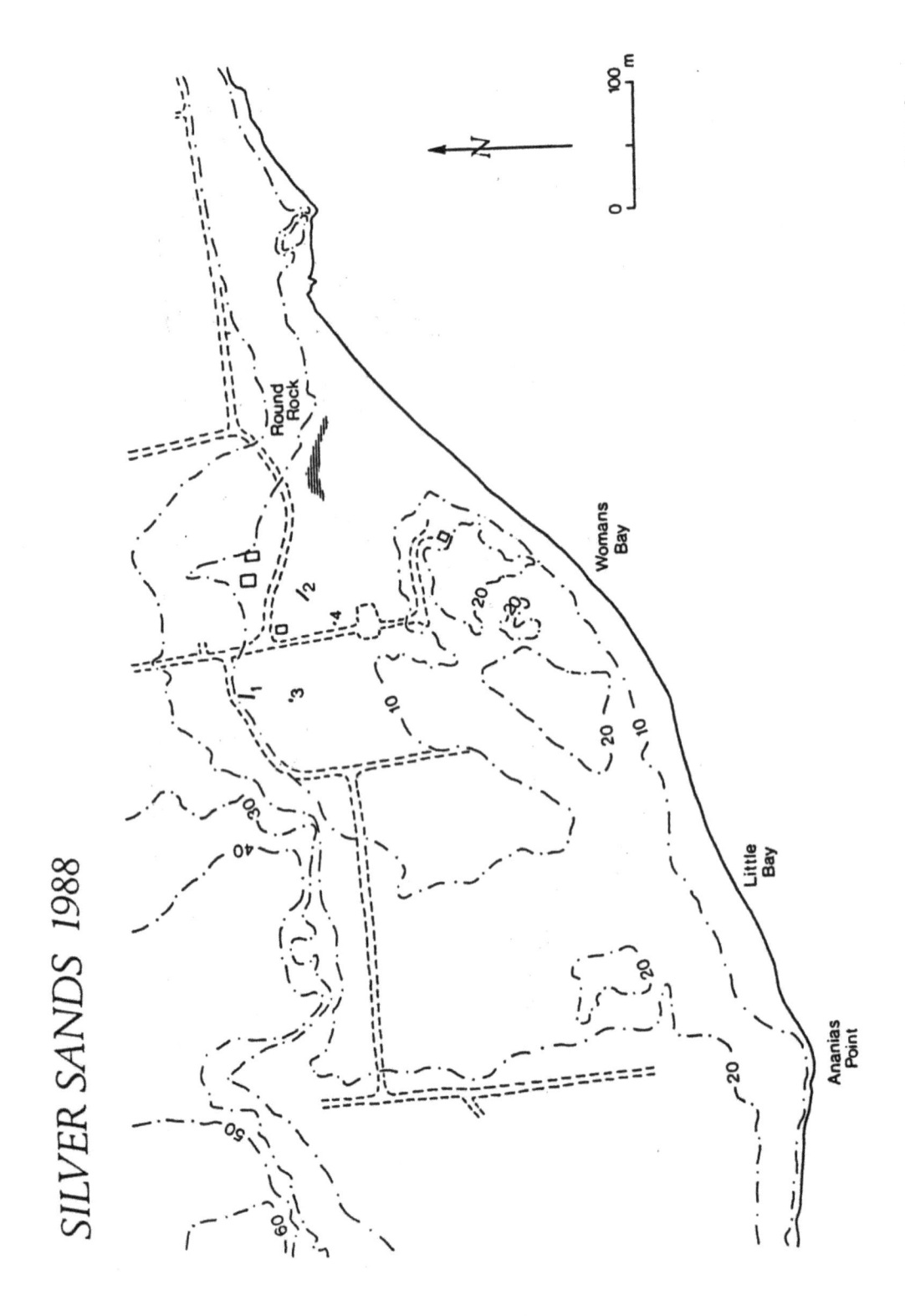

Figure 5. Silver Sands. General site plan and location of trenches excavated in 1988. The area around trench 3 was a salt marsh in prehistoric times.

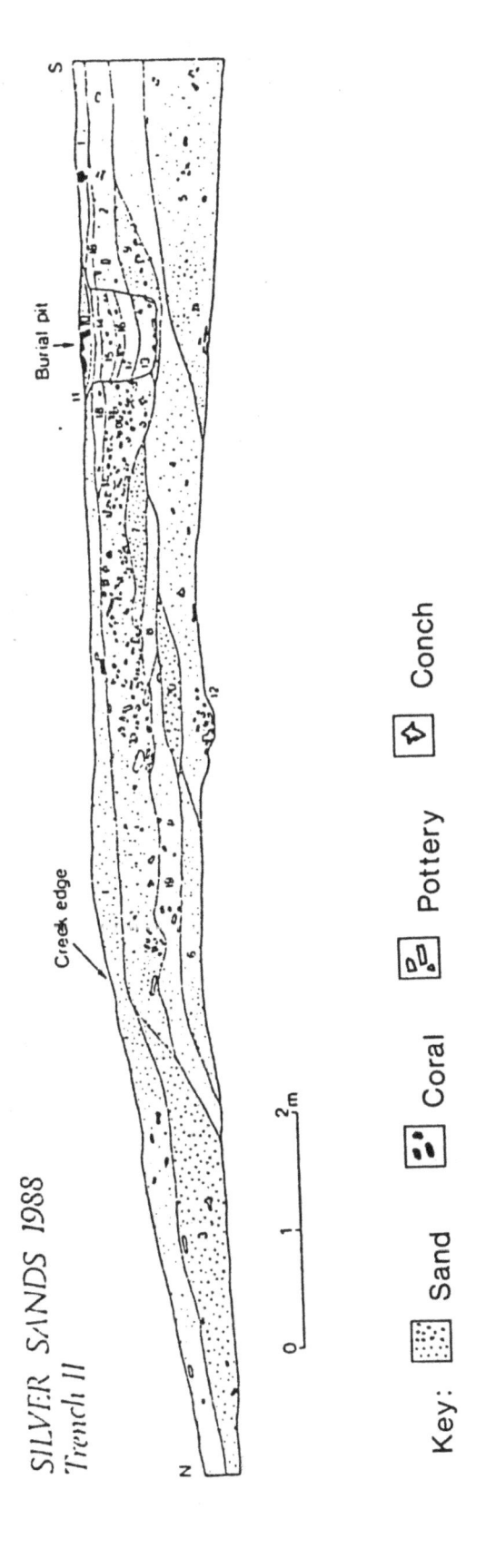

Figure 6. Silver Sands. Trench 2. Section through burial pit cutting midden deposited on former marine creek edge.

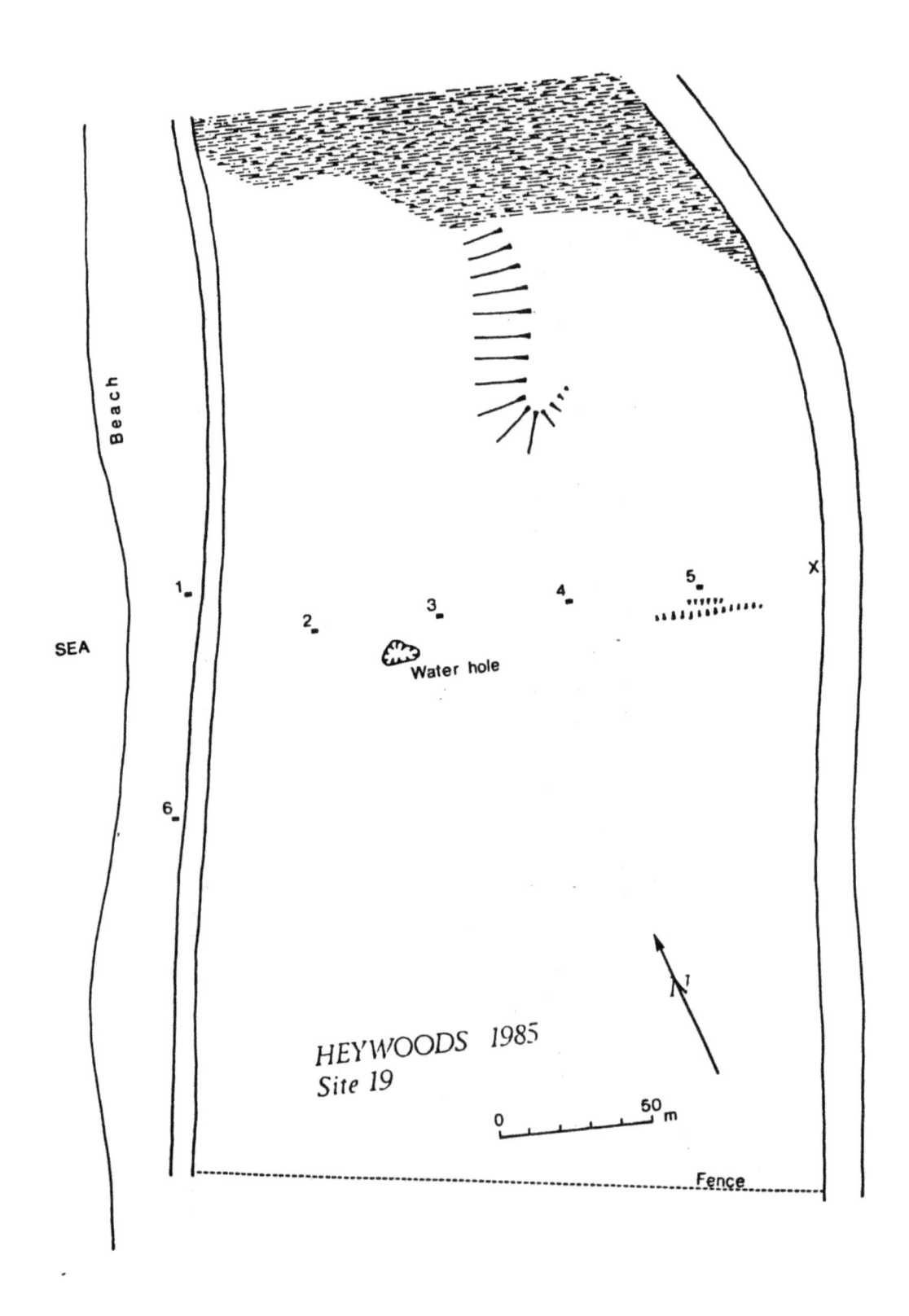

Figure 7. Heywoods. General site plan and location of trenches excavated in 1985. The area around trenches 4 and 5 was a salt marsh in prehistoric times.

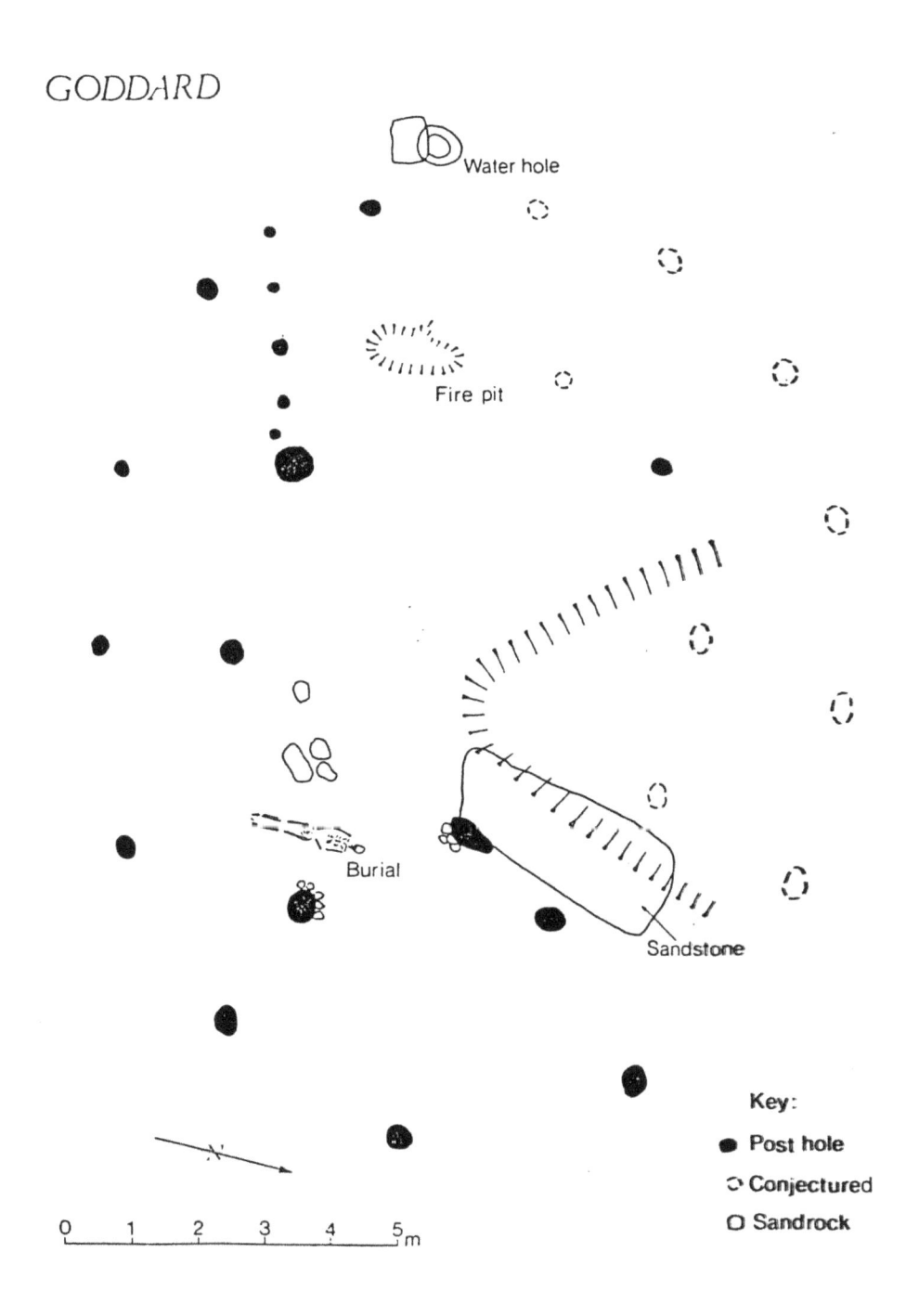

Figure 8. Goddard. Plan of post-built house excavated in 1986 (from Hackenberger 1987). Dashed postholes are conjectured by the author.

HILLCREST 1988

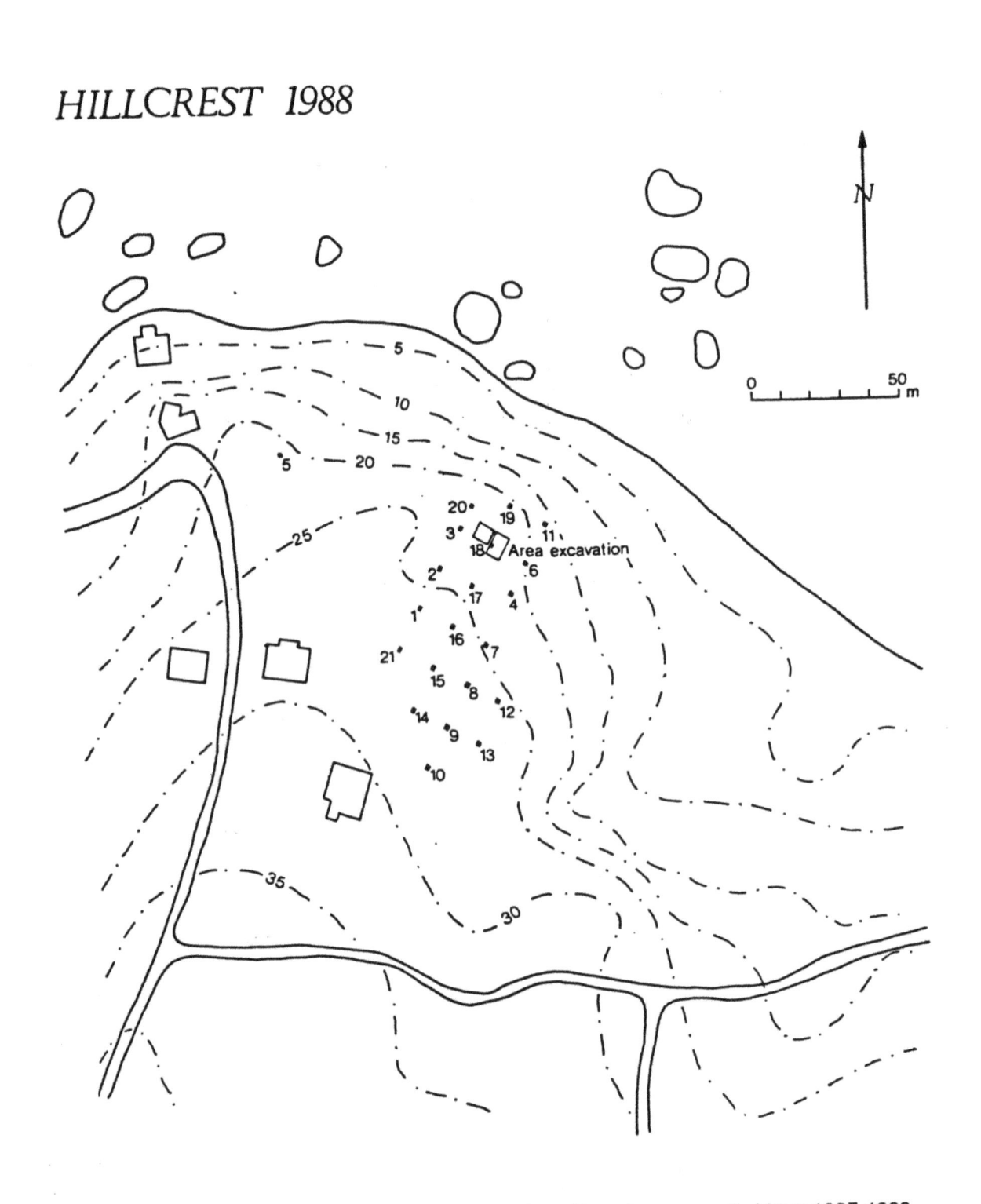

Figure 9. Hillcrest. General site plan and location of trenches excavated from 1985-1988.

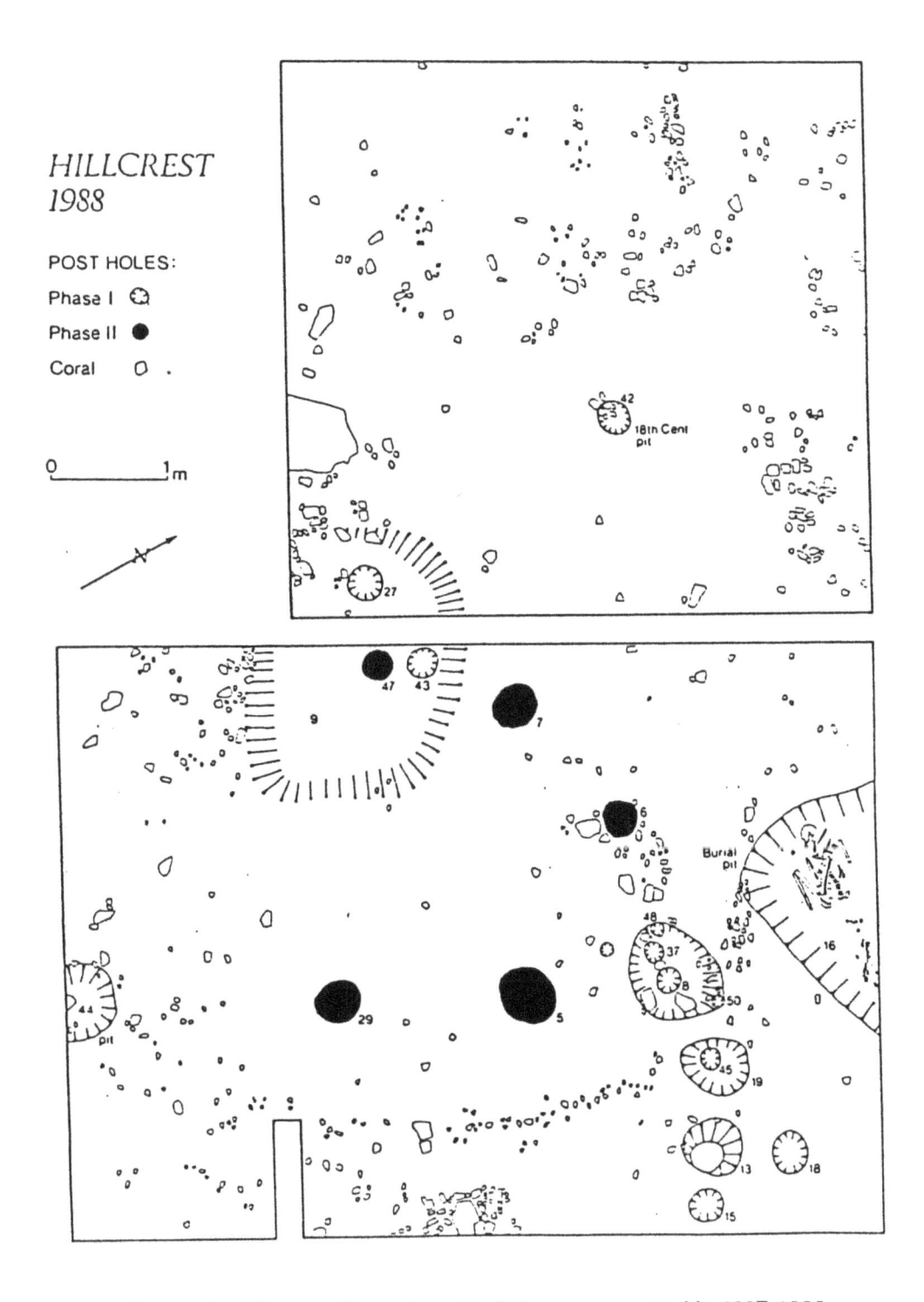

Figure 10. Hillcrest. Plan of post-built house excavated in 1987-1988.

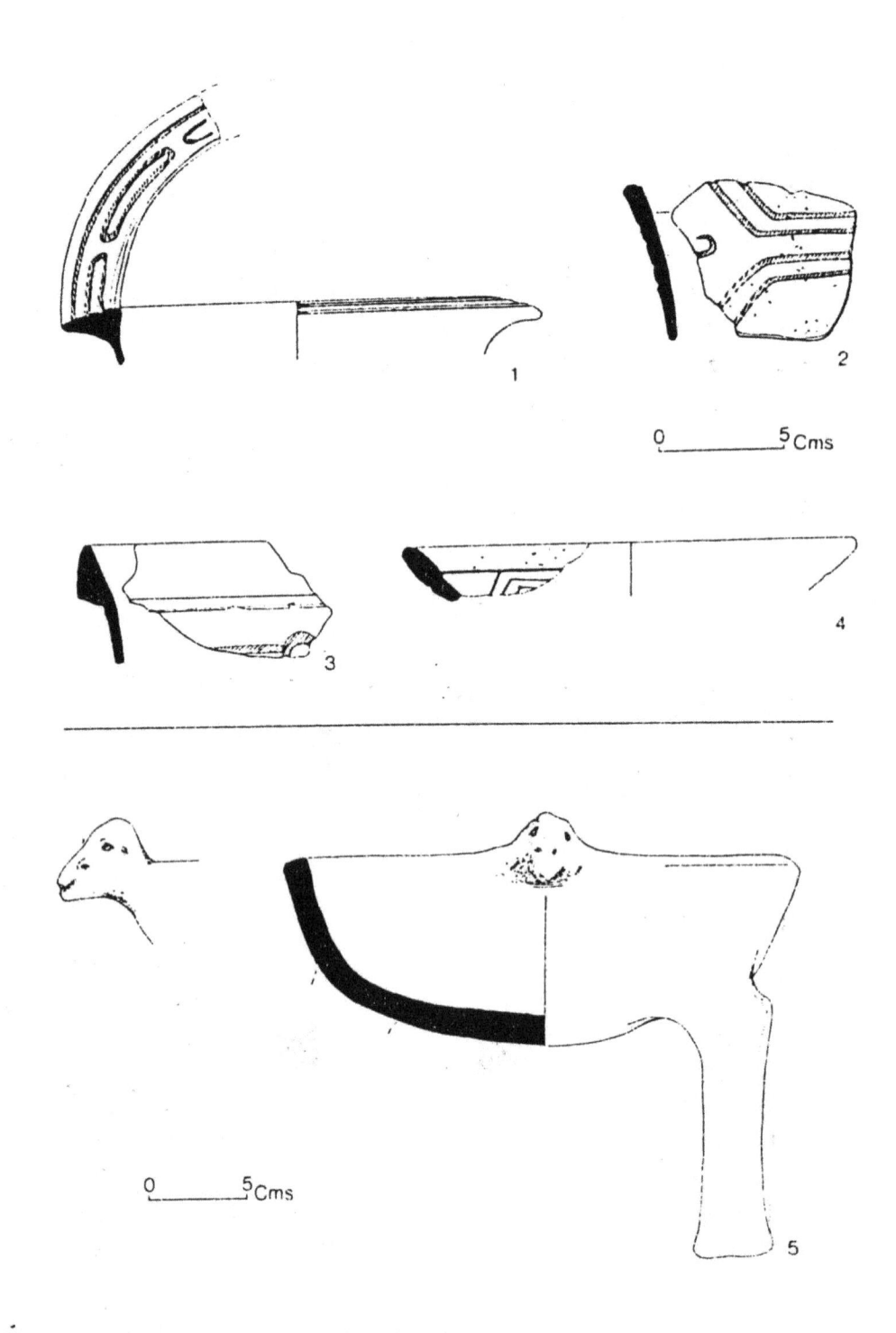

Figure 11. Barbados pottery styles. 1-4: Saladoid/Barrancoid; 5: Suazoid. (Drawn by Lys Drewett).

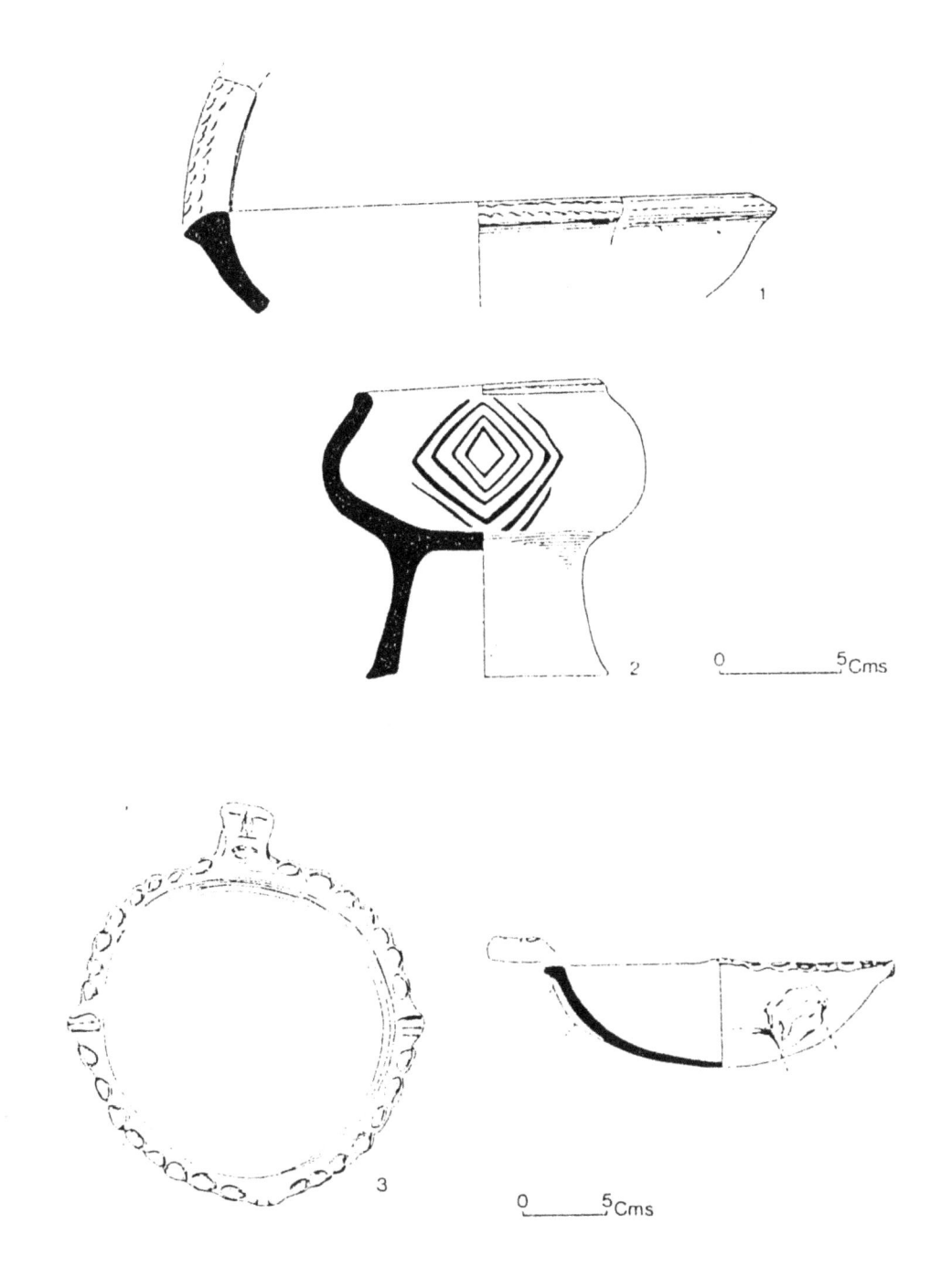

Figure 12. Barbados pottery styles. 1: Suazoid; 2-3: Troumassoid/Suazoid. (Drawn by Lys Drewett).

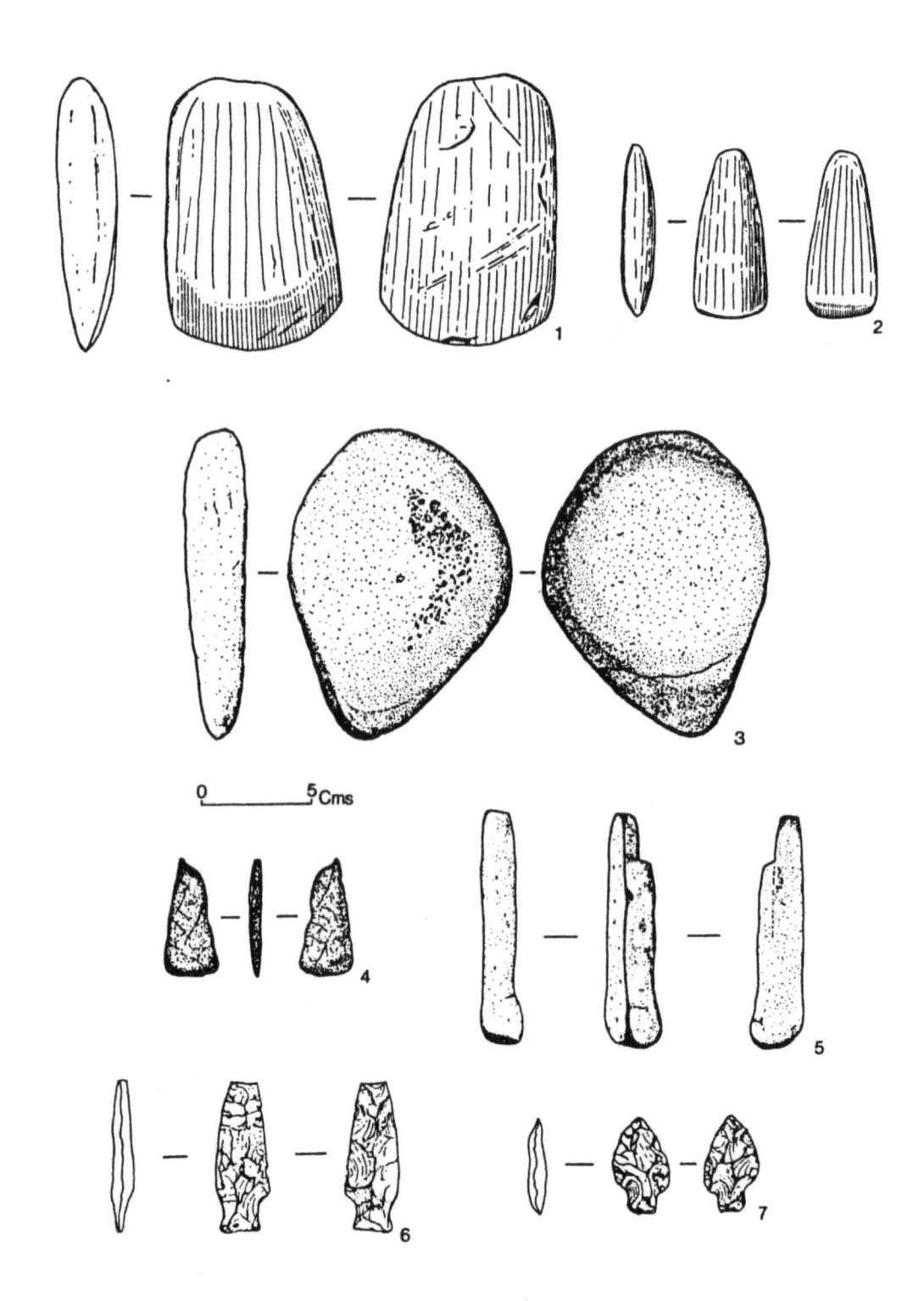

Figure 13. Barbados stone tools. 1-2: axes; 3: polisher; 4: 'knife'; 5: wedge shaped polisher; 6-7: projectile points. (Drawn by Duncan Lees).

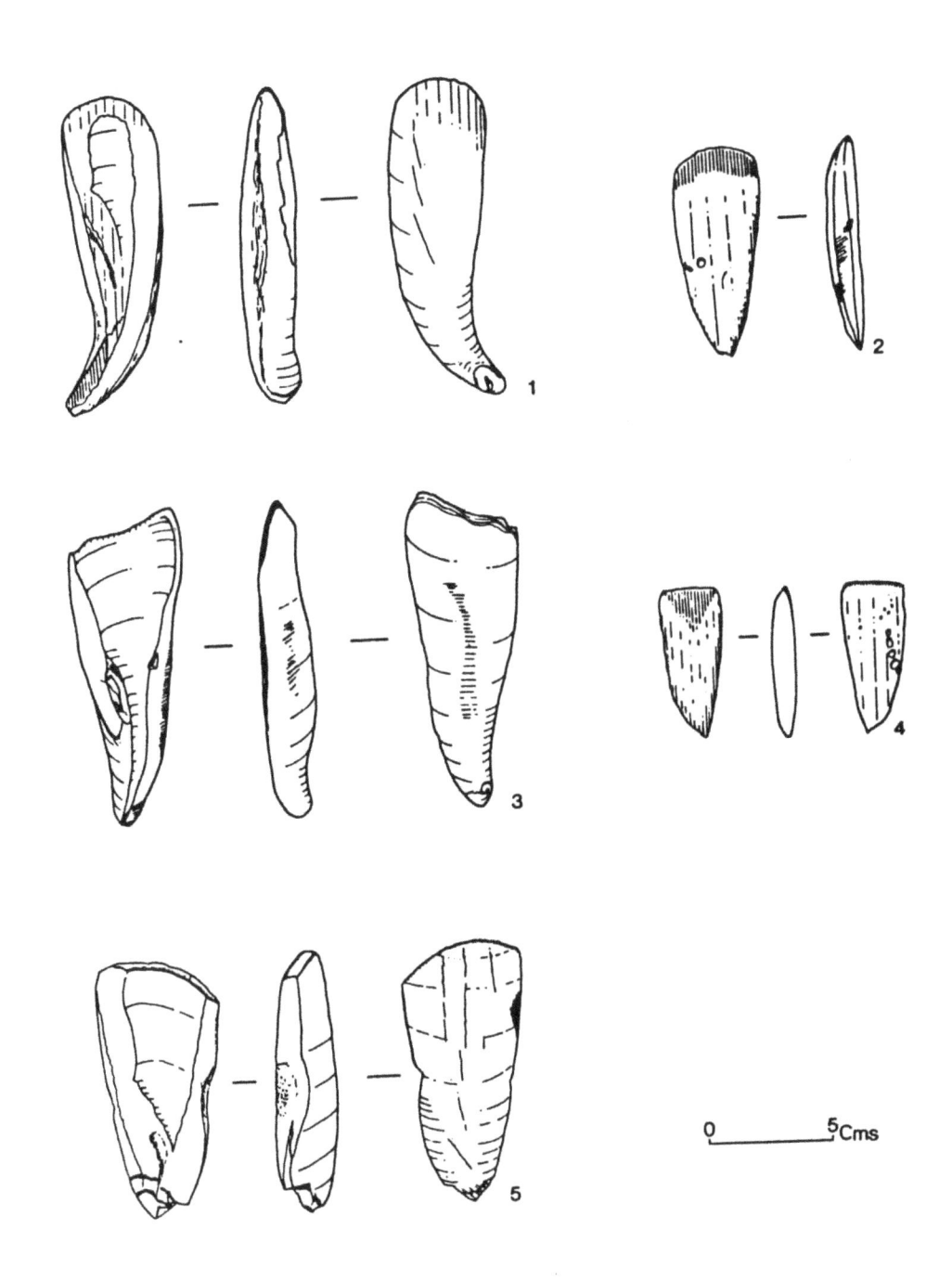

Figure 14. Barbados shell tools. (Drawn by Christopher Place).

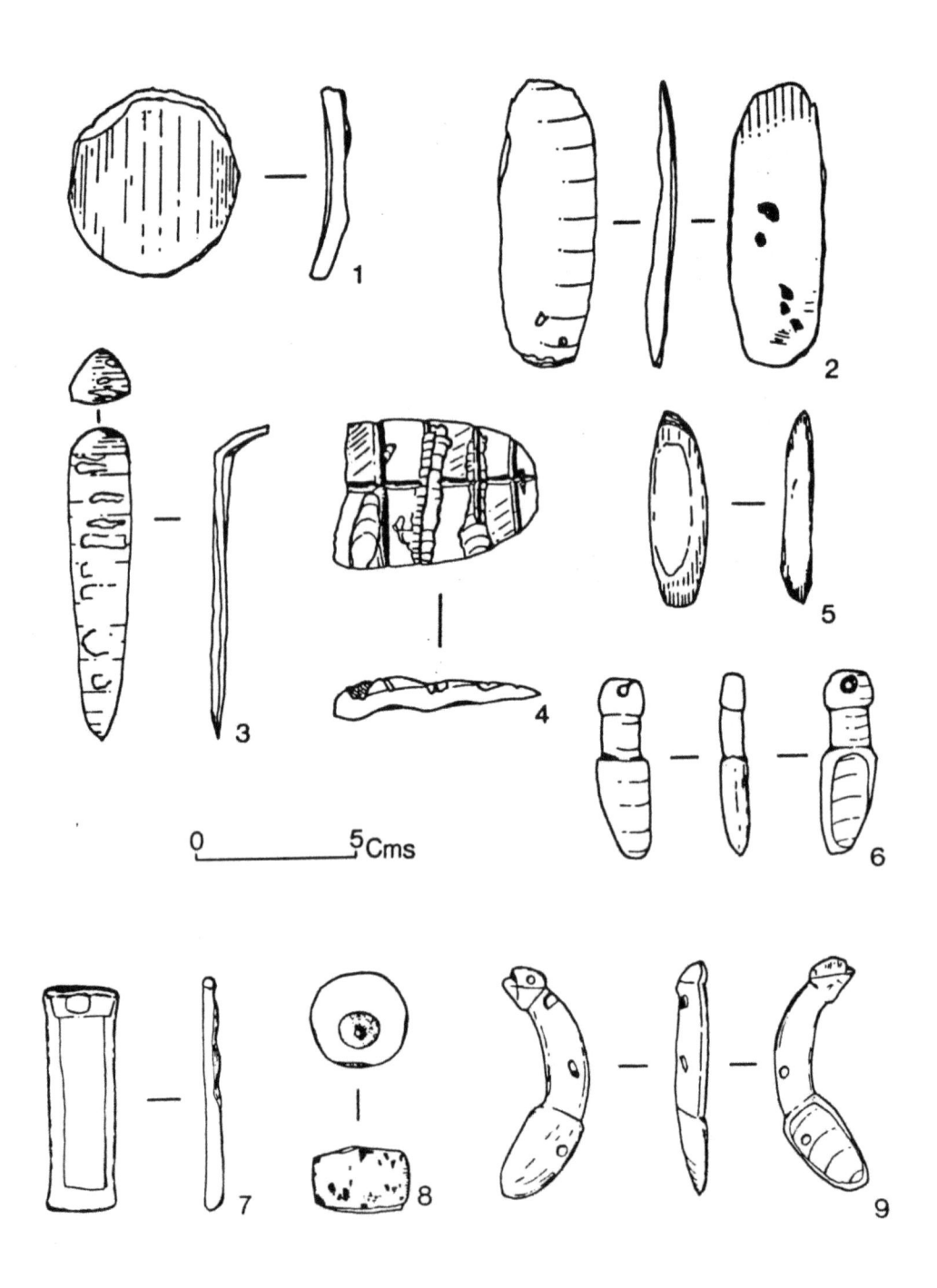

Figure 15. Barbados shell objects. (Drawn by Christopher Place).

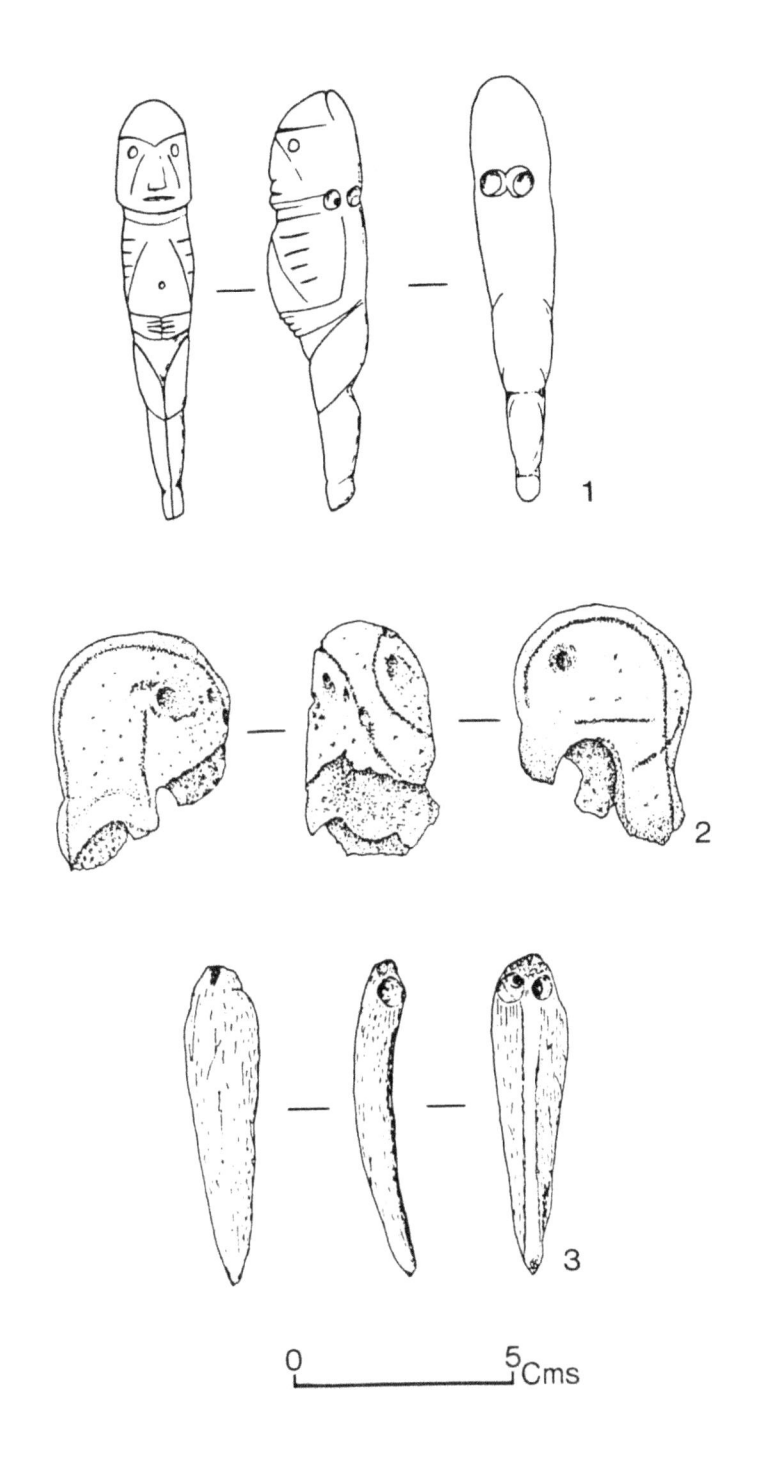

Figure 16. Barbados carved shell (No. 1), stone (No. 2), and turtle shell (No. 3). (Drawn by Christopher Place).

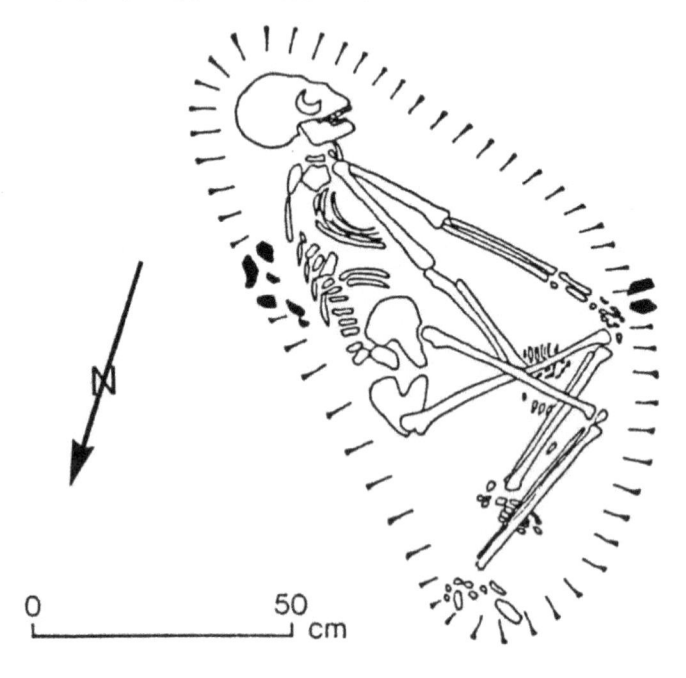

Figure 17. Silver Sands. Crouched burial of Suazoid date.

TRANSITION FROM A TERRESTRIAL TO A MARITIME ECONOMY:

A NEW VIEW OF THE CRAB/SHELL DICHOTOMY

William F. Keegan

ABSTRACT

Faunal assemblages from Island Arawak sites exhibit a shift from terrestrial to marine sources of animal protein through time. It has been hypothesized that: (1) the initial emphasis of terrestrial prey reflects a continuation of the riverine/tropical forest economy of the South American homeland; and (2) the subsequent shift to marine protein sources reflects the optimal path of diet-breadth expansion. This paper presents a brief review of the research design developed to examine these propositions, and summarizes the available results of ongoing investigations.

INTRODUCTION

Fifty-five years ago, Froelich Rainey (1935) uncovered archaeological deposits in Puerto Rico in which land crabs and painted pottery were common. These deposits presented a marked contrast to overlying deposits in which marine mollusks and unpainted pottery were predominant. Rainey reasoned that these distinct assemblages represented two separate migrations into the West Indies: a "Crab Culture" that was replaced by a "Shell Culture." Although this was a reasonable interpretation at the time, subsequent research has documented an unbroken chain of cultural development between Rainey's Crab and Shell Cultures (Rouse and Allaire 1978; Goodwin 1979; Davis 1988).

Recent efforts to explain the so-called Crab/Shell dichotomy have emphasized either cultural or non-cultural factors. The latter perspective characterizes Carbone's (1980) efforts to demonstrate that the shift resulted from the demise of crab populations keyed to a regional change in climate. If a region-wide change in climate was the primary stimulus, then the shift should occur simultaneously on every island. This hypothesis has been rejected because the timing of the shift varies throughout the West Indies (Davis 1988).

A model of cultural causation has been proposed by Christopher Goodwin based on his investigations on St. Kitts (1979, 1980). Goodwin presents a detailed ecological argument that implicates human population growth and increasing local human population densities as motivating the observed shift in dietary protein sources. Goodwin's conclusion that population growth was responsible for the shift is supported by the available evidence. Yet his conclusion begs two significant questions. First, why would a population allow its numbers to grow beyond its subsistence base? And second, why choose marine mollusks? The former question has haunted the social sciences since the days of Thomas Malthus, so Goodwin need not be held accountable. The latter has attracted most recent attention.

Alick Jones (1985) recently used the analysis of several column samples from the Indian Creek site, Antigua, to review questions surrounding the crab/shell transition. Jones adopted a somewhat eclectic approach and identified a variety of "factors" that probably influenced the direction and timing of this transition. He concludes that "his data from excavations of shellfish middens are best interpreted in terms of a non-cultural optimal foraging model" (Jones 1985:532). Jones did not, however, undertake an optimal foraging analysis of his data.

The present study, initiated independently in the investigation of the prehistoric colonization of the Bahamas, has picked up the trails that were blazed by Rainey, Carbone, Goodwin, and Jones. Specifically, this author has developed and implemented a research design that specifies the interdependence of economy and demography (Keegan 1985; Keegan and Butler 1987). The present paper begins with a brief review of the research design, and ends with a discussion of the expectations generated by this methodology as they concern subsistence changes during the prehistoric colonization of the Caribbean islands. Working conclusions are suggested based upon these preliminary results.

RESEARCH DESIGN

The present research design employs three levels of analysis. At the most abstract level are theories of subsistence behavior that describe an idealized structure of subsistence decision making. This general level is operationalized with models of economic efficiency that place empirical observations within the framework of abstract theory. Zooarchaeological and paleobotanical techniques are used to specify the dietary items in the economic models. Finally, the predictions of the models are used to define consumption profiles, with the accuracy of these profiles ("diet reconstructions") evaluated with osteochemical techniques (Keegan and DeNiro 1988; Keegan 1989).

THEORIES OF SUBSISTENCE BEHAVIOR

A direct link between anthropology, economics, and ecology is found in the economic definition of life-history strategies as the allocation of scarce means (e.g., time, energy, space, information) among the competing biological processes of growth, maintenance, and reproduction (Gadgil and Bossert 1970). This definition justifies the use of the economic technique known as equilibrium analysis to study adaptive strategies. Equilibrium analysis posits a dynamic equilibrium between supply and demand, expressed in units of price and quantity (Hirshliefer 1980; Keegan 1985). It is at this level of analysis that changes in the factors of demand (e.g., population growth) and/or in the factors of supply (e.g., foraging efficiency) interact to determine the position of the supply-demand equilibrium (Keegan and Butler 1987). Cultural responses to changes in this equilibrium are observed as changes in the factors of production -- including food choice, productive technology, and the organization of production. In sum, subsistence behavior or subsistence strategies reflect this higher-order equilibrium of supply and demand (Earle 1980; Keegan 1985).

MODELS OF FORAGING EFFICIENCY

Theories of human subsistence behavior have been operationalized with models developed in microeconomics and in evolutionary ecology. Since optimal foraging theory has been widely discussed in the literature it will not be reviewed here (see Winterhalder and Smith 1981; Smith 1983; Keegan 1986a). Instead, it must suffice to state that optimal foraging models require the specification of a goal, a currency, a set of constraints, and a set of options; in other words, the "sufficient parameters" of the more abstract equilibrium analysis (Levins 1966).

It should also be noted that the use of optimal foraging models in anthropology has been wrongly criticized on the misplaced belief that these are animal or non-cultural models. In fact, optimal foraging theory is better described as an extension of price theory (microeconomics) that was developed to investigate non-market economies. The foundation of optimal foraging theory, the marginal-value theorem, is also the basis for utility theory in microeconomics (cf. Charnov and Orians 1973; Hirshleifer 1980:Chapter 2).

Formal ethnoeconomic studies have come to emphasize cost-minimization as the most typical *goal* of subsistence economies (Earle 1980; Johnson and Behrens 1982; Keegan 1986a). Stated more explicitly, subsistence decisions are evaluated with respect to the goal: satisfy currency wants at the minimum cost of currency production.

In studies of foraging behavior, a nutritional *currency* is usually employed, and Calories have been used as the primary currency for examining forager decision making (Reidhead 1980; Winterhalder 1981; Keene 1982). Studies of extant tropical forest societies, societies which have production strategies that are similar to those proposed for the prehistoric Caribbean, have emphasized the importance of protein as a limiting currency (Ross 1978; Roosevelt 1980; Keegan 1986a). In the present study, both Calories and protein are evaluated.

Constraints are factors that limit an individual's ability to capture the currency (e.g., technology, resource distributions and abundance). When a time-allocation framework is used to quantify currency capture, then time can serve as the sum of constraints. Finally, *options* are the various food types that could be incorporated into the subsistence economy.

Optimal foraging models, as developed in ecology, provide very specific predictions concerning when shifts in time allocation between discrete resource patches and in diet breadth will occur. The models direct attention to changes at the margin, and it is in the identification and explanation of marginal shifts that larger-scale changes in subsistence production have their roots.

CONSUMPTION PROFILES

Given sufficient data, optimal foraging models could be used to predict the proportional contribution of every individual food type to the optimal diet. In practice, this level of specificity has only been attempted in linear-programming analyses (e.g., Reidhead 1980; Johnson and Behrens 1982; Keene 1982). However, since linear-programming analysis examines changes in *average* (versus *marginal*) return rates, the results of linear-programming analyses typically do not match long-term, diachronic patterns of subsistence change (Reidhead 1980).

Even where such specificity is possible, it will be of limited use if we are unable to evaluate the degree to which the optimal diet accurately characterizes prehistoric subsistence behavior. Unfortunately, direct archaeological tests of theoretical predictions are often constrained by both preservational biases and the limits of inferential techniques. It is, for example, possible to identify the root crops in Classic Taino gardens from ethnohistorical sources, but these cultigens are not easily distinguished in archaeological deposits and their measurement is limited to that of presence or absence rather than proportional contribution.

To some degree the problem of preservational biases can be circumvented through osteochemical analyses. Stable isotope and trace-element methods provide the means for evaluating prehistoric consumption practices in particular instances. These techniques are not, however, sufficient to distinguish between every individual food type in the diet, and we must therefore limit our interpretations to distinctions between food groups. In this regard, osteochemical techniques do not provide a direct reconstruction of diet in the sense that a diet is the sum of contributions from individual food types. Rather, osteochemical techniques identify consumption profiles which reflect the relative contributions of different food groups.

CARIBBEAN SUBSISTENCE CHANGE: TERRESTRIAL/MARINE TRANSITION

The optimal foraging analysis of prehistoric Caribbean subsistence behavior begins with the identification of the food types that comprised the dietary options (what others have called the "menu"). This initial task is accomplished through reference to ethnohistorical accounts, through the ethnobotanical study of wild-plant use and horticultural production, and through the zooarchaeological analysis of excavated faunal assemblages (Sauer 1966; Wing 1969; Fortuna 1978; Sullivan 1981; Wing and Reitz 1982; Wing and Scudder 1983; deFrance 1988a, 1988b). The result is a list of edible foods that were consumed in some unspecified quantities at some time in the past. Next, the nutritional composition of every food type is estimated. These estimations have, to date, been accomplished primarily through reference to measurements made on similar food types (Keegan 1985); more direct nutritional assays are presently being undertaken.

Finally, food types are ranked according to their marginal rates of currency return. These rankings are accomplished by estimating the amount of time required to capture, process, and consume (i.e., handle) one item of each food type (Table 1). Handling times have been estimated for the Lucayan Taino of the Bahamas in a variety of experimental procurement, processing, and behavioral-ecological studies (Keegan 1985, 1986b). These Bahamian studies form a data base from which marginal-return rankings can be developed for the ongoing Puerto Rican study (Keegan and DeNiro 1988).

The rankings developed in the Bahamas study suggest that terrestrial foods (e.g., mammals, crabs, cultigens, iguana) have significantly higher return rates than do their marine counterparts (Table 1). There are exceptions to this general rule, but armed only with the resource rankings it would not be surprising to observe diets based entirely on terrestrial resources. A terrestrial diet only seems surprising when one considers the location of Puerto Rico -- a relatively small island in the center of the West Indies.

The consumption practices of prehistoric Caribbean societies are being evaluated using stable isotope analysis. The carbon and nitrogen isotopic compositions of modern and archaeological examples of prehistoric food groups - terrestrial animals, cultivated roots and tubers, maize, marine fishes, and marine mollusks - have been measured. In addition, bone collagen extracted from one Saladoid period Puerto Rican and 17 Lucayan Taino individuals have also been characterized (Figure 1) (Keegan and DeNiro 1988). This sample is presently being expanded, and specific studies of Saladoid and Ostionoid period diets are being conducted.

The isotopic analysis completed to date identified four discrete consumption profiles (Keegan and DeNiro 1988). First, the individual from Saladoid period Puerto Rico, who may represent the earliest phase of island-Arawak colonization (Rouse and Allaire 1978), has a consumption profile that is characterized by a 93±7% reliance on terrestrial foods. Additional samples from the Maisabel site are being analyzed to determine whether or not this consumption profile is typical of Saladoid period individuals.

Second, three of the Lucayans have consumption profiles that are characterized by a similar, but less pronounced, emphasis on terrestrial foods. Third, the majority of Lucayans (n=11) have consumption profiles that are characterized by almost equal contributions of marine and terrestrial food types. Finally, three of the Lucayans have consumption profiles that are characterized by a 66 to 74±7% contribution of marine food types. However, since the isotopic signature of maize falls within the range of marine food types, an undetermined contribution of maize may also be reflected in the consumption profiles of these individuals. Other osteochemical techniques are being explored to distinguish the relative contributions of maize and marine food types.

Finally, population growth and expansion merit consideration. The author has demonstrated, using simple equations from population biology, that the Arawakan-speaking colonists of the West Indies probably maintained exponential growth rates during periods of expansion and that the majority of the Lesser Antilles may have been bypassed or settled only temporarily during the initial Saladoid expansion (Keegan 1985).

If one extends Roosevelt's (1980) analysis of Saladoid peoples on the Orinoco River into the Lesser Antilles a remarkable coincidence occurs. Using an estimated population growth rate from Parmana and comparing that to Goodwin's data from St. Kitts, the author found the estimates to be identical (r=0.50%). This coincidence led to the question, if Roosevelt observed a shift in protein sources when the population density doubled from about 1.5 to 3.0/km^2 in Parmana, did anything similar happen on St. Kitts? In Parmana the shift involved a dramatic increase in maize in the diet (Roosevelt 1980); on St. Kitts the shift from land crabs to marine mollusks is estimated to have occurred at an equivalent doubling point. Obviously we are relying on a heavy dose of "all else being equal." Nonetheless, it is worth investigating economic continuity during the Saladoid (i.e., the return rates are the same, only the food-resource *options* are different), along with taking a renewed look at the inter-island contemporaneity of the crab/shell transition. This time contemporaneity is defined in terms of population densities rather than absolute dates.

CONCLUSIONS

The pattern that is emerging from the application of abstract theory linked to specific empirical tests is of an economically efficient colonizing population. A population that is able to maintain rapid growth by expanding into unoccupied or underutilized (undercapitalized) islands. Independent tests confirm that the population was growing rapidly (perhaps even exponentially), that initial population distributions maintained low local population densities, and that subsistence activities were focused on the highest ranked food items.

When the highest ranked food items were no longer available in quantities sufficient to satisfy *total* currency requirements, then diet breadth expanded in the expected direction to incorporate marine sources of protein. This shift is, in every respect, an expansion of diet breadth. High-ranked resources continue to comprise a small, but nutritionally important, component of the diet through time. The isotopic analysis of the Maisabel skeletons, combined with zooarchaeological, ethnobotanical, and other archaeological investigations, are directed toward testing hypotheses that were deduced from abstract theory and partially tested with complementary data from elsewhere in the West Indies.

REFERENCES CITED

Carbone, V. A.
   1980   Some Problems in Cultural Paleoecology in the Caribbean Area. *Proceedings of the International Congress for the Study of the Pre-Columbian Cultures of the Lesser Antilles* 8:98-126. Tempe.

Charnov, E.L. and G.H. Orians
   1973   Optimal Foraging: Some Theoretical Explanations. Ms. on file, Department of Biology, University of Utah, Salt Lake City.

Davis, D. D.
   1988   Coastal Biogeography and Human Subsistence: Examples from the West Indies. *Archaeology of Eastern North America* 16:177-185.

deFrance, S. D.
   1988a   *Zooarchaeological Investigations of Subsistence Strategies at the Maisabel Site, Puerto Rico.* Unpublished Master's paper, Department of Anthropology, University of Florida, Gainesville.

   1988b   Saladoid and Ostionoid Subsistence Adaptations: Zooarchaeological Data from a Coastal Occupation on Puerto Rico. Paper presented at the 53rd Annual Meeting of the Society for American Archaeology, Phoenix.

DeNiro, M. J. and C.A. Hastorf
   1985   Alteration of $^{15}N/^{14}N$ and $^{13}C/^{12}C$ Ratios of Plant Matter During the Initial Stages of Diagenesis: Studies Utilizing Archaeological Specimens from Peru. *Geochimica et Cosmochimica Acta* 49:97-115.

Earle, Timothy K.
   1980   A Model of Subsistence Change. In *Modeling Change in Prehistoric Subsistence Economies*, edited by T.K. Earle and A.L. Christenson, pp. 1-29. Academic Press, New York.

Fortuna, L.
   1978   Analisis polinico de Sanate Abajo. *Boletin del Museo del Hombre Dominicano* 10:125-130.

Gadgil, M. and W. H. Bossert
   1970   Life Historical Consequences of Natural Selection. *The American Naturalist* 104:1-24.

Goodwin, R. C.
   1979   *The Prehistoric Cultural Ecology of St. Kitts, West Indies: A Case Study in Island Archaeology.* PhD dissertation, Arizona State University. University Microfilms, Ann Arbor.

   1980   Demographic Change and the Crab-Shell Dichotomy. *Proceedings of the International Congress for the Study of the Pre-Columbian Cultures of the Lesser Antilles* 8:45-68. Tempe.

Hirshleifer, J.
   1980   *Price Theory and Applications.* 2nd ed. Prentice-Hall, Englewood Cliffs.

Johnson, A. and C. A. Behrens
    1982 Nutritional Criteria in Machiguenga Food Production Decisions: A Linear-Programming Analysis. *Human Ecology* 10:167-189.

Jones, A. R.
    1985 Dietary Change and Human Population at Indian Creek, Antigua. *American Antiquity* 50:518-536.

Keegan, W. F.
    1985 *Dynamic Horticulturalists: Population Expansion in the Prehistoric Bahamas.* Ph.D. dissertation, University of California, Los Angeles. University Microfilms, Ann Arbor.

    1986a The Optimal Foraging Analysis of Horticultural Production. *American Anthropologist* 88:92-107.

    1986b The Ecology of Lucayan Arawak Fishing Practices. *American Antiquity* 51:816-825.

    1989 Stable Isotope Analysis of Prehistoric Diet. In *Reconstruction of Life From the Skeleton*, edited by M.Y. Iscan and K.A.R. Kennedy. Alan R. Liss, New York, in press.

Keegan, W.F. and B.M. Butler
    1987 The Microeconomic Logic of Horticultural Intensification in the Eastern Woodlands. In *Emergent Horticultural Economies of the Eastern Woodlands*, edited by W.F. Keegan, pp. 109-127. Center for Archaeological Investigations, Occasional Paper 7. Southern Illinois University, Carbondale.

Keegan, W. F. and M. J. DeNiro
    1988 Stable Carbon- and Nitrogen-Isotope Ratios of Bone Collagen Used to Study Coral-Reef and Terrestrial Components of Prehistoric Bahamian Diet. *American Antiquity* 53:320-336.

Keene, A. S.
    1982 *Prehistoric Foraging in a Temperate Forest: A Linear Programming Model.* Academic Press, New York.

Levins, R.
    1966 The Strategy of Model Building in Population Biology. *American Scientist* 54:421-431.

Rainey, F. G.
    1935 A New Prehistoric Culture in Puerto Rico. *Proceedings of the National Academy of Science* 21:12-16.

Reidhead, V. R.
    1980 The Economics of Subsistence Change: A Test of an Optimization Model. In *Modeling Change in Prehistoric Subsistence Economies*, edited by T. K. Earle and A. L. Christenson, pp. 141-186. Academic Press, New York.

Roosevelt, A. C.
    1980 *Parmana, Prehistoric Maize and Manioc Subsistence along the Amazon and Orinoco.* Academic Press, New York.

Ross, E. B.
    1978 Food Taboos, Diet, and Hunting Strategy: The Adaptation to Animals in Amazon

Cultural Ecology. *Current Anthropology* 19:1-36.

Rouse, I. and L. Allaire
    1978   Caribbean. In *Chronologies in New World Archaeology*, edited by R.E. Taylor and C. Meighan, pp. 431-481. Academic Press, New York.

Sauer, C. O.
    1966   *The Early Spanish Main*. University of California Press, Berkeley.

Smith, E. A.
    1983   Anthropological Applications of Optimal Foraging Theory: A Critical Review. *Current Anthropology* 24:625-651.

Sullivan, S. D.
    1981   *Prehistoric Patterns of Exploitation and Colonization in the Turks and Caicos Islands*. Ph.D. dissertation, University of Illinois, Urbana-Champaign. University Microfilms, Ann Arbor.

Wing, E. S.
    1969   Vertebrate Remains Excavated from San Salvador Island, Bahamas. *Caribbean Journal of Science* 9:25-29.

Wing, E. S. and E. J. Reitz
    1982   Prehistoric Fishing Communities of the Caribbean. *Journal of New World Archaeology* 5:13-32.

Wing, E. S. and S. J. Scudder
    1983   Animal Exploitation by Prehistoric People Living on a Tropical Marine Edge. In *Animals and Archaeology: 2. Shell Middens, Fishes and Birds*, edited by C. Grigson and J. Clutton-Brock, pp. 197-210. B.A.R. International Series 183. Oxford.

Winterhalder, B.
    1981   Optimal Foraging Strategies and Hunter-Gatherer Research in Anthropology: Theory and Models. In *Hunter-Gatherer Foraging Strategies*, edited by B. Winterhalder and E. A. Smith, pp. 13-35. University of Chicago Press, Chicago.

Winterhalder, B. and E. A. Smith
    1981   *Hunter-Gatherer Foraging Strategies*. University of Chicago Press, Chicago.

Table 1. Return Rates and Rankings of Lucayan Taino Food Types and Food Groups (from Keegan 1985).

Food Sources	Average Weight/ Individual (kg)	Kcal/ kg	Grams Protein kg	Handling Time (hr/kg)	Pop. Density (kg/ha)	E/h	gP/h	Rank E/h	Rank gP/h
Green Turtles (Chelonia mydas)	19.0	1300	2.2	0.026	2609	50,000	84	1	1
Hutia (Geocapromys sp.)	1.4	1500	1.5	0.12	21	12,500	13	2	5
Land Crab (Cardisoma sp.)	0.2	900	1.7	0.10	2000	9,000	17	3	3
Queen Conch (Strombus gigas)	0.17	800	1.3	0.09	850	8,889	14	4	4
Rock Iguana (Cyclura carinata)	0.7	2000	2.4	0.24	15	8,333	10	5	6
Horticulture root crops maize	-- --	-- --	-- --	---- ----	-- --	5,000 ----	-- 20	6 -	1 2
All Fishes	0.25	1000	1.9	0.22	----	4,545	9	7	7
West Indian Top Shell (Cittarium pica)	0.035	800	1.3	0.25	1750	3,200	5	8	8
Chiton sp.	0.005	800	1.3	0.5	500	1,600	3	9	9
Codakia orbicularis	0.01	800	1.3	1.39	4000	576	1	10	10
Nerites (Nerita sp.)	0.002	800	1.3	1.4	400	471	<1	11	11

Note: E/h is Calories per handling hour; gP/h is grams of protein per handling hour.

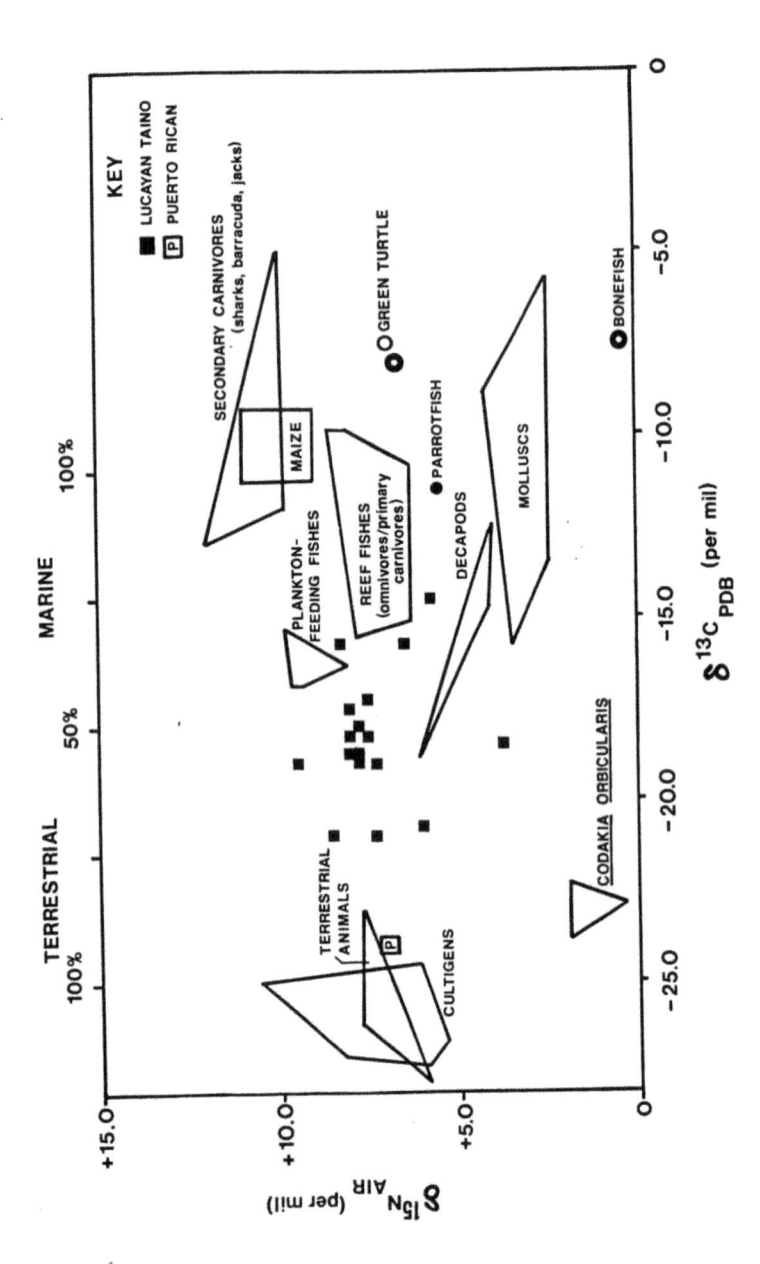

Figure 1. d^{13}C and d^{15}N values of the consumed portions of foods and of the diets of Lucayan Taino individuals (from Keegan and DeNiro 1988). Food values are represented by polygons for groups for which at least three specimens were sampled in which case the polygons cover the extreme values, by a square for maize, in which case we added ±1 per mil to the mean d^{13}C and d^{15}N values reported in DeNiro and Hastorf (1985), and by points for cases in which only one or two specimens were analyzed.

ENVIRONMENTAL DIVERSITY AND MARITIME ADAPTATIONS IN THE CARIBBEAN AREA

David R. Watters and Irving Rouse

ABSTRACT

The Caribbean Sea is the dominant feature of the Caribbean area and contains a diverse range of marine and estuarine habitats. The maritime component of cultural adaptations in the prehistoric Caribbean has received relatively limited attention from archaeologists working in the region. A research strategy combining a seaward perspective on maritime adaptations with the previously dominant landward orientation provides an effective approach to interpreting Caribbean prehistory. The significance of maritime adaptations and the reliance on marine and estuarine resources were factors that varied temporally and spatially, and from one cultural heritage to another.

INTRODUCTION

This symposium volume deals with lifeways and adaptive strategies of early ceramic groups in the Caribbean. Not too many years ago, such a symposium would have been structured and organized in a quite different manner. Papers would have been derived from and based upon research on the "Saladoid" peoples rather than the more general "early ceramic groups," and would have focused on those peoples' cultural heritages. Few papers would have dealt, in any depth, with the topics of lifeways and adaptive strategies because of the lack of research on those subjects. In one sense, the current volume reviews some of the more recent research trends in Caribbean prehistory studies. In yet another sense, it highlights the "revised thinking" about prior studies that has been going on in Caribbean prehistory studies during the past decade or so.

Elsewhere, Watters (1982) argued that Caribbean archaeologists should familiarize themselves with research in Oceania, another insular area of the world where some similar issues and problems are being investigated. Kirch and Hunt's (1988) very recent review of the "Lapita Cultural Complex" of Melanesia and western Polynesia, representing the earliest evidence of occupation by ceramic-bearing peoples in the southwest Pacific, has numerous implications for the renewed dialogue about the Caribbean's "early ceramic groups." Kirch's (1988) summary chapter on Lapitoid "problems and issues," with its discussion of origins, dispersal, economy, style and variability of material culture, long-distance exchange, society, and what happened to Lapitoid peoples, brings to mind many of the questions confronting Caribbean archaeologists.[1]

The Oceanists' research on problems of origin and dispersal has been limited largely to the Lapitoid period, despite the existence of oral traditions about subsequent events that need to be checked archaeologically. Unfortunately, the Lapitoid peoples abandoned pottery as they colonized the central Pacific and evolved into the Polynesioid peoples, and the latter have left few stylistically significant artifacts of other kinds that can be substituted for ceramics. Caribbeanists do not suffer from this disadvantage, except when working with the Archaic age before the appearance of pottery, and, as a result, have been able to make greater progress in investigating cultural heritages.

On the other hand, Oceanists have reached a higher level of sophistication in studying artifact functions, ecological adaptation, society, and long-distance exchange. They have taken advantage of a wealth of ethnohistorical and ethnographic information not available in the Caribbean area, where so many of the natives became extinct soon after the discovery of the New World.

Oceanists project their knowledge of the historic and contemporary natives' exploitation of marine resources back through prehistoric Polynesioid peoples to the original Lapitoid settlers of the central Pacific. Caribbeanists tend instead to attribute their own landward orientation to the Native Americans. They have paid relatively little attention to maritime adaptations except in studying the smaller islands of the Lesser Antilles, where land area is limited. This pervasive "terrestrial bias" is further discussed elsewhere (Watters 1981, 1982, 1983; Rouse 1982:48-52, 1986:128, this volume).[2]

In a subtle way, the approach to maritime adaptation issues taken by the authors in Kirch and Hunt's (1988) work provides an interesting juxtaposition to the treatment of the same issues in the Caribbean. Few of those authors deal exclusively with issues of maritime adaptations, but virtually every chapter, regardless of topic, includes some discussion of aspects of maritime adaptations that relate to the broader subject matter being presented. Maritime adaptations are not viewed as separate or isolated components of Lapita culture, but instead are interpreted as an integral part of a broader based adaptive strategy. Although a quite similar strategy has been proposed for the Caribbean (Watters 1982), very little research that *integrates* maritime adaptations has been attempted or accomplished. Thus, the "Lapitoid approach" markedly contrasts with Caribbean prehistory studies.

CARIBBEAN PERSPECTIVES

The Caribbean Sea is the dominant feature of the Caribbean area. Fronting the Caribbean Sea are the continental and insular landmasses of Central and South America and the Greater and Lesser Antilles. From an oceanographic viewpoint, the Caribbean Sea is the central feature of the area while the landmasses surrounding it are peripheral. West and Augelli (1976:xiv) acknowledge the prominence of the Caribbean Sea when they apply the fully appropriate term *Caribbean America* to its bordering landmasses. Similarly, the United Nations Environment Programme (United Nations 1980) lists Caribbean South America, Caribbean Central America, and Insular Caribbean as the three land sectors that border the Caribbean Sea, within what is termed the "Wider Caribbean Area" (encompassing the Caribbean Sea and Gulf of Mexico).

In view of the prominence of the Caribbean Sea, one might presume that research on the region's prehistory would include a substantial and sustained commitment to issues and questions involving maritime adaptations of the indigenous peoples. In reality, research on maritime adaptations in Caribbean prehistory can be characterized, at best, as sporadic; more often it is neglected or ignored. Research projects have rarely embraced a "seaward perspective," in which the investigation of maritime adaptations is included as an integral part of a broader research strategy. Research devoted explicitly to the study of maritime adaptation issues is even rarer. Similarly, study of a host of ocean processes that have affected the archaeological record in the Caribbean has generated little interest.

The Caribbean Islands are often characterized as "stepping stones" because of their strategic location between North and South America, and as "laboratories" because they are bounded, circumscribed entities. Similar comments have been made about other island groups throughout the world (see Keegan and Diamond 1987 for a recent review). A "landward orientation" is implicit in such statements because the study area of interest is from the coast *inward*, and not from the coast *outward* toward the ocean. A landward view tends to emphasize terrestrial and freshwater environments, whereas a seaward perspective emphasizes marine and estuarine environments.

Landward and seaward perspectives actually complement one another, as the Kirch and Hunt (1988) volume demonstrates. They are not mutually exclusive, and a research strategy that takes into account both viewpoints is a far more logical approach to interpreting Caribbean prehistory. This paper, which emphasizes the diversity of marine environments in the Caribbean and the maritime aspects of cultural adaptations of the region's indigenous peoples, does so intentionally and explicitly in order to counterbalance a perceived terrestrial bias and preoccupation with a landward orientation.

ENVIRONMENTAL DIVERSITY

A fundamental distinction in environmental diversity can be made between continental mainlands with their closely related continental islands (e.g, South America and Trinidad) and the oceanic islands of the Caribbean Sea (e.g., Greater and Lesser Antilles and the Bahamas).[3] In the tropical western Atlantic, the Caribbean Islands are unique in that they constitute the only major oceanic archipelago available for colonization by prehistoric peoples. Such island arcs are more commonly encountered in the Pacific Ocean than the Atlantic.

The continental or oceanic character of an island directly relates to its environmental diversity, with oceanic islands usually exhibiting much less diversity in terms of terrestrial habitats and biota. Marine and estuarine environments, being beyond the confines of the island's bounded landmass, can be remarkably diverse. Although they can be diverse, these environments are not uniform because they are subject to their own constraints, including such things as variation in salinity or bathymetry.

Environmental diversity on continental or oceanic islands involves more than just proximity to a continent, although that is important. Other significant factors include island size, its geologic and oceanographic histories, soils, surrounding waters and banks, bathymetry, and position with respect to air and water currents, as well as a host of factors related to an organism's capability to disperse.

Area-Shoreline Ratio

The relationship between an island's total land area and its shoreline is illustrative. Table 1 shows total area, extent of shoreline, and the ratio between the two for six Caribbean islands; Venezuela's shoreline (note that it is shorter than Cuba's) is included for comparison. One pattern that is evident for the six islands is that greater total area corresponds with greater shoreline extent. That simply indicates a larger island tends to have a longer shoreline, a logical relationship that is less than profound.

Of considerable interest, however, is the variation seen in area-shoreline ratios for the six islands. Table 1 shows that these ratios differ significantly from island to island, ranging from 41.05:1 for Cuba to 2.34:1 for Montserrat. There are 41.05 km^2 of land area suitable for terrestrial environments for every 1 km of shoreline on Cuba, while on Montserrat there are only 2.34 km^2 of land area for each 1 km of shoreline. Thus, the land area available for terrestrial environments on Montserrat is far less than on Cuba, for each 1 km of shoreline. The ratios for moderate sized islands (Jamaica and Trinidad) are consistently higher than those of the smaller islands of St. Lucia, Barbados, and Montserrat with the lowest area-shoreline ratios.

An area to shoreline ratio is a crude measurement that does not take into account a number of complicating variables. For example, an island's shape can affect the ratio with a linear island having less land area than a spherical one when shorelines are held constant. An island with a significantly indented coast (e.g., embayments) will have more shoreline than one without indentations. Also, data presented in Table 1 are derived from current configurations and do not take into account changes in island area or shoreline that may have occurred since aboriginal occupation. Vertical displacement of land (uplift or subsidence) or water (rising or dropping sea level) can expand or reduce an island's area as well as extend or diminish its shoreline length.

Marine and Estuarine Environments

As noted previously, marine and estuarine environments are not uniformly distributed in the Caribbean, and there are many factors that contribute to the occurrence of such habitats. Generally speaking, ocean waters tend to facilitate dispersal of marine biotas across an archipelago but act as a barrier to movement of terrestrial organisms. This is why biogeographic studies focus on terrestrial lifeforms and only rarely include marine organisms (Watters 1989). Three examples -- coral reefs, shallow water shelves, and mangal formations -- illustrate the diversity and nonuniform distribution of marine and estuarine environments.

Coral reefs are a case in point. It has been noted that "most coral reef development in the Atlantic Ocean is restricted to the Caribbean and adjacent areas in southern Florida and the Bahamas" (Milliman 1973:2). Although reefs occur in the Caribbean Sea near continents and islands and on shallow banks, their distribution is patchy or scattered. Proper conditions for reef development do not occur uniformly throughout the Caribbean. Adey and Burke's (1976, 1977) studies of eastern Caribbean coral reefs confirm the variation in distribution. One interesting correlation (Figure 1) is a strong tendency for greater reef development on smaller, low islands with decreased rainfall and limited runoff, whereas volcanic islands with eroding shores and heavy sediment transport generally do not show extensive reef formation (Adey and Burke 1976:108).

Coral reefs support a great variety of organisms, many of which were exploited by prehistoric peoples (see Wing and Reitz 1982). It is especially noteworthy that many reef-dwelling species are widely distributed and have broad ranges. This means that similar reef faunas tend to recur wherever coral reefs are present in the insular Caribbean, and when coral reefs occurred near prehistoric habitation sites, the archaeological remains of the reef-dwelling species often are similar.

The absence or scarcity of reefs near an island acted as a limiting factor or environmental constraint for humans since reef resources either were not available or were minimally so. Evidence for variation in faunal remains from islands with few reefs and those with many is reflected in the archaeological record, such as with vertebrate remains from "reef-rich" Barbuda and "reef-poor" Montserrat in the Lesser Antilles (Steadman et al. 1984; Watters et al. 1984).

There is also significant variation in the amount and extent of shallow water shelves bordering islands and continents in the Caribbean. Cuba, with extensive stretches of shallow water along the south, west, and part of the north coast, has shelves more expansive than any other Greater Antilles island. Some of the Virgin Islands and many islands in the Bahamas are surrounded by significant shelves, while Venezuela has a diminutive shelf except near Trinidad and the Gulf of Maracaibo. Although there are notable exceptions, the shelves surrounding the volcanic islands of the Lesser Antilles in most cases are more restricted than those around limestone islands in the outer arc (Figure 2). The presence of shallow water shelves is an important factor in the development of reefs, sea grass beds, and other marine or estuarine habitats.

Yet, what could be the shelves' most significant role in Caribbean prehistory is a largely unrealized potential at this time. The shelves may hold evidence of early occupation of the region in the form of inundated archaeological sites (Nicholson 1976a; Ruppé 1980). Such sites could occur *if* the region was occupied when sea level was lower and the shelves were above water, and *if* the inhabitants occupied the exposed land that subsequently was submerged by rising seas. Depending on the depth of the shelves and the drop in sea level, the amount of emergent land would have varied greatly among the islands. It is also worth noting that current shoals (e.g., the Saba Bank west of that island) may have been exposed as "new" islands in the past. Perhaps the most critical *"if,"* however, is the question of whether such sites would have withstood the impact of a transgressing sea to the extent that they can be detected, located, and examined, either today or in the future using new techniques (Watters 1981).

Following Chapman (1977:1), the term "mangal" in this paper signifies mangrove formations in general, while "mangrove" is reserved for designating individual genera and species. Mangal is widely but patchily distributed in the Caribbean today, with some mangrove genera having restricted ranges while others are widespread (West 1977). Present distribution of mangal is very different from what existed previously. Environmental factors controlled the occurrence of mangal in the past, but it is clear that the current distribution is largely an artifact of human intervention and habitat destruction. For example, Puerto Rico probably has only one-fourth of its original mangal area remaining today, and of the three-quarters destroyed, much has been lost relatively recently (National Oceanic and Atmospheric Administration 1978:61).

The potential importance of mangal formations for Caribbean prehistory, especially in regard to population movements into the region, has been recognized by some authors (e.g., Barrau and Montbrun 1978). Veloz Maggiolo (1980; Veloz Maggiolo and Vega 1982) regards exploitation of mangal resources as a key indicator of the Ortoiroid migration into the Caribbean from Trinidad. Their Saladoid successors and the Casimiroid peoples who came from Middle America also relied on these resources, though less heavily (Rouse and Alegría 1989; Moore 1982). Although data are equivocal, mangal formations, because they shelter a variety of exploitable finfish, shellfish, and crab species, may have played a more significant role in maritime adaptations than generally has been appreciated. Mangal formations also have contributed to changes in the configurations of islands through time, due to their ability to trap sediments and gradually extend a shoreline seaward. They also act as a buffer to high seas and thus reduce coastal flooding and erosion, a fact demonstrated dramatically today to some Caribbean nations that have allowed the destruction of their mangal formations.

Coral reefs, shallow water shelves, and mangal formations have been presented as three examples of the diversity of marine and estuarine environments in the Caribbean. Other examples, such as the distribution of sea grass beds, could be equally enlightening. For the three examples chosen, each in its own way relates to different maritime adaptation issues involving the Caribbean's indigenous peoples. However, environmental diversity tends to highlight the *spatial* aspects of maritime adaptations. Maritime adaptations also have a *temporal* viewpoint because human response to environmental constraints differed through time in the Caribbean area. Thus, maritime adaptation issues are even broader in scope than what has been suggested so far.

MARITIME ADAPTATION ISSUES

The significance of maritime aspects of cultural adaptations in Caribbean prehistory is not merely a function of diversity in the marine and estuarine environments. Environments do not "determine" or "force" human populations to follow one particular adaptive strategy, but environmental constraints do limit the range of potential adaptive strategies for human populations. For populations on islands that are agriculturally marginal because of unreliable or limited freshwater sources, increased use of marine resources for subsistence purposes would be one strategy for coping with the environmental constraint. Creation of impoundment areas to ensure adequate water supplies to enhance crop productivity could be another effective adaptive strategy. In either case, the environmental constraint (i.e., limited freshwater resources) is the same but the adaptive strategy in terms of human behavior or response differs.

Nature is not the only constraining factor. Each people or local population is further restricted by its culture, that is, by the lifeways inherited from its ancestors. Progressive members of the population devise and promote new ways of coping with the local environment; conservatives struggle to maintain the status quo. The two groups eventually compromise short of the optimal strategies.

Each people's decision is also affected by its contacts with neighboring peoples and cultures. It may, for example, decide to trade for scarce resources instead of attempting to obtain them locally, or it may be prevented from doing so by sociopolitical factors. In effect, a people adapts to its human as well as its natural environment (Rouse 1986:165-166, this volume).

It is not sufficient, therefore, to study maritime adaptation issues in isolation. They must be understood in culture-historical perspective and in temporal and spatial contexts, as the following discussions of travel, settlement patterns, and subsistence will illustrate.

Travel

The fundamental maritime adaptation issue among oceanic populations is the ability to travel by sea. Without it, the Lapitoid peoples would not have been able to colonize the Pacific Islands nor the Saladoid peoples, the West Indies.

According to present knowledge, the Lapitoid peoples arose in Melanesia during the second millennium B.C. and expanded into western Polynesia during the first millennium, halting at the point where the larger, more closely spaced islands of their homeland gave way to the tiny, dispersed islands of the Central Pacific. They remained in this frontier zone for a thousand years before learning how to sail the broad expanses of water in central and eastern Polynesia against the prevailing winds and to colonize its isolated islands (Rouse 1986:30-35).

The seafaring ability thus developed has become a major issue in Oceanic archaeology. It is being investigated by studying travel among the surviving natives, by the fortunate discovery of a canoe dating from the period of transition between the Lapitoid and Polynesioid cultures, by computer simulation of conditions at that time, and by experimental voyages in native-type canoes (Rouse 1986:40-42).

The Saladoid peoples appear to have originated in the Orinoco Valley during the third or second millennium B.C. and to have expanded to the Guiana coast and the nearby island of Trinidad during the first millennium. There, they established a frontier zone, in which they learned how to travel in the open sea. With this skill, they were able shortly before the time of Christ to advance through the small islands of the Lesser Antilles and establish a new frontier in Puerto Rico, the first large island in the Greater Antilles. They halted in that transitional zone for another half millennium, adapting to its longer shoreline, greater landmass, and denser Archaic age population before being able to proceed into the larger, more heavily populated islands beyond it (Rouse, this volume).

One paper in the present volume discusses a parallel early Ceramic age expansion from the western coast of Venezuela to the continental island of Curaçao during the middle of the first century A.D. (Haviser, this volume). The Dabajuroid Indians who carried out this expansion must also have acquired maritime skills, but they were unable to use them to move farther out to sea, as the Saladoid peoples had done before them, because their part of the Caribbean Basin lacked a chain of oceanic islands like the Lesser Antilles, through which they could have proceeded into the Greater Antilles. They were limited to coastal migration, eastward into Saladoid territory and westward towards Central America (Arvelo B. 1987).

While Caribbeanists have long been interested in the effect of the prevailing winds, currents, and other features of the natural environment on movements like these (Fewkes 1914, Hostos 1922, Ricketson 1940), they have paid relatively little attention to the skills needed to carry them out (McKusick 1960 and Nicholson 1976b are exceptions). Most authors have tacitly assumed that, since Europeans had the requisite ability, the Indians did too. Yet no evidence has been adduced that the Indians had sails, let alone the ability to tack against the wind, as Europeans did. We need to emulate our Oceanic colleagues' studies of seafaring equipment and practices and to apply the resultant knowledge to our interpretations of the archaeological remains.

Settlement Patterns

The settlement patterns of the Caribbean must also be understood in spatial, temporal, and cultural contexts. Dwelling sites in the small islands of the Lesser Antilles and the Bahamas are distributed along the coast and only rarely are more than 1 km from the shoreline. This distribution occurs regardless of time and applies to both Archaic and Ceramic settlements.

In the large islands of the Greater Antilles, on the contrary, the distribution of sites varies through space and time. The dwelling sites of the Coroso people, who inhabited Puerto Rico during the Archaic age, are coastal, but the contemporaneous Casimiroid sites of Hispaniola and Cuba are also widely distributed through the interior, so much so that Koslowski (1980:70) has suggested seasonal movement between the coast and the interior.[4] These facts are consistent with the presumed origins of the two groups, the Corosans in the small islands of the Lesser Antilles and the Casimiroids in the river valleys of Middle America (Rouse 1986:129-134).

As for the Ceramic age, the early Saladoid sites of Puerto Rico are limited to the coastal plain, late Saladoid sites also occur in the foothills, and settlement was gradually extended into the mountains during the subsequent Ostionoid periods (Rouse 1952:566-571).[5] The site distributions in Hispaniola, Jamaica, and Cuba are not so well known, but there is reason to believe that the Ostionoid Indians who brought the early Ceramic age to those islands followed two main routes, one along the south coast of Hispaniola to Jamaica and the other through the great east-west valleys of northern Hispaniola to Cuba (Rouse 1986:144). In Jamaica, the migrants expanded into the interior, as in Puerto Rico. The Indians of central Cuba preferred hilltop sites some distance inland (Rouse 1942:Figure 9).

More detailed, period by period surveys of the sites in the larger islands of the Greater Antilles are needed to substantiate and expand these conclusions. Only Moore's research in southern Haiti reaches the standard set in Puerto Rico and central Cuba (Moore 1984).

Subsistence

Most of the Archaic age groups that occupied the Insular Caribbean, perhaps as far back as the fifth millennium B.C., are believed to have relied heavily on marine resources because of their coastal settlement locations, proximity to reefs and rocky headlands, and the faunal remains recovered from their sites. They are generally regarded as not having practiced horticulture, though they did eat zamia and other wild plant foods (Veloz Maggiolo and Vega 1982:36). Also, it is generally thought that the depauperate nature of the terrestrial fauna would have permitted but limited hunting or gathering of land animals, a point that actually is questionable given the importance of land crabs for groups occupying the Caribbean later.[6] Almost by default, the Archaic groups are seen as "maritime adapted."

The Archaic sites in the interior of Hispaniola and Cuba are an exception to this rule. In the absence of shells that would have neutralized soil acidity, these sites have yielded few faunal and floral remains. Their inhabitants may be expected to have had a terrestrial orientation, taking advantage of the relatively rich supply of animals, birds, freshwater fish, and food plants available in the interiors of the two largest islands.

The Saladoid peoples are generally believed to have brought a horticulturally based subsistence strategy into the Lesser Antilles and Puerto Rico at the beginning of the Ceramic age. The proximity of their dwelling sites to land suitable for cultivation and the presence of griddles, which their historic descendants used to prepare manioc, support this view.

What is also interesting is a shift in protein sources observed in the archaeological record. The Saladoid Indians who lived on the South American coast and in the adjacent part of the Lesser Antilles obtained their protein primarily from fish, shellfish, birds, and land animals, without making much use of crabs (Rouse, this volume). Large numbers of land crabs were added to the diet in the northern part of the Lesser Antilles and in Puerto Rico, so much so that Rainey (1940) referred to the Saladoid remains of Puerto Rico as a Crab culture.

Rainey also noted a stratigraphic variation in the distribution of land crabs and marine shellfish in Puerto Rico, with the former being heavily represented in lower, Saladoid levels but largely replaced by mollusk remains in the upper, Ostionoid levels. This has been interpreted as evidence for a subsistence strategy change to terrestrial protein sources from the maritime sources used by the previous Archaic age population. A recent study by Elizabeth Wing (1989) of the faunal remains from the Hacienda Grande site in Puerto Rico shows, however, that the Saladoid inhabitants relied equally on terrestrial and maritime sources.

The Ostionoid Indians continued to depend primarily upon horticulture when they finally expanded beyond the Saladoid frontier into Hispaniola, Jamaica, the Bahamas, and most of Cuba, bringing the Ceramic age to those islands. Veloz Maggiolo (1983:18) notes that they relied more heavily on agriculture in the fertile interior valleys of Hispaniola than on the north coast, where soils were poorer and seafood was more readily available. Maritime subsistence strategies became even more important as they moved into the Bahamas, where good farmland was less common and the climate in the north was too cool for the growth of manioc, their primary crop (Sears and Sullivan 1978:23).

What is rarely addressed for early ceramic groups in the Caribbean is spatial variation in maritime adaptations. Yet, given the diversity of environments, both terrestrial and marine, in the prehistoric Caribbean, there is every reason to believe that early ceramic groups faced different environmental constraints when colonizing the different islands. Area-shoreline ratios for "large versus small" islands point this out at a gross level, while variation in reef, shelf, and mangal distributions pertains at an island-specific level.

Given the environmental diversity and constraints, one would expect to observe a range or suite of adaptive strategies coming into play on various islands rather than having one strategy apply to all islands. On reef-rich Barbuda with an abundance of marine resources, the maritime portion of the adaptive strategy should prevail, whereas on Montserrat, which has productive soil but few reefs, the horticultural component should dominate. This does not mean that crops were ignored on Barbuda or that marine resources were ignored on Montserrat, but instead that one part of the subsistence strategy was *emphasized* on each island.

CONCLUSION

The "seaward orientation" of some Ceramic age peoples in the Greater Antilles was noted by Rouse (1951:260-262) almost forty years ago, when he correlated the distribution of certain ceramic styles with passages between islands. Thus, pottery in western Hispaniola was more similar to pottery of eastern Cuba, across the Windward passage, than to pottery of eastern Hispaniola. Rouse (1982) attributes this distribution to the fact that the passages facilitated interaction among seafaring people while the island landmasses acted as barriers.

Initially, the island landmass acted as an environmental constraint, but people later overcame that constraint and settled the interior of the islands. Thus, the orientation shifted through time, with a decreasing seaward and increasing landward emphasis. This pattern points out the importance of viewing the orientations as complementary rather than mutually exclusive.

Adoption of a research strategy that melds landward and seaward perspectives is a logical approach to interpreting Caribbean prehistory. The maritime component of cultural adaptations should not be separated out and analyzed as an isolated phenomenon. Instead, emphasis should be on the overall cultural adaptation, with the maritime component being but one part of the adaptive strategy, in some cases of minor importance but in others a prominent one.

NOTES

1. The terms "Lapitoid" and "Polynesioid," which are not accepted by all Oceanists, are used herein for terminological consistency with respect to "Saladoid," and follow Rouse (1986:30-35).

2. Watters's (1983) article in the *Proceedings of the Ninth International Congress for the Study of Pre-Columbian Cultures of the Lesser Antilles* is missing four pages from the middle of the submitted manuscript.

3. The Greater Antilles are characterized as oceanic in this paper. However, debate about the continental or oceanic character of all or part of the Greater Antilles has occurred among geologists and biogeographers twice in the twentieth century. The most recent debate centers on the "vicariance hypothesis" (Rosen 1975). Pregill (1981) provides arguments against this hypothesis.

4. Rouse's terminology for the Archaic age series in the Caribbean is used here in place of Veloz Maggiolo's.

5. Here, we use Rouse's revised terminology for the Ceramic age series, in which Ostionoid is extended to include the series previously called Elenoid, Meillacoid, and Chicoid, and the latter are reduced to the status of subseries (Rouse 1986:134-151).

6. Whether land crabs can be classed as truly terrestrial resouces is somewhat equivocal because some species prefer to inhabit coastal mangal stands, an arguably estuarine environment. Yet, they also occur inland at locations well removed from the coast, a situation that supports the terrestrial designation. They definitely are not marine crabs.

Acknowledgments. This is an extensively revised version of a paper with the same title presented by the authors in the New World Maritime Adaptations Symposium at the 48th Annual Meeting of the Society for American Archaeology, Pittsburgh, Pennsylvania, April 1983. The authors wish to acknowledge the comments and discussion of the participants in that symposium. They are also indebted to Richard Scaglion for advice on writing the section on area-shoreline ratio.

REFERENCES CITED

Adey, Walter H. and Randolph B. Burke
    1976   Holocene Bioherms (Algal Ridges and Bank-Barrier Reefs) of the Eastern Caribbean. *Geological Society of America Bulletin* 87(1):95-109.

    1977   Holocene Bioherms of Lesser Antilles -- Geologic Control of Development. In *Reefs and Related Carbonates -- Ecology and Sedimentology*, edited by Stanley H. Frost, Malcom P. Weiss, and John B. Saunders, pp. 67-81. Studies in Geology, vol. 4. American Association of Petroleum Geologists, Tulsa.

Arvelo B., Liliam M.
    1987   *Un modelo de poblamiénto prehispánico para la cuenca del Lago de Maracaibo.* Unpublished Master's thesis, Department of Anthropology, Instituto Venezolano de Investigaciones Científicas, Caracas.

Barrau, Jacques and Christian Montbrun
    1978   La mangrove et l'insertion humaine dans les écosystème insulaires des Petites Antilles: Le cas de la Martinique et de la Guadeloupe. *Social Sciences Information* 17(6):897-919.

Chapman, V. J.
    1977   Introduction. In *Ecosystems of the World 1: Wet Coastal Ecosystems*, edited by V. J. Chapman, pp. 1-29. Elsevier, Amsterdam.

Defense Mapping Agency Hydrographic/Topographic Center
    1980   *Anegada Passage with Adjacent Islands.* Chart 25600, 44th ed., scale 1:250,000. Defence Mapping Agency Hydrographic/Topographic Center, Washington, D.C.

Eastern Caribbean Natural Area Management Program
    1980a   *Barbuda Preliminary Data Atlas.* Eastern Caribbean Natural Area Management Program, St. Croix, U.S. Virgin Islands.

    1980b   *Montserrat Preliminary Data Atlas.* Eastern Caribbean Natural Area Management Program, St. Croix, U. S. Virgin Islands.

Fewkes, Jesse Walter
    1914   Relations of Aboriginal Culture and Environment in the Lesser Antilles. *Bulletin of the American Geographical Society* 46:662-678.

Hostos, Adolfo de
    1922   Notes on West Indian Hydrography in its Relation to Prehistoric Migrations. *Annaes, 20th Congress, International Congress of Americanists* 1:239-250. Rio de Janeiro.

Houghton Mifflin
    1979   *The International Geographic Encyclopedia and Atlas.* Houghton Mifflin, Boston.

Keegan, William F. and Jared M. Diamond
   1987   Colonization of Islands by Humans: A Biogeographical Perspective. In *Advances in Archaeological Method and Theory*, vol. 10, edited by Michael B. Schiffer, pp. 49-92. Academic Press, New York.

Kirch, Patrick V.
   1988   Problems and Issues in Lapita Archaeology. In *Archaeology of the Lapita Cultural Complex: A Critical Review*, edited by Patrick V. Kirch and Terry L. Hunt, pp. 157-165. Thomas Burke Memorial Washington State Museum Research Report No. 5. Seattle.

Kirch, Patrick V. and Terry L. Hunt (editors)
   1988   *Archaeology of the Lapita Cultural Complex: A Critical Review*. Thomas Burke Memorial Washington State Museum Research Report No. 5. Seattle.

Koslowski, Janusz K. .
   1980   In Search of the Evolutionary Pattern of the Preceramic Cultures of the Caribbean. *Boletín del Museo del Hombre Dominicano* 13: 61-79.

McKusick, Marshall B.
   1960   *Aboriginal Canoes in the West Indies*. Yale University Publications in Anthropology No. 63. New Haven.

Milliman, John D.
   1973   Caribbean Coral Reefs. In *Biology and Geology of Coral Reefs*, vol. 1, edited by O. A. Jones and R. Endean, pp. 1-50, 401-410. Academic Press, New York.

Moore, Clark
   1982   Investigation of Preceramic Sites on Ile à Vache, Haiti. *The Florida Anthropologist* 35(4):186-199.

   1984   Inventaire des sites archéologiques dans la Péninsule Sud d'Haïti. *Bulletin du Bureau National d'Ethnologie* 2: 65-83.

National Oceanic and Atmospheric Administration
   1978   *Puerto Rico Coastal Management Program and Final Environmental Impact Statement*. Office of Coastal Zone Management, National Oceanic and Atmospheric Administration, Washington, D.C.

Nicholson, Desmond V.
   1976a The Importance of Sea-Levels -- Caribbean Archaeology. *Journal of the Virgin Islands Archaeological Society* 3:19-23.

   1976b Pre-Columbian Seafaring Capabilities in the Lesser Antilles. *Proceedings of the International Congress for the Study of Pre-Columbian Cultures of the Lesser Antilles* 6:98-105. Gainesville.

Pregill, Gregory K.
   1981   An Appraisal of the Vicariance Hypothesis and Its Application to West Indian Terrestrial Vertebrates. *Systematic Zoology* 30:145-155.

Rainey, Froelich G.
   1940   *Porto Rican Archaeology*. Scientific Survey of Porto Rico and the Virgin Islands, vol. XVIII-part 1. The New York Academy of Sciences, New York.

Ricketson, Oliver G., Jr.
    1940   An Outline of the Basic Physical Factors Affecting Middle America. In *The Maya and Their Neighbors*, edited by Clarence L. Hay, Ralph L. Linton, Samuel K. Lothrop, Harry L. Shapiro, and George C. Vaillant, pp. 10-31. D. Appleton-Century, New York.

Rosen, D.
    1975   A Vicariance Model of Caribbean Biogeography. *Systematic Zoology* 24:431-464.

Rouse, Irving
    1942   *Archeology of the Maniabón Hills, Cuba.* Yale University Publications in Anthropology No. 26. New Haven.

    1951   Areas and Periods of Culture in the Greater Antilles. *Southwestern Journal of Anthropology* 7:248-265.

    1952   *Porto Rican Prehistory.* Scientific Survey of Porto Rico and the Virgin Islands, vol. XVIII-parts 3 and 4. The New York Academy of Sciences, New York.

    1982   Ceramic and Religious Development in the Greater Antilles. *Journal of New World Archaeology* 5(2):45-55.

    1986   *Migrations in Prehistory: Inferring Population Movement from Cultural Remains.* Yale University Press, New Haven.

Rouse, Irving and Ricardo E. Alegría
    1989   *Excavations at María de la Cruz and Hacienda Grande, Loiza, Puerto Rico.* Yale University Publications in Anthropology, New Haven, in press.

Ruppé, Reynold J.
    1980   Sea-Level Rise and Caribbean Prehistory. *Proceedings of the International Congress for the Study of the Pre-Columbian Cultures of the Lesser Antilles* 8:331-337. Tempe.

Sears, William H. and Shaun O. Sullivan
    1978   Bahamas Prehistory. *American Antiquity* 43:3-25.

Steadman, David W., David R. Watters, Elizabeth J. Reitz, and Gregory K. Pregill
    1984   Vertebrates from Archaeological Sites on Montserrat, West Indies. *Annals of Carnegie Museum* 53:1-29.

United Nations Environment Programme
    1980   *Marine and Coastal Area Development in the Wider Caribbean: Overview Study.* UNEP/CEPAL/WG.48/INF.14, November 1, 1980. United Nations Environment Programme, New York.

Veloz Maggiolo, Marcio
    1980   *Las sociedades arcaicas de Santo Domingo.* Museo del Hombre Dominicano and Fundación García Arévalo, Santo Domingo.

    1983   Para una definición de la cultura Taína. In *Las culturas de América en la época del descubrimiento: Seminario sobre la investigación de la cultura Taína*, pp.15-21. Comisión Nacional para la Celebración del V Centenario del Descubrimiento de América, Madrid.

Veloz Maggiolo, Marcio and Bernardo Vega
    1982 The Antillean Preceramic: A New Approximation. *Journal of New World Archaeology* 5(2):33-44.

Watters, David R.
    1981 Linking Oceanography to Prehistoric Archaeology. *Oceanus* 24(2):11-19.

    1982 Relating Oceanography to Antillean Archaeology: Implications from Oceania. *Journal of New World Archaeology* 5(2):3-12.

    1983 Assessing the Ocean's Roles in Antillean Archaeology. *Proceedings of the International Congress for the Study of the Pre-Columbian Cultures of the Lesser Antilles* 9:531-541. Montréal.

    1989 Archaeological Implications for Lesser Antilles Biogeography: The Small Island Perspective. In *Biogeography of the West Indies: Past, Present, and Future*, edited by Charles Woods. E. J. Brill, Leiden, in press.

Watters, David R., Elizabeth J. Reitz, David W. Steadman, and Gregory K. Pregill
    1984 Vertebrates from Archaeological Sites on Barbuda, West Indies. *Annals of Carnegie Museum* 53:383-412.

West, Robert C.
    1977 Tidal Salt-Marsh and Mangal Formations of Middle and South America. In *Ecosystems of the World 1: Wet Coastal Ecosystems*, edited by V. J. Chapman, pp. 198-213. Elsevier, Amsterdam.

West, Robert C. and John P. Augelli
    1976 *Middle America: Its Lands and Peoples*. 2nd ed. Prentice-Hall, Englewood Cliffs.

Wing, Elizabeth S.
    1989 Animal Remains from the Hacienda Grande Site. Appendix to *Excavations at María de la Cruz and Hacienda Grande, Loiza, Puerto Rico* by Irving Rouse and Ricardo E. Alegría. Yale University Publications in Anthropology, New Haven, in press.

Wing, Elizabeth S. and Elizabeth J. Reitz
    1982 Prehistoric Fishing Communities of the Caribbean. *Journal of New World Archaeology* 5(2):13-32.

Table 1. Area to Shoreline Ratios for Six Caribbean Islands.

Island	Area (km^2)[a]	Shoreline (km)[b]	Area-Shoreline Ratio
Cuba	114,524	2,790	41.05:1
Jamaica	10,961	564	19.43:1
Trinidad	4,828	390	12.38:1
St. Lucia	616	103	5.98:1
Barbados	430	88	4.89:1
Montserrat	98	42	2.34:1
Venezuela	—	2,000	—

[a] Data from Houghton Mifflin (1979).

[b] Measured from maps and charts of islands (approximate).

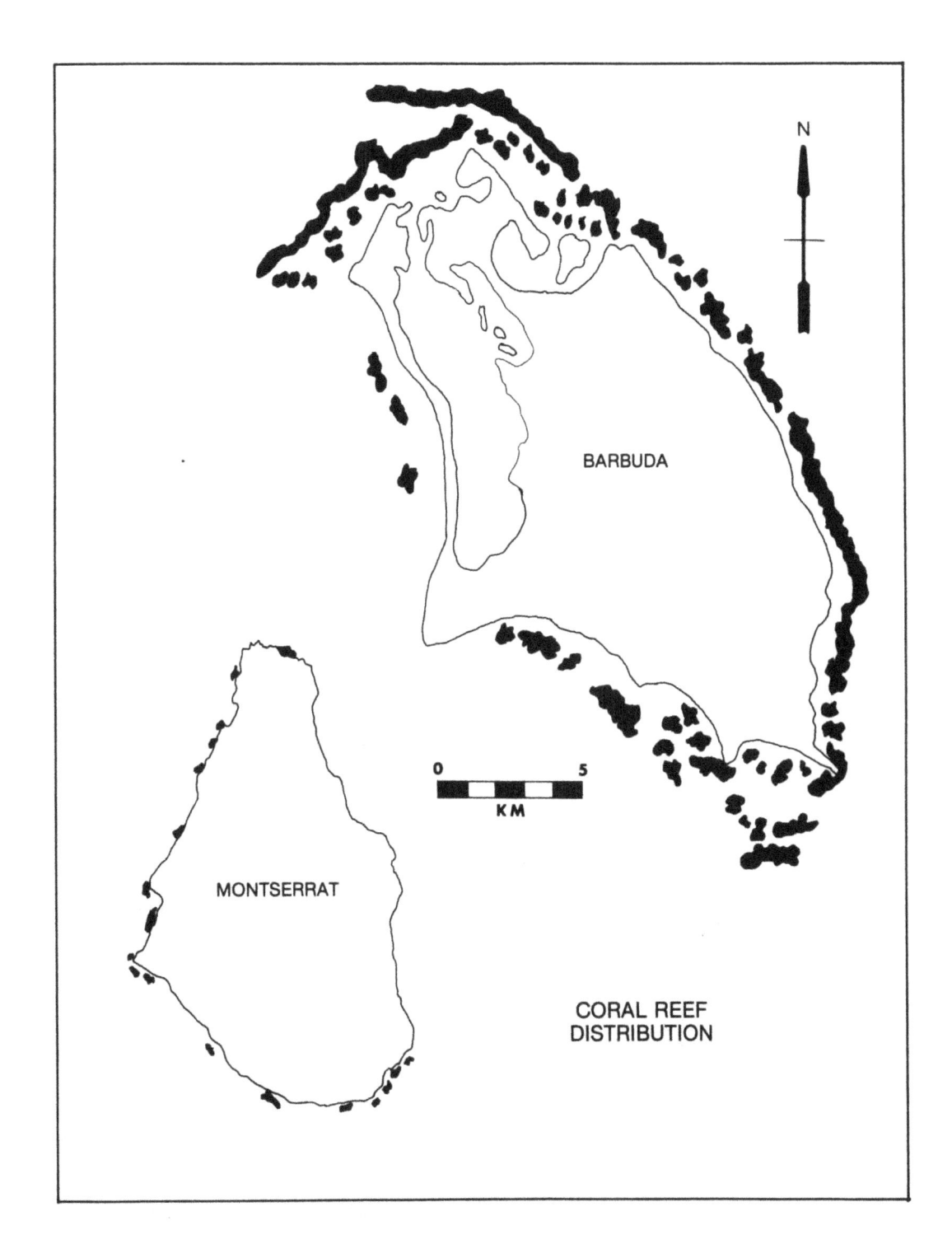

Figure 1. Distribution of living coral reefs around Barbuda and Montserrat, northern Lesser Antilles. Barbuda, a low-lying limestone island with extensive shallow water shelves, has much greater reef development than Montserrat, a volcanic island with limited shelves. They are located about 100 km apart. [Source: Eastern Caribbean Natural Area Management Program 1980a and b].

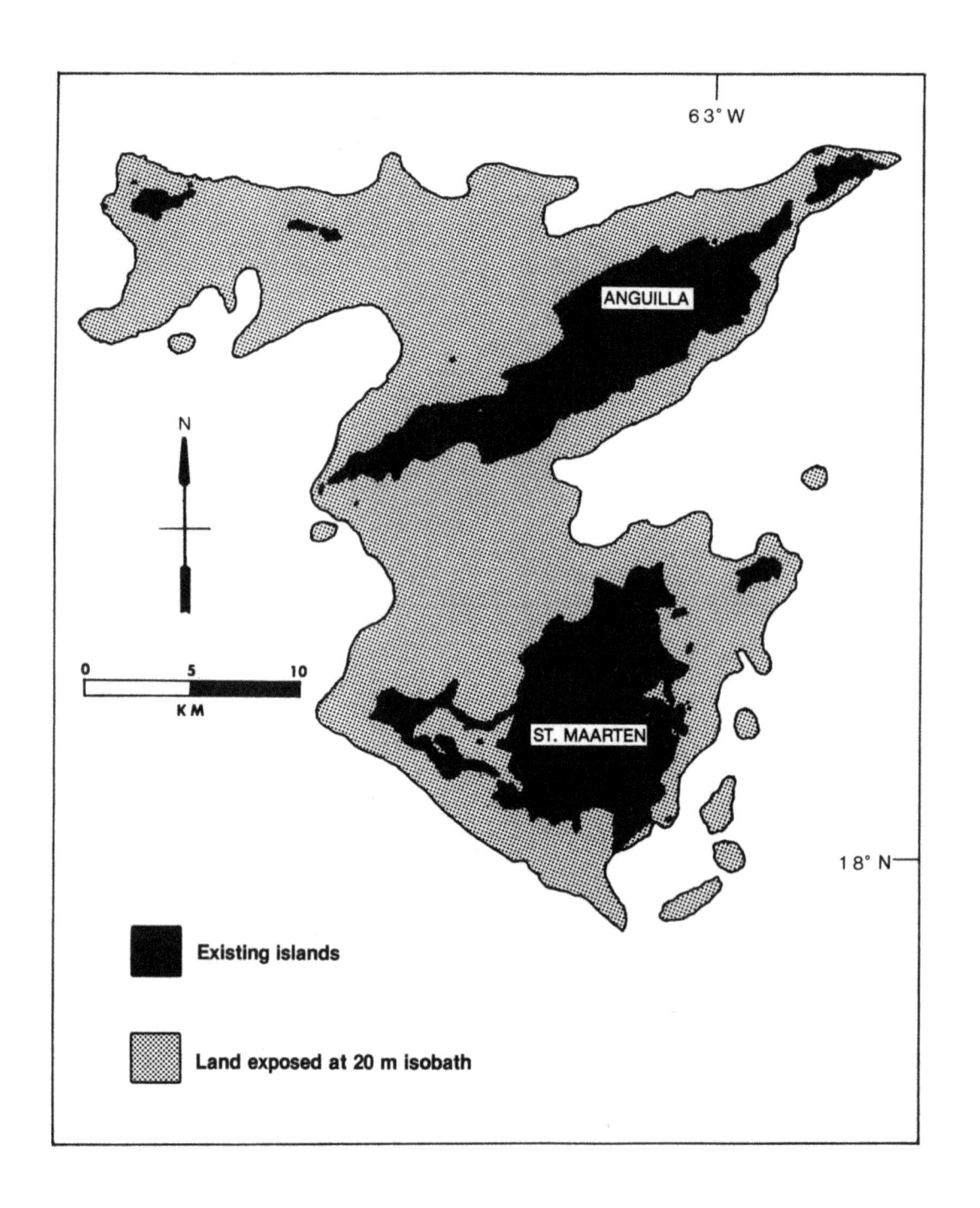

Figure 2. The expanse of presently submerged land around Anguilla and St. Maarten that would be exposed if sea-level dropped to the 20m isobath. [Source: Defense Mapping Agency Hydrographic/Topographic Center 1980].

PART 2:

VOLCANISM AND ARCHAEOLOGY

VOLCANIC CHRONOLOGY

AND THE EARLY SALADOID OCCUPATION OF MARTINIQUE

Louis Allaire

ABSTRACT

Recent geological work on the chronology of Mt. Pelée's volcanic eruptions introduces a new perspective on the dating and circumstances of the initial agricultural colonization of Martinique by Cedrosan Saladoid peoples. This paper discusses the significance of the volcanological evidence for the identification of volcanic tephra layers uncovered in the stratigraphy of the Vivé and Fond Brûlé archaeological sites. In the context of a revised dating of Saladoid expansion towards the Lesser Antilles that may go back to the fifth century B.C., alternative chronological interpretations allowed by radiometric determinations are also explored.

INTRODUCTION

Over 50 years have elapsed since the first report on a Saladoid site of Martinique was published in 1937. Its author, Father Delawarde (1937), reported on the discovery of pottery fragments from the northeast coast of the island near Marigot, a locality that was soon to be known as the "Arawak capital" of Martinique (Pinchon 1952). Delawarde's early paper was essentially descriptive, his most astute observation being perhaps that the vessels' shapes were reminiscent of "our modern spittoons" (Delawarde 1937). Since 1937, however, some 30 archaeological sites belonging to the various phases of the Saladoid series, the earliest pottery of the Lesser Antilles, have been identified (Pinchon 1952; H. Petitjean Roget 1975), and more than 50 titles have appeared in some form of publication on that particular style and period alone (the most significant of which will be cited in the following discussions). These contributions vary greatly in substance and scholarly qualities and, with very few exceptions, none of the excavations were the work of professionally trained archaeologists.[1]

In view of this situation, we cannot avoid asking today whether anything of significance has resulted from these 50 years of archaeological research in Martinique, especially on the early ceramic and agricultural colonization of this Windward Island. Indeed, a comprehensive synthesis of the accumulated evidence has still to be compiled. Nevertheless, the present picture leaves no doubt that early Saladoid developments in Martinique followed the pattern established elsewhere in the Windward Islands. The earliest Saladoid manifestation, with its fine, delicate pottery whose decoration includes the diagnostic zoned-incised cross-hatched incisions, the white-on-red painting and the simple modeled-incised adornos, has long been labelled locally as the "Horizon I" style (Petitjean Roget 1970)[2] as the earliest ceramics so far identified on the island. This early style is now assigned to the Cedrosan subseries of the Saladoid that extends from Trinidad to Puerto Rico, and which is assumed to have been introduced by the migration of the first agricultural people to the West Indies. It is those Cedrosan sites that are so often associated with layers of abundant remains of crabs (Rouse, this volume).

This initial Cedrosan subseries maintains its distinctive stylistic features until about the middle of the fourth century A.D., and this is certainly the case in Martinique (Allaire 1973; Rouse and Allaire 1978), when a more elaborate expression of the Saladoid style emerges rapidly. This new manifestation is characterized by modeled-incised decoration, more complex vessel shapes and a profusion of white-on-red painted designs. This particular style is known in Martinique as that of the "Horizon II"; it has more recently been designated as a separate Palo Secan subseries (Irving Rouse, personal communication 1989); these changes may be traced to the style of the expanding Barrancoid series on the mainland. Horizon II in Martinique, as well as elsewhere in the Lesser Antilles, actually may be stylistically more complex, as is suggested by the assemblages from such sites as Vivé II (Lehouillier 1974) as opposed to the more elaborate Diamant collection (Petitjean Roget 1968, 1970). We obviously need more detailed site reports and stylistic analyses before definitive conclusions can be reached. Yet, there is no doubt that if the Horizon I/Cedrosan ceramics represent a Classic expression of Saladoid stylistic evolution, the Horizon II/Secan varieties are certainly representative of its baroque stage. Eventually, by ca. A.D. 650, typical Saladoid decoration gives way to an entirely new series of styles known as the Troumassoid, based essentially in the Windward Islands. Contemporaneous developments in the Leeward Islands are still even today poorly known; they are assumed to belong to the Elenan subseries of the Ostionoid according to Rouse's recent chronological system (Rouse 1986).

In Martinique, Horizon I sites, which are the major subject of this paper, have so far shown to be all exclusively located along the fertile northeast coast of the island, right at the base of the famous Mt. Pelée volcano where its gentle eastern slopes are today one of the island's major agricultural areas (Figures 1 and 2). This is one of the most humid inhabited areas of Martinique; with annual precipitation of between 2,000 and 3,000 mm (Lasserre 1977), where in addition, repeated deposits of fresh volcanic ashes have boosted its natural productivity to unusually high levels. This is also the area of dense tropical rain forest that offers optimum conditions for a slash-and-burn garden agriculture as was typical of its early historical population, the Island Caribs.

So far, only six Horizon I or Cedrosan sites are known in Martinique from the published reports (Pinchon 1952; Petitjean Roget 1970; Petitjean Roget 1975). These include, (Figure 1) from north to south, the sites of Moulin l'Etang (Fayaud 1976), Vivé (Mattioni 1979; Bullen and Mattioni 1972), Fond Brûlé (Mattioni 1982), Adoration (Delawarde 1937; Haag 1965),[3] and Lasalle (Revert in Harcourt 1952). In addition, a small surface collection obtained by myself from a building project just above the Fond St-Jacques Bay in 1971, as part of an early unpublished survey, includes early stylistic features that may be assigned to the Horizon I (Figure 3).[4] All these sites also contain a later Horizon II component.[5] Much is still to be learned about this Horizon I culture and adaptation. That its people had selected the best agricultural section of the island is revealing of their main subsistance base, and the abundant remains of clay griddles in their ceramic remains is reliable evidence that they cultivated bitter manioc as a staple food.[6] Unfortunately, little else can be reconstructed of their subsistence because of the unusual lack of any faunal remains from the sites including, neither shells nor animal bones (whereas typical early Saladoid sites elsewhere in the West Indies consist essentially of middens with abundant faunal remains, including the ubiquitous crab claws). This unusual situation may be due to the high levels of soil acidity, constant humidity, effects of nearby sea spray, and the recent introduction of chemical fertilizers (Revert, in Harcourt 1952).[7] Although there is little doubt that the people of the Horizon I also hunted, fished, and collected shellfish for food, it must be pointed out that the particular conditions of the northeast coast with its rough open Atlantic battered shores, almost continuous high cliff shoreline, cobble beaches, and lack of mangrove swamps is relatively unfavorable for fishing and shellfish collecting. This is in sharp contrast to the conditions encountered further south along that coast.

That some of the sites are the remains of large villages is well illustrated by the occupation floor uncovered by Mattioni (1979) in his Vivé I level.[8] More precise identifications of settlement types are difficult for other sites, which consist of multiple midden deposits visible as surface scatters in freshly ploughed sugar cane or banana fields. It is, for instance, still impossible to determine whether these six or seven sites, whose distances between each other vary between hardly 2.0 km to not more then 5.0 km, and average a mere 3.0 km, were all occupied simultaneously or represent chronological differences resulting from periodic village relocations. To learn more about the Horizon I occupational sequence, we must await the detailed stylistic analyses based on the abundant decoration of the ceramic assemblages that will allow for more precise comparisons and for seriating sites in their proper chronological order.

Despite so many gaps in our knowledge of the Horizon I occupation of Martinique, especially as it relates to the agricultural colonization of the island, one particular aspect received a significant amount of attention, and this since the earliest investigations. Early local investigators, especially Father Delawarde and the naturalist Eugene Revert (in Harcourt 1952) noted a close association in many sites between the archaeological remains and volcanic deposits from eruptions of the Mt. Pelée volcano, towering to 1,400 m over the northern part of Martinique, within a mere seven or eight kilometers from the Horizon I sites located on the northeast coast of the island. The occurrence of tephra deposits (any ashes, granular fragments or lapilli, and pumice ejected from the volcano and redeposited over the landscape) was nowhere so striking as the layer discovered in the early 1970s by Mario Mattioni (1979) at the Vivé site. There, a 45 cm deep layer of white ashes and lapilli was found to have covered the extensive and rich occupation floor of a Horizon I settlement (Vivé I). The eruption responsible for these deposits may have destroyed the village and thus forced its abandonment by the inhabitants (Figure 4). Moreover, the site was unique for the presence of a subsequent archaeological component, belonging to the Horizon II style, and dated to the fifth century A.D. (Lehouillier 1974). Indeed, no site other than Vivé was able to conjure up so vividly the volcanic hazards to which the early agricultural settlers of Mt. Pelée's fertile slopes had at all times been exposed. Inspired by Vivé, Mattioni was able to pursue his investigations of this volcanic occurrence; he was successful in discovering a second site, Fond Brûlé, located in the same general area where a volcanic layer separated two Saladoid occupations (Mattioni 1982). A similar context was later identified at the Moulin l'Etang site, the northernmost Horizon I occupation (Fayaud 1976).

At the time Mattioni was investigating Vivé and Fond Brûlé, little was known of the recent eruptive history of Mt. Pelée corresponding to the period of human occupation. That is, approximately the last 2,000 years, beyond the well known events responsible for the catastrophic destruction of the town of St-Pierre on the western side of the island in May of 1902 and the extermination of its nearly 30,000 inhabitants. This still remains one of the deadliest eruptions of the twentieth century (Westercamp 1987). In the 1960s, a single radiocarbon date for a prehistoric eruption had been available to archaeologists. This date of A.D. 295±150 was published by the geologist, Grunewald (1964), in his study of Martinique (Figure 5). It was derived from a lignite fragment (a coal-like ancient piece of wood preserved in volcanic deposits) from a locality close to the vent area, and at considerable distance from the Vivé site. Despite the tentative nature of the association, this date appeared at the time convenient for assigning an age to the Vivé volcanic layer, especially in the context of what was then known of the dating of Horizon I occupations, then assigned to the second century A.D., and of the Horizon II, to the fifth century A.D.

THE VOLCANIC CHRONOLOGY

AND ITS ARCHAEOLOGICAL MANIFESTATIONS

The first chronological work on the recent eruption sequence of Mt. Pelée was presented in the 1970s by geologists Roobol and Smith (1976) who also included references to volcanic deposits found in archaeological context (Roobol et al. 1976), but it is only the more recent works of Westercamp and Traineau (1983) that have provided a more complete and detailed sequence based on substantial radiometric dating that may be correlated with archaeological chronologies (Figure 5).

The most famous recent eruption of Mt. Pelée is obviously the 1902 disaster (Westercamp 1987). Indeed, the type of pyroclastic eruption that destroyed St-Pierre has given its name to similar typical explosions of *nuées ardentes* (e.g., clouds of incandescent ashes and gases) that flow down the slopes of the volcano carrying ashes and blocks, filling valleys and destroying everything in their path. These so-called *Pelean eruptions* are not associated with lava flows, nor is the other major type of earlier eruption of Mt. Pelée, designated as *Plinian* (from the famous Vesuvius eruptions), which is associated with extremely violent destruction of the volcano itself, and the widespread distribution of destructive pumice and ash flows (Bullard 1976).

The recent volcanological studies mentioned above now suggest that Mt. Pelée's eruptions occurred in cycles of approximately 250 years over the last 5,000 years (Westercamp and Traineau 1983). Within the chronological framework of Saladoid occupations, the period beginning around 500 B.C. is characterized essentially by Plinian-type eruptions, whereas the more recent and typical Pelean or *nuées ardentes* eruptions appear only after A.D. 1000.

Interestingly, perhaps the most unsuspected result of Westercamp and Traineau's (1983:169) recent chronology was to show that even in comparison with the major 1902 disaster of St-Pierre, the most powerful eruption of the entire 5,000 year sequence had occurred shortly before the time of Christ, that is, at the very beginnings of Saladoid expansion to the West Indies. This unique series of eruptions seems to have consisted of essentially three separate occurrences separated by perhaps not more than 20 years. Martinique must certainly have experienced an especially severe century of repeated and especially destructive volcanism affecting the northern half of the island at precisely the time of its initial agricultural colonization. Westercamp and Traineau (1983) assign an average date of 70±140 B.C. to the main eruption that they designate as the Third Plinian eruption (or P3). This is based on six "precise" radiocarbon dates which are not listed individually in the published report but suggest a possible time range spanning the period between 210 B.C. to A.D. 70. It may be noted that the geologists, however, do not emphasize this potential time range, focusing instead on the median date of 70 B.C. This may explain a discrepancy with the earlier sequence advanced by Roobol and Smith (1976), which only identified two distinct eruptions within that time bracket: one dated to 195 B.C. and the other to 65 B.C. (Figure 5). We may assume that Roobol and Smith's evidence pertained to the same eruptive sequence as Westercamp and Traineau's P3 occurrence. There is no doubt, however, that this major Plinian eruption left abundant traces over the entire northern half of the island, consisting essentially of pumice and tephra. Of special interest to archaeologists is an unusual eastward distribution of pumice and ash flows as opposed to the more typical westward pattern of airfall deposits caused by the prevailing winds (Figure 6). Geologists certainly all agree, however, that the Plinian 3 eruptions were potentially "very destructive" and "a serious hazard" for any inhabitants within an area of 10 to 12 km from the vents (Westercamp and Traineau 1983:171).

The powerful Third Plinian (P3) eruptions were followed some 250 years later by a lesser, albeit more complex, volcanic event that began with an isolated *nuée ardente* (incandescent cloud) eruption (designated as NMP) and dated to A.D. 210±80 (A.D. 130-290). Shortly thereafter occurred a renewal of Plinian activity (designated as P2) dating to A.D. 280±60 (A.D. 220-340), which also spread pumice and ashes toward the east, filling valleys along the eastern slope of the mountain (Figure 6) (Westercamp and Traineau 1983:171).

It is this third century A.D. eruption, with its particular eastward direction, that is most likely correlated with the volcanic layer at Vivé. As described by Mattioni (1979:Fig. 3), this 45 cm absolutely sterile level occurs between 90 and 35 cm from the site's surface, covering the brown sandy layer of the Vivé I occupation. It consists essentially of a deposit of pumice and lapilli fragments ranging in size from 1.0 to 4.0 cm. The layer is a light yellow or whitish color that contrasts with the uppermost layer of brown soil mixed with tephra (Figure 4), which is associated with Horizon II remains. Although there is no reference in the recent volcanic sequence to the date of A.D. 295 used by Mattioni for dating his volcanic layer at Vivé, the date itself nevertheless appeared strikingly consistent with the radiocarbon dating of an early Saladoid occupation consisting of a substantial occupation floor that may represent the actual abandonment of the site caused by the eruption. The actual radiocarbon date for Vivé I is A.D. 220±100, later calibrated to A.D. 260 (Schvoerer et al. 1985), could be interpreted as being essentially contemporaneous with any of the existing radiometric dates for these third century eruptions, and especially P2 with its eastward tephra deposits (Figure 5). The direct association of an early Cedrosan occupation with a layer of volcanic deposit is not limited to Vivé.

The Fond Brûlé site, located on the edges of the first small coastal river 3 km south of Vivé (Figure 1), and within a stone's throw from the beach, was also excavated extensively by Mattioni (1982) beginning in 1977. The site revealed a similar occurrence of volcanic deposits separating two archaeological levels belonging, as at Vivé, to Horizons I and II. The nature of the tephra there varies somewhat from Vivé according to Mattioni's descriptions. The Fond Brûlé deposit shows a darker yellowish coloration and consists essentially of a fine pumice stratum occurring between 118 and 77 cm below the surface of the excavated area (Figure 7). Moreover, the lower part of the layer seems to have been affected by variations of the water table. Since the remains at Fond Brûlé are found at the foot of a slope, it is believed that much of the volcanic deposits might have resulted from colluvium rather than from the primary airfall deposition as seems to be the case at Vivé. The volcanic layer overlying a Horizon I deposit also uncovered in test excavations at Moulin l'Etang, the first Horizon I site located some 5.0 km north of Vivé (Figure 1), cannot be determined more precisely because of the incomplete information available in the short unpublished report (Fayaud 1976).

Of the geologists who have recently studied Mt. Pelée's volcanic activity, only Roobol and Smith (1976) include any reference to the archaeological evidence, which they use as a major element of their chronological interpretations. Unfortunately, no geologist was able to record the actual volcanic layers at either Vivé or Fond Brûlé, but Roobol and Smith, with the assistance of the archaeologist Henri Petitjean Roget (Roobol et al. 1976), nevertheless were able to investigate the available evidence from the immediate vicinity of these and other later archaeological sites, which at the time of their visits had been backfilled. This certainly limits the precise evaluation of in situ deposits in such complex situations as that of soils and terrains associated with human occupations, and Roobol and Smith (1979) are cautious to warn against hasty interpretations, especially when sites occur at some distance from the vents, in areas usually affected by extensive erosion and reworking of sediments such as the coastline of the island and its small river valleys.

Roobol and Smith's examination of soil profiles from the vicinity of the Vivé and Fond Brûlé sites (more precisely the south side of Vivé and a gravel quarry at the mouth of the nearby Capot River) is summarized in Figure 9. They were able to verify the presence of the Vivé lapilli layer between two soil layers at both places. On the south side of Vivé, however, the two distinctive archaeological layers occurred in a mixed soil context overlying the block and ash layer of an earlier Pelean eruption (Figure 9D). The same admixture resulting from soil erosion was also encountered on the hill behind the Fond Brûlé site where potsherds are found over the yellow ash deposits and pumice fragments of a Plinian eruption (Figure 9E) apparently similar to the deposits uncovered in the site by Mattioni (1982). These observations warrant caution in assessing the significance of volcanic deposits at Vivé and Fond Brûlé. These layers of apparently different constitutions certainly both cover similar early Cedrosan remains but there are as yet no detailed typological reports for either site and still less any substantial comparative analysis of the two assemblages. The geological correlation of the two volcanic layers must also be considered at best tentative as Roobol et al. (1976) are also careful to emphasize.

CHRONOLOGICAL IMPLICATIONS

The volcanic chronology for the last 2,000 years becomes fully significant when it is considered in the perspective of recent advances in dating the original Saladoid expansion to the West Indies. Until a few years ago, the initial Saladoid occupation of the West Indies could not be traced to an earlier date than the first century B.C. (Rouse and Allaire 1978). In this last year only, a series of radiocarbon dates from the Leeward Islands of Montserrat and St. Martin (see Rouse, this volume), have now pushed back the possible time of this initial migration to even before 500 B.C. The significance of these chronological revisions is the subject of Rouse's paper in this volume. For Martinique, however, an assessment of the available dates must be set in the context of the recent volcanic chronology.

As part of his excavations at Fond Brûlé, Mattioni had obtained two radiocarbon determinations from charcoal samples that had proved to be of unexpectedly early age, that is, 265±115 B.C. and 530±140 B.C. (uncalibrated). For this reason both dates were rejected as inconsistent with the then accepted dating for Cedrosan sites on Martinique, and consequently, the dates were not published. Instead, Mattioni resubmitted the samples for reanalysis at different laboratories with, this time, more conservative, albeit, somewhat late results that ranged between 150±210 B.C. and A.D. 320±210 (Schvoerer et al. 1985). Because of these discrepancies, Mattioni initiated a project of thermoluminescence dating which, however, was to suffer technically from two consecutive hurricanes, in 1979 and 1980, a fact that must be considered in the evaluation of the results published by Schvoerer and his colleagues (1985) of three determinations that range between A.D. 805 and 60 B.C.

In the context of the recent dates from Montserrat and St. Martin mentioned above, as well as early B.C. dates for Puerto Rico and Trinidad (Rouse, this volume) the early radiocarbon and thermoluminescence determinations for Fond Brûlé need to be reconsidered. Alternative chronological sequences are summarized in Figure 10. Contrary to the "traditional," more conservative interpretation (Figure 10,A), which places Horizon I in the second century A.D. and the P3 eruptions at ca. 70 B.C. (Westercamp and Traineau 1983), that is, before the arrival of Saladoid settlers, it is important to consider the possibility of an earlier P3 manifestation in the second century B.C. as allowed by the error margin in the radiometric determinations (Figure 5) as well as an initial Saladoid (Cedrosan) expansion occurring before or during the P3 period of activity (Figure 10,B). This volcanic event may have prevented an early occupation of Martinique, especially if one is not convinced by the validity of the B.C. dates obtained by Mattioni for Fond Brûlé. Alternatively, if one accepts an early occurrence of Horizon I at Fond Brûlé (Figure 10,C) and identifies its overlying volcanic deposits as those of the P3 eruptions, we may be able to argue for a later Vivé I occupation with its own distinctive P2 deposits as postulated by Mattioni. A fourth possibility is to lump all Horizon I sites into the third century B.C. and to assign all volcanic deposits to P3 tephra (Figure 10,D). This scenario includes a protracted depopulation of the island until the time of the Horizon II settlements in the fourth century A.D. The last alternative considers the Lasalle site, which is dated to A.D. 180±100 and not associated with volcanic deposits, therefore unaffected by contemporaneous volcanic eruptions further north along the coast, to be an early survival of Horizon I culture, thus bridging the gap between P3 and the appearance of the Horizon II occupations (Figure 10,E).

Certainly, in view of the evidence compiled by Westercamp and Traineau (1983) one is tempted to argue that only an eruption of such dispersal and magnitude as P3 could have resulted in lasting tephra deposits in areas of active erosion and terrain modifications as the immediate coastal shoreline where the sites are located. Yet, since there is nothing to challenge the dating of Horizon II occupations that overlie the volcanic layers or occur elsewhere on the same part of the coast, to anywhere but a period between A.D. 400 to 600, we would be left with a problematical hiatus to fill, unless other Cedrosan sites, such as Adoration or Lasalle, the latter with its own radiocarbon date of A.D. 180±100 would remain representative of the first three centuries A.D. occupations. Unfortunately, although volcanic deposits were noted early in direct but mixed associations with the archaeological remains at the Lasalle and Marigot sites (Revert in Harcourt 1952; Delawarde 1937)[9] the area south of Fond Brûlé along the east coast was not included in the recent geological studies.

What seems quite beyond dispute, however, is that the early Saladoid colonists of the Lesser Antilles, in their progress through the islands sometime in the last centuries B.C., certainly must have witnessed and experienced in some ways the effects of the catastrophic series of Third Plinian eruptions, which must have remained active for more than half a century. Judging from the widespread distribution of its tephra (Figure 6), it is not diffcult to imagine the extent of the devastation it would have created over almost the entire northern half of Martinique, that it would have covered under a blanket of several meters of ashes and pumice, destroying or damaging much of the vegetation in its wake, and, we may also assume, making this entire part of the island totally uninhabitable for decades.

For the human settlements of the northeast coast, less than 12 km from the volcano's vent, the effects would have been nothing less than catastrophic. In the villages, buildings would have collapsed, and gardens would have been buried and much of the plants killed. It is difficult to evaluate the effects on human lives. No human remains have yet been found in association with volcanic deposits, and it must therefore be assumed that the people had time to flee. Other hazards associated with Plinian eruptions must be considered: torrential rains and flash floods, lightening, and earthquakes, all of which could have taken human lives. The effects of such eruptions are not limited to humans; indeed, not only plants but animals would have been affected and even fishing grounds disrupted, thus depriving a surviving population of game and fish (Blong 1987). Benefits from volcanic eruptions must also be considered. Vegetation may survive less than one meter of ashes, and rapid rejuvenation may result in the gardens where productivity would be greatly enhanced by the increased fertility produced by the volcanic deposits. However, this is relative to the severity of the eruption, and the repeated paroxysms of the Third Plinian eruptions occurring at 20 year intervals might have caused more lasting devastation and destruction.

One must certainly remain cautious in evaluating the significance of the volcanic chronology in the context of a revised dating of Saladoid expansion to the Lesser Antilles, especially from the viewpoint of Martinique. Despite its potential for future research, the situation is far from having received the attention and exhaustive investigation it deserves. The study of prehistoric volcanism and its impact on ancient human populations of El Salvador in Central America by Payson Sheets (1983) and his colleagues is a model that still has to be emulated in Martinique as well as other islands of the Lesser Antilles, such as Guadeloupe and St. Vincent, which also witnessed prehistoric eruptions.[10]

In this context, archaeologists may be at most allowed only to speculate on the potential significance of the volcanic chronology and its correlation with archaeological sites. That volcanic eruptions were witnessed or experienced by the earliest agricultural settlers of Martinique and adjacent islands is a fact that can certainly not be denied. We may also be allowed to question whether there already was an established human population on Martinique's northeast coast at the time of the Third Plinian eruptions. It is possible that the earliest Cedrosan settlements occurred instead after the protracted period of volcanic activity due to adverse conditions that may have prevented or deterred early colonists from landing or even approaching Martinique.

That the northeast coast, because of its fertility and despite its exposure to volcanic hazards, was eventually the most desirable beachhead selected by the initial colonists for their agricultural settlements is strongly suggested by site distribution. The more immediate origin of these early settlers is in itself another problem; the stretch of the northeast coast occupied by early Cedrosan sites faces directly toward the island of Dominica to the north. This situation does not suggest any close relationships with the islands to the south and especially St. Lucia from where colonists would probably instead have preferred the extensive southern beaches -- and especially Diamant with its small enclosed coastal plain -- as their intitial landing place.[11]

There is no doubt either that the limited radiocarbon dates for Martinique reveal some discontinuity after ca. A.D. 350 that may be interpreted as a rather sudden introduction of the Horizon II occupation, both on the northeast coast and elsewhere on Martinique, after ca. A.D. 450, and through the fifth and seventh centuries. This hiatus is itself suggestive of the result of volcanic hazards, certainly this time those of the eastward expansion of the Second Plinian eruption (P2) which may have caused the island to be abandoned, dispersing its inhabitants toward the South, or toward Dominica or even St. Lucia.

In addition to the physical devastation resulting from the volcanic activity, the mental repercussions may have been equally severe. Volcanic activity affecting traditional societies often finds an expression in religious beliefs and myths (Blong 1987). In our attempts to uncover the meaning of early Cedrosan culture on Martinique archaeologists must take into account the existence of such tremendous forces that must have been perceived as supernatural by the early islanders. The full effects of volcanic activity on these populations may not simply have been limited to the rare catastrophic eruptions; one would like to imagine that a mere grumbling from the mighty Mt. Pelée would have had dire consequences for the normal existence of the peoples living under its shadow.

NOTES

1. Exceptions include limited tests by Haag (1965) at the Adoration site, and his examinations of Father Pinchon's collections. Irving Rouse (personal communication 1972) visited Martinique and surveyed sites there in 1950. Among local archaeologists, Eugène Revert was a geographer and teacher by profession, and Father Pinchon was a biologist and naturalist. More recently, the botanist Jacques Barrau was able to examine several early sites, on which he comments in a publication (Barrau and Montbrun 1978). Early Saladoid collections, especially those excavated by Revert at Lasalle in the 1930s, were described and published in France by Raoul D'Harcourt (1952), an Americanist with the Musée de l'Homme in Paris. For a history of archaeological research on Martinique, see Jacques Petitjean Roget (1970).

2. More precisely, the full expression should read "Horizon Arawak I" because of the popular assumption that Saladoid ceramics were produced by an Arawak ethnic group as opposed to later ceramic series believed to be the work of a Carib ethnic group. An association between the spread of the Saladoid series and the proto-Arawakan language group and later Arawakan dialects has, however, received serious consideration among many archaeologists. I may add, incidentally, that there is no equivalent of the Huecan subseries of Vieques and Puerto Rico in Martinique (see Rouse, this volume), and that a preceramic occupation suggested by the Boutbois and Le Godinot collections (Allaire and Mattioni 1983) is still at best tentative, yet not to be rejected in view of similarities with Archaic age sites of Central America and elsewhere in the Caribbean.

3. This Adoration site is located just north above the town of Marigot; it may be the place investigated by Delawarde (1937) in his pioneer publication. Archaeological remains have, however, been found at other places in the immediate vicinity, such as under the village itself, as I discovered in my own survey of 1971. Other Saladoid sites are also mentioned by

d'Harcourt (1952), but it is not possible to say whether they belong to Horizons I or II.

4. I was able with the help of Mario Mattioni to conduct limited test excavations and a surface collection at the large Séguineau site located halfway between Adoration and Fond Brûlé, in December 1983. No Horizon I component could be identified in the abundant surface remains and their distribution. The stratigraphic test also failed to uncover a volcanic layer while only providing a hint of a Horizon I occupation. The situation of that site on top of a promontory that would have been exposed to active erosion may explain the absence of volcanic deposits. Beginning in 1971, I was able in the course of my work on Martinique to survey and repeatedly visit the Horizon I sites mentioned in the text. I was also able to open small stratigraphic tests at Fond Brûlé, and have assembled surface collections from all these sites except Vivé.

5. Horizon II occupations, which are twice as numerous as those of the Horizon I on the northeast coast of Martinique, also appear to have experienced severe volcanic eruptions that are likely to have brought substantial destruction and loss of life on the northeast coast, according to geologists Roobol and Smith (quoted in Petitjean Roget 1975). Roobol and Smith (1976) have found evidence of a Plinian eruption radiocarbon dated to A.D. 444±60 (Figure 5) and have observed similar manifestations in a soil profile covering a Horizon II occupation radiocarbon dated to the sixth century A.D. (Petitjean Roget 1970) at the Grande Anse site located across the small river from Fond Brûlé.

6. Even in view of the lack of botanical remains, it is unlikely that the fragments of clay griddles uncovered in all Horizon I sites might have been used for baking maize cakes (DeBoer 1975) instead of the expected cassava made with bitter manioc. The general cultural context and historical relationship with the tropical lowlands of South America, as well as the ethnographic analogy with the early historical Island Carib, strongly support that bitter manioc was indeed the agricultural staple in the West Indies. There is hardly a reference to maize cultivation in the early historical chronicles. In this context, several large grinding stones uncovered on the Vivé I occupation floor by Mattioni (1979), and the lack of identifiable *manos*, must be interpreted as having served for the processing of other foodstuffs or materials. These heavy implements might also have been used for fashioning and sharpening stone or shell axes as frequent grooves indicate on the concave grinding surfaces.

7. Revert (in d'Harcourt 1952) found hardly a fistful of identifiable animal bones at Lasalle; Mattioni (1979), however, in addition to a few poorly preserved burials, uncovered a complete manatee mandible as well as one from a dog in his Vivé I component (Mattioni 1973; Mattioni and Bullen 1974).

8. The fertile, low river bottom surrounding the Vivé site was later extensively sampled by Mario Mattioni (personal communication 1983) in 1983. Unfortunately, the results of this investigation have not so far been published. Remains from both Horizons I and II occupations were encountered throughout.

9. Delawarde (1937) had noted the occurrence of pottery fragments at Marigot in a layer heavily mixed with pumice. Likewise, the geographer Revert (in d'Harcourt 1952) had observed that the ceramics at Lasalle occurred over a sterile volcanic deposit containing pumice fragments of a type he links to a tephra that covers most of the landforms from Marigot in the north, to St. Joseph further south towards the interior of the island. This area is unfortunately not included in recent volcanological studies.

10. The Kingston Post Office site on St. Vincent, according to Ripley and Adelaide Bullen (Bullen and Bullen 1972:94), revealed a "stratigraphic situation . . . exactly like that at the Vivé site on Martinique," with its 18 in layer of sterile volcanic "tuff" separating two occupation layers. The lowest layer was radiocarbon dated to A.D. 160±100 and consists of a Cedrosan component. As the Bullens suggest, volcanism in St. Vincent may have been simultaneous

with that of Martinique. Effects of more recent volcanic activity on St. Vincent's landscape and people are described by Bullard (1976). Like Martinique, St. Vincent offers a promising field for the joint investigations of archaeologists and volcanologists.

11. As part of a survey project sponsored by Mattioni and the Direction des Antiquités in Martinique, I was able in 1983 to carry out a small test excavation at the large and much plundered Diamant site on the south coast of Martinique. Although the site has been more associated with Horizon II and later archaeological occupations, the test trench revealed an undisturbed deposit just above the sterile white sands of the original beach (below 80 cm from the surface). This level contained a small ceramic assemblage that may qualify as Horizon I or very Early Horizon II; it was, moreover, associated with abundant crab claws, the typical context of early Cedrosan sites in the Lesser Antilles and Puerto Rico. No volcanic deposits from Mt. Pelée have ever been reported for the southern part of the island; local volcanism in the south is ancient and predates the time of its human occupation. This early occupation at Diamant raises the possibility of an independent beachhead settlement from St. Lucia to the south. Unfortunately, no early Cedrosan sites have so far been reported for that island.

Acknowledgments. Since my research has focussed primarily on the post-Saladoid occupation of Martinique, my acquaintance with Saladoid sites and archaeology on the island owes much to their major investigators there such as Jacques Petitjean Roget and his son Henri, as well as Mario Mattioni, the excavator of Vivé and Fond Brûlé. Thanks to them I was able to visit most of the sites, collect from the surface and examine their extensive collections. I have also greatly benefitted from discussions and correspondence with the authority, Irving Rouse, from the time of my student years until just before submitting the final version of this paper.

REFERENCES CITED

Allaire, Louis
    1973 *Vers une préhistoire des Petites Antilles.* Travaux du Centre de Recherches Caraibes, Universite de Montréal.

Allaire, Louis and Mario Mattioni
    1983 Boutbois et Le Godinot: deux gisements acéramiques de la Martinique. *Proceedings of the International Congress for the Study of the Pre-Columbian Cultures of the Lesser Antilles* 9:27-38. Montréal.

Barrau, Jacques et Christian Montbrun
    1978 La mangrove et l'insertion humaine dans les écosystemes insulaires des Petites Antilles: le cas de la Martinique et de la Guadeloupe. *Social Science Information* 17:897-919.

Blong, R. J.
    1987 *Volcanic Hazards: A Sourcebook on the Effects of Eruptions.* Academic Press, New York.

Bullard, Fred M.
    1976 *Volcanoes of the Earth.* University of Texas Press, Austin.

Bullen, Ripley P., and Adelaide K. Bullen
    1972 *Archaeological Investigations on St. Vincent and the Grenadines, West Indies.* American Studies Report No. 8. The William L. Bryant Foundation, Gainesville.

Bullen, Ripley P. and Mario Mattioni
    1972   Some Ceramic Variations at Vivé, Martinique. *Atti del Congresso Internazionale degli Americanisti* XL:225-229. Roma-Genoa.

DeBoer, Warren R.
    1975   The Archaeological Evidence for Manioc Cultivation: A Cautionary Note. *American Antiquity* 40:419-432.

Delawarde, J.-B.
    1937   *Préhistoire martiniquaise: les gisements du Prêcheur et de Marigot.* Imprimerie Officielle, Fort-de-France.

Fayaud, Rene-Louis
    1976   Rapport final et de synthèse des deux premiers sondages effectués au lieudit "Moulin l'Etang", commune de Basse-Point, Martinique. Ms. on file, Dépôt de Fouilles, Direction des Antiquités, Fort-de-France.

Grunewald, Henri
    1964   *Géologie de la Martinique.* Imprimerie Nationale, Paris.

Haag, William A.
    1965   Pottery Typology in Certain Lesser Antilles. *American Antiquity* 31:242-245.

Harcourt, Raoul d'
    1952   Collections archéologiques martiniquaises du Musée de l'Homme. *Journal de la Société des Américanistes de Paris* n.s. 41:353-381.

Lasserre, Guy (editor)
    1977   *Atlas de la Martinique.* Institut de Géographie Natinal, Paris.

Lehouillier, Richard
    1974   *Classification du matérial céramique de Vivé II, Martinique.* Unpublished Master's thesis, Departement d'Anthropologie, Universite de Montréal.

Mattioni, Mario
    1973   *Troisième compte-rendu des fouilles au lieudit Vivé: les canidés.* Musée Départemental, Fort-de-France.

    1979   *Salvage Excavations at the Vivé site, Martinique: Final Report..* University of Manitoba Anthropology Papers No. 23. Winnipeg.

    1982   *Salvage Excavations at the Fond Brûlé Site, Martinique: Final Report.* University of Manitoba Anthropology Papers No. 27. Winnipeg.

Mattioni, Mario and Ripley P. Bullen
    1974   Precolumbian dogs in the Lesser and Greater Antilles. *Proceedings of the International Congress for the Study of Pre-columbian Cultures of the Lesser Antilles* 5:162-165. Antigua.

Petitjean Roget, Henri
    1975   *Contributions à l'étude de la préhistoire des Petites Antilles.* Thèse présentée à l'Ecole Pratique des Hautes Etudes, Paris.

Petitjean Roget, Jacques
    1968   Etude d'un Horizon Arawak et proto-Arawak à la Martinique à partir du niveau II du Diamant. *Proceedings of the International Congress for the Study of Pre-Columbian Cultures in the Lesser Antilles* 2:61-68. St. Ann's Garrison, Barbados.

    1970   L'Archéologie martiniquaise. *Parallèles* 36/37:4-47.

Pinchon, Robert
    1952   Introduction à l'archéologie martiniquaise. *Journal de la Société des Américanistes de Paris* n. s. 41:305-352.

Roobol, M. J., H. Petitjean Roget, and A. L. Smith
    1976   Mt. Pelée and the Island Population of Martinique. *Proceedings of the International Congress for the Study of Pre-Columbian Cultures of the Lesser Antilles* 6:46-53. Gainesville.

Roobol, M. J. and A. L. Smith
    1976   Mount Pelée, Martinique: A Pattern of Alternating Eruptive Styles. *Geology* 4:521-524.

Rouse, Irving
    1986   *Migrations in Prehistory: Inferring Population Movement from Cultural Remains.* Yale University Press, New Haven.

Rouse, Irving and Louis Allaire
    1978   Caribbean. In *Chronologies in New World Archaeology*, edited by R.E. Taylor and Clement W. Meighan, pp. 431-481. Academic Press, New York.

Schvoerer, Max, P. Guilbert, F. Bechtel, Mario Mattioni, and J. Evin
    1985   Des hommes en Martinique vingt siècles avant Christophe Colomb? *Proceedings of the International Congress for the Study of the Pre-Columbian Cultures of the Lesser Antilles* 10:369-397. Montréal.

Sheets, Payson D. (editor)
    1983.   *Archaeology and Volcanism in Central America: The Zapotitan Valley of El Salvador.* University of Texas Press, Austin.

Westercamp, Denis
    1987   L'éruption de la Montage Pelée. *La Recherche* 18:914-923.

Westercamp, Denis and H. Traineau
    1983   The Past 5000 Years of Volcanic Activity at Mt. Pelée, Martinique (F.W.I.): Implications for Assessment of Volcanic Hazards. *Journal of Volcanological and Geothermal Research* 17:159-185.

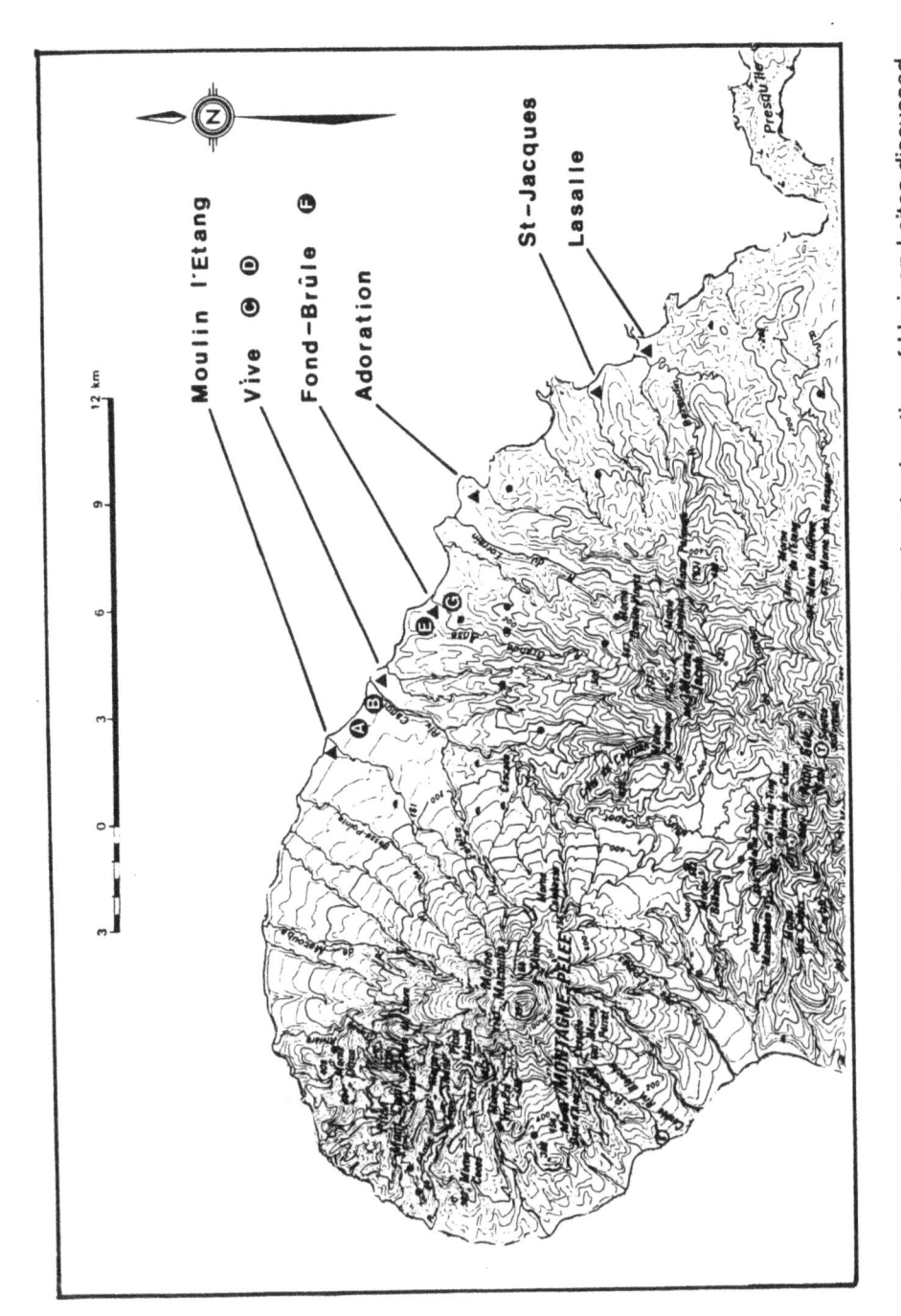

Figure 1. Mt. Pelée and the northern part of Martinique showing the location of Horizon I sites discussed in the text. Letters indicate the locations of volcanic stratigraphic profiles presented in Figure 9.

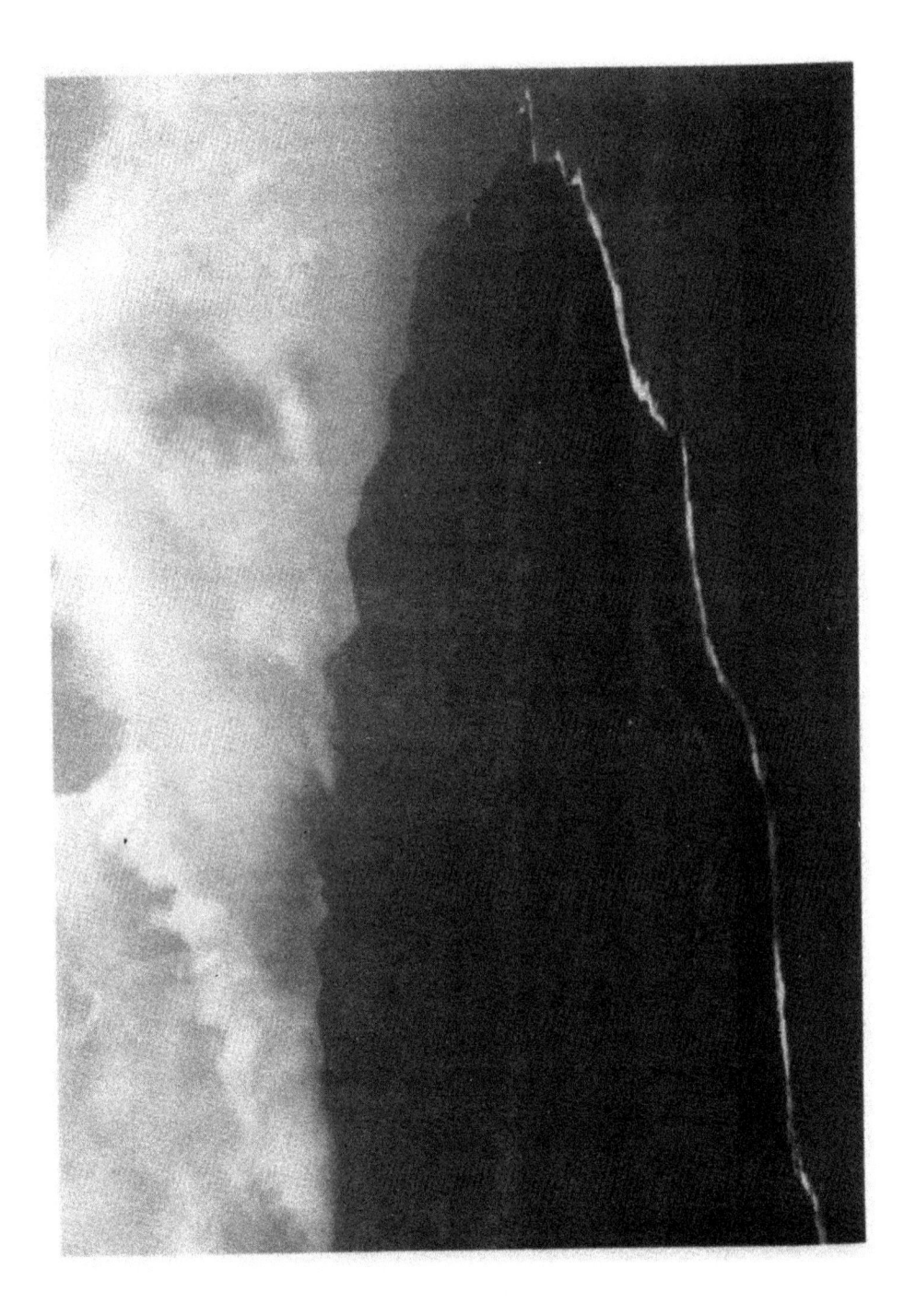

Figure 2. The northeast coast of Martinique and Mt. Pelée in the background from the air.

Figure 3. Artifacts from a surface collection of the St.-Jacques site including diagnostic Horizon I types: zoned incised cross-hatching, fine line incising, white-on-red painting, as well as the general thinness of the ware and lack of heavy flange developments.

Figure 4. The tephra layer at Vivé represented by the light colored deposit of pumice and lapilli. Photographed after the closure of the 1971 excavations.

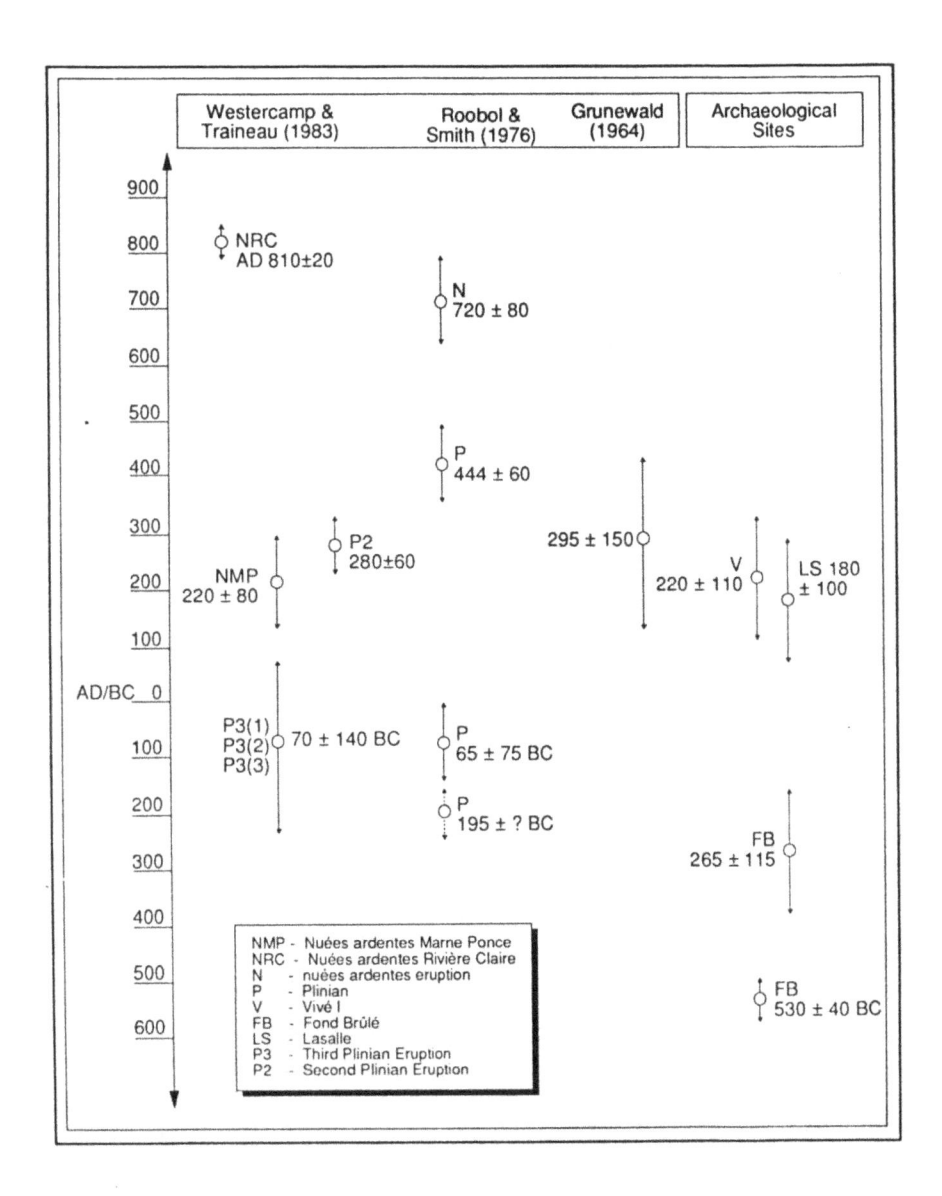

Figure 5. Comparative radiocarbon dated sequences for the later chronology of Mt. Pelée eruptions corresponding to the period of Horizon I and Horizon II occupations including selected significant radiocarbon dates from archaeological sites.

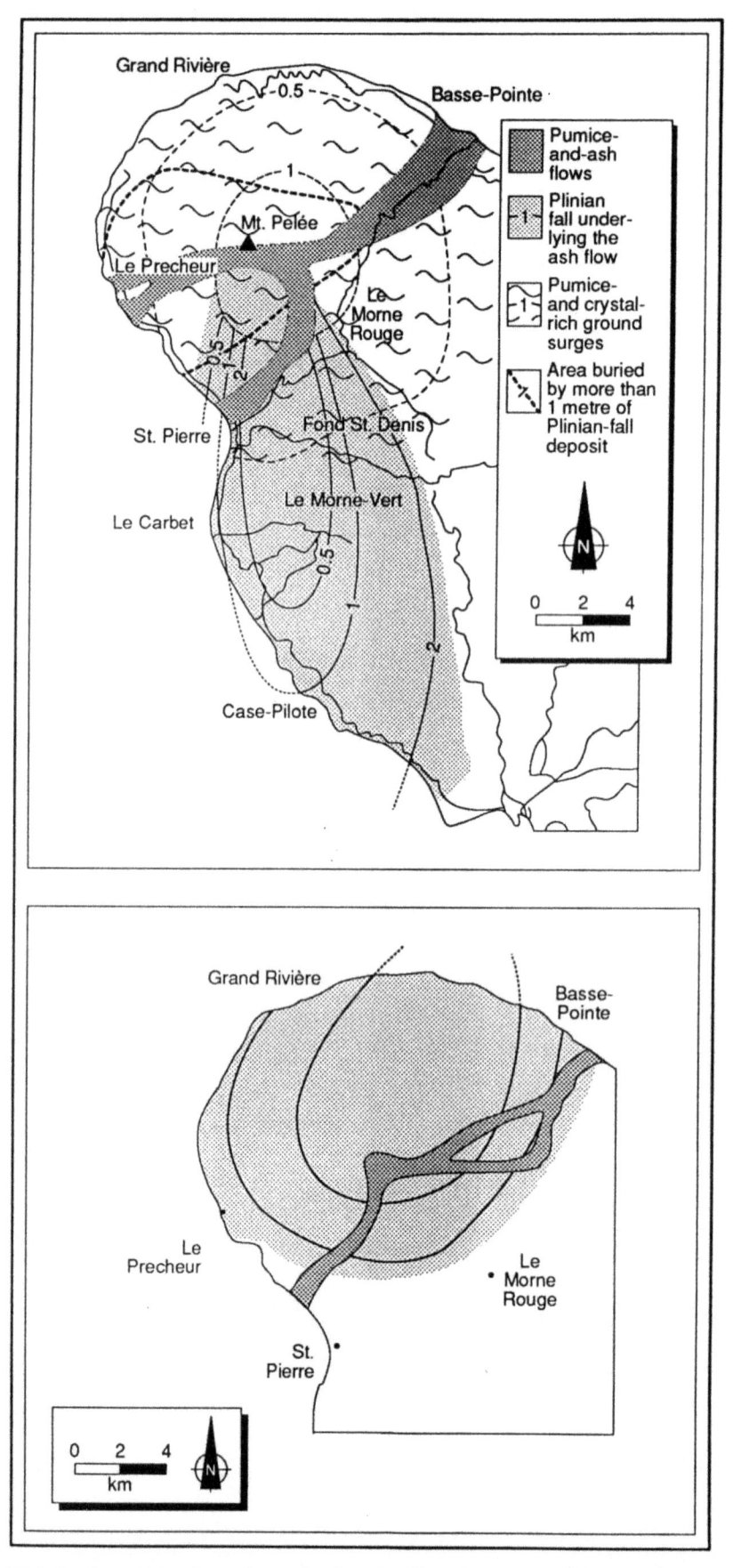

Figure 6. Distribution of tephra deposits for the Third (top) and Second (bottom) Plinian eruptions of Mt. Pelée, Martinique (after Westercamp and Traineau 1983).

Figure 7. Representative stratigraphic profile of the Fond Brûlé site (1983) showing the Horizon I occupation level (lower step) below the heavy ash and pumice deposits (middle step).

Figure 8. Location of the Fond Brûlé archaeological deposits showing the reworking hazards to which the terrain is exposed, both from the hill behind the site and from river erosion.

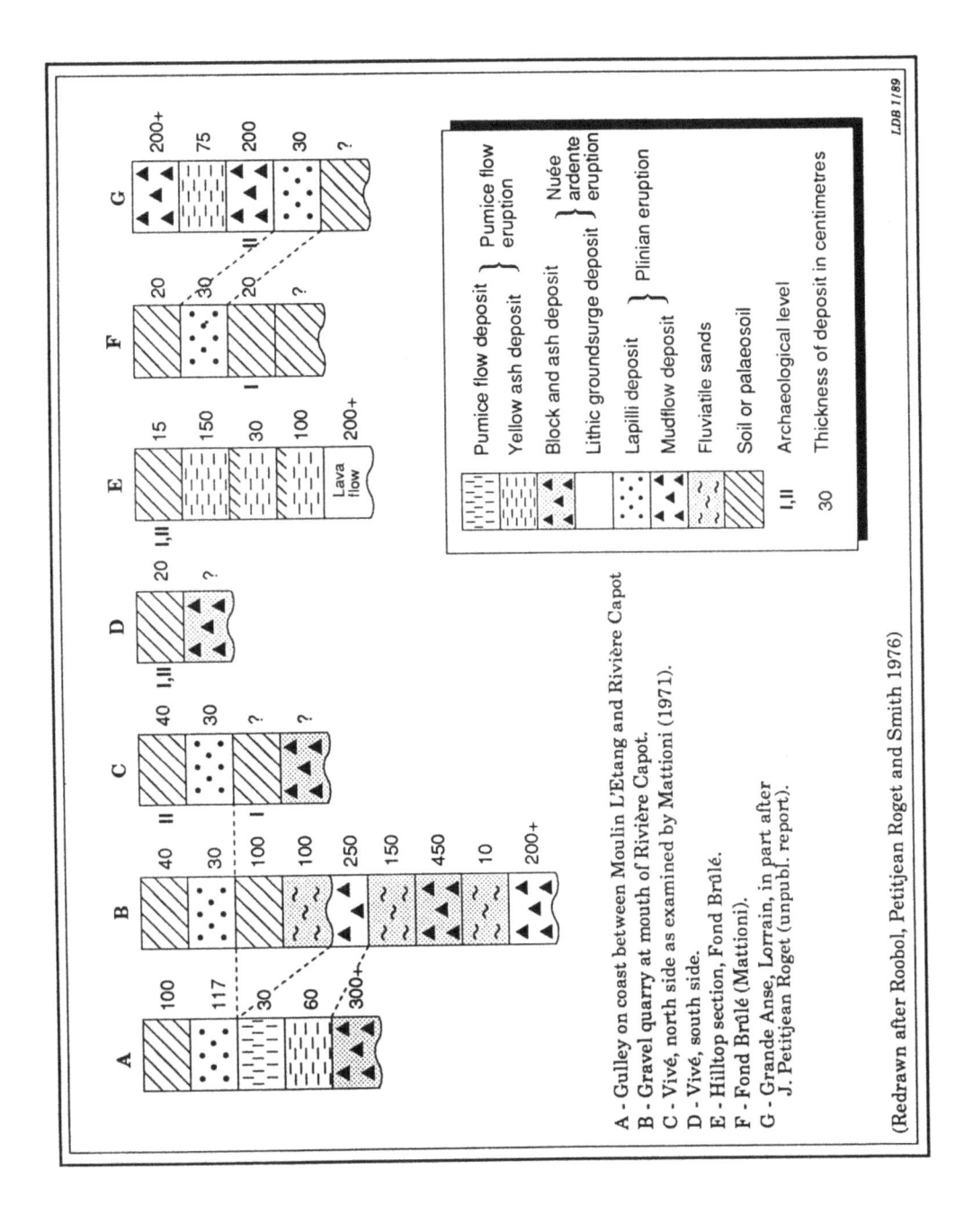

Figure 9. Recent volcanic stratigraphy of Vivé and Fond Brûlé and their immediate vicinity.

A - Gulley on coast between Moulin L'Etang and Rivière Capot
B - Gravel quarry at mouth of Rivière Capot.
C - Vivé, north side as examined by Mattioni (1971).
D - Vivé, south side.
E - Hilltop section, Fond Brûlé.
F - Fond Brûlé (Mattioni).
G - Grande Anse, Lorrain, in part after J. Petitjean Roget (unpubl. report).

(Redrawn after Roobol, Petitjean Roget and Smith 1976)

Legend:
- Pumice flow deposit } Pumice flow eruption
- Yellow ash deposit
- Block and ash deposit } Nuée ardente eruption
- Lithic groundsurge deposit } Plinian eruption
- Lapilli deposit
- Mudflow deposit
- Fluviatile sands
- Soil or palaeosoil
- I, II Archaeological level
- 30   Thickness of deposit in centimetres

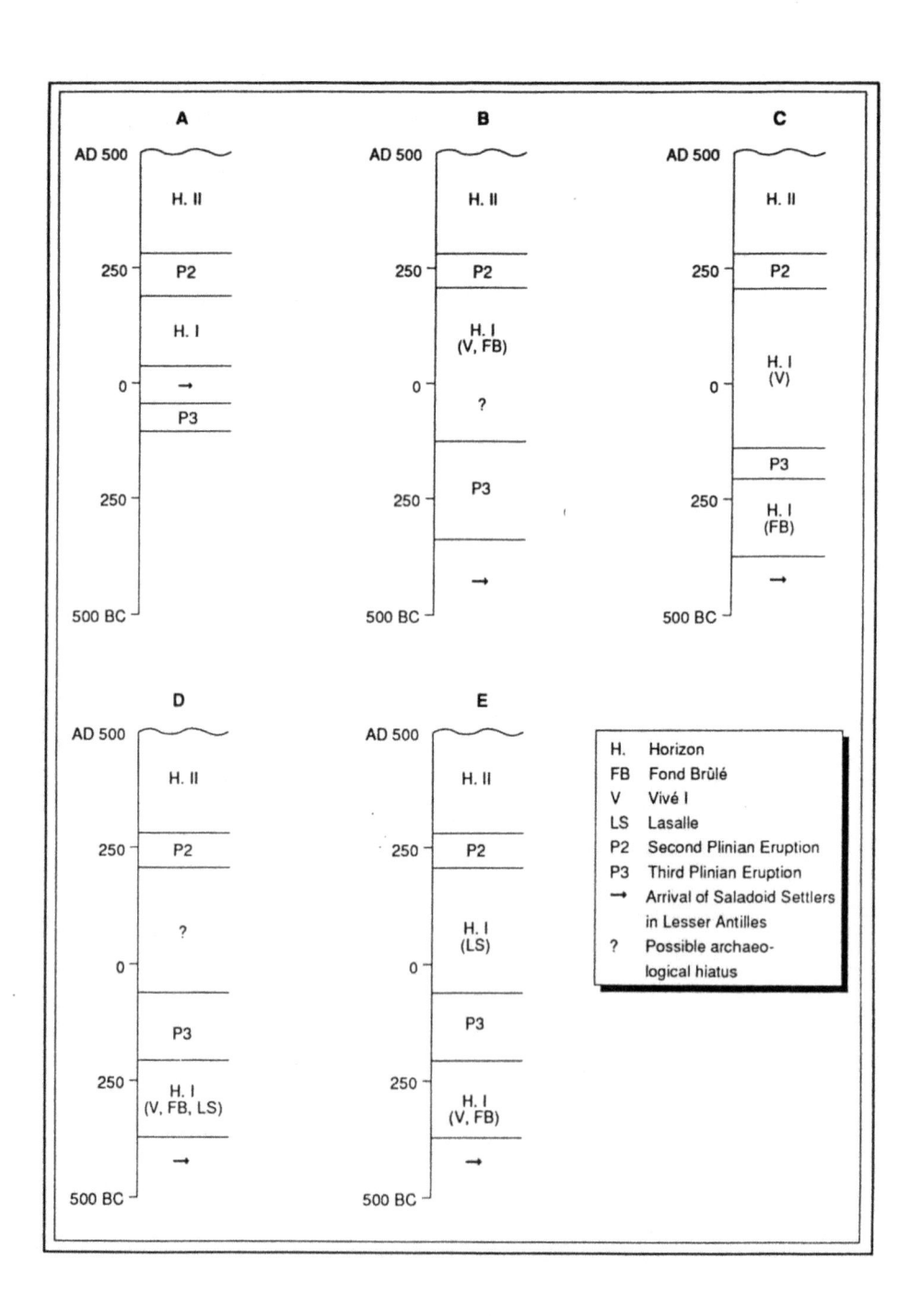

Figure 10. Alternative models of chronological interpretations for the Horizon I (Early Cedrosan) occupation of Martinique and the beginnings of its agricultural settlements.

PART 3:

SITE STRUCTURE

AND

COMMUNITY ORGANIZATION

THE INTERNAL ORGANIZATION OF A PIONEER SETTLEMENT

IN THE LESSER ANTILLES:

THE SALADOID GOLDEN ROCK SITE ON ST. EUSTATIUS, NETHERLANDS ANTILLES

Aad H. Versteeg

ABSTRACT

The investigation of the midden and adjacent areas of the Golden Rock site (from 1984-1988, 2,800 m^2) yields four functional areas. A yard area has a central position within the settlement. Three circular structures are situated in it: two have diameters of ca. 7.5 m, the other is a large 19 m diameter *maloca*. The two smaller houses are slightly older than the *maloca*. The midden (dump area) and a burial area are situated side-by-side south of the yard. A ceremonial area, north of the yard, is made up of two pottery caches, a stone cache and one skeleton with a burial gift. The site dates to the fifth to seventh centuries A.D.

INTRODUCTION

Most prehistoric excavation programs in the Caribbean have concentrated on midden areas of the sites, i.e. on refuse heaps or dumps of former villages. As clear-cut stratigraphy usually is lacking in the dumps, it is difficult to conclude on time depth and demographic aspects of the ancient settlement. Similar problems arise for understanding the social organization and activity patterns of the population of such settlements.

The present archaeological project of the Leiden State University investigated one habitation cluster (dump + surrounding areas, where the houses of the people who produced the refuse were located) of a Saladoid settlement on St. Eustatius. The shape, size, and number of houses in such a cluster is believed to yield a set of data of direct importance for understanding the way the Saladoid people organized their village. It has been demonstrated that a relation exists between social organization and village organization (e.g. Hugh-Jones 1985).

Demographic aspects can be studied better on the basis of a village floor plan, than on the basis of the refuse, as is done in some studies in this area (e.g. Roosevelt 1980). The floor plans of houses on St. Eustatius yield information on other issues as well, such as that of cultural continuity: was there a continuity of house shape, settlement organization, and social organization from early Saladoid times in Venezuela (cf. Roosevelt 1980) and in the Lesser and Greater Antilles during the first millenium A.D. up to late prehistoric times in the Lesser Antilles? How do the parameters compare of the Saladoid sites and those related to them of the sub-present and present Tropical Forest Indian settlements of Amazonia? Some of these questions can now be answered; the data of many more prehistoric sites in the above-mentioned regions are necessary to answer all these questions.

For an understanding of the data obtained in St. Eustatius it is important to note the diversity in the physical environment of the Lesser Antilles that was available to the Precolumbian settlers. Therefore, I will first discuss the Lesser Antilles as a physical environment and then the specific position of St. Eustatius within this context.

THE LESSER ANTILLES

The Lesser Antilles consist of hundreds of islands between Tobago to the south and Puerto Rico to the north. The islands differ considerably in size, altitude and rainfall, flora, and fauna (Beard 1949; Blume 1968), and therefore, in attractiveness for groups of horticulturally based Indian settlers. Compared to the mainland the islands are relatively dry, except for some patches with higher elevations. The size and altitude of an island directly determines the amount of precipitation, and the presence of streams or rivers.

Guadeloupe, Martinique, and Dominica are the largest (Table 1), and the highest (Table 2) of the islands between Tobago and Puerto Rico. These three islands have permanent freshwater streams and micro-environments that vary from relatively wet to dry.

Faunal species diversity of the islands is low compared to the South American mainland. Furthermore, the smaller an island the lower are the values for species diversity and abundance (Keegan and Diamond 1987). Only the large islands offer a wide variety of freshwater fishes and turtles (Wing and Reitz 1982). The coastal and marine resources of the islands, however, are rich and it is no wonder that the Saladoid population used these to obtain their animal protein (deFrance, this volume) as is clear from the archaeological finds. A considerable amount of readjustment was required in order to exploit efficiently the marine resources for the first generations of Saladoid settlers in the Caribbean islands.

To what extent the islands yielded fewer species of plants useful for such purposes as construction, rope, medicine, gums, etc. is not clear from the archaeological record. The human introduction of such plants from the mainland partially may have overcome this. The aguti (*Dasyprocta aguti*) is an example of a faunal introduction by the Indians (Wing 1983). Another strategy may have been the development of long distance trade networks, such as claimed by Rouse (1983) for the period of Barrancoid influence in the Lesser Antilles.

ST. EUSTATIUS WITHIN THE LESSER ANTILLES

St. Eustatius is one of the smaller islands (Figure 1) of the Lesser Antilles, measuring only 21 km^2 (Figure 2). It is the twenty-third largest and eleventh tallest of the Lesser Antilles. Its soil is relatively porous, it has no freshwater streams that flow year-round, and there are no mangrove swamps. It is striking that indigenous palms are lacking today (Stoffers 1956), in contrast to the neighboring islands of St. Kitts (Beard 1949), and Saba (Stoffers 1956). The 600 m high peak of the Quill volcanoe of St. Eustatius creates some relatively wet micro-environments. Coastal and marine resources are rich on the windward coast, which features a coral bay supporting numerous fish species and a beach where turtles used to nest until recently. The leeward coast has a beach too; today concentrations of shellfish, among which *Cittarium pica* is predominant, are found at the rocky coast, north of the leeward beach.

As far as we know, St. Eustatius was not settled in the first centuries A.D. by the first groups of Saladoid immigrants into the Antilles. The earliest evidence of Indian occupation on St. Eustatius exists in the Golden Rock site, which dates to the fifth and sixth centuries A.D.

THE GOLDEN ROCK SITE

Golden Rock is located on the central plain of St. Eustatius (Figure 2). The site consists of five midden deposits, which are dispersed at roughly 100-300 m intervals (Figure 3). The deposits are situated on the flattest part of the island around the present airfield, roughly 1 km from both the leeward and windward coasts. The five clusters were discovered and mapped in 1923 (Josselin deJong 1947). All of the clusters contain an identical style of Saladoid pottery, suggesting that the clusters were inhabited more or less simultaneously.

One of the clusters, Golden Rock-1 (GR-1), was excavated between 1984 and 1988 by a team from the Leiden State University. The purpose of the excavation is to provide insight into a Saladoid series settlement, its organizational pattern and the corresponding social organization. To obtain this information most of the midden and its surroundings were excavated. The analysis currently is underway so the present paper is a progress report. Excavations at GR-1 will be continued in 1989.

GR-1 STRUCTURES

A midden of ca. 20 x 30 m is situated in an east-west direction in the southern section of GR-1 (the grey area in Figures 4 and 5). More than two-thirds of the midden was excavated by hand in 4 x 4 m pits. This midden represents the dump of the houses located just to the north of it. A wide variety of refuse and Saladoid artifacts was recovered, including pottery, worked and unworked shells, stone, coral, animal bones, concentrations of charcoal, and coprolites. No typological distinctions were found between the artifacts from the lowest levels of the midden and those from the top; only slight quantitative differences were noted. This midden indicates that no hiatus occurred during the occupation of GR-1. For a more detailed discussion of the content of the midden and of C-14 dating results the reader is referred to Versteeg (1987).

The large excavation pits around the midden area (Figures 4 and 5) were excavated by machine, followed by shovel scraping. This procedure revealed hundreds of features visible in the horizontally scraped surface. The features are discernible in a light-colored layer at a depth of 60-70 cm below the pre-excavation surface. All features were vertically cut: the content was screened through 2.8 mm mesh (Versteeg 1987:8). Features originating from prehistoric activities could be separated from (sub)recent ones on the basis of artifact content and the soil color in the features, although the origin of some remain uncertain. For a detailed discussion of the problem see Schinkel (1988).

The prehistoric features occur in three categories of depth related to a hard layer in the subsoil: the tuff. This concrete-like layer is situated roughly 30 cm below the light-colored layer mentioned above (ca. 90-100 cm below the pre-excavation surface). The tuff layer is visible in Figures 6 and 7. One category of features reaches through the tuff, or, at locations where the tuff is not present, is deeper than 100 cm. The second category of features has a similar depth as the tuff, and uses the tuff as a floor. The third category consists of shallow features, reaching less than 30 cm below the light-colored layer (less than 90 cm total depth).

The surface that existed during the Indian occupation has only been preserved below the midden. So much refuse accumulated there during habitation that later post-depositional processes did not destroy the old surface in this section of GR-1.

At the location of structure C (Figure 5) the level of the pre-excavation surface is about that of the Indian period. However, plowing and subsequent erosion and accumulation processes during the Colonial period destroyed the old surface (and with it the house floor) completely. Between the Indian and Colonial uses of this terrain some artifacts from the surface accumulated in artifact traps such as postpipes of the postholes (see Figures 6 and 7). At the location of structure B (Figure 4) the surface during the Indian occupation was slightly higher than the pre-excavation surface (for more details see Schinkel 1988).

All features of the first and deepest category are postholes belonging to round configurations (structures A, B, and C; Figures 4 and 5). These structures are interpreted to be three round houses. In earlier publications only structures B and C have been reported (Versteeg 1987). Structures B and C were recognized during the fieldwork. It was during a later, detailed study of all GR-1 features that Schinkel (1988) discovered a third round structure (A in Figure 4), intersecting structure C. The characteristics of the fill of the postholes (color, uniformity of the texture, lack of large pieces of charcoal) set the postholes of structure A apart from those of structure C. Schinkel (1988) demonstrates convincingly that A represents an older phase of occupation than C, although no indications were found for a hiatus between the phases. Data from the midden (see above) suggest an uninterrpted occupation of GR-1. Apart from the differences mentioned above, layout and shape of the postholes of structures A, B, and C are similar.

The postholes all are very deep: the average depth of the postholes of structure A, not taking into account those of the extensions, is 1.68 m, of structure B 1.81 m, and of structure C 2.33 m. The largest structure, of which the roof was heaviest, has the deepest postholes, interpreted as the strongest posts. Except in structure B, the postholes of the central posts are less deep than those of the outer circle; the latter carry most of the weight of a conical roof (see Table 3 for different depths of the excavated postholes of structures A, B, and C). The figures given above, and also those of Table 3, indicate the difference between the lowest point of the excavated posthole and the surface in Indian times.

The shape of the postholes is asymmetrical: the upper section is characterized by a sloping part to allow for easier introduction of the heavy and long post into the posthole. The rest of the posthole was dug vertically by the Indians, from the hard tuff layer to the deepest point. During introduction of the post into the posthole, the post was hinged around the hard tuff layer (see Figure 6 for the sloping section and the rounded off hinge point).

Structures A and B have extensions. Two deep postholes were found north and south of the circle of eight postholes of structure B. Structure A has a similar extension at the north side, but the postholes are not very deep. At the south side of structure A no postholes were found, but the situation in the field at this spot made the identification of features very difficult. Probably these two postholes were not seen during the excavation, or they were already dug away in prehistoric times by the Indians, when they dug the postholes for the nearby central posts of structure C. A similar situation exists at the northwest side of structure A, where two postholes were not seen during the excavation. The extensions probably had roofs, at least those of structure B, as sturdy posts are suggested by the deep postholes of the extensions (average 1.56 m).

All three structures have one (A and B) or two (C) rows of postholes in a semi-circular configuration. All are postholes of category 2, just reaching to the tuff. Some of the posts of these postholes rested on the tuff, and left a clear imprint in it behind. The depth of these postholes is 90-100 cm below the surface of the Indian period. These semi-circular configurations are all oriented north-south. They may have had the function of windscreens, to give some protection to those carrying out activities between windscreen and house. Three have an apex to the east, the direction of the prevailing wind; one belonging to structure C has an apex to the west. The protection here is offered more by the house than by the semi-circular configuration: the latter provides a fenced-in area, duplicating the situation existing at the east side of the house. Perhaps the symmetry obtained in this way was the important factor: see below for the ceremonial functions ascribed to such large roundhouses.

The areas between house and windscreen probably were not roofed: the distance between wall and semi-circular configuration is too large in structures A and B, and the postholes of the semi-circular configurations of C are much less deep than those of the opposite house wall, suggesting that the posts in the less deep postholes did not carry the weight of the roof.

Structure C belongs to a younger phase than structure A. In theory structure B may belong to both phases or to one of them. However, the existing evidence indicates a relation to structure A, and not to C. The characteristics of the posthole fills of structure B are similar to those of A (see above). Large pieces of charcoal in the postholes of structure C indicate that the house was burned; neither of the structures A nor B have similar pieces of charcoal in the postholes.

The layouts of structures A and B (7 m and 7.5 m diameters, respectively), the shapes of the extensions, and the semi-circular configurations at the east sides are common characteristics of both structures. The only difference between A and B is the heavy central post (deep posthole) of B and the two less massive central posts (less deep postholes) of A. This evidence is the basis for combining structure A with structure B in the same occupational phase of GR-1.

Structure C is interpreted to be a *maloca*, a large round communal house, in which more than one nuclear family lived. The presence of a *maloca* at GR-1 in the second phase occupation is an indication for increased cultural complexity. In the ethnographic literature the relationship of such *malocas* to cosmologic concepts and symbolism is stressed (e.g. Wilbert 1981), as well as the front entrance to a plaza and the rear exit to a dump (Hugh-Jones 1985).

Given the striking similarity between the floor plan of the St. Eustatius *maloca* and modern similar structures in northwest South America a cultural continuity for such a house shape/village layout seems plausible. Because such a concept existed in St. Eustatius in a sixth century A.D. Saladoid village, it is of utmost interest to know how are far back in time we can chart this house shape/village layout pattern, especially in the context of Saladoid pottery that has been traced to ca. 2000 B.C. in the Central Orinoco (Roosevelt 1980).

The number of inhabitants of such *malocas* differs in the ethnographic literature. Schinkel (1988) has summed up several parallels; he suggests that the best figures for the number of inhabitants of the Statian houses are between 6 and 3 m^2 per person, indicating (based on Casselberry 1974) that for the *maloca* 6 m^2 per person is more probable, and for the smaller structures (A and B) each person was allocated 3 m^2. Based upon these data roughly 15-20 individuals occupied structure A, 14-16 people inhabited structure B, and structure C housed 45-50 occupants.

BURIALS AND CEREMONIAL AREA

South of the houses five buried individuals were found (Burials 1-4; Figures 4 and 5). Burial 2 contained two individuals. Different postures of the dead were noted (cf. Figure 8 and Versteeg 1987:Figure 8). Burial 1 contained the best preserved skeleton (Versteeg 1987:Figure 8); it was found nearest to the calcium-rich midden deposits. It is a man who died at an age of 55-60 years. There are no indications to which phase of occupation Burials 1 and 2 belong. Orientation of these graves is southwest-northeast. Currently, the University of Groningen is analyzing the stable isotopes of the bone collagen of the St. Eustatius skeletons. This research includes the dating of the skeletons by accelerator mass spectrometry.

Burial 4 has a clear relationship to the *maloca*, and so, to the younger phase of occupation of GR-1. It is a woman of about 18 years and positioned roughly in a north-south orientation (Maat and Smits 1987). The burial pit was dug slightly later than the postholes of the *maloca*. A woman of 23-40 years old was buried in grave 3 (Figure 8). This grave has the same orientation as grave 4. The woman was buried slightly later than that of Burial 4 (Schinkel 1988), so Burial 3 also belongs to the younger phase of occupation. None of these dead were buried in a careful manner. All skeletons exhibit different postures, which accords with the notion that the "backsides" of the houses were used for dumping activities.

One carefully prepared burial was found to the north of the houses: an approximate 14 year old individual was buried there below a large upturned pottery vessel. A neat burial pit had been made on the hard tuff floor (number 5 in Figures 4 and 5).

The total number of dead found in the large, completely investigated area at GR-1 is small compared to the number of people associated with the *maloca*, both earlier period houses, and the period of occupation during which the midden accumulated. Probably the remains of all who died were not buried in the GR-1 cluster, but either elsewhere in the settlement (possibly in the postulated plaza [see below]) or they were disposed of outside of the settlement.

North of the houses, in the direction of the other Golden Rock habitation clusters, two caches were in pits dug down to the tuff subsoil. Both caches (6 and 8 in Figures 4 and 5) contained beautiful pottery vessels: a red-and-white painted bowl, a zoned incised crosshatched bowl, and a vessel surmounted by nubbins (Figure 11; Figure 10 shows one of the caches and the tuff floor). In the same general area a large well-polished stone was found (9 in Figures 4 and 5). Except for the stone, neat circular pits were dug for these caches into the tuff floor.

Given the careful treatment of the burial in this portion of the midden and the way the caches were prepared agree with how space is used in the fronts of ethnographically observed *malocas*. Evidently this is the ceremonial area of GR-1. As the *maloca* was built on the spot of the earlier house A, the internal division of the settlement probably was similar during the younger and older phases of occupation.

Further, a rectangular structure (D in Figures 4 and 5) was found in the ceremonial area (Schinkel 1988). The postholes of this structure belong to categories 2 and 3 (maximum of 90-100 cm below the surface in Indian times); so this structure is much lighter than the three round ones. It is striking that this structure, featuring right angles, has a windscreen at right angles, while the round structures have curved windscreens. Judging from its location, this rectangular structure had a ceremonial function. Its floor plan, differing from that of the houses in the living area also suggests a different function than the round houses. There is no indication whether it belongs to the earlier or later or both occupational phases. None of the postholes of this structure contained charcoal so it did not burn down with the *maloca*.

In the same general area as the rectangular structure a semi-circular arrangement of postholes was found, belonging to category 3 (E in Figures 4 and 5). Up to now we have not been able to excavate an adjacent area to determine whether or not it is a full circle of posts. The function of this structure is not clear. Given its location it may be a ceremonial structure. However, if it was situated outside of the ceremonial area it may have been a workshed related to the nearby structure B. The ethnographic literature supplies parallels for such light constructions in close proximity to a large residence. Often such structures are worksheds.

CONCLUSIONS

The excavations of the GR-1 area yielded many new data: The Saladoid pioneers on this island built two types of round houses. One is small and probably housed about 15 people. The other is a large communal house, referred to as a *maloca* in the ethnographic literature, and which accomodated more than 30 occupants. Two periods of occupation were distinguished at GR-1: two round houses (each about 7 m in diameter) existed during the first phase in the fifth century A.D.; the second phase is represented by the large communal house, or the *maloca*. The evidence suggests a continuous occupation between both phases. The houses were well-built sturdy structures with conical roofs. Undoubtedly, they were designed for considerable periods of continuous use.

Two types of burials were found: carelessly prepared burials next to the dump and a carefully inhumated individual with a burial gift in the ceremonial area of the midden. People in this portion of the village were buried with various degrees of care in two areas of the settlement, which suggests that Saladoid communities were less egalitarian than is generally supposed (see also Siegel, this volume).

A plaza is presumed to have existed on the flattest part of the island (the location of the present airport!), around which the five Golden Rock clusters are positioned. The ceremonial area of GR-1 is situated between the plaza and the houses. Behind the houses is the dump and the majority of the burials. This implies a frontside to the north and a backside to the south for the houses. The *maloca* had a north and a south entrance providing access to the ceremonial and dump areas, respectively. Ethnographic observations suggest that a "dance path" existed between the entrance and exit (Hugh-Jones 1985). Burial 4, next to this hypothesized "dance path," has the same north-south orientation.

The village organization, as displayed in Golden Rock, agrees well with ethnographic descriptions of some of the unacculturated tropical forest villages in northwest South America, precisely the region from which the Saladoid colonists of the Caribbean islands originated. The St. Eustatius data indicate that a well-established tradition of village organization was present and maintained by these pioneering populations.

The paucity of natural resources on St. Eustatius explains why it was not settled until the fifth century A.D., whereas other nearby islands already had been occupied by Saladoid colonists for centuries. With the abandonment of the Golden Rock village, St. Eustatius was unpopulated until late in prehistory.

Data of Goodwin (1979), Rouse (1976), and Davis (1988) indicate that the neighboring islands of St. Kitts and Antigua were occupied continuously from the early Saldoid period to the late prehistoric times. The relatively high carrying capacities of these larger islands could support larger populations than St. Eustatius. Regional mate and commodity exchange are to be expected as a necessity for the population of a small island like St. Eustatius (cf. Vayda and Rappaport 1963). The most probable islands for such an exchange network are St. Kitts and Antigua, both of which had long periods of Saladoid occupations. Finally, for the immediate origin of the Statian Indian populations these and other of the larger neighboring islands may offer clues. A detailed study of the Saladoid sites on the surrounding islands will supply answers to these questions.

REFERENCES CITED

Beard, J.S.
1949 *The Natural Vegetation of the Windward and Leeward Islands*. Oxford Forestry Memoirs 21. Clarendon Press, Oxford.

Blume, H.
1968 *Westindien in Uberblick*. Westermann, Braunsweich.

Casselberry, S.E.
1974 Further Refinement of Formulae for Determining Population from Floor Area. *World Archaeology* 6:117-123.

Davis, D.D.
1988 Calibration of the Ceramic Period Chronology for Antigua, West Indies. *Southeastern Archaeology* 7:52-60.

Goodwin, R.C.
1979 *The Prehistoric Cultural Ecology of St. Kitts, West Indies: A Case Study in Island Archaeology*. Ph.D. dissertation, Arizona State University. University Microfilms, Ann Arbor.

Hugh-Jones, S.
1985 The Maloca: A World in a House. In *The Hidden Peoples of the Amazon* by E. Carmichael, S. Hugh-Jones, B. Moser and D. Tayler, pp. 76-93. British Museum Publications, London.

Josselin deJong, J.P.B.
1947 *Archaeological Material from Saba and St. Eustatius*. Mededelingen Rijksmuseum voor Volkenkunde 1. Brill, Leiden.

Keegan, W.F. and J.M. Diamond
1987 Colonization of Islands by Humans: A Biogeographical Perspective. In *Advances in Archaeological Method and Theory*, vol. 10, edited by M.B. Schiffer, pp. 49-92. Academic Press, New York.

Maat, G.J.R. and E. Smits
1987 Physical Anthropological Report Pre-Columbian Remains from St. Eustatius, Part II. Ms. on file, Institute of Prehistory, Leiden State University, Leiden.

Roosevelt, A.C.
1980 *Parmana: Prehistoric Maize and Manioc Subsistence along the Amazon and Orinoco*. Academic Press, New York.

Rouse, I.
1976 The Saladoid Sequence on Antigua and its Aftermath. *Proceedings of the International Congress for the Study of Pre-Columbian Cultures of the Lesser Antilles* 6:35-41. Gainesville.

1983 Diffusion and Interaction in the Orinoco Valley and on the Coast. *Proceedings of the International Congress for the Study of the Pre-Columbian Cultures of the Lesser Antilles* 9:3-13. Montréal.

Schinkel, C.
    1988   Statian Structures. Features of the Saladoid Site Golden Rock, St. Eustatius, Netherlands Antilles. Ms. on file, Institute of Prehistory, Leiden State University, Leiden.

Stoffers, A.L.
    1956   *The Vegetation of the Netherlands Antilles*. Publications of the Foundation for Scientific Research in Surinam and the Netherlands Antilles 15. Nigaoff, The Hague.

Vayda, A.P. and R.A. Rappaport
    1963   Island Cultures. In *Man's Place in an Island Ecosystem: A Symposium*, edited by F.R. Fosberg, pp. 133-144. Bishop Museum Press, Honolulu.

Versteeg, A.H.
    1987   *Methods and Preliminary Results of an Archaeological Salvage Project on St. Eustatius, Netherlands Antilles*. Report of the Institute of Archaeology and Anthropology of the Netherlands Antilles 4. Willemstad, Curaçao.

Wilbert, J.
    1981   Warao Cosmology and Yekuana Roundhouse Symbolism. *Journal of Latin American Lore* 7(1):37-72.

Wing, E.S.
    1983   Human Adaptation to the West Indian Environments. Paper presented at the Meetings of the Institute for Iberoamerican Cooperation, Madrid.

Wing, E.S. and E.J. Reitz
    1982   Prehistoric Fishing Communities of the Caribbean. *Journal of New World Archaeology* 5(2):13-32.

Table 1. Rank Order of Island Sizes (Large to Small) Between Tobago and Puerto Rico.

Rank	Island	Size (km^2)[a]
1	Guadeloupe	1434-1603
2	Martinique	984-1090
3	Dominica	787-790
4	St. Lucia	603
5	Barbados	430
6	St. Vincent	337-389
7	Grenada	311-345
8	Antigua	280
9	St. Croix	212
10	St. Kitts	173-176
11	Marie Galante	150-155
12	Barbuda	160-161
13	Vieques	132
14	Nevis	98-130
15	Anguilla	91
16	St. Martin	86
17	Montserrat	84-98
18	St. Thomas	83
19	Tortola	62
20	St. John	49
21	Cariacou	34
22	Culebra	28
23	St. Eustatius	21
24	Bequia	18
25	Saba	10

[a] Some islands have a size range listed due to inconsistencies across publications.

Table 2. Highest Elevations of the Islands (Large to Small) Between Tobago and Puerto Rico that are 400 Meters and Above.

Rank	Island	Altitude (m)[a]
1	Guadeloupe	1467-1484
2	Dominica	1422-1447
3	Martinique	1397
4	St. Kitts	1156-1315
5	St. Vincent	1179-1234
6	St. Lucia	950-1032
7	Nevis	985-996
8	Montserrat	914
9	Saba	870
10	Grenada	840
11	St. Eustatius	600
12	Tortola	518
13	St. Thomas	465
14	St. Martin	424
15	Antigua	400

[a] Some islands have a size range listed due to inconsistencies across publications.

Table 3. Depth of Postholes Between Lowest Point of Posthole
and Reconstructed Prehistoric Surface for the Three Roundhouses.

STRUCTURE A		STRUCTURE B		STRUCTURE C	
Posthole	Depth (cm)	Posthole	Depth (cm)	Posthole	Depth (cm)
Central	149	Central	200	Central	210
	95				219
Outer Circle	202	Outer Circle	185	Outer Circle	271
	161		170		217
	·350		194		250
	190		170		377
	115		196		190
	105		155		230
			170		217
			185		252
					232
					113
					216
					205
					320
					240
					200
					190
Extension	103	Extension	123	Inner Circle	300
	83		162		220
			170		332
			170		285
					186
					232
					148
					197

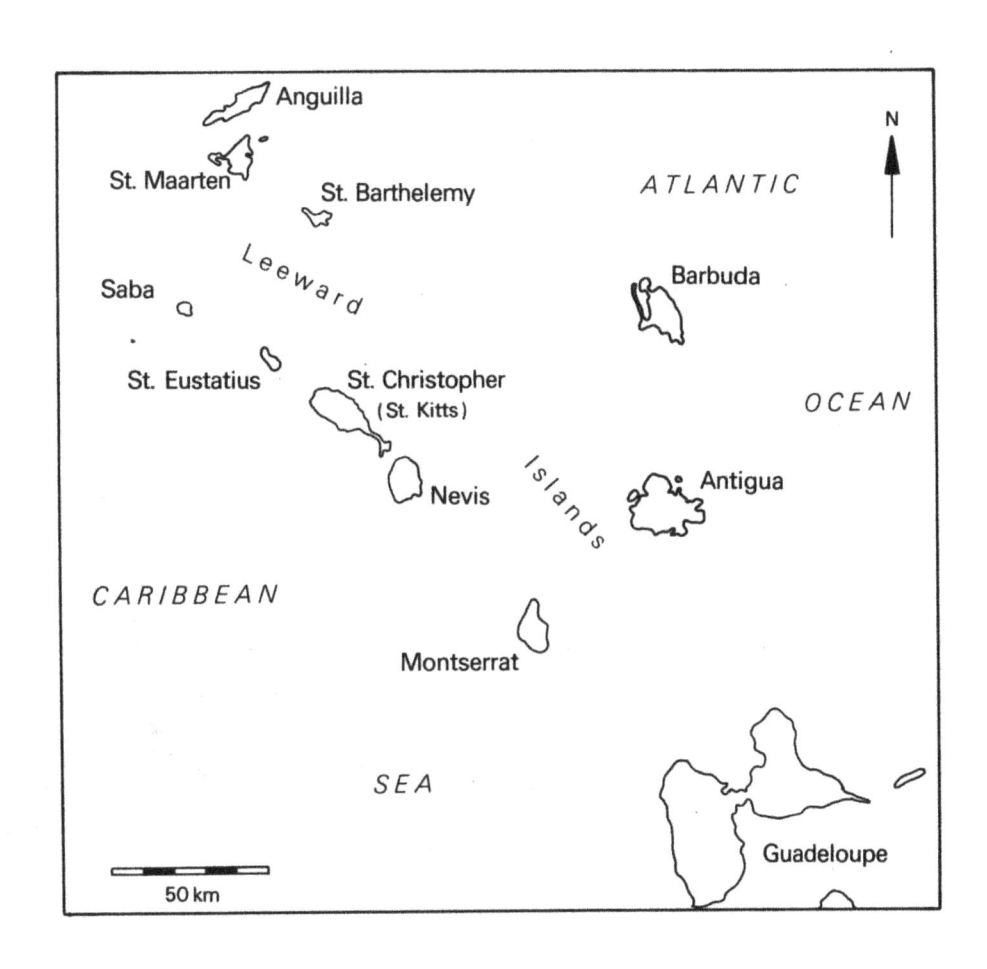

Figure 1. St. Eustatius and surrounding islands.

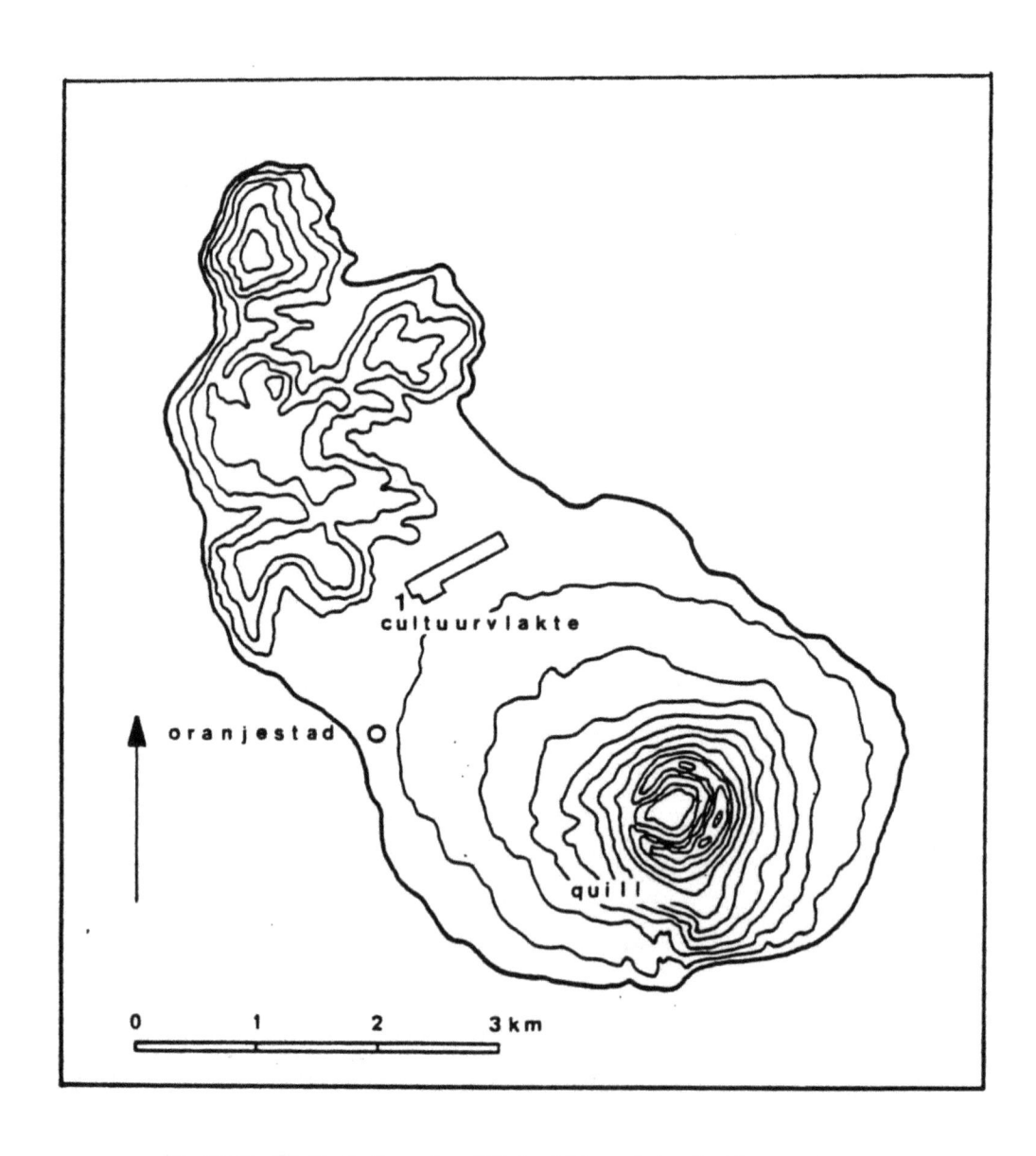

Figure 2. St. Eustatius. 1 = GR-1 midden of the Golden Rock site.

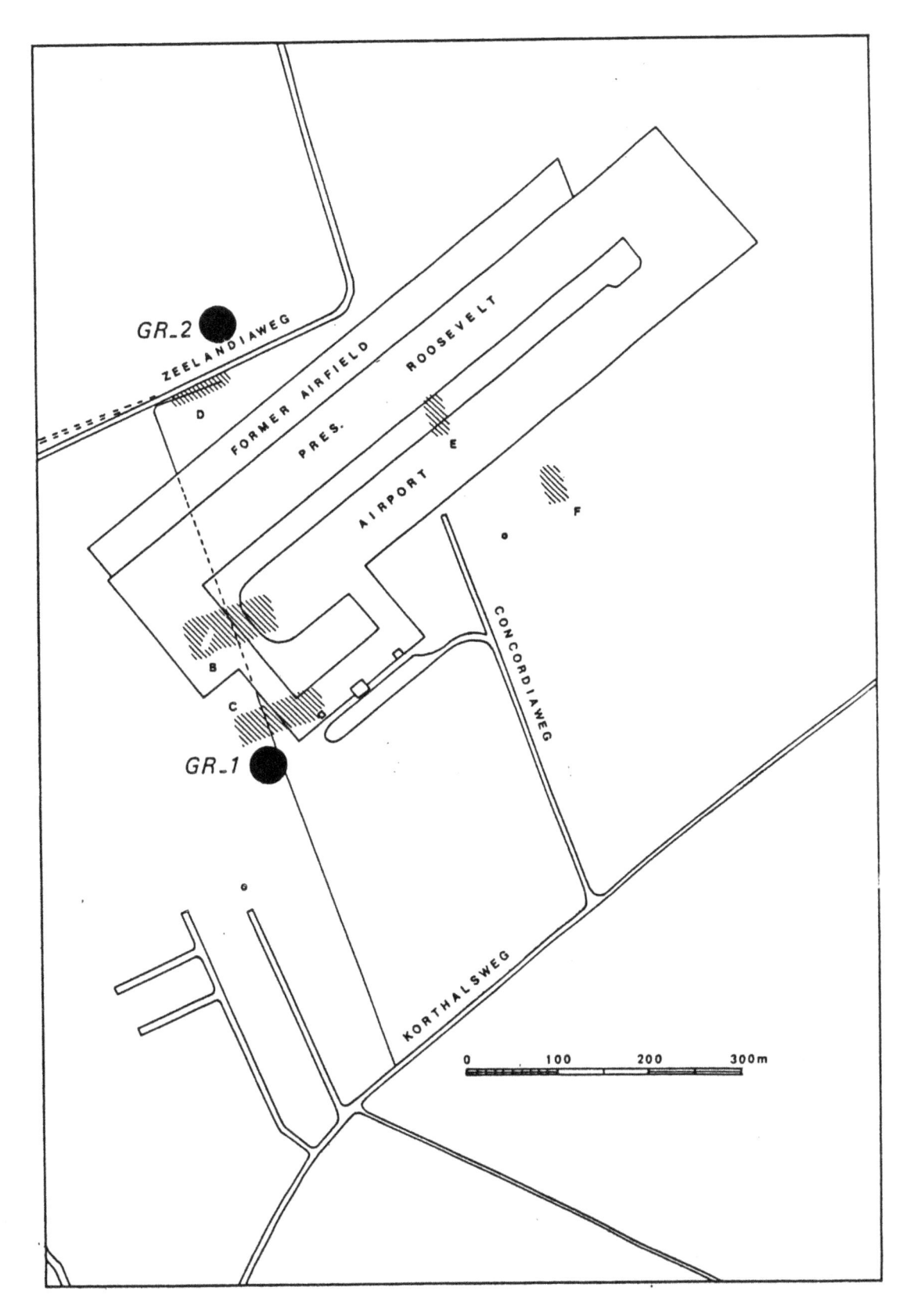

Figure 3. Golden Rock site and surroundings. B, C, D, E, and F are the middens of the site indicated by Josselin deJong (1947).

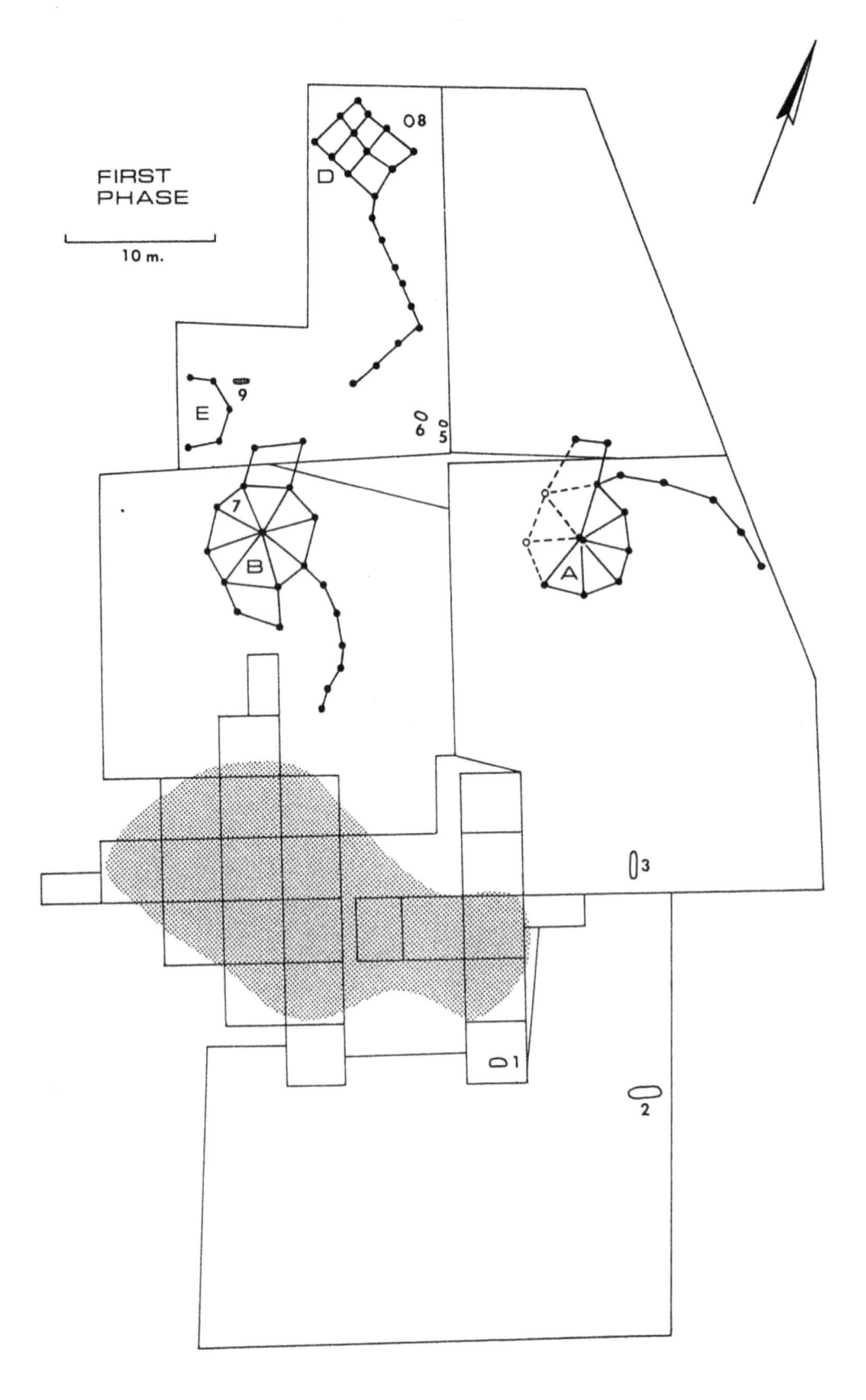

Figure 4. First (older) phase of the GR-1 midden.

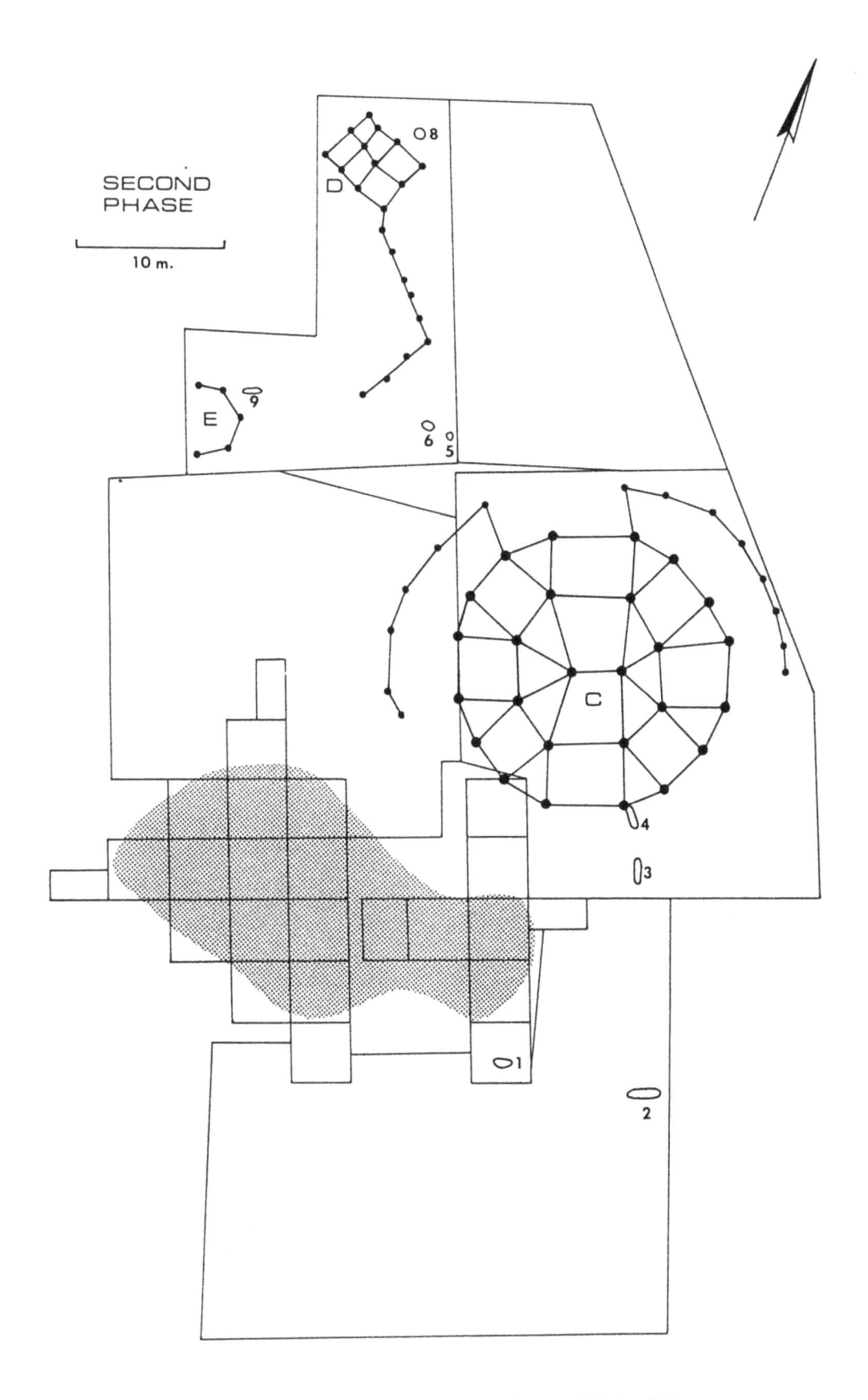

Figure 5. Second (younger) phase of the GR-1 midden.

Figure 6. Posthole of the outer circle of the *maloca*. The sloping portion of the posthole is where the post was inserted into the hole. Notice the dent at the left side of the postmold, just below the concrete-like tuff layer, caused by the heavy post. The rounded hinge point defines the right side of the postmold. The visible surface is made by the machine; it is ca. 70 cm below the surface in Indian times.

Figure 7. Posthole of the outer circle of the *maloca*, excavated from the present surface. The sloping part is not visible from this perspective. Depth of the posthole in Indian times was 271 cm.

Figure 8. Burial 3, a woman of 23-40 years of age. Pathology: hyperostosis. This burial is associated with the younger phase of the occupation.

Figure 9. Excavated surface at the location of the *maloca*.

Figure 10. Cache number 6 (see Figures 4 and 5).

Figure 11. One of the four vessels found in cache number 6. It has an orifice diameter of 14 cm and a maximum height of 9.9 cm.

SITE STRUCTURE, DEMOGRAPHY, AND SOCIAL COMPLEXITY IN THE EARLY CERAMIC AGE OF THE CARIBBEAN

Peter E. Siegel

ABSTRACT

Using site structural data in combination with demographic inferences a model is developed for political centralization in the early Ceramic age of the Caribbean. The Maisabel site structure includes a series of Saladoid mounded middens arranged in a concentric pattern surrounding a cemetery. Based upon the elaborate artifacts found within the mounded middens and the careful spatial arrangement of the middens with the cemetery it is suggested that together these features (mounded middens and cemetery) represent a ceremonial complex. The ceremonial complex is interpreted to be a physical representation of the ancestor cult observed in many lowland South Amerindian groups, and as such is a symbol of the religious and political centralization process that is occurring at this time. The Maisabel site is located along the final frontier of the Saladoid expansion, and the prehistoric settlement occupants are likely to have been involved in an agonistic interaction with the indigenous Archaic age hunter-gatherer-fisher populations. Subsequent group consolidation by the Saladoid farmers results in the initial stage of social complexity ultimately producing the Taino chiefdoms observed at the time of Spanish contact.

INTRODUCTION

The study of prehistoric behavior, demography, and the organization of activities has only recently become a domain of interest amongst some archaeologists working in the Caribbean and Amazon Basins. Yet given research in such areas as the development and spread of food intensification processes (Roosevelt 1980), demographic expansion (Keegan 1985), and changes in social organization (Rouse 1985) it is necessary to consider as well the lifeways and activity patterns of the people involved in these large-scale events.

In order to retrieve data appropriate for answering questions relevant for behavior and demography it is necessary that sites be excavated differently than what has been the case traditionally. Rather than placing trenches only in the thickest midden deposits it is important to investigate the areal extent of cultural debris and to ascertain, if possible, various functional areas of the prehistoric settlement.

To this end, a large early Ceramic age site, called Maisabel, was excavated by the Centro de Investigaciones Indígenas de Puerto Rico. Details of the sampling design and the overall site structure are presented elsewhere (Siegel and Bernstein 1987), thus I will only briefly review these now.

Maisabel is located on the north coast of Puerto Rico, roughly 30 km west of San Juan (Figures 1 and 2). Based upon the results of a two-stage sampling program the area of the site has been determined to be nearly 20 ha. Further, we know that there are a series of Saladoid mounded middens carefully placed in a horse-shoe configuration surrounding the central portion of the site (Figure 3). Centered amongst the mounded middens, but in a low artifact density section of the site is a cemetery that apparently spans the Saladoid and the Ostionoid occupations. In between the two largest mounded middens was discovered a house area.

Based upon artifact styles and radiocarbon dates the house represents an Ostionoid occupation (Table 1).

In this paper I will use an ethnographic analogue from lowland South America as a basis for inferring the demographic structure of the Maisabel house and compare this with the Saladoid Golden Rock house located on St. Eustatius. The demographic and site structural characteristics will then be used to discuss the process of sociopolitical centralization in the early Ceramic age of the Caribbean.

THE HOUSE

Given the amount of area exposed in our excavations it is clear that the Ostionoid house is quite large. Unfortunately, due to time constraints in the field we were unable to unearth the entire structure. However, based upon the orientation of a large ditch feature delimiting the house, the presence of a number of other features, and an entry way we may offer a reconstruction of at least the house form and approximate size (Figure 4). These data, in combination with an appropriate ethnographic analogue, may be used to estimate the number of occupants residing in the structure.

The long-axis of the house follows a northeast - southwest line. Based upon the ditch feature orientation, the width of the house is approximately 14 m. It is clear that the house takes an oblong rather than a round form.[1] The communal long house is a traditional house type among some lowland Amerindian horticultural societies in northern South America [e.g., Cubeo (Goldman 1979); Panare (Dumont 1976); Tukano (Jackson 1983)]. As such, the houses generally are organized along sib lines, with a number of related sibs constituting a phratry.

Morphologically, the ethnographically-observed communal long houses have a central corridor parallel with the long-axis of the structure. On either side of the corridor is a series of apartments. Each apartment is the residence of a nuclear family. A regular pattern, apparently, for the placement of main entrances to these kinds of structures is at the center of a wall (Figure 5). Whether the entry way is on a long or short wall varies, but it is always at the center of a given wall (Steward and Faron 1959:329, 352; Jackson 1983:34).

If we examine the Maisabel house plan from this perspective we may attempt to reconstruct the original size of the structure. Figure 6 shows the sections of the ditch feature actually excavated. In Figure 7 we see these sections connected. Then, using the computer graphics program, "Draw it Again Sam..." (Redburn 1986) the sections of the ditch feature excavated were horizontally flipped (Figure 8). Using the photo of the Witoto Indians communal house published in Steward and Faron (1959:352; Figure 9) and assuming the standing figure is six feet tall we may estimate that the entrance to the Witoto house is 10 feet wide. I used this figure as a basis for inferring the size of the Maisabel house entrance, which determined where the horizontally flipped drainage ditch should be placed (Figure 10). At this point, we then have enough of the house outlines to attempt the reconstruction of the original house area. Using a compensating polar planimeter I estimated the house area to be 576 m^2.[2]

This figure may be used to estimate the number of occupants by referring to ethnographically collected data on number of household occupants associated with structure area. Statistics are available on the demographic and architectural organization of a group of lowland South American Indians called the Waiwai, located in southern Guyana on the Brazilian border (Siegel 1987).

I have indirect material cultural evidence that the Waiwai are an appropriate ethnographic analogue for comparing with the prehistoric occupants of Maisabel. There are some unique elements of the prehistoric artifact assemblage from Maisabel that clearly are derivative of the same types of artifacts observed being used by the Taino Indians at the time of Spanish contact. The best examples of this are the small three-pointed objects, locally referred to as *zemis* (Figure 11). Furthermore, the Antillean ethnohistoric literature contains numerous citations and drawings of perishable artifacts, which are still in use today among the Waiwai (Oviedo y Valdés 1851-1855; Sheldon 1820:Plate14). Such objects include bitter manioc grater boards, squeezers, and sifters. By relating the imperishable prehistoric artifacts to the same category of objects in use by the ethnohistorically observed groups cultural continuity is documented in Puerto Rico. Then by relating the perishable artifacts of the ethnohistorically observed peoples in Puerto Rico with the same objects in use today among the Waiwai I establish a cultural link in this dimension (Roth 1924, 1929; Evans and Meggers 1960; Yde 1965). Logically then I suggest that the prehistoric Maisabel occupants share in the same material cultural tradition as do the present day Waiwai.

Aboriginally, and until roughly 30 years ago, the Waiwai lived in large communal houses (Fock 1963; Yde 1965; Figure 12). As a result of missionary intervention the Waiwai now generally live in single nuclear family dwellings (Mentore 1984). However, they maintain the original household structure by spatial propinquity of the individual nuclear families (resulting in house compounds of related nuclear families). Statistically, this pattern is very clear. The Pearson's correlation coefficient between nuclear family size and associated house floor area is 0.66 (Figure 13), whereas the correlation coefficient for household size and associated house floor area is 0.98 (Figure 14).[3] The latter regression equation may be used as a predictor for number of house occupants based upon floor area.

Looking now at the Maisabel house we see that 576 m^2 is much larger than the largest Waiwai household house area. This is not surprising given the smaller overall area of the Waiwai village compared to Maisabel. Plotting the 576 m^2 on the least-squares regression line generates a figure of roughly 60 associated individuals (Figure 15). Using the Waiwai demographic organization this represents five households and 12 nuclear families (12 people/household, 5 people/nuclear family).

It is useful to compare the Maisabel house with any other excavated Ceramic age structures from the Caribbean. One of the best documented structures is located in the Golden Rock site on St. Eustatius (Versteeg and Effert 1987; Versteeg 1987; Versteeg, this volume). This is a large round house, referred to as a *maloca* by Versteeg (1987). Based upon radiocarbon dates and artifact styles Versteeg places the entire site into a late Saladoid context.

Using the compensating polar planimeter I measured the area of the Golden Rock house to be 285 m^2. This value is commensurate with the largest Waiwai household house area producing a figure of roughly 30 occupants (Figure 15). Again, using the Waiwai data this represents two to three households and six nuclear families. This is half the size of the Maisabel structure.

SOCIOPOLITICAL CENTRALIZATION

IN THE EARLY CERAMIC AGE OF THE CARIBBEAN

Using these figures and structural characteristics of early Ceramic age sites in the Caribbean I would like to offer some general observations regarding the processes of cultural change and political consolidation in this region. Before presenting these observations, however, I want to make clear my assumptions. I take as given that the earliest Saladoid migrants were based upon a simple clan or possibly a lineage social and political organization. Upon settling into the various Antillean islands there was an in situ process of sociocultural change, in certain areas, ultimately resulting in the Taino chiefdoms observed at the time of European contact. Therefore, the logical questions to be addressed are what were the factors initiating this cultural evolutionary process, when did they occur, and what are the archaeological correlates?

As Rouse has abundantly documented, the earliest Saladoid sites are located in the Orinoco Valley of Venezuela (Rouse 1952, 1964, 1977, 1981, 1982, 1983, 1985, 1986; Rouse and Cruxent 1963; Rouse and Allaire 1978; Rouse et al. 1985). In the first millenium B.C. Saladoid groups began migrating into the Antilles and the Guianas (Rouse 1986:134-136). Shortly before the time of Christ Saladoid peoples had arrived in Puerto Rico and Hispaniola.

Based upon radiocarbon dates Rouse indicates that there are a series of five frontiers between Ceramic and Archaic age groups in the Caribbean. Behind each of the first three of these frontiers are located Saladoid sites. Frontiers 4 and 5 are represented by Ostionoid sites (Rouse 1986:144-148). Frontier #3 is the final frontier for the Saladoid expansion (Rouse 1986:Figure 24, this volume:Figure 4).

I believe that it is at this frontier where the process of sociopolitical consolidation begins in the early Ceramic age of the Caribbean. The context of this change occurs not in the Saladoid heartland, but on the Saladoid frontier (Rouse 1986:178). The frontier is the stage for the centralization process because it is within this context that the Saladoid farmers are faced with a structural opposition that requires social consolidation. The structural opposition, in this case, is represented by the indigenous Archaic age hunter-gatherer-fisherer populations, who were likely to be competing with the Saladoid colonists for the narrow band of coastal plain defining the periphery of the islands.

There is a small amount of evidence thusfar suggesting that the social environment for the early Ceramic age population in Puerto Rico was not entirely peaceful. (Puerto Rico corresponds to the area near frontier #3 in Rouse's [1986:135] plotting of the Ceramic-Archaic age boundaries in the Caribbean.) From the Maisabel site, for instance, there are two burials exhibiting clear signs of violent death. Burial #4 has a mantarey stingray spine projectile point embedded in the rib-cage (Figure 16) and burial #17's lower-right arm was severed (Figure 17), while his upper-right humerus has distinct sawing or cutting marks (Figure 18, perhaps battle wounds). Further, at the Hacienda Grande site, a burial was recovered with a stingray spine embedded in the cranial vault. Of course, it is impossible to say whether these individuals met their demise from the local native groups or from other members of the same colonizing group.

Roe (this volume) argues (based upon current ethnographic evidence "in a now pacified and depopulated lowland") that inter-ethnic agonism was the likely cause for the Saladoid migration, and by extension the source of hostilities between groups once they arrived in the Caribbean. I agree that inter-ethnic competition on the mainland of South America was a likely mechanism for the initial peopling of the Caribbean by early Ceramic age groups. (Alternatively, Rouse argues that separate populations represented by the Barrancoids and later the Arauquinoids moving into the Orinoco Valley pushed the Saladoids into the Lesser Antilles, who were thus responding to "external rather than internal conditions" [Rouse 1986:181].) However, I don't think that it is appropriate to make an analogy between the nature of present day agonistic interactions on the mainland of South America and prehistoric agonistic interactions in the Caribbean. On the mainland of South America related groups may be trading with each other one day and raiding each other the next. For instance, the Parukoto Indians nearly wiped out the Brazilian Waiwai in the latter part of the ninteenth century, and barely twenty years later the two groups had established trade and marriage connections (Farabee 1916:226-230, 1924:183; Fock 1963:6-7). The two groups share in a mutually understandable system of give and take.[4]

The mutually understandable system is governed by rules of social structure and group identity. These rules define alignments and points of cleavage. In a high density lowland (during prehistoric times) sets of related ethnic groups would coalesce (like confederacies), in times of warfare, in opposition to *other* sets of ethnic groups. Fock with regard to the Waiwai makes a similar observation: "The Carib dialect and major groups do not appear to possess any political importance for the Waiwai *today*, but can possibly during warlike periods have exercised an influence on the composition of leagues" (Fock 1963:236; emphasis added).

As the Saladoid peoples moved into the islands of the Caribbean they were confronted by a very different native population than what they were accustomed to in South America. Sociocultural distance was much higher between the colonists and the colonized than among the colonists. Following rules of social structure and group identity, therefore, the differences between the competing ethnic groups entering the Caribbean islands (Ceramic age populations) become less important when faced with a very different but large and well-organized opposition (Archaic age populations). This is what I mean by structural opposition between the Ceramic and Archaic age populations on frontier #3.[5]

If there are hostile activities transpiring at this time they are more likely to be occurring between the colonists and the colonized rather than among the colonists. Given that there are hostile pressures from the native Archaic age populations the selective advantage for the Saladoid groups is to coalesce into large settlements for protection. In doing so, however, mechanisms need to be instituted that counteract the forces pushing for social fissioning.

CEREMONIAL COMPLEX

What we see at some of the Saladoid sites in Puerto Rico that have been documented in sufficient detail is a circular configuration of mounded middens located in the center of the site (Figure 3; see also Rainey [1940:77]). Generally, it had been considered that these mounded middens represent accumulations of refuse associated with individual households. However, the fill of these middens generally contain the most elaborate artifacts produced by the Saladoid artisans. Further, the fragments of the ceramic vessels found are often very large, thus indicative of primary refuse. It is true that there is also a large amount of mundane material within these middens. This consists of animal bones, invertebrate hard parts, utilitarian ceramic wares, etc. However, the ratio of elaborately produced items to general everyday items is much higher in the mounded middens than the off-midden units excavated. For these reasons, I believe that the mounded middens are not simply refuse heaps, but are ceremonial features.

At this point I need to define terms. As Schiffer (1972, 1976, 1987) has well documented there are a variety of refuse types, each associated with specific behaviors. In discussing the structure of a site we are effectively addressing the processes and mechanisms by which artifacts came to be deposited where we find them. Figure 19 displays a classification of refuse types and disposal processes, with which archaeologists frequently deal. This scheme is not meant to be all inclusive. It simply highlights the importance of being clear in our assessments of archaeological deposits.

As we see, "mounded midden" is one type of primary ceremonial refuse. I am concerned here only with the discard to refuse portions of the "flow model...to view the life history of any element" in the archaeological record (Schiffer 1972:157). In other words, I *assume* that various aspects of the archaeological record have gone through variable use trajectories. However, once items have entered the archaeological context *how* do we accurately identify the resulting refuse types? Therefore, objects found in the mounded middens undoubtedly had a long life history prior to final deposition. But, this material is still considered to be primary refuse because it is the output of an activity occurring on the location of the mounded midden. For instance, an elaborately carved greenstone amulet is placed into the mounded midden in the context of the ancestor cult. The mounded midden becomes an activity area associated with the ritual. Durable elements found in this area resulting from the ceremonial activities are a form of primary refuse associated with "ritual discard" (Schiffer 1987:79).

Schiffer, in a general discussion of ritual caches distinguishes the offertory or votive cache: "such caches appear to represent the (often periodic) placement of artifacts in a special location, perhaps as an *offering*" (Schiffer 1987:80; emphasis in original). This, I believe, characterizes well the mounded middens at Maisabel with one qualification: I would not consider these features to be "caches." A cache implies a localized deposit of objects that are secreted away from general knowledge. To the contrary, the mounded middens are prominently displayed in the center of the site and probably were loci for public gatherings. I suspect that all members of the Saladoid community knew very well what was contained within the mounded middens.

Unfortunately, human behavior, and thus the archaeological record, is not so neat as to generate nicely partitioned and distinct "activity areas." There is a tremendous amount of overlap and mixing of materials resulting from different activities. Thus, in the mounded middens we find in addition to the sumptuary items a large amount of mundane materials. This material is secondary refuse, which has been deposited in a separate location from where it was used. In my terminology a mounded midden is defined as the combination of secondary refuse consisting of mundane material and sumptuary items deposited in a ritual/ceremonial context (Figure 20).

I have selected six excavation units to illustrate this relationship. Three units are from mounded middens and three are off-midden units. Count/weight ratios were calculated for the ceramic sherds by level and then by unit (Table 2). There is a clear difference in the ratios from the mounded vs. non-mounded midden contexts. With few exceptions the mounded midden unit values are much lower than the off-mounded midden units, level by level (Figure 21). The first levels of all the units display high values. This reflects the comminution factor of the plow when the field was under cultivation during the historic period.

The pattern is even more pronounced when we examine the mean sherd count/weight ratios by excavation unit. The three mounded midden units have lower values than the off-mounded midden units (Figure 22). The mounded middens are repositories for large amounts of primary refuse (in addition to secondary refuse).

The elaborately produced items from the same six units used for the sherd count/weight ratios are presented here. These items are divided by raw material: ceramic, stone, shell, bone, and coral. Within each of these raw material categories a finer breakdown of the artifacts is presented (Table 3).

For ceramic vessels, elaboration is considered in terms of surface treatment characteristics and certain aspects of secondary shape modifications (Table 3). A range of groundstone, shell, bone, and coral artifacts are also considered here to be "elaborate items" (Table 3).

Figures 23 and 24 display the distribution of elaborate ceramic attributes. Figure 23 shows elaborate surface treatment in grams/m^3 and Figure 24 exhibits the number of secondary shape features/m^3. In both of these Figures it is seen that attributes associated with sumptuary ceramic artifacts are much more frequent in mounded versus off-mounded midden units. The same pattern holds for elaborate groundstone and shell/coral artifacts (Figures 25 and 26 respectively). These data suggest that a specialized end-of-cycle funneling of sumptuary items is occurring in a ritual context (for a Mesoamerican example of ritual end-of-cycle dumping see Ekholm [1984]).

Initially, I termed the mounded middens as "planned constructions," or mounds. However, this phrase implies a certain amount of planning and coordinated work. If there was an active work program of constructing mounds over a relatively short period of time we would expect to see mounds filled not with artifacts but simply earth. In this case, the mound stratigraphy should reveal this type of construction by discerning individual "basket loadings" (Vin Steponaitis, personal communication 1988).

I still believe that the mounded middens are a result of planned activity beyond simple refuse disposal. However this planning and type of "construction" relates more to long term and cosmological factors than to notions of physical features (like mounds) per se. In other words, the immediate goal is not to produce "mounds" (which would then require a concerted effort of earth moving [Erasmus 1965]), but to deposit certain classes of artifacts in specified places. An alternative explanation for the mounded middens is that they are simply the output of household activities. While I believe that a large amount of the material is secondarily deposited everyday debris, a considerable portion of these deposits consists of *primary* offertory refuse. This offertory material is not output from casual household activities.

As I argue below, the funneling of elaborate artifacts into the mounded middens is undoubtedly related to the burial ceremonies and the ancestor cult. Ceremonies, therefore, relating to the ancestor cult are not conceived of as discrete, isolated acts but are part of a continuous process within the dimension of cosmological time. The archaeological correlates of this ceremonial behavior are large quantities of sumptuous artifacts within localized deposits. From Mounded Midden 1 (large circular north midden) we have a series of radiocarbon dates that span the Saladoid period (Table 4). It is clear from these dates that the Saladoid occupants used this area for hundreds of years.

Located in the central portion of the site, ringed by the mounded middens, is a cemetery. In the few excavation units placed here I recovered 23 burials. I am convinced that there are many more burials here, perhaps hundreds; the size of this portion of the site is roughly equivalent to the area of a football field. The ages for the burials seem to be primarily Saladoid, but there is one Monserrate (Saladoid/Ostionoid transitional phase) and possibly a few Ostionoid burials. I am suggesting at this point that the mounded middens and the cemetery together represent a ceremonial complex of sorts. I do not think that it is coincidental that the cemetery is at the precise center of the site. This central portion of the site thus may be a visual, spatial, social, and cosmological focal point for the early Ceramic age occupants of Maisabel. I believe that this may accord with the ancestor cults associated with many of the South American lowland Indian groups (Goldman 1979:190-202; Jackson 1983:200-201, 209-210; Crocker 1985:117).

Concentric social space is a very strong organizing principle for South Amerindian lowland societies (Lathrap 1970:133; Roosevelt 1987:171). As Roe (1987) exhaustively demonstrates, the village, and its circular form is a microcosm of the cosmos. At the center of a village often is where the *maloca* (communal house) is located. The *maloca*, and its internal organization, also becomes a model of the macrocosm (Siskind 1973:49; Wilbert 1981; Roe 1982:136-139, 1987:10-11; Jackson 1983:204). I would argue that the concentricity observed in the distribution of the Maisabel mounded middens is an expression of the same world view. However, instead of a communal house located at the center of the "universe" there is a cemetery. Death, burial rites, and interment are strongly associated with rebirth, renewal, and propagation. Elizabeth Traube working among the Mambai on the island of Timor in eastern Indonesia makes a similar observation:

> Life is not a free-floating vitality to be forcibly obtained, irrevocably possessed, but is rather the perishable product of a cycle of exchanges. What closes each exchange cycle and opens a new one is death, the final countergift. Death is at once a means of recompense and a technique of renewal, or, put slightly differently, dying is conceived of as an obligation contracted through living [Traube 1986:11].

We see this same concept in Amerindian notions of death and rebirth. Peter Roe indicates that the:

> aboriginal Shipibo-Conibo buried both adults and children in a flexed or semifetal position in burial urns, which...correspond to a kind of ceramic womb. Thus the very act of burial also was an act of impregnation of the earth with the spirits of the dead, who were going to be born again [Roe 1982:116].

Jean Jackson on the Tukanoans:

> Although Tukanoans at death are spoken of as being permanently removed to their ancestral homes located in specifiable areas of the Vaupés region, dead-people spirits are also reincarnated as energy - as life - and remain on this level. It is significant that Pamüri wi, the name of the Bará ancestral house, refers to rebirth. One translation of this name is "the house where our ancestors were born." It also refers to the birth of present-day Bará, or more specifically, rebirth: metamorphosis and reincarnation [Jackson 1983:209].

In these examples we see that time becomes circular, and that death is simply one phase in a continuous process. Burial rites and interment are acts that highlight important points of the process. By placing the cemetery at the center of the universe (village=universe) death becomes a sacred, knowable, and therefore controllable dimension of time. The ancestor cult thus is a major organizing principle for the sociocultural system. As such, it is at once a descriptive and explanatory model for the participants. In this context of continuous and cyclical world view we see that cosmology recapitulates genealogy, and vice versa.

Among the Panare Indians in the middle Orinoco Valley, ceramic vessels are ritually broken at mourning ceremonies when a death has occurred (Dumont 1976:140-141). If the mounded middens at Maisabel are in fact associated with an ancestor cult (spatial association of the middens with cemetery) possibly there is a similar activity here, whereby the elaborate ceramic vessels are ritually "killed" in mourning ceremonies. (This activity will result in low ceramic count/weight ratios. See Table 2 and Figure 21 for mounded versus off-mounded midden count/weight ratios.)

As discussed earlier I believe that the Saladoid groups located on frontier #3 coalesced into large settlements in response to hostilities from the resident Archaic age populations. The coalescing of several groups (clans or lineages? into a phratry?) in large permanent villages undoubtedly would necessitate a social organization with a more authoritative base than that provided by a headman or bigman.[6] What we may be observing in sites like Maisabel are the beginnings of a consolidation process that ultimately resulted in fully developed chiefdoms (Taino) with the associated architecture (ball courts).[7] We should expect that in the beginning stages of the sociopolitical consolidation there would be architecture that is commensurate with these early stages. The basic cosmology and world view (which includes a developed ancestor cult) would already have been present in the Saladoid culture from their Orinocan origins. With the increase in social complexity required on the Saladoid frontier the authoritative figure (chief?) simply formalizes the religious institutions with specified locations for depositing sumptuary items (our mounded middens) and a prepared burial ground.[8]

Fried's (1967:120) discussion of kinship relations in ranked society is relevant here. He argues that an "ideology of kinship" dominates ranked society, which is contrasted with an "ideology of coresidence" for egalitarian (or specifically band) societies. The ceremonial complex is a "monument" to the ancestor cult, and by extension emphasizes the political authority in the kinship relations.

The Maisabel ceremonial complex, therefore, may be a codifying system for the changing social institutions at this time. The caretakers and organizers of this centralized, sacred space mediate between nature and supernature to use Dumont's (1976) terminology. Likewise, internal dissension is ameliorated by this organizational structure. Thus, it is my feeling that in the earliest stages of Saladoid political consolidation the individuals vested with religious authority also served in an adjudication capacity, within the existing kinship structure. The ceremonial center of the site reflects a more complex (i.e., differentiated and specialized) level of social integration and regulation than what was characteristic of Saladoid social organization prior to the migration from South America.[9] The ceremonial complex is symbolic of this centralization of the religious and political authority. Thus, what we may be observing is a subtle shift in political organization from a relatively egalitarian to a simple rank society.[10] The impetus for this shift, in Puerto Rico, is probably based on a certain degree of warfare (or fear of it), which resulted from the competition with the native Archaic groups for access to coastal resources.

This model of social complexity relates to a large body of literature dealing with political evolution. Elements of social circumscription (Carneiro 1970) in combination with warfare (Webster 1975, 1976; Kirch 1984) are conditions that may result in group consolidation, increasing levels of population density, and concomitant social inequality (Fried 1967; Polgar 1975; Segraves 1982; Cohen 1985). DeBoer's (1981) discussion of buffer zones in Amazonian cultural history may have some relevance for the Saladoid frontier settlements found in the Caribbean. If the known distribution of large Saladoid sites in the Caribbean is not an artifact of sampling bias then it would appear that along the final Saladoid frontier large settlements were maintained for protection against other cultural groups. This does not necessarily represent a "buffer zone" in DeBoer's sense of the term, but it is a contact between two hostile groups.

A MODEL FOR SOCIOPOLITICAL COMPLEXITY

IN THE SALADOID PERIOD

In a provocative discussion of Taino chiefdoms Samuel Wilson (1988) offers some inferences into the process of increasing societal complexity. Wilson argues that sociopolitical authority was centralized or concentrated into fewer numbers of lineages. This process occurred within the structure of the kinship system; namely inheritance and succession patterns in combination with marriage rules were manipulated to consolidate power and authority:

> A significant outcome of the practice of elite intermarriage was the creation of overarching kinship ties which connected the elite strata of the various Taino cacicazgos. Exogamous marriages among the Taino elite linked large-scale descent groups, and disrupted the prior pattern of ranked or "conical" descent groups [Wilson 1988: Conclusion p. 8].

Furthermore, powerful caciques could accrue *and* consolidate greater amounts of power by practicing polygamy on a large scale (Wilson 1988: Conclusion p. 10).

Wilson suggests that the manipulations in the kinship structure were undoubtedly involved in transforming the relatively egalitarian Saladoid horticulturalists into the complex chiefdoms known as the Taino (Wilson 1988: Conclusions p. 12-13). Wilson's discussion is provocative if not speculative with regard to this span of time, especially given that he relies exclusively on ethnohistoric data. He terms his synchronic analysis of Taino society "the microprocesses of sociopolitical change," which is contrasted with "the prime movers or large scale processes often discussed in the archaeological literature." Evidently, Wilson equates any diachronic or long-term analysis of culture change as a prime-mover argument. Confounding prime-mover arguments with any diachronic analysis unfortunately disregards the long-term and systemic approaches to change that clearly recognize the multivariate (contra univariate or prime mover) nature of culture (Flannery 1972; Plog 1974; Wright 1977; Redman 1978).

Finally, Wilson's study begs the question: *Why* did culture change? He presents a detailed description of Taino society and *how* power and authority were consolidated into fewer lineages, but what were the motivating circumstances? Moreover, it is not clear to me why Wilson considers certain factors (his "historical trends") as distinct and secondary to specific kinship practices, which he claims are in fact transformative *process*. Thus, according to Wilson population growth, population pressure, intergroup competition, etc. are evidence for such "processes" as elite intermarriage, descent-line concentration, formation of cacique confederacies (1988: Conclusion p. 20).

Wilson's analysis leads to the question finally "Why did complex chiefdoms emerge in the Caribbean?" (Wilson 1988: Conclusion p.17), which he answers by saying that archaeological research devoted to the centuries prior to European contact is needed.

A recent theoretical position statement on social typology has been presented by John Hoopes (Habicht-Mauche et al.1987; Hoopes 1988). The concept of the "complex tribe" is offered as an alternative trajectory to the models of chiefdom formation in the anthropological literature (or sometimes as an addition to it). Hoopes contrasts Fried's (1967) model of egalitarian-ranked-stratified-state society with Services's (1975) band-tribe-chiefdom-state model: "Service's categories are based upon levels of social integration and centralization, qualities which are only indirectly related to Fried's degrees of social differentiation and the emergence of social classes" (Hoopes 1988:2). For this reason Hoopes argues that applying "the term chiefdom to societies with any recognizable degree of social differentiation has greatly limited its utility" (p.2).

Hoopes posits that there are cultures which conduct communal activities, have status variation, but no centralized authority. He argues that in these cases it is incorrect to identify the cultures as chiefdoms, but instead should be termed "complex tribes": "societies which have evidence for sophisticated community activity and the characteristics of ranked society, but which do not appear to have been organized around the office of a paramount, centralized authority" (Hoopes 1988:2-3). The notion of complex tribe provides an important interpretive framework for a particular sociopolitical category.

I believe that the "complex tribe" characterizes well the sociopolitical organization represented by the Saladoid groups located along frontier #3. Decision-making authority is not centralized within a single chiefly lineage, but status differentiation is clearly represented (in the burials)[11] and the involvement with the ceremonial complex signifies a more integrated community organization than a simple tribe.

However, if the frontier Saladoid situation is an example of a complex tribe it is one which eventually gives way to a more centralized decision-making authority and clear status differentiation based on ascription. This departs from Hoopes's expectation that the organizational characteristics of complex tribes will counteract tendencies towards the centralization of political authority: "adaptive advantages of segmentation would have worked against the conditions encouraging centralization" (Hoopes 1988:10).

The fact remains in Antillean archaeology that the ethnohistorically observed Classic Taino Indians maintained complex chiefdoms, which ultimately were derived (in an evolutionary sense) from the Saladoid cultures (Wilson 1988). Thus, for the frontier Saladoid, the complex tribe social form did not "diffuse centralizing tendencies" (Hoopes 1988:13), but instead provided an organizing framework for the following period (Ostionoid) of rapid centralization. In a sense, the complex tribe represents a "preadaptation" for the period of political consolidation resulting in chiefdoms (see Spencer [1987:378-379] for a discussion of "preadaptation" in connection with political evolution).

As noted earlier we get the first evidence of the construction of ball courts during the Ostionoid period (Alegría 1983:150; Robinson et al.1985:33, 40). The political implications of the ball courts are discussed elsewhere (Alegría 1983; Wilson 1988: Conclusion pp. 11-12), but it is clear that they represent a centralization of decision-making authority. I would argue that qualitatively we are dealing with a very different form of decision-making with the emergence of the ball courts than what was present during the previous Saladoid period. This should not be taken, however, as an endorsement for a Saladoid displacement by a [different] Ostionoid population. It means simply that there is an abrupt shift in the nature of power relations and authority structure from the complex tribal Saladoid society to the simple chiefdoms that emerge during the Ostionoid period.

In this context, therefore, the complex tribe represents an intermediate stage, in an evolutionary sense, between simple tribe and simple chiefdom. Whether the organizational changes are continuous or abrupt is not clear, but my feeling is that elements of both (continuous and discontinuous change) are involved. The shift from a simple to complex tribal form of organization probably occurs smoothly in response to proximate factors. Hoopes (1988:10) clearly points out the flexible nature of tribal segmentary organization. Lineages may coalesce or fission depending on local circumstances. However, the shift from complex tribe to simple chiefdom (in the cases where this evolutionary shift occurs) probably has more to do with an abrupt rather than a smooth change. Possibly the combination of several factors will produce a threshold beyond which a chiefdom type of sociopolitical organization is likely to result (Earle 1987:281; Spencer 1987:380-381). Such factors probably include status competition between tribal segments (households, lineages, etc.), formidable opposition from other groups, increasing rigidity of territorial boundaries, etc. If only one of these factors is present then a chiefdom is unlikely to form. In the event, however, that a number of these factors coincide, spatially and temporally, possibly an abrupt shift will occur whereby political authority and decision-making become centralized within say one powerful lineage. Charles Spencer makes a similar observation with regard to the transition from a big man leadership to a centralized political authority:

> I suggest that the permanent appearance of chiefly organization comes about when effective big man leadership happens to converge with a host of propitious contextual factors (such as institutionalized social differentiation, sanctification of leadership roles, intervillage elite alliances, interregional exchange or warfare) so that a new design...is...born...and persists, with the consequence that...the centralized political region, emerges as an important unit for future selection [Spencer 1987:380-381].[12]

From an emic/cultural perspective the ruling lineage (and therefore everybody else as well) will maintain a connection to the values of the pre-existing complex tribe. This may be a legitimizing strategy of the emergent chief and his lineage (Figure 27).[13] Therefore, the pre-existing cosmology and world view is still maintained and the same deities are worshipped. However, the new chief and his kin become the interpreters and caretakers of the world view. Possibly this is when the realm of cosmology and world view shifts from simply the status of myth, story, legend, and state-of-mind to also a "concrete" or physical locus within the village that the chief and his kind may control: ball courts and other monumental architecture become strategic political resources controlled by chiefly lineages.[14]

SUMMARY AND CONCLUSIONS

The results of the Maisabel research indicate that the earliest Saladoid occupants provided the basic village groundplan, upon which later groups built. The core of the village plan includes a ceremonial complex represented by carefully positioned mounded middens surrounding a centrally-located cemetery. It is argued here that the ceremonial complex observed in Maisabel is a physical representation of the ancestor cult that is a basis for the cosmologies of many lowland South Amerindian groups. Further, the ceremonial complex is directly associated with an increase in societal complexity leading to ranked society, and ultimately resulting in the fully developed chiefdoms, known as the Taino, which were observed by the Spaniards at the time of contact in the fifteenth and sixteenth centuries.

The pressures that induced this political consolidation are related to the processes of frontier settlements. I do not think it is coincidental that we are observing the beginnings of centralization in the Ceramic age of the Caribbean along the final frontier of the Saladoid expansion, rather than in the Saladoid heartland. It is at this frontier where we should expect to find the greatest structural opposition to the Saladoid colonists, in the form of the Archaic age hunters and gatherers. In the face of organized opposition the Saladoid peoples consolidated into large villages, setting the stage for all of the attendant social problems that result from relatively high population densities.

Finally, the population estimates for the Golden Rock and Maisabel houses are informative with regard to group size. The Golden Rock house is late Saladoid (fifth century A.D.), whereas the Maisabel house is early Ostionoid (roughly eigth century A.D.). My prediction is that when we find Saladoid houses in Puerto Rico they will approximate the size of the larger early Ostionoid house found in Maisabel, rather than the smaller Saladoid house from Golden Rock. The reason for this is that St. Eustatius is well behind the final Saladoid frontier, thus not in close contact with large competitive cultural groups. Village sizes should be smaller and pressure for consolidation should be minimal in such places as St. Eustatius compared to Puerto Rico. I would like to close this paper by suggesting that frontier settlements are one of numerous settings for observing the processes of societal complexity and political consolidation.

NOTES

1. The number of prehistoric structures available for comparison in the Caribbean is pitifully small. Aad Versteeg (this volume) has a complete late Saladoid house, which is round (this will be discussed in detail later). Steven Hackenberger (1987) working on the island of Barbados recovered a portion of an early Saladoid house in the Goddard site. Based upon the post-hole distribution Hackenberger suggests that the house is circular to oval in shape (see also Drewett, this volume). Espenshade (1987) working at the PO-21 site in the Cerrillos Valley near Ponce, Puerto Rico reports the finding of 13 prehistoric post-stains, dating to the early Ostionoid period. Espenshade (1987:155) interprets the post distribution to be part of an oval house roughly 8 m x 6 m in area. However, examining the plan map of the feature locations (Espenshade 1987:Figure 29) indicates that this reconstruction is based on absolutely no discernible patterning or systematic analysis of the features. Espenshade (1987:143) does say that the evidence is extremely tenuous and that other reconstructions are entirely possible. Finally, working in the lowland South American Early Formative Valdivia site of Real Alto, Lathrap and his students recovered 28 prehistoric houses through a number of occupational phases. Zeidler (1984:211-222) conducted a detailed analysis of the house sizes and shapes. By examining the length/width ratios of the structures Zeidler concludes that "the data suggest

an overall stability in elliptical shapes"(Zeidler 1984:218).

2. I realize that this strategy and the resulting figures border on the speculative until the entire structure has been excavated. Given this qualification, however, I feel that the reconstructive analysis is still useful. Aad Versteeg (personal communication 1988) pointed out that the calculated floor area will be considerably different depending on if the roof overhang is included or not. The drainage ditch represents the periphery of the structure *including* the roof overhang. The problem with trying to compute floor area minus the roof overhang is in knowing how large the overhang might have been. The Waiwai house floor areas (discussed in the body of the text) were computed using the drainage ditches as floor delimitors. In this regard, therefore, the two contexts (Maisabel and Shepariymo) are comparable.

3. A household consists of several related nuclear families. The house compound is the physical locus within the settlement for the basic social, economic, and demographic unit (or household), and where many of the household activities are conducted. Of course there are many activities organized along household lines that are performed outside of the house compound. The majority of these activities are economically based, such as tending to agricultural plots, hunting game, and gathering firewood, and are short-term. The same pattern of household and house compound organization has been noted for the Shipibo Indians in the montaña of eastern Peru (DeBoer and Lathrap 1979; Roe 1980; Roe and Siegel 1982; Siegel and Roe 1986:99).

4. Chagnon's (1968) description of the Yanomamö alliance and raiding patterns is an extraordinarily graphic testimony to this process. If we were to project this same system into the high density lowland of the prehistoric context it is not difficult to imagine less successful groups "hitting the road" (or the river and ocean to be more accurate) and heading off to the Lesser Antilles.

5. I believe that these social mechanisms operating on the final frontier of the Saladoid expansion may have some relevance for the Cedrosan/Huecan Saladoid issue. As Rouse (this volume) indicates the La Hueca and Hacienda Grande peoples coexisted from the second century B.C. to the third century A.D. However, by A.D. 300 La Hueca, as a style (and the Huecan Saladoid subseries), disappears leaving Cedrosan Saladoid (Hacienda Grande and Cuevas in Puerto Rico, and Prosperity and Coral Bay-Longford in the Virgin Islands [Morse, this volume]).

The inter-ethnic agonism powering the movement of Saladoid groups up the island chain may have operated as Roe suggests. It thus behooves these groups to maintain their ethnic identity in numerous ways, including the "messaging" through stylistic differences in material culture (Wobst 1977; Conkey 1978:62-66; Wiessner 1983:256-257). However, once confronted with alien and potentially hostile opponents, the inter-ethnic agonisms among the Saladoid groups become inter-ethnic alliances. It now behooves the groups to minimize ethnic differences and to reinforce inter-group solidarity. Given this selective pressure, the La Hueca style (and Huecan Saladoid subseries) is discontinued as group boundaries become more inclusive in response to the Casimiroid threat.

6. Rouse has suggested that the Archaic age populations residing on the large islands of Puerto Rico, Hispaniola, Jamaica, and Cuba would represent a more formidable opposition to the Saladoid migrants than the native populations occupying the smaller islands of the Lesser Antilles. Possibly for this reason the Saladoid expansion ended where it did [Irving Rouse, personal communication 1988; see also Bullen and Bullen (1976:8)].

It is important to note here that technologically the Saladoid colonists were probably not significantly superior to the native Archaic groups. The Ceramic and Archaic age groups were pre-industrial. Thus, it is not a foregone conclusion that the Saladoid migrants would simply "plow through" territories inhabited by the native populations.

Dennell (1985) makes this same observation regarding the Neolithic expansion into the Mesolithic territory in prehistoric Europe. Further, Dennell indicates that archaeologists often assume, incorrectly, that the cultural stages or epochs have immutable temporal boundaries:

> From the very onset of prehistoric studies in Europe, the frontier between hunter-gatherers and early farmers was drawn in *chronological* rather than *spatial* terms...Some of these stages overlapped in different parts of Europe [Dennell 1985:114; emphasis in original].

This same awareness is important to keep in mind for the Caribbean prehistoric context (see Rouse's paper in this volume). The Saladoid colonists were not moving into an empty territory and the nature of the interactions between them and the natives most certainly had some effect on settlement location, access to certain resources, and social organization.

It would be interesting to examine the cultural response of the Archaic age hunter-gatherer-fisher populations to the Ceramic age groups. One might expect that the Ceramic *and* Archaic age populations on either side of frontier #3 were complexifying in tandem for the same reasons. This is another issue requiring careful excavations of Archaic age sites.

7. Ricardo Alegría discusses the possible origins for the ball game in the West Indies. The earliest good evidence for structural ball courts dates to the Ostionoid period (ca. A.D. 700). Olsen (1974:33-34) presents what he sees as evidence for a ball court in the Saladoid deposits of the Indian Creek site on Antigua. Alegría (1983:121-122), however, disputes Olsen's evidence, pointing out its speculative nature.

Whether there are one or more origins for the rubber ball game in the Americas is unknown. Alegría (1983:153-156) presents a balanced appraisal of the alternative possibilities and concludes that there is just not enough data available at this time to offer an answer.

Regardless if the game was independently invented in different areas or derived from one source I believe that it probably entered the West Indies from South America with the Saladoid expansion (see also Stern 1949:98-101). There are numerous aspects of the archaeological record supporting the contention that the shift from the Saladoid to the Ostionoid periods represents an in situ cultural development. My expectation is that the in situ development, as reflected by the material culture, also occurs in the sociopolitical and religious realms of the culture.

There is some evidence that the ball courts were associated with burial ceremonies and ancestor worship (Fewkes 1907:82-83; Alegría 1983:63). In his excavations of the ball courts at Utuado, Puerto Rico Fewkes found 10 skeletons associated with one of the plazas. He concluded that "large numbers of the dead were buried just outside the dance courts and that the elaborate *areitos*, or mortuary dances, were held in the latter" (Fewkes 1907:83).

My line of reasoning, albeitly tenuous, is as follows: The ball courts are associated with ceremonial activities, among which ancestor worship is important (Alegría 1983:63). The late prehistoric and contact period ball courts are monumental in scale, clearly associated with the centralization of decision-making authority and strong status differentiation. Prior to the shift in power relations, whereby authority was distributed along kinship lines monumental architecture was absent. However, the discrete localities (our mounded middens), where sumptuary items were funneled, and the cemetery may have been functionally isomorphic to the Taino ball courts. By Taino times centralization, specialization, and integration developed to the point that ball courts and cemeteries are associated with distinct sets of activities and authority structures. Thus, the ball courts are primarily secular in orientation, associated with political authority, decision-making, and status differentiation. The cemeteries, on the other hand, deal exclusively with mourning ceremonies and the ancestor cult. These activities, however, play a prominent role with the secular correlates of the ball game. Admittedly, this model is conjectural, but I believe that it is in accord with other bodies of information regarding cultural change and continuity in the Caribbean.

8. Correlated with the relationship between the ceremonial complex and the ancestor cult is the observation that a cemetery "provides an association with the dead", which "becomes a part of community life and continuity with the past" (Price and Brown 1985:12). Price and Brown (1985:12) further note that a burial ground emphasizes a territorial claim by the group (see also Charles and Buikstra 1983:124), which is likely to be observed in other aspects of the archaeological record relating to "increased identity signaling and boundary defense." In this regard, it is important to note that there are a series of petroglyphs carefully carved into the horizontal bedding plane of the beach rock fronting the Maisabel site, which may be part of the territorial marking system of the settlement occupants (see also Roe 1987:42). Ethnographically, the Tucanoan-speaking Cubeo were observed using strategically placed petroglyphs as markers delimiting tribal boundaries (Goldman 1979:8, 44).

9. There is very little evidence available at this point concerning Saladoid settlement organization in South America. Roosevelt (1980:217-225), however, does present some figures on prehistoric site size and associated population levels (derived from ethnographic data) in the Orinoco Valley. For the Saladoid phases (La Gruta, Ronquín, and Ronquín Sombra) the areas for the habitation sites range from 1.50 to 1.70 ha. Indian Creek, a Saladoid site located on the island of Antigua, also has areal information available. Based upon Rouse's (1974:167,169) excavation and site map the size of Indian Creek is 4.67 ha. The area of Maisabel is 17.23 ha (Siegel and Bernstein 1987:Table 1). If we assume that larger Saladoid sites reflect greater degree of societal complexity then Maisabel should be more complexly organized than La Gruta, Ronquín, and Indian Creek. Based upon this small handful of sites, for which we have areal information it appears that in the Lesser Antilles and the mainland of South America Saladoid settlements were much smaller, and by extension less complexly organized than those located in Puerto Rico.

I must add here that by presenting the relationship between settlement size and social complexity I am not raising the hoary issue of causality at this point. Whether the intrinsic rate of growth results in a population size that "triggers" a necessary change in social complexity, or, conversely changes in the social, political, and economic spheres produce concomitant changes in complexity is a problem requiring further research (Dumond 1965; Carneiro 1967; Cowgill 1975; Drennan 1987). I would just like to say, however, that given available evidence at this time the observed shifts in social complexity are probably re-organizational responses to sociopolitical factors in the Caribbean rather than simply to increasing population size.

10. Whether the shift is gradual or discontinuous is not clear. Recent studies in the development of complex systems suggest that there are thresholds along a dimension of organizational structure. When a threshold is reached, either through endogenous or exogenous factors, then there will be an abrupt change in the organizational structure of the system (Peebles and Kus 1977:427; Johnson 1978, 1982).

11. Thirty-five human burials were found distributed across two distinct sections of the site. In the center of the site, an area termed the "cemetery," I recovered 23 burials. The remaining burials were found in the house area discussed earlier. The majority of the burials were found without any grave offerings. However, several were accompanied by ceramic vessels. These individuals include adults (men and women) and children (Budinoff 1987).

If grave offerings are considered to be an indicator of relative status position in life then the Maisabel burial sample suggests that differentiation was based on ascribed status distinctions (especially given that a handful of children were afforded preferential burial treatment). Furthermore, some individuals were accorded more careful post-mortem treatment than others. However, since no grave goods were associated with these burials it is not obvious whether they are Saladoid or Ostionoid individuals. An accelerator mass spectrometry dating analysis currently is being conducted for these individuals and will be reported on later (Siegel 1988).

12. Spencer's point about a "centralized political region" is important for the discussion of chiefdom development. At this stage in Caribbean archaeology there have been very few *systematic* surveys, and none for the goal of documenting sociopolitical centralization. If we may consider for the moment, however, sites that are known I may offer at least a suggestion for the process.

Archaeological and ethnohistoric data for the Taino context indicate that the society was organized into a sociopolitical hierarchy, with primary, secondary, and possibly tertiary centers of authority. In Puerto Rico, for instance, there are at least 79 ball courts/plazas distributed across 72 sites (Alegría 1983:115). Thirty-nine of these features are rectangular-shaped courts likely to have been used for the ceremonial ball game and range in size from roughly 100 m^2 to 4,100 m^2 (Alegría 1983:117, Figure 31). These courts, however, are not from a single slice of time. They range from A.D. 700 to 1500, with a great proliferation occurring during the period from A.D. 1000-1500 (Alegría 1983; Robinson et al. 1985). I would argue that the distinct size ranking in the Taino ceremonial centers reflects a carefully prescribed chain of command in their sociopolitical organization.

In addition to the ceremonial centers, there are hamlets and villages. Very little is known about the internal organization and variability that exists in these non-ceremonial sites. In the Ostionoid period there are ball courts and ceremonial centers but they are smaller and less variable in size than the Taino ones. This suggests that there was less verticality in the political hierarchy of the Ostionoid society compared to the Taino society.

Finally, there is no good evidence for a "centralized political region" during the Saladoid period. The known Saladoid sites in Puerto Rico are relatively evenly dispersed around the perimeter of the island, except for the west coast (Rouse, this volume). Furthermore, the available information does not indicate any ranking in terms of relative settlement size.

There is tantalizing evidence, however, from the artifact inventories of these Saladoid sites. All of them contain a similar repetoire of Saladoid material culture, including white-on-red painted pottery, zic ware, three-pointers, shell beads, groundstone adzes and bi-convex celts, etc. (see Rouse [1952, this volume] for a complete description of the Saladoid material culture inventory). However, there are two sites that stand out noticeably in terms of artifact inventories. These are Sorcé (Chanlatte Baik 1981; Chanlatte Baik and Narganes Storde 1983) and Punta Candelero (Rodríguez and Rivera 1987).

Sorcé has been intensively excavated for many years by Luis Chanlatte Baik and Yvonne Narganes Storde. They have recovered the full range of Saladoid artifacts, but in addition there are a number of elaborate items which are not found at all, or very rarely, in other sites. These consist largely of the elaborately carved and polished stone amulets and beads. Many of these objects are made out of exotic stone, such as amethyst.

Punta Candelero, recently discovered and excavated by Miguel Rodríguez (Rodríguez and Rivera 1987) also contains a large assemblage of the elaborate items identical to those found at Sorcé. An alternative explanation to what is presented in note 5 is that these sites represent the seat of a formative centralized political region. Sorcé, being on the island of Vieques, is well-protected from potential aggressors. Furthermore, the Pta. Candelero settlement may have served as a checkpoint, through which visitors were required to pass on their way to Vieques.

It is conceivable that Sorcé's political authority extended not only to Puerto Rico but also to the Saladoid settlements in the Virgin Islands. However, defining the limits of the political region will require careful comparative analysis of the assemblages from the region. There is a critical need at this stage in the Ceramic age archaeology of the Caribbean for *systematic* and *well-controlled* regional surveys for the goal of documenting and eventually explaining the process of political centralization. Without this necessary data base many of our discussions concerning political evolution will be no more than speculative musings.

13. Anna Roosevelt indicates that the same process occurred among the late prehistoric chiefdoms of the Lower Amazon: "chiefdoms had societal religious ideologies enhancing the position of elites through the worship of deified ancestors...There were specialists in charge of the religious houses and ceremonies, and also diviners and curers" (Roosevelt 1987:154).

14. Alegría aptly characterizes the situation:

The rubber ball game of the Taino is a clear indicator of the complexity of this society...The construction of the courts required some technological competence, specialists, and an organized political unity beyond the village. The labor force needed for the excavation of the courts, the construction of earth embankments, and the alignments of stones required a powerful chief, as well as a society with a food surplus to sustain the laborers who were constructing the courts [Alegría 1983:5-6].

Acknowledgments. The Maisabel Archaeological Project has been funded entirely by the Centro de Investigaciones Indígenas de Puerto Rico. I would like to thank Dave Bernstein and Al Dekin for constructive input into this paper. Figures 1 and 2 were prepared by Beth Carter, Figures 3 and 4 by Luis Roca and Associates, and Figures 21, 23-26 by Tim Roberts. I would particularly like to thank Peter Roe, Irving Rouse, Mike Schiffer, Charles Spencer, Vin Steponaitis, and Aad Versteeg for their comments on this work. I am especially grateful to Irving Rouse for his meticulous comments on numerous drafts of the paper, for which it is substantially improved. I am solely responsible for the interpretations and conclusions.

REFERENCES CITED

Alegría, Ricardo E.
   1983 *Ball Courts and Ceremonial Plazas in the West Indies*. Yale University Publications in Anthropology No. 79. New Haven.

Budinoff, Linda C.
   1987 An Osteological Analysis of the Human Burials Recovered from an Early Ceramic Site on the North Coast of Puerto Rico. Paper presented at the 12th International Congress for Caribbean Archaeology, Cayenne, French Guiana.

Bullen, Ripley P. and Adelaide A. Bullen
   1976 Culture Areas and Climaxes in Antillean Prehistory. *Proceedings of the International Congress for the Study of Pre-Columbian Cultures of the Lesser Antilles* 6:1-10. Gainesville.

Carneiro, Robert L.
   1967 On the Relationship between Size of Population and Complexity of Social Organization. *Southwestern Journal of Anthropology* 23:234-243.

1970   A Theory of the Origin of the State. *Science* 169:733-738.

Chagnon, Napoleon A.
1968   *Yanomamö: The Fierce People.* Holt, Rinehart and Winston, New York.

Chanlatte Baik, Luis A.
1981   *La Hueca y Sorcé (Vieques, Puerto Rico): Primeras migraciones agroalfareras antillanas: nuevo esquema para los procesos culturales de la arqueología antillana.* Privately printed, Dominican Republic.

Chanlatte Baik, Luis A. and Yvonne M. Narganes Storde
1983   *Vieques-Puerto Rico: asciento de una nueva cultura aborigen antillana.* Privately printed, Dominican Republic.

Charles, Douglas K. and Jane E. Buikstra
1983   Archaic Mortuary Sites in the Central Mississippi Drainage: Distribution, Structure, and Behavioral Implications. In *Archaic Hunters and Gatherers in the American Midwest*, edited by James L. Phillips and James A. Brown, pp.117-145. Academic Press, New York.

Cohen, Mark N.
1985   Prehistoric Hunter-Gatherers: The Meaning of Social Complexity. In *Prehistoric Hunter-Gatherers: The Emergence of Cultural Complexity*, edited by T. Douglas Price and James A. Brown, pp. 99-119. Academic Press, New York.

Conkey, Margaret W.
1978   Style and Information in Cultural Evolution: Toward a Predictive Model for the Paleolithic. In *Social Archeology: Beyond Subsistence and Dating*, edited by Charles L. Redman, Mary Jane Berman, Edward V. Curtin, William T. Langhorne Jr., Nina M. Versaggi, and Jeffery C. Wanser, pp. 61-85. Academic Press, New York.

Cowgill, George L.
1975   On Causes and Consequences of Ancient and Modern Population Changes. *American Anthropologist* 77:505-525.

Crocker, Jon C.
1985   *Vital Souls: Bororo Cosmology, Natural Symbolism, and Shamanism.* University of Arizona Press, Tuscon.

DeBoer, Warren R.
1981   Buffer Zones in the Cultural Ecology of Aboriginal Amazonia: An Ethnohistorical Approach. *American Antiquity* 46:364-377.

DeBoer, Warren R. and Donald W. Lathrap
1979   The Making and Breaking of Shipibo-Conibo Ceramics. In *Ethnoarchaeology: Implications of Ethnography for Archaeology*, edited by Carol Kramer, pp. 102-138. Columbia University Press, New York.

Dennell, Robin W.
1985   The Hunter-Gatherer/Agricultural Frontier in Prehistoric Temperate Europe. In *The Archaeology of Frontiers and Boundaries*, edited by Stanton W. Green and Stephen M. Perlman, pp. 113-139. Academic Press, New York.

Drennan, Robert D.
   1987 Regional Demography in Chiefdoms. In *Chiefdoms in the Americas,* edited by Robert D. Drennan and Carlos A. Uribe, pp.307-324. University Press of America, Lanham, Maryland.

Dumond, Donald E.
   1965 Population Growth and Cultural Change. *Southwestern Journal of Anthropology* 21:302-324.

Dumont, Jean-Paul
   1976 *Under the Rainbow: Nature and Supernature Among the Panare Indians.* University of Texas Press, Austin.

Earle, Timothy K.
   1987 Chiefdoms in Archaeological and Ethnohistorical Perspective. *Annual Review of Anthropology* 16:279-308.

Ekholm, Susanna M.
   1984 When Refuse Isn't Garbage: Mesoamerican End-of-Cycle Ceremonial Refuse. Paper presented at the 49th Annual Meeting of the Society for American Archaeology, Portland, Oregon.

Erasmus, Charles J.
   1965 Monument Building: Some Field Experiments. *Southwestern Journal of Anthropology* 21:277-301.

Espenshade, Christopher T.
   1987 *Data Recovery Excavations at Site PO-21 Cerrillos River Valley, Puerto Rico.* Garrow & Associates. Submitted to the United States Army Corps of Engineers, Jacksonville District. Copies available from State Historic Preservation Office, San Juan, Puerto Rico.

Evans, Clifford and Betty J. Meggers
   1960 *Archaeological Investigations in British Guiana.* Bureau of American Ethnology Bulletin No.177. Smithsonian Institution. Government Printing Office, Washington, D.C.

Farabee, William C.
   1916 The Amazon Expedition of the University Museum. *The Museum Journal* 7:209-244.

   1924 *The Central Caribs.* Anthropological Publications Vol. X. The University Museum, University of Pennsylvania, Philadelphia.

Fewkes, Jesse Walter
   1907 *The Aborigines of Porto Rico and Neighboring Islands.* Bureau of American Ethnology Bulletin No. 25. Smithsonian Institution, 1903-1904, pp. 1-220. Government Printing Office, Washington, D.C.

Flannery, Kent V.
   1972 The Cultural Evolution of Civilizations. *Annual Review of Ecology and Systematics* 3:399-426.

Fock, Niels
   1963 *Waiwai: Religion and Society of an Amazonian Tribe.* Nationalmuseets Skrifter, Etnografisk Række No.VIII. The National Museum of Copenhagen, Denmark.

Fried, Morton H.
   1967 *The Evolution of Political Society: An Essay in Political Anthropology.* Random House, New York.

Goldman, Irving
   1979 *The Cubeo Indians of the Northwest Amazon.* 2nd ed. University of Illinois Press, Urbana.

Habicht-Mauche, Judith, John Hoopes, and Michael Geselowitz
   1987 Where's the Chief?: The Archaeology of Complex Tribes. Paper presented at the 52nd Annual Meeting of the Society for American Archaeology, Toronto.

Hackenberger, Steven
   1987 Archaeological Investigations, Barbados, West Indies 1986. Paper presented at the 12th International Congress for Caribbean Archaeology, Cayenne, French Guiana.

Hoopes, John W.
   1988 The Complex Tribe in Prehistory: Sociopolitical Organization in the Archaeological Record. Paper presented at the 53rd Annual Meeting of the Society for American Archaeology, Phoenix.

Jackson, Jean E.
   1983 *The Fish People: Linguistic Exogamy and Tukanoan Identity in Northwest Amazonia.* Cambridge University Press, New York.

Johnson, Gregory A.
   1978 Information Sources and the Development of Decision-Making Organizations. In *Social Archeology: Beyond Subsistence and Dating,* edited by Charles L. Redman, Mary Jane Berman, Edward V. Curtin, William T. Langhorne Jr., Nina M. Versaggi, and Jeffery C. Wanser, pp.87-112. Academic Press, New York.

   1982 Organizational Structure and Scalar Stress. In *Theory and Explanation in Archaeology: The Southampton Conference,* edited by Colin Renfrew, Michael J. Rowlands, and Barbara A. Segraves, pp. 389-421. Academic Press, New York.

Keegan, William F.
   1985 *Dynamic Horticulturalists: Population Expansion in the Prehistoric Bahamas.* Ph.D. dissertation, University of California, Los Angeles. University Microfilms, Ann Arbor.

Kirch, Patrick V.
   1984 *The Evolution of Polynesian Chiefdoms.* Cambridge University Press, New York.

Lathrap, Donald W.
   1970 *The Upper Amazon.* Thames and Hudson, London.

Mentore, George P.
   1984 *Shepariymo: The Political Economy of a Waiwai Village.* Unpublished Ph.D. dissertation, Graduate School in Arts and Social Studies, University of Sussex, Sussex, England.

Olsen, Fred
   1974 *Indian Creek: Arawak Site on Antigua, West Indies.* University of Oklahoma Press, Norman.

Oviedo y Valdés, Gonzalo Fernández de
1851-1855 *Historía general y natural de las Indias, islas y tierra firma de la mar océan.* 4 vols. José Amador de los Rios, Madrid.

Peebles, Christopher S. and Susan M. Kus
1977 Some Archaeological Correlates of Ranked Societies. *American Antiquity* 42:421-448.

Plog, Fred T.
1974 *The Study of Prehistoric Change.* Academic Press, New York.

Polgar, Steven (editor)
1975 *Population, Ecology, and Social Evolution.* Mouton, The Hague.

Price, T. Douglas and James A. Brown
1985 Aspects of Hunter-Gatherer Complexity. In *Prehistoric Hunter-Gatherers: The Emergence of Cultural Complexity*, edited by T. Douglas Price and James A. Brown, pp. 3-20. Academic Press, New York.

Rainey, Froelich G.
1940 *Porto Rican Archaeology.* Scientific Survey of Porto Rico and the Virgin Islands, vol. XVIII-part 1. The New York Academy of Sciences, New York.

Redburn, Kendall
1986 *Draw it Again Sam....* Aba Software, Frazer, Pennsylvania.

Redman, Charles L.
1978 Mesopotamian Urban Ecology: The Systemic Context of the Emergence of Urbanism. In *Social Archeology: Beyond Subsistence and Dating*, edited by Charles L. Redman, Mary Jane Berman, Edward V. Curtin, William T. Langhorne Jr., Nina M. Versaggi, and Jeffery C. Wanser, pp.329-347. Academic Press, New York.

Robinson, Linda S., Emily R. Lundberg, and Jeffery B. Walker
1985 *Archaeological Data Recovery at El Bronce, Puerto Rico Final Report, Phase 2.* Archaeological Services. Submitted to United States Army Corps of Engineers, Jacksonville District. Copies available from State Historic Preservation Office, San Juan, Puerto Rico.

Rodríguez, Miguel and Virginia Rivera
1987 Puerto Rico and the Caribbean Pre-Saladoid "Crosshatch Connection." Paper presented at the 12th International Congress for Caribbean Archaeology, Cayenne, French Guiana.

Roe, Peter G.
1980 Art and Residence Among the Shipibo Indians of Peru: A Study in Microacculturation. *American Anthropologist* 82:42-71.

1982 *The Cosmic Zygote: Cosmology in the Amazon Basin.* Rutgers University Press, New Brunswick.

1987 Village Spatial Organization in the South Amerindian Lowlands: Evidence from Ethnoarchaeology. Paper presented at the 52nd Annual Meeting of the Society for American Archaeology, Toronto.

1987 The Petroglyphs of Maisabel: A Study in Methodology. Paper presented at the 12th International Congress of Caribbean Archaeology, Cayenne, French Guiana.

Roe, Peter G. and Peter E. Siegel
1982 The Life History of a Shipibo Compound: Ethnoarchaeology in the Peruvian Montaña. *Journal of Archaeology and Anthropology* 5:94-118.

Roosevelt, Anna C.
1980 *Parmana: Prehistoric Maize and Manioc Subsistence along the Amazon and Orinoco.* Academic Press, New York.

1987 Chiefdoms in the Amazon and Orinoco. In *Chiefdoms in the Americas*, edited by Robert D. Drennan and Carlos A. Uribe, pp.153-185. University Press of America, Lanham, Maryland.

Roth, Walter E.
1924 *An Introductory Study of the Arts, Crafts, and Customs of the Guiana Indians.* Bureau of American Ethnology Bulletin No. 38. Smithsonian Institution, 1916-1917. Government Printing Office, Washington, D.C.

1929 *Additional Studies of the Arts, Crafts, and Customs of the Guiana Indians.* Bureau of American Ethnology Bulletin No. 91. Smithsonian Institution. Government Printing Office, Washington, D.C.

Rouse, Irving
1952 *Porto Rican Prehistory: Introduction; Excavations in the West and North.* Scientific Survey of Porto Rico and the Virgin Islands, vol. XVIII-part 3. The New York Academy of Sciences, New York.

1964 Prehistory of the West Indies. *Science* 144:499-513.

1974 The Indian Creek Excavations. *Proceedings of the International Congress for the Study of Pre-Columbian Cultures of the Lesser Antilles* 5:166-176. Antigua.

1977 Pattern and Process in West Indian Archaeology. *World Archaeology* 9:1-11.

1981 Origin of the Ostionoid Series: Migration or Interaction? Paper presented in the Symposium on Problems of Antillean Archeology, Universidad Católica, Ponce, Puerto Rico.

1982 Ceramic and Religious Development in the Greater Antilles. *Journal of New World Archaeology* 5(2):45-55.

1983 Diffusion and Interaction in the Orinoco Valley and on the Coast. *Proceedings of the International Congress for the Study of the Pre-Columbian Cultures of the Lesser Antilles* 9:3-14. Montréal.

1985 Social, Linguistic, and Stylistic Plurality in the West Indies. Paper presented at the 11th International Congress for Caribbean Archaeology, San Juan, Puerto Rico.

1986 *Migrations in Prehistory: Inferring Population Movement from Cultural Remains.* Yale University Press, New Haven.

Rouse, Irving and José M. Cruxent
1963 *Venezuelan Archaeology.* Yale University Press, New Haven.

Rouse, Irving and Louis Allaire
   1978   Caribbean. In *Chronologies in New World Archaeology*, edited by R.E. Taylor and Clement W. Meighan, pp.431-481. Academic Press, New York.

Rouse, Irving, Louis Allaire, and Aad Boomert
   1985   Eastern Venezuela, the Guianas, and the West Indies. Ms. prepared for an unpublished volume, *Chronologies in South American Archaeology*, compiled by Clement W. Meighan. Department of Anthropology, University of California, Los Angeles.

Schiffer, Michael B.
   1972   Archaeological Context and Systemic Context. *American Antiquity* 37:156-165.

   1976   *Behavioral Archeology*. Academic Press, New York.

   1987   *Formation Processes of the Archaeological Record*. University of New Mexico Press, Albuquerque.

Segraves, Barbara Abbott
   1982   Central Elements in the Construction of a General Theory of the Evolution of Societal Complexity. In *Theory and Explanation in Archaeology: The Southampton Conference*, edited by Colin Renfrew, Michael J. Rowlands, and Barbara A. Segraves, pp.287-300. Academic Press, New York.

Service, Elman R.
   1975   *Origins of the State and Civilization*. Norton, New York.

Sheldon, William
   1820   Brief Account of the Caraibs, who Inhabited the Antilles. *Transactions of the American Antiquarian Society* 1:365-433.

Siegel, Peter E.
   1987   Small Village Demographic and Architectural Organization: An Example from the Tropical Lowlands. Paper presented at the 52nd Annual Meeting of the Society for American Archaeology, Toronto.

   1988   Occupational History of an Early Ceramic Age Settlement on the North Coast of Puerto Rico. Grant #BNS-8822317, Proposal Submitted to the Archaeology Program, National Science Foundation. Washington, D.C.

Siegel, Peter E. and Peter G. Roe
   1986   Shipibo Archaeo-Ethnography: Site Formation Processes and Archaeological Interpretation. *World Archaeology* 18:96-115.

Siegel, Peter E. and David J. Bernstein
   1987   Sampling for Site Structure and Spatial Organization in the Saladoid: A Case Study. Paper presented at the 12th International Congress of Caribbean Archaeology, Cayenne, French Guiana.

Siskind, Janet
   1973   *To Hunt in the Morning*. Oxford University Press, New York.

Spencer, Charles S.
   1987   Rethinking the Chiefdom. In *Chiefdoms in the Americas*, edited by Robert D. Drennan and Carlos A. Uribe, pp.369-390. University Press of America, Lanham, Maryland.

Stern, Theodore
   1949   *The Rubber-Ball Games of the Americas.* Monographs of the American Ethnological Society No.17. University of Washington Press, Seattle.

Steward, Julian H. and Louis C. Faron
   1959   *Native Peoples of South America.* McGraw-Hill, New York.

Stuiver, Minze and Paula J. Reimer
   1986   A Computer Program for Radiocarbon Age Calibration. *Radiocarbon* 28:1022-1030.

Traube, Elizabeth G.
   1986   *Cosmology and Social Life: Ritual Exchange among the Mambai of East Timor.* University of Chicago Press, Chicago.

Versteeg, A.H.
   1987   Saladoid Houses and Functional Areas Around Them: The Golden Rock Site on St. Eustatius (Netherlands Antilles). Paper presented at the 12th International Congress of Caribbean Archaeology, Cayenne, French Guiana.

Versteeg, A.H. and F.R. Effert
   1987   *Golden Rock: The First Indian Village on St. Eustatius.* St. Eustatius Historical Foundation No.1.

Webster, David
   1975   Warfare and the Evolution of the State: A Reconsideration. *American Antiquity* 40:464-470.

   1976   *Warfare and the Evolution of the State: A Perspective from the Maya Lowlands.* Miscellaneous Series No.19. Museum of Anthropology, University of Northern Colorado, Greeley.

Wiessner, Polly
   1983   Style and Social Information in Kalahari San Projectile Points. *American Antiquity* 48:253-276.

Wilbert, Johannes
   1981   Warao Cosmology and Yekuana Roundhouse Symbolism. *Journal of Latin American Lore* 7(1):37-72.

Wilson, Samuel M.
   1988   Hispaniola: The Chiefdoms of the Caribbean in the Early Years of European Contact. Ms. on file, Department of Anthropology, University of Chicago.

Wobst, H. Martin
   1977   Stylistic Behavior and Information Exchange. In *Papers for the Director: Research Essays in Honor of James B. Griffin*, edited by Charles E. Cleland, pp.317-342. Anthropological Papers No. 61. Museum of Anthropology, University of Michigan, Ann Arbor.

Wright, Henry T.
   1977   Recent Research on the Origin of the State. *Annual Review of Anthropology* 6:379-397.

Yde, Jens
   1965   *Material Culture of the Waiwái.* Nationalmuseets Skrifter, Etnografisk Række No. X. The National Museum of Copenhagen, Denmark.

Zeidler, James A.
   1984   *Social Space in Valdivia Society: Community Patterning and Domestic Structure at Real Alto, 3000-2000 B.C.* Ph.D. dissertation, University of Illinois, Champaign-Urbana. University Microfilms, Ann Arbor.

Table 1. Radiocarbon Dates Associated with the House.

Lab Sample Number	Uncorrected Age (B.P.)	Uncorrected Age (B.C./A.D.)	Calibrated Age[a] (B.P.)	Calibrated Age (B.C./A.D.)	Calibrated Age Range ± 2 sigma
Beta-17631	1530±90	A.D. 420	1406	A.D. 544	A.D. 268-660
Beta-17641	1440±70	A.D. 510	1329	A.D. 621	A.D. 440-680
Beta-17635	1360±70	A.D. 590	1290	A.D. 660	A.D. 560-790
Beta-17633	1310±60	A.D. 640	1273	A.D. 677	A.D. 630-870
Beta-17640	1300±70	A.D. 650	1269	A.D. 681	A.D. 620-890
Beta-17638	1260±60	A.D. 690	1225[b]	A.D. 725	A.D. 650-890
			1215[b]	A.D. 735	
			1184[b]	A.D. 766	
Beta-17636	1160±70	A.D. 790	1064	A.D. 886	A.D. 680-1010
Beta-17639	1150±70	A.D. 800	1061	A.D. 889	A.D. 680-1020
Beta-17634	1140±60	A.D. 810	1059	A.D. 891	A.D. 723-1010
Beta-17632	1070±70	A.D. 880	970	A.D. 980	A.D. 790-1113
Beta-15007	1040±50	A.D. 910	951	A.D. 999	A.D. 890-1040

[a] The radiocarbon dates were calibrated using Method A of the program CALIB written by Stuiver and Reimer (1986). The reported lab error multiplier is 1.0.

[b] Radiocarbon count rate in this portion of the dendrochronology calibration curve does not give a unique value.

Table 2. Ceramic Count/Weight Ratios Listed by Square and Level for Three Mounded and Three Off-Mounded Midden Excavation Units. Notice that the ratios generally are much lower in the mound units. This relationship is most apparent when we examine the mean count/weight ratios listed at the bottom of the chart. These figures support the notion that the mounds are repositories for primary deposits, compared to off-mound contexts, which contain secondary refuse.

DEPTH cm below ground surface	MOUNDED MIDDEN UNITS			OFF-MOUNDED MIDDEN UNITS		
	N96W13	N112W88	S36W18	N52E50	N32E32	N84E72
0-20	0.269	0.273	0.243	0.307	0.262	0.271
20-30	0.213	0.175	0.069	0.322	0.190	0.217
30-40	0.158	0.142	0.128	0.270	0.172	0.194
40-50	0.142	0.108	0.114	0.231	0.220	0.207
50-60	0.126	0.109	0.103	0.255	0.269	0.188
60-70	0.094	0.130	0.095		0.000	0.000
70-80	0.132	0.142	0.105		0.220	0.216
80-90	0.168	0.385	0.093			
90-100	0.145	0.231	0.109			
100-110	0.130	0.141	0.148			
110-120	0.142		0.043			
120-130	0.178					
130-140	0.265					
$\bar{x}$ potct / $\bar{x}$ potwt	0.169	0.159	0.117	0.278	0.212	0.221

Table 3. Artifacts Considered to be Elaborate in the Discussion of Sumptuary Items.

CERAMIC SURFACE TREATMENT	CERAMIC SECONDARY SHAPE FEATURES	SHELL/CORAL/ BONE ARTIFACTS	GROUNDSTONE ARTIFACTS
Zoned-incised and crosshatched	D-shaped handle	Bead	Biconvex celt/ plano-convex adze
White slip	Loop-shaped handle	Three-pointer (*zemi*)	Celt/adze fragment
White-on-red paint	Tabular lug handle	Gouge	Hammerstone
	Appliqué button	Axe	Amulet
Red-on-unslipped	Spout	Hoe	Bead
Incised	Effigy	Chisel	Three-pointer
Polychrome	Carena	Disc	Net sinker
Unspecified	Exterior lip flange	Carved figure	Mano
	Interior lip flange	Projectile point	Metate
	Internally thickened rim	Amulet	Abrader
	Appliqué point	Unspecified	Carved figure
	Disc	Unidentifiable	Unspecified
	Unspecified		Unidentifiable
	Unidentifiable		

Table 4. Radiocarbon Dates from Mounded Midden 1.

Lab Sample Number	Uncorrected Age (B.P.)	Uncorrected Age (B.C./A.D.)	Calibrated Age[a] (B.P.)	Calibrated Age (B.C./A.D.)	Calibrated Age Range ± 2 sigma
Beta-14999[b]	3370±60	1420 B.C.	3630	1681 B.C.	1875-1520 B.C.
Beta-14998[b]	2810±70	860 B.C.	2934[c] 2904[c] 2893[c]	985 B.C. 955 B.C. 944 B.C.	1212-820 B.C.
Beta-14996[b]	2300±80	350 B.C.	2341	392 B.C.	755-180 B.C.
Beta-14380	2060±60	110 B.C.	2045	96 B.C.	341 B.C.-A.D. 70
Beta-14381	1960±90	10 B.C.	1922[c] 1905[c] 1899[c]	A.D. 28 A.D. 45 A.D. 51	189 B.C.-A.D. 240
Beta-14993	1810±60	A.D. 140	1729	A.D. 221	A.D. 70-374
Beta-14997	1810±70	A.D. 140	1729	A.D. 221	A.D. 60-390
Beta-14992	1660±100	A.D. 290	1552	A.D. 398	A.D. 130-610
Beta-15000	1190±90	A.D. 760	1120[c] 1091[c]	A.D. 830 A.D. 859	A.D. 660-1020

[a] The radiocarbon dates were calibrated using Method A of the program CALIB written by Stuiver and Reimer (1986). The reported lab error multiplier is 1.0.

[b] These samples were recovered from below the culture-bearing deposits and thus are not associated with any of the prehistoric occupations at the site.

[c] Radiocarbon count rate in this portion of the dendrochronology calibration curve does not give a unique value.

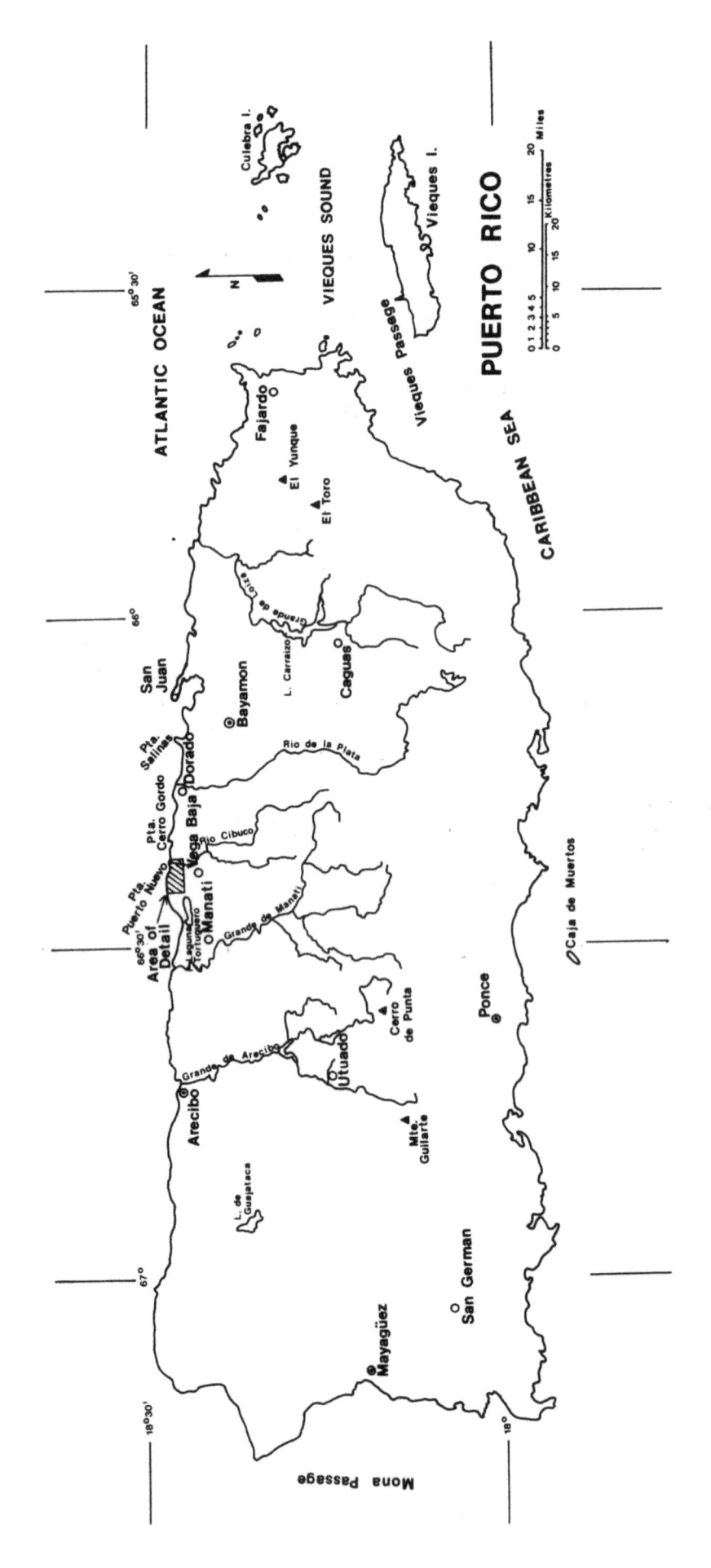

Figure 1. Map of Puerto Rico showing the location of the study area. Maisabel is located in the Puerto Nuevo ward of Vaga Baja, roughly 30 km west of San Juan.

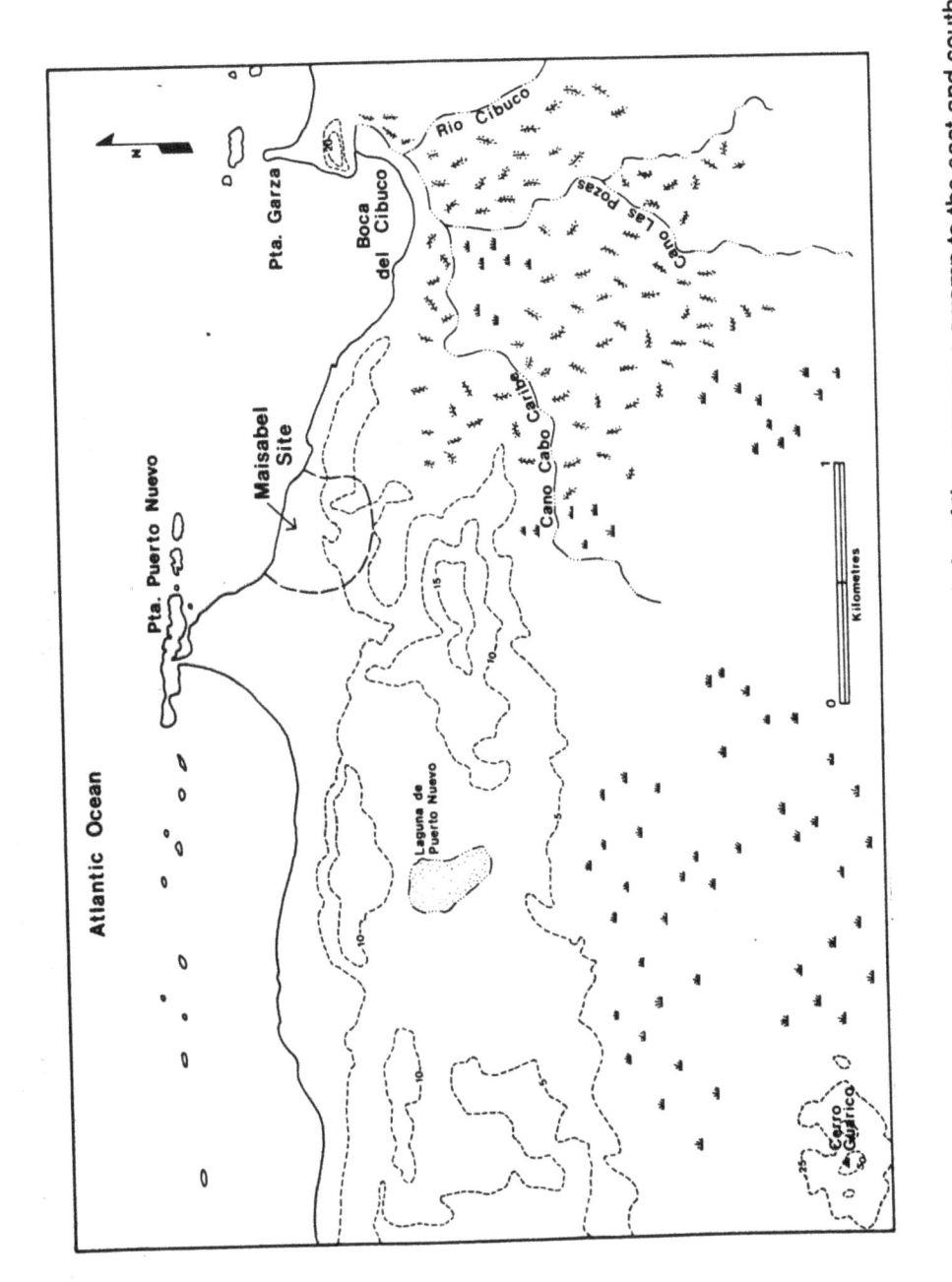

Figure 2. Detail of the Maisabel setting. Notice the proximity of the mangrove swamp to the east and south of the site and the Río Cibuco to the east.

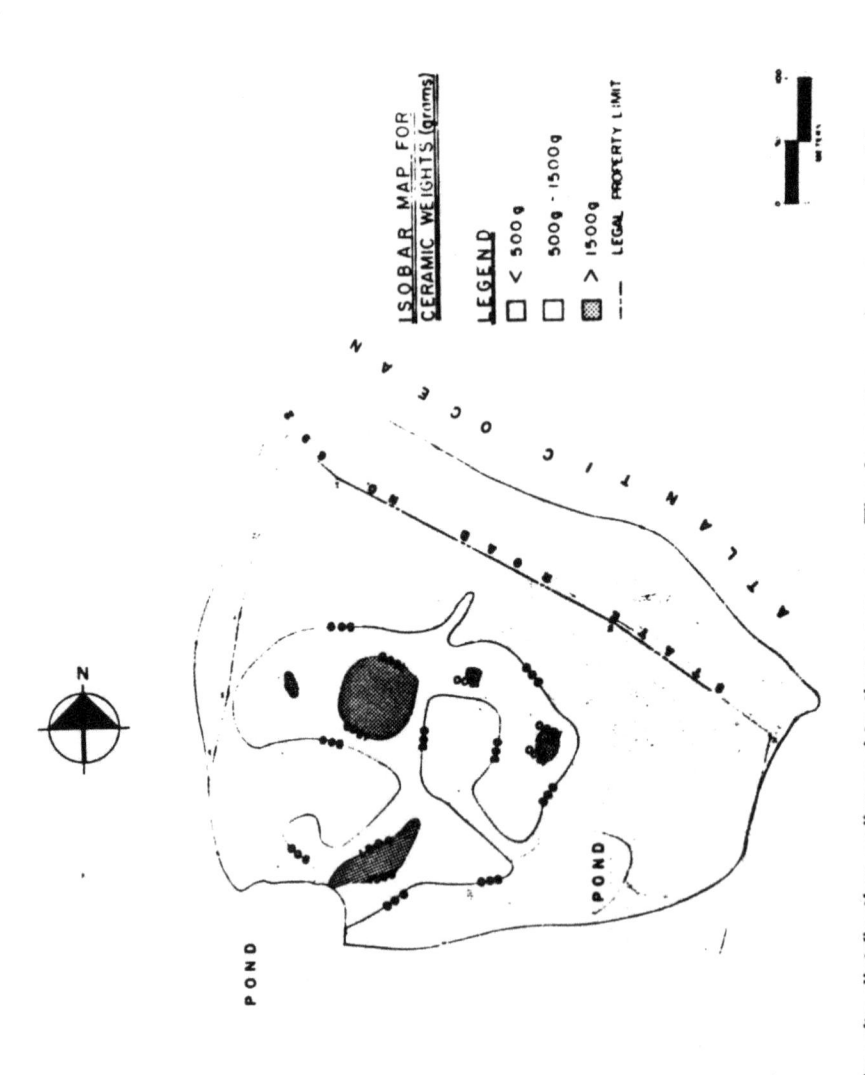

Figure 3. Ceramic density distribution collapsed to three groups. The largest area is represented by auger pits containing less than 500 g of pottery. The intermediate sized area (white on the map) is the zone where each auger pit produced pottery weighing 500 - 1500 g. The smallest zone generated pottery in excess of 1500 g per machine pit. The spatial distribution of these "hotspots" produces a rough circular pattern in the center of the site.

Figure 4. Macroblock map displaying the features. Notice the long, curvilinear ditch feature (F #101: denoted by hachuring). The eastern terminus of this feature is located in N44E1 and is clearly terminated by a large limestone slab. This limestone slab is interpreted to be a plug helping to minimize water from draining out of the ditch and into the house.

Figure 5. Drawing presented in Steward and Faron (1959:329) showing the Tupinambá longhouses. Notice that each house has an entrance centered along a wall.

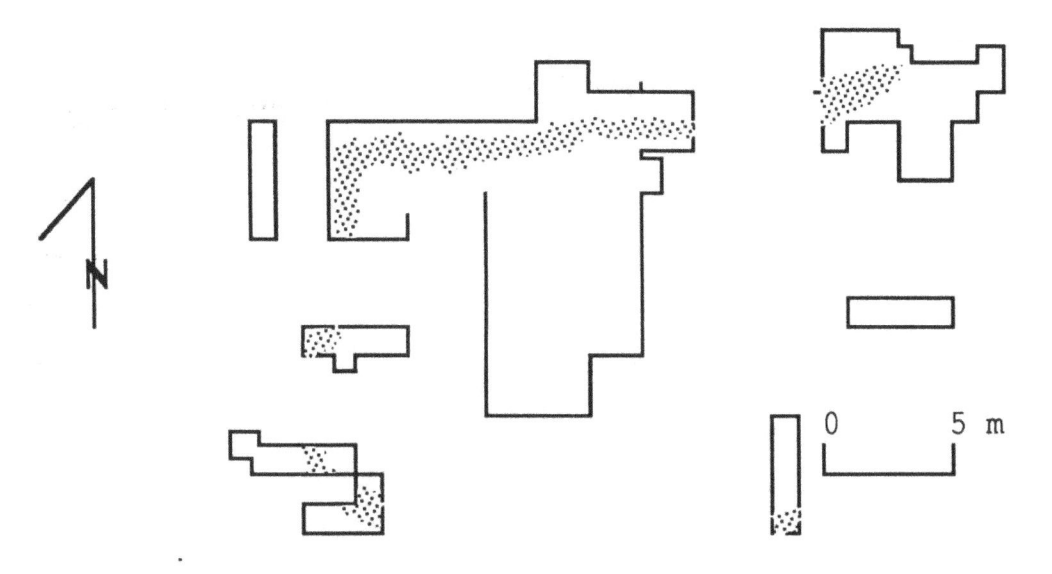

Figure 6. Map of macroblock showing the portions of the ditch feature (stippling) excavated.

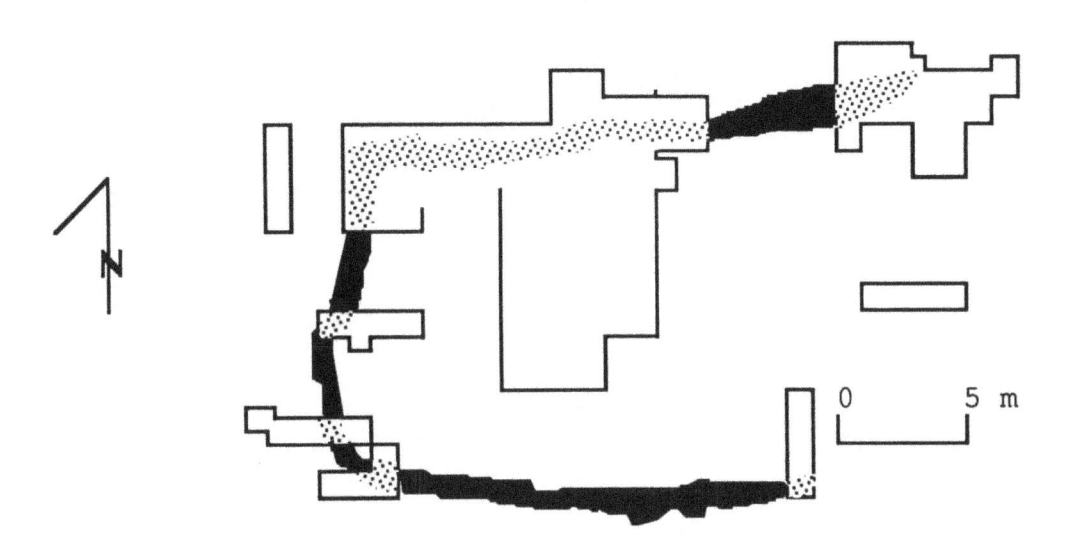

Figure 7. Map of macroblock showing the portions of the ditch feature excavated (stippling) connected by blackened areas.

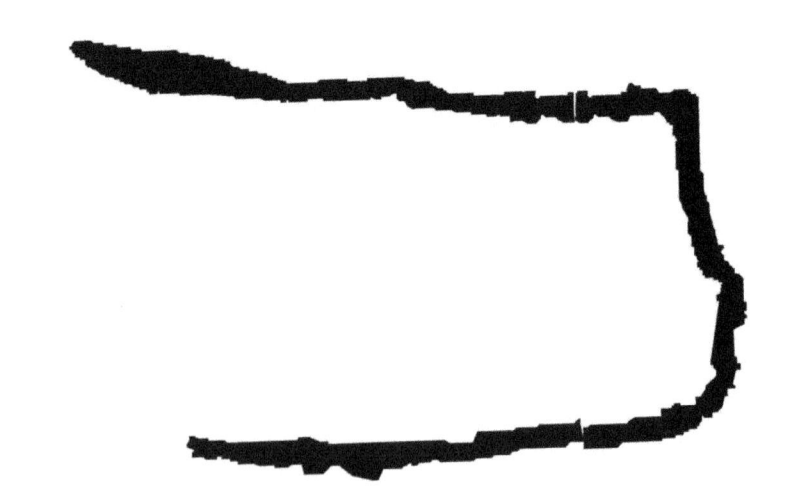

Figure 8. Map showing the excavated and connected portions of the ditch feature as they appear horizontally flipped. See Figure 7 for scale.

Figure 9. Photo presented in Steward and Faron (1959:359) of a communal Witoto house. If we assume that the standing figure is six feet tall then the entrance to this house is roughly 10 feet across.

Figure 10. Combining Figures 6-8 with the 10 foot entrance width based upon the Witoto house produces this map. I realize that this reconstructive exercise is somewhat speculative until the entire area of concern has been excavated. However, given the unambiguous nature of the portions of ditch feature recovered, the large number of other features found within the arc of the ditch, and characteristics of ethnographically observed longhouses I believe that the speculative aspect of the exercise has been minimized sufficiently to allow me to proceed with the analysis of the structure area.

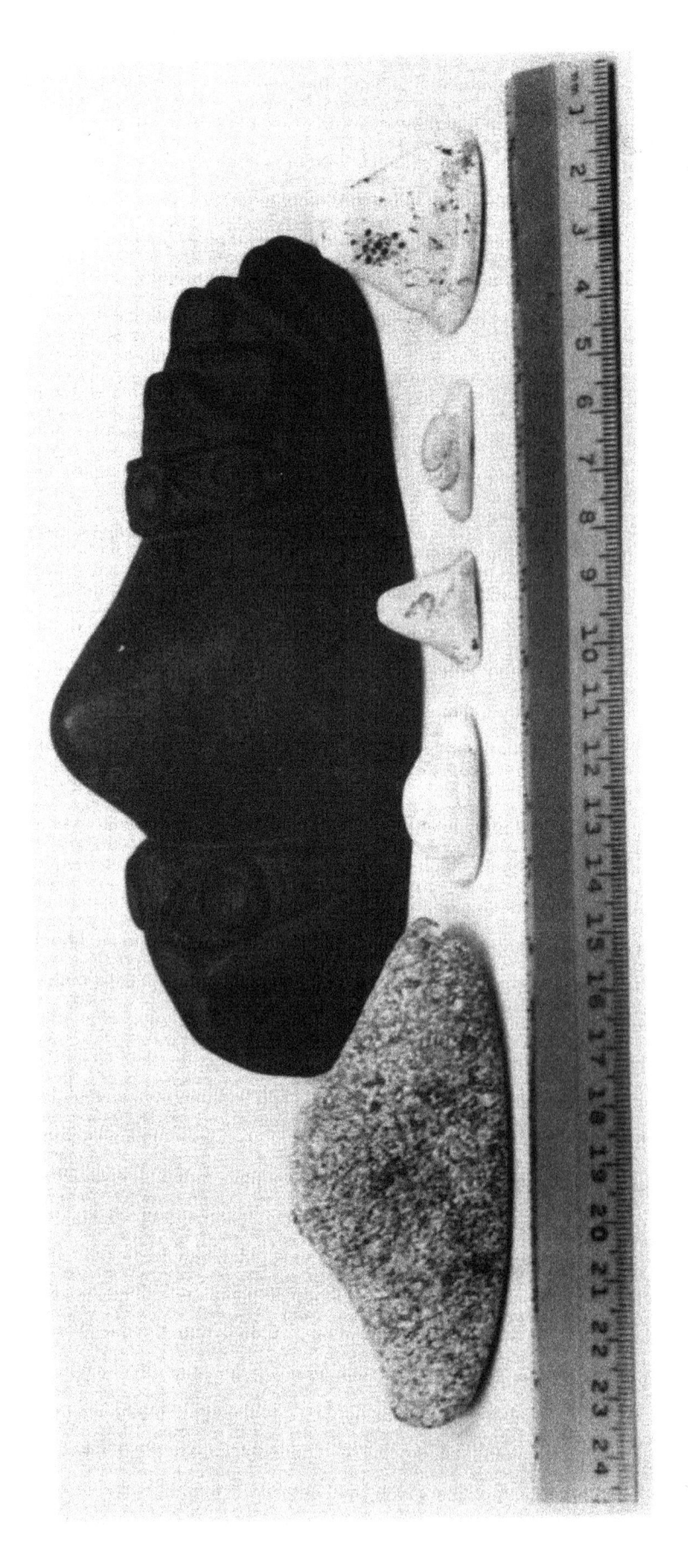

Figure 11. In the foreground of this photograph are five three-pointers recovered from Saladoid contexts in the Maisabel site. In the background is a replica of a Taino three-pointer. Even though the Taino three-pointer is much larger than the Saladoid three-pointers the similarities between both groups is clear.

Figure 12. Waiwai communal house in 1955. (From Yde 1965:153)

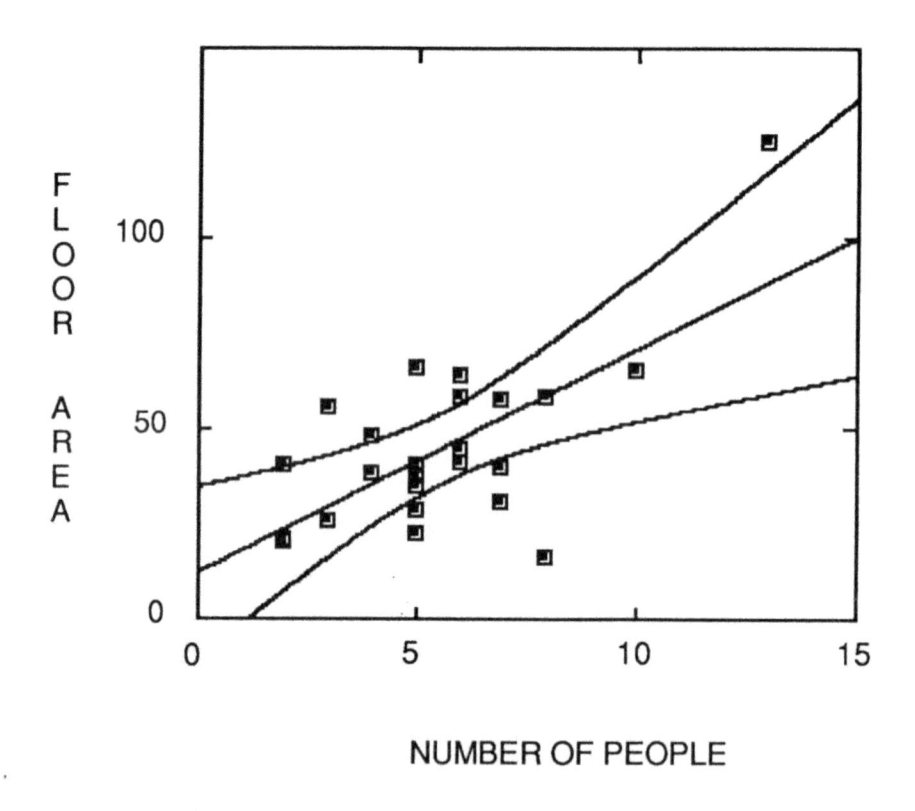

Figure 13. Relationship between floor area (m^2) of nuclear family houses with respect to number of people per house. The 95% confidence interval is plotted to emphasize the wide distribution of points around the least-squares regression line. n=24, r=0.66, r^2=0.44.

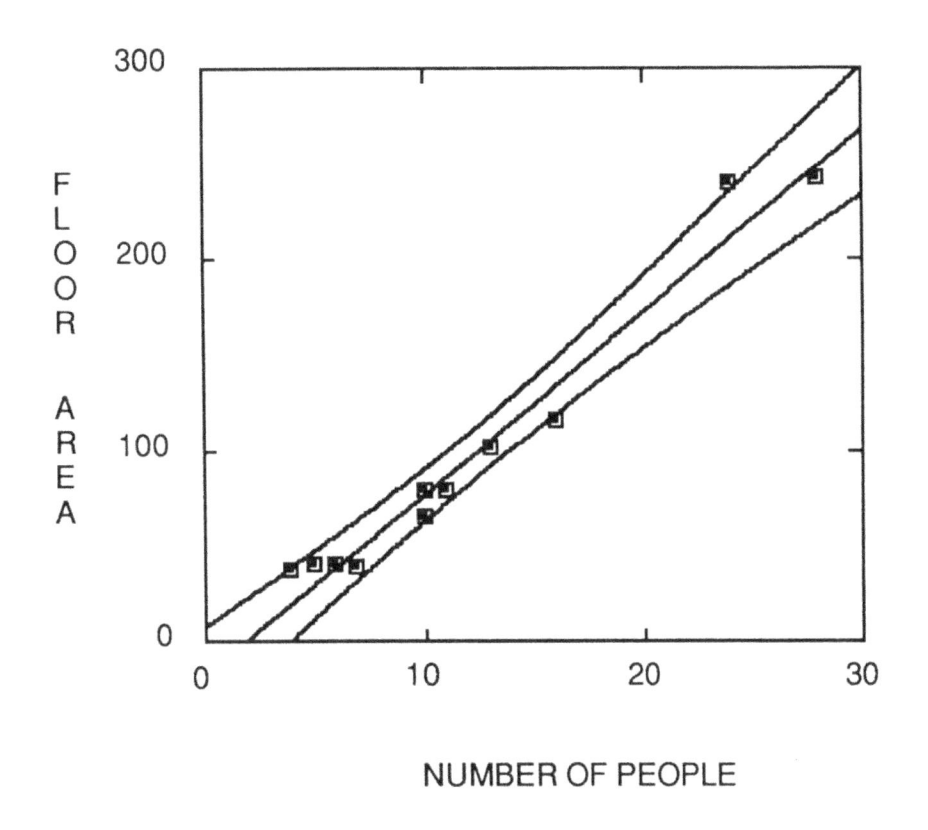

Figure 14. Relationship between household house floor areas (m^2) and number of occupants. Notice the tighter spread of points with respect to the least-squares regression line compared to figure 14. n=11, r=0.98, r^2=0.96.

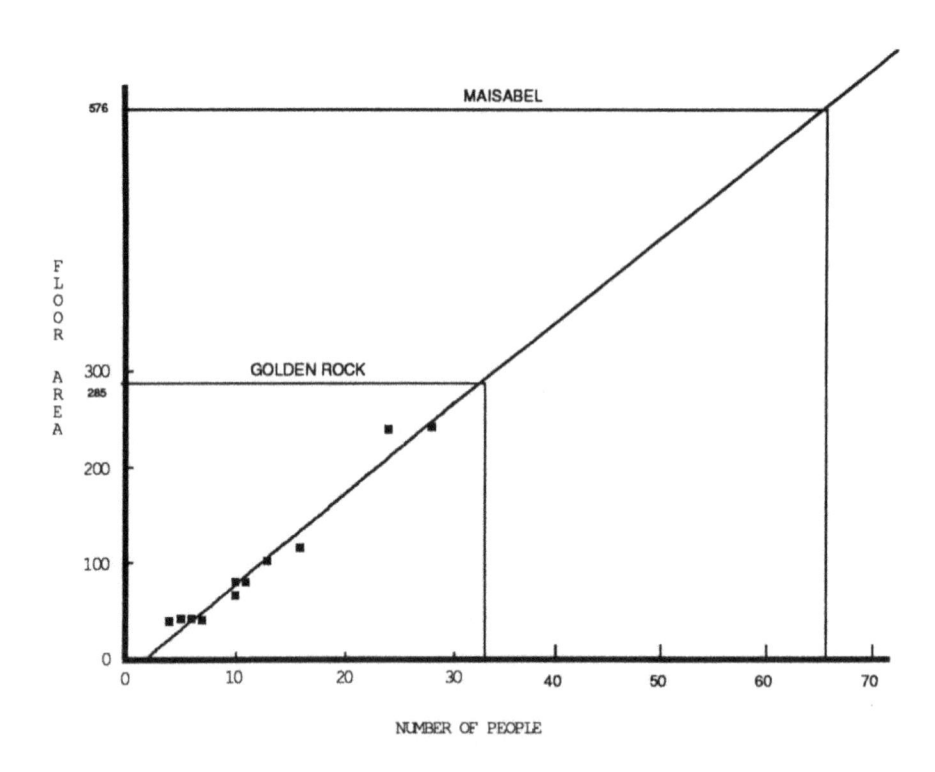

Figure 15. Using the regression equation displayed in Figure 14, the floor areas (m^2) of the communal houses recovered from the Golden Rock and Maisabel sites are plotted to determine roughly the number of people occupying each of the structures. Notice that the Maisabel house is approximately twice as large as the Golden Rock house.

Figure 16. Burial #4 as it was recovered in the field. This individual is in a flexed fetal position lying on his right side (male, older than 45 years). Notice the stingray spine projectile point parallel with the ribs.

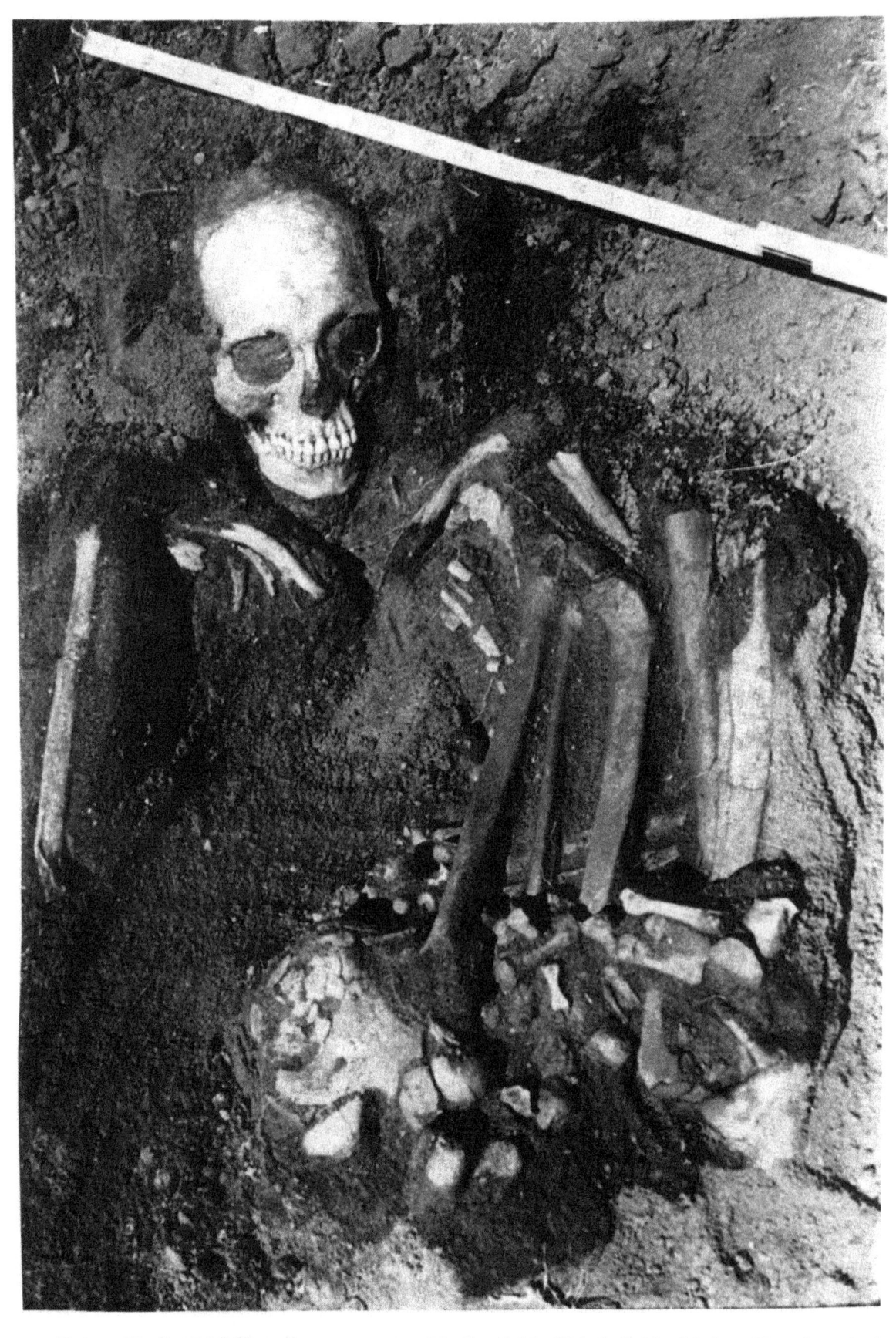

Figure 17. Burial #17 as it was recovered in the field. This individual is in a flexed seated position (male, 25-30 years). Most of the bones of this individual were present, except for the lower right arm.

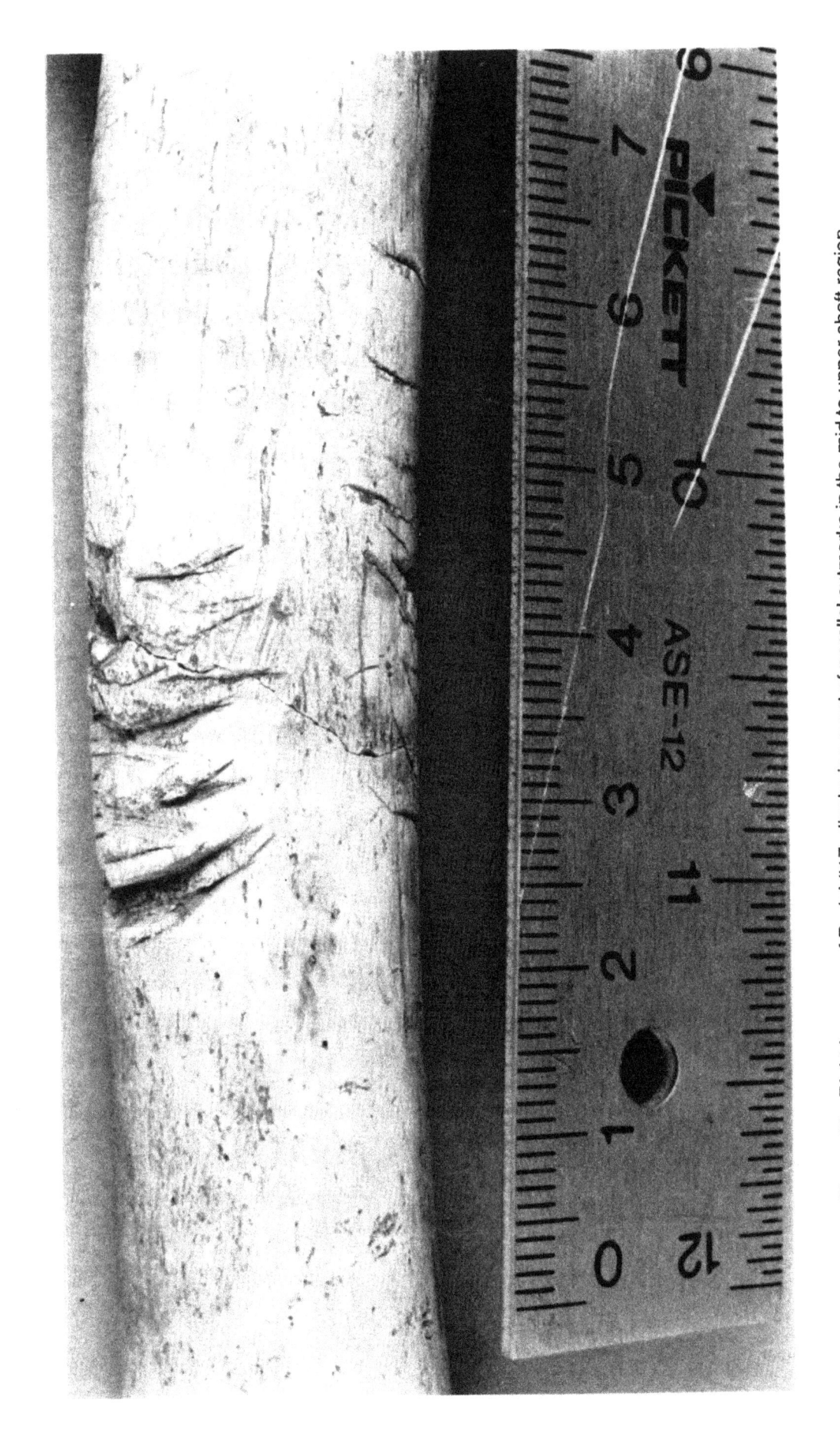

Figure 18. Right humerus of Burial #17, displaying a set of parallel cutmarks in the mid to upper shaft region of the bone.

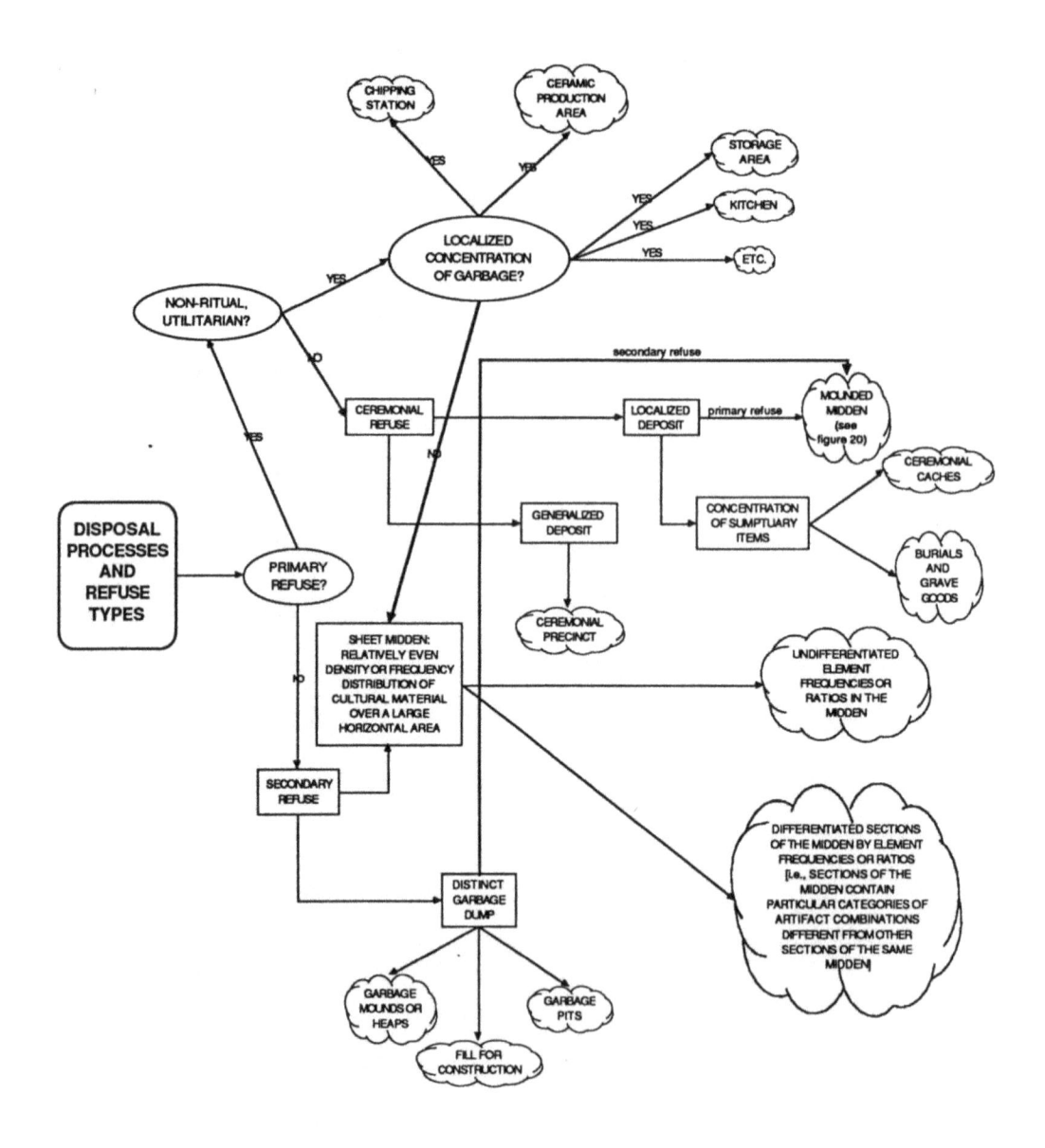

Figure 19. A general classification of disposal processes and refuse types dealt with by archaeologists. This scheme is not meant to be all inclusive. It points out the complexity of archaeological deposits and the importance of being clear in our terminological definitions.

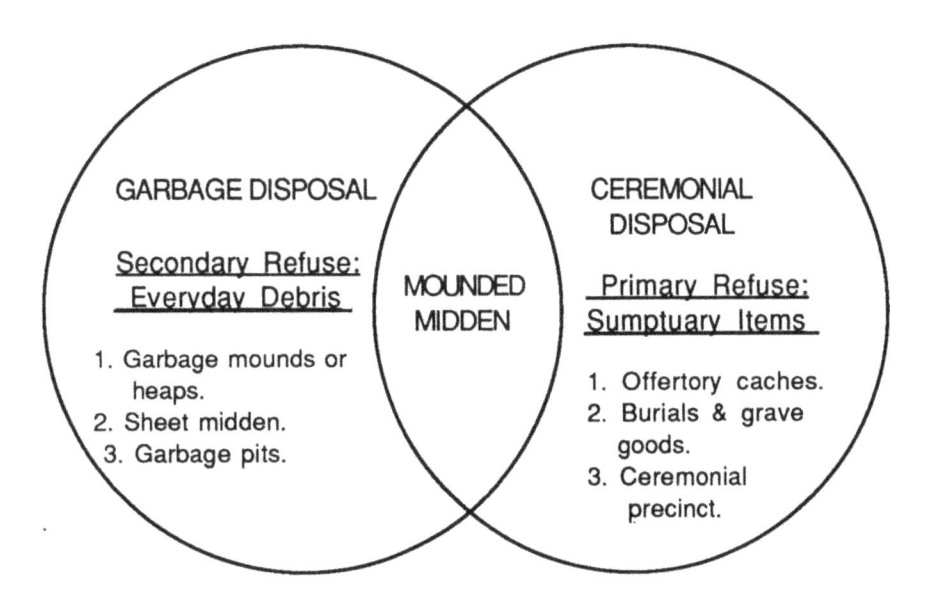

```
GARBAGE DISPOSAL                          CEREMONIAL
                                          DISPOSAL
Secondary Refuse:        MOUNDED          Primary Refuse:
 Everyday Debris         MIDDEN           Sumptuary Items

1. Garbage mounds or                      1. Offertory caches.
   heaps.                                 2. Burials & grave
2. Sheet midden.                             goods.
3. Garbage pits.                          3. Ceremonial
                                             precinct.
```

Figure 20. The refuse type, "mounded midden," is characterized by the intersection of primary ceremonial refuse and secondary everyday debris. If one of these two components is missing from the midden then it will be considered a different refuse type.

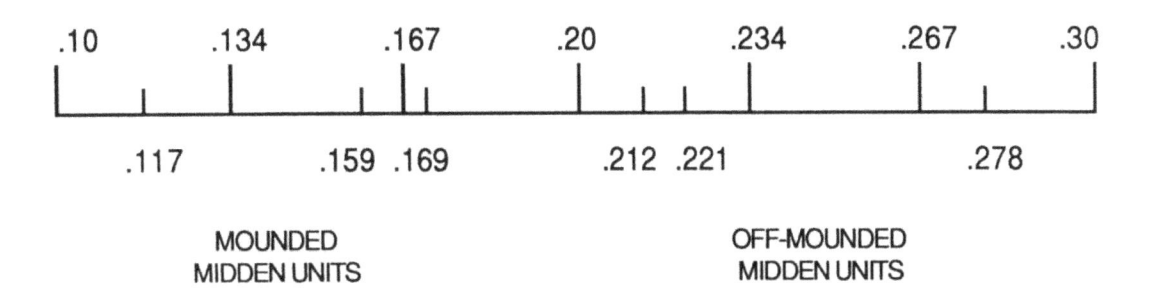

```
.10      .134     .167      .20      .234     .267     .30
 |────|───|────|──||────|────|───|────|────|────|────|
    .117       .159 .169     .212 .221          .278

       MOUNDED                         OFF-MOUNDED
     MIDDEN UNITS                      MIDDEN UNITS
```

Figure 22. The mean count/weight ratios of the mounded midden and off-mounded midden units. Notice that the mound unit values are clustered in the lower portion of the scale, while the off-mound values are located at the greater end of the scale.

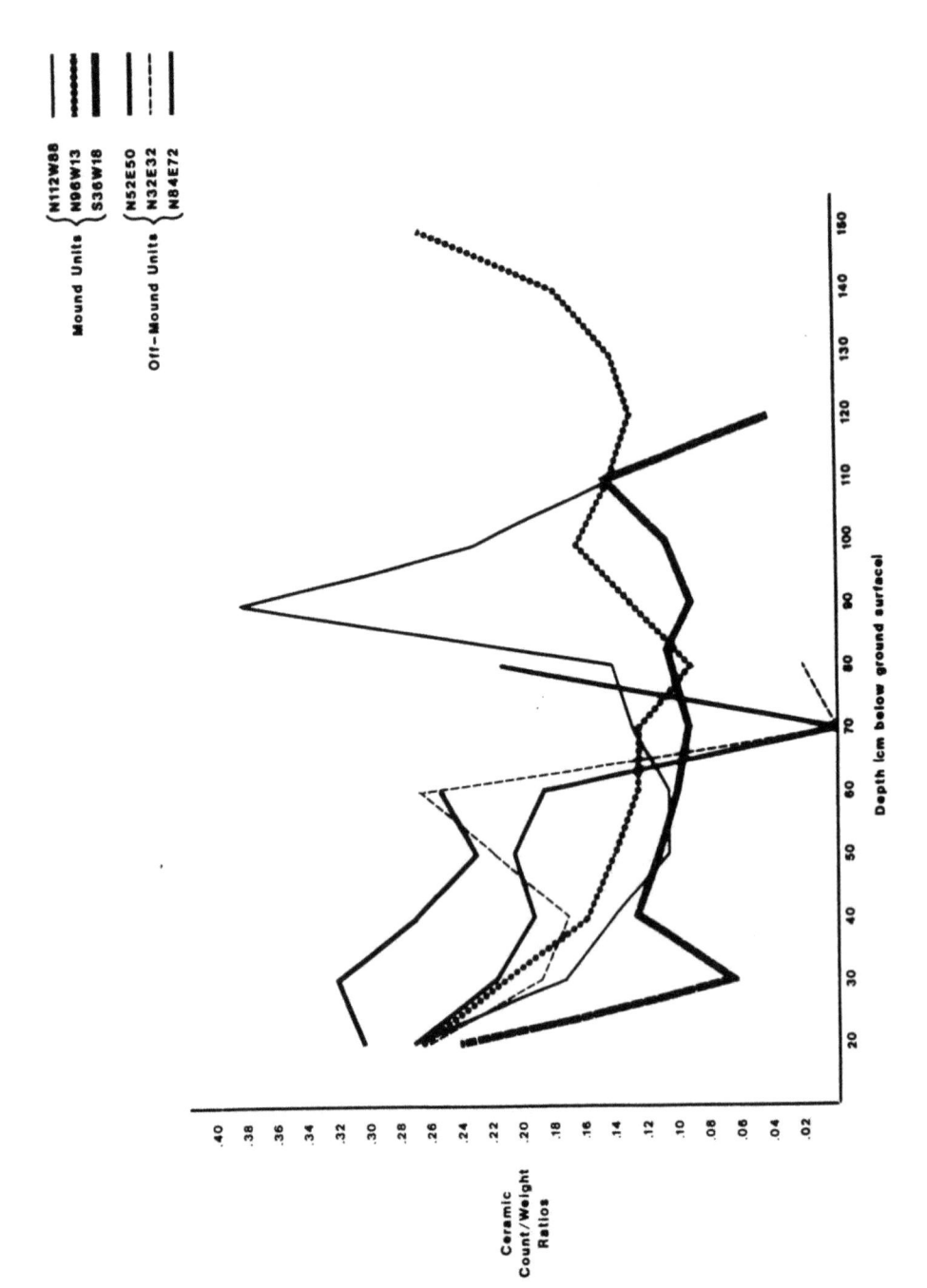

Figure 21. Ceramic count/weight ratios plotted by level for each of three on- and off-mounded midden units. The mounded midden values generally are lower than the off-mounded midden ratios.

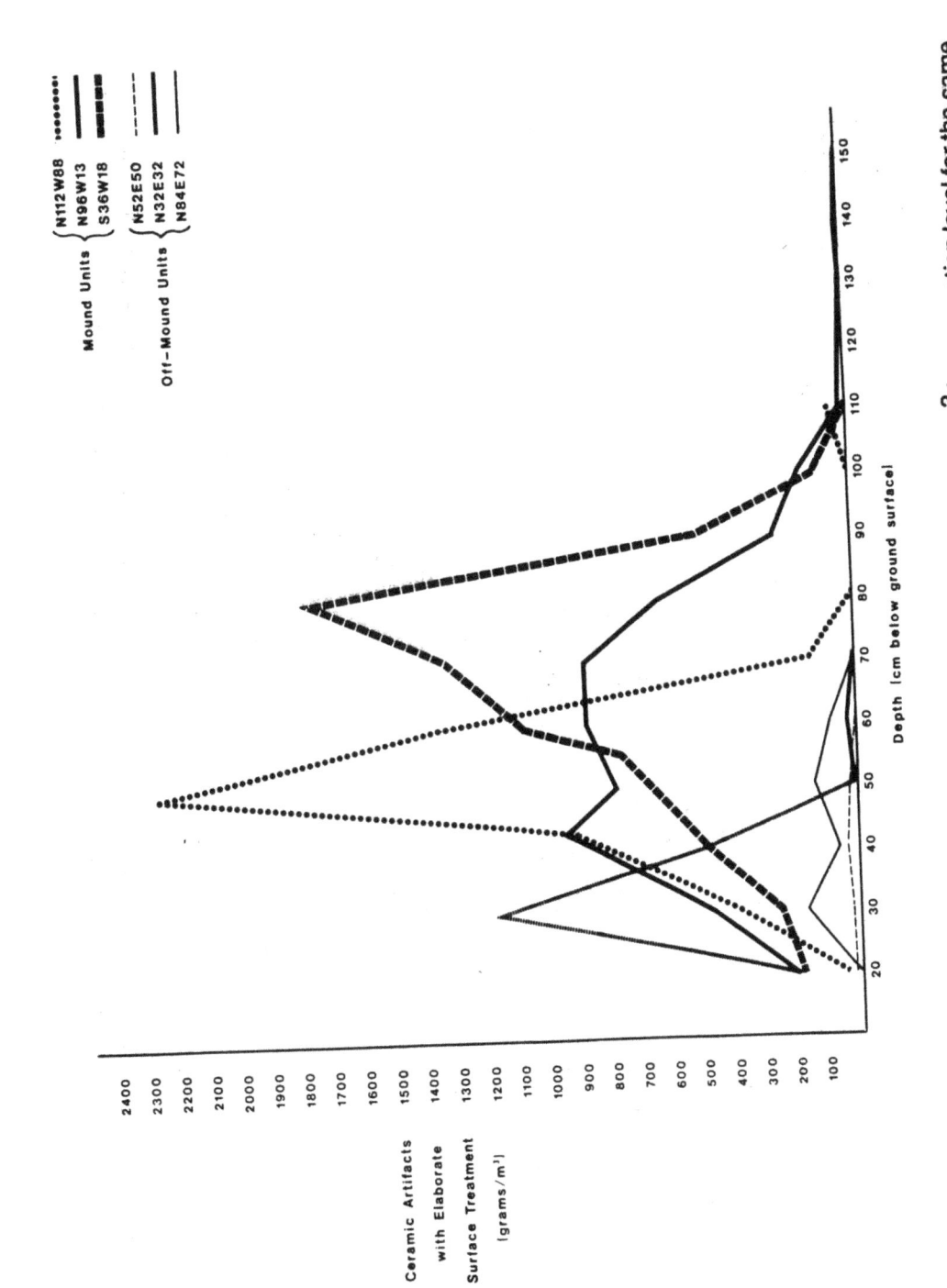

Figure 23. Ceramic artifacts with elaborate surface treatment plotted in g/m³ by excavation level for the same six units shown in Figure 21. The mounded midden units clearly have more decorated pottery than the off-midden units.

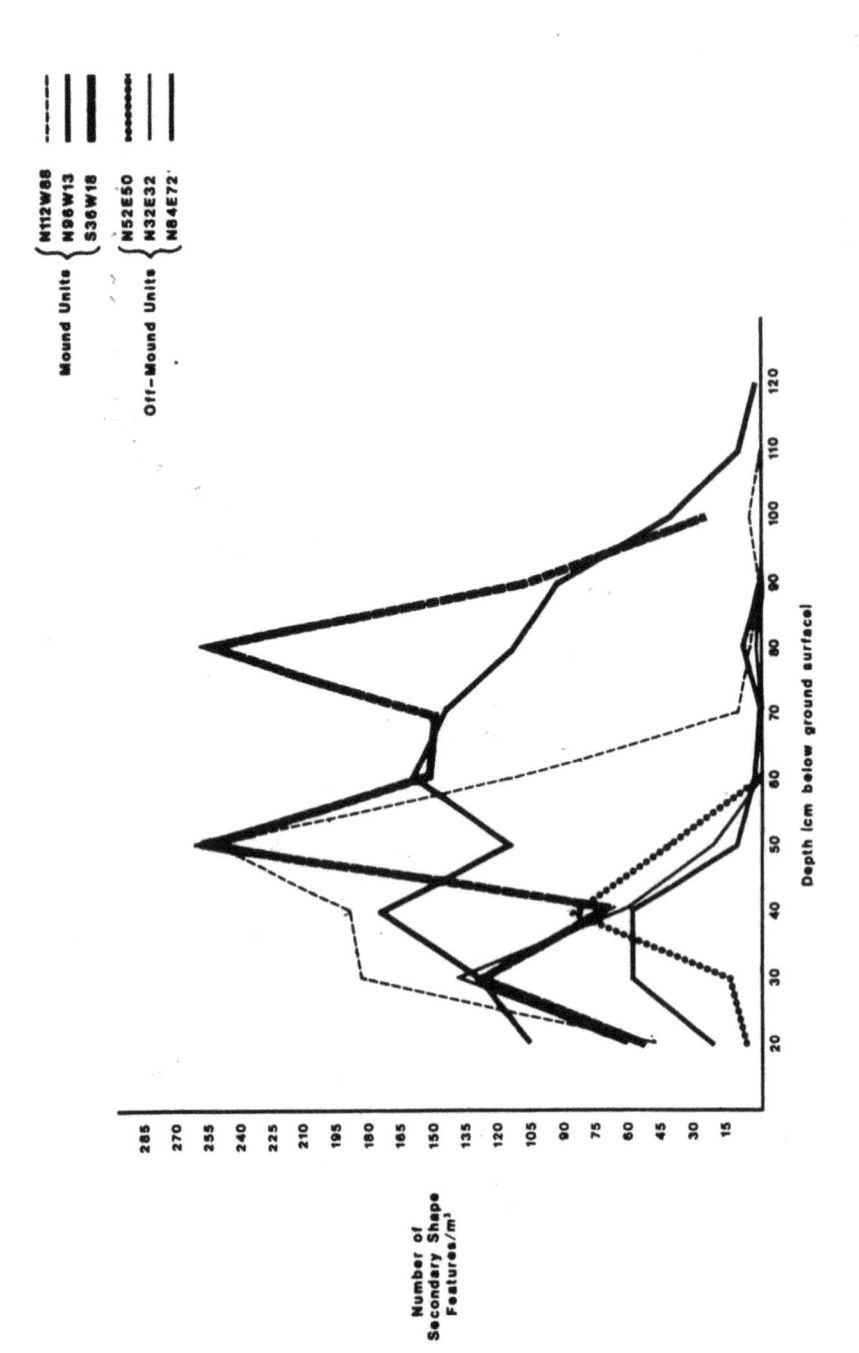

Figure 24. Number of ceramic secondary shape features/m³ plotted by excavation level for the same six units shown in Figure 21. Again, the mounded midden units generally overshadow the off-mounded midden units.

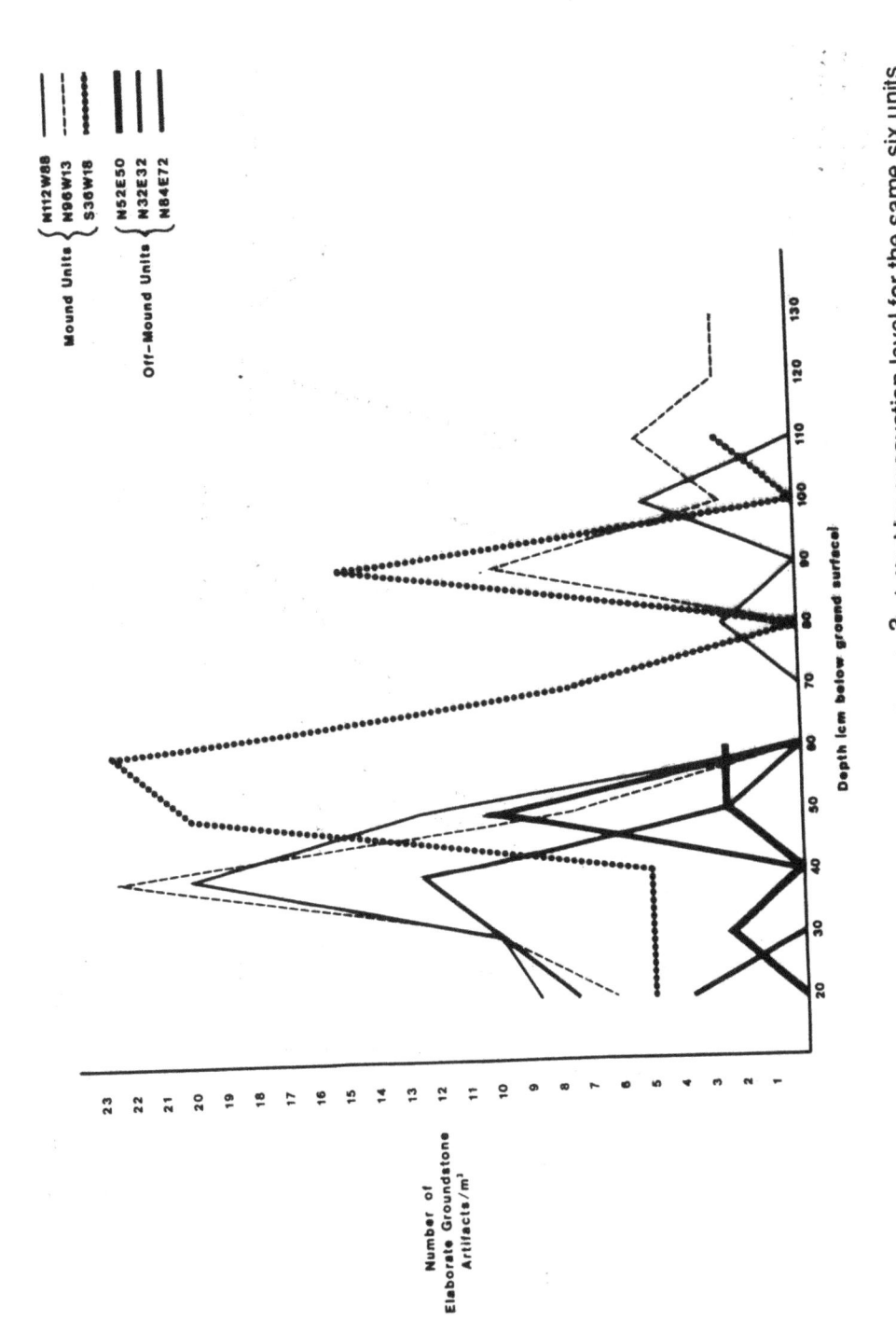

Figure 25. Number of elaborate groundstone artifacts/m^3 plotted by excavation level for the same six units shown in Figure 21. The same pattern holds as for the previously plotted relationships.

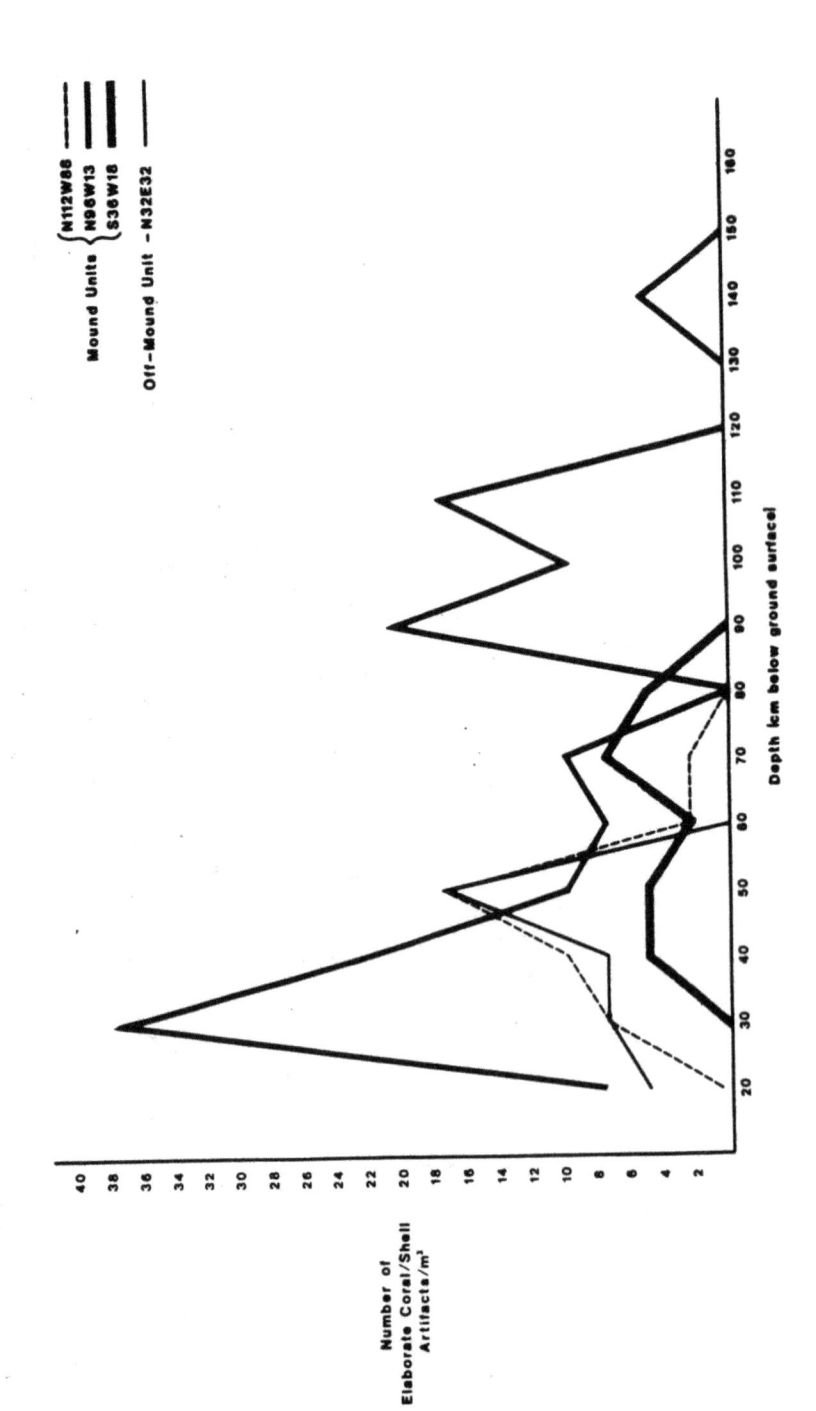

Figure 26. Number of elaborate coral/shell artifacts/m^3 plotted by excavation level for one off-mounded and three mounded midden units. In this case only one of the three off-mounded midden units examined here, had any elaborate coral or shell artifacts.

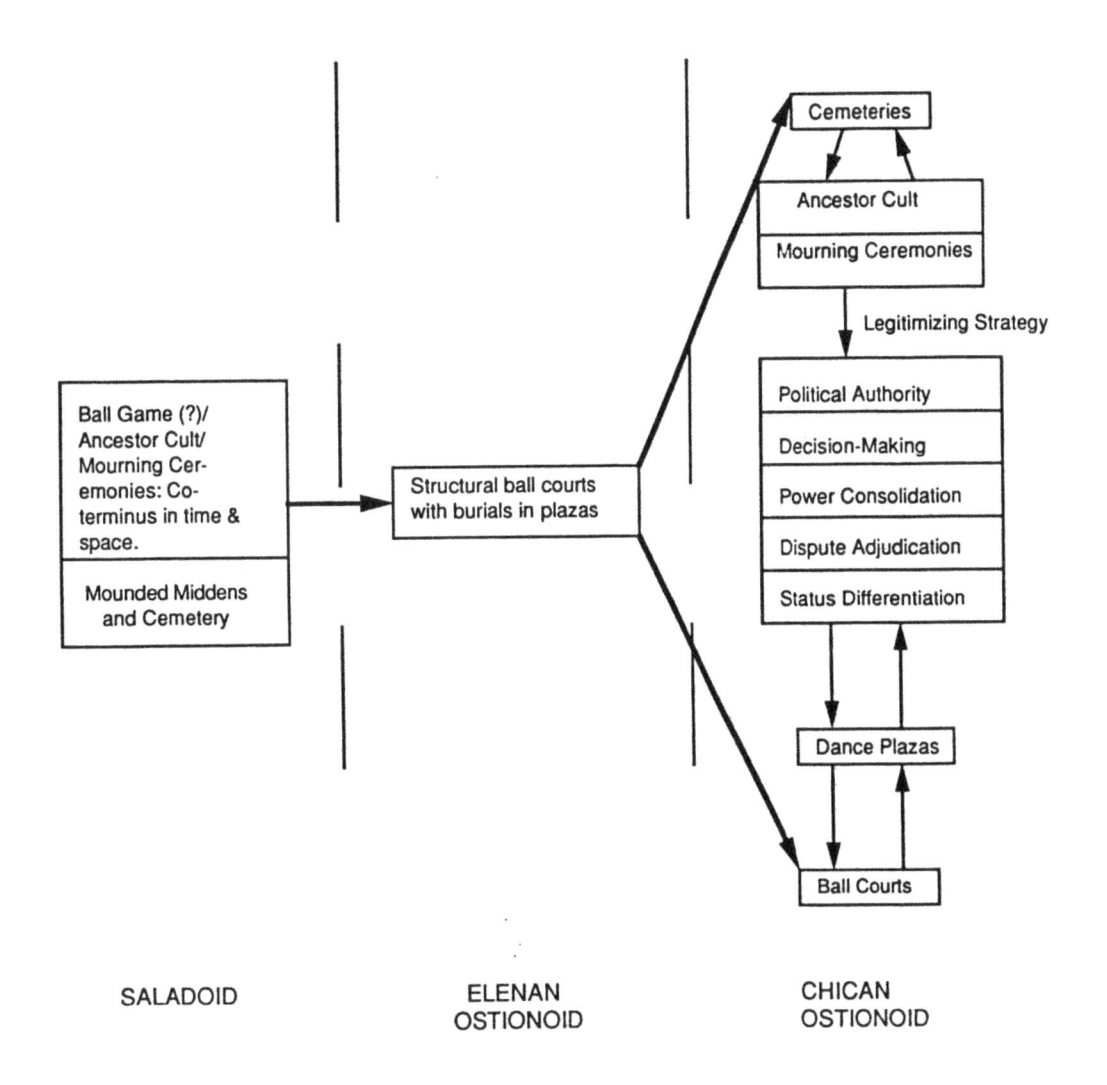

Figure 27. This model charts the development of the rubber ball game in connection with sociopolitical consolidation from the Saladoid through the protohistoric and Contact periods. Note that the ball game during the Saladoid period is listed with a question mark. There is no solid evidence for structural ball courts at this time. It could be (and I would argue that it is very likely) that the ball game was being played during the Saladoid period. Part of the sociopolitical changes resulting in the Ostionoid series are the construction of structural ball courts. At this time the ball courts and cemeteries are one in the same. The best example of this are the Ostionoid ball courts located in the large ceremonial center of Tibes, Puerto Rico. In the plaza of the largest ball court 188 burials were found. Finally, sociopolitical consolidation resulted in a differentiation and specialization of certain social control functions. Ball courts and cemeteries are no longer spatially synchronous, and are associated with distinct authority structures. The ancestor cult, which is focused on the cemetery becomes a legitimizing mechanism of the chiefly lineages in order to consolidate power. The ball court, and thus the activities associated with it, is the physical manifestation of political authority.

PART 4:

CERAMIC STYLE, POPULATION MOVEMENT, AND INTERACTION

THE ZONED INCISED CROSSHATCH (ZIC) WARE OF EARLY PRECOLUMBIAN CERAMIC AGE SITES IN PUERTO RICO AND VIEQUES ISLAND

Miguel Rodríguez

ABSTRACT

The geographic distribution and cultural association of the zoned incised crosshatch (ZIC) pottery is reviewed for the early Ceramic age sites of Puerto Rico and Vieques Island. Two basic patterns are observed: first, ZIC pottery mixed (albeit as a minority ceramic ware) with the predominantly painted pottery of the Hacienda Grande and Cuevas styles; and second, ZIC pottery as a distinctive ceramic style (La Hueca) in horizontally and vertically segregated deposits, though in close proximity or under Hacienda Grande and Cuevas deposits. Both patterns are concurrent in some sites on the north coast of Puerto Rico and on both sides of the Vieques Sound region. Additional research is required to clarify conflicting data on the chronology of the ZIC pottery, its local diffusion routes and possible stylistic influences of this pottery on later ceramic developments in the Greater Antilles.

INTRODUCTION

The purpose of this paper is to review the current state of knowledge concerning the geographic distribution, cultural associations, and stratigraphic context of the zoned incised crosshatched (ZIC) ware[1] found in early Precolumbian sites in Puerto Rico and the neighboring island of Vieques. The data I will present are derived from the published archaeological literature, unpublished studies, personal communications and the preliminary findings of field work still in progress.

Although it is limited to findings in the northeastern corner of the Caribbean, this study is relevant to the whole context of regional archaeology. From an ecological and geographical standpoint, Puerto Rico and Vieques are the linking units between the Lesser and the Greater Antilles. Furthermore, the current resurgence of the old controversy relating to the relationship of the ZIC ware to the first migrations of pottery-making, horticultural peoples from South America is based specifically upon recent findings from these islands (Chanlatte and Narganes 1980; Chanlatte 1983; Rodríguez and Rivera 1987).[2]

THE ZIC WARE

In 1934 the archaeologist Froelich Rainey (1940) identified, for the first time in Puerto Rico, ZIC ware sherds. He collected these samples from the deepest "Crab Culture" levels in the Precolumbian sites of Canas, Ponce, on the south coast, and Monserrate, Luquillo, on the northeastern coast of the island[3] (see Figure 1 for the locations of the sites mentioned in the text). The number of specimens he recovered was relatively low. For example, only 11 of the 859 sherds he excavated from the "Crab Culture" levels of the Canas site were ZIC ware sherds.[4] Rainey grouped them together under his sub-classification "b," i.e., incised designs applied after firing (which would actually make them engraving), under his "Plain Brown Ware" major category (Rainey 1940:57, [see Figure 2]). From this moment on, the ZIC ware became one of the diagnostic ceramic characteristics of the "Crab Culture," identified by Rainey as the material remains of the earliest ceramic-bearing insular settlers of the Caribbean.

Rainey also noted the clear stylistic association of this ware with that of the Lesser Antilles and the coast of Venezuela. This relationship helped to establish the first model of settlement of the Caribbean Basin as being a northbound migratory movement departing from the coast of Venezuela, first for the islands of the Lesser, and then for the Greater Antilles.

Following Rainey, the archaeologist Irving Rouse excavated 44 additional sites in Puerto Rico and the neighboring islands of Vieques and Mona.[5] Rouse also investigated new sites where he identified certain sherds that he believed to be intrusive, or trade sherds, from the Lesser Antilles. These were: two sherds from the Las Cucharas site in the vicinity of the town of Lajas on the southwest coast, that he associated with the Cedros style from Trinidad (Rouse 1952:401-402); one sherd from Coto, the Isabela site on the northwest coast, that he linked with the Palo Seco style also from Trinidad (1952:432-433); and one sherd from Cayo Santiago, a small key off the eastern coast, near the town of Humacao, that he related to both the Palo Seco and the Cedros styles (1952:553).

Besides these four sherds, Rouse acquired four additional presumed trade sherds from local residents that he also related to the styles of the Lesser Antilles. Three of these, two from Buenos Aires, Coamo, and one from the Canas site, Ponce, he classified within the Cedros style, while the fourth, from Carmen, Salinas, Rouse related to the Palo Seco style (Rouse 1952:544).

Even though Rouse did not make specific descriptions of these specimens, he considered that certain unpainted incised crosshatched sherds found in Puerto Rico were reminiscent of the Cedros style in Trinidad (Rouse 1952:339). Thus, it is possible to infer that the fragments recovered from the new sites of Las Cucharas, Cayo Santiago and Buenos Aires were indeed ZIC sherds.[6]

Based upon his research in Puerto Rico, Rouse reformulated the ceramic style associated with Rainey's "Crab Culture" and named it "Cuevas" because he believed that his Cuevas site, on the north coast, was more representative of the earliest pottery-making migrants to Puerto Rico than Rainey's Canas site (1952:413-417). In Rouse's early pottery diffusion model, the "Cuevas" style corresponded to Period II of his chronology for Caribbean prehistory. This Cuevas style was subdivided into two phases: (a) an early phase with polychrome painting, elaborate white-on-red painted designs and incised decoration, and (b) a later phase with only simple white-on-red painted designs at the beginning and just plain and polished pottery for the rest of the phase (1952:339).[7]

According to Rouse, the few specimens of ZIC decoration found at any one site, as well as the small number of sites with ZIC ware around the island, argued against the inclusion of this variation as one of the basic elements defining the "Crab Culture" in general and his "Cuevas" style in particular.[8] Although he repeatedly designated them as being intrusive or "Cedros" trade sherds, (thus not considering this ware to be of local manufacture), the ZIC variation was included in Period IIa of the "Cuevas" style, and one ZIC sherd from Canas was included as part of the sample sherds in a plate visually summarizing the "Cuevas" style (1952:443, Pl. 2j).

During the succeeding decades the archaeologist Ricardo Alegría conducted extensive excavations in three large coastal sites in the northeastern section of Puerto Rico: Monserrate, Luquillo; Hacienda Grande, Loíza (Alegría 1965); and El Convento in San Juan (Pons de Alegría 1973). These sites yielded abundant ceramics with elaborate ZIC designs associated with the early Period IIa "Cuevas" style. Based on the stratigraphic and stylistic analysis of his finds at the Hacienda Grande site, Alegría included the ZIC ware in his definition of a new early ceramic complex of the "Igneri" culture. This "Hacienda Grande" complex corresponded to the earliest ceramic-manufacturing and horticulturalist inhabitants of the Caribbean.

According to Alegría (1965:246-249) his new "Hacienda Grande" pottery style included polychrome painting and elaborate bichrome white-on-red designs on inverted bell-shaped vessels, as well as curvilinear incised designs and ZIC ware (Figure 3). Regarding ZIC ware, Alegría's findings made two facts evident: First, the ZIC ware from his Hacienda Grande excavations was stratigraphically associated with all of the early elements of Igneri culture. Second, because of its abundance, ZIC ware must have been locally produced and not "intrusive" or "trade sherds" from the Lesser Antilles.

In the addendum to the preface of his 1952 (pp. 308-309) monograph and by 1964 separately (p. 509), Rouse recognized these new findings from Loíza and inserted Hacienda Grande as the earliest style of the Saladoid series; that is, he placed it before his now redefined Cuevas style. He also reviewed his concept of the ZIC ware as intrusive or trade ware from the Lesser Antilles and revised it to include local production. This review also led Rouse to upgrade the importance of the ZIC ware. Indeed, he selected it as a time marker for the entry of the earliest poottery-making settlers in the Caribbean islands, including Puerto Rico.[9]

The El Convento site, located in Old San Juan underneath two sixteenth century historic buildings, is one of the key sites for the study of ZIC ware in Puerto Rico. Archaeological excavations at the El Convento site were conducted under Alegría's supervision during the course of a major restoration project of the historic structures. The recovered ceramic artifacts were analyzed from a stylistic and technological perspective by Pons de Alegría (1973). In this site, the ZIC ware appears to be as important as the polychrome and the white-on-red painted wares. However, due to the fact that the site had been disturbed for centuries by the historic buildings, the different wares were excavated mixed together within the same levels (Pons de Alegría 1973: 126).[10]

In the wake of the well-publicized findings of Alegría's original work at Hacienda Grande, a considerable number of amateurs and collectors conducted unsupervised digging at the site. One of them, George Warreck, a former University of Puerto Rico professor, obtained samples of ZIC ware sherds, mostly from the northwestern quadrant of the site (George Warreck, personal communication 1975). Warreck's information suggests that the ZIC ware might have been spatially segregated at Hacienda Grande, that is, it may have been the predominant component in specific sectors of the site.[11] Warreck also published a classification of 655 ZIC sherds from Hacienda Grande (Warreck 1972:3-5).

The decade of the 1970s began with the initiation of important long-term research projects in Puerto Rico, some of them relevant to the present subject. In Las Flores, Coamo (close to the site of Buenos Aires where two possible ZIC sherds were previously identified by Rouse), Ortíz Aguilú (1975) found some ZIC ware fragments in close association with Hacienda Grande style potsherds (Juan José Ortíz Aguilú, personal communication 1978). In addition, the Collores, Juana Díaz site, also on the southcentral coast, which earlier had been excavated by Rainey (and his collection studied by Rouse [1952]), became again the subject of controlled excavations by myself (Rodríguez 1983). There, in association with Cuevas style artifacts (the second and final style of the now redesignated Cedrosan Saladoid subseries [Rouse1986]), we found two ZIC sherds (Rodríguez 1983:128, Figure 23a).

Another site, Puerta de Tierra, San Juan (also previously worked by Rouse), was excavated extensively under the direction of Gus Pantel of the Fundación Arqueológica de Puerto Rico in 1987. Although his findings have not been published, I know of various fragments of ZIC ware that were collected from the eroded and mixed surface levels of that site.[12] Even though these sherds were found within disturbed levels, and thus lack a clear stratigraphic and cultural context, they are nevertheless important because they again, as in Collores, hint at the association of some ZIC ware sherds with the later Cuevas component, rather than with the Hacienda Grande component.

Towards the end of the decade, the Centro de Investigaciones Arqueológicas of the University of Puerto Rico Museum began a long-term field project at the sites of Tecla, Guayanilla, on the southern coast of Puerto Rico, and Sorcé, located on the southwestern coast of the neighboring island of Vieques (Chanlatte 1976, 1983; Chanlatte and Narganes 1980). Both of these sites are large Cedrosan Saladoid settlements in whose ceramic collections there are some ZIC decorated fragments next to typical polychrome and white-on-red (WOR) sherds.

At first, the relatively low number of ZIC sherds found at both Tecla and Sorcé confirmed the vertical stratigraphic associations of this ware originally described from the Canas, Monserrate, Hacienda Grande and El Convento sites. However, all this changed with the discovery of a large purely ZIC ware component at the "La Hueca" southern sector of the Sorcé site in Vieques by Chanlatte.[13] As a result of Chanlatte's excavation, the hoary controversy of the ZIC ware and its archaeological implications was reopened and took a new turn. During a number of years Chanlatte and Narganes (1980,1983) announced the identification of a new agro-ceramic "cultural complex," which they designated "La Hueca." According to these investigators some of the main characteristics of the La Hueca Cultural Complex are: the exclusive presence of ZIC ware, elaborate effigy and "snuff"-inhaling ceremonial vessels and a highly sophisticated lapidary industry composed of microbeads, carved zoomorphic amulets and pendants made of semi-precious exotic stones. The horizontal segregation of the exclusive ZIC ware deposits in the La Hueca sector from the typical Hacienda Grande mixed painted and ZIC ware components at the Sorcé site confirmed the separate identity of the ZIC assemblage.[14]

In recent years the Centro de Investigaciones Indígenas de Puerto Rico has undertaken a multidisciplinary research project at the north coastal site of Maisabel, Vega Baja (Siegel 1986, this volume; Siegel and Bernstein 1987; Siegel and Roe 1987). According to published reports the Maisabel site is another example where ZIC sherds are found in Hacienda Grande contexts.[15]

The discovery of a new site located in Punta Candelero, Humacao, on the southeastern coast of Puerto Rico was announced by its amateur discoverer in 1986 (Rivera 1986). Between 1987 and 1988 it was tested and extensively excavated under my supervision (Rodríguez and Rivera 1987; Rodríguez 1988). The site, located on the western side of the Vieques Sound area, opposite from, and under certain conditions within sight of the Sorcé-La Hueca site on the island of Vieques, also has two distinct vertically and horizontally segregated ceramic components: ZIC ware (Figures 4-6), and Cuevas, the latter being found always in the top levels of the main ZIC ware deposits. On the basis of the new findings the purely segregated ZIC ware is now redefined by Rouse as a separate La Hueca style, which co-existed in the Cedrosan Saladoid subseries alongside Hacienda Grande and the other initial Saladoid styles from the West Indies (Irving Rouse, personal communication 1987).

However, until the present no Hacienda Grande component has been found at the site of Punta Candelero or in its immediate vicinity, although a later Monserrate style ceramic component (the first of the Elenan Ostionoid subseries) is present in the southeastern section of the site. This is yet another departure from the previous vertical and horizontal stratigraphic associations of the ZIC ware with the Hacienda Grande style WOR sherds in most of the other major and well documented sites of Puerto Rico such as Canas, Monserrate, Hacienda Grande, El Convento, Sorcé-La Hueca and Maisabel.

In relation to the C-14 dating of the site, we were able to obtain during our first testing in 1987 two C-14 dates ranging between 250 B.C. and A.D. 10 in association with the ZIC ware, some of the earliest dates for a ceramic site in Puerto Rico (Table 1). But a new set of seven C-14 dates are surprisingly late, ranging between A.D. 560 and 1340. They were obtained during our 1988 field season (Table 1). Also, a date ranging between A.D. 1030 and 1190 was recovered, which relates to the Cuevas ware. Chanlatte's twelve published C-14 dates for La Hueca style of the Sorcé-La Hueca site, range between 75 B.C. and A.D. 325 (Chanlatte and Narganes 1983:65-66). But a set of eight new C-14 dates obtained in 1987 from a section of the original Midden Z of La Hueca extended between A.D. 1080 and 1510 (Luis Chanlatte, personal communication 1989). Obviously, the C-14 dating analysis of the horizontally segregated ZIC ware deposits from La Hueca and Punta Candelero is not clear and will have to await further studies.[16]

Besides these documented sites, I have been able to confirm the existence of ZIC ware in at least three other coastal sites in Puerto Rico. This information has been obtained through a combination of systematic testing, surface visual inspection, and interviews with local and amateur informants. These three additional sites are Ensenada, Rincón (Rodríguez 1985), facing the Mona Passage in the westernmost tip of the island (Figure 7), Guamaní, Guayama (Rodríguez 1987) on the southeastern coast, and Victor Rojas, located under the old section of the city of Arecibo on the northwestern coast. There is no definite information now available regarding the vertical or horizontal stratigraphic relationships of the ZIC samples within these three sites, nor of their cultural contexts. However, in all three sites there are also Hacienda Grande ceramic style samples.

CONCLUSIONS

My research has identified ZIC ware from 17 sites in Puerto Rico and the neighboring island of Vieques. In terms of the total sample of sites, 17 is a high number, especially when one takes into account the relative lack of knowledge about the regional distribution of this ceramic ware in the Lesser and Greater Antilles.[17]

In addition, ZIC ware is well represented throughout this part of the Greater Antilles and adjacent portions of the Lesser Antilles (Puerto Rico and Vieques respectively). There are six sites with ZIC ware along the northern coast of Puerto Rico, seven along the southern coast, one on the western coast and the remaining three in the east, on both sides of the Vieques Sound area. Most of these are coastal sites, close to stands of mangroves and in direct association with fertile sandy soils, but no extensive exploitation of shellfish is reported. This is the typical settlement pattern for all the early pottery-making and horticulturalist groups on the island.

The strongest concentration of the ZIC ware appears to be on the eastern and northern areas of Puerto Rico, where this pottery is associated with Hacienda Grande deposits at the Sorcé-La Hueca, Monserrate, Hacienda Grande and El Convento sites. It is also spatially segregated in horizontally distinct, exclusive deposits within or close to Saladoid (early and late) settlements in Sorcé-La Hueca and Punta Candelero (and possibly also in Hacienda Grande and El Convento). It is also in this region that the ZIC ware appears to be most numerous, have its greatest stylistic complexity and to be found in what looks like the context of ceremonial and religous practices and an extensive trade network system.

In contrast, there seems to be an attenuated presence of ZIC ware on the south and west coast of Puerto Rico. In those regions, ZIC ware is usually reduced to a few sherds within both early and late Cedrosan Saladoid contexts. This latter pattern may very well lead to a reapplication of the intrusive and/or "trade ware" concept, but not from the Lesser Antilles, where it is thought to have persisted later than in the Greater Antilles (Rouse, personal communication 1989), but rather from the larger sites of La Hueca and Punta Candelero to the east, if the late C-14 dates from these sites are verified.

The present distributional evidence suggests the possibility of two cultural patterns for the ZIC ware in Puerto Rico: one in association with the Hacienda Grande and Cuevas styles as a minority ware, and the other as a distinctive ceramic style (La Hueca style). However in that latter case the ZIC ware maintains some sort of relationship with Cedrosan Saladoid components.[18]

It is possible that both patterns originated elsewhere before arriving to the northeastern Caribbean. Upon reaching the islands of Vieques and Puerto Rico the movement of people comprising the "La Hueca" ZIC-type materials divided into two main routes. Perhaps the major east-to-west route of diffusion was along the north coast of Puerto Rico, with a subsidiary, and possibly later, movement along the southern coast. Tantalizing uncertainties as to the temporal duration of the ZIC ware and its ultimate fate await further investigations.

NOTES

1. I am using "ware" in a very general sense in this paper to include the whole range of plain, punctated, modeled and linear incised pottery which is associated with the ZIC pottery, rather than just the specific zoned incised material. Thus my usage corresponds to that of a "ceramic assemblage or complex," rather than a "ware" within a particular "style" as Rouse uses it.

2. For a regional and theoretical review of the ZIC ware controversy see: Lathrap (1970); Harris (1978); Chanlatte and Narganes (1980, 1983); Rouse (1982, 1986); Chanlatte (1983, 1984); Roe (1985); Rodríguez and Rivera (1987).

3. These and other Puerto Rican sites were excavated by Rainey as part of the major scientific survey of the island organized under the auspices of the Peabody Museum, Yale University, the American Museum of Natural History in New York, and in cooperation with the University of Puerto Rico, and published by the New York Academy of Sciences.

4. During the course of research in the collections of the Peabody Museum of Yale University in 1984, I had the opportunity to examine the ZIC sherds Rainey recovered. These sherds belong to sections of the angular labial flanges of rounded, open bowls. In some examples they appeared in combination with appliqué nubbins and tabular handles (Figure 2).

5. This project was conducted between 1936 and 1938 under the auspices of the Caribbean Anthropological Program of the Peabody Museum of Yale University and the University of Puerto Rico.

6. Although Rouse could have been referring to either the plain, zic incised or painted pottery of the Cedros style, there are reasons for arguing that it was the similarity of the zic incised pottery obtained in some Puerto Rican sites that caught his attention. First, plain and painted pottery of a similar cast already existed in a local form at both the Canas site and in his own Cuevas materials. Therefore, why go to Trinidad for a prototype when local examples existed? My suggestion that some of these sherds were zic incised needs to be checked in the Yale collections. I did check those ZIC sherds from Canas and Monserrate during my visit to Yale in 1985.

7. From his early research in Puerto Rico and other islands, Rouse established the basic model of the Precolumbian peopling of the Caribbean and its cultural chronology that is still in use by most researchers regionally. In addition, he systematically defined the concepts and nomenclature for the major aboriginal ceramic styles, and the series to which they pertained in

Puerto Rico as well as in the rest of the Greater Antilles, the Lesser Antilles and adjacent regions of South America.

8. The relatively low number of ZIC sherds produced by the early excavations can be explained in many ways. In the case of Rainey's extensive excavations, one might suggest that since the samples were selected and classified by hand in the field, it is possible that many of the ZIC specimens were discarded as being undecorated (plain) domestic ware. Without washing and a thorough examination, ZIC ware sherds can often pass for plain ware. Rouse's excavations, although more carefully conducted, were designed to establish chronology. Therefore, they were limited to a few "telephone booth" test pits (four or eight two meter square sections). In most of these sites the early "Cuevas" component (later designated as "Hacienda Grande") was spatially restricted or missing altogether. While field or laboratory identification problems cannot be ruled out, it therefore seems most likely that ZIC sherds were not present in Rouse's test pits simply because either his pits missed the ZIC middens or those deposits did not exist at the sites.

9. As a result of Alegría's findings, Rouse modified his chronological cultural model by replacing his Period IIa of the Igneri culture (his Cuevas style) with the Hacienda Grande phase or style. Henceforth, his Cuevas style would be placed within Period IIb. Added to other early local styles from the Lesser Antilles and Venezuela, the Hacienda Grande and the Cuevas styles then came to comprise the Saladoid series.

My paraphrase of Rouse's changing perception of the material does not reflect all the alterations that he has gone through confronting the actual material. As such, it conveys a schematic picture of his attempts to wrestle with the complexities of the material and does not do full justice to his conceptual flexibility. For example, Rouse went through three stages, not two, in his recognition of the Hacienda Grande style departing from his original formulation of Cuevas as confronted by Alegría's findings. He first noted higher percentages of zic incisions in Alegría's sample than he found in his own Cuevas pottery. This led him to believe as of 1952 (in his addendum to the introduction of his monograph, not in the text) that Alegría's new find was a different variant of Cuevas, rather than two phases within the Cuevas style as his 1952 text had it. By 1964 Rouse had "seen enough of Alegría's pottery to realize that it represented a separate style rather than a variant of my Cuevas style" (Rouse, personal communication 1989). This entire sequence is relevant because it parallels Rouse's current thinking about the La Hueca style, "which I first considered to be a variant on the Hacienda Grande style and later recognized as a separate style in its own right" (Rouse, personal communication 1989).

10. It was from a study of the ZIC designs in the El Covento site that their great variety came to be recognized for the first time in Puerto Rico. For example, the zoomorphic sculptural elements (also referred to as "elephant trunk" body projections-see Figures 3 and 4) and other novel decorative elements like the zoned incisions without crosshatching, parallel lines of punctations, and clusters of short incised lines, were noted (Pons de Alegría 1973:Plates 47 and 55). All of these decorative devices were later to be associated with the ZIC ware from the La Hueca and Punta Candelero sites.

11. Roe (1985) referred to a possible confirmation of this spatial segregation of ZIC ware within the Hacienda Grande site based on the unpublished findings of Chanlatte's test excavations of 1970 under the auspices of the University of Puerto Rico Museum.

12. The author worked as a field and laboratory supervisor on this project and so has first-hand information regarding the materials recovered.

13. The site of Sorcé proper is defined by a series of large refuse deposits forming a half circle opened toward the bed of the Urbano River. The adjoining site of La Hueca is also

defined by a series of mounds arrayed in a semi-circle opening to the Urbano River, but they are somewhat smaller and individually more distinct than the Sorcé middens. In fact, a topographic map made by the author for Chanlatte and Narganes (1983:127) revealed that both sites together formed a capital "M" opening to the river since they "collide," or interpenetrate, in the middle. For that reason, Sorcé-La Hueca should be regarded as one large site with two horizontally segregated components.

14. There are still many questions as to what that separate identity might mean. Why is ZIC ware spatially segregated from WOR Saladoid pottery in some contexts and associated with it in others? Some of the papers in this collection deal with this connundrum (Roe, this volume; Rouse, this volume; Siegel, this volume).

15. Yet, an amateur, Héctor Rivera, a portion of whose Maisabel collection was purchased by the Centro de Investigaciones Indígenas de Puerto Rico as a comparative sample, indicated to the author that most of the ZIC ware in his collection, and in other amateur collections from this site, was obtained from the deepest levels of a particular section of the site (Rivera, personal communication 1985). Heretofore, this sector has been avoided by the CIIPR excavations precisely because of its disturbed nature (Peter Roe, personal communication 1989), but it is possible that additional studies of this area could yield important information on the spatial segregation of ZIC ware at the Maisabel site. On the other hand, looting may have already obliterated the possibility of such a study.

16. Clearly there are a number of issues in the C-14 dating of early ceramic sites in Puerto Rico and Vieques that potentially complicate any discussion such as this. For example, there are also very early C-14 dates for Hacienda Grande materials suggesting that they may be at least as old as the ostensibly prior La Hueca materials of Chanlatte's first formulations (see Rouse, this volume)

17. In fact, there are only seven known sites in Puerto Rico and the island of Vieques where polychrome pottery, one of the diagnostic elements of the Hacienda Grande ceramic style, is found. These are: Canas, Monserrate, Hacienda Grande, El Convento, Tecla, Sorcé-La Hueca, and Maisabel. To repeat, and in contrast to this picture, ZIC sherds are known from 17 sites.

18. Chanlatte has pointed out the possible stylistic and technological differentiation between the ZIC ware associated with the Hacienda Grande and the horizontally segregated ZIC ware within what is now defined as La Hueca style from La Hueca and Punta Candelero. I concur with Chanlatte's observation.

REFERENCES CITED

Alegría, Ricardo E.
   1965   On Puerto Rican Archaeology. *American Antiquity* 31:246-249.

Chanlatte Baik, Luis A.
   1976   *Cultura Igneri:Investigaciones en Guayanilla, Puerto Rico. Tecla II, Parte I.* Investigaciones 5. Museo del Hombre Dominicano y Fundación García-Arévelo, Santo Domingo.

   1983   Sorcé-Vieques: Climax cultural del Igneri y su participación en los procesos socioculturales Antillanos. *Proceedings of the International Congress for the Study of the Pre-Columbian Cultures of the Lesser Antilles* 9:73-95. Montréal.

1984 *Arqueología de Vieques. Catálogo de exposición.* 2nd ed. Centro de Investigaciones Arqueológicas, Universidad de Puerto Rico, Río Piedras.

Chanlatte Baik, Luis A. e Yvonne M. Narganes Storde
1980 La Hueca, Vieques: nuevo complejo cultural agroalfarero en la arqueología Antillana. *Proceedings of the International Congress for the Study of the Pre-Columbian Cultures of the Lesser Antilles* 8:501-523. Tempe.

1983 *Vieques, Puerto Rico: asiento de una nueva cultura aborigen Antillana.* Impresora Corporán, Santo Domingo.

Harris, Peter O'Brien
1978 A Revised Chronological Framework for the Ceramic Age in Trinidad and Tobago. *Proceedings of the International Congress for the Study of the Pre-Columbian Cultures of the Lesser Antilles* 7:47-54. Montréal.

Lathrap, Donald W.
1970 *The Upper Amazon.* Praeger, New York.

Ortíz Aguilú, Juan José
1975 Las Flores-An Early Ostionoid Village in South-Central Puerto Rico. Paper presented at the 6th International Congress for the Study of the Pre-Columbian Cultures of the Lesser Antilles, Guadaloupe.

Pons de Alegría, Carmen A.
1973 *The Igneri Ceramic from the Site of the Convent of San Domingo: A Study of Style and Form.* Unpublished Master's thesis, Department of American Studies, State University of New York, Buffalo.

Rainey, Froelich G.
1940 *Porto Rican Archaeology.* Scientific Survey of Puerto Rico and the Virgin Islands, vol. XVIII-part 1. The New York Academy of Sciences, New York.

Rivera, Héctor
1986 Un trascendental hallazgo arqueológico en Humacao. *El Mundo* Martes, 1 de Julio:26.

Rodríguez, Miguel
1983 *Prehistoria de Collores.* Unpublished Master's thesis, Centro de Estudios Avanzados de Puerto Rico y el Caribe, San Juan.

1985 *Stage 1A Archaeological Report for the Rincón Intercepting Sewer, Rincón, Puerto Rico.* Submitted to Roberto Rexach Cintrón and Associates. Copies available from the State Historic Preservation Office, San Juan.

1987 *Stage II Archaeological Report for the Guamaní Site in Guayama STP, Guayama, Puerto Rico.* Submitted to the Puerto Rico Aqueduct and Sewer Authority. Copies available from the Institute of Puerto Rican Culture, San Juan.

1988 *Informe final preliminar, excavaciones en Punta Candelero, Palmas del Mar, Humacao, P.R.* Submitted to Palmas del Mar Co. Copies available from the Institute of Puerto Rican Culture, San Juan.

Rodríguez, Miguel and Virginia Rivera
    1987   Puerto Rico and the Caribbean Pre-Saladoid "Crosshatch Connection." Paper presented at the 12th International Congress for Caribbean Archaeology, Cayenne, French Guiana.

Roe, Peter G.
    1985   A Preliminary Report on the 1980 and 1982 Field Seasons at Hacienda Grande (12 PSj7-5): Overview of Site History, Mapping and Excavations. *Proceedings of the International Congress for the Study of the Pre-Columbian Cultures of the Lesser Antilles* 10:151-180, 206-224. Montréal.

Rouse, Irving
    1952   *Porto Rican Prehistory: Introduction; Excavations in the West and North.* Scientific Survey of Puerto Rico and the Virgin Islands, vol. XVIII-part 3. The New York Academy of Sciences, New York.

    1964   Prehistory of the West Indies. *Science* 144:499-513.

    1982   Ceramic and Religous Development in the Greater Antilles. *Journal of New World Archaeology* 5(2):45-55.

    1986   *Migrations in Prehistory: Inferring Population Movements from Cultural Remains.* Yale University Press, New Haven.

Siegel, Peter E.
    1986   The Maisabel Project. *Arqueología* 2(1):20-21.

Siegel, Peter E. and David J. Bernstein
    1987   Sampling for Site Structure and Spatial Organization in the Saladoid: A Case Study. Paper presented at the 12th International Congress for Caribbean Archaeology, Cayenne.

Siegel, Peter E. and Peter G. Roe
    1987   The Maisabel Archaeological Project: A Long Term, Multi-Disciplinary Investigation. Paper presented at the 12th International Congress for Caribbean Archaeology, Cayenne.

Warreck. George
    1972   The Cross-Hatch Designs of the Hacienda Grande Style. *Boletín Informativo, Fundación Antropológica, Arqueológica e Histórica de Puerto Rico* 1(2):3-5.

Table 1. Radiocarbon Dates for the La Hueca Style (Separate ZIC Ware) from the Punta Candelero Site, Humacao, Puerto Rico.

Lab Sample Number	Material	Excavation Unit	Age (B.P.)[a]	Median Date (B.C./A.D.)	Age Range (B.C./A.D.)
I-14,979[b]	*Strombus*	Test C, .80-.90[c]	2120±80	170 B.C.	250-90 B.C.
I-14,978[b]	Charcoal	Test A, .60-.70	2020±80	70 B.C.	150 B.C.-A.D. 10
I-15,408	Charcoal	Unit J, .60-.70	1310±80	A.D. 640	A.D. 560-720
I-15,410	Charcoal	Unit F4, .40-.50	1260±80	A.D. 690	A.D. 610-770
I-15,409	Charcoal	Unit L, .40-.50	1230±80	A.D. 720	A.D. 640-800
I-15,431	*Strombus*	Unit C, .80-.90	1220±80	A.D. 730	A.D. 650-810
I-15,432	Charcoal	Unit I, .70-.80	1000±110	A.D. 950	A.D. 840-1060
I-15,429	*Strombus*	Unit L2, .80-.90	860±80	A.D. 1090	A.D. 1010-1170
I-15,407	Charcoal	Unit F, .60-.70	690±80	A.D. 1260	A.D. 1180-1340

[a] These dates are uncorrected.

[b] Dates obtained during 1987 testings. The rest are from 1988.

[c] Meters below ground surface.

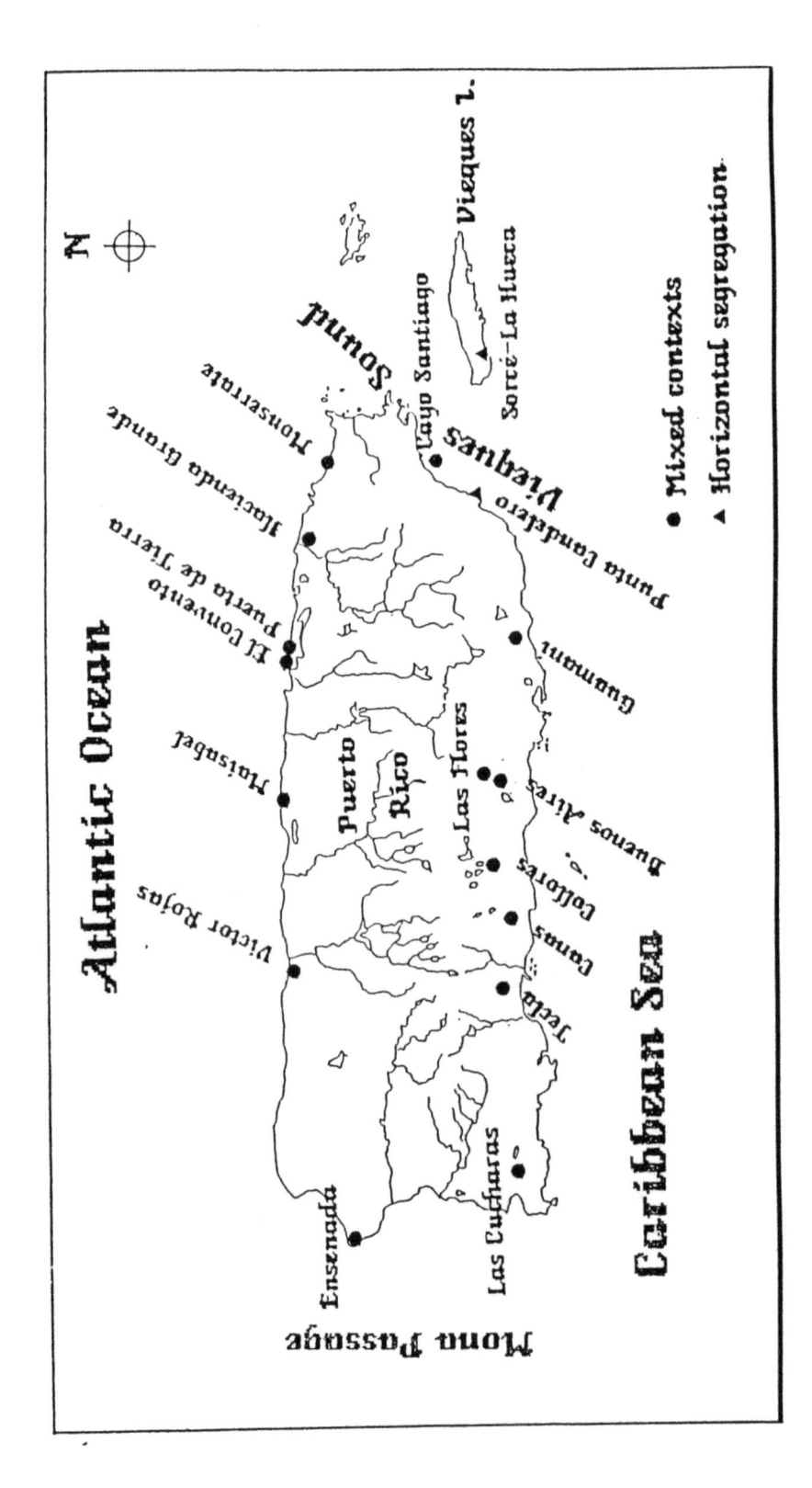

Figure 1. Locations of sites with zoned incised crosshatched (ZIC) pottery specimens in Puerto Rico and Vieques Island.

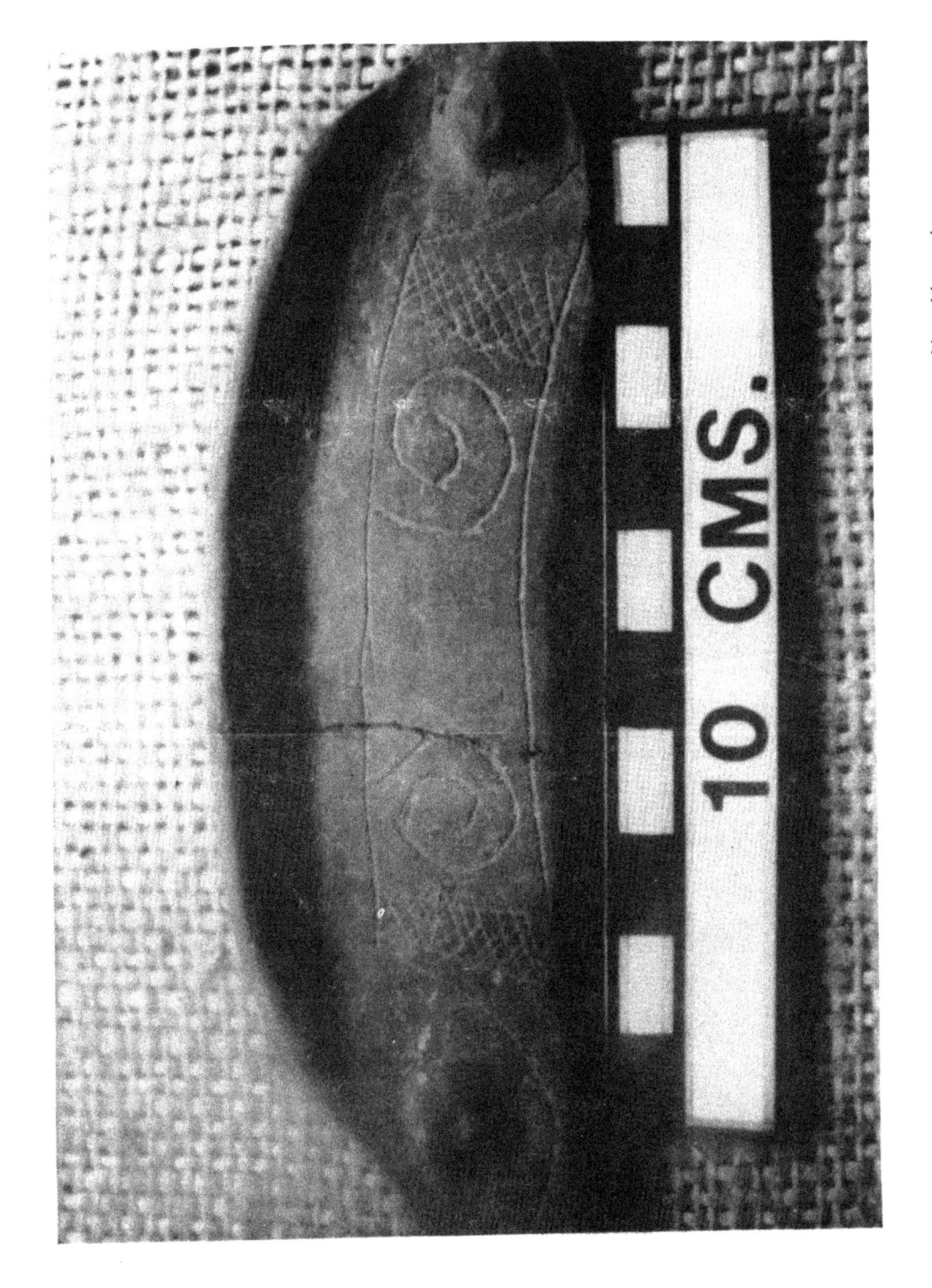

Figure 2. ZIC sherd from Canas, Ponce (Yale Peabody Museum, New Haven).

Figure 3. ZIC sherds from Hacienda Grande, Loíza (University of Turabo Museum, Gurabo).

Figure 4. Modeled body projections from ZIC effigy vessels, Punta Candelero, Humacao.

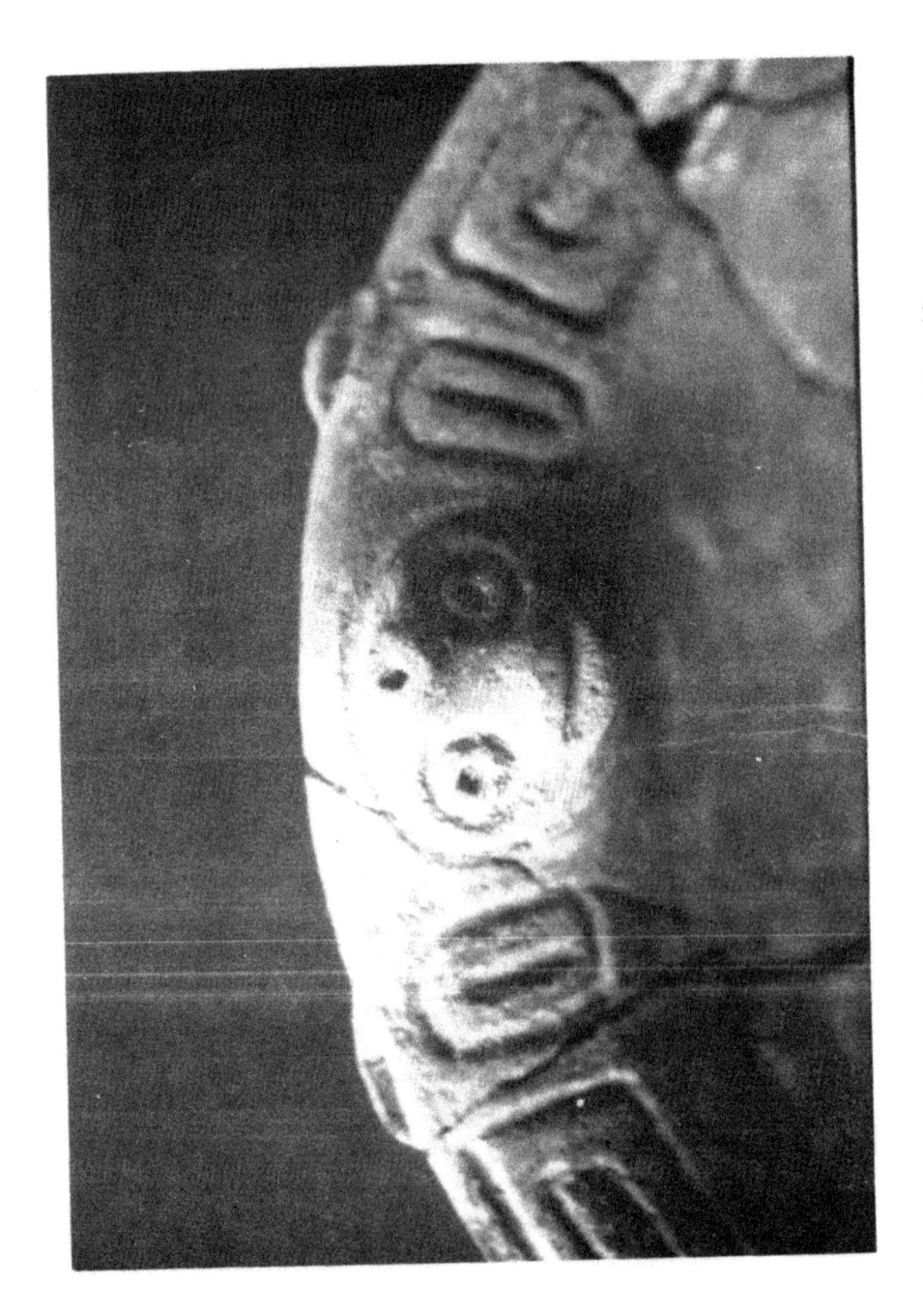

Figure 5. Zoned incised without crosshatch from Punta Candelero, Humacao.

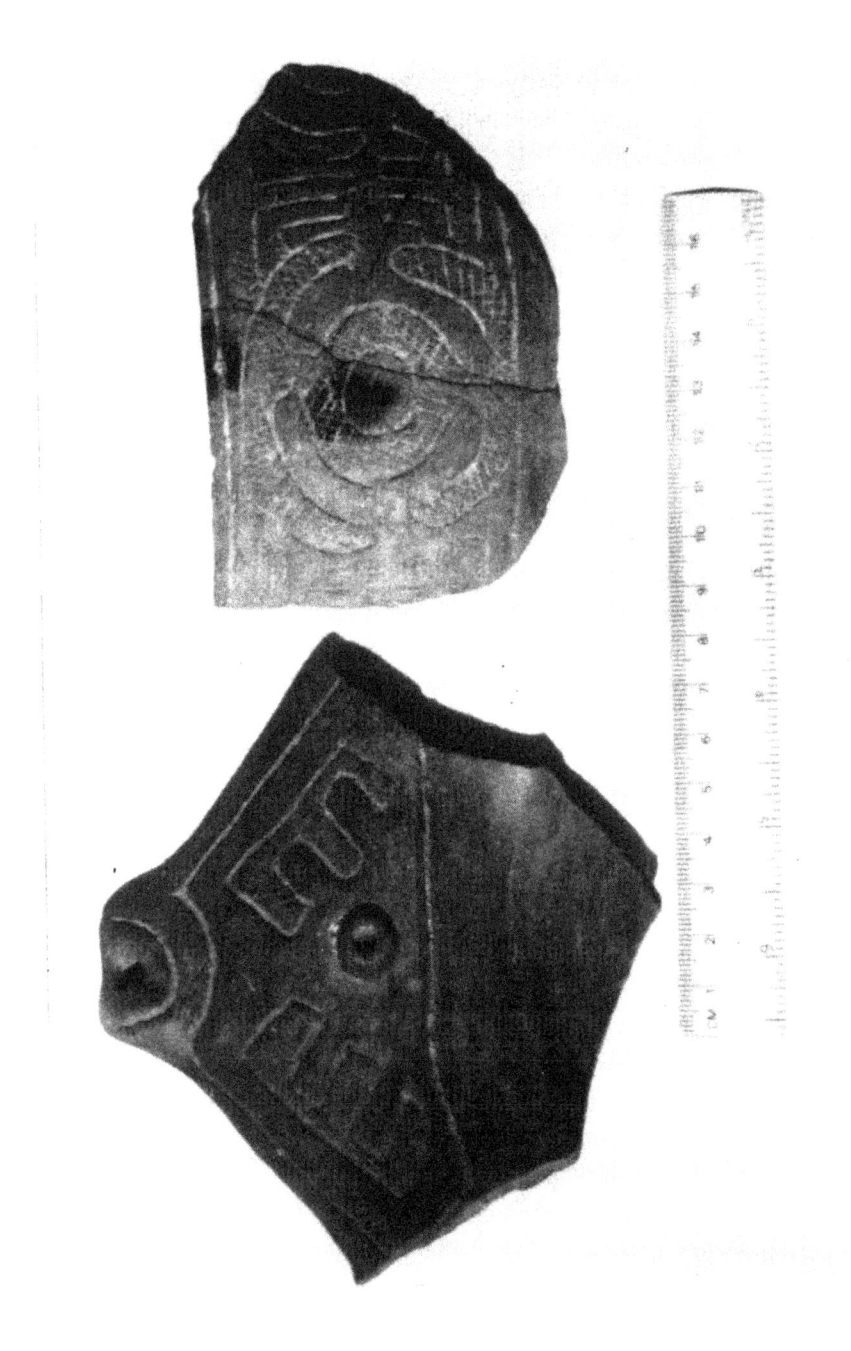

Figure 6. ZIC examples from Punta Candelero, Humacao.

Figure 7. ZIC sherds from Ensenada, Rincón (University of Turabo Museum, Gurabo).

A GRAMMATICAL ANALYSIS OF CEDROSAN SALADOID VESSEL FORM CATEGORIES AND SURFACE DECORATION: AESTHETIC AND TECHNICAL STYLES IN EARLY ANTILLEAN CERAMICS

Peter G. Roe

ABSTRACT

A generative grammatical analysis of the vessel forms and the surface decoration of Antillean Saladoid pottery suggests that the two complexes hitherto defined for Puerto Rico and Vieques: Cedrosan Saladoid (Hacienda Grande and Cuevas styles or phases), and the La Hueca Cultural Complex, are so closely related that the latter may be redesignated the "La Hueca style or phase" of the Cedrosan Saladoid series. This affinity exists despite their areal segregation at certain sites such as Sorcé and Punta Candelero. A settlement model of the Antilles from the mainland suggests an "agonistic engine" driving the migration process that might explain the segregation of these culturally-related groups (represented by the Hacienda Grande and La Hueca styles). Competitive exclusion and absorption of the La Huecan populations by the Hacienda Grande ethnic group via raiding for women could explain the mixture of La Hueca traits in Hacienda Grande sites such as the medial "Linear Incised Ware" of the Hacienda Grande style. This ware may represent a fusion between La Hueca incised and Hacienda Grande painted decoration. Both styles are characterized by evidence of recent arrival from and close connection with the mainland. They represent "personal presentation" material cultures suggestive of a tribal level of sociopolitical integration conveyed by village craft specialists quite unlike the "public power" material culture of the Taíno chiefdoms of contact times.

PROLOGUE

In this paper, I will conduct a preliminary enquiry into "paleo-aesthetics." That is, the rich stylistic information present in the prehistoric Cedrosan Saladoid[1] pottery of Puerto Rico (Figure 1) can yield information on the ancient technical and aesthetic styles that governed its makers. All too often pottery, one of the chief "index fossils" of culture, is treated as a fragmented typological "given," rather than as a culturally conditioned set of decisions about artisan's conceptual "targets," or prototypes, and their extensions (Kempton 1981; Roe 1987c). Usually ignored as well are the technical styles (Lechtman and Merrill 1977) within which the artisan operates, as is any concern for the artisan's knowledge and his/her behavioral implementation ("competence/ performance") of craft processes and raw materials. Lastly, it has only been with the relatively recent development of ethno-archaeology[2] that the total performative context has been addressed for a craft's articulation with other crafts, the economic system, the social structure and the world view of a culture (Miller 1985).

This contextual approach is particularly important in South Amerindian arts and crafts, and in the Caribbean systems derived from them (Roe 1987b), where the individual artifact is a "microcosm of the macrocosm" (Roe 1987a, 1988a). In this technical and aesthetic style the artifact symbolically represents in its typological aspect, and recapitulates in its processual fabrication/use contexts, the pervasive animism of the world view of the groups that create it. Almost all artifacts are conceived of as the mythic transforms of proto-cultural animal symbols. Many skills as well are viewed as the property of such creatures, generously given to, or stolen by, humans in beginning time (Whitten and Whitten 1988).

This is why so many of the vessel forms are really zoomorphic effigies, miniature "utilitarian sculptures" in clay (Figure 2a,b). Perhaps this also explains why figurines (both solid and hollow), representational adornos and pectorals are so common in this pottery.[3] This heavy symbolic/semiotic "loading" of artifacts and artifactual process makes it possible to reconstruct the larger system of which the individual artifact is but a concrete manifestation. I will follow this holistic approach here by attempting to wring the maximum of information from these fragments of the past.

This systemic perspective stands in stark contrast to the "artifact physics" approach common in modern archaeology. In the latter highly "etic" mode the archaeologist is often content to portray the accidental fragments he/she encounters (potsherds), rather than attempting to reconstruct the cultural wholes (pots) from which they are derived. It appears to have escaped the attention of most archaeologists that Amerindians did not manufacture potsherds; they made pottery. The problem is compounded when these isolated potsherds are presented in a manuscript without their attendant orientation, either as plane-view line drawings (like so many pretty sea shells, cf. Duprat 1974:76; Dávila 1979:Figure 2), plane-view and unoriented profiles (Figueredo 1980:Figures 1,2) or, as is frequently the case in the Caribbean, muddy (read nearly opaque due to poor printing technology) plates. Thus, if one tries to understand the regional early Saladoid styles of the Caribbean, one will usually look in vain for good detailed drawings of whole vessels (González 1984 to the contrary notwithstanding).

A notable exception are the beautiful drawings of H. Petitjean-Roget (1976a; 1976b; 1978). Yet even his renderings emphasize more the aesthetic than the scientific aspects of the ceramics, in the sense that they are cursive and are depicted either in three-quarter view (1975, II:70),[4] or are only partial profile section drawings (1975, II:50).[5] Thus the need is clear for methods of portrayal that actually convey information about pottery rather than interminable, redundant, and ultimately useless verbal descriptions. The same can be said of even attractive photographs of fragments. I will try to partially correct this "desert of depiction" by presenting accurate section drawings, originally done in 1:1 scale and photographically reduced, of the pottery I will be discussing.

For the same reasons of comprehensibility, I will present complete pots, even when reconstruction is required. In those cases where, on the basis of further evidence, some of these hypothetical reconstructions may turn out to be in error, they represent heuristic devices, predictions about form and decoration based on an operationalized model, which are intended to be either confirmed or disconfirmed. In other words, if in one view archaeology is the science of using dead informants, what one needs to produce, on the basis of often fragmentary physical evidence, are predictions of the concepts that lay behind the "paleo-behavior." Such predictions can then be tested against new discoveries as the corpus grows (Roe 1973:119).

Further, by employing a newly operationalized method of generative grammatical analysis of vessel shape and surface decoration, I suggest a possible resolution of several current conflicting hypotheses about multiple migrations to the islands of Puerto Rico and Vieques by the first waves of pottery-using, horticultural peoples from South America. Stylistic analysis of pottery therefore provides an independent data set to other information derived from intra- and inter-site artifact and feature spatial analysis, faunal identification or radiochronometric dating to shed light on conflicting theories.

Since the Saladoid pottery represents some of the most elaborate and aesthetically-compelling material culture ever created by South American Indians, an investigation of it will help to answer anthropological culture-historical questions about the temporal priority in time, and cultural affiliation of these archaeological assemblages. It will also add "flesh to the arid artifactual bones" by inquiring into the motivation, aesthetic judgements, and executional skill of these ancient island artists. Ultimately, such an approach can document the rich diversity of a native tradition from the inside by conducting a kind of aesthetic "dialogue with the dead." Viewed as a complement to cultural ecology, such techniques will ultimately invest these early arrivals to the Caribbean with greater reality and empathy than just an analysis of objects as "givens."

INTRODUCTION

Antillean, or Cedrosan, Saladoid, is the earliest pottery of the first waves of horticultural populations to reach the Antilles in the first several centuries B.C. It is some of the most elaborate ceramics produced in the prehistoric New World, a fact that is normally overlooked in museum exhibitions since few whole pots have been found in this region compared with the vast quantities recovered from Peru or Mexico. Indeed, in both the complexity of vessel form categories and the playful way they were combined, as well as the intricacy of the white-on-red painting and its other battery of surface decorative techniques (false bichrome,[6] true polychrome,[7] false negative,[8] pre- and post-fire painting/crusting,[9] pattern burnishing,[10] cross-hatched incision and engraving,[11] excision,[12] smudging,[13] zoomorphic and anthropomorphic,[14] modeled and appliqued,[15] solid and hollow adornos and figurines[16]), Antillean Saladoid actually surpasses the mainland style for which it is named.

Why is this pottery so elaborate? This "hyper-development" is a direct result of an extensive and rapidly developed "interaction sphere"[17] dating from the initial, explosive radiation of horticultural societies of a "Tropical Forest" adaptation (Lathrap 1970) along the main rivers of the Amazonian-Orinocan systems. This sphere dates as far back into the "Formative" to the seventh or eighth millennia B.C., based on indirect plant domestication data, or the fourth millenium B.C., based on a scattering of early circum-Amazonian ceramic cultures (Raymond 1988:288). The sphere stretched from the mouth of the Amazon to the montaña of Ecuador and Peru of the Amazonian system (Raymond 1988:293, 300, Note 3). From thence it encompassed the eastern Colombian Andean outliers and the Orinoco during the third millenium B.C. (Roosevelt 1980; Rouse et al.1985), as well as the surrounding areas of the coastal sections of the Guianas.[18]

Finally, this interaction sphere extended outward into the Caribbean as far as the eastern tip of Hispañola coterminous with Cedrosan Saladoid expansion. Within this region, culturally cognate, but ethnically diverse, competing populations moved and interacted rapidly to generate regions of high information density. Long distance travel over water turned the *whole eastern Caribbean* into a "canalized" avenue for Saladoid expansion, a narrow set of island stepping stones circumscribed laterally by water.

AN "AGONISTIC ENGINE" MODEL OF

CULTURAL INTERACTION AMONG EARLY HORTICULTURALISTS

Within this tightly delimited area new, mainly osteological (Budinoff 1987), evidence hints at an "agonistic engine" of multi-ethnic group competiton as one possible driving force behind this pattern of migrations. The closest analog to this spatial jostling in ethnographic times is the raiding for women. In the recent past of the South American lowlands, such raiding most often occurred against other groups that were *similar to*, but often smaller in scale, than an aggressive horticultural society. It was a stylized, and ritualized, "dialog of death" (Roe 1982a). Therefore, I am more concerned about the possible *internal* relations of the horticulturalist groups (La

Hueca/Hacienda Grande), within the Lesser Antilles and the Greater Antilles, than with the *external* relations between the already-resident Archaic populations on Puerto Rico and the arriving Saladoid sub-groups. This by no means excludes the real possibility of the latter (Siegel, this volume) as a complicating social factor.[19]

However, for the purposes of this paper, I suggest that it was more probably the competition between the similar and culturally-related horticultural groups, rather than just the agonistic interaction of dissimilar groups across the frontier, that was the driving force behind the frontier. I emphasize inter-horticultural group raiding because of my ethnographic studies of current lowland South Amerindians (Roe 1976, 1980, 1981, 1982b). These investigations indicate that mutual influence and cultural borrowing tends to occur, as does armed competition, between culturally similar groups.[20] Their cognate ideological systems, including both technical and artistic styles (in this case pottery traditions), produce mutual intelligibility if not amity. Today, for example, in the Peruvian montaña the Shipibo and the Conibo, dialectically-differentiated riverine Panoans, are intermarrying and consolidating cultural similarities as a segmentary-oppositional response to impinging Western (mestizo) colonists. Yet in the early contact and pre-contact period these two "similar" cultural groups were locked in deadly combat, and mutual raiding for women was common (Roe 1982a).

Yet even antagonistic groups borrow from each other. I affirm that before borrowing can occur there must already be an internal grammatical similarity between the interacting cultural systems. Cultural diffusion is not like the common cold, one does not catch it through simple propinquity. Such a point has already been made with regard to material cultural styles by Muller (1971), and demonstrated by my studies of Shipibo/Cuna ethnoaesthetics (Roe 1976).

Therefore, I look back down the islands and emphasize the greater informational recombinatorial possibilites of interacting and competing horticultural populations of similar cultural affiliation. This is my explanation for why Antillean Saladoid pottery reached the apogee of ceramic development it achieved. This reason may also be why the "epi-Saladoid" and post-Saladoid cultures could not sustain and extend that achievement. "Ceramic devolution" was inevitable once the interaction system these pottery traditions depended upon to drive the engine of style was ruptured by a cessation of long-distance trade.[21]

A contributing factor along with the severing of trade connections was the inevitable narrowing of vision in later times as a result of the restriction of interaction. This "cultural myopia" was itself a product of the very success of that local ecological adaptation. As Rouse has pointed out (1982) interaction centered on the watery spaces (straits or passages) between islands. In later times it might have just become confined to those adjacent islands and no longer continued along the whole series of spread-out islands as it had done earlier.[22]

At the time of the first ceramic-bearing cultures, I thus conceive of the Caribbean as a kind of "inverted main-river" analogue. The main-river habitat in the South American lowlands is an area of extreme information density due to high rates of social interaction between different competing ethnic groups. Movement within it tends to assume a "toothpaste tube" pattern of groups, each social and cultural group being like a differently colored segment of paste. Each segment (group) maintains its spatial interrelationships with neighboring units as the whole string is squeezed from the tube. This "phase coherence" characterizes flood plain migration because the ethnic groups (each of which are a "people" in Rouse's terminology) are moving linearly along the watercourses, hemmed in by laterally fringing jungle on old alluvial land and separated by "no-man's lands" from the next groups, up- and down-river (DeBoer 1981a; Myers 1976; Raymond 1988:298, 300, Note 5).[23] Current ethnographic evidence confirms this picture wherever agonistic inter-ethnic relations still obtain (Mentore 1985; Roe 1987a). This early and pre-contact pattern belies the accepted picture of peaceful natives in a now pacified and depopulated lowland.

I argue that the ancient Antillean groups also moved in a linear fashion, only this time following a stream of land (the island chains) laterally hemmed in by water, rather than a stream of water canalized by land. To employ another metaphor, this "hydraulic" theory is congruent with the role attributed to the Barrancoid series "pushing" the Saladoid series populations out into Trinidad and the Lesser Antilles (Rouse et al. 1985). In both cases of "geographical circumscriptive inversion" the historical "losers" are forced to the margins of the system and bypassed. In the Amazonian-Orinocan systems this "marginality" meant the upper tributaries and interfluves (Raymond 1988:289), while in the Antilles it became the windward islands in the Lesser Antilles (Watters et al. 1984:390) and the mountainous interior and isolated peninsulas of the Greater Antilles where "Archaic" populations perhaps remained until contact (Rouse 1982, 1986).

This linear-centralized and canalized system[24] is important in cultural development, not just in migratory patterns. Such is the case because the center, with its higher interaction rates, produces more "information," thus enabling the machine of style to reach greater recombinatorial and creative complexity within it. Intense social interaction permits the various style cycles involved to turn over quickly and produce the diversity of Saladoid expressions we see in the Antilles.[25] Restated, this means that the more information is available, the greater recombinatorial freedom individual artists will have to create more complex art (Roe 1979, 1981) within the interacting groups that compose a local system. Also, by dominating scarce resources, certain of these groups have the technological control to realize that art. DeBoer (1981b), for example, has shown how only by controlling access to hundreds of linear kilometers of river and tributary frontage, can the modern Shipibo obtain the complex raw materials that makes polychrome pottery possible.

The sophistication of Antillean Saladoid pottery is even greater and the geological poverty (especially of the smaller islands in the Lesser Antilles) more marked than on *tierra firme*. Therefore lateral raw material trade and procurement was perhaps of even greater significance in the Antilles than on the mainland. This rapid movement through the Antilles and the high rates of contact involved, (the whole prestige good exchange system as represented by the lapidary art [Sued-Badillo 1978], and the evidence from it of long-distance trade in raw materials coupled with local manufacture [Rodríguez, this volume]) set the stage for the complexity of Cedrosan Saladoid (Roe 1985; Roe et al. 1985).

MATERIAL CULTURAL EVIDENCE FOR THE RAPIDITY

OF ISLAND COLONIZATION AND MAINLAND INTERACTION

There is abundant artifactual evidence for the speed of these migrations, a fact in itself that argues for some agonistic engine driving population movement.[26] For example, the steadily increasing antiquity of early Saladoid cultures near the western terminus of their expansion in Puerto Rico and eastern Dominican Republic at 200-100 B.C., speeds up the process of migration from Trinidad (the Cedros complex there dating to 190 B.C. [Rouse et al. 1985]) by at least a century, making it a virtually "instantaneous" (in archaeological time) process. In addition, evidence in both pottery technology and iconography attests to a still-fresh memory (or connection) with the mainland in the Puerto Rican Hacienda Grande and La Hueca styles.

Ceramic potrests, or *topia*, are the classic evidence for "culture lag" in the domain of ceramic technology. They come in solid (Roe et al. 1985, from the Monserrate site, Puerto Rico) and hollow (Figure 21a, from the La Hueca component at the Sorcé site, Vieques) concave-hourglass and convex barrel-shaped variants (Figures 21b, c, from the Hacienda Grande component at the Sorcé site, Vieques). Like such functional "absurdities"[27] as ceramic pestles (Raymond et al. 1975:Figures 28h-j), these *topia* derive from a necessary technological adaptation to a stoneless, alluvial, lowland setting in the Amazonian-Orinocan basins. Their continued presence in the Greater Antilles, which are blessed with a super-abundance of locally available and suitable metamorphic and igneous river cobbles, is a clear instance of these newly arrived Saladoid groups still not having completely adjusted to the local resources of an insular environment.

This same process of "culture lag" is also evident from the culinary remains. Thus, initially there is a dependence on large, easily accessible life-forms as sources of protein to supplement the manioc the first immigrants brought with them. The ease with which these life forms, like the blue land crab (*Cardisoma guanami*) and the gastropod *Cittarium pica*, could be procured and the susceptibility of those creatures to over-exploitation (Goodwin 1980) bespeaks a lack of adaptation to the unique energetic properties of an insular environment,[28] and hence the recentness of the colonist's arrival from a *tierra firme* origin.

It is surely no coincidence that at the same time local culinary readjustment occurs (maritime, shellfish resources displacing land crabs), the ceramic *topias* drop out of the ceramic inventory. They are presumably replaced by the locally available river cobbles.

The same phenomenon of "the body being in the Antilles, the mind still back in *tierra firme*," typical of pioneers anywhere, is also mirrored in the sculptural iconography on Saladoid ceramic vessels. Both in hollow ceramic figurines and in adornos for vessel rims, we encounter a range of realistically depicted mainland fauna identifiable to the species level! We have coatis and caiman, Capuchin monkeys (Figure 22), Capybaras (Figure 23) and leaf-nosed bats (Figure 24), in addition to dogs (Figure 20b) and a magnificent hollow tapir effigy (Figures 4-6) jar of disturbingly west coast South American cast (specifically the Ecuadorian [Machallila-Chorrera], and the North Peruvian Coast). Parenthetically, this latter form is congruent with other early ceramic traits such as effigy-head stirrup-spouts (Figure 13) and deformed, carinated bat effigy bowls (Figure 25, La Huecan style) that attest to an extensive mainland interaction sphere. Of course, local fauna, like the land crab (González 1984:Figure 20), and marine fauna are also portrayed. Examples of the latter are: the common category of marine turtle effigy vessels (Figure 3), manatees (Figure 26), and the Hacienda Grande (Figure 27) and later (Monserratean) manta ray trays (Figure 28).

However, later ceramic evolution witnesses a dropping out of these realistic sculptural ceramic adornments and sees their replacement with generalized fantastic creatures (variously called "bats," "dogs," and "monkies").[29] This occurs at the same time that the *topia* disappear and the "Crab/Shell" dichotomy (now better regarded as a continuum) shifts to the shell end of the spectrum. Clearly, by that time (the various "Pre-Taino" cultures like Elenoid/ Ostionoid= "Elenan Ostionoid/Ostionan Ostionoid") the notion that a vessel should have theriomorphic handles, often opposed (Figure 29), thus turning the whole bowl into an effigy, was still current but any memory of specific lowland South American fauna had long since been erased by time, the severing of trade and travel links with the mainland and a concomitant localized "settling in."

Recentness of arrival into the Antilles is congruent with the maintenance of continuing links with the mainland. The presence of semi-precious stone exogenous to the Caribbean (amethyst) in the prestige artifacts suggests a continuing access to the mainland[30] coupled with local manufacture (Chanlatte 1983a:40). The existence of another such lapidary manufacturing center in Monserrate (Harrington 1924) in the Lesser Antilles provides a link in that prestige trade with the mainland. If these Indians were skilled enough to get to the Antilles, they certainly would have been capable of returning to the mainland at will.

BRIEF HISTORY OF SALADOID RESEARCH

IN PUERTO RICO AND VIEQUES

While the definition of this Antillean climax of the potter's art is currently based on stylistic distinctions, it was first recognized as a contrasting pattern in food remains. Rainey initially came across this distinctive pattern of deposition, and the fine pottery with which it was associated, at the sites of Canas, Coto and Monserrate on the northeast coast of Puerto Rico (Rainey 1940). Since I have also excavated the latter site (Roe et al. 1985), I will subject it to a closer examination.

The site was first visited by Froelich G. Rainey in 1934 and again, for a shorter period, in 1935. He found a surface scatter of ceramic and shell debris near the beach over an area roughly 300 m long by 200 m wide (Rainey 1940:75). Back from the beach rising gently to a meter or 1.5 m above the sand were five mounds, which he designated with the letters: A, B, C, D, and E.

Monserrate formed a basis[31] for Rainey's precocious definition of the distinction between cultural phases based on the faunal remains of meals, "indirect artifacts" (byproducts of behavior, not the intended behavior), rather than exclusively on direct artifacts (pottery or lithic implement styles).[32] Thus, his formulation presaged the modern archaeological concern for environmental reconstruction and the inferring of subsistence strategies.

In one of the mounds he discovered shell refuse clearly stratified on top of debris rich in blue land crab (*Cardisoma guanhumi*) claws (1940:80). He correlated this disjunction with differences in material culture to reconstruct an earlier "Crab Culture," characterized by fine quality, frequently "bell-shaped" ceramics with white-on-red painted decoration (Figure 30), D-shaped handles, and plano-convex "axes" (actually adzes), and a later overlying "Shell Culture." The latter utilized shell for artifacts as well as food resources, had lower quality ceramics chiefly characterized by modeled adornos, and petalloid "celts" (actually axes) (1940:92). He favored the cultural mechanism of site-unit intrusion, through migration, of different groups of people who supplanted the earlier Crab Culture occupants, to explain these differences. Perhaps it is not accidental that this reconstruction echoes "Urnfield People" and "Beaker Folk" successionary migratory models then current in European prehistory. Repeated migrations had a better name in archaeology than they do today when the fashion is to opt instead for local development and in situ evolution through local ecological adaptation. Ironically, through his emphasis on dietary shift, Rainey provided the very ammunition for later theories of in situ adjustment, even though he emphasized the "migration model."

In terms of the other dimension, diachronic ordering, a shallow time perspective, a kind of "Taíno Tyranny," dominated Puerto Rican culture history. Chronicler accounts from the fifteenth and sixteenth centuries colored any discussion of prehistory. This "short chronology" was only beginning to be lifted during these days before C-14 dating and still endures on the popular level, where many people express surprise that there were any Indians before the Taíno. The tendency was to see the island's past as a single undifferentiated Taíno occupation! Adolfo de Hostos hinted at a pre-Taíno occupation based on his excavations at Cabo Rojo (1919) in Ostionoid contexts. While de Hostos did not recognize Saladoid pottery as being older than his pre-Taíno "red ware," another collector, Montalvo Guenard, later showed the white-on-red pottery he had found at Canas to Rainey before the latter visited Monserrate and encountered the same pottery. It eventually became the basis of Rouse's (1952) "Cuevas" style, the first of the recognized sub-phases within Antillean Saladoid pottery, but *not* the first in terms of temporal priority. It was precisely in hopes of following up on Rainey's discovery of a "pre-Taíno" stratigraphic superposition at Monserrate that Alegría selected the site for further massive excavations and confirmed Rainey's stratigraphic discoveries (Alegría 1947a:5, 1947b).

Rouse, in his study of Rainey's materials, as well as the material he excavated from many sites in Puerto Rico, recognized the white-on-red pottery as representing the earliest pottery on the island and designated it "Cuevas" after the type-site (Rouse 1952). However, Alegría's excavations at Monserrate and Hacienda Grande, during which he discovered yet more elaborate pottery, some with cross-hatchured decoration, as well as small stone amulets and other artifacts, led him to postulate a new phase anterior to Cuevas, which he designated "Hacienda Grande" (Alegría 1965; Pons de Alegría 1978). Rouse accepted this new phase and placed both Hacienda Grande and Cuevas within the Saladoid series based on their similarity to the Saladero type-site on the lower Orinoco River in Venezuela, which also had this mixture of white-on-red painting and *painted*,[33] not *incised-engraved*, cross-hatchured decoration (Rouse 1964:508).

These stylistic affinities and a pattern of corresponding C-14 dates led Rouse to postulate a step-like progressive migration of "Neo-Indian" Saladoid populations into the Greater Antilles from South America. They came via Trinidad and the stepping-stone islands of the Lesser Antilles (Rouse 1952). While originally arranged in a neat "sloping horizon," or "series," of Saladoid styles, which demonstrated their progressively later spread out into the Antilles from the Orinocan region of mainland South America (Rouse and Alegría 1978), there is currently much ferment within this cultural reconstruction (Rodríguez, this volume).

A recent series of unexpectedly early dates for the arrival of this pottery in Puerto Rico (Rouse and Alegría 1989; Rouse, this volume), some obtained by Peter Siegel and myself from two sites on the north coast, Hacienda Grande and Maisabel, now open the possibility of much quicker colonization than was first imagined. Alternatively, they hint at a "reverse movement" back down the Lesser Antilles from the Greater Antilles to account for stylistic differences and similarities between Greater Antillean Saladoid, like the Hacienda Grande phase, and the latter Saladoid and Early Elenan phases of the Virgin Islands.

Additionally, a direct challenge to this whole regional chronology, as developed by Rouse based on his work in Venezuela and throughout the Caribbean, has been put forth by Chanlatte (1979, 1981, 1983a,b, 1984, 1985a,b, 1986, 1987) on the basis of his work at several sites in Vieques and Puerto Rico. Chanlatte postulates an earlier, and perhaps direct, migration of horticultural societies than the Hacienda Grande "Saladoid" occupation. This he has labeled "La Hueca" and compared it with the "Guapoid" *style* of coastal Venezuela (Chanlatte and Narganes 1980:514). In other contexts, he has referred to La Hueca materials as "Huecoid," but appears to use the "oid" suffix without the implication of membership in a series as Rouse does (this volume), since each was based on single sites (La Hueca in Vieques [now joined by Punta Candelero] and Río Guapo in Venezuela). While it contains material originally included within the white-on-red painted pottery of the Saladoid complexes (Alegría 1965), he and Narganes (Chanlatte and Narganes 1980, 1986) describe it as being very different from the Saladoid materials, not only in ceramics but also in lithic artifacts and dietary patterns (Narganes 1985).

Since 1979 Chanlatte has coupled the ambitious "oid" designation with the more conservative designation of the "La Hueca Cultural Complex" (but perhaps more to break from Rouse's system by substituting "Agro-I" for La Hueca and "Agro-II" for Hacienda Grande than from uncertainty as to whether it formed a series-like horizontal and vertical cultural unit). Since 1985 he has also designated it as a "Phase" (Chanlatte 1985b:10). I will opt for Chanlatte's more conservative *complejo cultural* solution and equate this "complex" with my "La Hueca style" (Rouse's "Huecan subseries" of the Cedrosan Saladoid series, this volume).

The key to Chanlatte's recognition that the "Huecoid" materials represent a different population movement into the Antilles than the Hacienda Grande style was his discovery of the spatial segregation of the La Hueca component in seven small mounds on a natural terrace near the sea in the Sorcé site of Vieques. These mounds are located a short distance from the Hacienda Grande component, a large continuous semi-circular midden on an upper terrace of that same site (Chanlatte and Narganes 1986:127). Based on conversations with Chanlatte in 1980, as we walked over the Sorcé site (Luis Chanlatte, personal communication 1980), he finds a curious disparity in the assemblages from the two areas. Although this disparity has not been documented statistically Chanlatte affirmed that he found the curious "dog" adorno handles of the La Hueca bowls (Figure 31) in the La Hueca mounds and in the Hacienda Grande midden, while *no* elaborate white-on-red (WOR) painted sherds were found in the La Huecan mounds.

Such an association, if confirmed, would point to both a curious pattern of "Pre-Columbian pothunting," or collecting of intrinsically interesting pottery by the Hacienda Grande peoples, and also indirect evidence for relative chronology. In other words, the only explanation for why this "collecting" was unidirectional (why no beautiful WOR sherds on the La Hueca middens?) was that the La Hueca mounds were already abandoned when the HG midden was being occupied. This inference is congruent with the size and pattern of the respective middens. Small, isolated mounds bespeak a modest occupation, or an occupation of short duration, while the immense HG midden looks like a continuous midden built up in a semi-circular manner by laterally-coalescing individual mounds. Such a depositional pattern could be the result of dense populations forcing propinquity, or long-duration occupation, or both.

Siegel's and my own fieldwork at the huge multi-component site of Maisabel in Vega Baja, Puerto Rico (Siegel 1986, this volume; Siegel and Bernstein 1987; Siegel and Roe 1987) provides a close analogue in the semi-circular organization of individual mounds, as did Rainey's, Alegría's and my own work at the Monserrate site (Roe et al. 1985). Yet the large series of C-14 dates that Chanlatte obtained for both components at the Sorcé/La Hueca sites reveals that the two deposits were virtually contemporary within the first sigma of error (Chanlatte and Narganes 1986:65-66) and the recent spate of very late C-14 dates from both La Hueca and Punta Candelero (Rodríguez, this volume) makes the situation even more confusing!

One possible reconstruction of the social events that might have produced this Sorcé/La Hueca pattern could have been a small (relative to the HG people) "advance party" of La Hueca style Saladoid populations that briefly occupied the lower portion of the site. Then, perhaps within such a short period of time that it is masked by the standard deviation ranges in the C-14 determinations (less than a century) a "main force" of culturally-distinct "pursuing" HG Saladoid populations displaced those La Hueca populations and initiated a long-term occupation. During that occupation some HG people picked up intriguing decorated potsherds from the abandoned La Hueca middens rather like Bunzel (1972:80) has documented for modern Hopi picking up Sikyatki Polychrome sherds as a source of artistic inspiration.

Meanwhile, numerous technical deficiencies in Chanlatte's presentation (problems with an initial lack of topographic maps, rapid rates of excavation, a paucity of feature and stratigraphy presentation and a lack of comparative statistics and artifact provenience and a naive use of radiometric dating, coupled with a disinterest in the utilitarian ware which is *very* similar to HG utilitarian ware, thus exaggerating the differences within the fine ware, etc.) led to a skepticism about Chanlatte's claims. The similarities between utilitarian wares of the two complexes, as well as the fact that earlier investigators like Rouse and Alegría always found the two wares mixed within their own excavations (although this could reflect technical difficulties of their own--long trenches over undulating topography, thick artificial stratigraphic units cross-cutting cultural depositions--thus explaining this co-occurrence as a result of mechanical mixture). Clearly a lack of similarly isolated sites in the Lesser Antilles, and the late dating of the putative "ancestral site," Río Guapo (Rouse, this volume), made Chanlatte's use of a "Guapoid" or a "Huecoid" series improbable (Rouse 1982:45).

Further, a number of previously anomalous C-14 dates from Puerto Rico (from Alegría's El Convento excavations [Pons de Alegría 1973, 1976], and my excavations at Hacienda Grande [Rouse, this volume]) were joined by similar determinations from Siegel's excavations at Maisabel, all in secure HG contexts, verified that the Hacienda Grande arrival in Puerto Rico was earlier than 100 B.C.! Since this was over a century before the supposedly "earlier" La Hueca migration,[34] doubt was even cast on the temporal priority of the "La Hueca Cultural Complex."

These difficulties, plus the direct challenge to a carefully laid out region-wide chronological schema that a separate and earlier "migration" into the Antilles represented, explain Rouse's initial reluctance to recognize the La Hueca materials as representing a separate "people." His first reconstruction attributed the spatial segregation of the La Hueca materials at the Sorcé site to religious usage.[35] Perhaps Chanlatte's mound represented a house or a temple with a special religious "ware"[36] (Rouse 1982). Certainly, we know from ethnographic contexts that a ritual ware can be so different from a domestic ware that it can scarcely be recognized as the product of the same people (Bunzel 1972:84, on the Zuni). However, the explanation of an isolated mound as a "temple" remnant became suspect when there turned out to be seven mounds. That began to look like a settlement. Moreover, the uni-directional overlap of wares Chanlatte verbally described was difficult to explain. (Why wouldn't one find at least one WOR sherd on the La Hueca middens if they were just different wares in a contemporaneous village?)

The sheer bulk of Chanlatte's finds, and their spectacular character,[37] lent them a special significance that seemed to argue for more than just the status of a specialized religious ware, especially when one factored in the lapidary art[38] and putative faunal assemblage differences. Thus, during the discussion session at the tenth International Congress in Martinique in 1983 Rouse first proposed a model that he further elaborated at the following congress in 1985 in Puerto Rico (1985b). Perhaps, in this view, with which I concur, there were multiple cultural groups, or "peoples," involved in this initial Cedrosan Saladoid migration into the Caribbean. Maybe different styles emphasized the two intrinsic strains within the Saladoid series present from the earliest documented times on the Middle Orinoco (a "painterly" Ronqun tendency and a "plastic" Barrancas tendency); one the post-fired crusted, highlighted cross-hatch and plastic decorated "La Hueca" materials and the other the pre-fire, white-on-red Hacienda Grande ceramics.

Meanwhile, Chanlatte returned to the site of Tecla in Guayanilla, the site of his earlier Puerto Rican excavations (Chanlatte 1976), to search for a segregated La Hueca component in Tecla I, the Hacienda Grande component at the site. He wanted to see if the Vieques situation could be duplicated in Puerto Rico. But during fairly extensive excavations in 1984 and 1985 Chanlatte was unable to locate one (Chanlatte 1986).

The reality of a separate complex of early ceramic materials spatially segregated from Hacienda Grande deposits in Puerto Rico, and perhaps earlier in time, was finally demonstrated through the *saqueador* ("pot-hunter") discovery of a shallow La Hueca site in Humacao, eastern Puerto Rico, called "Buena Vista" (Chanlatte and Narganes 1986:5; Rivera 1986). Later, Rodríguez and Rivera, who had worked with Chanlatte in the HG midden at Sorcé and executed his topographic map of the La Hueca and Sorcé sectors, visited the new site (1987), which they redesignated "Punta Candelero" after the peninsula on which it was located. They conducted salvage excavations in the sandy midden in the wake of the *saqueadores* and are continuing operations there.

The discovery of this site on the grounds of the Palmas del Mar resort is important since it represents the first independent confirmation of Chanlatte's prediction that a spatial segregation of styles would also be found in Puerto Rico. Punta Candelero reinforces the separate cultural identity of the people who left this deposit spatially segregated from any of the larger Hacienda Grande sites (Rodríguez, this volume). Rodríguez and Rivera also provided radiochronometric confirmation of the common pattern of finding La Hueca style ZIC sherds in the lower levels of Hacienda Grande sites by obtaining a C-14 date on charcoal of 70 B.C. (the shell date is earlier, at 170 B.C.). These dates place Punta Candelero contemporary with the earliest huge HG sites elsewhere on the island. They are also earlier than those obtained from the La Hueca component in Sorcé, Vieques. Indeed, the earliest of these dates slightly antedates the most recent, and earliest, Hacienda Grande determinations.[39]

Rodríguez has allowed me to examine these materials and both he and Rivera have presented them at the 12th Congress in French Guiana in 1987 (see also Rodríguez, this volume). These materials repeat the caste of Chanlatte's La Hueca specimens, in terms of ceramics, faunal assemblages (a different *hutía* (agouti-like) rodent for La Hueca, *Heteropsomys insulanus* than for Hacienda Grande, *Isolobodon puertoricenses*),[40] and lapidary art (Rodríguez and Rivera 1987).

However, the Punta Candelero ceramics are also indisputably Saladoid in their utilitarian wares. The "aryballoid-like" jar type pictured in Figure 32b and c, for example, can be found in either the Hacienda Grande and Cuevas styles or in the La Hueca contexts. The only difference between the Cuevas and La Hueca specimens Rodríguez showed me from his Punta Candelero collections was the slightly softer carinas of the La Hueca specimens, their somewhat more asymmetrical execution and their distinctive grey, rather than brown (Cuevan) paste. These detailed similarities in the largely-unpublished utilitarian wares between the two pottery complexes (compare also a La Hueca utilitarian campaniform, Figure 33a, with a Hacienda Grande campaniform, 33b- one from La Hueca, the other from Sorcé) can be taken as indicating a shared "Saladoid" culturally cognate status. I will pursue these similarities in a more detailed and formal manner below.

Rodríguez and Rivera (1987) initially suggested a "Cross-hatch Horizon" (rather like Meggers and Evans's 1961:375-378 "Zoned Hachure Horizon") to link the La Hueca materials of Punta Candelero with similar, but far-flung similar examples. In this they agreed with Chanlatte and Narganes (1986:4), who related the La Hueca style to much earlier labial-flanged and post-fire crusted pottery like Early Tutishcainyo in the Peruvian montaña and early plastic decorated pottery in Colombia like Puerto Hormiga. Is this a reformulation of the hoary "Saladoid/Barrancoid" contrast with Hacienda Grande being aligned to Saladero and Ronquín, La Gruta (1986:7)? I remember this solution of an independent, perhaps direct (or at least bypassing Trinidad), "ancestral-Barrancoid" migration to the Antilles precociously offered by Lathrap when I was a graduate student of his in the early 1970s!

THE ELEPHANT (ADORNO) AND THE BLIND MEN:

MANY SOLUTIONS TO THE LA HUECA "PROBLEM"

My hypothesis completes the set of logical possibilities between the positions of the various archaeologists who have thus tried to explain the formal and decorative variability within the ceramic assemblages of the first horticulturalist immigrants to the Greater Antilles. Temporal priority goes to Alegría and Rouse's first position: (1) that there is just one series, the Saladoid series, of which the earliest style present in the Greater Antilles, the Hacienda Grande style, has both WOR and ZIC modes. These modes are found on distinct functional wares of the ceramic repertory of the same cultural group. Then Chanlatte's and Rodríguez's current position emerged: (2) The ZIC decorative type is spatially segregated from the WOR type, at least initially, and together with other traits which form a distinct cultural complex, signals the prior arrival of another, non-Saladoid, group, named after the type site of La Hueca. Indeed, ZIC decoration shared by mainland assemblages such as Río Guapo on the coast of Venezuela, suggests a "Huecoid" series (or at least a "La Hueca" stylistic manifestation of a "Guapoid" series, or, lastly, co-membership within a "Crosshatch Horizon."

Based on the discovery of spatial segregation between ZIC and WOR modes at the site of La Hueca/Sorcé in Vieques, Rouse and Alegría first offered an explanation that: (3) the ZIC modes appeared as a complex, or ware, characteristic of a specialized social style, perhaps of religious specialists/structures spatially segregated from the residential ZIC and WOR middens, where special activities and patterns of discard occurred. Then, subsequent to the discovery of the same segregated pattern at the Punta Candelero site in Puerto Rico, Rouse offered his current "compromise" solution: (4) the elevation of the ZIC ware from a style to the *possibility* of a Huecan Saladoid subseries, on equal footing with a Cedrosan Saladoid subseries that encompassed, among others, the Hacienda Grande pottery style or material cultural phase, but still within the Saladoid series.

In my original formulation of these pottery relationships (Roe 1988c), I went back to Rouse's earlier emphasis on "style," and (5) accepted the shared Saladoid affinities of both the La Hueca style ZIC ware and the Hacienda Grande ZIC ware, while also suggesting certain differences, to designate them both as "sub-styles" within the Cedrosan Saladoid series conceived as a regional style. Yet another possibility, and based on his excavations at the Maisabel site, Peter Siegel (personal communication 1988), suggests (6) "...that La Hueca is a *style* on equal footing with the HG *style*, which when combined with the other known Saladoid *styles* in the Antilles comprise the Cedrosan Saladoid subseries."

Pondering Siegel's suggestion, Rodríguez's latest formulation (this volume), which deletes the "Crosshatch Horizon" argument but retains the impression of a distinct cultural identity for La Hueca, and Rouse's most recent (this volume) reconstruction of La Hueca as representing the material remains of a distinct "people," I offer the following schema: (7) That the close similarities in vessel form and surface decorative modes and dimensions between La Hueca and Hacienda Grande, coupled with their initial spatial segregation, argues for a social, as well as a cultural reconstruction. Ethnicity may be expressed in their later intermixing in the "linear incised ware," and the eventual disappearance of La Hueca without descendant styles, but the continuance of Hacienda Grande modes and dimensions into Cuevas and early Elenan Ostionoid (I reject the very late dates for La Hueca, as do Chanlatte and Rodríguez, but for other reasons), and the movement of those styles into what was the La Hueca "core region," the Vieques Sound.

Therefore, I suggest that the La Hueca and Hacienda Grande styles are the material expressions, in pottery, of two closely related "cultural groups" within the Cedrosan Saladoid subseries that saw each other, (using lowland South American ethnographic analogy) as competing "ethnic groups." Perhaps via raiding for wives, the La Hueca group became absorbed into Hacienda Grande, and acculturated as potters to produce the "linear incised" ware. This continued until the tradition reverted to its painterly core and incision dropped out completely, attesting to a "fused" Cuevan Saladoid subseries as "epi-Saladoid."

As of the last International Congress (the 12th, 1987) of Caribbean Archaeology, held in Cayenne, French Guiana, Chanlatte's position has begun to gather strength, particularly among the French investigators of the Lesser Antilles as they too discover similar complexes within previously undifferentiated pottery collections. At the same time, Rouse's space-time reconstruction has gotten more complex, and therefore probably also closer to messy historical reality, as he has worked with the notions of the social and cultural complexities that can arise along and across frontiers and boundaries (Rouse 1986, this volume). Rather than proposing lock-step movements, or monolithic "migratory waves," the conceptual door is now open to consider the movements of individuals (immigration), trade, raiding, and many other interactions of multiple, and possibly competing, ethnic groups.

With this schema I, like Rouse, deny Chanlatte's earlier insistence that La Hueca represents a different series. On the other hand, I assign each style to competing ethnic groups,[41] thus accepting Chanlatte's and Rodríguez's argument about their spatial and social segregation, while holding in abeyance their insistence on the temporal priority of the La Hueca style materials until more evidence is available, particularly from the Lesser Antilles.[42] At the same time, I agree with Siegel that La Hueca and Hacienda Grande are really styles within the same subseries, and not the remains of separate subseries as Rouse currently argues.

Because of its great complexity, and the information about cultural norms and variation that it easily conveys, pottery "style" (both in the technological sense, and in the more generally accepted aesthetic sense) is uniquely suited to answering many of these questions (Rouse 1982). This is so if, and only if, we can utilize a method allowing us to compare and contrast ceramic styles as a means of guaging possible cognate relationships between them.

THE LINEAR INCISED WARE: A TEST CASE

It is clearly too large a problem to re-evaluate all the pottery components of these arguments. Fortunately, Chanlatte has inadvertently offered a test hypothesis on a smaller, and operationally more manageable, scale which can help to decide between the various cultural reconstructions currently proposed. In a recent paper presented at the Association of Puerto Rican Anthropologists meeting in Dorado, Chanlatte (1987) suggests that some of the "Saladoid" types (in my terms, several vessel types with characteristic decorative and shape modes along similar dimensions which compose one of the wares within the Hacienda Grande style) may represent the overlap between the earlier cross-hatchured incised "Huecoid" ware with post-fired white crusting and the later white-on-red pre-fire painted Saladoid pottery. This ware consists of elaborate red-slipped pottery in a restricted range of small, carinated vessels (Figure 34). These hard, shiny (pebble-polished) vessels are decorated with "linear incision" and post-fired crusting in contrasting white paint. According to local convention I will designate this specialized (perhaps manioc beer serving) ware as the "linear incised ware" and make it the special focus of this paper.

The large scale excavations at the early Saladoid site of Maisabel (Ayes 1985; Rivera 1985), in Vega Baja, north coast of Puerto Rico, of which I am Co-Director (along with Siegel), and sponsored by the *Centro de Investigaciones Indígenas de Puerto Rico* (C.I.I.P.R.), of which I am Curator, has produced a huge sample within which the "linear incised ware" forms a significant component (Siegel 1986). Rouse has viewed this material and suggested that it represents an excellent opportunity to temporally locate this ware in its stratigraphic setting and to elucidate its position within the Saladoid series (Irving Rouse, personal communication 1986).

I developed a "generative grammatical" methodology (Roe 1980, 1982b, 1989), based on stylistic componential analysis (Roe 1975), to specify the degrees of similarity and difference between art styles in a variety of media, from textiles to pottery. When coupled with modal analysis (Raymond et al. 1975) it can compare both ceramic vessel form and surface decoration between traditions or series.

Therefore, one way of resolving the conflicting hypotheses about the earliest migrations to the Antilles is to use the linear incised ware as a basis for a generative grammatical study of both vessel form categories and surface decoration modes. The overarching problem is to chart the pattern of early migrations of horticultural populations from South America into the islands, test and evaluate conflicting theories about these movements, and measure the process of cultural and ecological adjustment of these *tierra firme* groups to an insular way of life.

A MODEL OF EARLY SALADOID OCCUPATION

OF THE GREATER ANTILLES

I evolved a model, based on excavations at five sites on the north and south coasts of Puerto Rico, to make some sense of the data for this initial peopling of the island. In broad terms, it begins with an initial rapid colonization by different, and perhaps mutually hostile,[43] Saladoid affiliated groups from South America. Still connected to the mainland by both trade and memory, they produced items, like *topias*, which only make sense in a lowland South American context and sculpt mainland jungle fauna, often identifiable to the species level, on their pottery. They crafted technologically complex pottery, whose many ingredients bespeak control of, or access to, dispersed island and mainland resources. In addition, their pottery was aesthetically sophisticated, alluding to a stylistic interaction sphere where information was great and readily communicated.

These apparently tribal-level groups had a material culture characterized by small, exquisitely-worked "personal presentation" items (mostly jewelry and fineware ceramics). In turn, this material culture implies an egalitarian and intimate (in terms of "personal space") level of social interaction. These items were made out of exotic[44] or dispersed raw materials and their manipulation, in diverse, complex and internally stereotyped components of both artifact form and surface embellishment, was based on a consumate knowledge of raw materials, elevated technical standards of workmanship, and finely developed connoisseurship. Such artifacts are clearly the products of highly skilled artists, and therefore individuals who were both expensive and rare, possibly peripatetic, to judge from the frequency of artifact repair and reuse.

These early Saladoid communities were intrusive pioneers into an alien landscape characterized by an impoverished island terrestrial fauna and a dispersed and possibly hostile resident preceramic population. The widely spaced distribution and large size of their communities (Figure 1) looks like a response to this uncertain situation. Their orientation to land resources, such as the land crab, or to easily-harvested, cyclically-concentrated near-shore molluscan fauna like *Cittarium pica* or the Nerites, testifies, in effect, to a lack of local subsistence expertise (Roe 1985; Roe et al. 1985).[45] The costly result of such simplified subsistence strategies was over-dependence on a few resources, the demographic collapse of such "target species" due to over-harvesting, and a consequent, and doubtlessly painful, ecological readjustment to a truly insular setting (Goodwin 1980).

As a partial by-product of the productivity of this system was the incipient shift from small-sized, exotic material constructed, "personal presentation" artistic goods to mass-produced, largely technical artifacts. To take just the two domains of the ceramic and lapidary arts I have already discussed: the concentration on technologically-limited spherical rather than technologically-complex stacked keeled shapes in later Puerto Rican complexes, and plastic rather than painted decoration (Figure 29), is related to the shift in stone work from small items of semi-precious stone to large items of local, and common, stone. Both are manifestations of a shift from a private "culture of refinement" to public displays of power within a hierarchically differentiating and, therefore socially segregated society. It is thus not coincidental that the ball game (González 1984; Questell 1983), with its associated ball court and monumental petroglyphic art becomes the durable symbols of this stage (Roe 1987b). These developments ultimately find full flower in the Taíno chiefdoms of proto-historic times (Alegría 1983).

A TECHNICAL AND AESTHETIC ANALYSIS OF EVOLUTION AND INTERACTION WITHIN GREATER ANTILLEAN SALADOID WARES

The core of the debate I am examining is Chanlatte's assertion that his "Huecoid" material is definitely *not* Saladoid. Yet, a study of the utilitarian ware from the two complexes, both in his collections from Vieques and in Rodríguez's collections from Puerto Rico, shows that the two styles are very similar. Both are clearly within the Saladoid vessel shape tradition. Additionally, there are typical Hacienda Grande Saladoid vessels which encorporate "La Hueca" style cross-hatchuring, but in a much more finely executed manner (compare Figure 35 or 38b with Figure 38a).[46]

Furthermore, this decoration occurs in the same design field on the same pedestal-based, flange-rimmed vessels, albeit of a slightly different shape (in the HG forms one finds broader, shorter, carinated and not rounded, rim extending outward in a horizontal manner versus slightly elevated LH forms). Figure 36b, drawn from a vessel recovered with a 100 B.C. C-14 date from the Hacienda Grande site by this author illustrates these similarities and differences as compared with Figure 36a, a typical "Huecoid" piece in the collections of the CIIPR.

Basically, the changes between these two vessels are reflective of changes in just four rules of vessel form generation within the same grammar: (1) the vessel width--alpha dimension is expanded in "b," (2) the vessel height--beta dimension is contracted in "b," (3) the labial flanged rim is canted out in a horizontal manner from an oblique orientation, and, (4) a carination is added below the sub-labial appliqued nubbin. One can show these systematic shifts by simply plotting each vessel on a flow-chart of vessel form generation based on a modal analysis of the vessel populations, to which these two specimens belong (Figure 37). Such a procedure operationalizes the question of just how "similar" or "different" each is by allowing the investigator to simply count shared dimensions and modes to yield an "index of comparability" for this vessel class (14 shared modes within 20 dimensions).

A plane view of the engraved labial flanged design fields of both vessels (Figure 38a,b) shows once again their close mutual similarities in such a way that one can systematically derive one from the other. In the manipulation of the dimensions width of labial flange--delta/width of interior vessel wall--gamma one can appreciate how Figure 38b differs from Figure 38a by simply increasing gamma and holding delta constant! Certain proportional changes then "automatically" happen as the vessel diameter increases, such as the increase in the width of the two nubbins (actually a kind of supra-labial flange tab, its linear dimension--epsilon) from narrow "a" to wider "b" with a resultant "saddle" between the nubbins of "b."

The workmanship of the technique of the two vessels is isomorphic with the degree of difficulty in vessel fabrication each step represents (short, wide, carinated forms with projecting elements are harder to realize in ceramics than tall, narrow and obliquely projecting, rounded forms). Predictably, the more "primitive" La Hueca specimen (Figure 36a) has sloppy *incision* (with line overlap) in a cross-hatched mode (Figure 38a), while the Hacienda Grande specimen (Figure 36b) has harder-to-execute *engraving* in a very careful cross-hatched mode with no missed line junctures or line overlap (Figure 38b).

Further, if one applies a generative grammatical analysis to the designs executed on each vessel, one sees how their relative complexity once more reflects their systemic relationships and differences. The simpler La Hueca piece shows the rotation of a straight line design element at right angles three times to produce a "C" motif in Figure 39a. Then, that motif is transversely reflected to produce an opposed-C design module (39a-1), which is then replicated by simple translation (39a-2) broken by a spacing of the module's width around the vessel's labial flange (39a-3,4), to generate a quadripartite design (Figure 38a).

The analogous Hacienda Grande vessel (Figure 38b) maintains its relative complexity over the La Hueca "historical prototype" (assuming for a moment that La Hueca predates Hacienda Grande)[47] by encorporating *two* design layouts within the same design field (the labial flange) through utilizing a rule of alternation. This requires *two* "derivational chains" (Figure 39b, left and right) from the same La Hueca "kernel statement" (39a, 1,2,3,4). This generative process involves, to look at the left chain (39b), a transverse reflection of the "C" motif, and then a fusion of the ends of the opposed "C"s via horizontal compression. Then, a deletion rule operates on the horizontally compressed line and it is erased yielding a squat open rectangle. On the right-hand derivational chain another "C" motif of opposed orientation is bifold-rotated and then replicated via translation. Once again compression, this time vertical, overlaps the resultant "S" modules, while a final deletion rule wipes out the overlapped lines to yield a squared meander design layout. Lastly, via a syntactical rule of design field organization (simple alternation) both design layouts are combined to yield a composite design layout (39c).

Thus, independent data sets from ceramic technology, vessel form generation and design construction (both plastic and graphic) demonstrate that both La Hueca and Hacienda Grande vessels of the same class belong to the same series. Moreover, they also demonstrate that the latter is consistently more complex than the former. I should emphasize that this distinction between La Hueca and Hacienda Grande crosshatching would be ignored by Chanlatte. Rather, to judge by his publications, he would typologically lump both the crude La Hueca and the more refined Hacienda Grande cross-hatching together under "cross-hatching" and then relate both to La Hueca.

Eventually, this Hacienda Grande cross-hatching is combined with pre-fire painting on typical Hacienda Grande *campaniform* (bell-shaped) vessels (Figure 35a,b). Then, these designs drop out of the successor phase to Hacienda Grande, the "Cuevas" tradition, while the white-on-red painting continues on other vessel shapes. I would suggest that this is so because the cross-hatching was not central to the Hacienda Grande tradition.[48] It had merely been "borrowed" from La Hueca (again, arguing for the moment from the point of view of La Hueca temporal priority). Rather, painting was central to the Hacienda Grande tradition[49] and therefore that was the decorative technique destined to survive to the very end. As Rouse points out in his paper in this volume, this displacement and eradication of La Hueca ZIC incision-engraving and the reappearance of red slip painting is also apparent in the Elenan Ostionoid series in the Virgin Islands. This pattern highlights the diachronic durability of the painterly tradition.

At the same time (ca. A.D. 300), the small La Hueca sites disappear while the large Hacienda Grande sites remain. One possible social implication of all this, drawing on lowland ethnographic parallels of wife-capture (Roe 1982a), where women are the potters, is that the Hacienda Grande populations absorbed some women from the closely-related La Hueca group, and their vessel shapes and surface decoration modes were incorporated into the Hacienda Grande style.[50] Simultaneously, as the fabrication norms of the Hacienda Grande group were higher than those of the La Hueca group, this new "borrowed" ware was executed in a finer manner on slightly different Hacienda Grande forms (Figure 35). Eventually, because this cross-hatchured style of decoration was not central to the white-on-red painted Hacienda Grande-Cuevas tradition, it dropped out as the descendants of the original captured women had now completely acculturated into the Hacienda Grande-Cuevas modes.

Parallel studies of cross-ethnic group aesthetics in cognate lowland Amerindian societies (Roe 1976, 1981) indicate that such aesthetic borrowing would have been likely to occur precisely because the two groups in question were culturally similar and had isomorphic canons of design and forms. Otherwise, a differently styled artifact simply represents "noise" to a dominant society, the product of barbarians. It will be regarded as ugly, and will be fated to be ignored or destroyed.

Crucial to this convoluted argument is the existence of an "intermediary" ware that encorporates elements of *both* the La Hueca style and the Hacienda Grande style of the Saladoid series. This is the so-called "linear-incised" ware. It is one of the wares within the Hacienda Grande style and is identified by linear incision (that is, incision that defines the "form-lines" of a design motif, rather than filling it in as in the case of ZIC) filled with post-fired kaolin (or talc) and limonite crusting, like La Hueca, but in a deeper, more finely-controlled "U"-shaped incision. This incision is cut into a well-polished pre-fire Hacienda Grande red slip.

Moreover, this decoration always occurs on elaborately, and exaggeratedly, carinated (González 1984:Figure 26) "flying saucer" (*plato voleador*)-style vessels (Figure 40), or on equally exaggerated and elegant "chalices" (Figure 41) with a concave middle section, an even more highly angled upper segment (Figure 42), and an additional corner point on the base. As a third representative of this specialized class, one finds the same recurved base and lower body (Figure 43a, b), but with the addition of an outcurving jar neck and unrestricted rim (43c, d). Figure 34 generates all these forms from the same components of dimensions and modes. Such clearly segmented and complex-silhouette vessels are characteristic only of the Hacienda Grande style.

I believe that it is no coincidence that all the design layouts on these vessels are on their upper surfaces. Indeed, these sharp carinations are present to produce relatively flat surfaces so that they can become design fields destined to be appreciated "globally" (that is, by viewing them from above as a whole), unlike the designs from the everted, *campaniform* vessels, such as Figure 30, which can only be appreciated as they were executed, in segments, from a vantage point perpendicular to the vessel form. Proof of this deduction is the lack of "plan ahead" problems in the global designs where the symmetrical inter-relationship of parts could be visually and simultaneously judged and their presence in the perpendicular designs where they could not.

Nearly all of these forms are small (Figures 40-43), thin-walled, extremely finely executed and of great aesthetic, almost "jewel-like," visual and tactile impact. Additionally, they are all constricted-orifice vessels with capacious little bodies that fit well within the hand. They are suitable only for liquids, and to judge by lowland South Amerindian ethnographic parallels, like the Shipibo Indian *quënpo* I have studied, these Saladoid cups would best have been suited for the presentation of manioc beer to honored guests.

Rather like the culturally-unrelated but formally-similar Japanese Tea Ceremony (Anderson 1987), where the participants are expected to utter a poem on the beauty of the cup's imperfections as they rotate it and take a sip, so too do South Amerindians lavish much care on cups and jars intended to offer valued drink to guests (Lathrap 1983). They do so as members of cultures in which both generosity and artistic skill are highly valued. Indeed, that is why the designs can only be appreciated "globally;" they are designed to be appreciated as one lifts the cup to one's mouth to quaff a drink!

A METHODOLOGY TO DECIPHER THE LANGUAGE OF THE CUPS: THE GENERATIVE GRAMMATICAL APPROACH

We have not yet utilized to the full the valuable ceramic evidence Saladoid pottery offers on these hypotheses. Only by using a powerful emic approach, which seeks to "communicate with the dead," in the sense that it tries to decipher their conceptual modes, postulate solutions while analyzing a corpus of material objects (in this case pottery), and predict similarities and differences the archaeologist might encounter in future excavations, can we hope to enter these ancient styles and view the intricacies of their styles from the inside out. The generative grammatical stylistic approach is one such attempt at operationalized connoisseurship.

It originated within the modal analytic framework of Rouse (1939), in which he divided vessels into their constituent "modes," or patterns of decisions, that the original artisan had to make to construct its various aspects of form. Lathrap (DeBoer and Lathrap 1979) then modified this program by further dividing these artifacts into "dimensions," or naturally ordered steps in fabrication, within which various modes are consciously selected. In this way, a routing diagram can be constructed that duplicates how an artisan constructs a pot,[51] first beginning with the base and then selecting one of several kinds of bases appropriate for the kind of vessel being made, then moving on to the lower vessel body and so on.

Then, building upon this scholarly tradition, several of Lathrap's students, myself included (Raymond et al. 1975), extended his method by incorporating the seminal work of Shepard (1971) on ceramic surface decorative symmetry rules.[52] We constructed a dimensional and modal analysis of *both* vessel shape categories and surface decoration. This analysis broke the artifacts into constituent elements (design elements) and postulated rules (design rules) that could parsimoniously account for the design layouts on vessels within an archaeological assemblage.[53] Such a method permits one to predict expectable new solutions in samples not yet recovered. I then further extended this method, as a check, to ethnographic populations (the Shipibo: Roe 1979, 1980) and in other domains of material culture (textile painting: Roe 1982b).

The method is now capable of generating chains of linked aesthetic solutions, sequential transformations of the style's elements and rules to form design "statements" (design layouts) composed of constituent motifs (design compounds) placed within the culturally-circumscribed appropriate areas of the artifact to be decorated (design fields). Since it can generate a series of designs out of a limited number of elements and rules this method can be designated a generative grammatical approach to the language of form and design. It is that approach which will be applied for the first time to Saladoid ceramics, specifically the "linear incised ware" to test the above-mentioned hypotheses about multiple ethnic groups in the first several centuries B.C. in the Caribbean.

THE EVIDENCE FROM VESSEL FORM CATEGORIES

Based on the extensive collections (ex-Castillo and ex-Guillermetz) that the CIIPR has, and from which I have drawn many of the specimens in figures, both La Hueca and Hacienda Grande style pottery can be broken into minimal elements of form (Figures 44, 45). Each one of these are the "modes" within the various dimensions of bases, lower vessel bodies, shoulders, necks, rims and lips that the pottery corpus reveals to be significant. One starts with vessel form because potters must first make vessels before they can decorate their surfaces.

The sharply segmented character of this pottery based upon stacking modular units lends itself to a grammatical analysis. For example, an elaborate Hacienda Grande Saladoid bottle (Figure 46) can be constructed out of some of the same parts (Figure 47) as the vessels of the linear incised ware (Figure 34). Furthermore, there is a significant amount of "play," or the formal recombination of vessel form elements to generate a series of similar vessels (in the case of the effigy version of the water/beer jars in Figure 48b), which are distinct stages in a "derivational chain" of vessel forms (Figure 49), analogous to various design layouts in an equally generative treatment of surface decoration.

"Play," within Cedrosan Saladoid vessel form generation highlights how a study of the process of vessel construction can shed light on the differential loci of "art" in a ceramic style. For some styles, that locus might be vessel shape, and for others, surface decoration. In the former, new modes along any dimension, or new dimensions, may be innovated and playfully recombined to generate a plethora of new shapes. One could, therefore, specify that such a style applies "rule creation behavior" (RCB) to vessel form construction. This may be illustrated by using a simpler archaeological tradition, like the vessel forms of the ninth century A.D. Cumancaya Tradition of the Peruvian jungle (Figure 50). Such a chart will look like the Antillean Saladoid situation, but it also highlights the differences in relative complexity. Even in a complex, biglobular, tradition such as Cumancaya, we do not find the number of vessel form dimensions we encounter in Cedrosan Saladoid. In particular, I have had to introduce a series of additional dimensions: "superior body, superior body neck" (Figures 44, 46)[54] to encompass the combinatorial possibilities of but one class of Puerto Rican Saladoid vessel, the large three-handled water/beer jar (Figure 49). Indeed, even further complexities are possible with this form through the addition of those "superior" segments to a basic jar (49c), handles onto those segments (49e), both vertical and horizontal nubbins on those upper handles (49a), etc. One has the impression that were the archaeological sample larger there would be an even greater number of dimensions, and modes, under each dimension than are currently known.

This is significant, since just to define art as elaboration of form beyond technical function, as is commonly the case in anthropology and archaeology (i.e., Maguet 1971), ignores *process* in favor of *end product*. This is a view antithetical to art, which emphasizes process over end product (art *is the process*), since the product may be ephemeral or non-existent. Does a dance step fossilize?[55]

Hence, one must also speak of creativity and novelty in the process. Something is not art just because it is ornate. If that ornate object is replicated in a *stereotyped* mode, without variation, then it cannot be art. One is reminded of José Ortega y Gasset's famous dictum, "in art, repetition is nothing." Such ornate repetition will create *artifice*, or artificial art of the sort one frequently encounters in airports, but not traditional art of the kind Amerindians produce.

If one simply replicates a technical aspect, such as vessel form (Figure 51), one produces the opposite of art, and the quintessence of technology, "Rule Replication Behavior," or RRB. Of course one follows an unerring trajectory, centered on the same cultural "target," if one is doing technology. Any deviation represents a waste of time or effort in the pursuit of an energy-efficient goal. In this contrast I do not include technological innovation within technology, but emphasize instead that such technical innovation has a marked affinity to the creative phase of art.

Therefore, Cedrosan Saladoid pottery is very complex because it represents a "double dose" of complexity, both vessel form and surface decoration are suitable domains for art. This also means that through a process of the "aesthetic imperative" (Roe 1979), Cedrosan Saladoid potters would have been open to the formal possibilities inherent in other, cognate traditions, such as La Hueca. The tendency of artists to push the envelope of style, or in Miller's (1985) terms, to systematically extend a prototype to create new prototypes, enables aspects of non-art to become art. Hence, the Hacienda Grande artists may "borrow" a new form, such as a pedestal-based, labial-flanged bowl, while processing it through their own vocabulary of carinated forms, rather like modern Shipibo potters who have archaistically innovated from ancient, ancestral Cumancaya vessel shapes (Roe 1976).

One index of ceramic similarity or difference between two styles within a series or a tradition, let us say La Hueca and Hacienda Grande,[56] can then be generated simply by counting dimensions, modes, elements and rules in common.[57] If one does this for the two pedestal-based, labial-flanged bowls in Figure 37, the results show close, but specifiable, differences. Moreover, the "linear-incised ware" bowls and jars of the Hacienda Grande style also emerge as a distinct "decisional complex" based on similar design component selections.

THE EVIDENCE FROM SURFACE DECORATION

The same process can be initiated with surface decoration (in this case painting and incision, Figure 52) after the forms on which it occurs have been analyzed and synthesized.[58] A generative grammatical methodology has been developed to analyze art styles that potentially can illuminate the relationships of the La Hueca and Hacienda Grande styles based on their incised and painted surface decoration dimensions and modes.

This approach postulates primitive design elements and design rules to construct acceptable graphic statements (design layouts) in various geometric styles. I have applied the method to (a) related modern South Amerindian ethnographic materials (Roe 1976, 1979, 1980, 1981), where both native aesthetic judgements and aesthetic artifact production can be used to evaluate the method, and (b) cognate South American lowland archaeological complexes (Raymond et al. 1975), where the postulation of hypothetical designs can later be confirmed or invalidated by new archaeological discoveries.

This method provides an insight into the debate of whether La Hueca is or is not Saladoid by showing how both styles and one ware within one style (Hacienda Grande style= Figure 52a; Linear Incised ware of the Hacienda Grande style=52b; and La Hueca style=52c) use the *same design grammar*, each of which *emphasizes variant forms of the same spiral motif*. That is, the bulk of Hacienda Grande cursive painted and incised designs are based on a spiral motif,[59] which with the addition of a "shank," a straight line departing from the spiral at 45 degrees, becomes a scroll. This scroll is then bifold-rotated to form various painted and "linear-incised" design layouts (Figures 40b, 41a,b).

If the scroll is oriented to 90 rather than 45 degrees, through simple rotation, and then transverse-reflected, it becomes an elongated motif of opposed curls. In turn, through continued simplification (via the application of contraction and deletion rules) it becomes an elongated lozenge with a parallel medial line. Then, pursuing further these inherent possibilities in many different derivational chains,[60] the two motifs can be combined (via a nesting rule) into the complex linear incised designs (Figure 42a) also found on this ware (Figure 43a).

Lastly, by following a separate line of reasoning, within the same over-arching style, the La Hueca potters created a simpler "T" motif. They did so, apparently, by further simplifying the opposed scrolls of the vertical (not 45 degree) motif so that they were schematic "Cs" (Figure 52a-c). Then, through a deletion rule and a contraction rule these elements were merged and rectangularized to form meander "T" patterns. In turn, some of these layouts become altered by the application of a vertical reflection rule to the "T" motifs to generate "I" motifs through translation (52c).

While there are fewer possibilities in the La Hueca style than in the Hacienda Grande style and its painted and linear incised wares, and hence greater uniformity in appearance (repetition of the same designs from pot to pot), the LH style manipulates the same elements and rules. The rectilinear construction of La Hueca designs is what distinguishes them, but even this is a result of the lower technical skills of La Hueca potters. Rectilinear designs are easier to execute than curvilinear ones.[61] This difficulty will later be replayed in the devolution of Hacienda Grande ceramics into Cuevas, where one can often distinguish the two by the cruder application of the paint and the rectilinear cast of Cuevas design layouts compared to their elegant and curvilinear Hacienda Grande precursors (Roe et al. 1985).

The design fields are similar in both the La Hueca and the Hacienda Grande complexes (labial flanges in particular). The only differences are that the La Hueca style decorates the *inside* of the vessel wall while the Hacienda Grande style embellishes the *outside* of the vessel (save in the case of open flat-based bowls, Figure 35). However, this difference is more apparent than real since the change in design field placement itself derives from a single alteration in the vessel form construction rules (the canting of a labial flange *inward* on La Hueca specimens (Figure 36) due to their greater fragility, versus canting the labial flange *outward* on the stronger Hacienda Grande paste. In short, a grammatical analysis of design construction on both La Hueca and Hacienda Grande styles highlights their *close similarities* and their *minor, and specifiable differences* in such a way as to argue for a *cognate Cedrosan Saladoid stylistic affiliation* to both styles. Moreover, the same analysis clarifies the intermediate character of the "Linear Incised Ware." Basically, this refers to the execution of "La Hueca-like designs" on Hacienda Grande shapes using a linear "La Hueca" design perception, but with post-fire Hacienda Grande technology. This shows that the synthesis between these two styles is the linear incised ware of the Hacienda Grande style because the incised designs it bears on a pre-fire red paste background are then coated with a post-fire crusting, à la La Hueca, in talc or kaolin.

This "highlighting" makes the Hacienda Grande designs stand out on the paste, like their white painted designs stand out on the same red paste in the same order (red first, white later). This explains why the Linear Incised ware can utilize visually ambiguous (where the creator/perceiver can mentally switch back and forth between visualizing figure-as-ground and ground-as-figure) motifs, particularly in the "stacked" multiple lozenge designs shown in Figure 52b. They are the perceptual analog of the "false negative" painted designs on Hacienda Grande WOR pots and, like them, require the aid of contrast (in the form of the added paint) to tease out figure from ground. In short, both Chanlatte is right (yes, they are different) and so are Alegría and Rouse (yes, they are also the same) with regard to the "cross-hatched" component of the Cedrosan Saladoid style.

Further, the general appearance of the geometric designs that grace both early styles display similar affinities to the Valdivia-Machalilla-Chorrerra sequence on the coast and interior of Ecuador (Lathrap et al. 1975) that we picked up in vessel form and sculptural decoration. Frequently, these similarities revolve around bifold-rotated and tranverse-reflected arrays of "T"-shaped motifs that may have their technical origin in plaited and twill-woven basketry and textiles. Indeed, there may be similar patterns of insight for the origin and iconography of these two traditions. Stahl (1985a, 1985b and 1986) argues that the comparable Valdivia figural and decorative ceramic style is based on hallucinogenic imagery, a sure stigmata of lowland affinity.

If both the vessel form and surface decoration similarities[62] between these early ceramic traditions are real, it would reinforce a picture of formative tropical forest interaction first charted by Lathrap (1970). Such interaction plausibly may be inferred for the whole region between the Peruvian montaña from the Ucayali to the Huallaga, and the Ecuadorian montaña and coast through the Orinoco[63] and Guianas out into the Antilles!

READING SOCIETY AND SOCIAL CHANGE OUT OF POTTERY

It may also be possible to divine something about social process from this material culture. Specifically, can the devolution of the pottery[64] in the Greater Antilles through time be counter-intuitively linked to the social "evolution" occurring at the same time, as reflected by the appearance of ball parks and monumental art in Pre-Taíno and Taíno times? After all, we normally believe that material and social complexification go hand-in-hand. "Media displacement" of art can help explain this apparent contradiction by signaling significant social shifts that were providing much of the impetus for this simultaneous evolutionary/devolutionary progression. In other words, perhaps not all media increase in complexity to mirror the increasing complexification in society. The devolution of one technology, here ceramics, may be linked with the evolution in another aspect of material culture, say monumental stone sculpture, which does reflect what is going on in society. Not only will the *locus* of art shift, so too will its *purpose*.

In the phenomenon of "media displacement," the locus of art can change from one medium to another as the society in which that art[65] operates changes. Thus, one can investigate specifically the relationship between art and ceramic and lithic artifacts at the beginning and end of the cultural continuum in the Greater Antilles. Initially art is expressed (in both the La Hueca and the Hacienda Grande styles) in small, superbly-executed and esthetically complex ceramic vessels and tiny, jewel-like stone carvings. The very scale of these finds and their sophistication prompts reconstructions about the societies that produced them.

Indeed, there has been some debate as to the nature of Saladoid society, with Dávila (1979:71) suggesting a simple tribal level of social integration, with some incipient hierarchy, and Carbone (1980:27) arguing for a greater degree of hierarchy based on the craft specialization and far-flung trade patterns evidenced by the complex Saladoid material culture.

Further, there is technological evidence (that has not yet been tested from a materials science perspective)[66] for a high degree of craft specialization, and hence social complexity to both support the costs of that specialization and utilize its products, within these early Antillean societies. Earthenware pottery has low tensile strength and modest compression strength. Therefore, a simpler tradition, like La Hueca or, in the even simpler successor styles of the Elenan/Ostionan Ostionoid or Chicoid series (Figure 29), should be characterized by a "primitive sphericity" to paraphrase Linné. That is, potters will maximize its strengths and minimize its weaknesses by tending to make their pots approximate the shape of a restricted, semi- closed spherical or ovoid "egg." It is no coincidence that the La Hueca forms emphasize round contours or that the latter Chicoid materials should uniformly display round bases and a simple shouldered "olla" (*cazuela*) shape.

In contrast, Cedrosan Saladoid potters defied earthenware pottery's limitations by maximizing skill and higher technology to approximate the tensile strength and complex shapes of metal! That is, many of its vessel shapes abound in corner-points (Shepard 1971), or carinations. These are sharp flexures in body contours. Coil-built pottery is fabricated in sections so that it can air-dry and stiffen, thus sustaining radical changes in the direction of the body contour. This generates problems in differential moisture content of the next superimposed section and, consequently, the fragility of the bond between the upper and the lower vessel body wall. Moreover, compression will rupture the vessels along these carination body joins, particularly when the join is made in such a way that the upper body section does not, contrary to sound practice, overlap the last coil of the underlying segment (Figure 43b). Even the simple air drying process which is a necessary prelude to firing will cause breakage as, for example, cracks develop around the interior of annular-based bowls with the discouraging result that the raised bottom literally "falls out."

If this is the case with one corner point, *a fortiori* the many such points that result from the aesthetics of Cedrosan Saladoid! This is a bias towards "verticality" among Hacienda Grande style potters, leading them to "stack" several body segments in the playful, recombinatorial fashion referred to earlier. In contrast, *all* the La Hueca forms (save the bottles) are simple, non-compound forms.

Moreover, body segments, which are technically appliqué, such as labial flanges and supra-flange tabs and adornos, further tempt gravitational fate by introducing yet additional points of tensile weakness. The fact that Cedrosan Saladoid potters could do this in *all* the dimensions of vessel construction argues most persuasively that pottery for them was not just another humble "domestic art," but represented instead a species of "utilitarian sculpture." The major vehicle for art in the Hacienda Grande style of the Cedrosan Saladoid was *pottery*, while for the La Huecan style the premier art form was doubtlessly *lapidary* corporeal *art*.[67] This, in turn, suggests that not everyone of the appropriate sex[68] was a potter, and that some potters were either more talented than others or more experienced in certain tasks.

Such differential specialization occurs in ethnographic lowland tribal societies like the Shipibo, one of the premier potting groups still practicing in South America. So great is the knowledge and experience required to make and successfully fire the huge (almost 2X1 m) beer jars, the *chomo ani* ("beer jar, big"), and so closely is such knowledge and experience related to age in such societies, that only a few, and renowned women in each large village can make them. Many smaller villages lack such specialists completely. Indeed, today these skills are in imminent danger of cultural extinction precisely because of their rarity. These specialists are widely renowned for their vessels. Their large pots find their way to other settlements via water transportation (which offsets their considerable weight). Such women will be "commissioned" to produce these large pots, which essentially are for the fiesta drinking bouts famous in the lowlands as a social integration mechanism felicitously combining entertainment, emotional release, military and marital alliance and trading functions.

Yet these older women are also wives and mothers and retain the full range of feminine duties within the sexual division of labor common in their society (they cook, clean, sweep, cultivate and harvest, etc.). In that sense they are like any other woman. Thus while they are specialists, these mature "master potters" are not full-time, supported, specialists. I will call such artisans "village specialists" to highlight their intermediate status between the "average practitioner," or "journeyman," on the one hand, and the "full-time occupational specialist" on the other. It is as such "village specialists" that I envision Hacienda Grande potters and La Hueca lapidary workers.

Specialization may also be addressed by employing a behavioral-chain approach (Schiffer 1972). That is, the story does not cease with the manufacture of an artifact to meet the cognitive demands of a prototype. It continues through the object's use-life trajectory and all the curational patterns appropriate to the culture that created it, including its repair, reuse, and ultimate disposition.

In my observations of on-going Amerindian systems, such as that of the Shipibo or Waiwai, I have noted an "aesthetic of the pristine" in operation. Probably because of an emphasis on craftsmanship in artifact fabrication and criticsm (the technical aspects of a pot are often the first aspects commented upon), this means that to be truly beautiful, or appropriate to use, an artifact must be brand new, or pristine. Ceramic artifacts that betray the traces of use or damage are quickly relegated to reuse categories such as holding temper or as coops for domesticates. Thus, there is no "aesthetic of the antique" such as in Western culture. An object is not more highly valued because it is old or betrays the passage of time in its dilapidated exterior.[69]

Such a bias for "newness" obtains in a society where skills are so widely distributed that new artifacts can be made at will to replace those damaged in use, or where the raw materials to make them are so abundant that replacement of damaged, destroyed, lost or exchanged items can be done cheaply or continuously. These are also the reasons why the "antique" is valued in our own skill-poor, machine cultures.

Hence, the discovery of the frequent repair or reuse of ceramic artifacts, in an attempt to extend their use-life, can be prima facie evidence that either skills were rare and expensive, or materials were rare and expensive, or both. I have seen many examples in large Saladoid collections, such as Chanlatte's, of vessels bearing matched perforations along fracture lines for string mending, or the lower body segments of complex-silhouette vessels that have broken along a coil line (just below the carination) which bear abraded upper coils, thus turning them into the "rims" of open bowls of the sort pictured in Figure 53. Repair and reuse indicators are congruent with the data from the dimensions of vessel shape and surface decoration to argue for a high degree of craft specialization in the production of Saladoid pottery.

Moreover, there is evidence from these and other dimensions that Hacienda Grande pottery was produced by a more sophisticated society than was La Hueca pottery.[70] In turn, that disparity in complexity provides an explanation for the incorporation of La Hueca modes into Hacienda Grande practice.

If we pick a scenario more akin to Carbone's hierarchical position, but still within a basically egalitarian framework for Saladoid society, the question emerges how did people value the characterisitics evident in the physical remains? I suggest that they did so within a intermediate type of social system between a simple tribe and the chiefdom, perhaps via a "big man" (such statuses of temporary "chiefship" like a war captain) model where individual achievements are sought, but their structural effects on stratification and/or ranking are rendered ephemeral because of redistribution mechanisms like feasting and ceremonial exchange. If such mechanisms as "social circumscription" (Chagnon 1983) existed within the narrow island chain from the Vieques Sound to the Lesser Antilles produced by the jostling of ethnic groups, then one could imagine a great deal of emphasis being placed on a material culture of "personal presentation" by emphasizing an individual's cultural aspirations or attainments.[71]

As in current Shipibo culture, the perception of an individual's "culturedness" is gained by being offered, or appreciating, small objects of exquisite workmanship (small because they are intended to be seen close up) that function "kinetically" as they are actually used during the course of the presentation. In other words, one should comment upon, and appreciate, a small, beautifully-painted beer mug as one drinks the proffered beer it contains. And as one does this the concealed clay pellets in its base will rattle as the cup is upended. It is really the *process* of presentation that is being elaborated as much as it is its end, and kinetic features like rattles in the base (or in Saladoid pottery, in hollow effigy handles, cf. Figure 23), which underscore that aspect of action through process. Not only was Saladoid pottery sculpture, but it was also "kinetic sculpture"!

But pottery makes a poor vehicle for the demonstration of power (not authority, which is based on culture)[72] since it is a technologically "democratic" medium (especially if it is earthenware and not porcelain, or if it is compared with metal containers cf., Miller 1985:74, 151). Everyone can own and make it on at least a journeyman level of ability and complexity.[73] Therefore, as Antillean society attained greater hierarchy in the "incipient chiefdoms" or "complex tribes" (Habicht-Mauche et al. 1987) of Pre-Taíno times, the locus of "art" shifts from pottery to large, static, stonework which demonstrates the power to mobilize and commission labor through its very weight or immobility. Moreover, being visible from a long distance away, this art of "public display" could be, and often is, crude in execution. Thus, we have petroglyphs and large sculpture out of common (not semi-precious or exotic) stone as one approaches the Taíno end of the cultural continuum. In Taíno times pottery is mass-produced at a simpler, stereotyped (in vessel categories and surface decoration modes), level and plastic (not painted) designs prevail.

Thus, we first see a "personal presentation" material culture reflective of egalitarian relations through its (a) small size, (b) jewel-like workmanship, (c) close inspection visibility, and, (d) kinetic (presentation process) features at the beginning of the sequence. Subsequently there is a process of "media displacement" in the art mirroring the increasing hierarchical sociopolitical relations through the characteristics of an increasingly "public display" nature of the material culture. This is evident through its (a) large size, (b) rude workmanship, (c) long-distance visibility, and, (d) static features at the end of the process of social evolution.

CONCLUSIONS

It should be emphasized that this approach to the archaeology of vessel form generation and surface decorative geometric patterning is very preliminary as it is based on "contextless" artifacts in collections. I will shortly apply the same technique to the well-documented stratigraphically-excavated materials from the CIIPR's Maisabel project. Only then will we be able to tie in the date of the appearance of the Linear Incised Ware to the Saladoid ceramic evolution on the island and test the model of ethnic interaction, as decipherable from ceramics, that I have advanced here.

However, this preliminary survey suggests that the "La Hueca" and "Hacienda Grande" ceramic styles are, contrary to Chanlatte, and *in agreement with Rouse* both within the Saladoid series. This is based on their mutual similarity, which is evident when one compares the utilitarian pottery within both complexes. Even specific fine ware forms, like the pedestal-based, labial- flanged bowl, are different, but in minor and specifiable ways. These similarities argue for a "cognate" status for both styles in everything from the rules of vessel proportion, to the specifics of design motif execution and construction.

Yet, contrary to Alegría, and to Rouse's early response, but not Rouse's reconstruction in this volume, I argue that La Hueca practice is recognizably distinct from Hacienda Grande in its implementation of cultural conventions. In this respect I am *in agreement with Chanlatte and Rodríguez*. These differences are present in specific kinds of vessels, such as the "bat effigy" vessels (Figure 25), or the "dog-handled bowls" (Figure 31). Moreover, La Hueca also differs, as Chanlatte has pointed out, with regard to the design fields appropriate for decoration in each system, although a great overlap does exist. My own studies using a componential/generative grammatical approach have isolated specific differences in the basic design elements and motifs used. While the La Hueca system utilizes the simpler-to-execute "T" modules, Hacienda Grande tends to utilize the more difficult-to-execute, and more variable, "C" modules. The sheer fact that *both complexes share the same grammar*, however, argues that they should either be considered, as Rouse advances herein, separate subseries within the same series, or as I (in agreement with Siegel) more conservatively suggest, styles within the same subseries.

The temporal relationships of these two styles is still somewhat unclear. While the pattern of C-14 dates suggests that they are contemporary, the greater technical sophistication and complexity of the Hacienda Grande style[74] argues that it may be a later development than the La Hueca style. Only the depositional situation and horizontal stratigraphy of the La Hueca/Sorcé site, which has yet to be documented statistically, as well as the tendency for La Hueca style material to be found in the earliest levels of sites with Hacienda Grande style components[75] hints at La Hueca priority.

My suggestion is that these two styles pertain not only to different, but closely-related, "peoples" in Rouse's sense, but that those "cultural groups" viewed each other as "ethnic groups" locked in agonistic interaction (perhaps raiding for women and ritual purposes, such as ritual cannibalism, corporeal human bone adornments, etc.) such as we see in the main-river and interfluvial regions of mainland South America. This would provide a suitable "engine" to explain both the rapid pace of colonization, the physical isolation of smaller La Hueca settlements and their differential adaptation as identifiable from contrasting faunal assemblages. Conflict or its threat also explains the rapid supplantation (through competitive exclusion) of the La Hueca people by a larger Hacienda Grande population.

My analysis tends to support Chanlatte's recent implied solution to this problem. The "linear incised" ware of the Hacienda Grande style appears to represent an assimilation of certain La Hueca modes into its canons. La Hueca post-fire crusting is retained, as is cross-hatched incision, but they are organized in both La Hueca "T" and Hacienda Grande "C" modular designs within linear incised form-lines. They are present in exquisitely-executed Hacienda Grande fashion on small, complex-silhouette, globally-conceived, specialized service ware, many perhaps beer mugs. A possible explanation of this curious pattern of ceramic influence is that the linear incised ware represents physical evidence of the assimilation of captured La Hueca female potters, and their descendants, within the more elaborate Hacienda Grande canons of taste and execution.

Such a melding of traditions was possible because the groups that raided each other and practiced wife-capture were really quite closely related culturally and linguistically. So close were their affinities that each group could appreciate, if not highly value, the design contributions and structure of the competing ethnic group's ceramic art and technology. Yet, because such La Hueca elements were not really central to the technological and aesthetic stylistic core of Hacienda Grande culture, this "medial ware" was destined for a short florescence and eventually drops out of later Saladoid art.[76] Its "last gasp" appears to be present in the post-fire highlighted linear incised designs of Tibes (Alvarado 1980; González 1984) "epi-Saladoid" ceramics (Figure 54).

In the progressive simplification over time of the Hacienda Grande successor styles, the "incised tradition" elements are lost while the "painted tradition" elements continue. They finally die in the red painted "false bichrome" of Monserratean and early Elenan Ostionoid ceramics, which had long since replaced the La Hueca style in its "homeland," the Vieques Sound culture area. By that time, presumably, one might speak of a thoroughly fused people with no internal "ethnic" distinctions (save perhaps in the regional difference between eastern Ostionoid [Elenan] and western Ostionoid [Ostionan] ceramics?). It was a society whose female potters had lost any "cultural memory" of their La Hueca precursors.

NOTES

1. In this paper I will be adopting Rouse's (1986:127, 134) most recent formulation of Vescelius's (1980) taxonomic terminology to Antillean or Insular Saladoid (see Bullen 1968, 1970) and Pons de Alegría 1979 for some earlier terminologies), but with Rouse's "series" definition. That is, I will be treating both "Huecoid," which I relabel "La Hueca," and "Hacienda Grande" as two styles, or phases, within the Cedrosan Saladoid Series (viewed as a series of "styles," not "complexes," [Rouse and Allaire 1978:438] to the contrary notwithstanding, since I am dealing primarily with pottery here).

2. An exception must be made for precocious early works of "ceramic sociology," to use Sackett's felicitous phrase, such as Bunzel's (1972) study of Acoma and Zuni potters.

3. I have already pointed out how artifacts like the common round, conical thatched-roof communal house, are microcosms of the macrocosm (the known universe and man's relationship to it) in current South Amerindian cultures, like the Guianan Carib (Ye'cuana, Waiwai, Wayana), that are culturally related to the ancient voyagers into the Caribbean (Roe

1987a). Other artifacts, like pottery or basketry, are also related to the animistic world view of that cosmology. Thus, not only are artifacts transformed animals themselves in mythic times, other artifacts like the design motifs that adorn them, are "copied" from reluctant "animal donors" in mythic times (Roe 1988a). This pattern of "technical/artistic animism" reaffirms both the relationship of humans to non-humans in mythic and shamanistic time, and the contrast with non-humans in current profane time.

There is also evidence that this pattern of dualistic thought is of the greatest antiquity. Thus in the Caribbean, in the early Saladoid era, we find the predictable association between these smaller artifacts, like baskets (a thatched hut is technically a "basket one lives in"), or pottery and housing type. This alignment can be specified in structuralist notation, if pots are to artifacts as huts are to artifacts (pots : artifacts :: huts : artifacts) and artifacts : transformed animals :: animals : naturefacts, then pots : transformed animals :: huts : transformed animals.

To cite but one concrete areal example, we find large, round communal huts of the mainland sort this ethnographic analogy is based on in St. Eustatius (Versteeg and Effert 1987:Figure 4), near Puerto Rico, and in Barbados (Hackenberger 1987) near the mainland. We also find separate smaller huts of an earlier occupation at the same site, both types equipped with wind screens made of poles radiating in a line from the structures in both the ethnographic Guianan present (Hurault 1961, for the ethnographic Wayana) and the Caribbean archaeological past (Versteeg, this volume; Versteeg and Effert 1987:Figure 4, on the Early Cedrosan Saladoid).

It may not be a coincidence that the little polygonal hut at the Golden Rock site on St. Eustatius looks like a ray in plane-view, with its curved, wind-screen "tail." The explanation for this apparent morphological act of analogy could be purely technological since that wind-screen is placed to shelter the inhabitants from the prevailing Westerlies. But a purely technological argument falls apart when one considers the windscreens attached to the large *maloca*. The anomaly is that there are "screens," not just one screen. There is one oriented to the prevailing winds, but there is a symmetrical one on the other side that has no such function. It is there, apparently, for reasons of pure symmetry. I suggest they turned the hut, in plane-view, into a sea turtle effigy!

Through ethnographic analogy, we discover a lowland symbolic association of women's wombs, hollowness, and containers (Roe 1982a). Thus we find that gourds and turtle shells are feminine symbols, and, in turn, feminine symbols carry the connotation of "home," or the residential unit as symbol of geneaological continuity and social identity, symbolized in the largest container of all, the communal hut. The modern Waiwai redundantly encode this association when they place a hollow gourd at the tip of the central house post as it protrudes from the apex of the conical roof of their round communal hut, or *muïmo*. There are early drawings that depict the same finials on the central house poles of contact-period Antillean huts!

Further, we find that turtle effigy bowls, or trays, are a common vessel form category in Cedrosan Saladoid (Figure 3). The same holds true at the Golden Rock site itself where an elegant Saladoid tray with its four "fin" adornos placed at the corners of the vessel betray it as a highly stylized sea turtle effigy (Versteeg and Effert 1987:Frontispiece). Moreover, we get the intentional interment of a Hawksbill turtle, the same species which is elsewhere portrayed in clay and in petroglyphs (Roe 1987b), in the same site (Versteeg and Effert 1987:Figure 10). Elsewhere in the Caribbean we know that animal intentional interment, like dogs (Chanlatte 1983a:Lámina 50), confers a special, perhaps ritual status, on those creatures (Walker 1984). All lines of evidence, therefore, intersect in a symbolic "kenning" (an indirect, highly metaphorical usage) of the communal hut as a symbolic sea turtle. Maybe, in other words, the structures are being "kenned" (cf. Roe 1974) as theriomorphs in an ultimate expression of the principles of "technical animism!

4. The same problem of three-quarter view depiction, sometimes without scale, exists in other attempts at portrayal of Cedrosan Saladoid vessel forms (Chanlatte 1976:149), or the profile views are too schematic, and without sectioning, to be of more than general use (1976:167). In such sources, attempts at reconstruction, salutory though they are, are sometimes inconsistent (1976:147, both "a" and "b" could be reconstructed but are not), or incorrect (1976:167f needs a rear set of flippers, but doesn't have them).

Another problem of having the artist, not the archaeologist, do the reconstructions is that the drawings may not be done correctly, as when a HG bird effigy vessel from Tibes similar to Figure 2 is reconstructed without its head (González 1984:Figure 7[a])! This results from naively assuming symmetry, which is always dangerous in this complex tradition, and the *effigy* nature of many depictions.

5. Although it must be pointed out that H. Petitjean Roget uses several pictorial devices that other investigators might do well to copy, such as cross-sectional profiles of adorno heads (1975, II:56) and cross-sectional and sub-component (width of adornos, depth from rim to carination, width of labial flange, etc.) dimensions of vessel parts indicated by linear brackets right on the drawing, rather than as a bar graph off to the side (the option chosen here).

Good drawings, although often idealized since they are rendered with mechanical means, and sometimes of only half-vessels, are also found in Mattioni's work on Martinique Saladoid (1976:13, Plate 1). However, he does provide synoptic vessel drawings for the style which are not the typical generalized outline conventions (1980:561, Figure 7), and sectioned drawings (1982:25), many times with both horizontal and vertical views (1979:33c). This salutory French Lesser Antillean tradition (to be continued by the fine renderings in Allaire's thesis of later materials) offers us the only relief from the dismal Greater Antillean tradition of scholarship (photographs are not a substitute for drawings, no matter how aesthetically reproduced [Rivera 1985]).

6. This is a late technique, often Monserratean, whereby the yellowish-kaolin paste forms a second "color," contrasting to an encircling rim and central interior bottom solid circle of red hematite pre-fire paint. In effect, two colors, bichrome, is thus created by a single color slip paint on a visually contrastive paste.

7. Rarely three colors are used on the interior of flat, flaring open bowls with direct rims. The white kaolin paint and a red hematite paint are applied along with a "salmon" colored orange or pink slip paint to form complex, scroll-based designs. Figueredo (1987:5) mentions a rare blue paint applied in a stripe under the rim of some St. Croix Cedrosan Saladoid vessels, but I have not yet seen this in Puerto Rico.

8. Designs may be applied with both positive (usually painting) and negative (usually resist) decorative techniques. Moreover, as an independent variable, this may be done with either positive or negative perceptual intent. When the former technique of application is used in the service of the latter point of perception, the resultant design may be termed "false negative." In the earliest Cedrosan Saladoid pottery, that of the Hacienda Grande style, this often takes the form of using massive areas of white over-paint, applied positively, to define a narrow band of red under-painting. In effect, this produces an elegant "negative"-appearing fine red line. Such lines are of the sort which are usually attained by negative resist techniques. Here, however, they are executed as a tour de force by employing the more difficult method of positive painting.

9. The possibility exists that all the incision and engraving, of both styles (La Hueca and Hacienda Grande) of early Insular, or Cedrosan, Saladoid pottery served as "surface roughening" to hold and retain post-fire painting (crusting) in a variety of fugitive colors: red (hematite), yellow (limonite) and white (talc). These colors served the aesthetic function of

providing contrast, out-lining the designs on which they appeared. It remains to be seen whether this use of post-fire painting has the same chronological implications (post-fire crusting, being technologically simpler and therefore anterior to pre-fire painting) that the post-fire/ pre-fire succession has in Paracas and other South Amerindian prehistoric styles.

Even in the wares with a predominance of pre-fire decoration there continues a minority usage of post-fire crusting in the form of thick, organic (carbon and tree resin-based) black paint. This viscous-looking crusting is applied to highlight features in effigies--such as the eyes and ears of the tapir effigy in Figures 4-6, or is drawn as a circumferential band on the waists of flared-rim, globular pots with white-on-red pre-fire painted designs (Figure 7).

10. Pattern burnishing is used differentially on Cedrosan Saladoid pottery to highlight adorno heads on labial-flanged bowls.

11. These two processes, incision and engraving, are invariably confused in the Caribbean literature. To adopt the distinction Shepard (1971) advances, *incision* is drawing lines in clay while the latter is still moist so that welts of displaced clay border the groove. *Engraving*, which is usually confounded with incision, is formed by drawing lines in clay that has already reached the leather-hard or drier stage. Engraving can also be executed in a post-fire mode, into the hard surface of the baked clay. In either mode, engraving leaves a macroscopic "burr" of shattered edges along the groove. Based on my initial studies of *collector* (not stratified) samples, these decorative modes appear to have stylistic implications since "La Hueca" style "cross-hatching" is usually incision, particularly in the bordering or outlining "form lines," while Hacienda Grande sub-style "cross-hatching" is usually engraving. The latter is in complementary distribution (absent when another technique is present) to "linear incision." "Linear incision is wide, groove-like, incision (Figure 8) with a square cross-section, carefully executed in a "global" manner (that is, looking from above) into small service ware.

12. Excision consists of the removal of broad areas of surface from a pot's design field as part of a design layout. It may be likened to removal of areas in linoleum block printing to create relief. Usually, excision is coupled with incision on the labial flanges of "linear incised" ware bowls (Figure 9). It is a rare mode of possible chronological import.

13. Smudging, as far as I know, has not yet been recognized in the Caribbean literature, although it clearly was a prominent decorative mode for the interior of moderately restricted (Figure 10) and unrestricted, or open, bowls and trays in Hacienda Grande style ceramics (Figure 11). Chanlatte recognized its post-fire nature and possible water-proofing function based on his excavations at Tecla, but erroneously ascribed the effect achieved to rubbing, not smudging (1976:53). Based on my own experimental archaeological work, and on my ethnographic observations of living Amerindian groups like the Shipibo who practice this technique, such decorative smudging is produced by burning resin-rich material under inverted vessels whose exteriors are protected by a resist material, such as wood ash. This leaves the interiors of the vessels with a smoky coating or residue. If such vessels are carefully pebble-polished before the smudging is done, as these prehistoric ceramics were, the resultant smudging will assume a lustrous, rather than a dull, contrastive color.

14. As in most "animistic" South Amerindian prehistoric styles, whether of early states like Chavín (Roe 1974, 1978), or contemporary tribal styles like those of the Shipibo (Roe 1976) and Waiwai (Roe 1988a), there is no hard-and-fast distinction between human and animal representations. This is so because there is a profound belief in "animal-human" transformation, both in mythic (beginning) time and in the shamanistic present. Hence, many depictions are truly "monstrous," that is, they consist of animal-human composite images. Similarly, where beliefs of "mythic attribution" are common ("we received the cultural gift of designs by copying the pelt markings of the Rainbow Dragon at the dawn of time"), as they are in many of these animistic systems, then there will also be a representational content behind

even geometric patterning. Just as one can show the transformation of a stylized anaconda into geometric zig-zag motifs on an early historic Piro cushma from the Peruvian montaña (Roe 1982a:Frontispiece), so too has Petitjean-Roget argued for the theriomorphic allusions, whether it be a tree frog (1976a) or a leaf-nosed bat (1976b), hidden in geometric Insular Saladoid pottery designs and adornos.

15. Pinch modeling and appliqué are combined in the fabrication of hollow effigy heads as the necks of jars (Figure 12) and bottles (Figure 13a-c); the former are anthropomorphic effigies, the latter are theriomorphic depictions. Appliqué, or the applying of fillets or strips of clay onto already-drier ceramic surfaces, was also used in a linear mode to build up "flat" depictions in low relief on the necks of jars and carinated bowls (Figure 14, felinized (?) "human" depictions). The latter representation shares decorative modes, like eye, eyebrow and mouth type, with an ophidian creature (Figure 15). Thus this typical "Saladoid being" concatenates feline (based on prominent teeth in certain mouth bands)-snake symbolism in a manner common to other early styles within the lowlands and highlands of early Formative times.

16. I define partial figurines (usually consisting of just the head and/or the upper torso--shoulder, arms and head, Figures 16a-b, 17), which are intended to decorate the labial flange, handle or rim design field of pottery, and serve as handles, as "adornos" (16c-d). These I distinguish from "figurines" (Figure 18), which were often free-standing.

17. It is clear that during these early Formative times the geographical barriers that segregated cultures in later periods, such as the Andean/Tropical Forest dichotomy, were less of a limiting factor in long-range migration and diffusion. Thus, there is a pattern of lowland "intrusion" across the Chamaya Highlands, where the Andes subside between Peru and Ecuador, from the *oriente* to the coast (Raymond 1988:281) and up the Huallaga (Raymond 1988:291) from the montaña to the Ceja and the highlands. The best evidence for this is in long-distance trade of exotic goods (Raymond 1988:290) and in the spread of early ceramic styles, including specific items like the stirrup-spout, labial-flanges, etc. (Raymond 1988:295). Even Andeanists, long committed to a kind of "cultural xenophobia" with regard to the lowlands, are recognizing the chronological priority of lowland pottery styles and their role in the introduction of the earliest pottery and attendant iconography into the Andes and the coast of Peru (Burger 1988: 312; Fung 1988:8; Keatinge 1988:306). We may see a dim reflection of this complex-silhouette, post-fire crusted, pre-fire painted and incised complex in the Cedrosan Saladoid of the Greater Antilles and its stirrup-spouted effigy vessels showing jungle fauna like tapirs (Figure 6), as well as in the spread of exotic semi-precious amulets depicting Andean Condors (Chanlatte and Narganes 1980:30).

Perhaps not coincidentally, we will also find specific iconographic symbols, such as jaguars and snakes, as well as the biochemical origins of that animal symbolism in the ritual use of hallucinogens, and specific canons of their representation, such as "kenning," "anatropic organization" (a form of composition whereby an image can be inverted yet still present upright images, cf., Burger 1988:118-120) (Figures 19, 20a) and dualism, in all the areas participating in this early "interaction sphere." I see this tissue of resemblances as peripheral expressions of the "age/area" role of the lowlands as the connecting link between later segregated regions as far afield as the coast of Western South America and the Caribbean.

18. Rouse (1985a), based on Boomert's Cedrosan Saladoid finds from Suriname, and historical linguistic reconstruction, argues for a "pincer's movement" of early ceramic-bearing populations around the Guiana Highlands rather than a simple east-to-west dispersal along the Orinoco. In turn, this proposed pattern of movement supports a central or lower Amazonian hearth of dispersal congruent with Lathrap's (1970) model.

19. Doubtless we have been the victims of a "false ethnographic analogy" (Wobst 1978) in visualizing prehistoric hunter-gatherers like the pitiful, and pacific, remnants pushed into marginal habitats who populate the ethnographic present. Expectations that the Antillean archaic populations would have had an equally low-density population, easily pushed aside by the intrusive horticulturalists, is belied in North America and in northern Europe (Price and Petersen 1987:113), where recent evidence is painting a contrary picture of dense, sedentary, and long-lived populations, the very success of which retarded the spread of horticulture into their zones. If the resident archaic populations in the Greater Antilles were as large and well organized as these other archaeological foragers, they could have formed an additional source of the agonism that is reflected in the osteological record (Siegel, this volume). Indeed, the limited penetration of the Saladoid groups into Hispañola may have reflected the difficulty they encountered in expanding against the resident archaic groups.

Clearly, by later times the competitive exclusion which I postulate for at least one of the migrating horticultural groups was also operative between the horticulturalists and the foragers. The latter retreated and took refuge in marginal habitats or zones, such as the rugged interior of the larger islands and their more remote peninsulas (Rouse, this volume).

20. As Irving Rouse has pointed out to me (personal communication 1988), I overlook an additional, intermediate possibility between these extremes. That is the "interaction between two populations only partially preadapted to each other, e.g., the Japanese vs. Westerners and the Hacienda Grande vs. the El Caimito peoples," the latter case he presents in his paper in this volume. While that case would seem to fall in the middle of this continuum, the former instance of the Japanese and the Westerners seems more a case of cultural similarity based on a kind of parallel cultural evolution out of an early shared feudal experience. It was also based on the isomorphisms between the Portuguese, in particular, and the Japanese at first contact (mutual respect derived from a similar military tradition, analogous statuses such as Hidalgos/Samurai, or Jesuit/Zen priests, etc.). Such cultural similarities go a long way to explaining the subsequent interaction of Japan with the West in comparison to the "cultural antipathy" displayed in Chinese or Korean/Western interactions.

21. My point here is that the complexity of artistic solutions is dependent upon a "high information" system produced by interacting, yet different artists and audiences. Once the ideas for making pottery were present the solutions could not have been sustained indefinitely at the initial levels of experimentation (in both vessel form and surface decoration) if it were not for continued interaction. I am not suggesting that Antillean populations had to constantly *relearn* the art of pottery manufacture by participation in the interaction sphere, just that the "audience" would have declined in diversity, as would the raw material diversity, thereby limiting the conceptual and material constitutents for ceramic complexity once the interaction sphere had collapsed. The archaeological record is full of technical and aesthetic systems that seem resistant to change due to extreme isolation, and rife with examples of rapid turnover at cultural centers where ideas and materials mesh in profusion.

22. As local adaptation replaced exotic materials with local materials, and increased the attractiveness of well-known habitats, there would have been less incentive to interact over great distances. Rather, interaction would have gradually assumed the pattern attested to in the contact chronicles, between adjacent islands, but not along whole island chains. The Puerto Rican Taíno knew a great deal about the Hispañolan chiefdoms, but little about the populations in the northern Lesser Antilles. If they had known more, we would not have such difficulty deciding who lived there, if anyone?

Cultural causality is always synergistic rather than mono-causal. Therefore this "ceramic devolution" was also a result of the changing role of the ceramic arts vis-à-vis more monumental and public media like petroglyphs and monoliths (Roe 1987b). As I argue in greater detail below, this material culture of "public display" was a result of the demographic growth and political complexification produced by that successful local adaptation.

23. Indeed, the difficulty in determining exactly who inhabited the northernmost islands between Puerto Rico and the more southerly Lesser Antilles in later prehistory that Rouse refers to in his paper (this volume) may reflect a similar "no-man's land," or buffer zone, between the agonistically interacting Island Caribs and the Taíno.

24. Lateral coastal movement, coupled with minimal interior colonization is another form of this canalized, "toothpaste-tube" model as Rouse's paper (this volume) shows for Saladoid migration toward the west along the northern coast of Venezuela. It also works well in the ethnographic present, as in the Guianas, where one frequently finds societies, indeed whole nation states, that are very wide but effectively only some forty kilometers deep (despite a much greater "jural depth" in the form of claimed borders). In such countries like Guyana and Suriname one finds former West African and East Indian populations clinging to the coast, their backs resolutely turned to the vast, Amerindian-inhabited interior (the Bush Negro populations in the middle range interior being the cultural product of a special case of agonistic flight and syncretic tribal reconstitution).

25. As Rouse adds (personal communication 1988): "the larger the population, the more information is likely to be generated. Greater land areas and larger interaction spheres can increase the population." Here, again, simple scale is an important "boundary condition" for stylistic complexity. In earlier times the scale was far-reaching space, inhabited by limited, but concentrated, populations. In later times it was human numbers, inhabiting smaller relative space. This is part of my explanation for "media displacement" in the material cultural locus of style. Nearly as much information probably existed in Pre-Taíno and Taíno times as it had in Saladoid times, but along different dimensions and focused on distinct levels. A profusion of rock art in Pre-Taíno and Taíno epochs, for example, takes the place of the earlier abundance of distinct vessel forms.

26. There were other factors influencing this rate of movement that would have produced more rapid movement through the Lesser Antilles than between the Greater Antilles. Two reasons might have accounted for this apart from inter-group agonistic relations. The first was the relative complexity of local ecology. The small islands of the Lesser Antilles, although diverse as a group, have extremely simple ecologies individually. The internally complex Greater Antilles, in contrast, have individually complicated ecologies. Therefore, adaptation could have occurred rapidly to the first, and slowly and tentatively to the second. This differential process of adaptation alone would regulate the speed of movement since local adaptation is necessary before the populations can build up on each island to a point where out-migration becomes necessary.

The second factor is also related to speed. This factor is the simple matter of scale, not complexity. As Siegel suggests,

> the sizes of the islands making up the Lesser Antilles are tiny. It doesn't take many people to settle on one of these islands before there's no more room or the carrying capacity is reached. Therefore, it might not be agonistic pressure forcing the migrants to put on their track shoes and hurtle through the islands, but simply that "x" number of families, clans or lineages can only fit on an island of "y" size. Thus, when "x" is reached for a given island, then the next island on the sequence is occupied. If the islands happened to be large, then I bet the migration would appear to be slower [Peter Siegel, personal communication 1988].

This seems highly plausible, and would explain the long "pauses" before new major islands were colonized as well as the prolonged period of time it took each to "fill up." However, this filling up is not a simple hydraulic process, but a real matter of jostling, and competing (as well as segmentally cooperating) social groups. Such competition and segmentary opposition (cooperating and coalescing internally to more successfully compete externally) is precisely what my "agonistic engine" postulates. Remember the Viking colonization of Greenland, Iceland and New Brunswick, produced as much by forced exile for excessive murders as by any exploring intent.

27. Siegel (personal communication 1988) suggests that these ceramic artifacts are not as much of a technological absurdity as I picture them to be:

> It seems to me that it makes more sense to have a potrest made out of ceramic, than stone, when the potrest is going to be subjected to high heat. Stone potrests that are holding up a ceramic griddle, for example, are likely to explode after some duration of heating. You wouldn't have this problem with ceramic potrests.

While this may be true, ceramic potrests have their own problems. Despite the selection of a different, more open, paste produced by larger temper size in an effort to limit cracking in the pre-fire drying (a greater problem for thick potrests than for the thinner pottery), the low-fire terracotta paste of the *topia* was subject to overfiring. This is notable in the hues of the iron oxides contained within the fire-dog paste and the tendency of that paste to spall off and crumble. This not only makes the archaeological specimens both fragmentary and fragile, it would have also limited the life-span of those in the "systemic context" as well.

In any event, this functional argument does not explain the eventual phasing out of ceramic potrests. An additional comment from Miguel Rodríguez (personal communication 1988), however, does vitiate my argument somewhat. He suggests, based on his experience, that *topia* are more common in Cuevas than they are in the Hacienda Grande style. This would be an anomaly since the Hacienda Grande style was associated with the first arrivals, who might be expected to have brought such traits from *tierra firme*. I can only suggest that this may be an artifact of sampling since the Cuevas assembalges are larger and more ubiquitous than the Hacienda Grande collections. While Rodríguez's assertion will have to be checked, note that the pattern of the association of *topia* with the early Saladoid phases still holds.

28. Siegel's comment (personal communication 1988) is pertinent here:

> This notion of terrestrial dietary emphasis of first migrants is, I think, mainly an artifact of sampling bias in archaeological projects that haven't used flotation. Once the data are properly collected we find that the earliest Saladoid migrants were in fact exploiting the marine resources *intensively* and extensively. This is clear from the Maisabel faunal analysis [see deFrance 1988, this volume].

While Siegel's recovery techniques and deFrance's studies have, in fact, increased the diversity of recorded Saladoid target species, they do not reverse the overwhelming evidence of the macro remains, which are still those compacted levels of disintegrated land crab remains and the highly visible emphasis on large gastropods, coupled with the lower frequency of smaller bivalves and univalves, which characterizes Saladoid levels in contrast to later levels. In addition to *pelagic* resources, the most obvious protein resources of the sea are the shallow water shellfish available to insular dwellers. Here the true "shell middens" of such sites as Punta Ostiones, more shell than earth, still stand in sharp contrast to even the "shell midden" levels of the Maisabel site, much less the Saladoid levels.

29. The reason why generalized, and fantastic creatures appear, rather than an increasing pictorial utilization of just local fauna as a reflection of the "settling in" process, may stem from both stylistic and material circumstances. As a result of the "style cycle" Antillean pottery was going through, exuberant and hurried modeling replaced careful moulding. This technique both made it more difficult to render realistic species and produced schematicization that

deleted representational cues or rendered them in "short-hand." Just as separate handles became mere appliqué crescents (Figure 29e), and heads featureless nubbins, so too did "realistic" animals turn into monstrous critters (29d).

The second reason may reflect the singular paucity of animals suitable for mythic depiction (that is, "species paragons," large or impressive exemplars of natural symbols) on these faunally impoverished islands. This natural limitation would only have been exacerbated by the increasing hunting that was probably making what small and unimpressive animals remained less visible or numerous.

30. The existence of raw materials like stones not found in the Caribbean, but present on the mainland, does not necessarily imply direct acquisition. These raw materials could also have arrived on the islands via some form of "up the line" exchange system like trading partners (present both among South Amerindians and in other world areal analogues, such as the *kula* ring of Melanesia), or some combination of both mechanisms (direct voyaging and indirect exchange). Either way, news, images and goods of the mainland filtered into the island chain.

31. "Rainey based the distinction primarily upon his previous excavations at Canas, where the stratigraphy was more distinct" (Rouse, personal communication 1988).

32. This distinction may be a bit strained, but it does signal a difference in degree, if not in kind. To differentiate both terms one must go back to ideas. The real "artifact" is the ethno-culinary classification system that selects certain species, or members of a species, as being "edible," and therefore worthy of being pursued, while relegating others to be "tabooed," and hence killed only accidentally or in pursuit of another goal (protecting a net, safe-guarding a harvest/herd, protecting one's life, etc.). After the animal is intentionally hunted, killed or captured, it is brought back to a processing area, its state (live/dead) and natural context altered, and its body processed (cleaned, depilated-defeathered-scaled, gutted and butchered, and most importantly from a "Culture/Nature" perspective, cooked), then preserved (smoked, salted), or eaten.

Any food remains are thus artifacts in both important senses of the term: intentional human modification and natural context alteration. Yet food remains are indirect artifacts at best since the goal lies in the food itself, not in the industrial or decorative use of the "means" of food, the body or its parts. However, once the fish mandible is selected as a scraper or engraver, or the spine modified as an awl, it becomes a "direct artifact," just like a similarly minimally-modified arrow cane arrowshaft, or a bird feather, now transformed as a headdress plume.

Such distinctions are important particularly for South Amerindians (and the Caribbean populations derived from them) because of the pervasiveness of "animistic technology" (to be considered below) in their material culture, as well as the admirable energy-material efficiency of that technology. This efficiency is attested to by the many "direct artifacts" that are also "naturefact transforms," natural things that become artifacts by a single processing step. A Waiwai hunter makes a "carrying bag" out of the skin of a Curassow by making just one incision in the head and peeling the skin inside-out to stuff the body in. Or he may hack off a palm frond to serve as either an impromptu lean-to, or a plaited burden basket destined for ephemeral use.

33. As Rouse notes (personal communication 1988), "(i)n my 1964 paper, I note only that the Orinocan pottery has *painted* cross-hatching. This is very different from the complex *zoned incised* crosshatching of the coastal and Antillean pottery. The distinction is the basis for my current differentiation of the Ronquinan and Cedrosan Saladoid subseries" (Rouse, this volume).

34. In the latest catalog, an even earlier date of 200 B.C. is projected for La Hueca, but the earliest C-14 date given is A.D. 5 (Chanlatte 1985b:5, 10). Some support for this is provided

by Rodríguez's single early date from Punta Candelero (Rodríguez, this volume). By simply citing ealiest and latest dates for both styles (without referencing the recent early HG dates and without regard for standard deviations, or for accounting for the considerable overlap at both the early and late ends of the temporal spectrum), Chanlatte suggests A.D. 5 to 275 for La Hueca (Agro-I) and A.D. 35 to 490 for Hacienda Grande (Agro-II) (1985b:5, 6). However, viewed statistically and with the full range of his dates in mind, these chronological reconstructions should be viewed as impressionistic at best.

35. There is a real difference in the percentages of the small snuff inhaladors and the incense burners between the La Hueca and the Hacienda Grande styles. Although both these artifact types are present in HG (González 1984:Figure 24; Pons de Alegría 1976), they are much more common in the LH assemblage (Rodríguez, personal communication 1989). Because of the hallucinogenic implications of this paraphernalia, certain differences in religious beliefs seem implied. But, these differences could be cultural and/or specialist related within the same series and do not necessarily signal membership in a different series.

36. My usage of terms is cognate with Rouse's, but the few differences do merit definition here. I suggest that a "style" is a particular systemic selection of the elements and rules of process, form and decoration (Roe 1989). It can be applied to both technical (effective=efficient) and aesthetic (affective) artifacts, thus generating various "art styles" and "technological styles." These styles are recognized by the differential patterns of choice between alternate possibilities on the attribute level (modes) of artifacts. Such statistical choices (an "everted" configuration, for example) occur within certain dimensions of form (of the "rim" on a ceramic vessel) as individual, but interacting, artisans and artists seek to realize specific cultural ideals, or "prototypes" (also called "types," i.e., a "manioc beer jar"). Scattergrams of attribute plots also define the overlaps between polar types within the real-world continuum of differential execution and realization. These "medial" clusters are a product of the "extension" process, "that particular vessel looks sorttah like a beer jar; yeah, its kindah like one").

Many styles are media based. Thus one can speak of a "lithic artifact style," or a "ceramic style," or a "feather-working style," etc. Alternatively, and frequently cross-cutting the media styles while knitting them together by common structural solutions and principles, are the functional styles. "Function" is broadly conceived to include *all* purposes: empirical (as culturally understood), religious, social-structural, economic, etc.

A particular constellation of related artifacts in a media or functional style may be given a name. In ceramics, such a constellation of different objects is called a "ware." Thus there may be many "wares" within a single ceramic "style." While "style" can be either an individual or a social phenomenon, a "ware" is by definition social.

37. There is some question as to the size of the La Hueca cultural group. On the one hand, the spectacular character of especially the lapidary work suggests numerous patrons to support the skills necessary to produce this "miniaturized" work. Moreover the seven mounds at the La Hueca site conjure up a picture of a substantial village. On the other hand, sophistication of material culture does not necessarily imply large numbers, nor is there any indication that all of the mounds at La Hueca were occupied at the same time. In similar Caribbean sites, such as Monserrate, we know that the settlement system was a "circulating pattern," that is, each mound was occupied at a slightly different time as the population moved about in a local setting (Roe et al. 1985).

Compared with the huge and deep sheet midden (see Siegel [this volume] for a definition of *sheet midden*) in the Hacienda Grande component at Sorcé, or even the more extensive Cuevas midden at Punta Candelero, the La Hueca deposits are shallow and unimpressive. For this reason, I suggest that the La Hueca group, whatever they were, were not as numerous, nor did they occupy their sites for the time the Hacienda Grande-Cuevas populations did.

38. Ricardo Alegría (personal communication 1989), for example, expresses surprise at the sheer quantity of small "amulets" and beads associated with the two La Hueca sites. This implies "excessive" production, perhaps aimed at trade. Yet one must ask what was the relevant artifact? Was the individual little "turtle" or "frog" amulet the cultural end product, or goal? If instead of being worn singly, as "amulets," these objects acted as beads within a necklace, and each necklace had hundreds of such zoomorphic beads, then the total number of artifacts (the whole necklace), perhaps only one per appropriate person (adult male?), would not appear "excessive." In that case it might not imply trade either. After all, many of the sculptural items of La Hueca are on such a small scale such that they could have co-occurred in corporeal art. In such a view the "extraordinary" lapidary production of the La Hueca artisans looks less extraordinary.

39. Rouse (this volume) is probably correct in stating that both the La Hueca and the Hacienda Grande styles date back to roughly 200 B.C. in the Vieques Sound area. However, there is a tendency for the LH dates to appear slightly earlier than the initial HG dates, continue contemporary with them, and terminate earlier than the end of HG dates at Sorcé-La Hueca (A.D. 5±80 [I-11,322]=LH; A.D. 35±80 [I-11,319]=HG), and comparing Punta Candelero (170 B.C.±80 [I-14,978]=LH) with Hacienda Grande (110 B.C.±70 [Beta-9970]=HG), El Convento (160 B.C.±80 [I-11,296]=HG) or Maisabel (110 B.C.±60 [Beta-14380]=HG) (Rouse and Alegría 1989).

Thus, it is still true that comparing all of the sites, or within the site where the styles are spatially segregated (Sorcé/La Hueca) the LH dates remain the earliest, if by a whisker. However, considering the difference in labs utilized, coupled with the small difference in initial dates and the subsequent overlapping dates, one might just as easily regard La Hueca as contemporary with Hacienda Grande. While this may seem to disconfirm my reconstruction of La Hueca being an "advance party" of Saladoid populations, I did suggest such a short period of time between the arrival of the LH people and the subsequent arrival of the HG people that it might be virtually masked by the overlap in C-14 dates.

As to the contemporaneity of dating at Sorcé/La Hueca, coupled with the asymmetrical pattern of finds reported for that site, the existence of two distinct cultural groups on the same site a matter of meters from one another is without precedent on this level of socio-political organization. Multi-ethnic settlements can and do exist for state-level societies, but not for tribal ones. The only exception on a tribal level are missionary-resettlement multi-ethnic villages (such as Shefarimo in Guyana with Trío, Waiwai and Wapishiana, or Shahuaya in Peru with Campa and Conibo, to name two sites where I have resided), but they are exclusively an artifact of post-contact times. Moreover, they always reveal considerable inter-ethnic friction attested to by spatial segregation (in Shefarimo the Wapishiana "alien tribals" occupied the periphery, the Waiwai core the center-cf., Siegel 1987, and in Shahuaya the Campa "alien tribals" were located across a small stream, joined to the Conibo core by a log bridge). Multi-ethnic villages do exist in close proximity, and maintain ritualized mutual visiting patterns in the Xingú, but even there the inter-village distances are on the order of kilometers, not meters.

Thus the pattern of dates from Sorcé/La Hueca argue for a contested, or "interdigitated" pattern of settlement and resettlement (via short term "pressured abandonments" rather than direct conflict since there is no evidence for fighting) until the issue was decided in the favor of the HG populations. However, that reconstruction directly contravenes the stated evidence of LH material on the HG middens but not the reverse. If both groups were cyclically reoccupying the site, one would expect some discarded HG material to have been picked up and redeposited in the LH middens, especially in view of the similarities between the styles and the elaborateness, and hence visual appeal, of the HG pottery. But that case is not supposed to have happened. Thus no clear-cut cultural reconstruction can account for what Chanlatte has reported for La Hueca/Sorcé. Only the physical isolation of the LH materials from any neighboring Hacienda Grande site which Rodríguez and Rivera have reported from the Punta Candelero site provides an intelligible cultural explanation. In that case contemporary, but isolated and perhaps mutually antagonistic (there is no HG "trade Ware" at the Punta Candelero site), and culturally distinct, ethnic groups provide a familiar parallel to countless segregated tribal villages in the ethnographic present.

40. As Siegel points out (personal communication 1988), even if these species identifications hold up statistically in a detailed faunal analysis of all the Punta Candelero La Hueca-associated fauna, and its comparison with the faunal assemblages from the Cuevas component at that site, or with the Cedrosan Saladoid assemblages from other sites (based on a study which is not yet done), such differences in faunal remains do not "...substantiate any claims regarding differences in adaptation [or culinary preferences, or even contrasting ethno-taxonomic culinary systems of permitted/prohibited game species] between Saladoid and 'Huecoid' peoples." This is because "(o)ne would need to conduct a range and distribution study of the hutía species, as they occurred naturally" and non-cultural (biological) variables might explain the discontinuous and mutually exclusive distribution of these early rodents:

Maybe there's (a) interspecific competition between hutía species resulting in geographically dispersed territories, or (b) maybe the hutía species simply are adapted to different types of habitats. Whatever the case, if the Punta Candelero folks are living in a place that *happens* to be near *Heteropsomys* hutía then the people will probably hunt that animal. This does not represent a different adaptive strategy compared to the HG folks hunting *Isolobodon* hutías. After all, they are all hunting hutías! [Peter Siegel, personal communication 1988]

Unfortunately for this objection, both forms of rodents are extinct in Puerto Rico (there were a few *Isolobodon* reported for Hispañola, but by now they too may be extinct. In any case no field studies have been done of them to study their range and preferred habitats-even assuming they have remained unaltered from a time before human pressure has affected their behavior).

The same patterns have been alleged, but not well documented, for the Sorcé/La Hueca site (Narganes 1985). Such a pattern would vitiate Siegel's objections. But yet another variable complicates the picture. Suppose the *Heteropsomys* were wild, and hence hunted, while the *Isolobodon* were domesticated, hence raised? Then the differences in life forms would certainly reflect differential adaptive strategies. The number of *Isolobodon* finds in Saladoid middens is certainly suggestive of domestication. Osteological studies probably could not resolve this issue, however, and we are left in a quandry. Clearly, not only more studies are needed, but better reports of whole faunal assemblages are required to see if these and other patterns emerge.

41. Rouse is technically correct in maintaining that one cannot speak of "ethnic groups" in archaeology, *sensu stricto*, but only of "peoples," since the latter is the sort of diachronic unit (a phase) which the tools of archaeology can appropriately unearth. Moreover, a "people," unlike an "ethnic group," does not require the kind of "empathetic" reasoning that ethnology can best provide (i.e., we don't know how an ancient population regarded themselves, or were regarded by others, that is, we have no direct access to their "ethno-anthropology," their ethnic classifications of humans, infra-humans and non-humans in Magaña's [1982] sense).

However, for the sake of creating a hypothetical model which can explain the current distribution of La Hueca/Hacienda Grande sites in time and space, and which may be tested archaeologically, I will employ ethnographic analogy with similar lowland riverine populations to suggest that these two peoples were competing ethnic groups such that the smaller group (La Hueca) could have been subject to acculturation and eventual cultural extinction on the part of the larger group (Hacienda Grande-Cuevas).

42. Another difficulty for my argument, at least at the present level of knowledge, is the lack of sites in the Lesser Antilles where La Hueca style pottery is found spatially segregated from Cedrosan Saladoid pottery. If my reconstruction of multiple cultural group migrations into the Antilles on the Saladoid level is to work one should find such sites all the way up the island chain to the Vieques Sound area. Isolated finds, especially in the lapidary art, from Trinidad and Monserrate, do parallel the La Hueca materials, but so far all the La Hueca ceramic specimens appear to come from mixed contexts. That is, both the recent excavations of Versteeg on St. Eustasius, and of Haviser on St. Martin, are like the earlier excavations on Puerto Rico (of Rainey, Alegría or Rouse), or the more recent excavations on Puerto Rico of Roe (Hacienda Grande and Maisabel) and Siegel (Maisabel). All of these excavations record La Hueca style pottery in association with Hacienda Grande style pottery, even though the LH pottery tends to be found in the lowest levels of the cuts.

However, many of the other excavations in the Lesser Antilles were either done by professionals during an earlier time of field technique development, or have been by amateurs. In both cases spatial control is an imponderable. Further, these are small islands thoroughly churned by even more intensive cultivation (most recently in sugar cane) than Puerto Rico or Vieques. All these circumstances could produce mechanical mixture in many sites. These might be partial explanations why it is that even though the Lesser Antilles have been more completely studied than any of the Greater Antilles we have not yet found similar sites to La Hueca and Punta Candelero there. Unfortunately, in archaeology the absence of finds means very little.

This paucity of La Hueca sites in the Lesser Antilles could also mean there never were any. It was precisely because of the lack of such linking sites between the mainland and the Vieques Sound region of eastern Puerto Rico, and the demonstrably late date of the putative "ancestral site" for La Hueca style pottery, Río Guapo, that Rouse (this volume) has concluded that the Huecan Saladoid originated within the Vieques Sound area itself. That is, he regards La Hueca as an autochthonous development behind the northwesternmost Cedrosan Saladoid frontier in the Greater Antilles. The Río Guapo style then becomes a probable case of "parallel stylistic evolution" along the western Saladoid frontier in northern South America, not connected by diffusion with the La Hueca style of Vieques and eastern Puerto Rico.

Only time and further excavations will determine which of these hypotheses are correct: (a) a separate migration of a distinct La Hueca cultural group slightly before, or in tandem with, a closely-related Hacienda Grande group, both within the Saladoid series (my hypothesis), or (b) a local development of a distinct La Hueca cultural group within the Vieques Sound culture area at the same time that the closely-related Hacienda Grande group, also within the Saladoid series, colonizes Puerto Rico (Rouse's revised hypothesis). Earlier hypotheses: that there was just a single cultural group with mixed traits migrating into the Greater Antilles (the original Alegría and Rouse reconstruction), or the view that a separate, and culturally unrelated (non-Saladoid) migration took place prior to the Saladoid migration (the original Chanlatte hypothesis, and to an extent, the evolving reconstruction of Rodríguez and Rivera) now seem less tenable, at least if the arguments about cultural affiliation that I advance in this paper are accepted.

43. Of course, inter-ethnic relations could also have been friendly, with intermarriage (as in the Northwest Amazon) or ritualized visiting and trading (as in the Guianas and the Xingú), being some mechanisms for non-agonistic interaction. For example, when the CIIPR expedition arrived to the remote Waiwai village of Shefarimo on the upper Essequibo River, Guyana, in 1985 we were housed in a hut that had just been constructed for the annual overland trading visit of the Trío Indians, related Caribs from Surinam to the east.

Perhaps both friendly and unfriendly relations occurred, but in synchronic or diachronic order. The lowland literature is replete with records of shifting alliances (as among the Yanomamö), where groups in friendly relations "regress" to raiding based on arguments (often over women), or once at war with each other "progress" to alliances via an intricate system of feasting-trading-conjoint raiding-marital alliances (Chagnon 1983). The absence of WOR sherds in the middens at La Hueca/Sorcé and Punta Candelero, and the presence of La Hueca style sherds at other sites like Hacienda Grande and Maisabel could mark these shifting patterns of trading/alliance/raiding.

However, the fact that the La Hueca style disappears around the third century A.D. while the Hacienda Grande-Cuevas tradition continues and occupies its sites (at Punta Candelero, for example), suggests that the La Hueca group was finally absorbed by force or threat of force on the part of the more numerous Hacienda Grande people. The lowland ethnographic literature is clear on this point, even the demands for "protection" of a smaller group by a larger group lead to the extraction of the most precious resource of all in the social continuity of the smaller group, women. With the women being abrogated social extinction soon follows. Alternatively, via raiding for women the enemy men were killed and the women absorbed by the conquering group (Roe 1982a). Either way the La Hueca style disappeared without descendants.

44. Chanlatte (personal communication 1986) affirms that geological identification has proved that at least the amethyest used as one of the raw materials in La Hueca lapidary art only occurs outside of the Caribbean, in the mainland of the Guianas.

45. Of course, since this culinary trajectory really inscribes a continuum, not the old dichotomy, as Saladoid groups moved inland from the coast they first substituted local analogous fauna for the coastal fauna before turning to new animal sources of protein. For example, the Cuevan Saladoid and Early Elenan Ostionoid Colón site, near Ponce, is located 12 kilometers inland on self-irrigated alluvium along a river that eventually debouches into the coast. Its faunal assemblage is unique in its preponderance of *freshwater* crabs, not the brackish-tolerant *Cardisoma*, of typical, and earlier, coastal Saladoid sites (Edgar Maíz, personal communication 1989). This local development I take to be a case of "culinary substitution" as the Saladoid and epi-Saladoid populations colonized the interior of the island.

46. As I explain elsewhere, for the type of analysis I am advocating to really be definitive, one has to study more than two specimens. *Modal* analysis *has* to be based on the comparative study of whole collections/assemblages by provenience units. In that case it differs from *typological* analysis, which can be limited to contextless individual specimens, precisely because modal anlaysis can reveal the full extent of *variation* within a collection rather than typologically cramming variants into rigid conceptual boxes of ideal Platonic "types." Since I believe the former to more powerful than the latter, I obviously advocate the comparative modal analysis of say 100 La Hueca pots with 100 Hacienda Grande pots. This is *not* such a study, but rather a *prospectus* for such a study. It is intended to show, based on my familiarity with the collections, *how* such a more comprehensive study should be done. In fact, that is why I identify my conclusions in this paper as *hypotheses*, they are intended to be confirmed or disconfirmed when the fuller study is carried out.

47. As in any "seriational" matter, the system can just as easily be inverted. What if HG predates LH? How would this alter my analysis? For one thing, rather than using a term like "evolve," I would have to substitute "devolve," while the basic analysis would remain the same, save for the direction of the derivational arrows. Thus, if I can derive Hacienda Grande from La Hueca, or La Hueca from Hacienda Grande, then how useful is the generative grammatical approach in the final analysis? What do I prove?

My response is that by demonstrating mutual commutability, I also show isomorphism (similar design elements, rules, compounds [motifs], fields and aesthetics). My aim here is *not*, in

Rouse's terms, "chronological archaeology" (one needs other information, such as technological evolutionary trends [is post-fire crusting always anterior to pre-fire painting?], stratigraphy [are the La Hueca sherds always in the very first levels of a Hacienda Grande site?], distributional evidence, and radiometric dating, to name only a few, to pursue chronology and decide which way is "up" in a formal seriation). Instead, my goal is "cultural archaeology" (what are the interrelationships of the "peoples" represented by the LH and HG material cultures), and "social archaeology," (what are the interrelationships of these "peoples" as "ethnic units" using ethnographic analogy as an explanatory device (because information as to ethnicity is not directly recoverable from archaeology save in those cases, as in the case of the Moche in Peru, where very elaborate representational iconography gives cues to "self" and "significant other" awareness, or in the case of countless other extinct cultures where written records or ethnohistorical and legendary documentation exists to provide this information). Thus my real goal here is simply to document the *similarity*, or the "mutual intelligibility on a stylistic level" of the La Hueca and Hacienda Grande pottery assemblages. This is part of a larger argument that they are both styles within the same subseries, the Cedrosan Saladoid subseries.

48. Rouse (1985b) made the same point in a different fashion when he suggested that the painted tradition was dominant in the Saladoid cultural plurality, as one language is in a duality of languages.

49. Speculatively, one might suggest that each ceramic tradition was reflecting the basic "structural core" of its own design tradition based on a perishable media. For La Hueca, and its rectilinear "C" and "T" modules, that media seems to be either basketry (the twill-weave nature of these designs is obvious) or weaving (complementary warp-patterning will achieve the same "twill" effect). In contrast, the cursive spirals of Hacienda Grande, together with its "false-negative" construction, hint at a painted style unconstrained by the "tyranny of warp-and-weft." That could either be painting on cotton clothing with vegetable dyes, or, more probably, body painting. Hollow human figurines are present in Hacienda Grande. Pons de Alegría (1983a:Figures 5, 10, 11) shows some elegant painted examples recovered from the El Convento site in Old San Juan. Their obvious nakedness and ligatures demonstrate the probability of body painting as a corporeal art in Saladoid society and provide a "media prototype" origin of the curvilinear motifs in Hacienda Grande art.

50. "This seems to me a good explanation for the La Hueca/Hacienda Grande succession in the Vieques Passage area. I don't know of any evidence that it took place elsewhere in Cedrosan Saladoid territory" (Irving Rouse, personal communication 1988).

51. A salutory local Caribbean effort to parallel this processual concern of modal analysis, albeit with a simpler quantitative goal, was pioneered by Goodwin and Thall (1983) on "Insular Saladoid" ceramics from the Sugar Factory Pier site on St. Kitts. In doing so they were able to document statistically a local "devolution" in ceramic technology on St. Kitts congruent with a similar process in Puerto Rico.

52. I should point out that this "modal" school is not the only species of formalism with roots in Shepard's work. The earlier work of Hardin (1983) and recent efforts by Washburn (Washburn and Crowe 1988) are but two more examples of the study of symmetry rules as applied to the structure of art design.

53. Rouse made a tentative step in this direction in his 1941 monograph, *Culture of the Ft. Liberté Region, Haiti*.

54. This is a case of formal "reduplication." Since I want to show this componentially, I have introduced these new body segments as separate modes within the body dimension. Were I to show this same phenomenon grammatically, I could indicate the same thing by specifying a "reduplication" rule for certain body modes, with allometric size and shape changes attendant

upon them. Parsimony, explanatory and predictive power and the illustrative purposes behind a description will dictate the choice between either of these approaches.

55. There is, of course, a whole feedback process between the conceptual formation of "targets," "prototypes," or "types" as the intentional goal of aesthetic and technical behavior and the raw materials and craft processes used to realize that goal. Speaking of the craft of traditional Japanese cabinet-making, Link (1975:22) has referred to this "intermediate stage" between the concept-as-intent, the raw materials and the finished "cultural product" as a form of communication. I would redefine this act of communion between the artisan and his raw materials and craft processes as "asymmetrical communication" (to distinguish it from the "symmetrical communication" that occurs between interacting organisms) since it is only metaphorically a two-way process. Animism aside, the Western view is that there is only one active will which is "reading into" the materials (in a Boasian sense) certain possibilities based on its immutable characteristics and "inherent perfectability" (1975:52). The materials and processes may be saying "you can do this," or "you can't do that" in a mystical sense, but not in an objective, or etic sense. This is not to belittle the fervent belief on the part of the best craftsmen and artists that such a conversation really occurs, only that scholarly, much less scientific, discourse is not equipped to affirm its objective existence.

Therefore, in a real sense the "media is the message" (always in part. Complex traditions tend to impose their will on the media, simpler, or perhaps just more sophisticated traditions tend to "go with the flow or grain" of the material and let it speak as much as the artisan's prior concept).

Regarding the "vehicle" of the medium itself, the "object," the investigator needs to remember that "physicality, which implies durability," a bias of the Western tradition, is a relative matter. An "ephemeral" dance step can be made a "fossil" by videotaping it, just as a "real" artifact, a mask, can be made "ephemeral" by destroying it to "liberate" the spirit encased in the mask after the ceremony is done (Myers 1988:16, on the Bora). For the same naive reason that we feel a dance step *must* be different from an oil painting because we believe that in the latter there is a "real" end product that can be examined or appreciated for what it is, the Western tradition long ignored masks made out of cloth, because they weren't "real" masks made out of good "substantial," wood (Weil 1971), or ignored the dance rituals that gave those masks life and cultural context because we found it difficult to bring them into the art gallery.

That is why "happenings" (performance art) were so revolutionary for Western art, they pointed up what we have traditionally ignored, that "art" or "craft" does not really lie in corporeal things; it is embodied in decisions that are actualized over time and space, some in physical form, and some in "formless" behavior, some for eternity (or at least as long as the museum exists, or the museum conservators can keep the artifact in one piece), and others for the moment.

This is the real philosophical debate between typology and modal analysis: what captures the cultural world better, "things" or the interaction of "intent" with "things," that is, *process*. Hence the charts and figures I present will imply process as well as end product. We are not dealing with sea shells; we are dealing with pottery.

56. I am treating "La Hueca" and "Hacienda Grande" as separate "styles" here. There were, of course, different functional "wares" within each style, such as the "utilitarian ware" (chiefly cooking forms) and the "fine" or "presentation" ware (chiefly drinking-snorting forms) in each. Because of its lack of painting (only crusting being used to supplement modeling and incision-impression), such a distinction is more difficult to establish in La Hueca than in Hacienda Grande. However, even in the former case the presence of adornos, which turn the whole vessel into an effigy (Figure 25), and the appearance of specialized features such as snuff tubes and spouts, as well as differential distribution of incision-impression heightened with crusting, all provide some information for inferring which of the vessels were utilitarian and

which were presentation.

There may also be more specialized "wares" within a ware, as is the case of the "linear incised ware," which is a sub-class of the fine ware of the Hacienda Grande style. It is identified by a restricted vocabulary of similar (highly carinated) forms, produced by a similar design perspective (global rather than perpendicular execution-appreciation), related to a particular putative function (kinetic presentation of intoxicating beverages in a ceremonial context, ie., the offering of manioc beer to honored guests, who are "cultured" enough to appreciate the act of offering, the beauty of the offering vessels, as well as the sentiments [generosity, non-aggressiveness] behind the offer, in addition to the tastiness, abundance and effectiveness of the beer). Moreover, it is decorated by a similar kind and range of decoration (linear-incised, post-fire crusted, single and multiply-banded spiral and curvilinear motifs).

Some of the fine wares in either style had "ritual" purposes (where stereotyped, repetitive, empirically non-instrumental (à la Maquet) and "parcelled out" (à la Lévi-Strauss) activities occur which are primarily directed at supernaturals, although other humans may be present and witness them (as in a ritual of propitiation to a deity), others had "ceremonial" aims (a similar series of acts, but where the primary "audience" consists of the other human witnesses, although supernaturals may also be present, as in the coronation of the King/Queen of England) (see Roe 1982a for these distinctions applied to verbal art).

Some forms, or types, within these wares had many "primary uses" (the original intended use), some had many "secondary uses" (supplemental uses, without modification), some were "reused" (modification coupled with a shift in intended use). Lastly, some were "repaired" (modified so that the original use may continue to be pursued in the face of entropy). All of these variables will affect the cultural role of pottery, and how it interacts with the roles of other media, such as monumental stone-carving.

Of course, there is another possibility, that the "La Hueca" style is really a "ware" within the Hacienda Grande style (Siegel, personal communication 1988), perhaps for a ritual purpose having to do with the offertory, and spatially segregated, burning and consumption of tobacco and hallucinogenic snuff. This is the position that Alegría (personal communication, 1989) still favors. For distributional and other reasons that I have referred to, I reject this option, as I do Chanlatte's position, that it indicates a radically different religious orientation from the Hacienda Grande population.

57. I do not do this statistically here because, as I have explained elsewhere, this is a *prospectus* for research, not the *results* of that research. While I have some basis for making these comparisons for artifacts within the Hacienda Grande and La Hueca assemblages, the two isolated assemblages of La Hueca/Sorcé and Punta Candelero have not yet been studied and described *as assemblages*. Rather, Chanlatte, in his extensive photo-documentation of selected vessels and parts thereof from his Tecla and La Hueca/Sorcé excavations, has presented his collections typologically, that is as isolated sherds/vessels. The excavated contexts of these objects, and their associations, have not been published. This is particularly the case with the less photogenic utilitarian ware from both styles. I have begun such a contextual study here, based on the drawings and photographs Chanlatte has kindly allowed me to do of many of his specimens, and Rodríguez has generously let me do with his unpublished materials, but the task is by no means concluded.

I expect, however, that since Rodríguez has taken my seminar in form and decoration analysis (Rodríguez 1983), and had earlier demonstrated an interest in "cultural whole" reconstruction on his own (Rodríguez, n.d.), that we will be in a position to do just what I outline in this paper (actually count and compare shared/contrasting La Hueca and Hacienda Grande dimensions and modes along those dimensions) once his analysis of the Punta Candelero assemblage is complete.

58. It does matter, analytically, that the design analysis be done after the form analysis, and not the other way around, because not only does such an order replicate the process the artisan goes through before the design is applied (a formalism, where possible, should follow the *order* of the process it seeks to paraphrase), but also because it is only after the forms come into being, or are visualized, that the *design fields* (the culturally permissable "decorateable" areas of an artifact [a jar neck], or a naturefact [the back of a human hand]) can be applied to them, and the *design layouts* (the "visual statement" composed of motifs and their attendant compositional rules) constructed to fill them.

59. While it is generally true that the Hacienda Grande style emphasizes the curvilinear spiral, and the La Hueca style the formally cognate rectilinearized scroll and lozenge (Rodríguez, this volume, Figures 2, 4, 6, 7a, 8), one does find rare examples of true spirals and half-circles in La Hueca ZIC incision just as one finds examples of LH "I" motifs in HG specimens (Figure 43d).

Rodríguez shows particularly interesting LH specimens (this volume, Figures 1 and 7b) with such motifs. Yet even on these examples note the wavering, rectangularized execution of the spirals and curves, in contrast to the sure, gracefully curving HG renditions. Such differences indicate unequal levels of practice, and consequentally, draftsmanship. Thus even the exceptions prove the rule.

60. A remarkably parallel, but historically unconnected, structural approach has been developed by Petitjean-Roget for the Antillean Saladoid pottery of Martinique and Guadeloupe (1973a, b). Based loosely on French structuralism, à la Lévi-Strauss in his "algebraic" aspects as applied to myth, Petitjean-Roget's system is also generative, and produces, like mine, derivational chains of conceptually linked solutions. The principal difference between his approach and mine is that Petitjean-Roget emphasizes the zoomorphic origin of these motifs (in the curled leg of a bactrian, cf., 1978:110), while my approach and the approach of my students (Cosme 1983; Hernández 1983; Maíz 1983; Pons de Alegría 1983b; Rivera 1983; Rodríguez 1983), treats Saladoid design as a formal problem. The two approaches are complementary.

In many ways, our abstract system is paralleled, again independently, by Jiménez (1972) in his design analysis section of Chicoid design layouts in Marcio Veloz's "Resumen tipológico de los complejos relacionables con Santo Domingo." His precocious attempt, unattributed in the manuscript, only lacks a systematic construction for all the various design layouts within every derivational chain of this "closed corpus" to exactly parallel our approach.

A related componential analytic technique that I developed can also be applied to complex figural art, such as the Elenan Ostionoid petroglyphs of Maisabel (Roe 1987b), or the even more sophisticated art of Chavín (Roe 1974). In all cases, an element and rule-based methodology can do much to wring both stylistic mechanics and iconography (in a "configurational" Kublerian sense) from extinct and living traditional styles.

61. The La Hueca potters partially compensated for this difficulty by making the bordering "formline" incisions when the clay was still relatively wet. This is *not* the case with the more finely executed Hacienda Grande "incision," which in many cases was done when the paste was much drier, and therefore actually qualifies as "engraving." However, even within the Hacienda Grande style of ZIC ware there are media and technique-based differences. As Rouse suggests :

> Within the Cedrosan Saladoid subseries...the same potters render(ed) both painted and ZIC wares (.) I've always thought the ZIC designs were rectilinear because these potters were executing them after the clay was dryer and harder, making it more difficult for them to produce curves while using their scratching technique [Irving Rouse,

personal communication 1988].

62. To repeat, these similarities are: complex, sharply-carinated silhouette, deformed effigy vessels, stirrup-spouted and labial flanged appliqué, annular bases and cross-hatched incision coupled with post-fired crusting.

63. Although ZIC pottery does *not* occur in the Orinoco Valley (Rouse, personal communication 1988).

64. I use the term "devolution" in connection with the pottery to imply a lessening in strength of paste (non-selected and unmodified local clay being substituted for prepared and selected clays and tempers), and a concomitant lowering of firing temperatures (probably by abandoning charcoal or the sophisticated differentiation of firewood and keying the separately procured wood types to succeeding stages in the time-temperature curve of the firing process), which systemically produced a weaker paste (less tensile strength, more reliance on compaction strength) and consequently an abandonment of (a) corner points of sharply inflected (carinated) forms in favor of the rounded forms of "primitive sphericity"), (b) appendages diverging at acute angles and for long distances relative to the vessel body (as in thin hollow-backed adornos, flanges, supra-flange tabs and annular bases) to be replaced by solid, simple adornos and appendages that tend toward appliqué (as in the widening of handles, the decrease of the interstitial space within the handle, and the plastering of the handle onto the vessel wall, ultimately producing vestigial appliqué handles as decorative, non-functional adornment), and (c) vessel body and appendage "stacking," and hence a drastic reduction in vessel form dimensions and total form vocabulary.

On the level of decoration, concomitant changes occur that indicate (a) lessened care and time spent on execution (line overlap, missed line junctures, line wobble, incision depth/width variation, (b) design structure simplification (dropping out of positive/negative play, increasing rectilinearization, breaking down of compound forms into their component parts-"reverse ontogeny") leading to, (c) repetition of the same design layouts, (d) restriction ("shrinking") of design fields in area and reduction in numbers of types, and (e) the replacement of high technology with low technology in media manipulation (i.e., loss of difficult-to-execute pre-fire slip painting [first abandoning polychrome, then bichrome, then false-bichrome, then overall "bath" replacing slip-paint] and its replacement with easy-to-execute wet-paste "surface roughening" (incision, impression, punctation), appliqué and modeling techniques. Figure 29 depicts the result of this relentless process, the Elenan Ostionoid and Esperanza pottery from El Bronce (near Ponce, Puerto Rico).

65. As I use the term "art," I must offer a cross-cultural definition of that much-written-of phenomenon which applies to these Antillean and related lowland South Amerindian styles. The more specific term "style" must also be defined. "Art" is a process, not a goal, where the *intent* (D'Azevedo 1958:711) is to create an "affecting presence" (Armstrong 1971), or psycho-socially stimulating event or thing directed to an audience (Munro 1963:419). Artistic cognition and behavior seeks to realize this intent by playfully (Huizinga 1950) manipulating the elements and rules of non-instrumental (in a simple Western "empirical" sense, cf., Maquet 1971:8) form. Paradoxically, these elements and rules, while actually the intentionally imposed "obstacles" of play, are also the *means* of expression because the artist finds pleasure in surmounting them (Miller 1973). It is the elaborating of subtle yet innovative solutions *within* the narrow frame of tradition that gives traditional art its vitality. It is something new within something old.

Behavioral skill (effort expended beyond technical necessity, Boas 1955:65) and redundancy (Bateson 1973:250) are combined to transmit both a conscious "message" and unconscious "information" about a possible order (Huxley 1977:182) in the world. Through insight, these novel and creative solutions seek to establish a state of "grace" unique to a self-reflective species (Bateson 1973:235).

Or, to be pithy, I could use a handy definition enunciated by Kaplan (1977:6) specifically for pottery, the subject under discussion here. In her sense, "art" implies "...those plastic and graphic forms elaborated beyond functional necessity through the skillful control of a medium to create an affect."

Taking a cue from Munro's realization that "(a)ll art is selection and emphasis, and selecting one thing means rejecting another" (1963:306), I assign to "style" that process of selection as a specific medium for the conveyance of *either* technology or art. The only method of selecting unambiguously between "technological style" (Lechtman and Merrill 1977) and "art style" is the *intent* of the producers of these contrasting approaches to the world. If the intent is *effective*, the selection produces technology (in either the Western empirical or the Malinowskian "magical" sense); if the intent is *affective* it produces an art style. A particular art style is therefore a cultural selection between the alternatives of form, function, significance and principle (with those four aspects of "innovation" linking art and technology as the other distinctions have contrasted them, cf. Barnett 1942) with the intent to affect an audience and transfer or exchange information with them (Wobst 1977:321).

To analyze further that unidimensional *archaeological* definition of "information" by Wobst, I will follow the more complex *ethnological* distinction offered by Jones (1973:268-269). In his sense, a message is the *intended* piece of information, whereas the information itself must be *inferred* from the message, possibly without the producer's conscious intent. In his words, "(t)he distinction is similar to that between reading off the message contained in a typed letter and inferring from the quality of the typing something about the secretarial skill of the typist."

Such a distinction is crucial for the "structuralist" stance to iconography (in my sense a system of signs and symbols in art) I have adopted in this paper. In other words, one might have understood the intended "message" of a Cedrosan Saladoid potter upon perceiving and appreciating the incised and painted designs upon an offered cup, that here was the hissing and fermenting beer of the cosmic anaconda, as coiled pot, an image ultimately derived from the "ophidian" symbolism of a hallucinatory encounter (assuming for a moment the perspectives of Gebhart-Sayer 1984; Roe 1988a and Stahl 1985a, 1985b, 1986). Since art is also "multivocal" one might have additionally perceived intended cultural messages about the social importance of generosity and the debts incurred upon its acceptance to create a social tie. If the individual who offered the beer was a comely young woman (to use regional ethnographic analogy), one could also infer messages about the "sexual" connotations of the offered beer, as well as related social-structural matters such as prospective marriage alliances.

On the other hand, as an archaeologist in an "etic" mode, one might infer "information" about the presence of highly skilled ceramic specialists in the society that produces such a vessel. One might also infer a "personal presentation" mode of material cultural and social interaction between individuals within that culture based on the same solicitous act. It is in this more complex sense of "message/information" that I will use "style" as the specific vehicle for the conveyance of artistic, technical, social and cosmological "communication."

66. For example, refiring and tensile strength tests could confirm or disconfirm my impression that La Hueca pottery is lower-fire than Hacienda Grande pottery. This is one of the problems that needs to be explored in Antillean ceramics.

67. To go back to the "ancestors," one of the ways of telling which of the media available to a culture are the locus of art is to see where the Veblerian (1953) "instinct of workmanship" is most in evidence. Where are the tour de forces in the material culture? Ever since Boas's demonstration of hidden effort in Plains Indian *parfletches* (1955), putting more time, effort and skill into something than is technically necessary has provided one of the definitions of art. That

is workmanship and "criteria of doneness and goodness are part and parcel of ...'workmanship'" (Link 1975:50-51), where "workmanship *is* the exercise of care, judgement and dexterity while engaging in a performance of technical behavior" (Link 1975:50-51). "Care" is signalled by emotional commitment to the project, "judgement" is the balancing of goals with the criteria of "standards of workmanship" specific to each technical (effective) process (Link 1975:52) and each aesthetic (affective) process.

Boas (1955:18) noted long ago that each culture emphasizes a different art in a different media, in accordance with the raw materials possibilities of their environment, their subsistence patterns and other life ways. Modern lowland South Amerindian ethnographers such as Kensinger (1975:69, on the Cashinahua), have noted the same thing. While ethnographers can use criteria to judge this "differential media development" beyond the ken of archaeologists (complexity in ethno-classificatory schema, plethora of names, prominent ritual and ceremonial contexts, verbal exegesis), archaeologists can pursue "premier domain" identification through the artifacts themselves.

The complex silhouettes, thin bodies and symmetrical cast of Hacienda Grande pottery embodies such workmanship and skill ("...the degree to which actors, by their behavior, achieve the standards of workmanship they have set for themselves" [Link 1975:55]) as a process of interaction with peers and critic = consumers. The relatively standardized forms within which creative solutions abound is evidence for the standards of workmanship.

In La Hueca the same criteria locate the premier art in the lapidary work. Here the number of different types of beads and amulets, the variety of stone and the exotic sources of some of the stone, the detailed workmanship, and the almost microscopic size (prima facie examples of tour de force) of many of the beads leads to the same conclusion.

Nevertheless, despite media differences, there is also a structural similarity between both styles. La Hueca and Hacienda Grande fixate upon small objects worn on the person (the lapidary art), or handled by the person (the ceramic art). All of these objects, regardless of stylistic affiliation, are used and appreciated in intimate (narrow personal space), yet visible contexts. Both styles, in short, betray the same culture of "personal presentation," albeit by utilizing different media.

68. There is the tendency to equate women with the making of pottery in the lowlands and lowland-derived cultures because that is the mode for the ethnographic present (male potters, such as those among the Ye'cuana, to the contary notwithstanding). Indeed, I have done so for part of my argument here. However, to heed Rouse's demand for multiple working hypotheses, we know also that when a task assumes the importance that I am attributing to Hacienda Grande pottery manufacture men are likely to appropriate it and include it within their own battery of tasks, as a reformulation of the traditional sexual division of labor. They will do so in search of greater social power (Mentore 1984, on the Waiwai; Roe 1987a). Thus, it would not surprise me if at least the Hacienda Grande style Saladoid potters were *male* rather than *female*, while I might suggest that the La Hueca potters were *female*.

There is no such ambiguity with regard to the lapidary arts. *Patterned* stonework (as against unpatterned stonework, such as Waiwai women employing bipolar percussion to produce variable flakes they *utilize*, but do not further modify, for grater teeth) is *always* a masculine province in current lowland ethnography. There is no reason to doubt that association in the archaeology. Therefore, *both* the Hacienda Grande and the La Hueca lapidary "village specialists" were most likely *male*, just as the products of that industry, the artifacts, were doubtlessly *masculine accoutrements*.

69. This is not necessarily a contradiction of what I have already said about the possibility of Hacienda Grande "pothunters" picking up La Hueca style sherds from the La Hueca area of the

Sorcé site. Those cases may have occurred for supernatural rather than primarily aesthetic reasons. Living South Amerindians, like the Shipibo, regard potsherds as the generalized power residences of the spirits of the ancients (Roe 1982a). Artisans in such groups may even archaistically innovate based on ancient pottery because they feel an affinity with the extinct populations as "ancestors" (Roe 1976). In other words, the Hacienda Grande people could have picked up the La Hueca sherds because they were "antiques," but without the "aesthetic of the antique." Perhaps they were culturally-related "power objects" with which the Hacienda Grande people felt some generalized affinity, rather than objects made precious merely because they were "old."

Alternatively, an aesthetic element could have been present in such Hacienda Grande-La Hueca cases, but as a manifestation of a pure interest in alien sculpture (the "aesthetic imperative"), rather than from any interest in these objects being "antiques."

70. While the greater complexity of La Hueca lapidary art than the corresponding Hacienda Grande art could indicate that both societies were equally complex, only that their premier arts existed in different material expressions (Siegel, personal communication 1988), I suggest that the larger number of different domains utilized and the greater apparent size of the supporting population gives pride of place to the Hacienda Grande style. In other words, one arbitrary way to determine social complexity, and therefore its sophistication, *archaeologically* is to count numbers of dimensions elaborated in the material culture, and then the numbers of types and modes along each dimension. Of course, this measure is subject to preservational bias (what if one culture had a very sophisticated feather art, and the other did not? All the feathers having disappeared, we cannot use this to weigh against other domains, like stoneworking, that does endure). This paper does not attempt such a comparative count, but my impression from surveying the respective collections is that were such a count to be done it would show greater complexity on the HG than the LH side.

Yet *sophistication* is defined by more than just greater relative *complexity*. It involves making more *subtle* distinctions as well as making *more* distinctions. In that sense I argue that there is no La Hueca analogue to the complex visual positive/negative play we see in Hacienda Grande pottery. Sculptural dualism is present in La Hueca as a kind of less sophisticated parallel ("anatropic organization," a form of "positive" pictorial reversibility where an adorno viewed right-side-up presents a different depiction than the same adorno viewed upside-down), but then it is also present in Hacienda Grande. La Hueca does have its novelties, such as an emphasis on miniaturization in the lapidary art or vessel wall deformation (the achieving of a compound shape by bending or pushing a vessel's walls before it is leather hard, cf., Figure 25) in the ceramics, but these innovations are more than outweighed by other Hacienda Grande dimensions such as an emphasis on kinetic features, reduplication and hollowness.

71. By "cultural aspirations" I imply a personal desire to *achieve* or *attain* statuses, and by "cultural attainments" the completion of that desire. Even in a simple tribal setting, Rabineau (1975:97) noted "...an apparent link between political leadership and aesthetic excellence, between thwarted political aspirations and a tendency to aesthetic extravagance." Her example from Cashinahua feather art comes from precisely the same sort of context that I am arguing for. This context is a material culture which is designed to be closely-visible within public (hence "political") presentational/performative contexts. She describes the interactions between the leaders of factions and the "pretenders" to such leadership as they and their followers express cultural notions of correct behavior through art canons.

These notions lead to certain judgements on the part of actors as to what constitutes an effective presentation in corporeal art within the political process, as well as the resultant aesthetic criticisms of the target audience. For example, while secure leaders choose decorative elements of the appropriate type and use them sparingly in their headdresses, aspirants tend to "overreach" by using inappropriately "valued" items like Harpy Eagle feathers on lower-than-appropriate categories of headdresses. Moreover, they compound their boorishness by using such elements exuberantly (Rabineau 1975:96). Hence "over-elaborateness" of material culture is opposed by the "golden mean" of restrained sumptuousness. These artifactual standards mirror the behavioral norms of the balanced and discrete non-coercive, consensus leader versus the ridiculed egocentric antagonist. In such cultures where "you are what you wear" or "you are what you use" the properties of highly visible artifacts will signal key cultural concerns for the achievement and maintenance of political aspirations, especially where kinship does not exclusively determine them. It is in that context that I regard these ancient artifacts as the "fossils" of political process.

72. My distinction here between "power" and "authority" is the standard anthropological one. Authority is the ability to induce other social beings to follow one's suggestions because they feel they should (mediated by such mechanisms as positive reciprocity and charisma), while "power" is the ability to make other social actors do what one wants, whether they desire to or not. Power, in other words, is based on coercion or the threat of it, while authority can manipulate more subtle factors such as admiration and guilt. Part of what confers authority is the cultural attainments one manifests through valued subsistence or ritual behavior. While power and authority often go hand-in-hand, the two are conceptually separate (as Rousseau demonstrated long ago in his essay on freedom).

Where "village specialists" of the sort envisioned in this paper produce highly valued items, there may be differential access to or control of the goods based *either* on power, or authority, or both. A shaman may garner impressive "gifts" for his cures just as a chief may demand such things as "contributions" from his followers. The archaeologist will not normally be able to distinguish between the two judged on distribution alone (let us say through association as grave goods). However, I argue he/she may be able to make such distinctions based on material, workmanship, type or scale. A one kilogram menhir of local stone adorned with a crude but highly visible petroglyph may say something different about the person or society which manipulated it than a one gram amulet carved painstakingly out of imported semi-precious stone.

73. Here I have shifted the locus of my discussion. Before I talked at length about how extraordinary early Saladoid pottery was, and how it must have been appreciated. It was precisely such fine pottery that not everybody could make. Hence it was the fine pottery that was coveted, not the utilitarian pottery made by and available to all. Now I suggest that as one progresses from one level of socio-cultural integration to another, while fine pottery can retain those connotations (witness black figure Greek ware or Moche and Nazca specimens), it is more likely to be superceded by other media that can better express power relations clearly.

74. Hacienda Grande has much greater complexity in design structure largely because of its use of pre-fire paint and the false negative, formline/filler distinctions painting makes possible; it also has a greater complexity of vessel categories because of its modular (component stacking) construction, as well as the existence of numerous vessel and figurine types not present in La Hueca.

75. At the moment this is based more on the oral tradition than on the basis of published reports. This situation, even if confirmed, could just as well indicate that either the La Hueca types were contemporary with the early Hacienda Grande settlements, and were obtained by them through trade or raiding (but then why no Hacienda Grande sherds in the two isolated La Hueca sites unless the relations were asymmetrical?), or that the La Hueca material was just a ware within the Hacienda Grande style. There are no documented contexts where La Hueca sherds *underlie* Hacienda Grande occupations. Indeed, as Siegel points out (personal communication 1988), "At Pta. Candelero, ZIC underlies Cuevas, thus supporting Rouse's contention that ZIC and HG are contemporaneous (if not the same thing)."

76. Of course, as a result of "ceramic devolution" many things drop out of the ceramic repetoire in later Saladoid (i.e., Cuevas) times. Thus, disappearance alone would not qualify the "linear incised" ware to be distinct from Hacienda Grande. However, I note that this ware is defined by a whole constellation of traits, not just its characteristic mode of surface decoration. Similar shape and size modes also form part of it and they do not seem to drop out at random, but at the same time.

Acknowledgments. I would like to thank the principal individuals and institutions involved in this preliminary study: Dr. Ricardo Alegría and Sra. Mela Pons de Alegría for their long-standing support and deep appreciation of Saladoid pottery, Dr. Irving Rouse for the benefits of his detailed criticism on an earlier draft of this paper, Sr. Luís Chanlatte for the generous placing of his unparalleled collections form Tecla and Sorcé at my disposal, Ms. Linda Robinson for giving me the reponsibility of Ceramic Consultant on her massive Caracoles project and thus broadening my familiarity with the later part of this ceramic sequence, and to Sr. Gaspar Roca, Director of the Centro de Investigaciones Indígenas de Puerto Rico, for his support for my study of the ex-Castillo collection, and for write-up time. To my former students (now esteemed colleagues) of the University of Delaware (Mr. Peter Siegel, now Ph.D. Candidate at the State University of New York at Binghamton) and the Centro de Estudios Avanzados de Puerto Rico y El Caribe (Sr. Miguel Rodríguez, Sr. Edgar Maíz, Sr. Juan González and Sr. Hernán Ortíz) I offer heartfelt thanks. Mr. Siegel, now Co-Director of the Maisabel Project, CIIPR, has given me much valuable criticism of an earlier draft of this study. Sr. Rodríguez has provided me with valuable access to his own slides and collections at the University of Turabo, and the benefit of his deep familiarity with Puerto Rican and Vieques ceramics. Sr. González put his Tibes materials at my disposal and Sr. Maíz has apprised me of his Colón excavations. To complete my familiarity with the middle of this sequence, Sr. Ortíz has worked with me on his Cuevas and Elenan Ostionoid materials from Ojo del Buey, Dorado. None of these individuals are, of course, responsible for the numerous errors I have doubtlessly perpetrated in this study.

REFERENCES CITED

Alegría, Ricardo E.
    1947a Nuevos hallazgos. *La Prensa* Sabado, 21 de Junio. New York.

    1947b Informe preliminar sobre la primera excavación del Centro de Investigaciónes Arqueológicas del UPR en la finca 'La Monserrate.' Ms. in possession of author.

    1965 On Puerto Rican Archaeology. *American Antiquity* 31:246-249.

    1983 *Ball Courts and Ceremonial Plazas in the West Indies*. Yale University Publications in Anthropology No.79. New Haven.

Alvarado, Pedro A.
    1980 *La cerámica del Centro Ceremonial de Tibes*. Unpublished Master's thesis, Centro de Estudios Avanzados de Puerto Rico y el Caribe, San Juan.

Anderson, Jennifer L.
    1987 Japanese Tea Ritual: Religion in Practice. *Man* n.s. 22:475-498.

Armstrong, Robert Plant
    1971 *The Affecting Presence: An Essay in Humanistic Anthropology*. University of Illinois Press, Urbana.

Ayes, Carlos M.
    1985 Excavaciónes arqueológicas en Maisabel. *El Metropolitano* 1(2):4, 16 de Agosto-15 de Septiembre de 1985. San Juan.

D'Azevedo, Warren L.
    1958 A Structural Approach to Esthetics: Toward a Definition of Art in Anthropology. *American Anthropologist* 60:702-714.

Barnett, Homer G.
    1942 Invention and Cultural Change. *American Anthropologist* 44:14-30.

Bateson, Gregory
    1973 Style, Grace, and Information in Primitive Art. In *Primitive Art & Society*, edited by Anthony Forge, pp. 235-255. Oxford University Press, Oxford and London.

Boas, Franz
    1955 *Primitive Art*. Reprinted. Dover Publications, New York. Originally published 1927.

Budinoff, Linda C.
    1987 An Osteological Analysis of the Human Burials Recovered From An Early Ceramic Site Located on the North Coast of Puerto Rico. Paper presented at the 12th International Congress of Caribbean Archeology, Cayenne, French Guiana.

Bullen, Ripley P.
    1968 Some Arawak Ceramic Variations Between Grenada, Barbados, St. Lucia, and Eastern Trinidad. *Proceedings of the International Congress for the Study of the Pre-Columbian Cultures of the Lesser Antilles* 2:81-86. Barbados.

    1970 The Archaeology of Grenada, West Indies, and the Spread of Ceramic People in the Antilles. *Proceedings of the International Congress for the Study of the Pre-Columbian*

Cultures of the Lesser Antilles 3:147-152. Grenada.

Bunzel, Ruth L.
   1972 *The Pueblo Potter: A Study of Creative Imagination in Primitive Art*. Reprinted. Dover Publications, New York. Originally published 1929.

Burger, Richard L.
   1988 Unity and Heterogeneity Within the Chavín Horizon. In *Peruvian Prehistory: An Overview of Pre-Inca and Inca Society*, edited by Richard W. Keatinge, pp. 99-144. Cambridge University Press, Cambridge.

Carbone, Victor A.
   1980 Puerto Rican Prehistory: An Outline. In *A Cultural Resources Reconnaissance of Five Projects in Puerto Rico*, edited by Ernest W. Seckinger, Jr., pp. 1-68. Submitted to the Jacksonville District Office, U.S. Army Corps of Engineers. Copies available from the State Historic Preservation Office, San Juan.

Chagnon, Napoleon A.
   1983 *Yanomamö: The Fierce People*. 3rd ed. Holt, Rinehart and Winston, New York.

Chanlatte Baik, Luis A.
   1976 *Cultura Igneri:Investigaciónes en Guayanilla, Puerto Rico, Tecla II, Parte I*. Investigaciónes 5. Museo del Hombre Dominicano y Fundación García Arvalo, Santo Domingo.

   1979 Excavaciónes arqueológicas en Vieques. *Revista del Museo de Antropología, Historia y Arte de la Universidad de Puerto Rico* 1(1):55-59.

   1981 *La Hueca y Sorcé (Vieques, Puerto Rico): Primeras migraciones agroalfareras Antillanas: Nuevo esquema para los procesos culturales de la arqueología Antillana*. Privately printed, Santo Domingo.

   1983a *Catálogo arqueología de Vieques: Exposición del 13 de Marzo al 22 de Abril de 1983*. Museo de Antropología, Historia y Arte, Universidad de Puerto Rico, Río Piedras.

   1983b Sorcé-Vieques: Climax cultural del Igneri y su participación en los procesos socioculturales Antillanos. *Proceedings of the International Congress for the Study of the Pre-Columbian Cultures of the Lesser Antilles* 9: 73-95. Montréal.

   1984 Nuevos descubrimientos arqueológicos en la isla de Vieques. *Revista del Instituto de Cultura Puertorriqueña* 23(86):29-36.

   1985a *Asentamiento poblacional Agro-I, complejo cultural, La Hueca, Vieques, Puerto Rico*. Privately printed, Santo Domingo.

   1985b *Catálogo arqueología de Guayanilla y Vieques: Exposición del 30 de Julio al 15 de Septiembre de 1985*. Museo de Antropología, Historia y Arte de la Universidad de Puerto Rico, Río Piedras.

   1986 Investigaciónes arqueológicas en Tecla, Guayanilla. *Arqueología* 2(1):22-23.

   1987 Nuevos descubrimientos en el sitio de Sorcé, Vieques. Paper presented at the semi-annual Meeting of the Association of Puerto Rican Anthropologists and Archaeologists, Dorado, Puerto Rico.

Chanlatte Baik, Luis A. and Yvonne M. Narganes Storde
  1980 La Hueca, Vieques: Nuevo complejo cultural agro-alfarero en la arqueología Antillanas. *Proceedings of the International Congress for the Study of the Pre-Columbian Cultures of the Lesser Antilles* 8:501-523. Tempe.

  1986 *Proceso y desarrollo de los primeros pobladores de Puerto Rico y las antillas.* Privately printed, San Juan.

Cosme, Rafael
  1983 La cultura Huecoide. Ms. in possession of author.

Dávila, Ovidio
  1979 La serie cultural Saladoide en la prehistoria de Puerto Rico. *Cuadernos Prehispánicos* 7:63-77.

DeBoer, Warren R.
  1981a Buffer Zones in the Cultural Ecology of Aboriginal Amazonia. *American Antiquity* 46:364-377.

  1981b The Machete and the Cross: Conibo Trade in the Late Seventeenth Century. In *Networks of the Past: Regional Interaction in Archaeology*, edited by Peter D. Francis, F. J. Kense, and P.G. Duke, pp. 31-47. The Archaeological Association of the University of Calgary, Calgary.

DeBoer, Warren R. and Donald W. Lathrap
  1979 The Making and Breaking of Shipibo-Conibo Ceramics. In *Ethnoarchaeology: Implications of Ethnography for Archaeology*, edited by Carol Kramer, pp. 102-138. Columbia University Press, New York.

deFrance, Susan D.
  1988 *Zooarchaeological Investigations of Subsistence Strategies At the Maisabel Site.* Unpublished Master's paper, Department of Anthropology, University of Florida, Gainesville.

Duprat, J.P.
  1974 Les themes de décoration de la poterie Arawak. *Proceedings of the International Congress for the Study of the Pre-Columbian Cultures of the Lesser Antilles* 5:72-81. Antigua.

Figueredo, Alfredo E.
  1980 Pottery from Gun Creek, Virgin Gorda. *Journal of the Virgin Islands Archaeological Society* 9:27-30.

  1987 Brief Introduction to the Prehistory of St. Croix, From Earliest Times to 1493. *Bulletin of the Society of Virgin Islands Historians* 1(1):4-10.

Fung Pineda, Rosa
  1988 The Late Preceramic and Initial Period. In *Peruvian Prehistory: An Overview of Pre-Inca and Inca Society*, edited by Richard W. Keatinge, pp. 67-96. Cambridge University Press, Cambridge.

Gebhart-Sayer, Angelika
  1984 *The Cosmos Encoiled: Indian Art of the Peruvian Amazon.* Exhibition Catalog. Center for Inter-American Relations, New York.

González Colón, Juan
    1984   *Tibes: Un centro ceremonial Indígena*. Unpublished Master's thesis, Centro de Estudios Avanzados de Puerto Rico y el Caribe, San Juan.

Goodwin, R. Christopher
    1980   Demographic Change and the Crab/Shell Dichotomy. *Proceedings of the International Congress for the Study of the Pre-Columbian Cultures of the Lesser Antilles* 8:45-67. Tempe.

Goodwin, R. Christopher and Peter F. Thall
    1983   Production Step Measures and Prehistoric Caribbean Ceramics: An Exploratory Study. *Proceedings of the International Congress for the Study of the Pre-Columbian Cultures of the Lesser Antilles* 9:301-323. Montréal.

Habicht-Mauche, Judith, John Hoopes and Michael Geselowitz
    1987   Where's the Chief?: The Archaeology of Complex Tribes. Paper presented at the 52nd Annual Meeting of the Society for American Archaeology, Toronto.

Hackenberger, Steven
    1987   Archaeological Investigations, 1986, Barbados, West Indies. Paper presented at the 12th International Congress of Caribbean Archaeology, Cayenne, French Guiana.

Hardin, Margaret Ann
    1983   The Structure of Tarascan Pottery Painting. In *Structure and Cognition in Art*, edited by Dorothy K. Washburn, pp. 8-24. Cambridge University Press, New York.

Harrington, Mark R.
    1924   A West Indian Gem Center. *Museum of the American Indian Heye Foundation Indian Notes* 1(4):184-189.

Hernández Rivera, Vctor
    1983   Analisis de diseños de la cerámica de la cultura Igneri (Saladoide) de Puerto Rico. Ms. in possession of author.

de Hostos, Adolfo
    1919   Prehistoric Porto Rican Ceramics. *American Anthropologist* 21:376-399.

Huizinga, Johan
    1950   *Homo Ludens: A Study of the Play Element in Culture*. Beacon Press, Boston.

Hurault, Jacques
    1961   Les indiens Oayana de la Guyane Francaise. *Journal de la Société des Américanistes*, Nouvelle Serie t.L:135-183.

Huxley, Aldous
    1977   *The Human Situation: Lectures at Santa Barbara by Aldous Huxley, 1959*. Edited by Piero Ferrucci. Harper & Row, New York.

Jiménez Lambertus, Abelardo
    1972   Design Analysis Section of Marcio Veloz Maggiolo's "Resumen tipolgico de los complejos relacionables con Santo Domingo."--unattributed in the manuscript. *Boletin del Museo del Hombre Dominicano* 1:47-56.

Jones, W.T.
   1973   Talking About Art and Primitive Society. In *Primitive Art & Society*, edited by Anthony Forge, pp. 256-277. Oxford University Press, Oxford and London.

Kaplan, Flora S.
   1977   Symbolism in Mexican Utilitarian Pottery. *Centerpoint* 2:33-41.

Keatinge, Richard W.
   1988   A Summary View of Peruvian Prehistory. In *Peruvian Prehistory: An Overview of Pre-Inca and Inca Society*, edited by Richard W. Keatinge, pp. 303-316. Cambridge University Press, Cambridge.

Kempton, Willett
   1981   *The Folk Classification of Ceramics: A Study of Cognitive Prototypes*. Academic Press, New York.

Kensinger, Kenneth
   1975   Studying the Cashinahua. In *The Cashinahua of Eastern Peru*, edited by Jane Powell Dwyer, pp. 9-85. Studies in Anthropology and Material Culture No. 1. The Haffenreffer Museum of Anthropology, Brown University, Bristol, Rhode Island.

Lathrap, Donald W.
   1970   *The Upper Amazon*. Praeger, New York.

   1983   Recent Shipibo-Conibo Ceramics and Their Implications for Archaeological Interpretations. In *Structure and Cognition in Art*, edited by Dorothy K. Washburn, pp. 25-39. Cambridge University Press, New York.

Lathrap, Donald W., Donald Collier and Helen Chandra
   1975   *Ancient Ecuador: Culture, Clay and Creativity 3000-300 B.C.* Exhibit Catalog. Field Museum of Natural History, Chicago.

Lechtman, Heather and Robert Merrill (editors)
   1977   *Material Culture: Styles, Organization, and Dynamics of Technology*. Proceedings of the 1975 Annual Meeting of the American Ethnological Society. West, St. Paul.

Link, Carol
   1975   *Japanese Cabinetmaking: A Dynamic System of Decisions and Interactions in a Technical Context*. Ph.D. dissertation, University of Illinois, Urbana. University Microfilms, Ann Arbor.

Magaña, Edmundo
   1982   Note on Ethnoanthropological Notions of the Guiana Indians. *Anthropologica* 24:215-233.

Maíz, Edgar J.
   1983   El análisis de la decoración incisa rellena con pintura y el 'Cross-Hatch' en el estilo Hacienda Grande de Puerto Rico. Ms. in possession of author.

Maquet, Jacques
   1971   *Introduction To Aesthetic Anthropology*. A McCaleb Module in Anthropology. Addison-Wesley, Reading.

Mattioni, Mario
  1976 Les grandes familles des formes du 'Saladoide Insulaire' au site de Vivé a la Martinique. *Proceedings of the International Congress for the Study of the Pre-Columbian Cultures of the Lesser Antilles* 6:11-13. Gainesville.

  1979 *Salvage Excavations at the Vivé Site, Martinique: Final Report.* Edited and translated by Louis Allaire. University of Manitoba Anthropology Papers 23. Winnipeg.

  1980 Salvage Excavations at the Fond-Brûlé Site, Martinique. *Proceedings of the International Congress for the Study of the Pre-Columbian Cultures of the Lesser Antilles* 8:553-566. Tempe.

  1982 *Salvage Excavations at the Fond Brûlé Site, Martinique: Final Report.* Edited and translated by Louis Allaire. University of Manitoba Anthropology Papers 27. Winnipeg.

Meggers, Betty J. and Clifford Evans, Jr.
  1961 An Experimental Formulation of Horizon Styles in the Tropical Forest Area of South America. In *Essays in Pre-Columbian Art and Archaeology*, edited by Samuel K. Lothrop and others, pp. 372-388. Harvard University Press, Cambridge.

Mentore, George P.
  1984 *Shepariymo: The Political Economy of a Waiwai Village.* Unpublished Ph.D. dissertation, Graduate School in Arts and Social Studies, University of Sussex, Sussex, England.

  1985 Report on the Centro de Investigaciones Indígenas de Puerto Rico's Expedition to the Brazilian Waiwai-1985. Ms. on file, Centro de Investigaciones Indígenas de Puerto Rico. San Juan.

Miller, Daniel
  1985 *Artefacts as Categories: A Study of Ceramic Variability in Central India.* Cambridge University Press, Cambridge.

Miller, Stephen
  1973 Ends, Means, and Galumphing: Some Leitmotifs of Play. *American Anthropologist* 75:87-98.

Muller, Jon
  1971 Style and Culture Contact. In *Man Across the Sea: Problems of Pre-Columbian Contacts*, edited by Carroll L. Riley, pp. 66-78. University of Texas Press, Austin.

Munro, Thomas
  1963 *Evolution in the Arts and Other Theories of Culture History.* Harry N. Abrams, New York.

Myers, Thomas P.
  1976 Defended Territories and No-Man's-Lands. *American Anthropologist* 78:354-355.

  1988 "Identical" Designs on Three Bora Artifacts. *Museum Anthropology* 12(2):14-19.

Narganes Storde, Yvonne M.
  1985 Restos faunísticos vertebrados de Sorcé, Vieques, Puerto Rico. *Proceedings of the International Congress for the Study of the Pre-Columbian Cultures of the Lesser Antilles* 10:251-264. Montréal.

Petitjean-Roget, Henri
    1975   *Contribution à l'étude de la Préhistoire des Petites Antilles I,II.* Unpublished Ph.D. dissertation, Ecole Pratique des Hautes Etudes, Paris.

    1976a Note sur le motif de la grenouille dans l'art Arawak des Petites Antilles. *Proceedings of the International Congress for the Study of the Pre-Columbian Cultures of the Lesser Antilles* 6:177-181. Gainesville.

    1976b Le theme de la chauve-souris frugivore dans l'art Arawak des Petites Antilles. *Proceedings of the International Congress for the Study of the Pre-Columbian Cultures of the Lesser Antilles* 6:182-186. Gainesville.

    1978   Note sur un vase Arawak trouve a la Martinique. *Proceedings of the International Congress for the Study of the Pre-Columbian Cultures of the Lesser Antilles* 7:99-115. Montréal.

Petitjean-Roget, Jacques and Henri Petitjean-Roget
    1973a Recherche d'une méthode pour l'étude de la décoration des céramiques précolombiennes de la Martinique. *Proceedings of the International Congress for the Study of the Pre-Columbian Cultures of the Lesser Antilles* 4:151-156. St. Lucia.

    1973b Etude comparative des tessons gravés ou incisés. *Proceedings of the International Congress for the Study of the Pre-Columbian Cultures of the Lesser Antilles* 4:157-173. St. Lucia.

Pons de Alegría, Carmen A.
    1973   *The Igneri Ceramic from the Site of the Convent of San Domingo: A Study of Style and Form.* Unpublished Master's thesis, Department of American Studies, State University of New York, Buffalo.

    1976   Saladoid 'Incense-Burners' from the Site of El Convento, Puerto Rico. *Proceedings of the International Congress for the Study of the Pre-Columbian Cultures of the Lesser Antilles* 6:272-275. Gainesville.

    1978   La cerámica saladoide y el problema de su terminología. *Review/Revista Interamericana* 8(3):400-404.

    1983a Las figuritas de barro de la cultura Saladoide de Puerto Rico. *Proceedings of the International Congress for the Study of the Pre-Columbian Cultures of the Lesser Antilles* 9:121-129. Montréal.

    1983b Un análisis de los diseños Saladoides. Ms. in possession of author.

Price, T. Douglas, Erik Brinch Petersen
    1987   A Mesolithic Camp in Denmark. *Scientific American* 256(3):112-121.

Questell Rodríguez, Eduardo
    1983   Tibes: Indian Cultural Heritage in Puerto Rico. *Qué Pasa* 35(5):6-9.

Rabineau, Phyllis
    1975   Artists and Leaders: The Social Context of Creativity in A Tropical Forest Culture. In *The Cashinahua of Eastern Peru*, edited by Jane Powell Dwyer, pp. 87-109. Studies in Anthropology and Material Culture 1. The Haffenreffer Museum of Anthropology, Brown University, Bristol, Rhode Island.

Rainey, Froelich G.
  1940   *Porto Rican Archaeology.* Scientific Survey of Porto Rico and the Virgin Islands, vol. XVIII-part 1. The New York Academy of Sciences, New York.

Raymond, J. Scott
  1988   A View From the Tropical Forest. In *Peruvian Prehistory: An Overview of Pre-Inca and Inca Society*, edited by Richard W. Keatinge, pp. 279-300. Cambridge University Press, Cambridge.

Raymond, J. Scott, Warren R. DeBoer and Peter G. Roe
  1975   *Cumancaya: A Peruvian Ceramic Tradition.* Occasional Papers 2. Department of Archaeology, University of Calgary, Calgary.

Rivera Aponte, Héctor
  1985   La cultura Igneri en Puerto Rico. *Geomundo* 9(3):224-229.

  1986   Un trascendental hallazgo arqueológico en Humacao. *El Mundo* Martes, 1 de Julio:26. San Juan.

Rivera Fontán, Juan A.
  1983   Análisis de diseños geométricos en la cerámica Saladoide del colección del Instituto de la Cultura Puertorriqueña. Ms. in possession of author.

Rodríguez López, Miguel
  n.d.   Dibujos de la cerámica Saladoide del sitio de Hacienda Grande, Puerto Rico. Ms. in possession of author.

  1983   Análisis de diseños geométricos en arqueología. Ms. in possession of author.

Rodríguez, Miguel and Virginia Rivera
  1987   Puerto Rico and the Caribbean Pre-Saladoid 'Crosshatch Connection.' Paper presented at the 12th International Congress of Caribbean Archaeology, Cayenne, French Guiana.

Roe, Peter G.
  1973   *Cumancaya: Archaeological Excavations and Ethnographic Analogy in the Peruvian Montaña.* Ph.D. dissertation, University of Illinois, Urbana. University Microfilms, Ann Arbor.

  1974   *A Further Exploration of the Rowe Chavín Seriation and Its Implications for North Central Coast Chronology.* Studies in Pre-Columbian Art and Archaeology 13. Dumbarton Oaks Research Library and Collections, Trustees for Harvard University, Washington, D.C.

  1975   Comparing Panoan Art Styles Through Componential Analysis. Paper presented at the 74th Annual Meeting of the American Anthropological Association, San Francisco.

  1976   Archaism, Form and Decoration: An Ethnographic and Archaeological Case Study from the Peruvian Montaña. *Ñawpa Pacha* 14:73-94, Plates. 26-29.

  1978   Recent Discoveries in Chavín Art: Some Speculations on Methodology and Significance in the Analysis of a Figural Style. *El Dorado* 3:1-41.

  1979   Marginal Men: Male Artists Among the Shipibo Indians of Peru. *Anthropologica* 21:189-221.

1980 Art and Residence Among the Shipibo Indians of Peru: A Study in Microacculturation. *American Anthropologist* 82:42-71.

1981 Aboriginal Tourists and Artistic Exchange Between the Pisquibo and the Shipibo: 'Trade Ware' in an Ethnographic Setting. In *Networks of the Past: Regional Interaction in Archaeology*, edited by Peter D. Francis, F.J. Kense and P.G. Duke, pp. 61-84. The Archaeological Association of the University of Calgary, Calgary.

1982a *The Cosmic Zygote: Cosmology in the Amazon Basin.* Rutgers University Press, New Brunswick.

1982b Ethnoaesthetics and Design Grammars: Shipibo Perceptions of Cognate Styles. Paper presented at the 81st Annual Meeting of the American Anthropological Association, Washington, D.C.

1985 A Preliminary Report on the 1980 and 1982 Field Seasons at Hacienda Grande (12 PSj7-5): Overview of Site History, Mapping and Excavations. *Proceedings of the International Congress for the Study of the Pre-Columbian Cultures of the Lesser Antilles* 10:151-180, 206-224. Montréal.

1987a Village Spatial Organization in the South Amerindian Lowlands: Evidence from Ethno-archaeology. Paper presented at the 52nd Annual Meeting of the Society for American Archaeology, Toronto.

1987b The Petroglyphs of Maisabel. Paper presented at the 12th International Congress of Caribbean Archaeology, Cayenne, French Guiana.

1987c Review of *The Folk Classification of Pottery*, by Willett Kempton. *North American Archaeologist* 8:343-356.

1988a Urfiri and the Acoro: The Dragon As the Origin of Designs in Shipibo and Waiwai Mythology. Paper presented at the 6th International Symposium on Latin American Indian Literatures, Guatemala City.

1988b The *Josho Nahuanbo* Are All Wet and Undercooked: Shipibo Views of the Whiteman and the Incas in Myth, Legend and History. In *Rethinking History and Myth: Indigenous South American Perspectives on the Past*, edited by Jonathan Hill, pp. 106-135. University of Illinois Press, Urbana.

1988c A Grammatical Analysis of Cedrosian Saladoid Vessel Form Category and Surface Decoration: Aesthetic and Technical Styles in Early Antillean Ceramics. Paper presented at the 53rd Annual Meeting of the Society for American Archaeology, Phoenix.

1989 Style and Culture: A Montage of Ethnological and Archaeological Approaches. In *Style, Society, and Person*, edited by Christopher Carr and Jill E. Neitzel. Cambridge University Press, New York, in press.

Roe, Peter G., Agamemnon Gus Pantel and Margaret B. Hamilton
1985 Monserrate Restudied: A Preliminary Report on the Excavation and Mapping, Lithic Artifact and Human Osteological Collections From the 1978 CEAPRC Field Season. Paper presented at the 11th International Congress of Caribbean Archaeology, San Juan, Puerto Rico.

Roosevelt, Anna Curtenius
   1980 *Parmana: Prehistoric Maize and Manioc Subsistence Along the Amazon and Orinoco.* Academic Press, New York.

Rouse, Irving
   1939 *Prehistory of Haiti: A Study in Method.* Yale University Publications in Anthropology No. 21. New Haven.

   1941 *Culture of the Ft. Libert Region, Haiti.* Yale University Publications in Anthropology No. 24. New Haven.

   1952 *Porto Rican Prehistory: Introduction; Excavations in the West and North.* Scientific Survey of Puerto Rico and the Virgin Islands, vol. XVIII-part 3. The New York Academy of Sciences, New York.

   1964 Prehistory of the West Indies. *Science* 144:499-513.

   1982 Ceramic and Religious Development in the Greater Antilles. *Journal of New World Archaeology* 5(2):45-55.

   1985a Arawakan Phylogeny, Caribbean Chronology, and Their Implications for the Study of Population Movement. Paper presented at the 34th Convención Anual de AsoVAC, Cumaná, Venezuela.

   1985b Social, Linguistic, and Stylistic Plurality in the West Indies. Paper presented at the 11th International Congress for Caribbean Archaeology, San Juan, Puerto Rico.

   1986 *Migrations in Prehistory: Inferring Population Movement From Cultural Remains.* Yale University Press, New Haven.

Rouse, Irving and Ricardo E. Alegría
   1978 Radiocarbon Dates from the West Indies. *Revista/Review Interamericana* 8:495-499.

   1989 *Excavations at María de la Cruz and Hacienda Grande, Loiza, Puerto Rico.* Yale University Publications in Anthropology. New Haven, in press.

Rouse, Irving and Louis Allaire
   1978 Caribbean. In *Chronologies in New World Archaeology*, edited by R.E. Taylor and Clement W. Meighan, pp. 431-481. Academic Press, New York.

Rouse, Irving, Louis Allaire, and Aad Boomert
   1985 The Chronology of Eastern Venezuela, Guianas, and the West Indies. Ms. prepared for an unpublished volume, *Chronologies in South American Archaeology*, compiled by Clement W. Meighan. Department of Anthropology, University of California, Los Angeles.

Schiffer, Michael B.
   1972 Archaeological Context and Systemic Context. *American Antiquity* 37:156-165.

Shepard, Anna O.
   1971 *Ceramics For the Archaeologist.* 5th ed. Carnegie Institution, Washington, D.C.

Siegel, Peter E.
   1986 The Maisabel Project. *Arqueología* 2(1):20-21.

1987 Small Village Demographic and Architectural Organization: An Example from the Tropical Lowlands. Paper presented at the 52nd Annual Meeting of the Society for American Archaeology, Toronto.

Siegel, Peter E. and David J. Bernstein
1987 Sampling for Site Structure and Spatial Organization in the Saladoid: A Case Study. Paper presented at the 12th International Congress of Caribbean Archaeology, Cayenne, French Guiana.

Siegel, Peter E. and Peter G. Roe
1987 The Maisabel Archaeological Project: A Long Term Multi-Disciplinary Investigation. Paper Presented at the 12th International Congress of Caribbean Archaeology, Cayenne, French Guiana.

Stahl, Peter W.
1985a Native American Cosmology in Archaeological Interpretation: Tropical Forest Cosmology and the Early Valdivia Phase at Loma Alta. In *Status, Structure and Stratification: Current Archaeological Reconstructions*, edited by Marc Thompson, Maria Teresa García, and Francois J. Kense, pp. 31-37. Proceedings of the Sixteenth Annual Conference of the Archaeological Association of the University of Calgary, Calgary.

1985b The Hallucinogenic Basis of Early Valdivia Phase Ceramic Bowl Iconography. *Journal of Psychoactive Drugs* 17(2):105-123.

1986 Hallucinatory Imagery and the Origin of Early South American Figurine Art. *World Archaeology* 18:134-150.

Sued Badillo, Jalil
1978 La industra lapidaria pretaína en las Antillas. *Revista/Review Interamericana* 8(3):429-462.

Veblen, Thorstein
1953 *The Theory of the Leisure Class*. Mentor Books, New York. Originally published 1899.

Versteeg, A.H. and F.R. Effert
1987 *Golden Rock: The First Indian Village on St. Eustatius*. St. Eustatius Historical Foundation No. 1.

Vescelius, Gary S.
1980 A Cultural Taxonomy for West Indian Archaeology. *Journal of the Virgin Islands Archaeological Society* 10:38-41.

Walker, Jeffrey B.
1984 A Preliminary Report on the Lithic and Osteological Remains from the 1980, 1981 and 1982 Field Seasons at Hacienda Grande (12 PSj7-5). *Proceedings of the International Congress for the Study of the Pre-Columbian Cultures of the Lesser Antilles* 10:181-224. Montréal.

Washburn, Dorothy K. and Donald W. Crowe
1988 *Symmetries of Culture: Theory and Practice of Plane Pattern Analysis*. University of Washington Press, Seattle.

Watters, David R., Elizabeth J. Reitz, David W. Steadman, and Gregory K. Pregill
    1984   Vertebrates from Archaeological Sites on Barbuda, West Indies. *Annals of the Carnegie Museum* 53(13):383-412.

Weil, Peter M.
    1971   The Masked Figure and Social Control: The Mandinka Case. *Africa* 41:279-293, Plates I,II.

Whitten, Dorothea S. and Norman E. Whitten Jr.
    1988   *From Myth to Creation: Art from Amazonian Ecuador*. University of Illinois Press, Urbana.

Wobst, H. Martin
    1977   Stylistic Behavior and Information Exchange. In *Papers for the Director: Research Essays in Honor of James B. Griffin*, edited by C.E. Cleland, pp. 317-342. Academic Press, New York.

    1978   The Archaeo-ethnology of Hunter-gatherers, or the Tyranny of the Ethnographic Record in Archaeology. *American Antiquity* 43:303-309.

KEY TO FIGURES

▨ Red, Pre-Fire Slip Paint

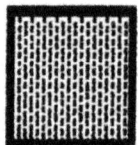

▦ Yellow, Pre-Fire Slip Paint

▩ Cross-hatched Incision/Engraving

☐ White, Pre-Fire Slip Paint

▓ Post-Fire Smudging

■ Black, Post-Fire Resin Crusting

Acronym Key

Centro de Estudios Avanzados de Puerto Rico y el Caribe	CEAPRC
Centro de Investigaciones Arqueológicas (UPR)	CIA
Centro de Investigaciones Indígenas de Puerto Rico	CIIPR
Universidad de Puerto Rico	UPR
Hacienda Grande	HG
White-on-Red Painting	WOR
Zoned Incision	ZIC

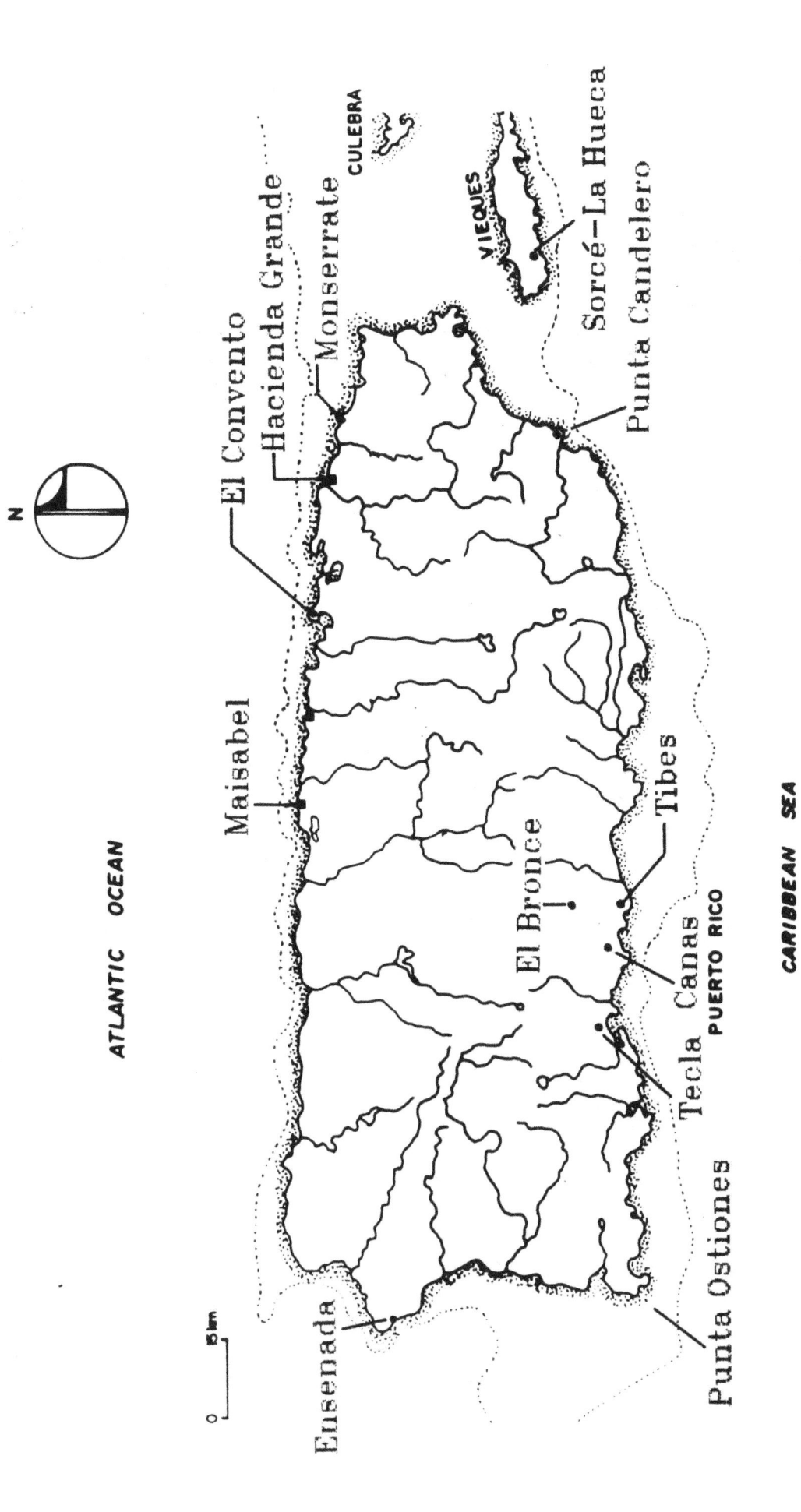

Figure 1. Puerto Rico and Vieques showing the principal early pottery sites.

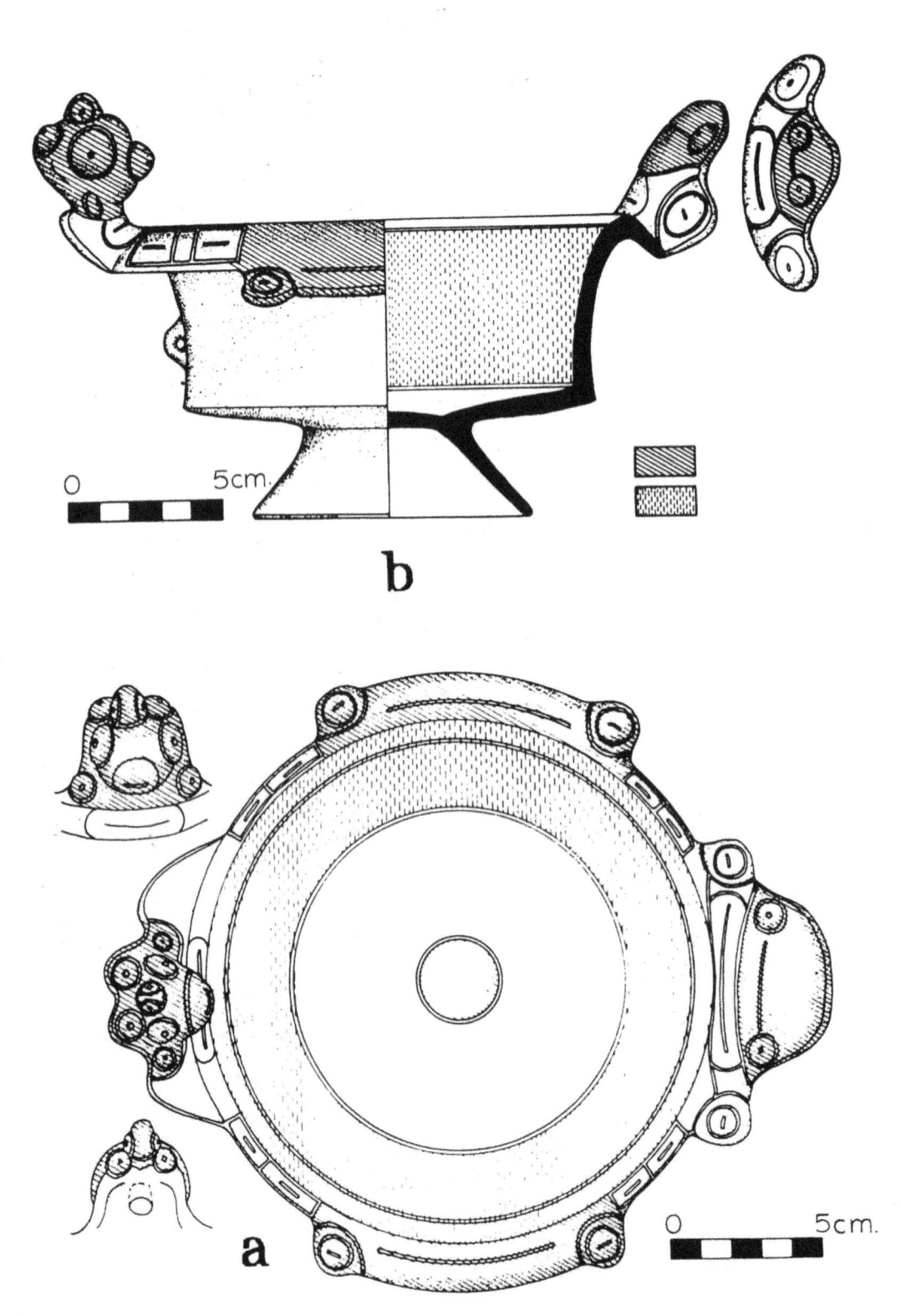

Figure 2. A Hacienda Grande Phase bird effigy annular-based bowl from the Tecla site in the Centro de Investigaciones Arqueológicos (CIA) collections, University of Puerto Rico (UPR). (a) A profile view of the vessel; the tail element is depicted in plane view. (b) A plane view with details showing the hollow-backed bird adorno's face and the back of its head.

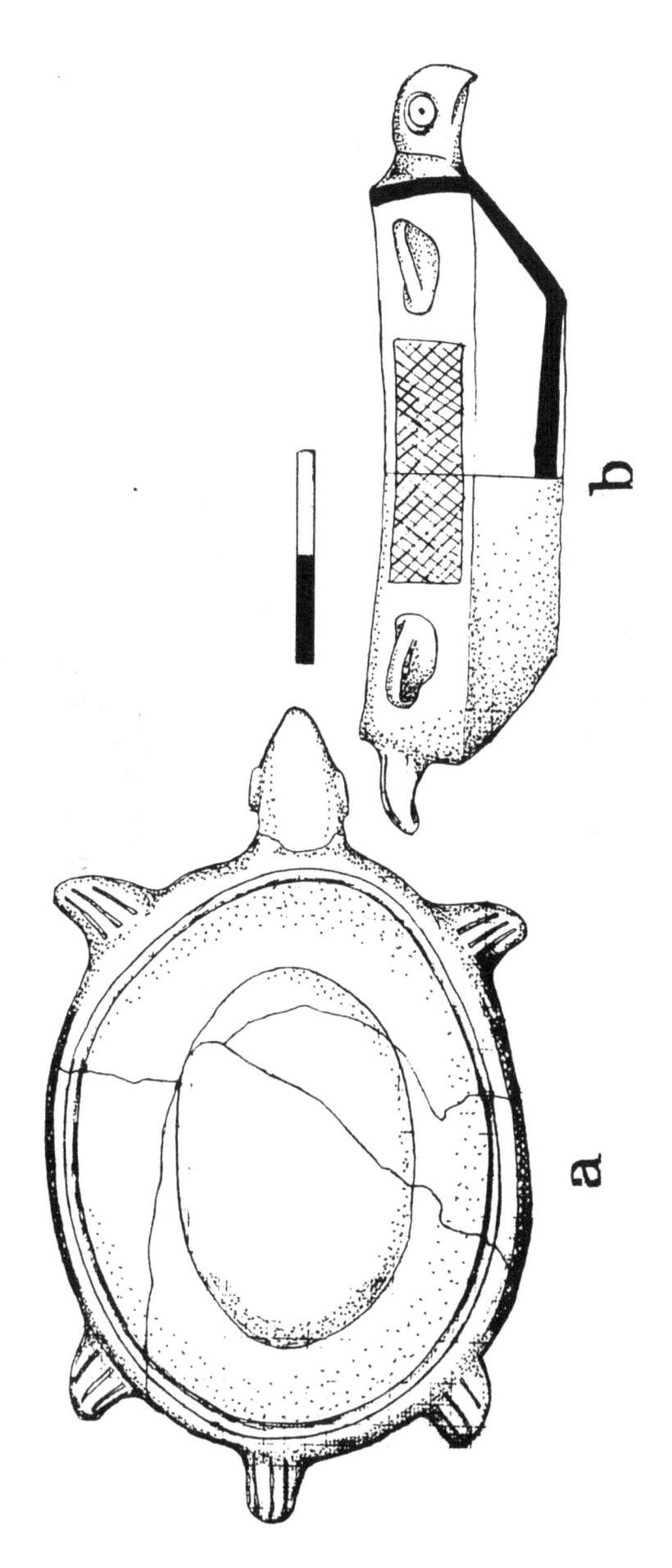

Figure 3. A Hacienda Grande phase Hawksbill Turtle effigy tray from the Centro de Investigaciones Indigenas de Puerto Rico (CIIPR) collections, (ex-Castillo, nos. P273 & P274), from the Hacienda Grande site. It has a cross-hatched panel. The head has been reconstructed based on similar examples. (a) A plane view. (b) A profile view.

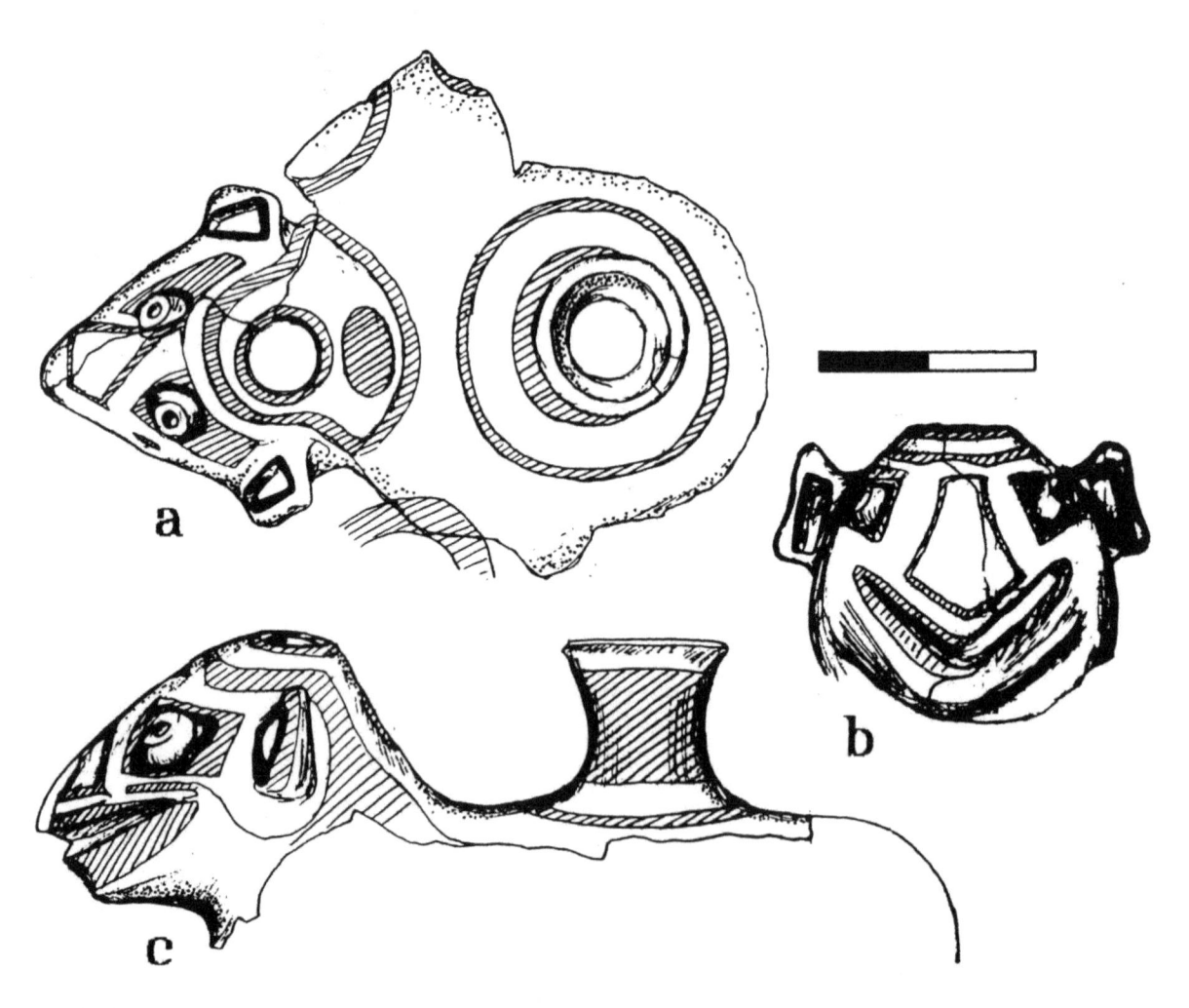

Figure 4. The Hacienda Grande phase hollow tapir effigy vessel with white-on-red (WOR) painting and black resin post-fire crusting highlighting the eyes and ears (CIIPR collections [ex-Castillo], Hacienda Grande site). (a) A plane view showing the spout on the head and the jar spout on the back. (b) A frontal view of the face. (c) A profile view showing the slight snout reconstruction.

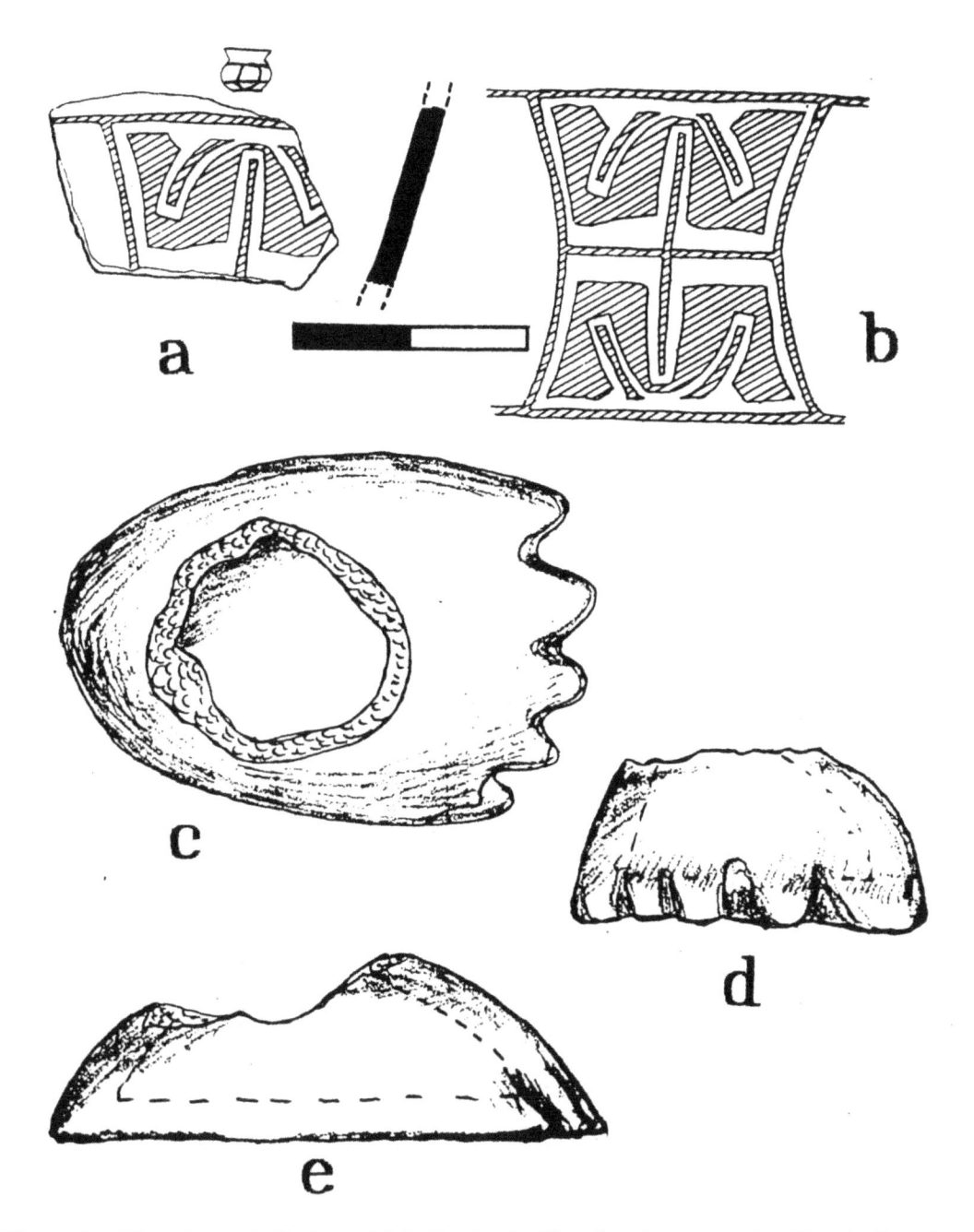

Figure 5. The elements that went into the tapir effigy figurine reconstruction, both painted (WOR) and sculptural. (a) A Hacienda Grande phase WOR sherd from the Hacienda Grande site. This sherd is from the body of a carinated jar, but of a design-field appropriate for the tapir's body (ex-Castillo, no. P4072). (b) A reconstruction of the design panel from the sherd. (c) A plane view of a Hacienda Grande phase animal hollow figurine foot (from the 1984 Centro de Estudios Avanzados de Puerto Rico y el Caribe (CEAPRC) excavations at the Hacienda Grande site [West 97/South 65, a 2X2 m square, 40-50 cm below ground surface]) of a type suitable for the tapir's feet. (d) A frontal view. (e) A profile view.

333

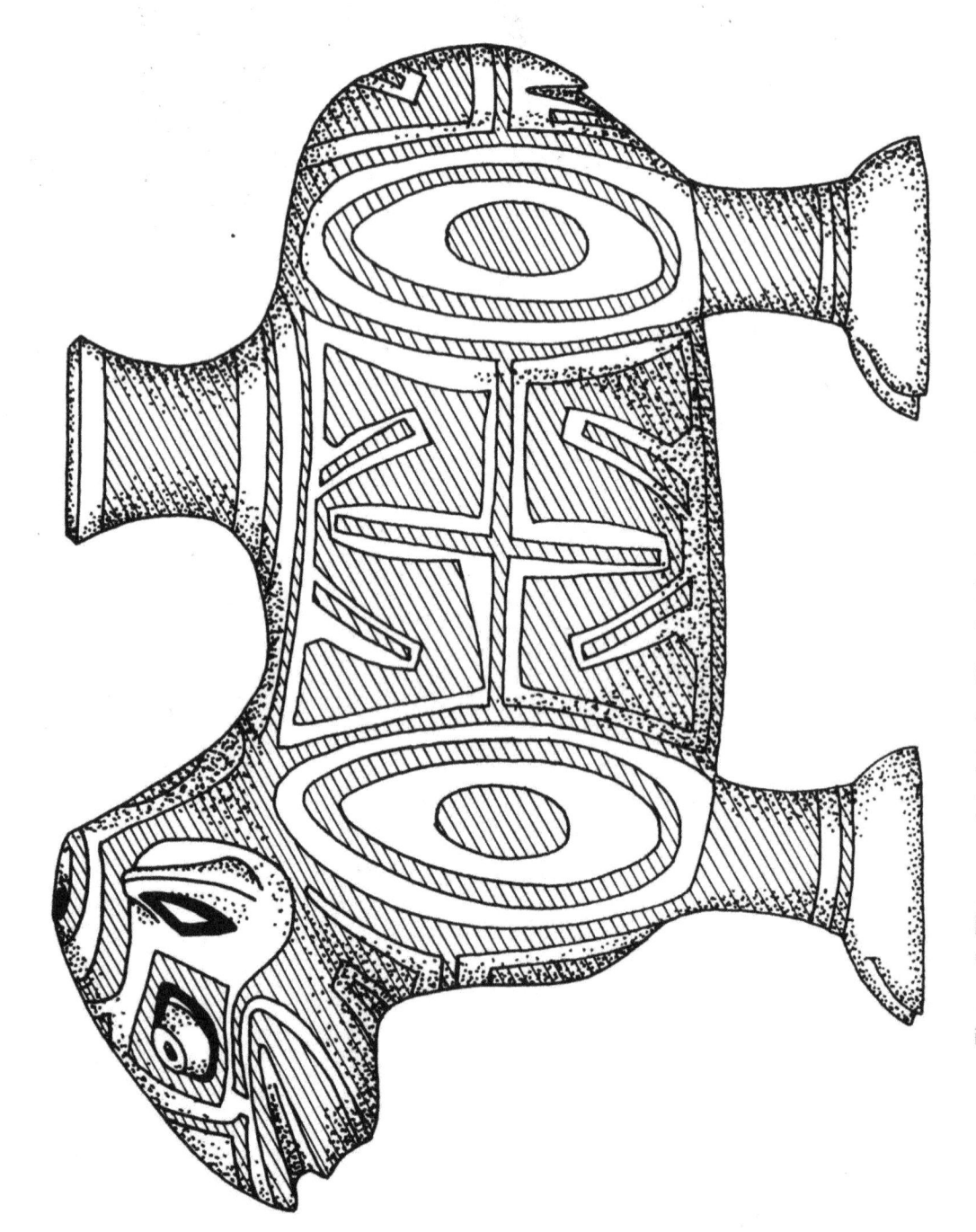

Figure 6. The completed tapir effigy bottle incorporating Figures 4 and 5 as elements. Another possibility for this effigy would have been as a carinated oblong bowl with a slightly concave flat base.

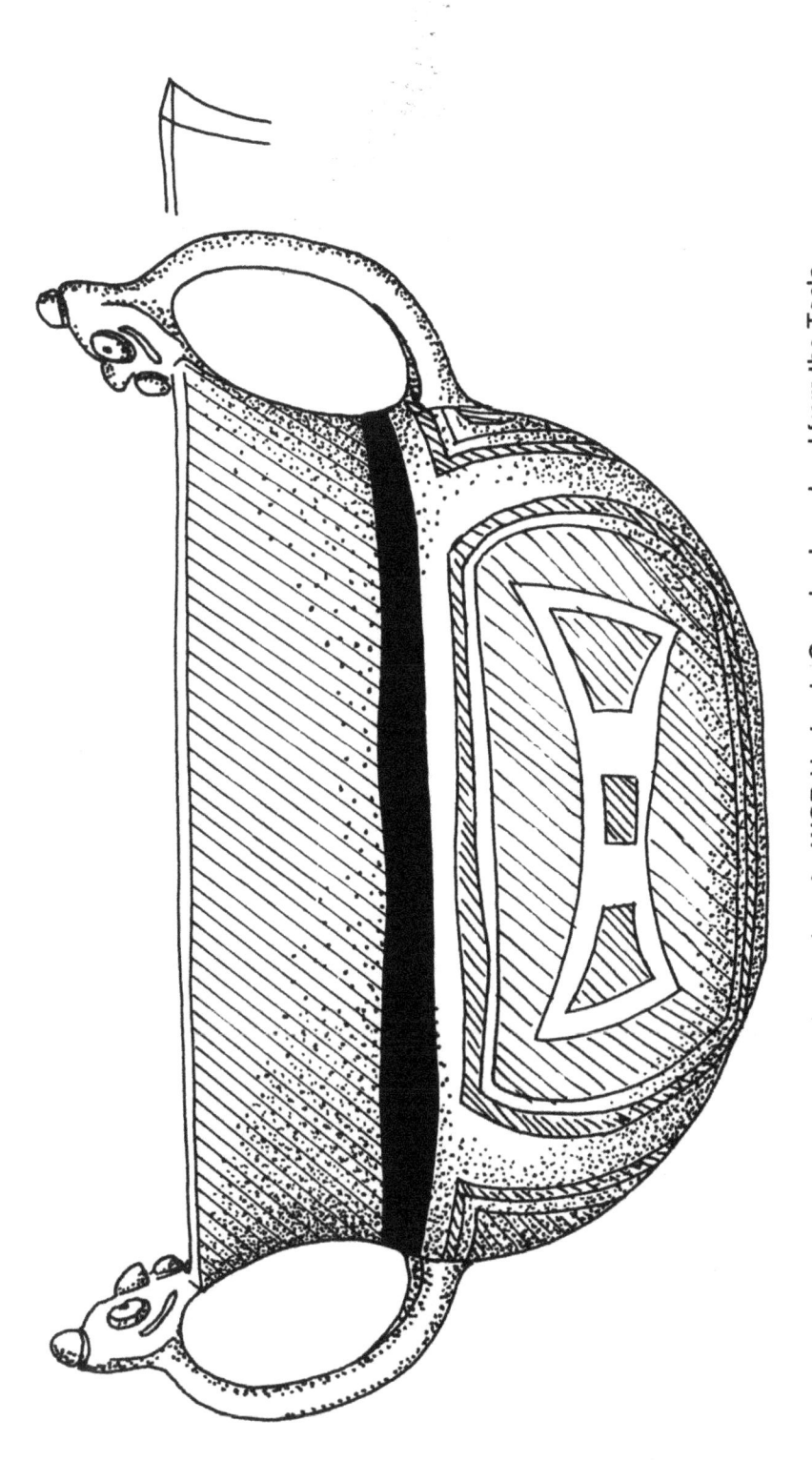

Figure 7. A slide projection tracing of a WOR Hacienda Grande phase bowl from the Tecla site in the collections of the CIA, UPR. The adornos have been reconstructed. Note the band of black resin post-fire crusting circling the vessel's waist.

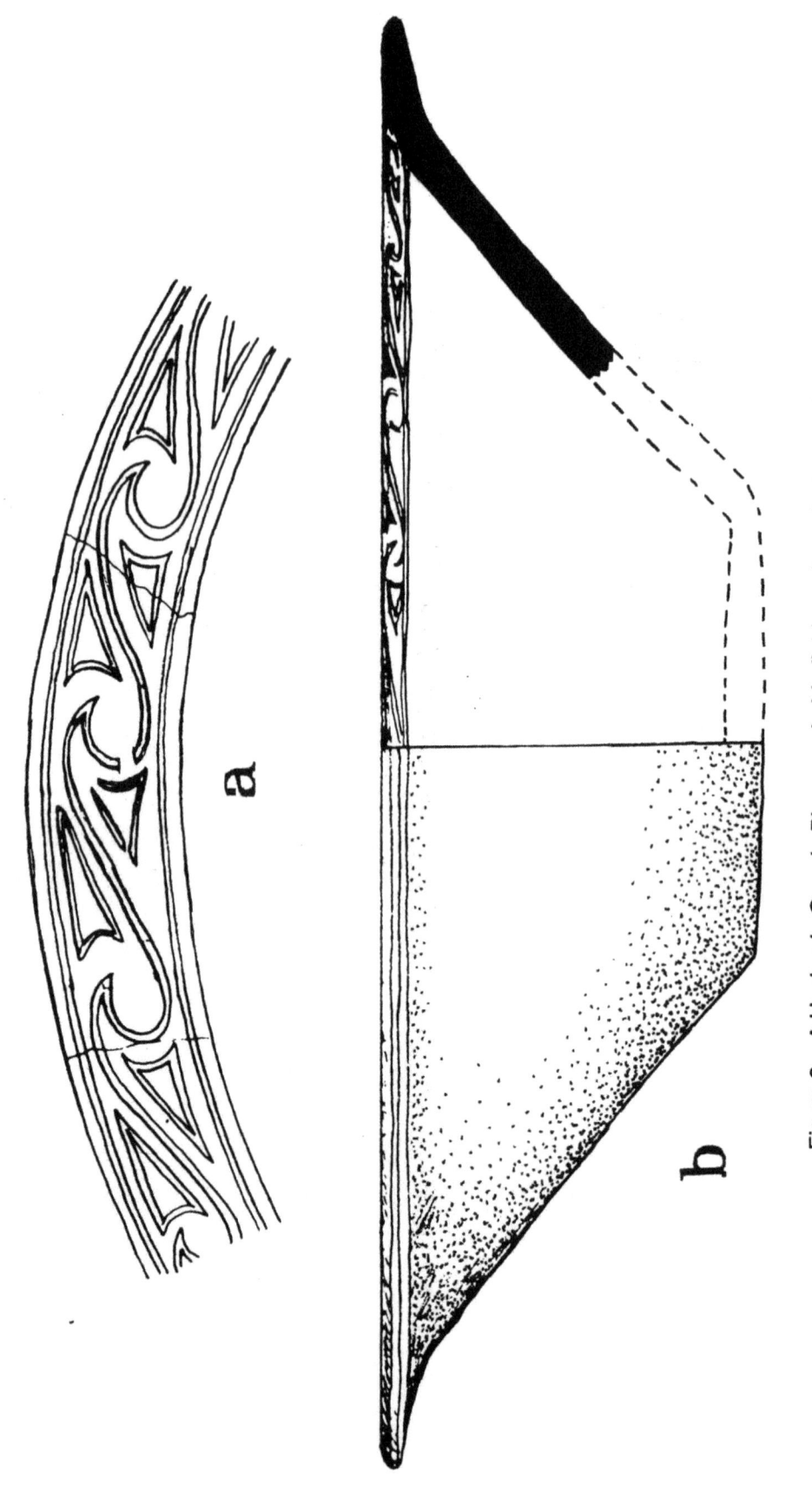

Figure 8. A Hacienda Grande Phase probable flat-based, out-flaring bowl with a labial flange on which is found linear incision, from the ex-Castillo collection (CIIPR). (a) A reconstruction of the curvilinear design layout found on the sherd. Note the broad, "u"-shaped incisions. (b) A profile view of the reconstructed bowl.

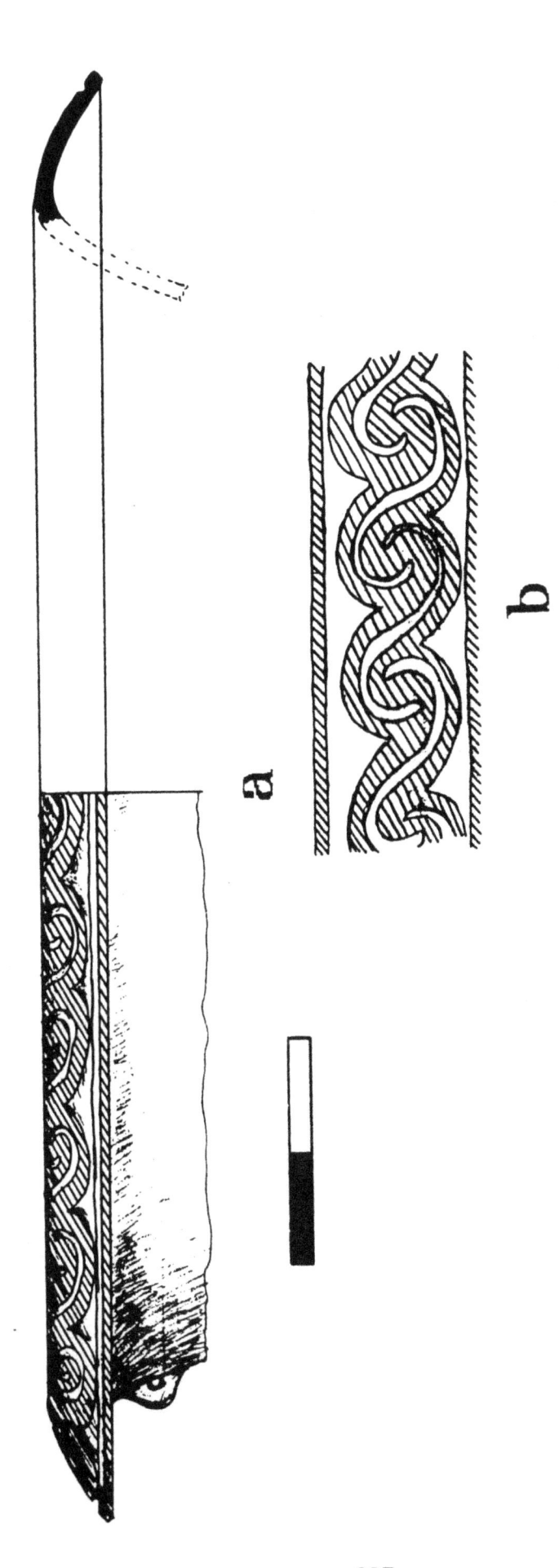

Figure 9. A Hacienda Grande phase WOR carinated pedestal-based bowl with a doubled-over labial flange decorated with linear incision and excision (ex-Castillo, no. P4361, Hacienda Grande site). (a) A profile view of the partially-reconstructed vessel. (b) A plane view of the curvilinear design layout.

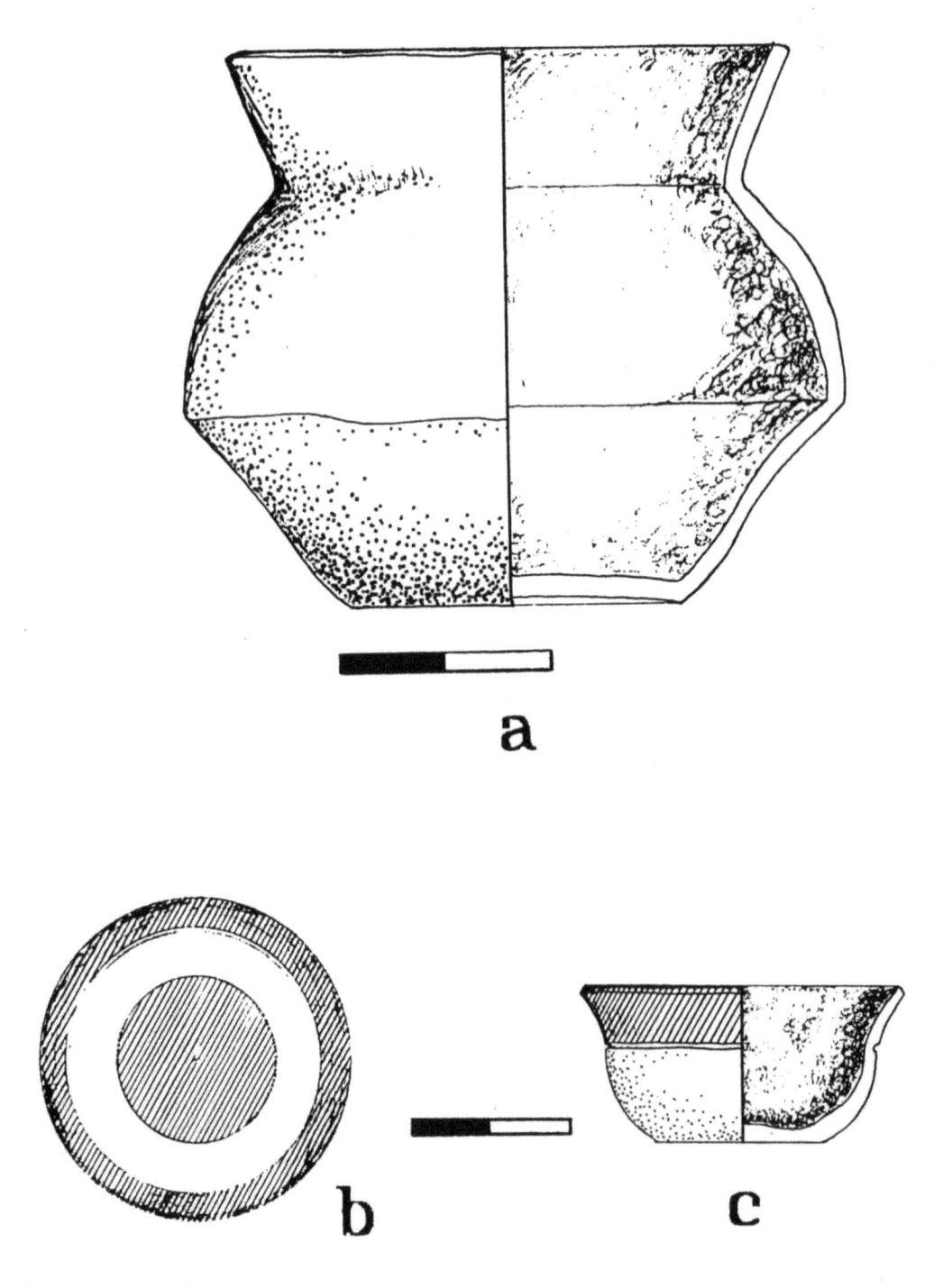

Figure 10. Small Cuevas Phase jars with smudged interiors. (a) A carinated plainware jar with smudged interior from the Maisabel site (ex-Blanco y Negro, CIIPR). (b) An interior plane-view of a small jar with smudged interior and a red-painted neck and rim band. This view shows the painted circle on the exterior of the base. This toy-sized pot is from the Hacienda Grande site (ex-Castillo, no. P29). (c) A profile view of "b" showing the raised, "dimple" base.

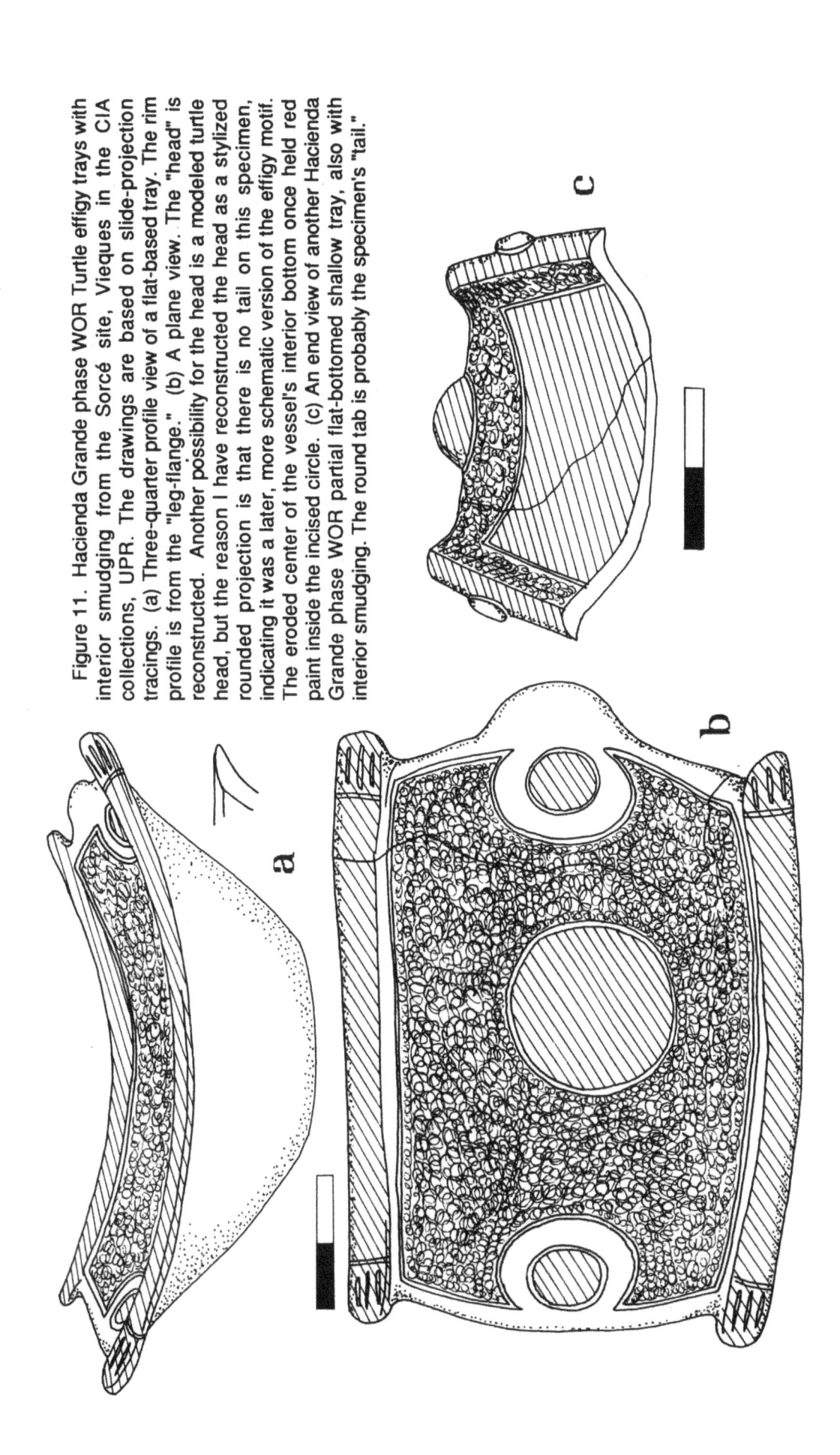

Figure 11. Hacienda Grande phase WOR Turtle effigy trays with interior smudging from the Sorcé site, Vieques in the CIA collections, UPR. The drawings are based on slide-projection tracings. (a) Three-quarter profile view of a flat-based tray. The rim profile is from the "leg-flange." (b) A plane view. The "head" is reconstructed. Another possibility for the head is a modeled turtle head, but the reason I have reconstructed the head as a stylized rounded projection is that there is no tail on this specimen, indicating it was a later, more schematic version of the effigy motif. The eroded center of the vessel's interior bottom once held red paint inside the incised circle. (c) An end view of another Hacienda Grande phase WOR partial flat-bottomed shallow tray, also with interior smudging. The round tab is probably the specimen's "tail."

339

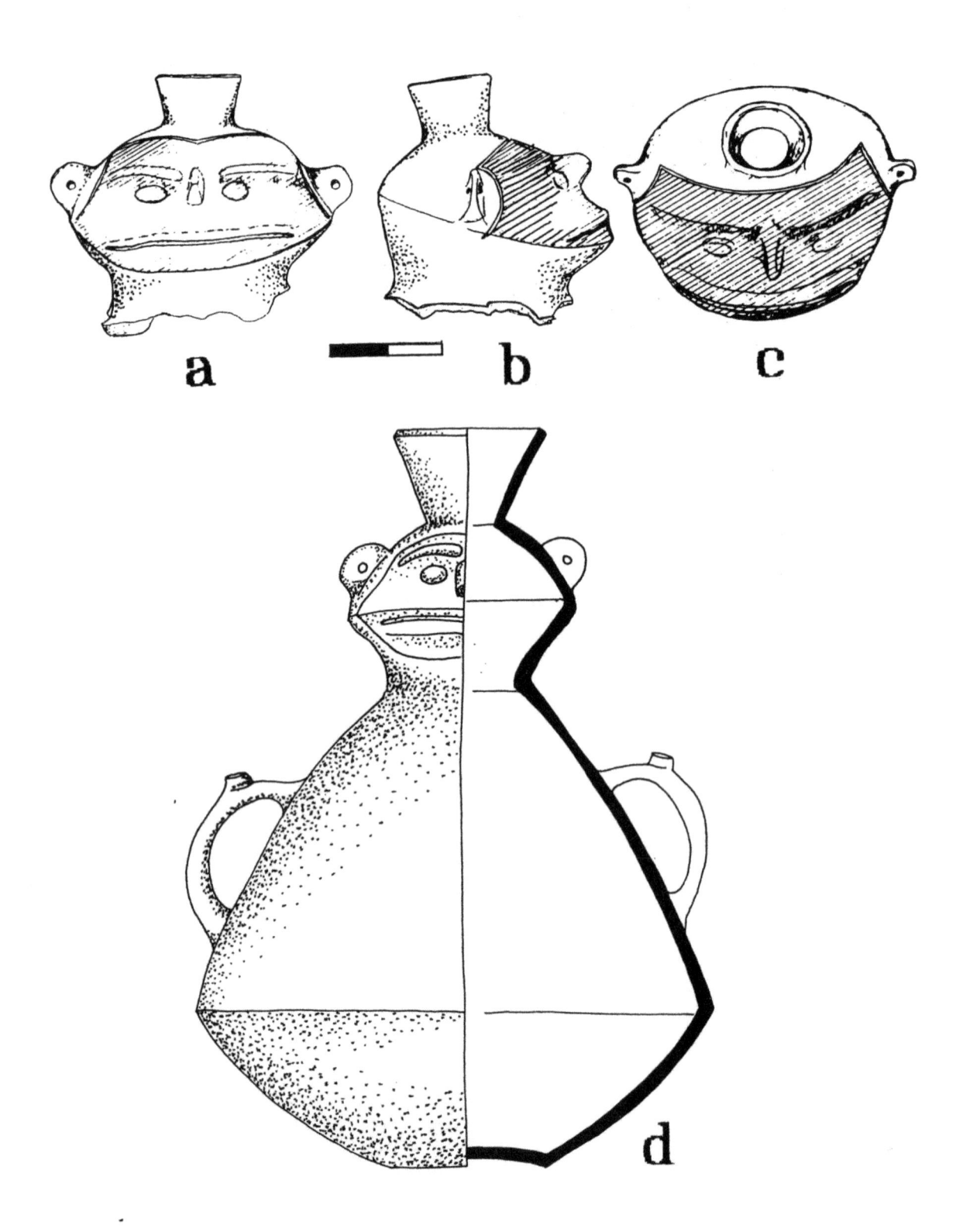

Figure 12. An anthropomorphic Hacienda Grande phase effigy jar neck and spout from the 1984 CEAPRC excavations at the Hacienda Grande site. This artifact, although broken, was a funerary offering for an adult flexed burial. (a) A frontal view. Note the perforated ears. (b) A profile view. (c) A plane-view showing the hair line and red painted face. (d) A reconstruction of the whole vessel.

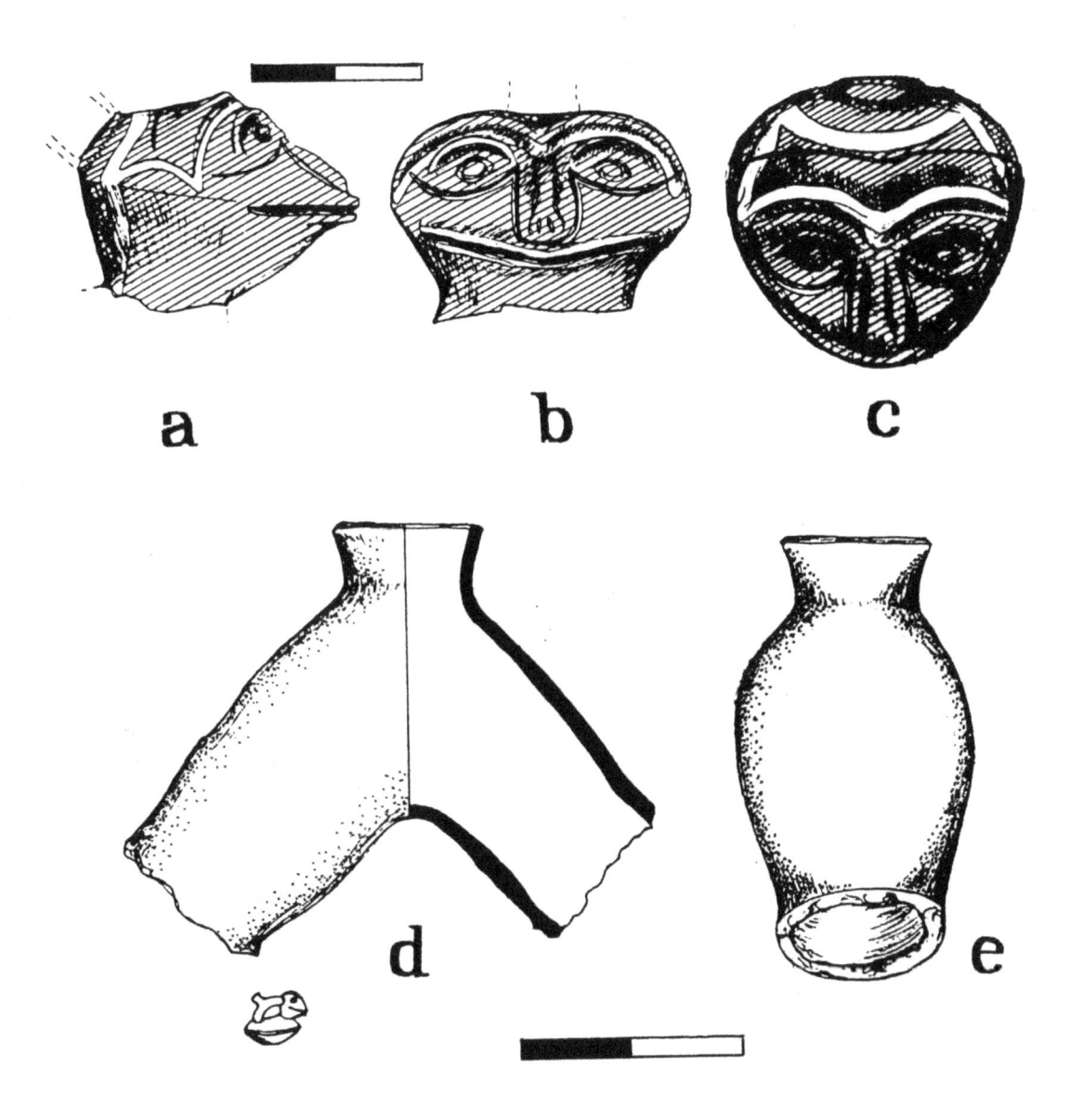

Figure 13. A Hacienda Grande phase WOR frog effigy head from a bottle together with the stirrup spout of the type that would have been attached to it. The effigy head was found during the course of the 1984 CEAPRC Hacienda Grande excavations which I directed (West 96/South 64). It was recovered from the east wall of that 2X2 m unit in association (again, although broken) with interment #3. (a) A profile view showing the hole for a stirrup-spout attachment at the rear of the head. (b) A frontal view. (c) A plane-view showing the fractured base hole for the stirrup-spout attachment. (d) A profile view of a stirrup-spout of the "right-angled" type suitable for attachment between an effigy head of the type figured in a-c and the body of a carinated, flat-based bowl (see small reconstruction drawing). (e) An end view of the stirrup-spout showing its bulbous contours.

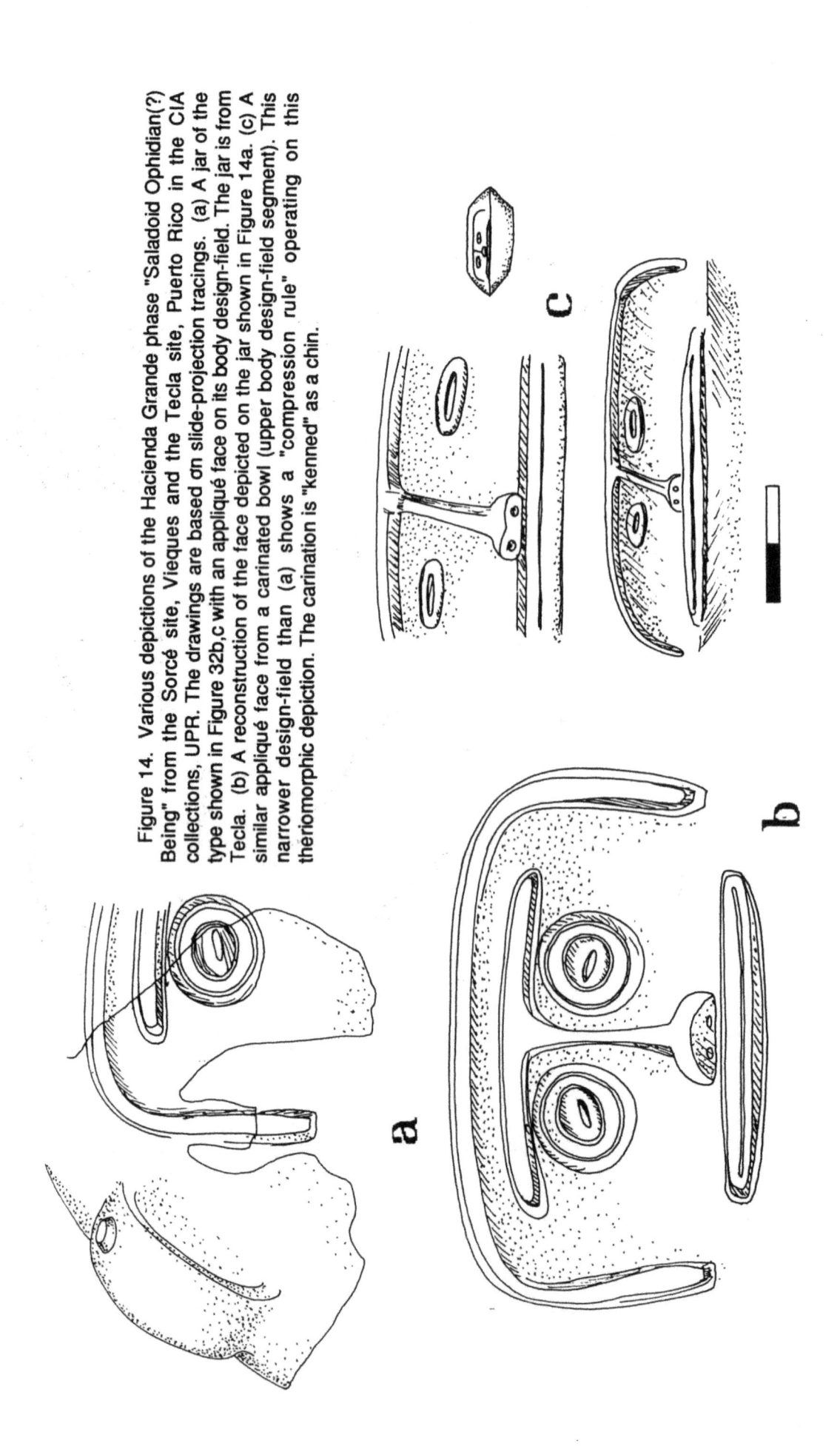

Figure 14. Various depictions of the Hacienda Grande phase "Saladoid Ophidian(?) Being" from the Sorcé site, Vieques and the Tecla site, Puerto Rico in the CIA collections, UPR. The drawings are based on slide-projection tracings. (a) A jar of the type shown in Figure 32b,c with an appliqué face on its body design-field. The jar is from Tecla. (b) A reconstruction of the face depicted on the jar shown in Figure 14a. (c) A similar appliqué face from a carinated bowl (upper body design-field segment). This narrower design-field than (a) shows a "compression rule" operating on this theriomorphic depiction. The carination is "kenned" as a chin.

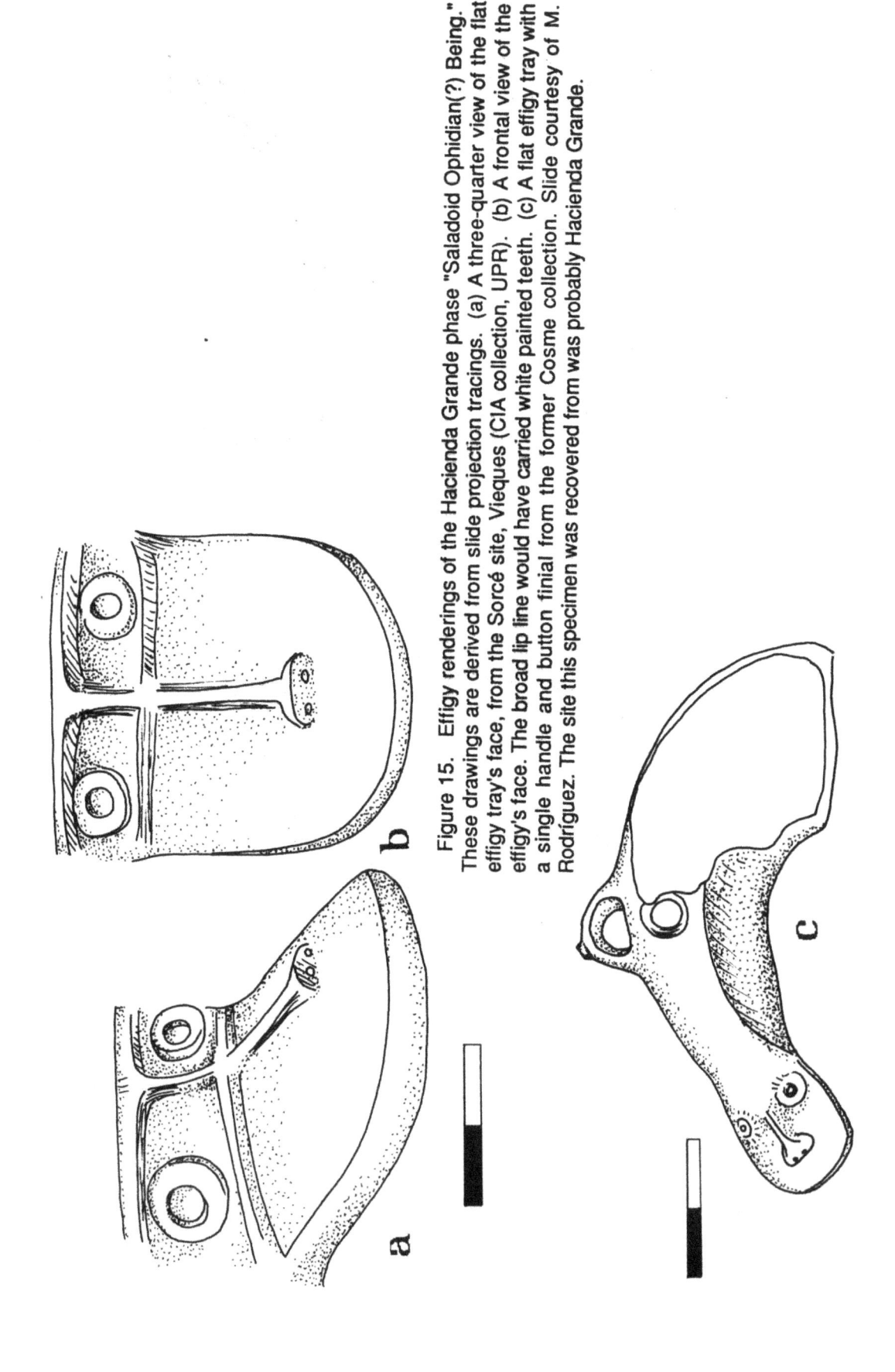

Figure 15. Effigy renderings of the Hacienda Grande phase "Saladoid Ophidian(?) Being." These drawings are derived from slide projection tracings. (a) A three-quarter view of the flat effigy tray's face, from the Sorcé site, Vieques (CIA collection, UPR). (b) A frontal view of the effigy's face. The broad lip line would have carried white painted teeth. (c) A flat effigy tray with a single handle and button finial from the former Cosme collection. Slide courtesy of M. Rodríguez. The site this specimen was recovered from was probably Hacienda Grande.

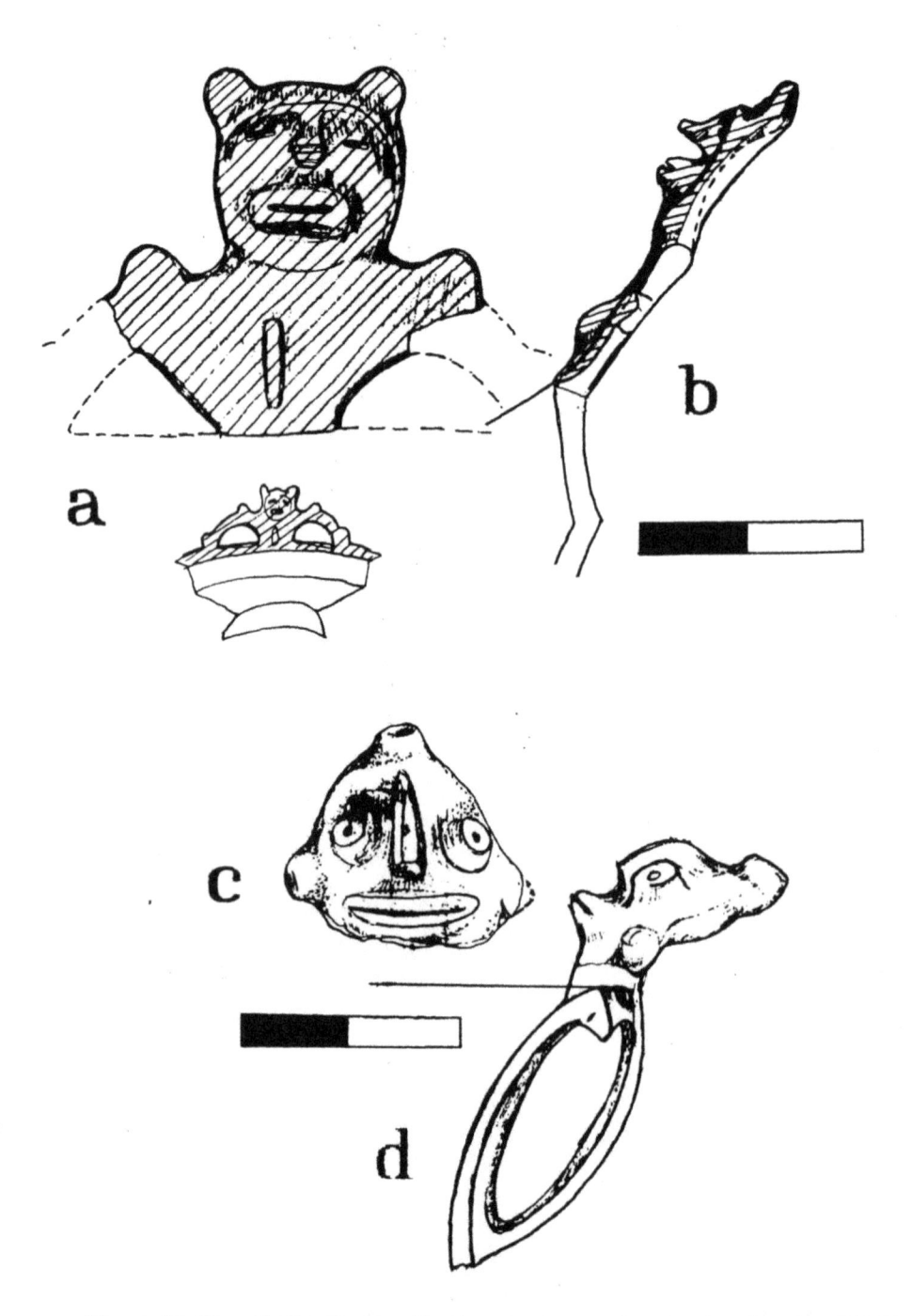

Figure 16. Two Hacienda Grande phase adornos from the ex-Castillo (CIIPR) collection of the Hacienda Grande site. (a) A frontal view of a flat "half-figure" red-painted anthropomorphic adorno built as a supra-labial flange rim lug on a carinated, pedestal-based bowl (cat. no. 140). (b) A profile view of this lug showing the characteristic hollow, or concave, back portion of the adorno's head. (c) A probable campaniform supra-vertical strap handle anthropomorphic adorno head. (d) A reconstruction, in profile view, of the handle on which the adorno served as a decorative lug.

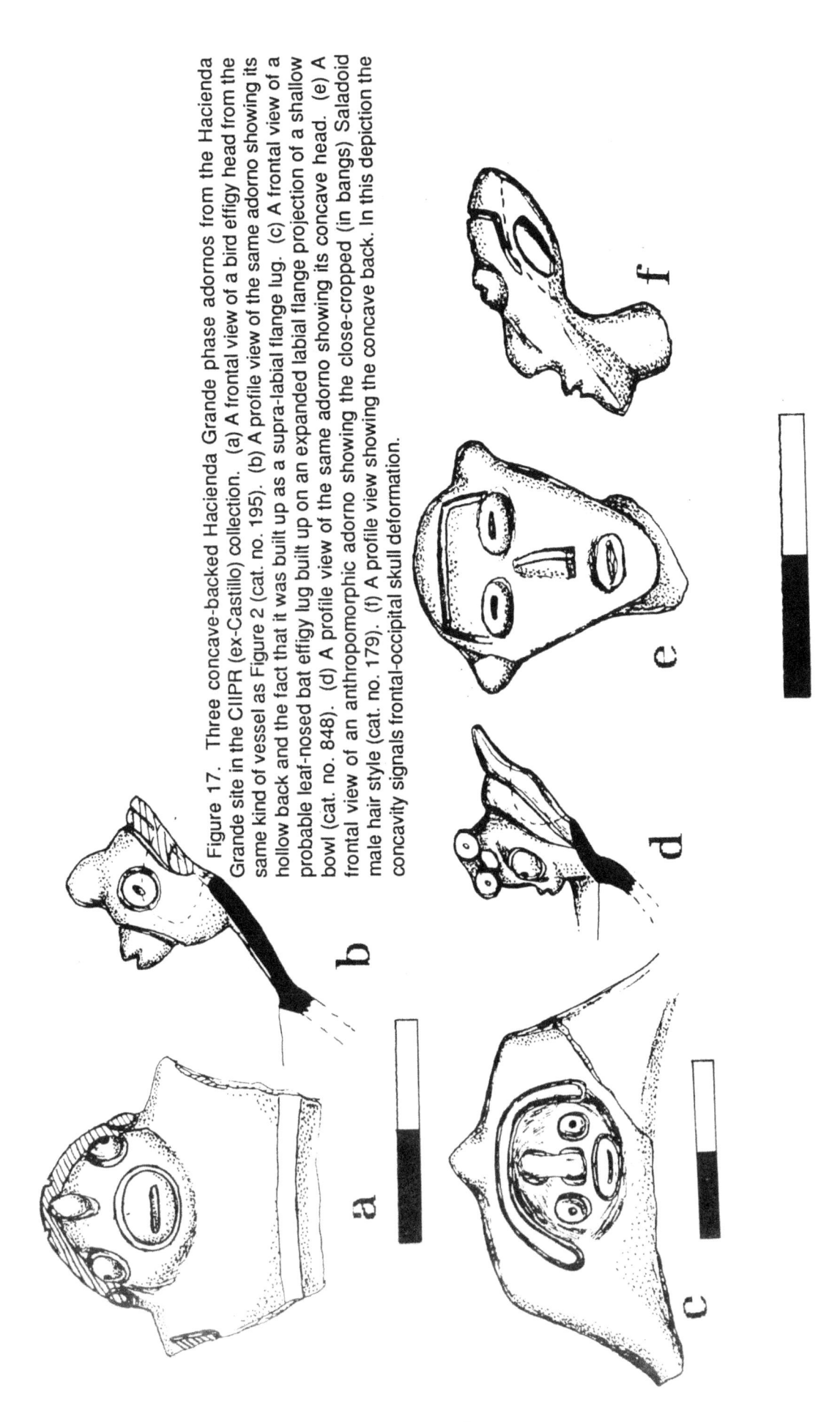

Figure 17. Three concave-backed Hacienda Grande phase adornos from the Hacienda Grande site in the CIIPR (ex-Castillo) collection. (a) A frontal view of a bird effigy head from the same kind of vessel as Figure 2 (cat. no. 195). (b) A profile view of the same adorno showing its hollow back and the fact that it was built up as a supra-labial flange lug. (c) A frontal view of a probable leaf-nosed bat effigy lug built up on an expanded labial flange projection of a shallow bowl (cat. no. 848). (d) A profile view of the same adorno showing its concave head. (e) A frontal view of an anthropomorphic adorno showing the close-cropped (in bangs) Saladoid male hair style (cat. no. 179). (f) A profile view showing the concave back. In this depiction the concavity signals frontal-occipital skull deformation.

345

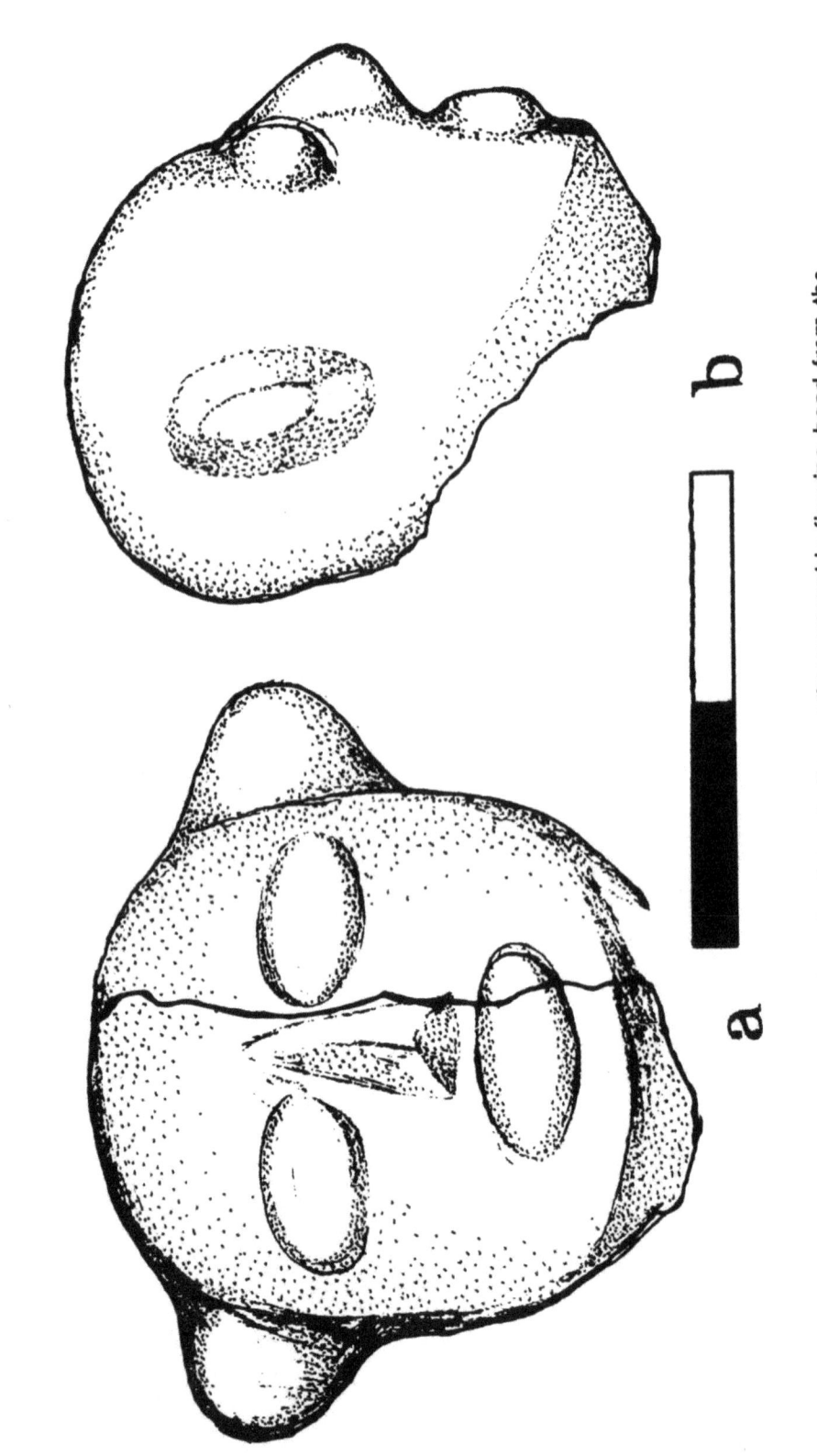

Figure 18. A Hacienda Grande phase hollow anthropomorphic figurine head from the Hacienda Grande site (CIIPR ex-Castillo collection, no. 329). (a) A frontal view the head with the right half reconstructed. All the details of the eyes and mouth would have been painted in with white paint (now fugitive). (b) A profile view of the intact side of the head.

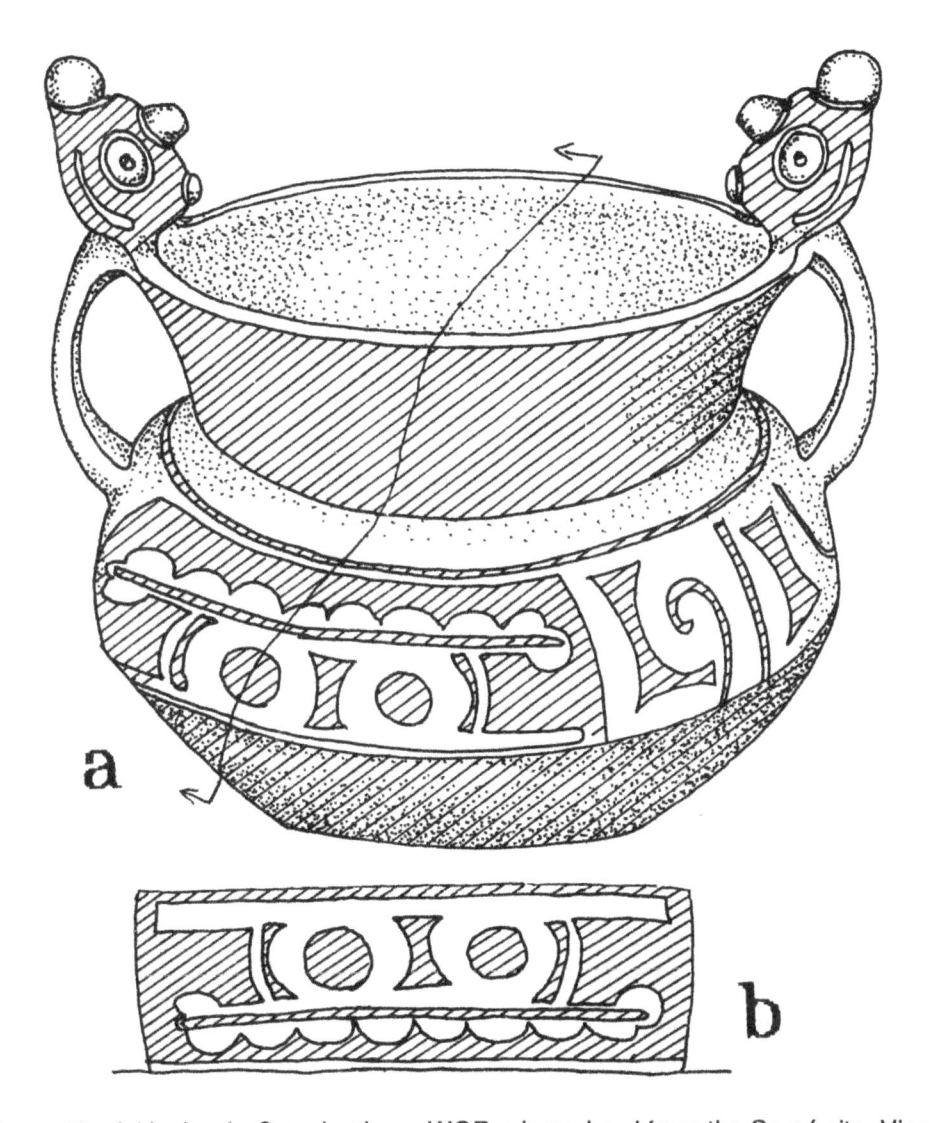

Figure 19. A Hacienda Grande phase WOR adorno bowl from the Sorcé site, Vieques in the CIA, UPR collection. This drawing is based on a slide projection tracing. (a) A tilted profile view. I have reconstructed the left half of the vessel. (b) I have inverted the painting of the "Goggle-Eyed Saladoid Being" to show that it was meant to be seen globally when viewing the orifice of the pot, which was "kenned" as the "mouth" of the being visible below its tooth-row. This pot shows "anatropic organization."

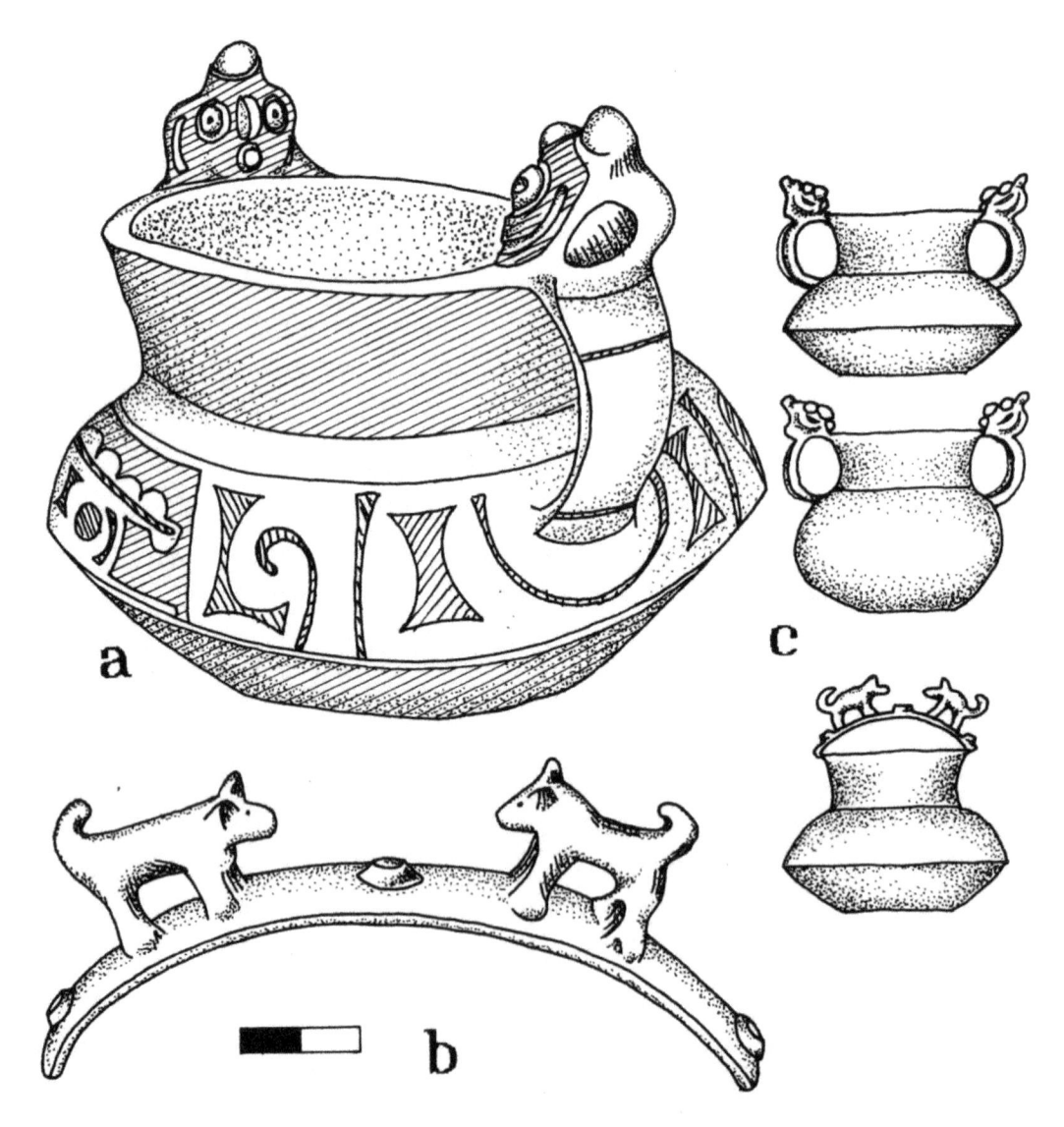

Figure 20. Some variations on the adorno and figurine-handled WOR Hacienda Grande Saladoid "waisted jar" vessel form based on slide-projection tracings. (a) A tilted three-quarter view of the same vessel as Figure 19 showing the "false negative" WOR painting on the upper body design-field segment and the hollow-backed adorno head style. (b) A "basket" handle with opposed dog figurines from the Hacienda Grande site (the former Cosme collection, slide courtesy of M. Rodríguez). Note the three decorative appliqué nubbins. (c) The three attachment possibilities for this "waisted jar" vessel form: two opposed vertical strap handles with adorno finials on a carinated body, on a rounded body, and as a basket handle with opposed figurine lugs on a probably carinated body.

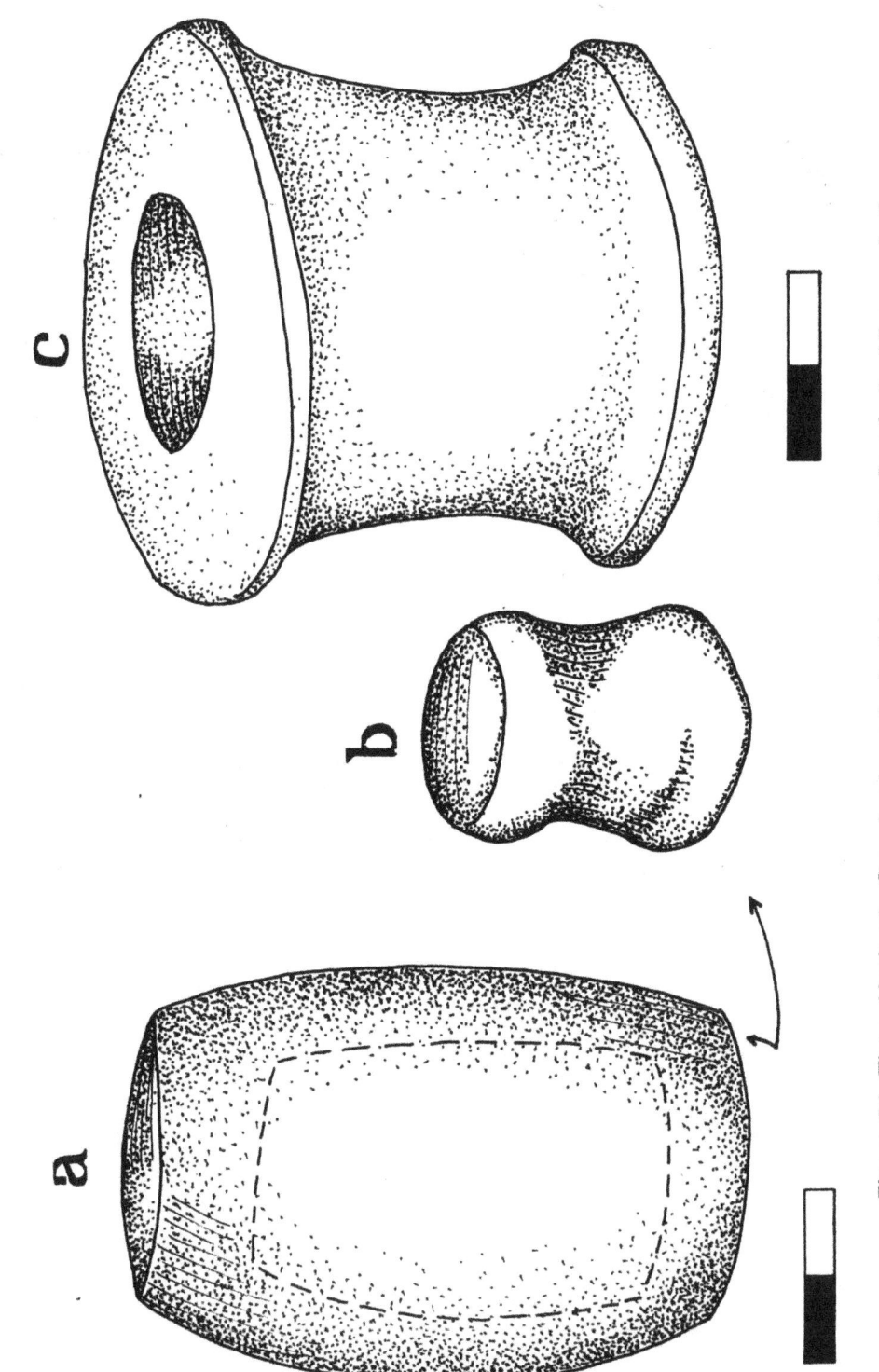

Figure 21. Three Hacienda Grande phase *topia* styles from the Sorcé site, Vieques, in the CIA collection, UPR. The drawings are based on slide projection tracings. (a) A hollow "barrel-shaped" variety, reconstructed. (b) A small, solid "hourglass-shaped" variant. (c) A hollow, "hourglass-shaped" variant.

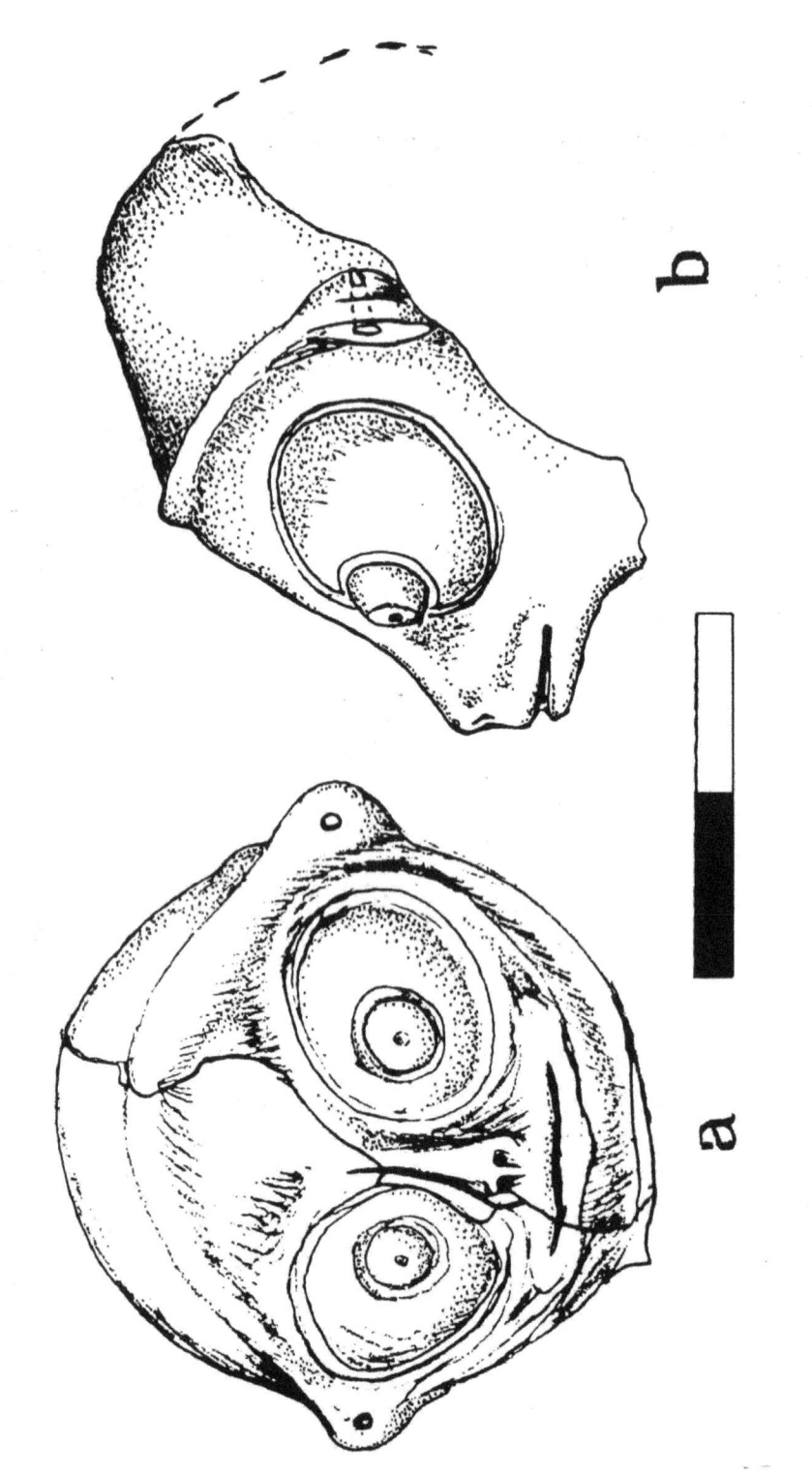

Figure 22. A capuchin monkey hollow effigy head from the Hacienda Grande phase and site in the CIIPR (ex-Castillo, no. 103) collections. (a) A frontal view, with the left side reconstructed. Note the perforations in the ears. (b) A profile view. The eyes have been pushed out from the interior before the encircling incisions and appliqued pupils were added. All of these hollow heads and bodies were built up by coiling with surface modeling, incison and appliqué were then added to define the features.

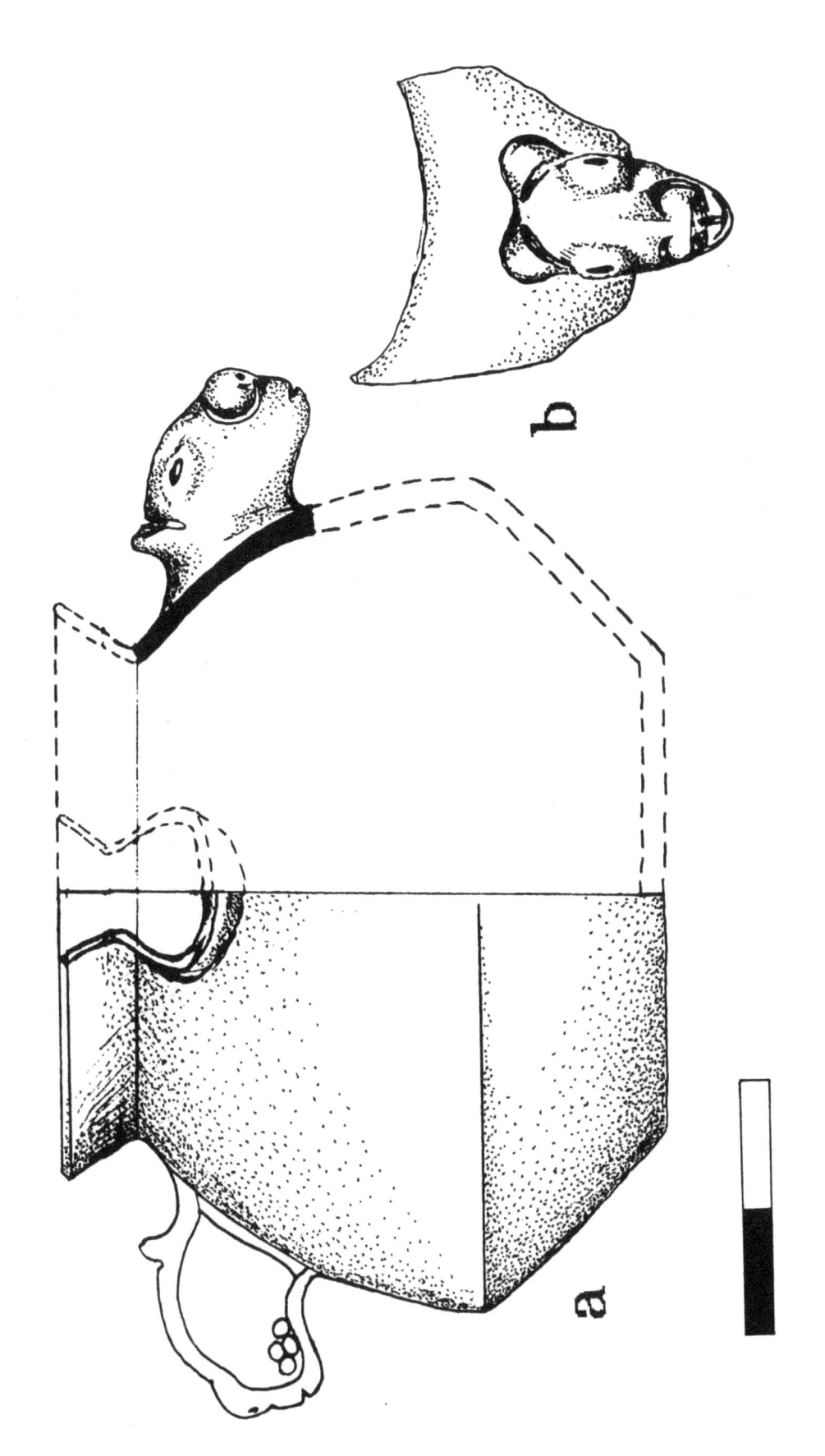

Figure 23. A rattle capybara, adorno, spouted jar from the Hacienda Grande site, the Hacienda Grande phase, in the CIIPR collections (ex-Castillo, no. 142). (a) A profile view, reconstructed using no. 888 as a model, showing the clay pellets inside the hollow adorno head. (b) A plane view of the adorno head on the upper portion of the vessel body.

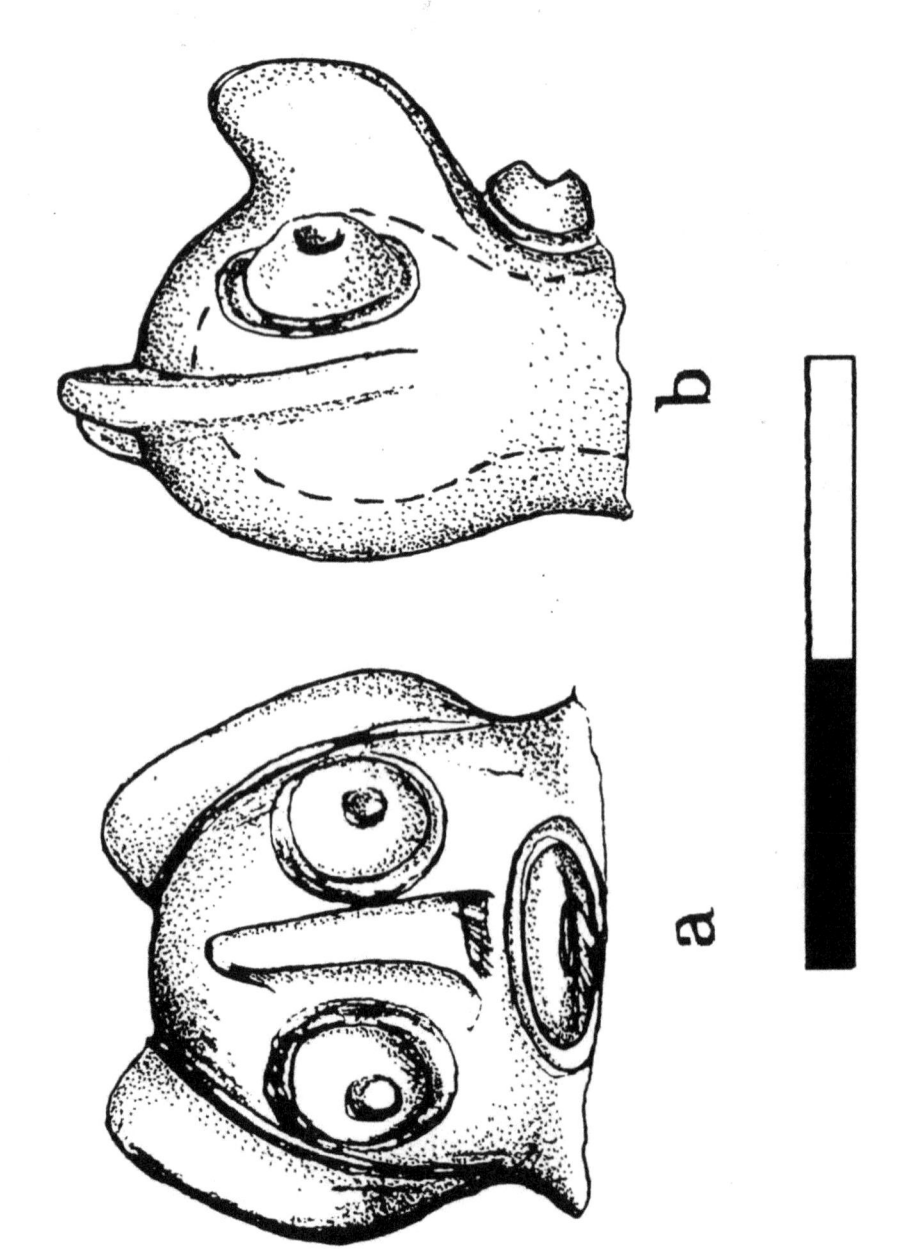

Figure 24. A hollow leaf-nosed bat effigy head from the Hacienda Grande phase type site of Hacienda Grande in the CIIPR (ex-Castillo, no. 148) collections. (a) A frontal view of the specimen. (b) A profile view depicting the hollow interior (using a broken line). Very probably this was a rattle shown in Figure 23.

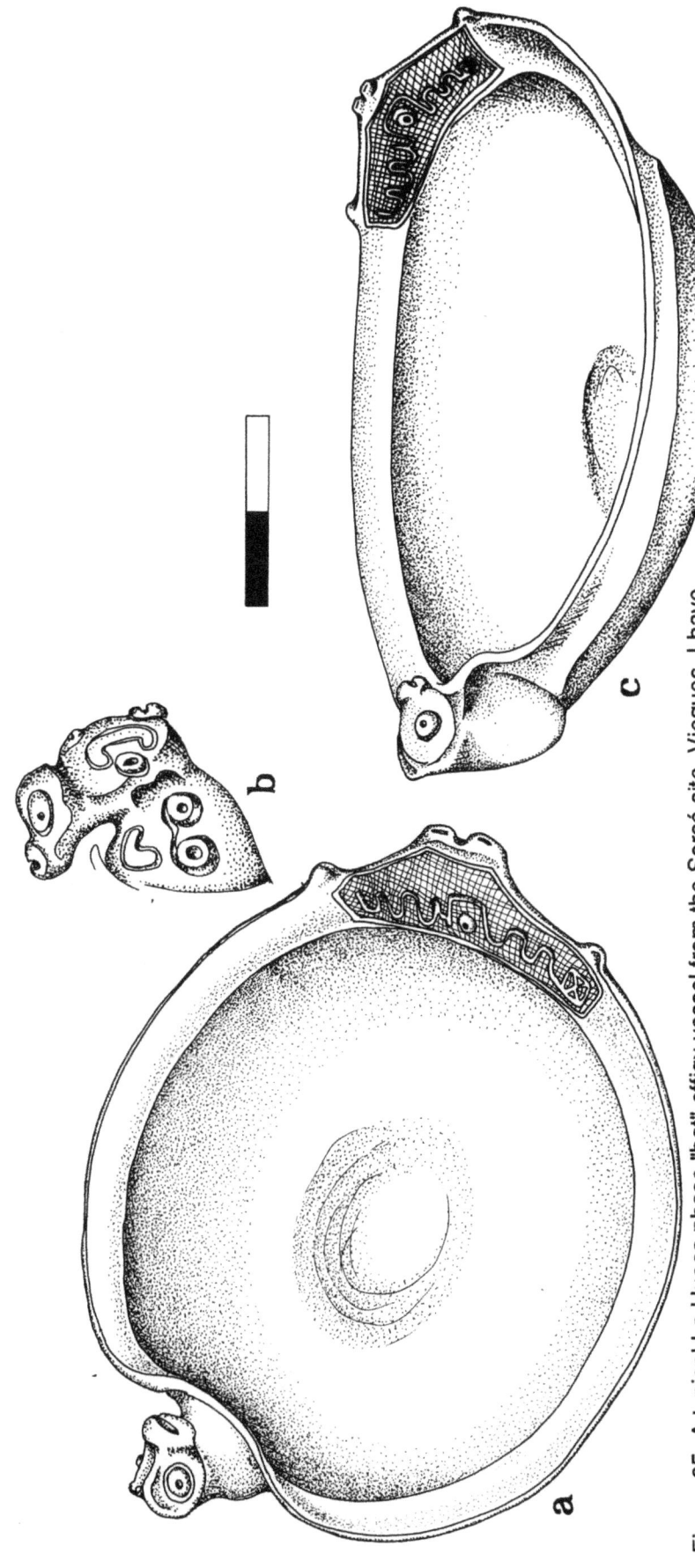

Figure 25. A typical La Hueca phase "bat" effigy vessel from the Sorcé site, Vieques. I have restored this vessel using slide projection tracings and comparable fragments, all in the CIA collections, UPR. (a) A three-quarter plane view of the vessel. Note the "wet paste deformation" that makes of the original circular bowl a heart-shaped set of "wings." This is accomplished by pressing in on the adorno when the paste of the vessel was still flexible, and pushing it into the interior of the pot. The nose of the bat head has been restored, as has its "tail," based on similar specimens. (b) A similar specimen from another vessel. All of these adornos were hollow semi-figurines. (c) A tilted three-quarter view demonstrating that the basic vessel form is a carinated, flat-based bowl with a concave upper body segment, a "quasi-campaniform."

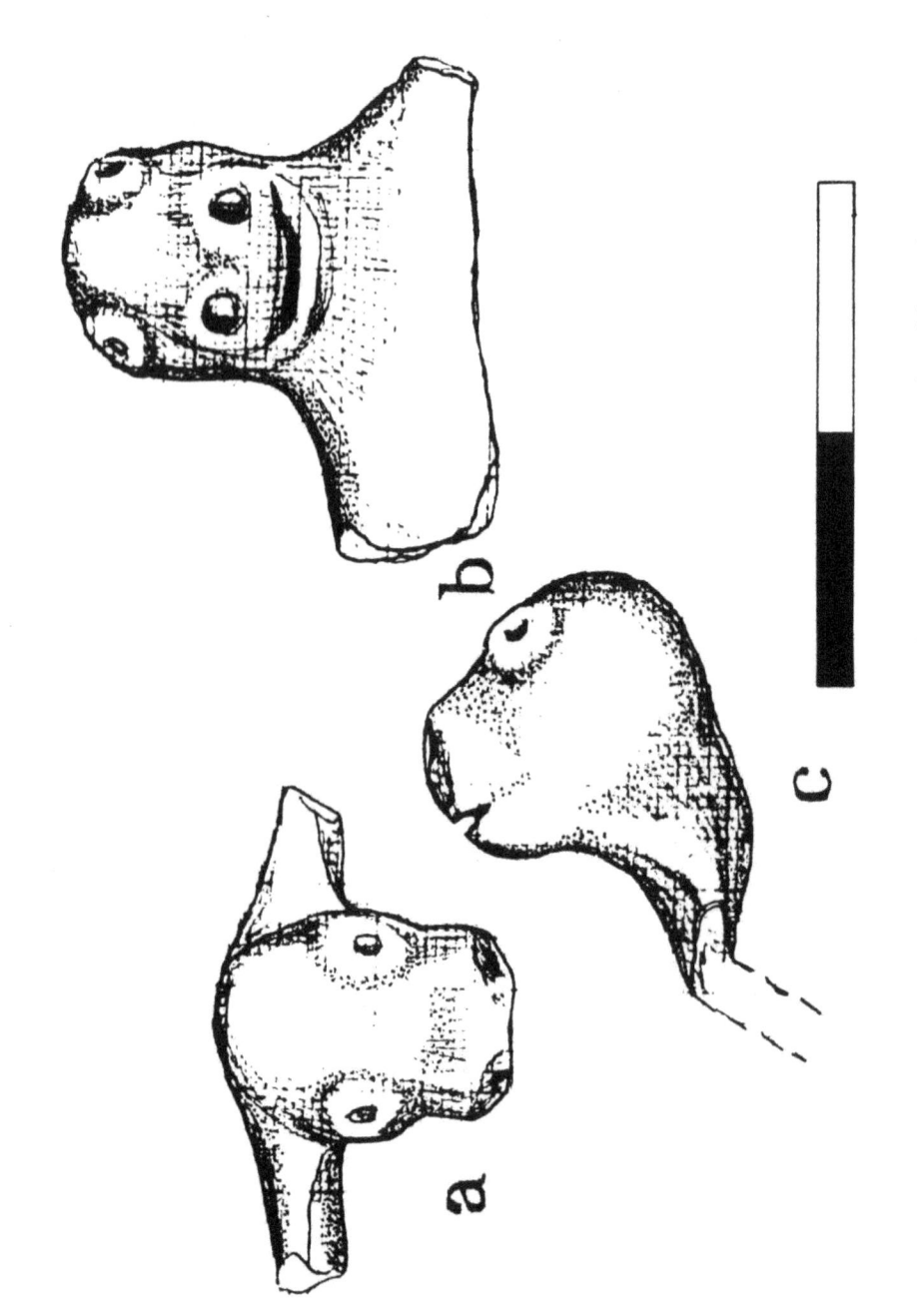

Figure 26. A manatee effigy as a solid Hacienda Grande phase adorno head from the type site. The specimen is from the CIIPR collections (ex-Castillo, no. 959). (a) A plane view. (b) A frontal view. (c) A side view.

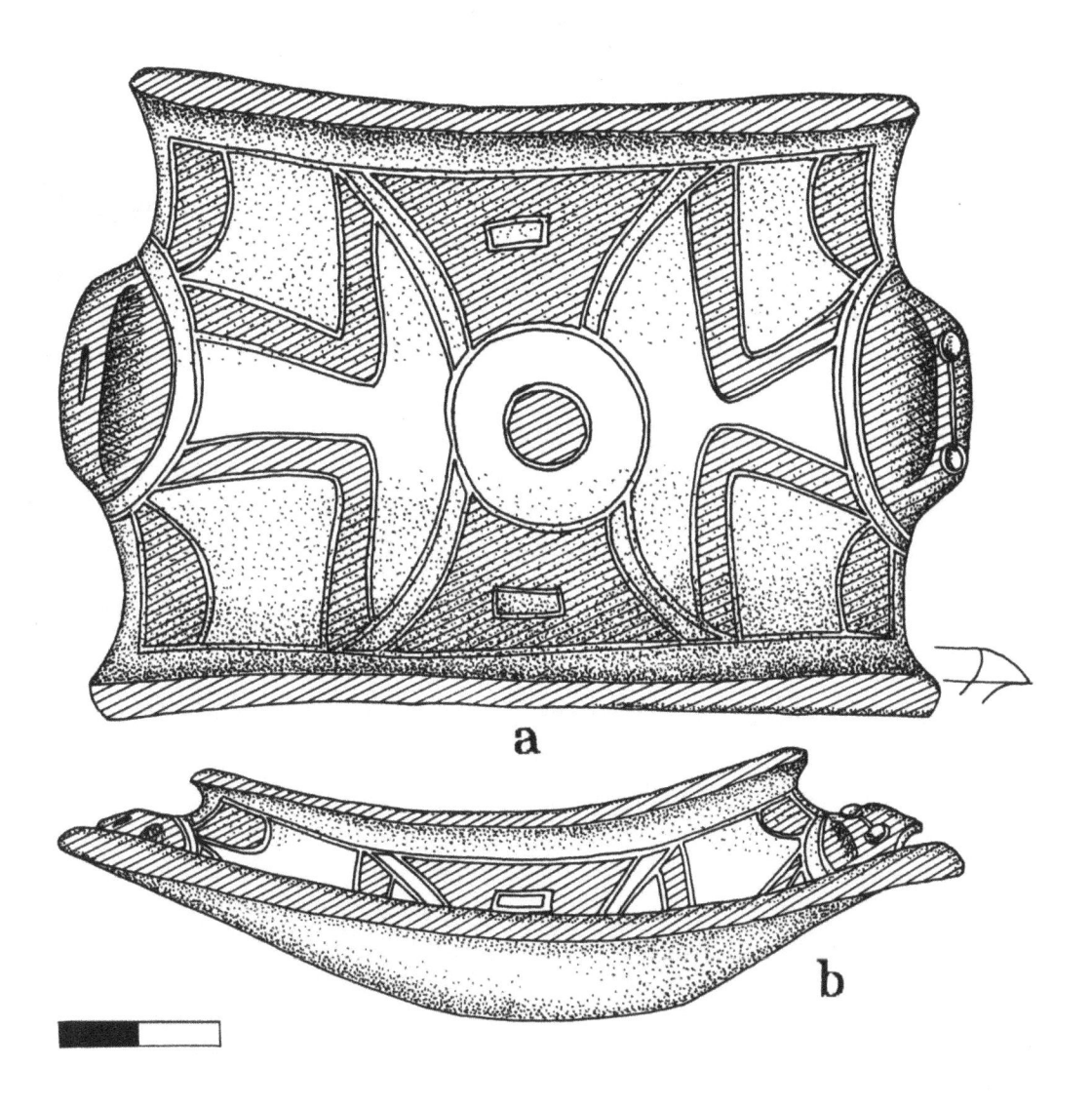

Figure 27. A "false bichrome" Saladoid "manta ray" effigy tray, probably from the Sorcé site, in the collection of Effrain Irrizary, Lajas. These drawings were prepared from slide projection tracings. The yellow paste provides a contrasting "second color" to the red paint zoned within linear incision. (a) A plane view with internally- and externally-thickened rim profile derived from the "wing" flange. (b) A tilted profile view showing the flat base.

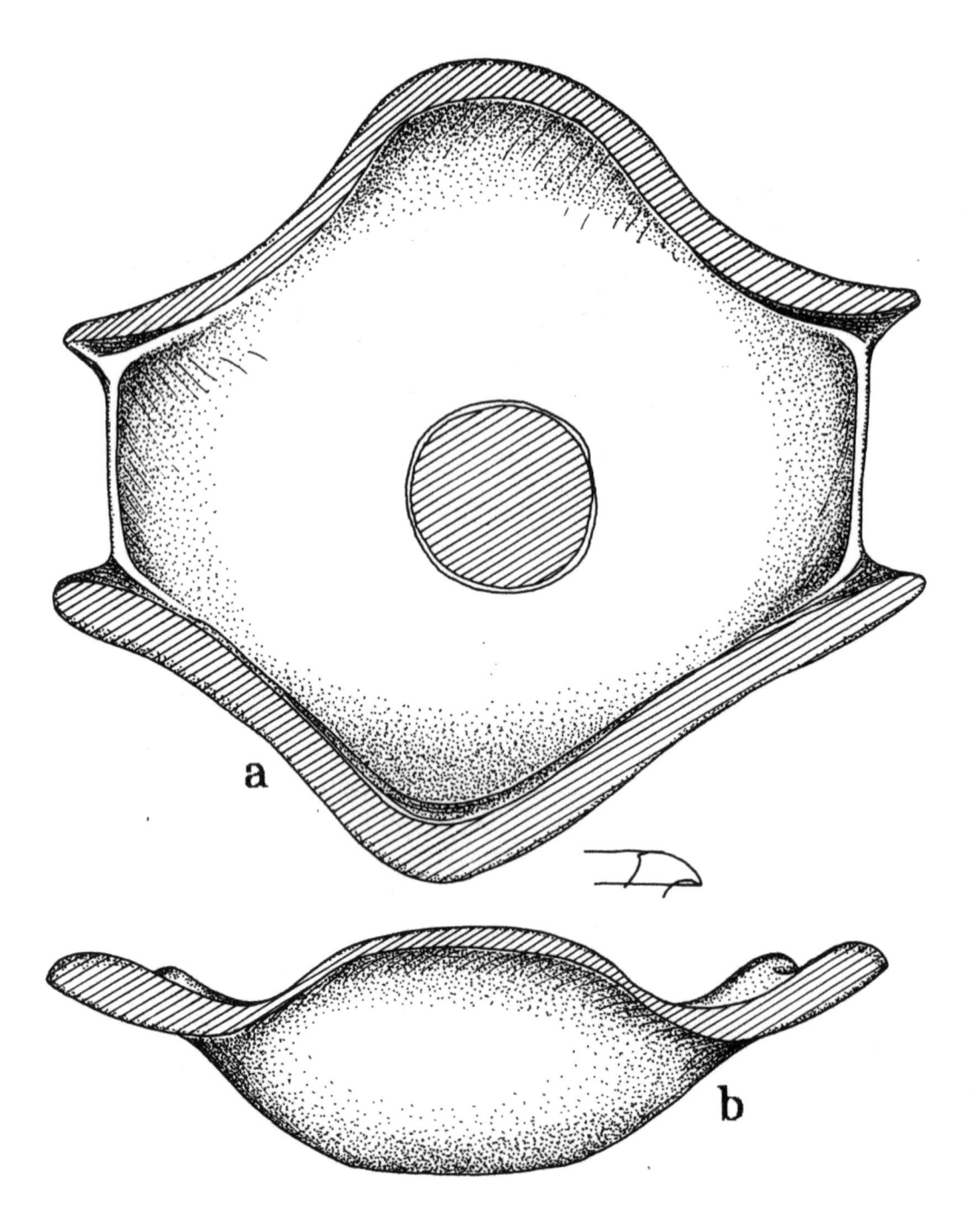

Figure 28. A Monserratean "manta ray" effigy bowl from the Sorcé site showing the progressive stylization of this once-theriomorphic type. This "false bichrome" piece is in the CIA collections of UPR. (a) A plane view. (b) A profile view showing the internally- and externally-thickened rim profile.

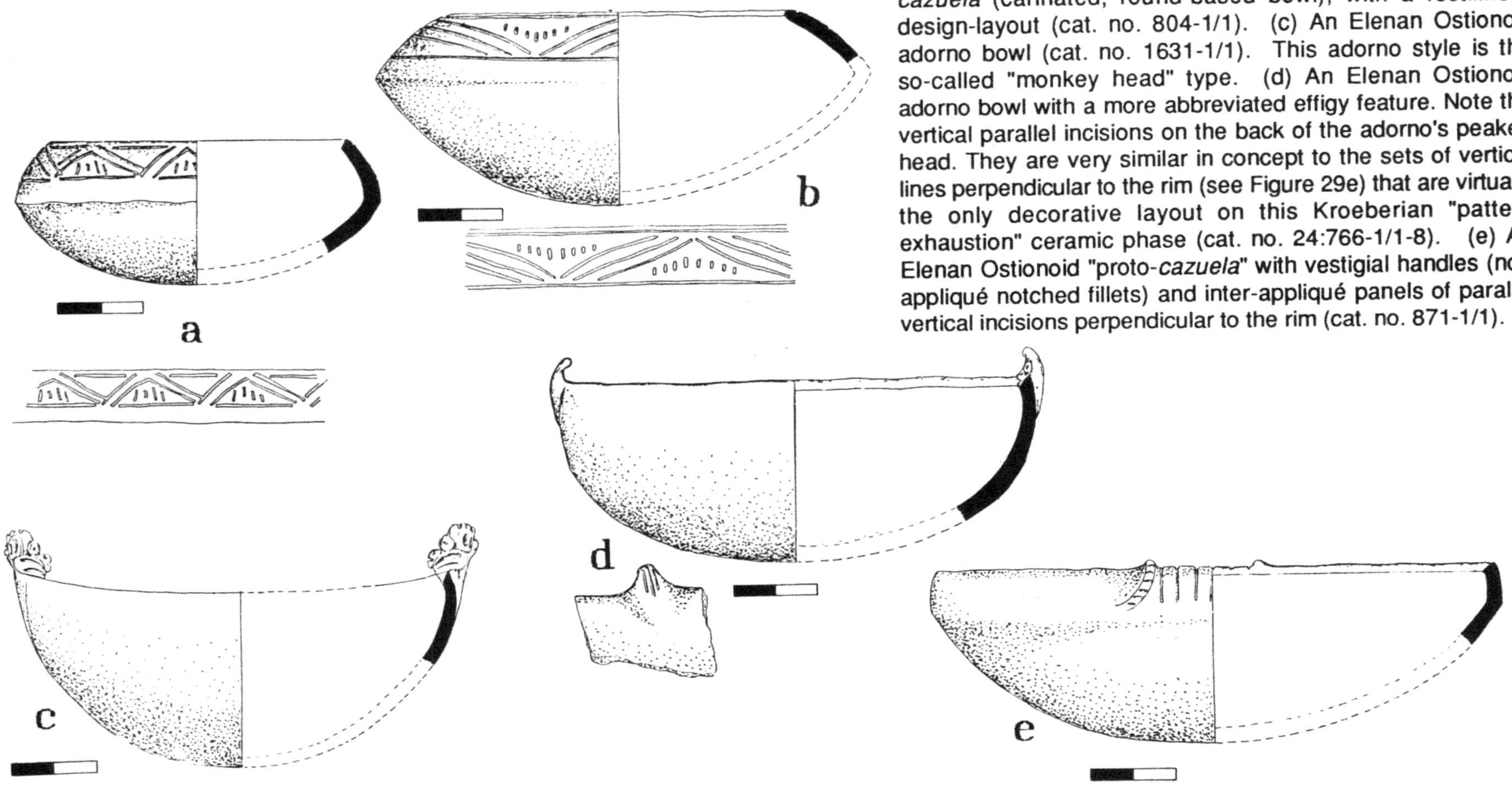

Figure 29. The triumph of "primitive sphericity" in later Puerto Rican ceramic "devolution" as witnessed in the El Bronce site collection: (a) An Esperanza phase *cazuela* with incised rectilinear decoration on the upper body design-field segment (cat. no. 24:421-1/1). (b) Another Esperanza phase *cazuela* (carinated, round-based bowl), with a rectilinear design-layout (cat. no. 804-1/1). (c) An Elenan Ostionoid adorno bowl (cat. no. 1631-1/1). This adorno style is the so-called "monkey head" type. (d) An Elenan Ostionoid adorno bowl with a more abbreviated effigy feature. Note the vertical parallel incisions on the back of the adorno's peaked head. They are very similar in concept to the sets of vertical lines perpendicular to the rim (see Figure 29e) that are virtually the only decorative layout on this Kroeberian "pattern exhaustion" ceramic phase (cat. no. 24:766-1/1-8). (e) An Elenan Ostionoid "proto-*cazuela*" with vestigial handles (now appliqué notched fillets) and inter-appliqué panels of parallel vertical incisions perpendicular to the rim (cat. no. 871-1/1).

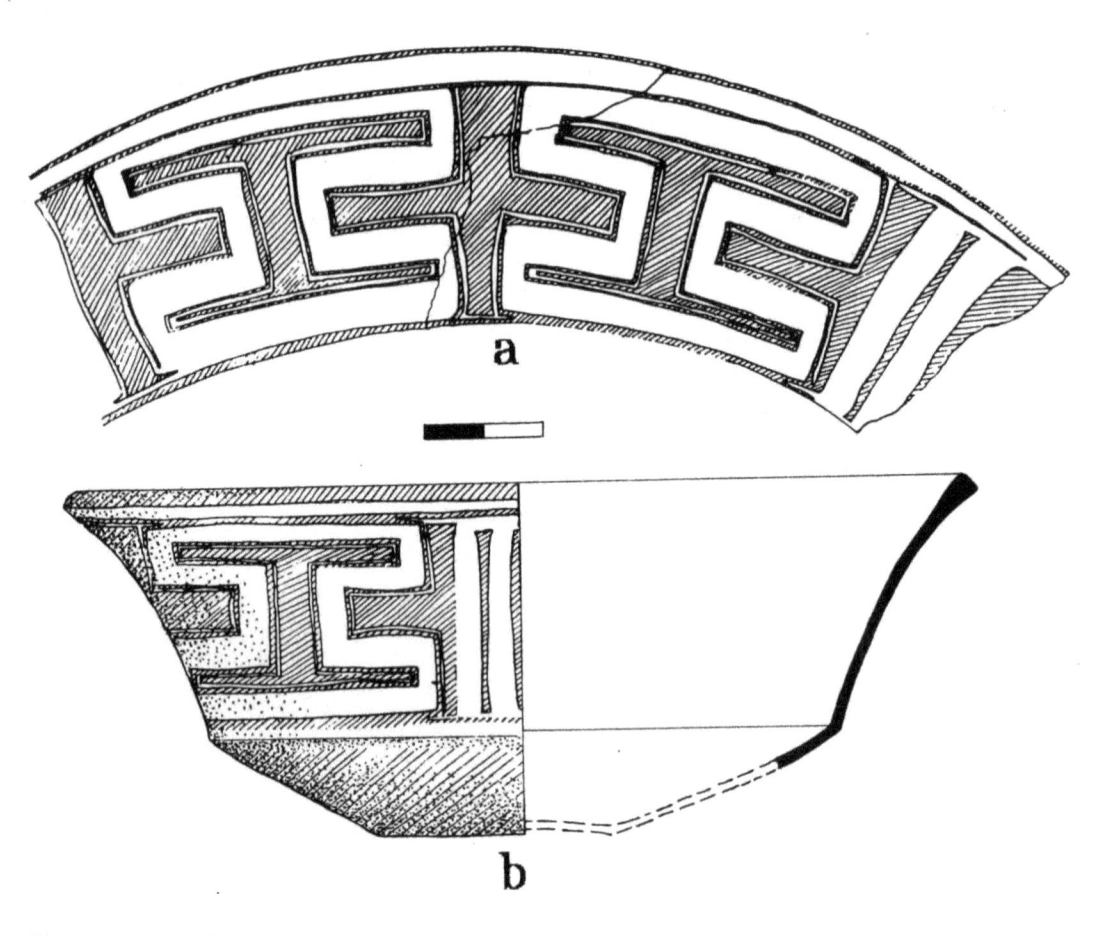

Figure 30. A late Hacienda Grande, Early Cuevas WOR campaniform from the Hacienda Grande site (CIIPR collections [ex-Castillo]). (a) The expanded and reconstructed rectilinear design-layout on the upper body design field of this vessel. This field was decorated by the artisan using a "perpendicular" mode of perception, envisioning the below-rim-above-carination field as a band. Hence many of the complete specimens of this type have "plan-ahead" crowding problems in the execution of their design-layouts. (b) A profile view of the specimen reconstructed from a large sherd.

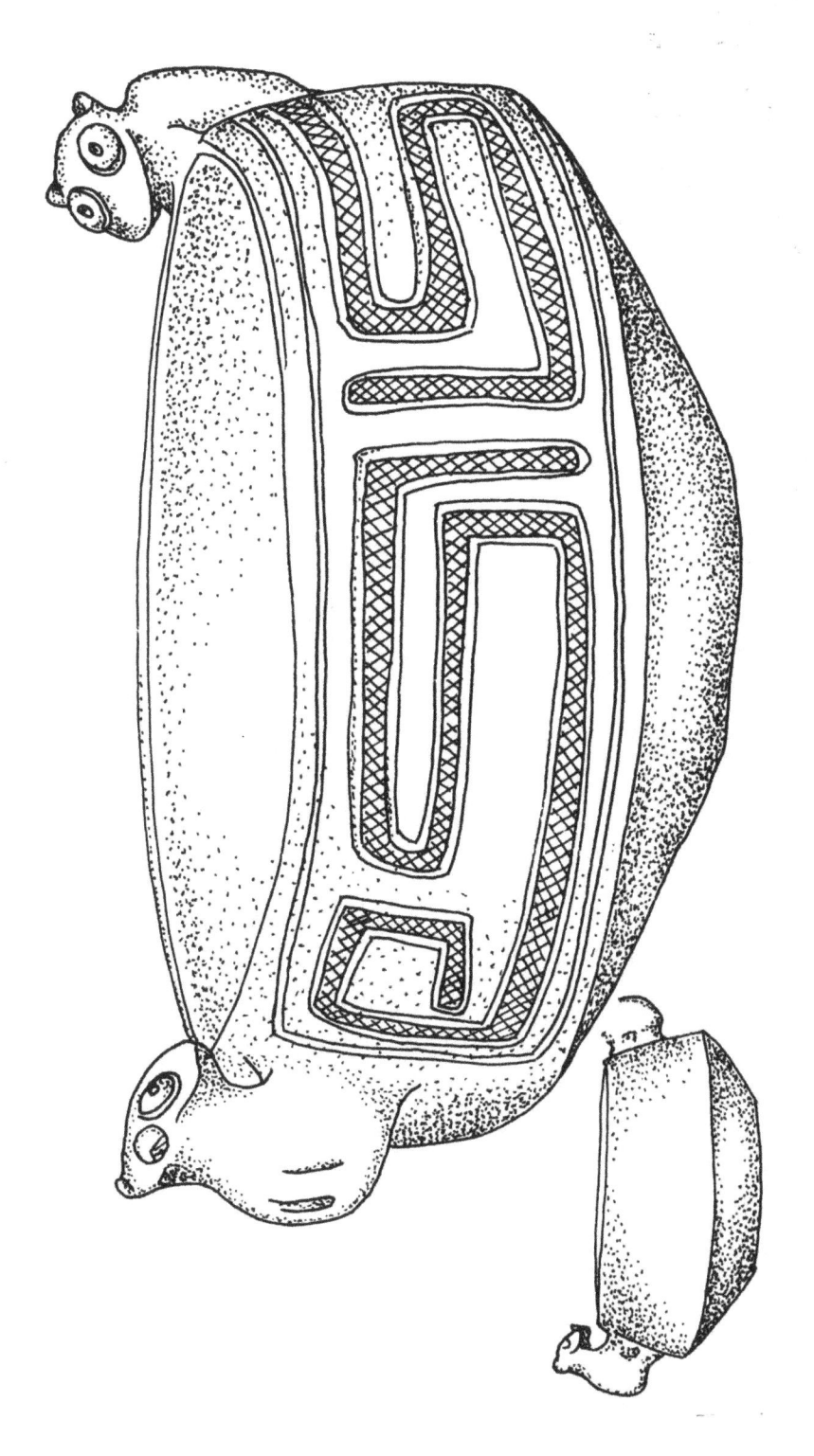

Figure 31. A typical La Hueca phase "dog adorno" bowl where the modeled solid dog figurines act as handles (the right handle is reconstructed). This cross-hatched vessel is drawn from a slide projection tracing (Sorcé site, collection of the CIA, UPR).

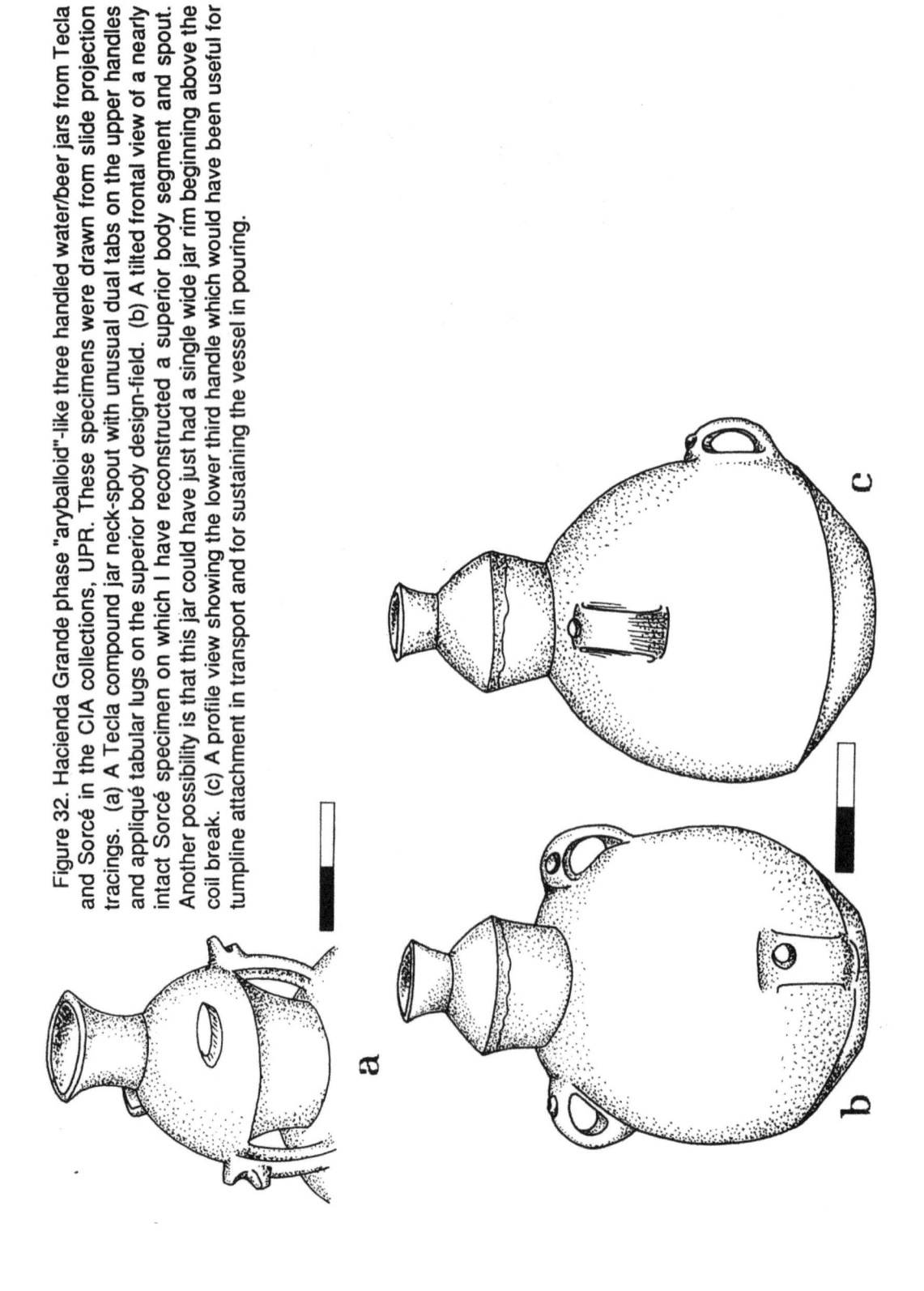

Figure 32. Hacienda Grande phase "aryballoid"-like three handled water/beer jars from Tecla and Sorcé in the CIA collections, UPR. These specimens were drawn from slide projection tracings. (a) A Tecla compound jar neck-spout with unusual dual tabs on the upper handles and appliqué tabular lugs on the superior body design-field. (b) A tilted frontal view of a nearly intact Sorcé specimen on which I have reconstructed a superior body segment and spout. Another possibility is that this jar could have just had a single wide jar rim beginning above the coil break. (c) A profile view showing the lower third handle which would have been useful for tumpline attachment in transport and for sustaining the vessel in pouring.

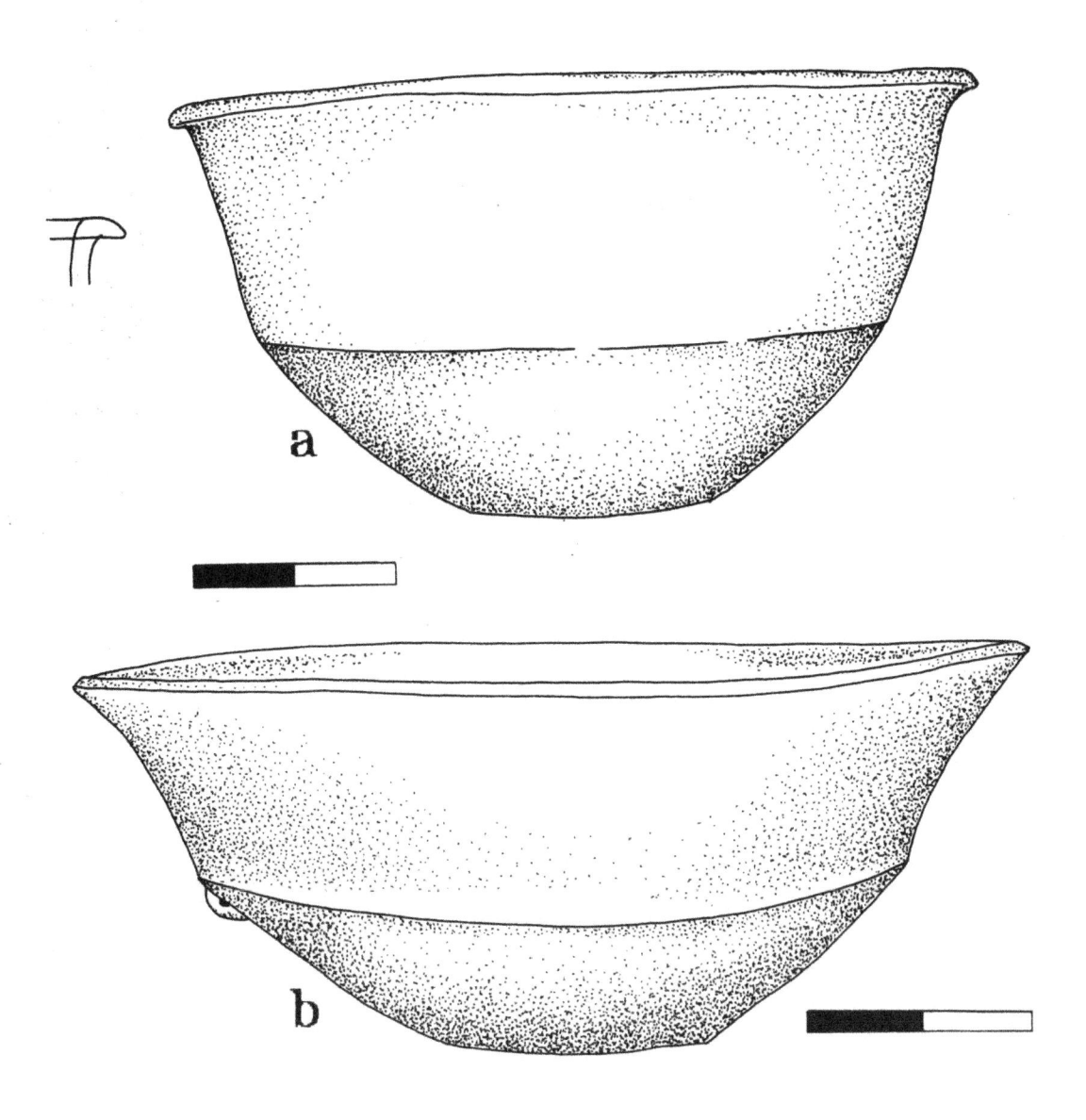

Figure 33. Vessel form similarities in the largely unillustrated utilitarian campaniform bowls from Sorcé's Cedrosan Saladoid Hacienda Grande and La Hueca phase components. Slide projection tracings made from CIA intact vessels, UPR. (a) A La Hueca piece. The principal differences between this style's rendition of the campaniform and the HG versions is the LH

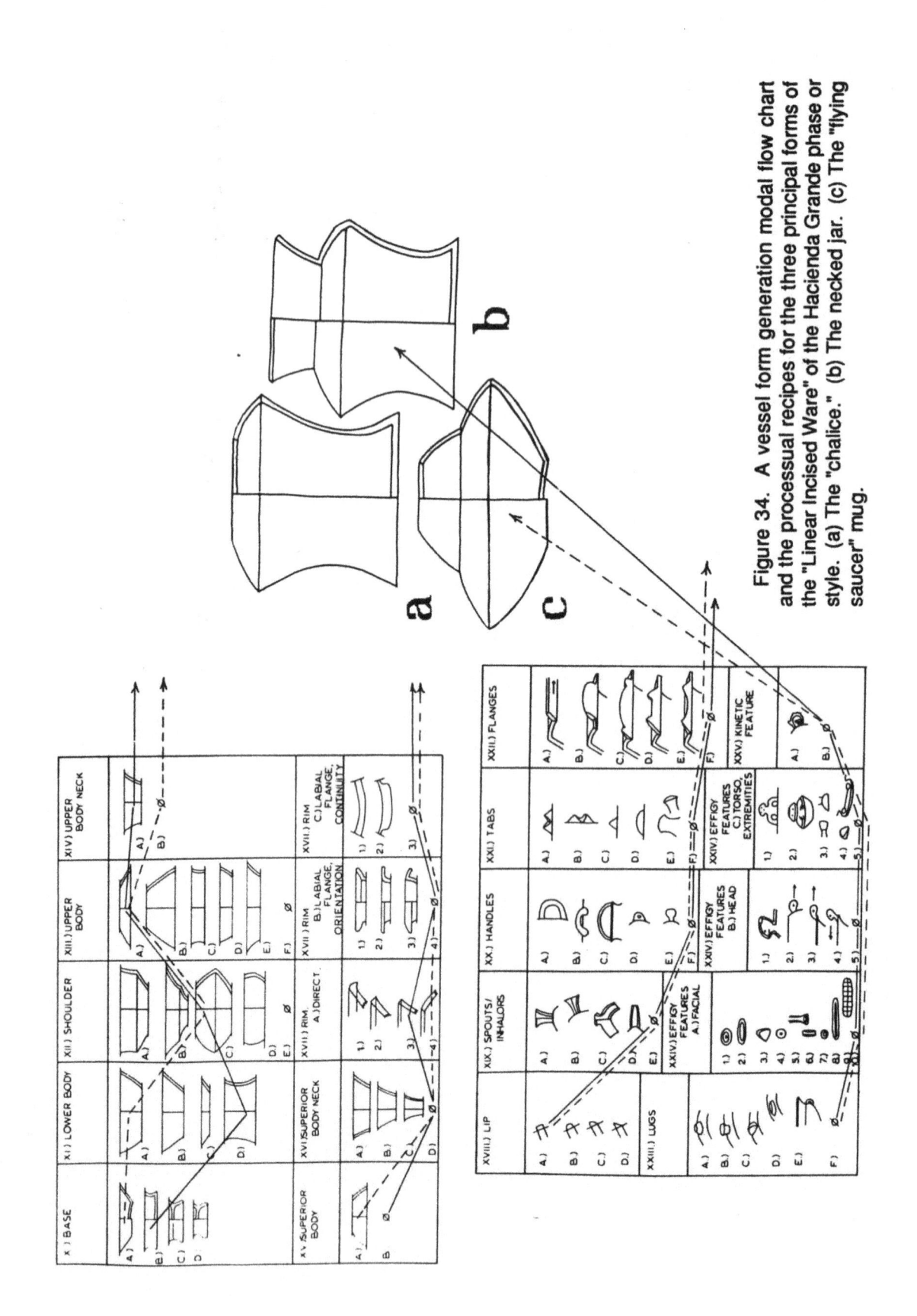

Figure 34. A vessel form generation modal flow chart and the processual recipes for the three principal forms of the "Linear Incised Ware" of the Hacienda Grande phase or style. (a) The "chalice." (b) The necked jar. (c) The "flying saucer" mug.

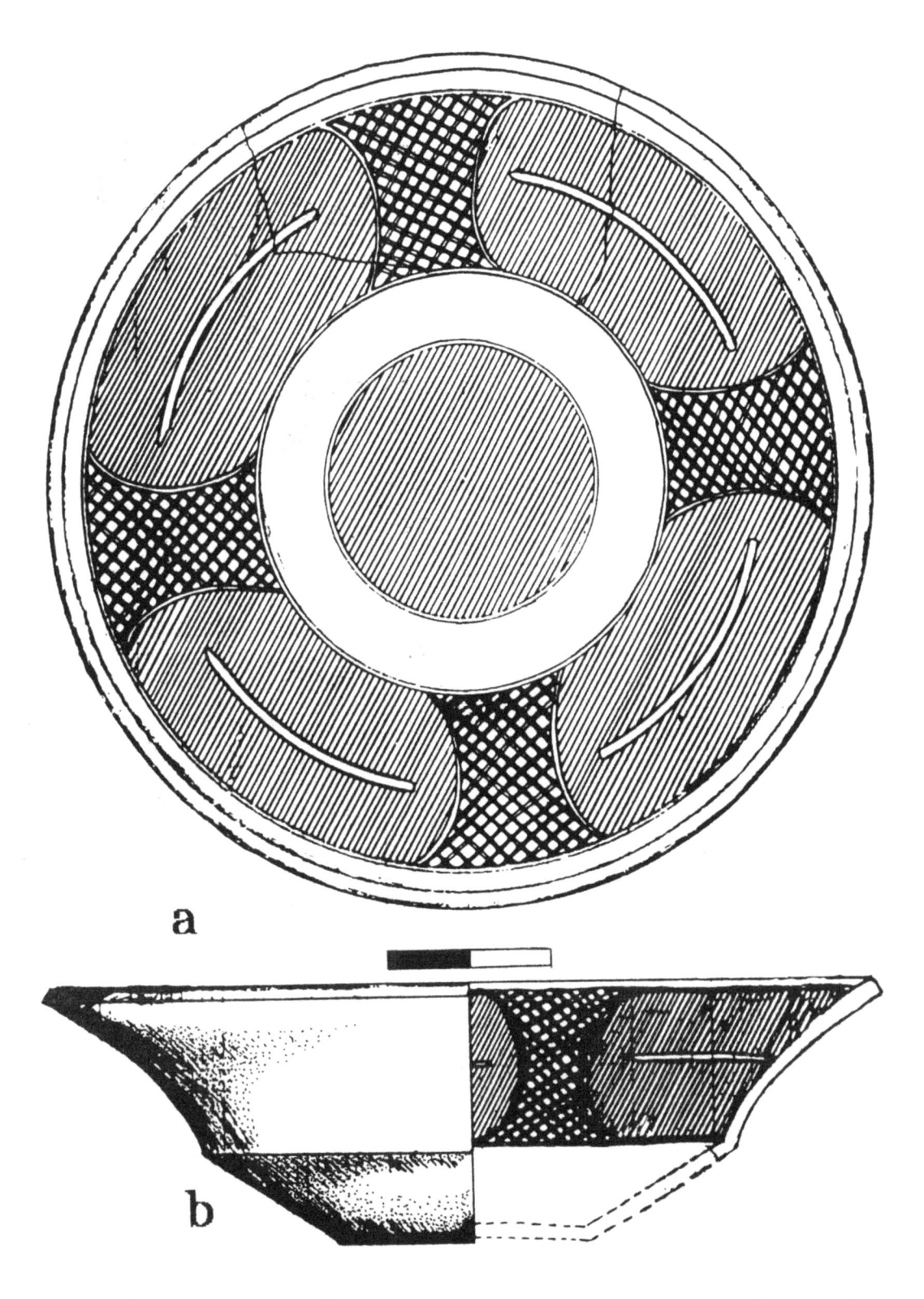

Figure 35. A small Hacienda Grande style ZIC campaniform open bowl from the Vacia Talega site in the collections of the CIIPR (ex-Castillo, no. P536). (a) A plane view of the interior showing the single sherd upon which this reconstruction is based. (b) A profile view.

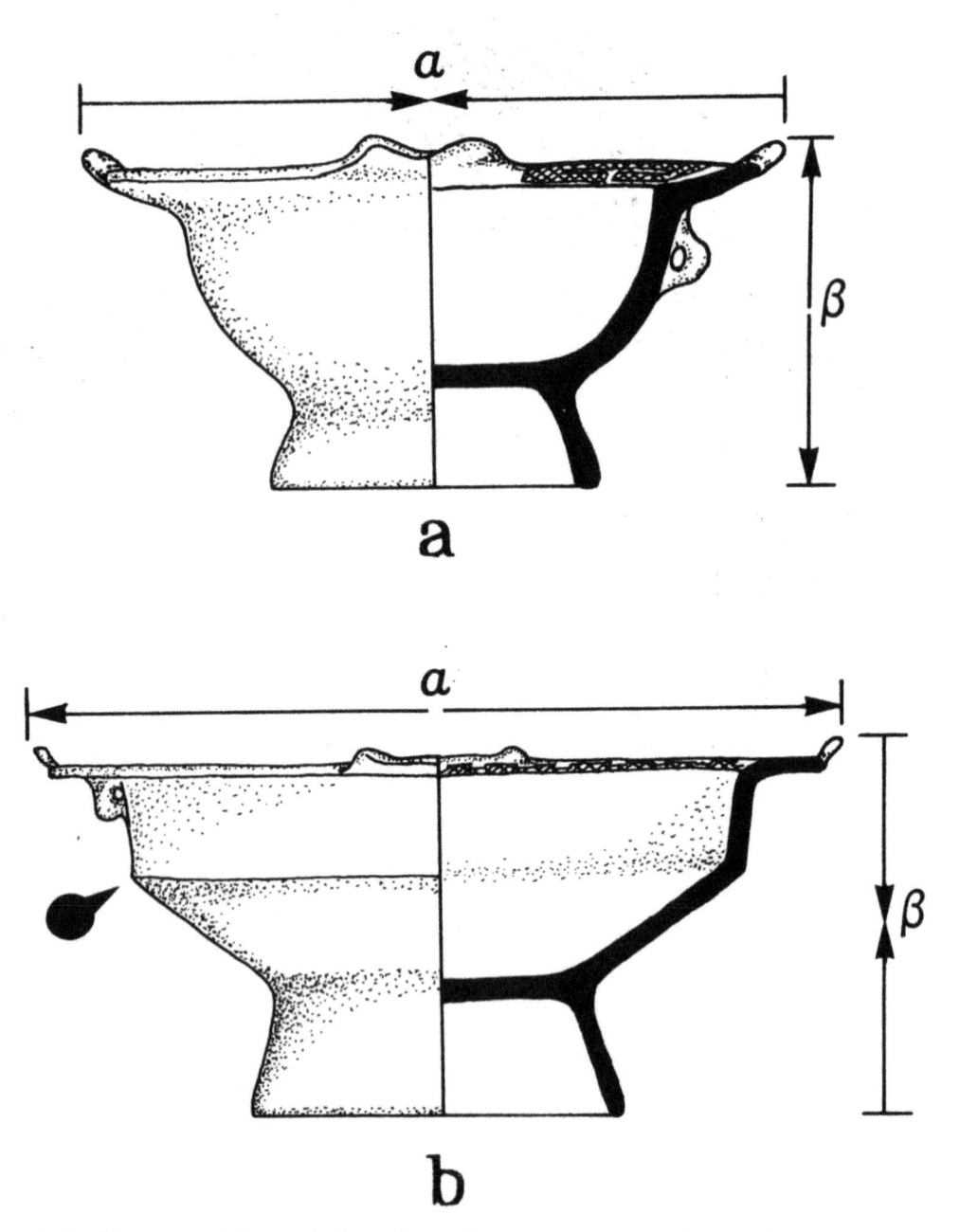

Figure 36. La Hueca and Hacienda Grande pedestal-based, labial-flanged bowls, the major dimensions of form variability. (a) The La Hueca specimen from the CIIPR collections (ex-Castillo, Hacienda Grande site). (b) The Hacienda Grande specimen from the 1984 CEAPRC excavations at Hacienda Grande.

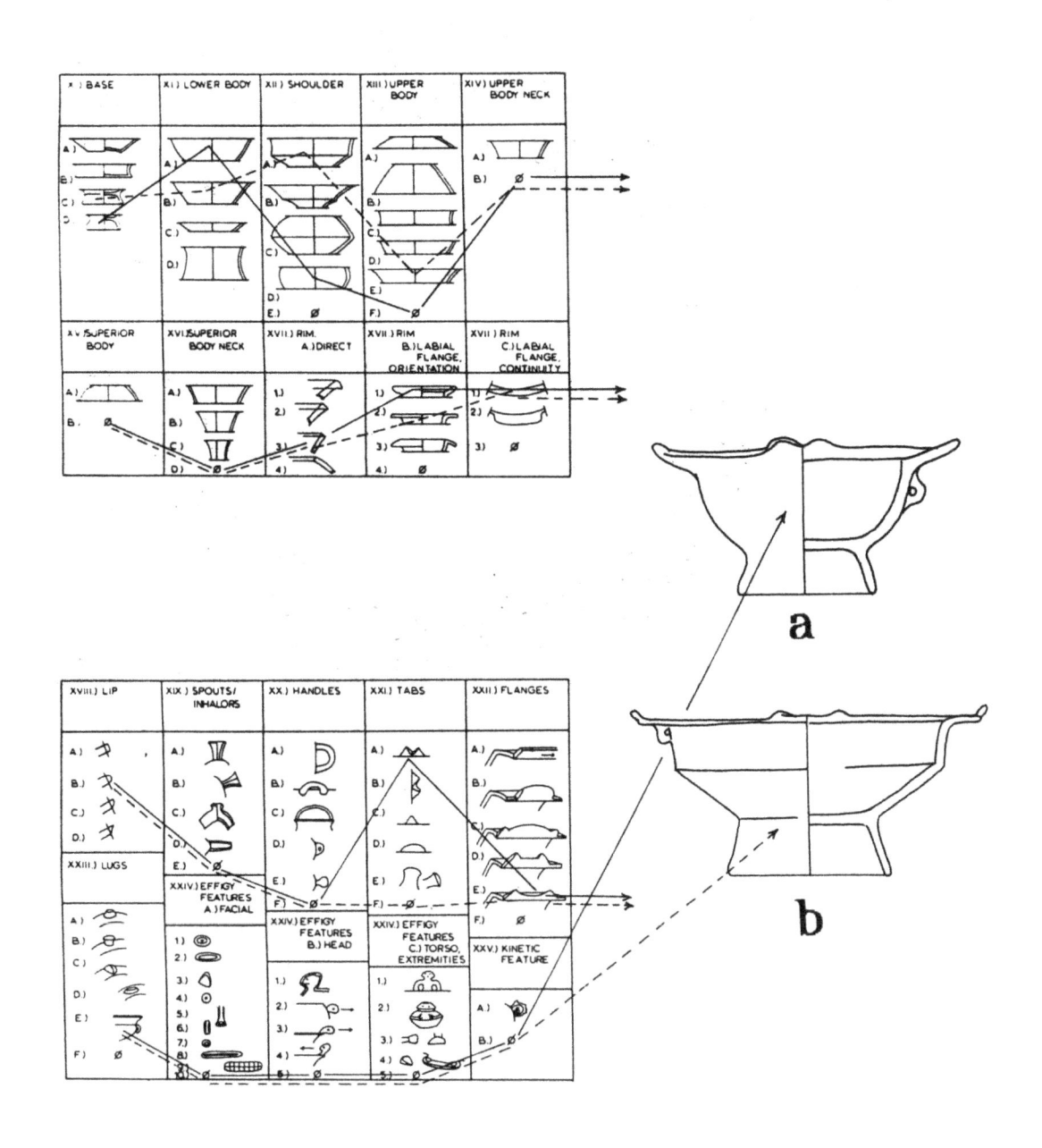

Figure 37. A vessel form generation modal flow chart and the processual recipes for La Hueca and Hacienda Grande pedestal-based, labial-flanged bowls.

Figure 38. Plane views of the La Hueca and Hacienda Grande pedestal-based, flanged bowls showing the major dimensions of design-field and design-layout variability. (a) The La Hueca specimen showing its comparatively sloppy execution. (b) The Hacienda Grande specimen showing its well-controlled cross-hatching.

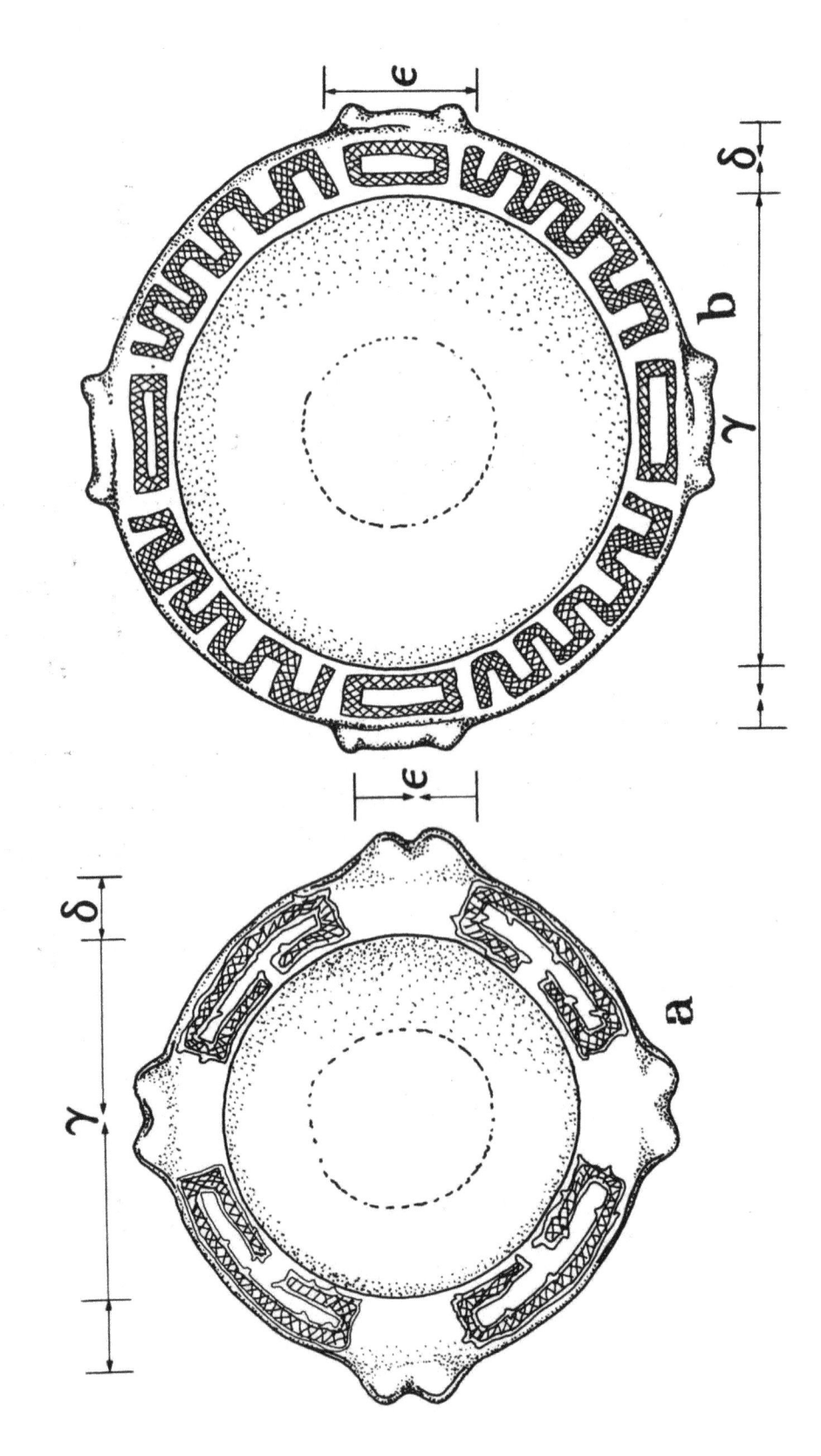

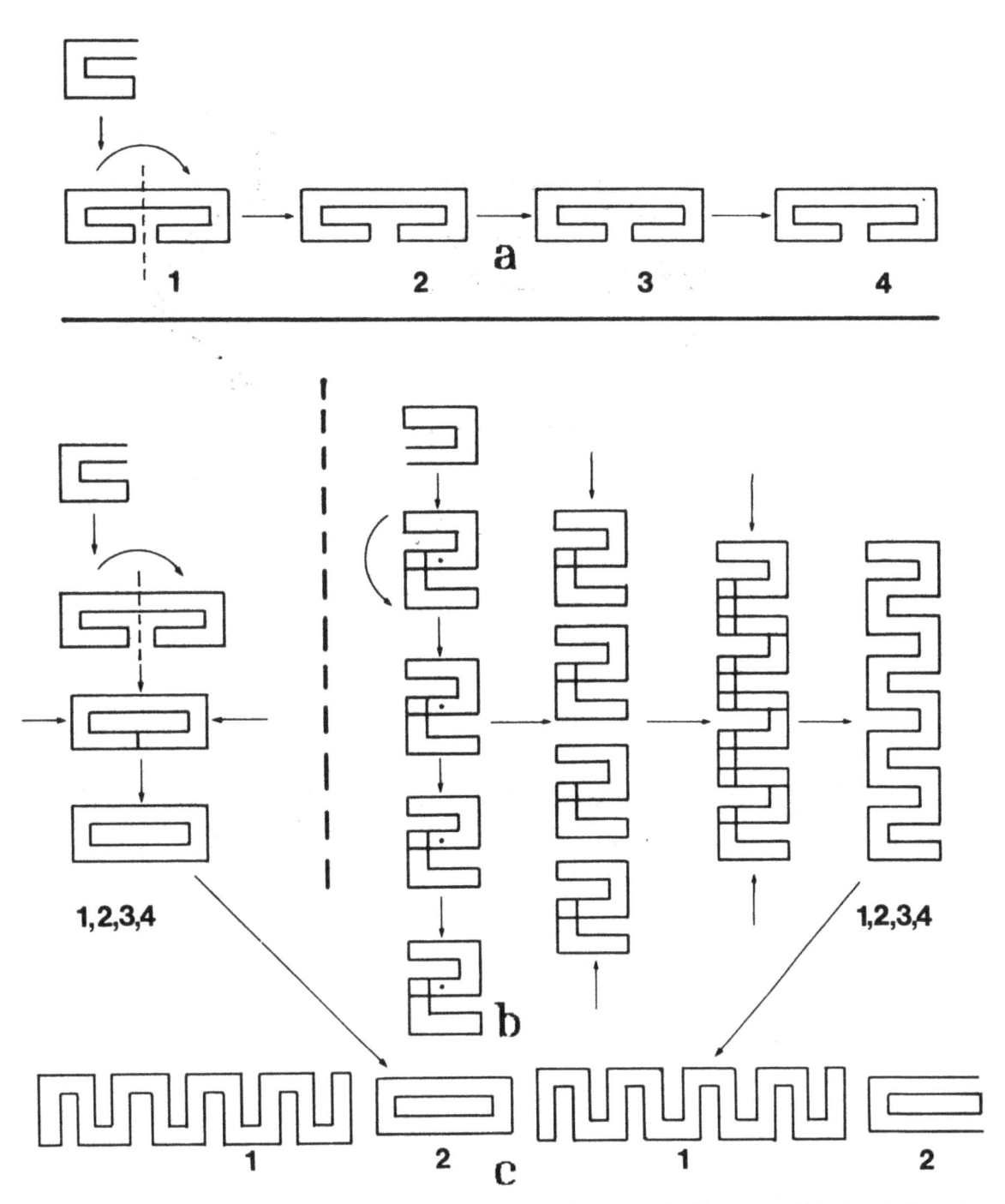

Figure 39. The generative grammatical derivation of cognate La Hueca and Hacienda Grande design-layouts on the similar fields of their respective labial-flanged, pedestal-based bowls. (a) A derivational chain of the La Hueca design-layout pictured in Figure 38a. (b) A set of two derivational chains for each "embedded" design motif set within the composite design-layout pictured in Figure 38b. (c) The resultant composite design-layout pictured in 38b, constructed using an "alternation" compositional band symmetry rule.

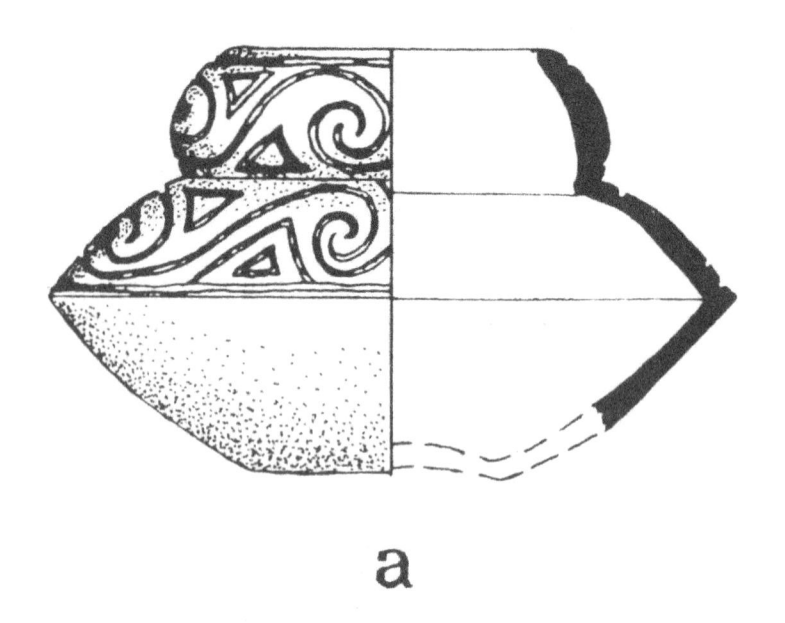

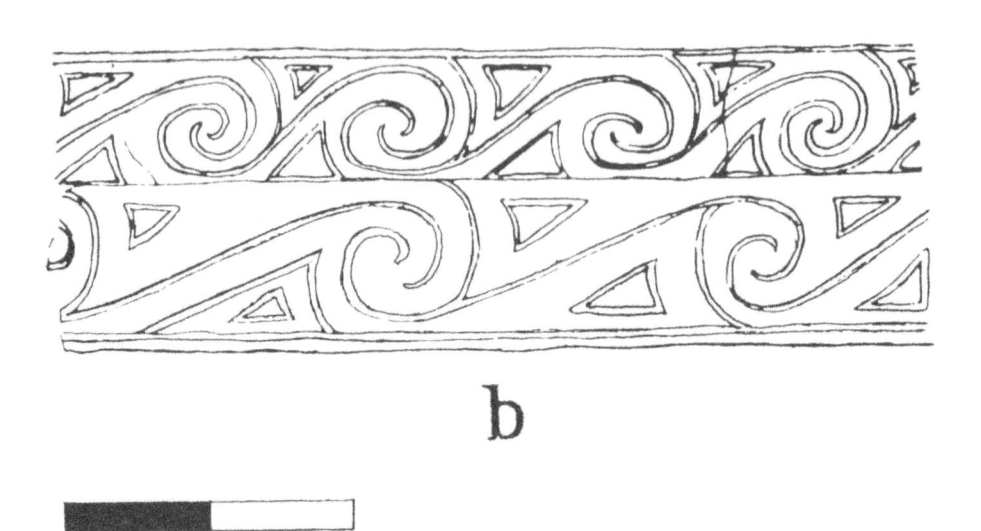

Figure 40. A small Hacienda Grande phase "flying saucer" mug in the "Linear Incised Ware" (CIIPR [ex-Castillo] collection, no. P4151, Hacienda Grande site). (a) This red-slipped specimen would have had white paint crusting in the incisions like no. P4498. (b) The two registers of the neck and upper body design-field curvilinear design-layouts "rolled out" from "a."

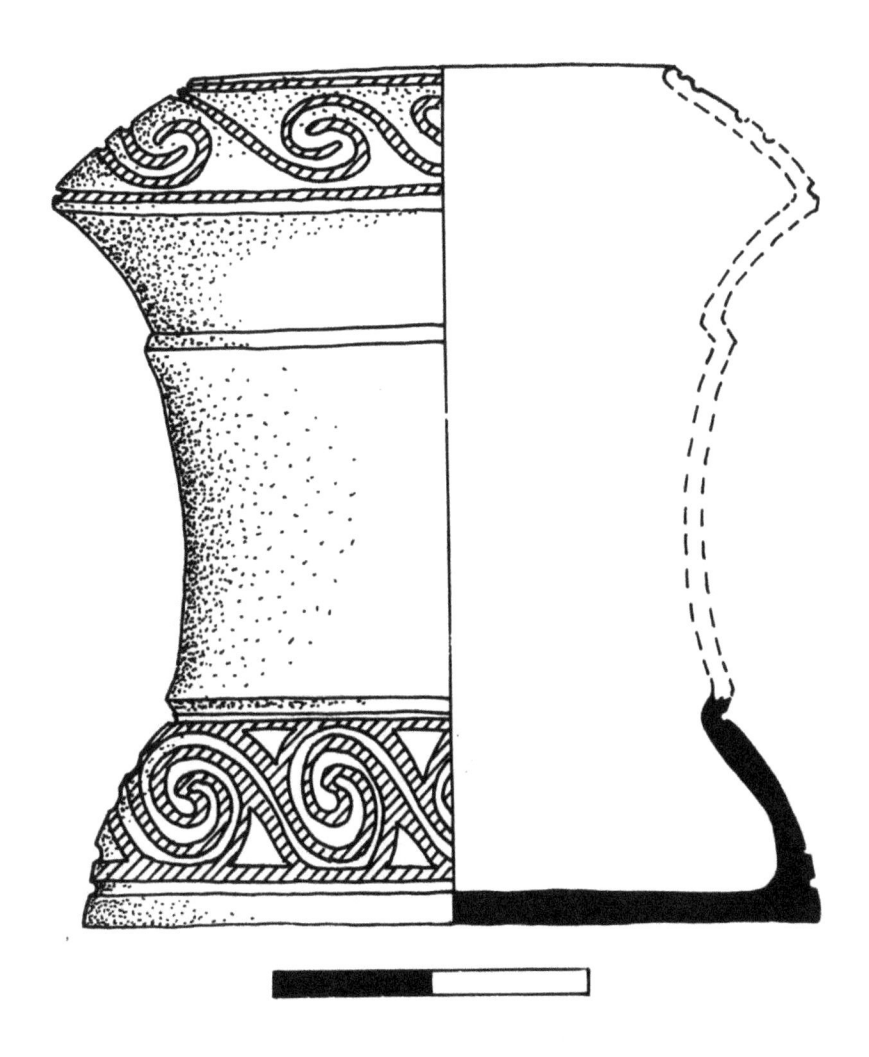

Figure 41. A deeply excised and incised, red slip-painted "chalice" in the "Linear Incised Ware" of the Hacienda Grande phase of the Cedrosan Saladoid subseries (CIIPR [ex-Castillo] collection, no. P2030, Hacienda Grande site). (a) A profile view showing the base from which the whole vessel was reconstructed. Figure 42 was used to determine the upper segment of this specimen. (b) The "rolled out" curvilinear design-layout from the in-sloping base design-field unique to this class of vessels.

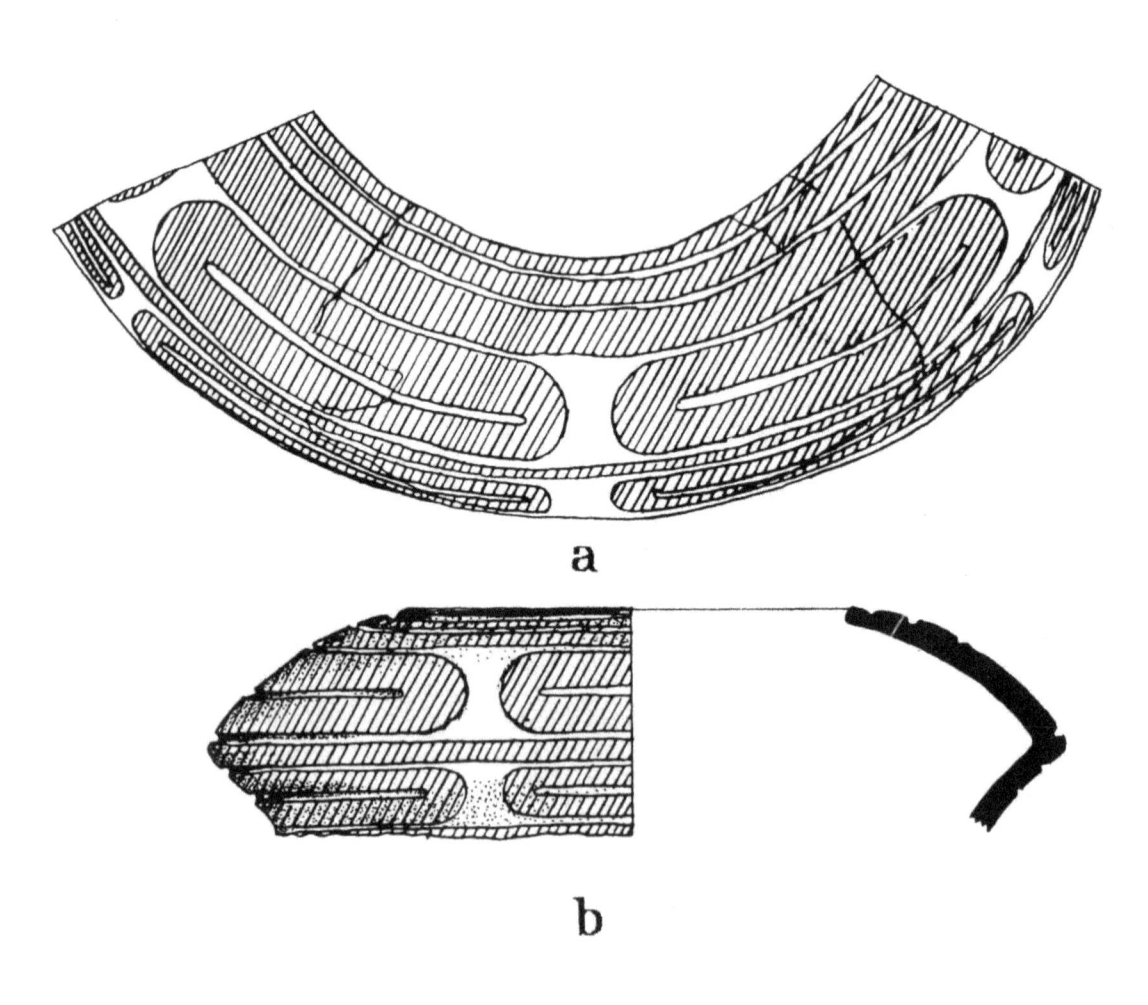

Figure 42. The upper segment of a similar red slip-painted, incised and excised, white filled "Linear Incised Ware" chalice (CIIPR [ex-Castillo] collection, no. P4211, Hacienda Grande site). (a) A "roll-out" of the design-layout, showing the size of the sherd used to reconstruct this

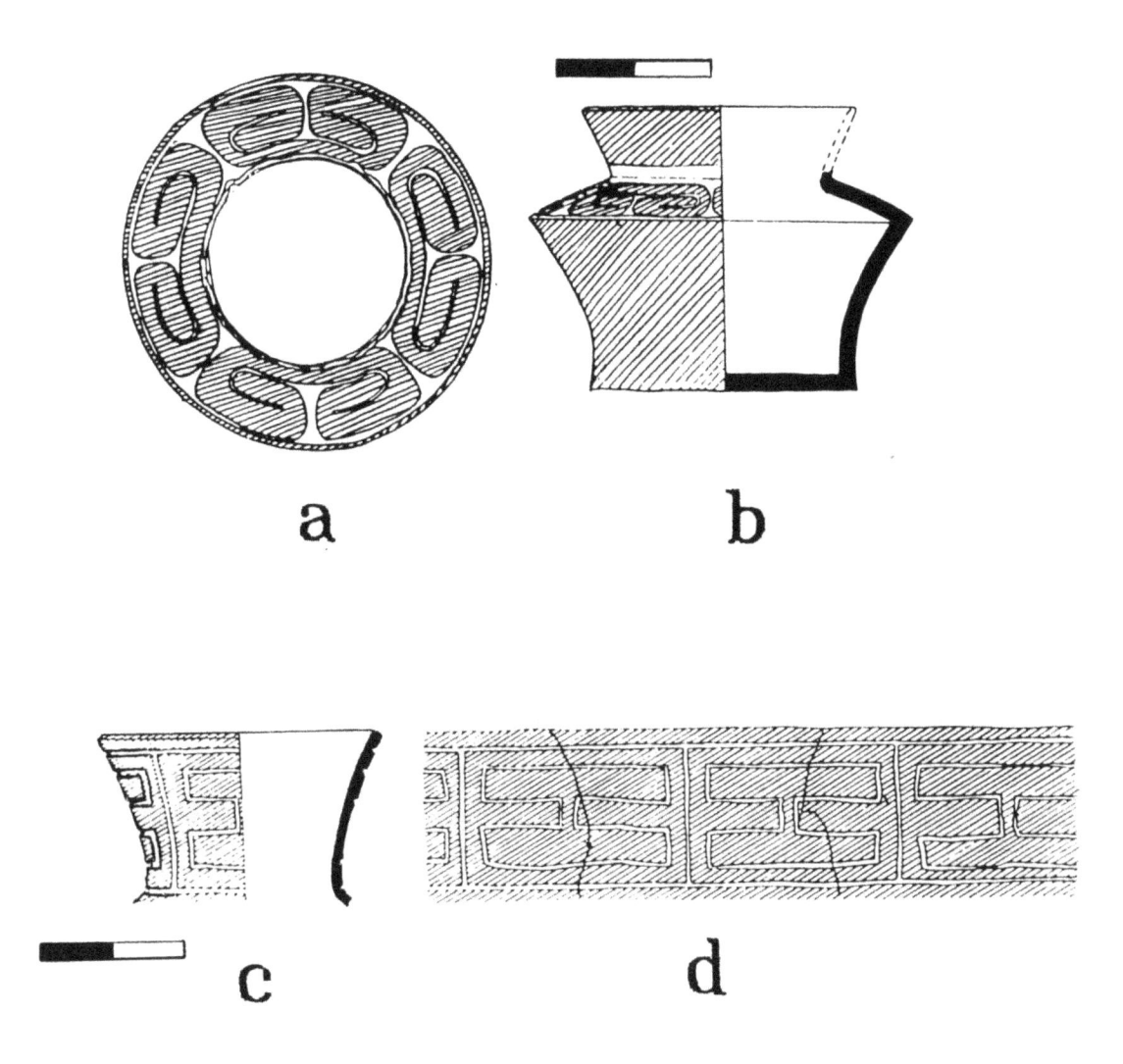

Figure 43. The last of the related forms of Hacienda Grande phase "Linear Incised Ware" vessel forms, the carinated jar with in-sloping base (CIIPR [ex-Castillo] collection, no. 382, Hacienda Grande site). (a) A plane-view of the upper body design-field within which the "globally-perceived" curvilinear design-layout is placed. (b) A profile view of the jar. Although this pottery is by far some of the most exquisite of the HG wares, a ware which is hard as stone, and rings like metal when it is struck, the artisan who made this particular vessel was not above an egregious error. Rather than overlapping the upper body on top of the carination, which would have given this form strength, "he" built it up attached to the inner *side* of the lower body. This foolish construction resulted in the compressional weakness that shattered the upper segment and was responsible for the loss of the jar neck. (c) A jar neck of similar type, but narrower diameter, to the neck that would have graced "b" above. This specimen is also from Hacienda Grande, of HG style (CIIPR collections [ex-Castillo]). (d) A "roll-out" and reconstruction of the aberrant *rectilinear* design-layout on this red-slipped incised piece.

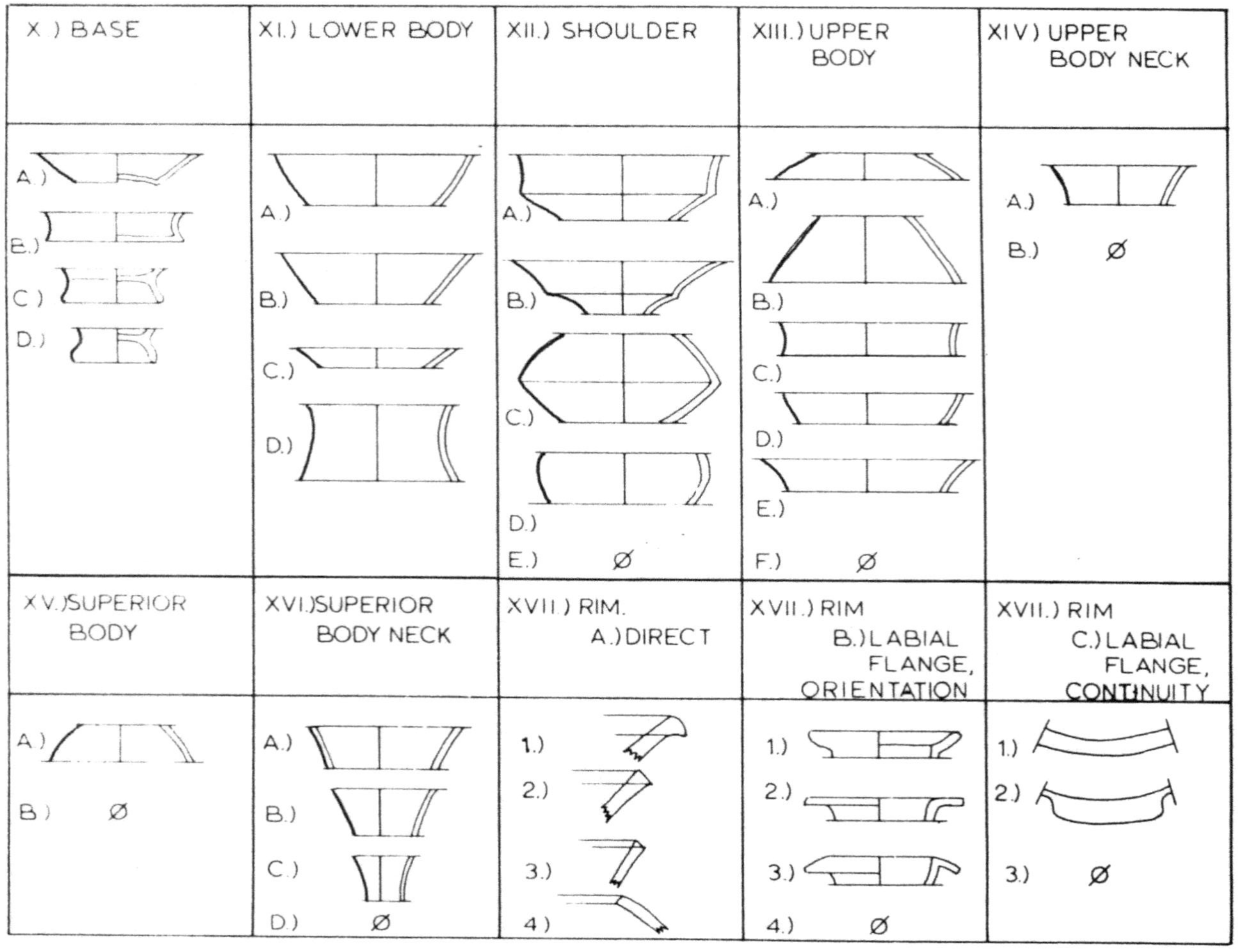

Figure 44. The vessel form generation table for the modal analysis of Cedrosan Saladoid shapes, dimensions X-XVII. This is part of the same chart employed in Figures 34 and 37.

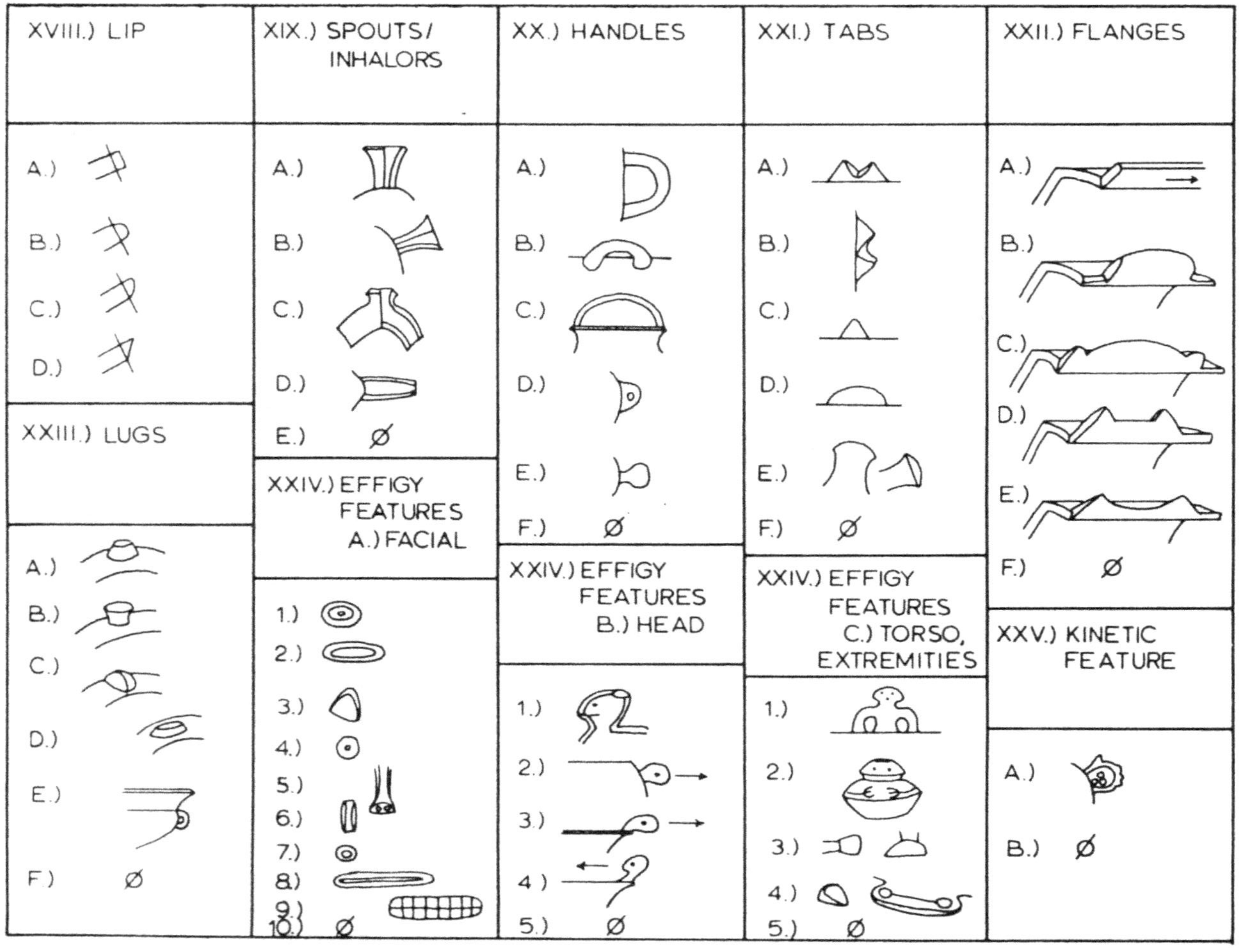

Figure 45. The vessel form generation table for the modal analysis of Cedrosan Saladoid shapes, dimensions XVIII-XXV. This is the other part of the same chart employed in Figures 34 and 37.

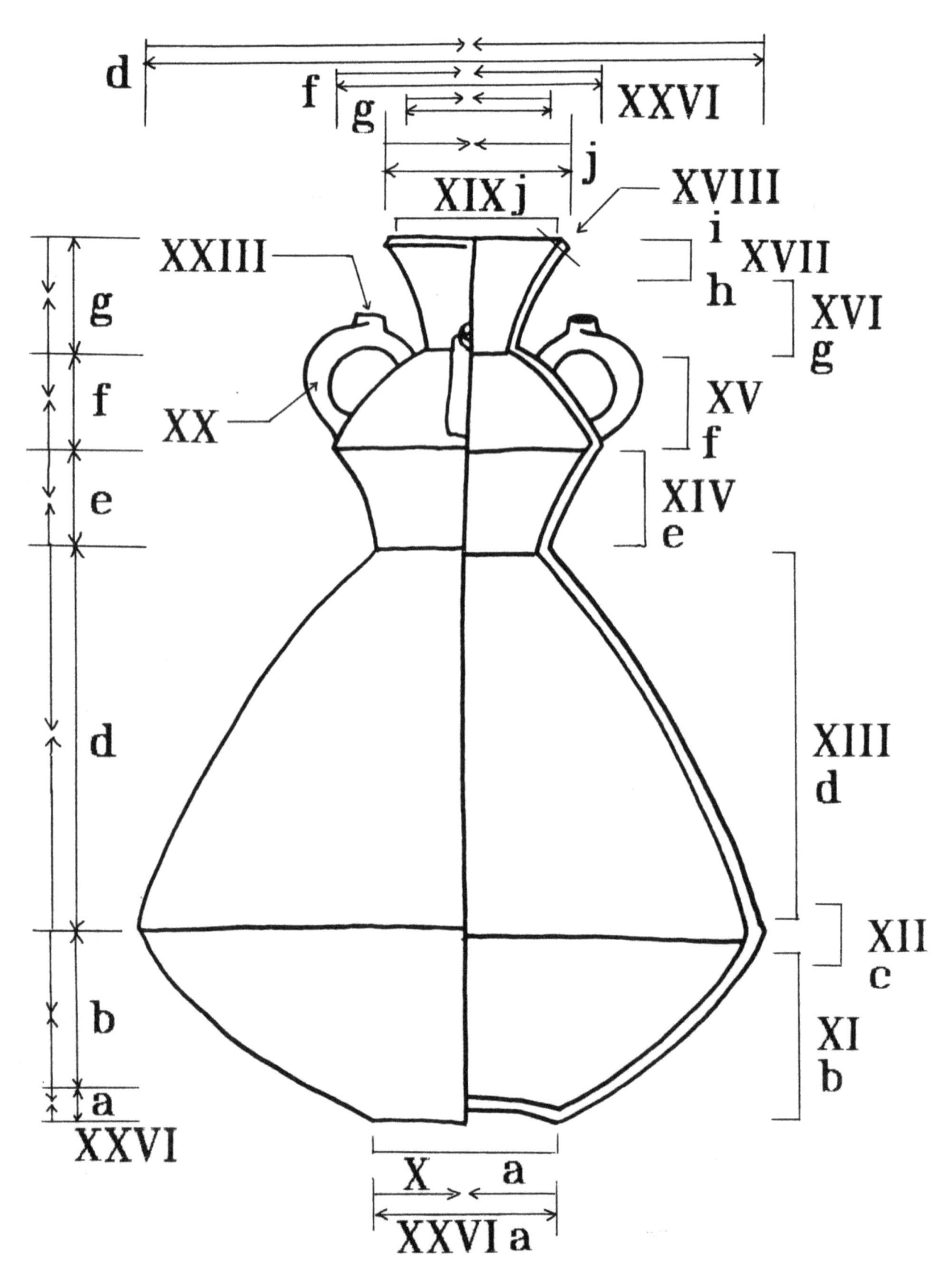

Figure 46. All the dimensions of Figures 44 and 45, using a complex HG jar form as an exemplar. The allometric shape changes that are entailed when size modes differ will "shrink" or "expand" these dimensions as needed (hence the bi-directional arrows).

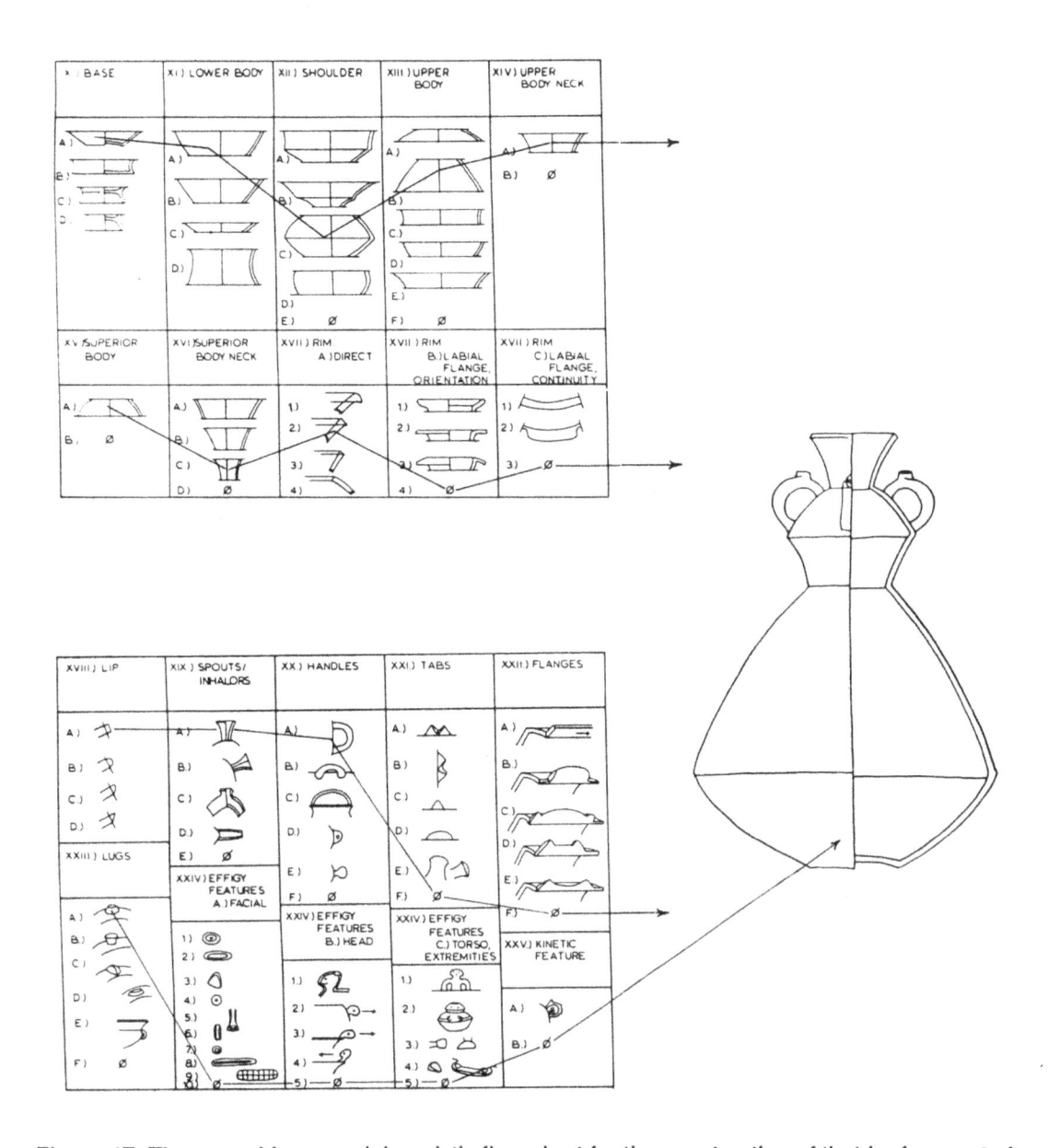

Figure 47. The vessel form modal analytic flow chart for the construction of that jar form out of the dimensions of the Cedrosan Saladoid subseries.

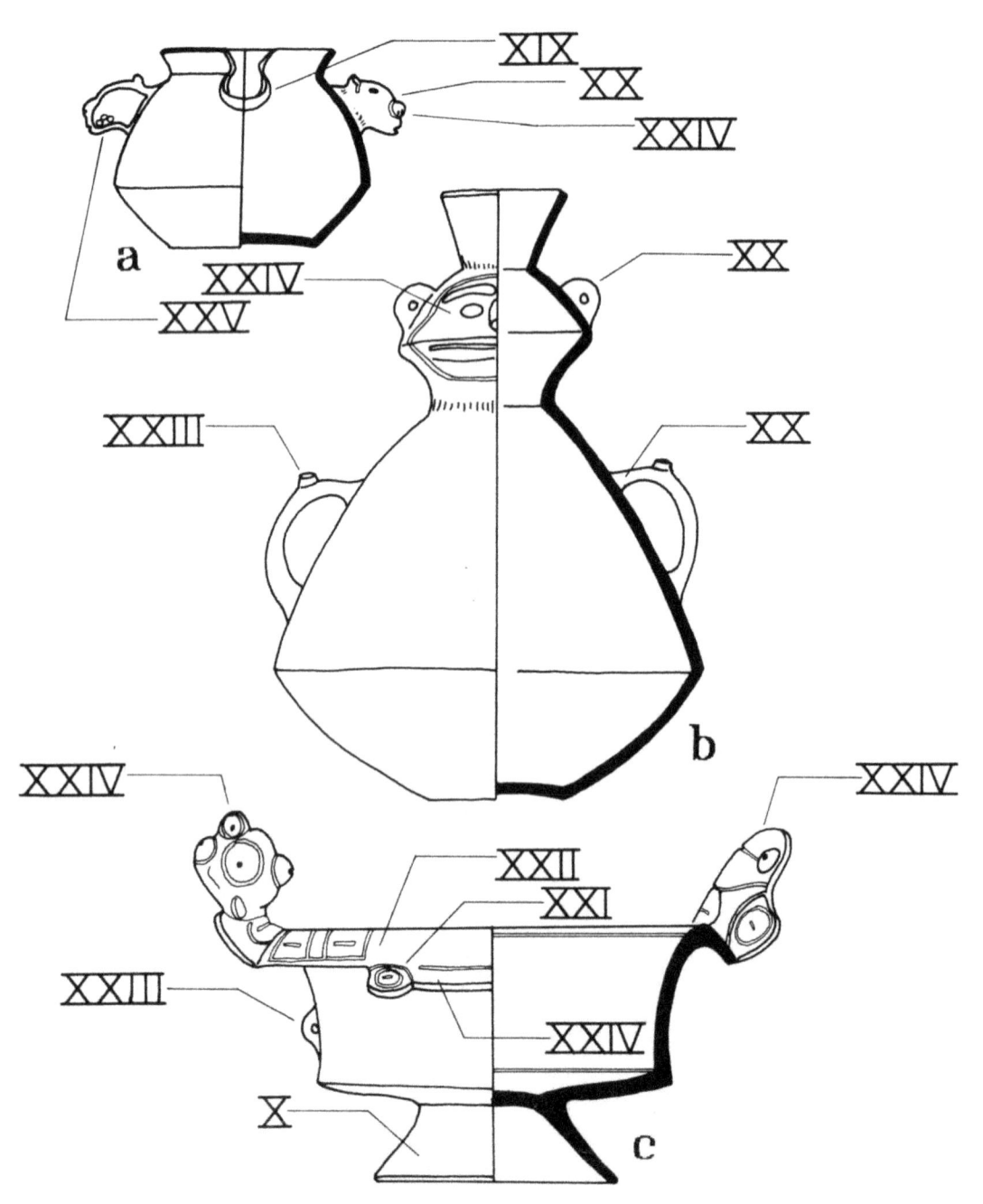

Figure 48. Three Hacienda Grande vessel forms showing the location of these specific form dimensions. (a) The rattling adorno jar. (b) The effigy jar. (c) The bird effigy, annular-based bowl.

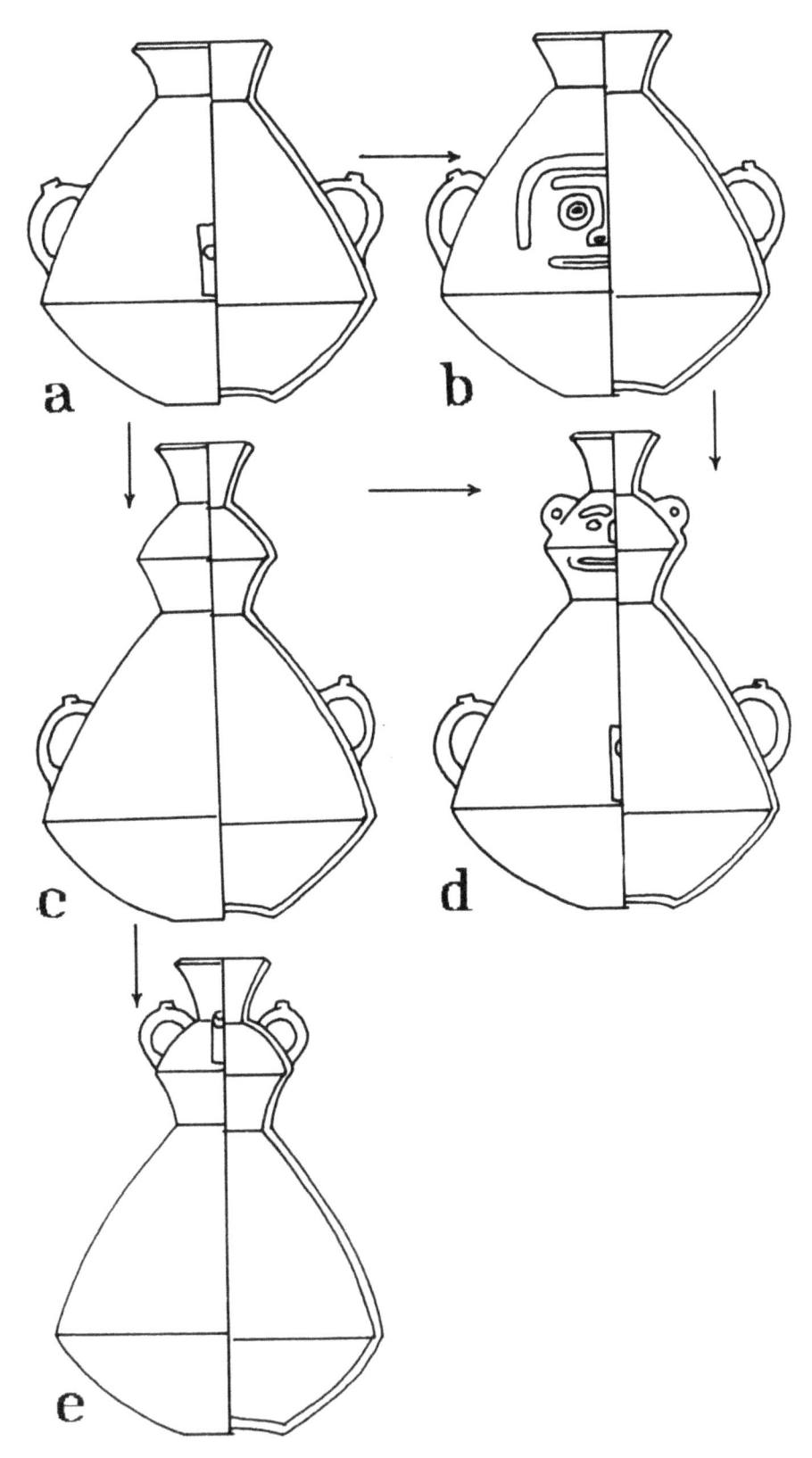

Figure 49. A "derivational chain" of Hacienda Grande jar forms. (a) The "aryballoid" jar. (b) The "pectoral" effigy aryballoid. (c) The "superior body" aryballoid. (d) The "superior body" effigy jar. (e) The "supra-superior body" handled jar.

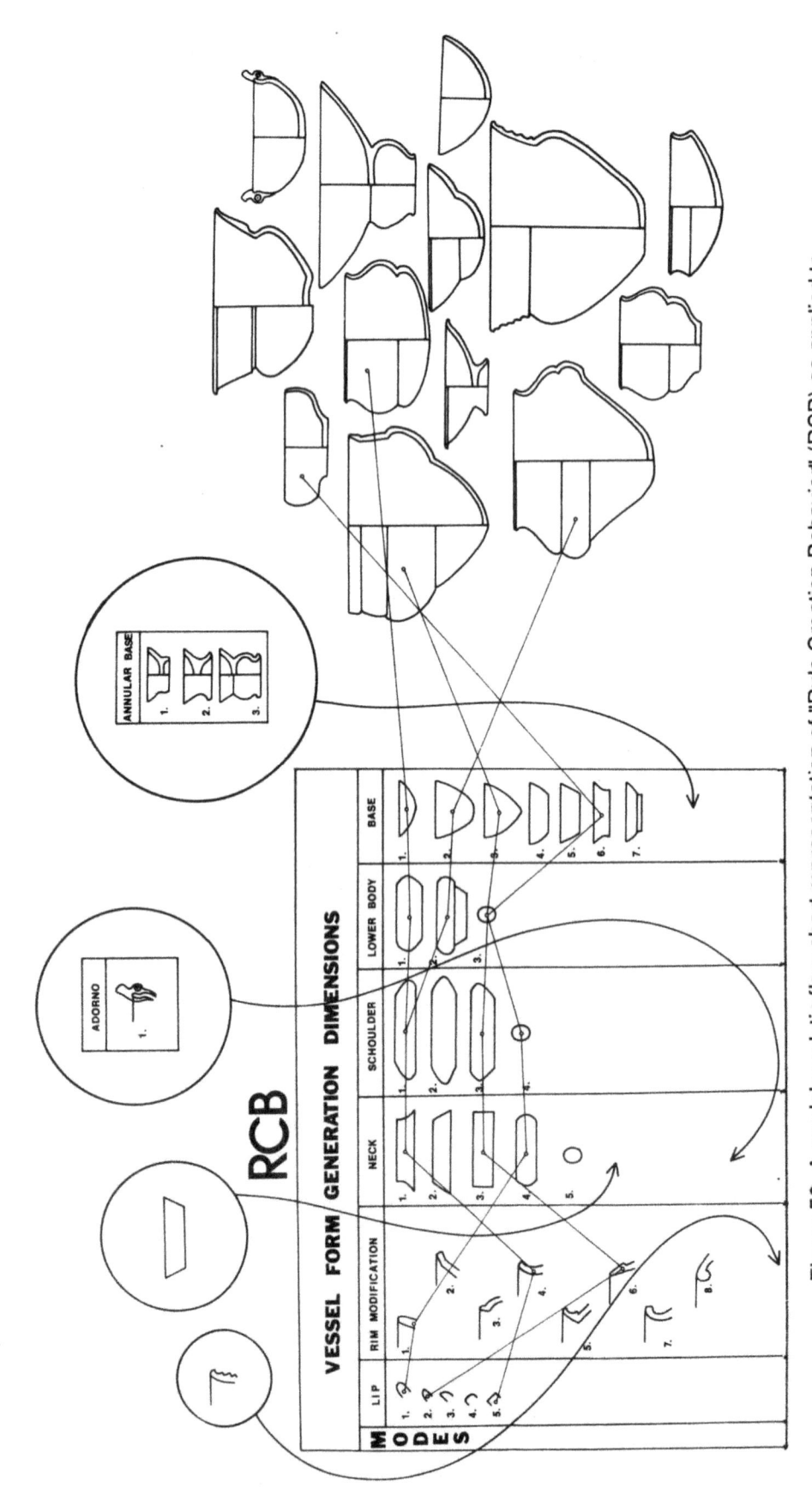

Figure 50. A modal analytic flow chart representation of "Rule Creation Behavior" (RCB) as applied to the simpler Cumancaya South American tradition. Note the oddly familiar adorno bowl, the annular-based bowls and the compound "stacked" forms which parallel their earlier Antillean Saladoid "distant cousin" forms (via the ancient traditions of the Ecuadorian montaña.)

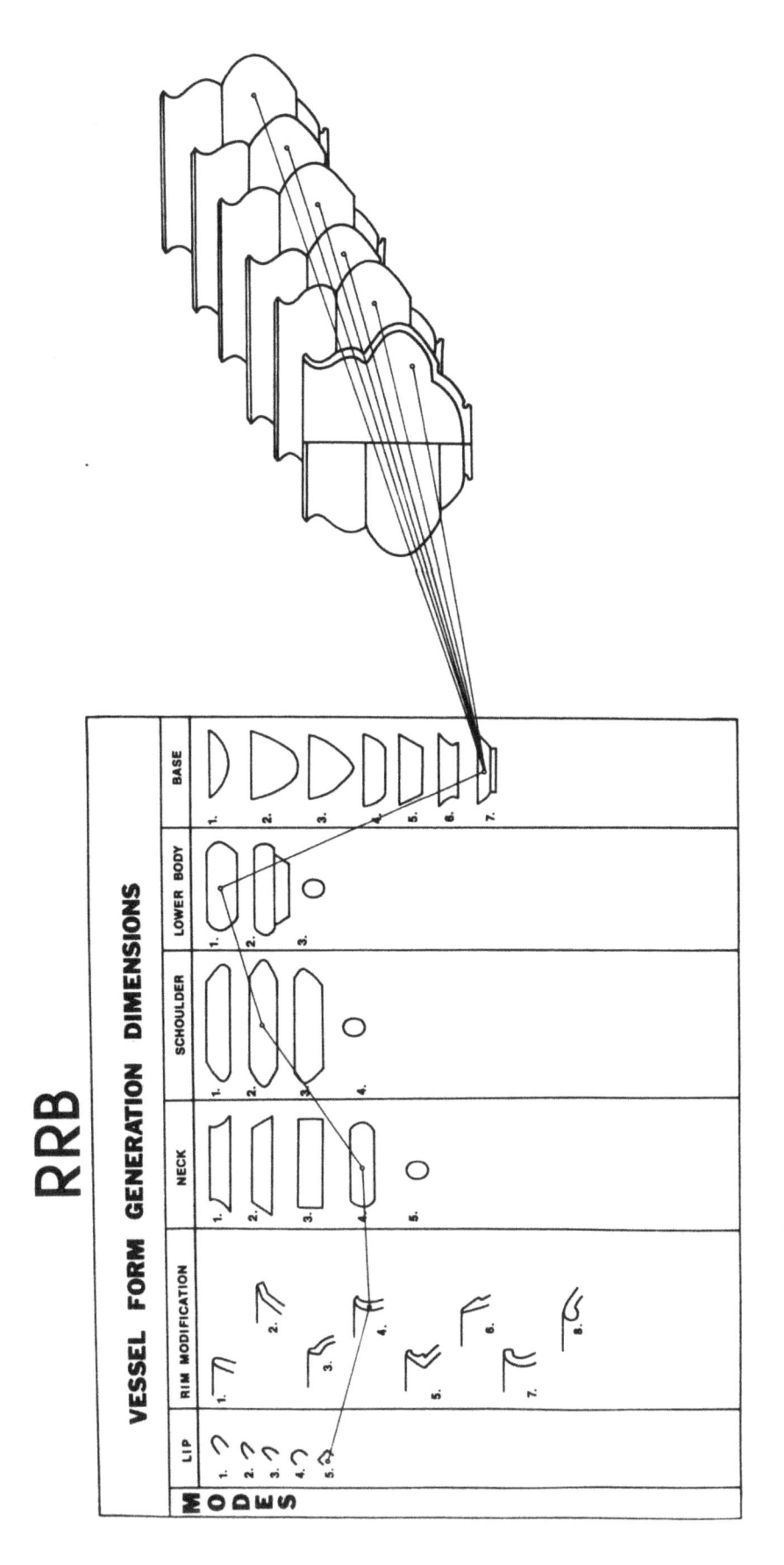

Figure 51. A modal analytic flow chart representation of "Rule Replication Behavior" (RRB), as applied to the generation of repeated examples of just one Cumancaya vessel form, a stacked jar.

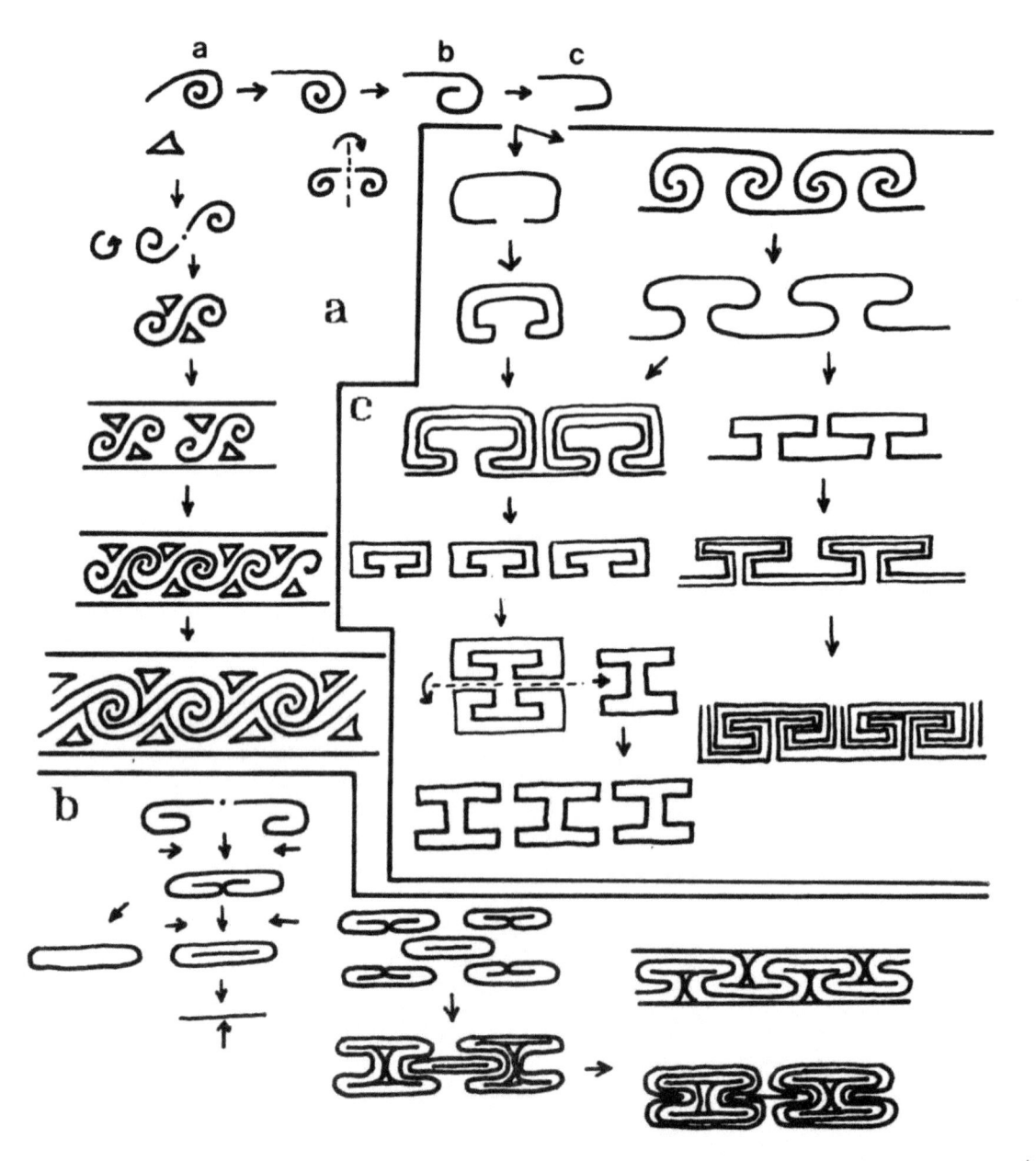

Figure 52. A synoptic set of derivational chains for the three classes of design-layouts characteristic of the Cedrosan Saladoid pottery discussed in this paper. (a) The curvilinear spiral-based WOR Hacienda Grande designs. (b) The incised and excised, red-painted and white-filled "Linear Incised Ware" designs of the HG style. (c) The rectilinear ZIC incised and post-fire crusted La Hueca style designs.

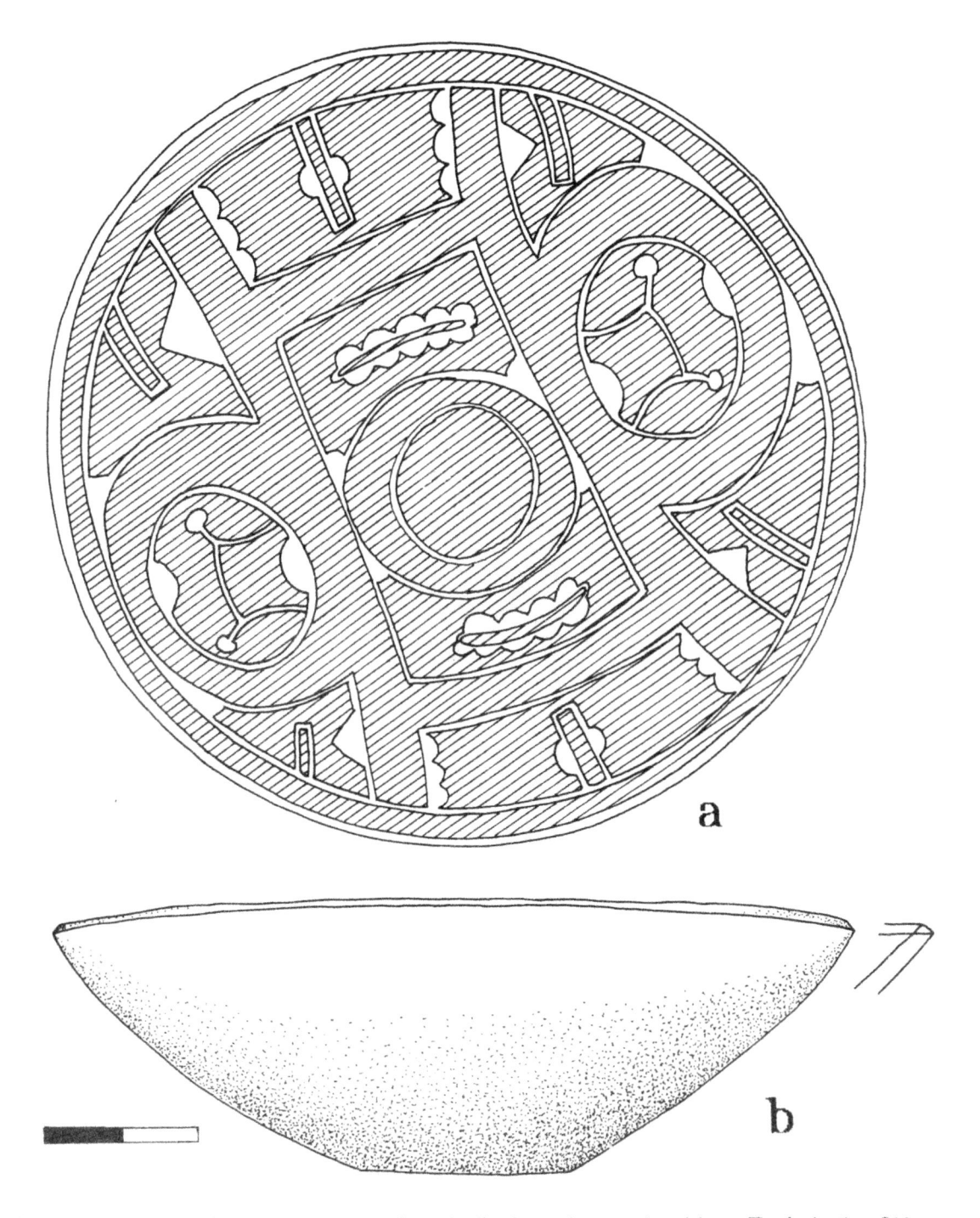

Figure 53. A "polychrome" Hacienda Grande flat-based, open bowl from Tecla in the CIA collections, UPR. An orange bath over the paste forms a third color. The other two are red and white. This vessel serves as the logo for the UPR's Centro de Investigaciones Arqueológicos (CIA), although with a few minor errors which are corrected in this slide projection tracing. (a) A plane view of the interior of the bowl with typical curvilinear HG decoration. (b) A profile view with rim enlargement.

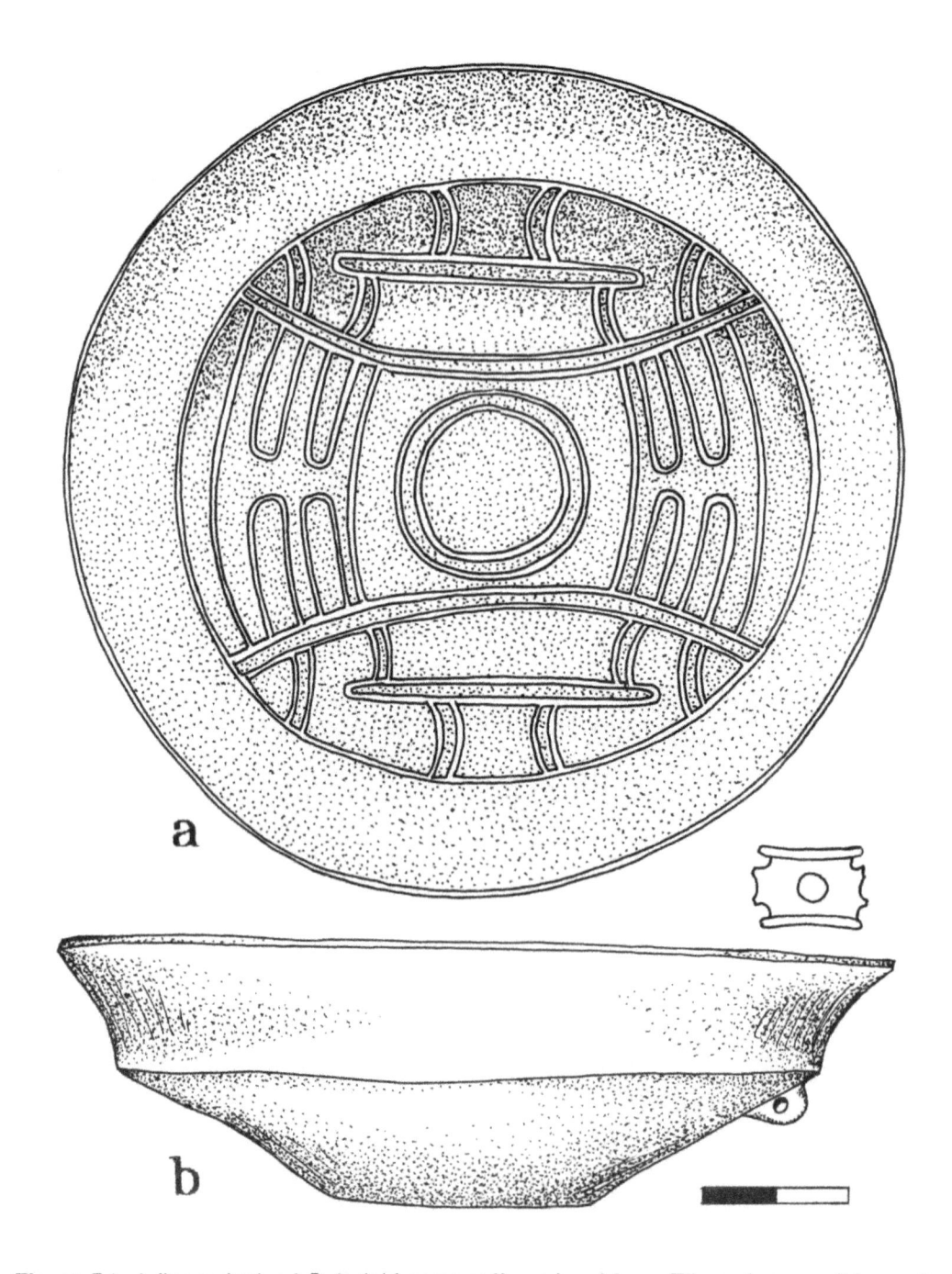

Figure 54. A linear incised Saladoid campaniform bowl from Tibes, from a slide projection tracing. An accurate cross-sectional drawing of this specimen can be found in González (1984). (a) A plane view of the interior of the bowl and its curious linear incised design. Note that it "kenns" the manta ray tray! Here is one type of vessel form portrayed schematically inside another, an unprecedented form of pictorial dualism. (b) A profile view of this vessel. Note the suspension nubbin.

PEOPLES AND CULTURES OF THE SALADOID FRONTIER
IN THE GREATER ANTILLES

Irving Rouse

ABSTRACT

The terms used by archaeologists to study peoples and cultures are defined and applied to the Saladoid frontier at the entry into the Greater Antilles. According to present evidence, this frontier lasted from 200 B.C. to A.D. 600. It was established by the Hacienda Grande people, whose ancestors had come from South America. Behind it lived the La Huecans, a divergent Saladoid population. Beyond it were the El Caimitos, an indigenous people that had apparently acquired pottery from the Hacienda Granders by the process of transculturation. During the second century A.D., Hacienda Grande culture expanded backward into La Hueca territory by means of acculturation and forward into El Caimito territory through population movement.

INTRODUCTION

Columbus encountered three ethnic groups in the West Indies: the Guanahatabeys (also known as Ciboneys) in western Cuba, the Tainos (alternatively called Arawaks) in the rest of the Greater Antilles and in the Bahamas, and the Island-Caribs in the southern part of the Lesser Antilles (Figure 1). The ethnohistorical evidence does not clearly indicate who inhabited the northern part of the Lesser Antilles, between the Tainos and the Island-Caribs.

Combined ethnohistorical and archaeological research has shown that the Guanahatabeys were a relict of the original Archaic age inhabitants of the archipelago. They still lived by food gathering, made their vessels of perishable materials rather than pottery, and were organized into bands rather than villages. They appear to have been pushed back into the far end of Cuba by the ancestors of the Tainos, who came from South America (Rouse l986:108-151).

The border zone, where the Tainos faced the Guanahatabeys, may be considered a frontier, like those subsequently established by the European settlers. It was occupied in the time of Columbus by the so-called Western Sub-Tainos, who extended from central Cuba into the Bahamas (Figure 2). The Classic Taino people lived back from the frontier in Hispaniola and Puerto Rico, with outliers on St. Croix Island in the American Virgins, Middle Caicos Island north of Haiti, and the eastern tip of Cuba. Allaire (1985a, 1985b) has inferred from the archaeological evidence that an Eastern Sub-Taino people occupied a second frontier in the northern part of the Lesser Antilles, separating the Classic Tainos from the Island-Caribs.

When encountered by Columbus, the Western and Eastern Sub-Tainos were in the Ceramic age (also known as Village Formative). They practiced agriculture and lived in relatively permanent villages, which have yielded no traces of public works. Each village was headed by a chief, who derived authority from personal deities known as *zemis*.

The Classic Taino people had advanced into the Formative age (alternatively called Temple Formative). These people constructed earth- and stone-lined plazas for use in public ceremonies and in ball games, kept figures of their zemis in the plazas and in temples constructed for the purpose, and were organized into hierarchical chiefdoms.

Elsewhere (Rouse 1983), I have traced the Taino/Guanahatabey frontier back into prehistory by following it along the boundary between the Ceramic and the Archaic ages on a chronological chart for the Greater Antilles (Figure 3). I found that it came into existence about A.D. 1000.

On the Greater Antillean chart and others for the Lesser Antilles and the adjacent mainland (Rouse 1983:Figures 2-4), I observed four previous Ceramic/Archaic age frontiers (Figure 4). Frontier 1, dating from the second millennium B.C., stood at the head of the Orinoco Delta. Frontier 2, which succeeded it during the first millennium B.C., was situated on the Guiana coast and in Trinidad. Frontier 3 emerged around the time of Christ on the east coast of Venezuela and in Puerto Rico. It was followed during the latter part of the first millennium A.D. by Frontier 4 on the eastern tip of Cuba. The historic frontier is fifth in the sequence.

This paper is concerned with Frontier 3, where the ancestors of the Tainos halted after reaching the Greater Antilles. It attempts to expand our knowledge of the peoples who lived on or near that frontier by delimiting them in time and space, comparing their cultures, and reconstructing their ancestries.

TERMINOLOGY

As used here, the term *people* refers to all the individuals who lived in a small, culturally homogenous area during a single, culturally defined period. A people is thus a human population, so tightly delimited in space and time that it may be said to have had a single culture.

Peoples are alternatively called *cultural groups* in order to distinguish them from *ethnic* and *social groups*. The three are defined differently: peoples by their cultures, ethnic groups by the cultural, linguistic, and/or racial traits through which their members identified themselves, and social groups by their personnel, organization, and functions. Consequently, each kind of group has to be studied separately, as in Figures 1 and 2.

We cannot expect to be able to identify the ethnic groups of Frontier 3. We lack written documents from which to infer the ways in which the West Indians divided themselves around the time of Christ.

On the other hand, cultural and social groups can and should be inferred from the archaeological remains of the time (Rouse 1986:3-13). The two need to be differentiated in the interest of clarity. Each people is organized into a variety of social groups, such as families, chiefdoms, and war parties, through which it carries out its activities. Some social groupings, such as trade networks, may extend beyond the boundaries of a people, defined as a local population; some may survive its demise.[1]

Each people has an overall set of artifacts, customs, and beliefs, which we call its *culture*, *focus*, or *phase*, and which we contrast with its *language*. Each social group, on the contrary, has a more limited range of cultural and linguistic traits, depending upon its composition and functions. The group's cultural traits are collectively known as its *subculture*.

A people and its culture may be viewed as the opposite sides of a coin, the people being the bearers of the culture (Rouse 1972:Figure 7). The relationship between a people and its culture is, however, more variable than the simile of a coin would indicate. Foreign individuals and social groups may move into a people's territory, become assimilated, and adopt its culture. If they move in large numbers, they may introduce enough of their own traits to produce a new culture or they may assimilate the local people and replace its culture with their own. Always, the nature of a people is determined by its culture. Whenever, therefore, a local population acquires a new culture, it becomes a new people.

A people's culture should not be confused with its *ceramic style* (alternatively called a *ceramic complex*). The latter concept was introduced from Peruvian into Caribbean archaeology by Howard (1947). It refers to the entire ceramic repertoire of a people, that is, to all the attributes of material, shape, and decoration that a local population built into its pottery during a single cultural period. Each style is defined by a unique set of attributes, which may also be used to identify its area and period and the people and culture who occupied them.

Caribbeanists have found ceramic styles to be particularly effective in identifying the peoples and cultures of the Ceramic and Formative ages because the artifactual assemblages of these ages consist mostly of potsherds. As in Peru, the styles and their peoples and cultures are plotted on chronological charts in order to determine their spatial and temporal boundaries. The plotting is based jointly upon the results of site surveys, stratigraphic excavation, seriation, and radiometric measurement.

The peoples in a chart who are reasonably contiguous and who resemble each other in style and culture are grouped into series and subseries, the series being designated by the suffix -oid and the subseries by the suffix -an. These heuristic devices enable us to identify local populations that shared a common heritage and to study the nature of their relationships.

Each style is divisible into *modes*, which are kinds of ceramic features, and *types*, which are kinds of pots and/or sherds. The types may be grouped into *wares* (also known as *series* of *types*). In addition, more widely distributed complexes of technological and stylistic norms, which we call *traditions* (or *horizons* if they are horizontal on a chronological chart), are inferred from the distributions of the modes, types, and wares. Like a ceramic style, each of these kinds of units is defined by a unique set of attributes of material, shape, and/or decoration. The attributes diagnostic of a mode, type, ware, or tradition, however, serve to identify the pottery, whereas the attributes diagnostic of a ceramic style identify the populations that produced the pottery (Rouse 1972:cf. Figures 4, 7).

Modes, types, wares, and traditions often extend from one style to another, cutting across the divisions of a chronological chart. They may be viewed as traits, capable of spreading from one style, people, and culture to another, through space, through time, or in both dimensions.

Caribbeanists refer to the spread of traits in this manner as *transculturation* (Ortiz 1947:ix-xiii). That process has to be distinguished from *population movement*, in which a foreign people displaces or assimilates the local people, and *acculturation*, in which the foreign people transmits its culture to the local people (Rouse 1986:11-12). Whole cultures, rather than individual traits, change in the latter two cases.

Traits such as modes, types, wares, and traditions can be inferred directly from one's archaeological remains, regardless of their proveniences. Ceramic styles, the peoples and cultures who possessed them, and their series and subseries must instead be inferred from the context of the specimens within sites, by comparing the assemblages of artifacts, ecofacts, and other features to be found there. Consequently, Willey, DiPeso, Ritchie, Rouse, Rowe, and Lathrap (1956:7-8) have coined the term *site-unit* to refer to styles, peoples and cultures, and series and subseries. They contrast this term with *trait-unit*, which denotes modes, types, wares, and traditions.[2]

The distinction between site- and trait-units is fundamental, and failure to recognize it has been the source of much confusion. For example, it is misleading to apply the simile of a coin to peoples and cultures without qualifying the comparison, as I have done above, because coins are trait-units, peoples and cultures are site-units, and the two change differently, as discussed in the Conclusions.

THE FRONTIER PEOPLES IN PUERTO RICO

Distributions

Our original radiocarbon measurements indicated that Frontier 3 was established in Puerto Rico during the second century A.D. (Rouse 1982a:Figure I). More recent measurements have pushed this event back into the second century B.C. (Rouse and Alegría 1989:Table 8). At that time, the Hacienda Grande people and culture made its appearance on the northern, western, and southern coasts of Puerto Rico and there established the new frontier (Figure 5). Evidence to be discussed below indicates that the Hacienda Granders subsequently advanced onto the eastern tip of Hispaniola, expanding the frontier through the rest of the Mona Passage area (Figure 3, top).

Behind the frontier, in the Vieques Passage area comprising Vieques Island and the eastern coast of Puerto Rico (Figure 5), lived the La Hueca people, who differed in culture (Chanlatte Baik 1981; Rodríguez and Rivera 1987). Still farther back, across the passage between Vieques and the Virgin Islands, were the Prosperity people, with a third culture (Morse, this volume).

According to the latest radiocarbon evidence (Rouse and Alegría 1989:Table 9), the La Hueca people arose in the Vieques Passage area during the second century B.C., simultaneously with Hacienda Grande people in the Mona Passage area, and gave way to the latter during the third century A.D. (Figures 3, 6). The Prosperity people is not so well dated, but may tentatively be said to have been contemporaneous with the entire span of the Hacienda Grande population (Morse, this volume).

Comparisons

The stylistic and cultural affiliations of the Hacienda Grande, La Hueca, and Prosperity peoples are indicated in the accompanying chronological chart by different kinds of shading (Figure 3). All three obviously belong to the Saladoid series because they resemble each other so closely. Their pottery is alike in paste, temper, and surface treatment; and they share numerous modes of shape and decoration, such as annular and flat bases, concavo-convex profiles, perforated lumps for suspending the vessels, rim flanges and tabs, peg-topped D-shaped handles, white and red paint, zoned incised crosshatching, and early Saladoid modeled-incised designs (Morse, this volume; Roe, this volume). They also share most types of artifacts, including bowls, bottles, griddles, incense burners, inhalers, stone and shell celts, three-pointed "zemis," and beads and amulets carved in stone, shell, and mother-of-pearl. Moreover, they have essentially the same settlement and subsistence patterns (cf., Chanlatte Baik and Narganes Storde 1983; Morse, this volume; Siegel, this volume).

Roe (this volume) has found through grammatical analysis that the Hacienda Grande and La Hueca styles are variations on a single theme. Statistical comparison of the two peoples in terms of their functional as well as their stylistic traits (as in Goodwin 1979 and Wilson 1987) is needed to determine whether the overall relationship between the two cultures is equally close. It would also be well to apply both procedures to the Prosperity style and culture as a control.

The Hacienda Grande and Prosperity styles have been grouped together in the Cedrosan division of the Saladoid series because both have its diagnostic combination of plainware, painted ware, and zic ware. (Zic is an acronym for zoned incised crosshatching.) The La Hueca style is assigned to a different, Huecan subseries because, while its plainware is similar, it lacks painted ware. Its potters used white and red paint only to fill the incisions in their zic ware. (For illustrations of the decorated wares, see Chanlatte Baik 1983.)

The two La Hueca-style sites, Sorcé and Punta Candelero, are also distinguished by bird-head pendants elaborately carved from an exotic kind of stone (Chanlatte Baik 1983:Plates 22-A, 22-B). Miguel Rodríguez López (personal communication 1988) has obtained evidence of their manufacture at Punta Candelero.[3] The only other known example comes from an indeterminate context in Trinidad (Fewkes 1907:Plate 56,*b*). Pendants of this type may have been objects of trade.

Ancestries

We should be able to reconstruct the ancestry of the Hacienda Grande and Prosperity styles, their peoples, and their cultures by studying the distribution of the Cedrosan Saladoid subseries, to which they belong. That subseries extends from Suriname (formerly Dutch Guiana) through Trinidad and Tobago in two directions: northward via the Lesser and the Greater Antilles into the Mona Passage area, and westward along the Venezuelan coast to Margarita Island (Figure 4). In both directions, it ends in Frontier 3.

Arie Boomert (personal communication 1983) has suggested that the Cedrosan Saladoid subseries arose on the Guiana coastal plain just east of the Orinoco Delta, and I have concluded that it radiated from there via Trinidad and Tobago, northward into the Antilles and westward along the coast of Venezuela (Rouse 1986:136-139). The hypothesis of origin in the Guianas needs further testing, but the northward and westward radiations have been validated by radiometric and stratigraphic analyses, as follows.

Two radiocarbon dates are known for Cedros, the type style in Trinidad. They indicate that the subseries arrived there before the time of Christ (Tables 1, 2). This conclusion is confirmed by the presence of Cedrosan Saladoid trade sherds in deposits of Barrancas-style pottery on the lower Orinoco River, dating from the first millennium B.C. Intrusive examples of the subseries' plain, painted, and zic wares have all been found in Barrancas-style assemblages.[4]

Three islands on the route north from Trinidad have yielded dates before the time of Christ (Table 1). It may be inferred from these dates that the Cedrosan Saladoid advance reached Martinique sometime between 530 and 150 B.C., Montserrat between 440 and 170 B.C., and St. Martin between 325 and 300 B.C.

The Martinique dates are the most convincing because they are products of an extensive series of thermoluminescence as well as radiocarbon measurements. Schvoerer et al. (1985:Table 5) conclude that the initial "Arawak Horizon I" occupation began about 200 B.C.[5] Research on the volcanic stratigraphy of Martinique is still inconclusive but supports their conclusion (Allaire, this volume).

The two dates from the Trant's site on Montserrat Island are the weakest (Table 1). They are 520 years apart, yet both come from the same Level 5 (David R. Watters, personal communication 1988). The accompanying trio of Radio Antilles dates are from a deeper level, 9, and are clustered between the fifth and the second centuries B.C. The two St. Martin dates, which are also from the bottom of their deposit, fall in the middle of that range (Haviser 1988:25).

If the overall pattern of B.C. dates is correct, the Cedrosan Saladoid peoples moved northward from Trinidad during the third century B.C. This agrees nicely with the evidence cited above that the Hacienda Granders, with whom the migration ended, arrived in Puerto Rico during the second century B.C.

The initial dates along the westward route are much later: A.D. 270 for Irapa on the Güiria Peninsula and A.D. 155 for El Mayal in the Carúpano area (Table 2). No dates are available for Margarita and its satellite islands, at the end of the western route, but Cedrosan Saladoid trade sherds have been found in a terminal Archaic age deposit on those islands, indicating that the subseries arrived there last of all, presumably after A.D. 300 (Rouse and Cruxent 1963:Figure 28).

The ancestry of the La Hueca style, people, and culture remains to be discussed. Only one other style can currently be assigned to the Huecan Saladoid subseries: Río Guapo in the Río Chico area of central Venezuela, beyond the end of the westward radiation of the Cedrosan Saladoid peoples (Rouse and Cruxent 1963:108-110).

Assignment of the Río Guapo style to the Huecan Saladoid subseries has been questioned because of an uncertainty about the nature of its pottery. According to its discoverer, José M. Cruxent (personal communication 1955), the pottery may have originally had painted designs and these may have been destroyed by unusually high ground water, as happened elsewhere in the Venezuelan Llanos. However, a true lack of painted ware is indicated by the nature of Río Guapo-style trade sherds in assemblages of El Palito-style pottery from a better drained area farther west. These sherds have only zic designs (Cruxent and Rouse 1958-59:86).

Assuming the Huecan Saladoid identification to be correct, Chanlatte Baik (1981:15) has inferred from it that there was a "Guapoid" or "Huecoid" migration from the central Venezuelan coast to Vieques Island. Such a migration would have had to proceed directly across the Caribbean Sea, since no Huecan Saladoid pottery has been found on any of the intervening islands. I doubt that the Río Guapo people possessed either the ability or the incentive to travel so far overseas in the absence of sails, which made long voyages possible in other parts of the world (Watters and Rouse, this volume).

More importantly, the Río Guapo style has a radiocarbon date of A.D. 320, and this is confirmed by measurements of A.D. 310 and A.D. 335 for the deposits of El Palito-style pottery farther west that have yielded zic-ware trade sherds (Table 3). Río Guapo is thus too recent to be ancestral to La Hueca.

Migration or the erosion of painted designs are not the only possible explanations for the similarities between the Río Guapo and La Hueca pottery. The two styles may have developed independently at the ends of the westward and northward radiations of the Cedrosan Saladoid subseries, in each case by abandonment of the latter's painted ware and retention of its plain and zic wares.

Further research in the Río Guapo area is needed to test the hypothesis of abandonment in the west.[6] The question of abandonment in the north is currently being investigated at the Hope Estate site on St. Martin. Several areas in that site have been found to contain only plain and zic wares. The assemblages from these areas are currently being radiocarbon dated in an effort to determine whether or not they are contemporaneous with the plain, painted, and zic ware assemblages that had previously been dated (Jay Haviser, personal communication 1988).[7]

If the variable distribution of painted ware at Hope Estate is not due to sampling error, that is, to work with assemblages that contain too few examples of painted and zic wares to yield meaningful results, the variability may indicate that one or more resident social groups had abandoned painted ware, creating a new subculture, and were about to move to Vieques Island, thereby transforming that subculture into the La Hueca culture. Alternatively, immigrants from South America may have introduced a new subculture or culture. I doubt that they did, for the following reasons.

It has recently become clear that the traditions of white-on-red painting and zic incision originated in different parts of the tropical lowlands, the former probably in the Orinoco Valley and the latter possibly in Amazonia (Rouse 1986:134-136; Pettijean Roget 1987). Present evidence indicates that the two traditions came together among the Cedrosan Saladoid peoples of the Dutch, British, and Venezuelan Guianas, who combined them with other ceramic traits to form a unique complex of plain, painted, and zic wares. Painted ware seems to have been dominant in this ceramic mix, just as one language or society is dominant in instances of linguistic or social plurality (Rouse 1985).

We have long known that the Cedrosan Saladoid potters carried their plurality of plain, painted, and zic wares with them as they radiated through Trinidad and Tobago into the Antilles and onto the east coast of Venezuela, and we have used this plurality to trace their expansion. Now we must address the question what happened to the plurality. The most obvious possibilities are abandonment of either painted or zic ware. We might expect the latter to have been dropped first, since the former was dominant in the mix. However, the first peoples known to have changed the mix, La Hueca in the north and Río Guapo in the west, both abandoned painted ware, thereby forming the Huecan subseries. Some time passed before the remaining Cedrosan peoples made the opposite choice, dropping zic ware and developing, for example, the Cuevas style in Puerto Rico and the Dominican Republic, which is terminal Saladoid (Figure 3).

If the original Huecan-Cedrosan divergence should be shown to have taken place in St. Martin, we would be able to say that peoples of both subseries participated in the subsequent Saladoid advance, the Huecans colonizing the Vieques Sound area and the Cedrosans the rest of Puerto Rico and the eastern tip of Hispaniola (Figure 3). It is not yet clear whether Huecans as well as Cedrosans settled in the Virgin Islands (Morse, this volume).

The La Hueca and Hacienda Grande peoples shared far too many of their ceramic and cultural traits for their ancestors to have diverged in South America. For example, both had the custom of feasting on crabs, which has not definitely been found south of Guadeloupe (Louis Allaire, personal communication 1989). The divergence must have taken place somewhere within the interaction sphere at the northern end of the migration route, among local populations who retained most of the traits of their Cedrosan ancestors because they had only recently separated and were still in close enough contact to mutually reinforce their ancestral heritage. It would therefore be advisable to search for other Huecan styles in the north, especially on the Virgin Islands, to date them, and to compare them in detail with the local Cedrosan styles in order to determine exactly where the divergence took place.

If the radiocarbon measurements for the Sorcé site are to be believed, the Hacienda Grande style spread back into the Vieques Passage area, against the flow of migration, during the third century A.D. (Rouse and Alegría 1989:Table 9). What caused this event? Hacienda Grande people may have moved in and assimilated the local population, or else the local potters may have been influenced by their neighbors to resume the production of painted ware. The last alternative is favored by an overlapping of the dates for the two styles at the Sorcé site (Figure 6) and by the survival of bird-head pendants into the Hacienda Grande period at Sorcé (Chanlatte Baik 1983:Plate 47-A).[8]

In drawing the foregoing conclusion, I may have overestimated the degree of similarity between the Hacienda Grande assemblages and the later Sorcé assemblages. Comparison of the two groups of assemblages with each other and with the Prosperity-style assemblages from the Virgin Islands might reveal enough differences among the three to justify treating the later occupation of the Sorcé site as a separate style, people, and culture within the Cedrosan Saladoid subseries. It could be called Sorcé.

THE FRONTIER PEOPLES IN HISPANIOLA

The westernmost occurrence of the Hacienda Grande style is at La Caleta near La Romana, across the Mona Passage from Puerto Rico (Figure 7). A radiocarbon date of ca. A.D. 240 (Rouse et al.1985:Table 4) indicates that Hacienda Granders settled there about the same time that their style spread eastward to Vieques (Figure 3). The westward expansion of the style must be due to population movement, for the La Caleta site has yielded no traces of admixture with the previous culture in the area.

That previous culture also had pottery, belonging to a style known as El Caimito (Figures 3, 7). It consists of simple hemispherical bowls with crude strap handles, rudimentary modeling, and curvilinear incised lines ending in punctations (Veloz Maggiolo et al. 1974:14,18-21). The excavators have obtained five radiocarbon dates ranging from 305 B.C.to A.D.120 (Rímoli and Nadal 1980:23).

A measurement of 360 B.C. from the rock shelter of Honduras del Oeste in the city of Santo Domingo, has also been attributed to the El Caimito culture by Rímoli and Nadal (1980:23). However, Morbán Laucer (1979:Table 2) reports that this date comes from a preceramic assemblage. Evidently, it was laid down by the El Porvenir people, belonging to the Casimiran Casimiroid subseries of the Archaic age (Figure 3). El Porvenir types found with it include long flint blades, double-bitted stone axes, and a stone vessel decorated with rectilinear incised designs and punctations (Rímoli and Nadal 1980:19-20).

A few potsherds were encountered in another, presumably later part of the same site. The excavators consider them to be trade ware (Rímoli and Nadal 1980:22). They are probably from the El Caimito people, who had arisen farther east in the meantime.

The El Caimito style is an enigma. I originally deferred judgement on it (Rouse 1982a:Figure 1) because its dates were much earlier than the then accepted dates for the first appearance of pottery in Puerto Rico and were based upon shell samples, which are considered less reliable than the charcoal samples used in Puerto Rico. Meggers and Evans (1983:Figure 7.11), on the other hand, thought it might be an offshoot of the Malambo style in Colombia. This assumes that the Malambo people established a colony on the island of Hispaniola, or that they transmitted elements of their style to the Hispaniolan Indians by interacting with them. Neither assumption makes sense to me because both would have required long overseas voyages against the prevailing winds and currents.

The El Caimito style needs to be reevaluated in the light of the new dates for the beginning of the Ceramic age in Puerto Rico. They make the Hacienda Grande and El Caimito styles contemporaneous and raise the possiblity of transculturation between the two styles.

Transculturation seems to me a better explanation of the situation than overseas diffusion from Colombia. Hacienda Grande pottery displays all the El Caimito traits noted above. They appear in cruder form on El Caimito pottery, as if they had been made by novices. The local, Courian Casimiroid artisans would have found it easier to copy Hacienda Grande modeling and incision than its painted and zic designs. Moreover, they would have been predisposed towards pottery in general and incision and punctation in particular by their tradition of making, incising, and punctating stone vessels, which began well before the time of Christ according to a recent radiocarbon measurement (Rouse 1982b:Plate 2,*E*; Rouse et al. 1985:Table 4).

The El Caimito pottery is accompanied by Casimiroid types of stone, bone, and shell artifacts (Veloz Maggiolo et al. l974:3-4). The only exceptions known to me are stone celts, which the El Caimito people may have obtained from the Hacienda Granders by trade. The settlement and subsistence patterns of the El Caimito people are likewise Casimiroid. Sites are relatively small, are often situated in the interior on rocky escarpments rich in wild plants and animals, and they lack clay griddles that would indicate the presence of agriculture (Veloz Maggiolo et al.1974:1-2). By contrast, the Malamboid peoples of Colombia and western Venezuela lived in large agricultural villages (Arvelo B. 1987).

CONCLUSIONS

Archaeologists who find similarities in culture between peoples in the West Indies and on the mainland frequently jump to the conclusion that the islanders migrated from the mainland, without considering other possible explanations for the similarities: (1) inheritance of traits from a common ancestor or (2) transculturation. The La Hueca and El Caimito peoples are cases in point. Both have been thought to have migrated from South America, but the evidence reviewed here indicates that they developed on either side of the Saladoid frontier in the Greater Antilles, as follows:

1. While La Hueca pottery is like that of Río Guapo in Venezuela, its makers cannot have come from there because their radiocarbon dates are much earlier than the Río Guapo dates. Instead, the two ceramic styles appear to be offshoots of successive Cedrosan Saladoid radiations from Trinidad: La Hueca, of a radiation northward through the Lesser Antilles during the first centuries B.C.; and Río Guapo, of a radiation westward along the coast of Venezuela during the first centuries A.D.

2. El Caimito pottery resembles that of Hacienda Grande in Puerto Rico as well as that of Malambo in Colombia. The latest radiometric evidence indicates that the three styles were contemporaneous. Since the non-ceramic traits accompanying El Caimito pottery are more like those of the local Archaic age, that pottery is better attributed to transculturation across the Saladoid frontier in the Greater Antilles than to overseas migration from Colombia.

Elsewhere (Rouse 1986:16,106), I have suggested that West Indian archaeology suffers from a "colonialist" bias. We have tended to project back into prehistory our ancestors' experience in introducing Western civilization to the islands, without giving sufficient thought to the alternative possibility of local development.

For example, Lovén (1935:2) simplistically assumed that the three ethnic groups encountered by Columbus, Guanahatabeys, Tainos, and Island-Caribs, all came from the mainland. He could have been right only if all three had reached the islands too recently to have been able to change their ethnic identities afterwards. Radiometric dating has proved him wrong; ethnic groups that arrived in the West Indies before the time of Christ can hardly have survived until the Historic age.

The colonialist bias has been reinforced by a tendency to base studies of population movement on trait- rather than site-units (see Terminology). Many Caribbeanists infer migrations from the distributions of individual modes, types, wares, and/or traditions. This procedure informs us about the origins of the traits, not about the ancestries of the populations who possessed them. To learn about ancestries, we must work instead with site-units, that is, with the peoples' styles of pottery, their cultures, and their series and subseries of styles and cultures.

For example, recent attempts to trace the Hacienda Grande and La Hueca peoples back to South America in terms of painted and zic wares respectively have shown only that both wares came from the Guiana coastal plain. To determine the origins of the two peoples, one must work instead with their entire ceramic styles and their total cultures. This procedure has demonstrated that both peoples developed in the Greater Antilles.

Similarly, Meggers and Evans (1983:307) have defined the term *Saladoid* solely by the presence of white-on-red painted pottery. They acknowledge that their definition is a departure from the original usage of the term. In effect, they have introduced a new meaning in order to be able to study the distribution of the Saladoid tradition of painting and to demonstrate its diffusion from the mainland. Persons interested in the peopling of the islands must work instead with the Saladoid series of styles and cultures and with its pertinent subseries, Cedrosan and Huecan.

The colonialist bias has also been reinforced by a misconception about the nature of human migrations. As noted above, we have tended to regard peoples and cultures as opposite sides of coins, able to move without change as coins do. On the contrary, a people is characterized by a variable set of practices, customs, and beliefs (Rouse 1972:Figure 11). As it moves, it selectively modifies these traits and thereby becomes differentiated into new peoples (Rouse 1986:175-182).

The process of differentiation is known as *divergent evolution* (Flannery and Marcus 1983). It is well illustrated by the proliferation of Saladoid peoples and cultures in the West Indies. The individuals and social groups who colonized each island or passage area adapted to its differing resources.[9] They also interacted more strongly among themselves than with their neighbors. Consequently, each local population developed its own unique set of cultural traits and thereby became a new people.

The La Hueca and Hacienda Grande peoples evolved in this manner during the course of the Saladoid expansion from the Lesser Antilles into Puerto Rico. The colonizers of the Vieques Sound area, at the entrance to Puerto Rico, became isolated in that area, where they were able to continue their previous adaptation to the small islands of the Lesser Antilles and consequently to develop the relatively rich La Hueca culture. The colonizers of the main part of Puerto Rico and the eastern tip of Hispaniola had to adapt to the differing resources and denser Archaic age populations in the large islands of the Greater Antilles. Under these frontier conditions, they developed the Hacienda Grande culture.

The La Huecans chose to forgo painted ware in favor of zic ware. By so doing, they became part of a new, Huecan Saladoid subseries. The Hacienda Granders and their immediate ancestors, the Prosperity people, chose to retain both zic and painted wares. As a result, they remained in the Cedrosan Saladoid subseries.

The Hacienda Granders became dominant with the passsage of time, presumably because they lived in a much larger area with more natural resources. Jointly with the Prosperity people, they influenced the La Hueca population to resume the production of painted ware, thereby causing that population to become acculturated to the Hacienda Grande culture, if not to a new culture within the Cedrosan Saladoid subseries.

Turning from the problem of selective inheritance of Saladoid traits to that of transculturation across the Saladoid frontier, I would note that this, too, resulted in divergence. The part of the Archaic age El Porvenir population that lived closest to the frontier, just across the Mona Passage from the Hacienda Grande people, developed its own El Caimito style of pottery under influence from the Hacienda Granders, and as a result separated itself from the rest of the El Porvenir people farther west in Hispaniola, who continued without pottery except for vessels that the El Caimito people traded to it.

In the chronological chart (Figure 3), I have had to assign the El Caimito people to the Ceramic age because of its ability to make pottery. Yet that people had a typically Archaic culture. This should not surprise us. Human populations are affected by the cultural as well as the natural conditions to which they are exposed.[10] If, therefore, a people of an earlier age encounters a people of a later age on a frontier where the two ages come together, the people of either age may adopt the traits of the other age that it finds useful.

Caribbean archaeologists have paid too little attention to the process of divergent evolution. It is not enough simply to plot the distributions of peoples' traits on maps in order to draw conclusions about the diffusion of traits. We should also be studying the genesis of each people and its culture. The questions to be answered include not only whence came the peoples' traits but also when, where, how, and why their cultures evolved from each other (Rouse 1972:Figure 6).

NOTES

1. In other words, peoples are chronological units, delimited in the dimensions of space and time, while societies are functional units, delimited in the dimension of form (Rouse 1972:Figure 1).

2. Willey et al. (1956:7-8) refer to the spread of traits from one culture to another as *trait-unit intrusion* and to the spread of one culture into the area of another as *site-unit intrusion*. The former term is synonymous with transculturation; the latter includes both population movement and acculturation.

3. I am indebted to Rodríguez López and his wife Virginia Rivera for showing me their Punta Candelero excavations and for sharing their conclusions with me.

4. Sanoja Obediente (1979:285) reports the presence of plainware trade sherds in his Barrancas-style assemblages. Karl Taube (personal communication 1985) has found examples of both painted and zic wares in previously unstudied Barrancas-style assemblages excavated by Cruxent and Rouse (I958-59:1:213-214).

5. My thanks are due to Louis Allaire for calling this reference to my attention.

6. Unfortunately, Cruxent was only able to obtain a small collection of potsherds from the Río Guapo site. It gives us an incomplete picture of the style and tells us little about the overall culture. Miguel Rodríguez López (personal communication 1988) has investigated the possibility of revisting the site in search of additional information. Based on discussions with people who know the area he reports that nothing is left there.

7. I would like to express my appreciation to Jay Haviser for keeping me informed about the progress of the Hope Estate research.

8. The significance of this information was pointed out to me by Ricardo E. Alegría.

9. For a discussion of the diversity of resources in the West Indies, see Watters and Rouse (this volume).

10. The El Caimito people may be said to have adapted to a change in the cultural conditions under which they lived. For an example of a people's adaptation to differences in natural conditions, see Veloz Maggiolo (I983:18).

REFERENCES CITED

Allaire, Louis
    1985a   The Archaelogy of the Caribbean. In *The Atlas of Archaeology*, edited by Christine Flon, pp. 370-371. G.K. Hall, Boston.

    1985b Some Comments on the Ethnic Identity of the Taino-Carib Frontier. In *Ethnicity and Culture*, edited by R. Auger, M.F. Glass, S. MacEachern, and P.H. McCartney, pp.127-133. Archaeological Association, University of Calgary, Calgary.

Arvelo B., Lilliam M.
    1987   *Un modelo de poblamiento prehispánico para la Cuenca del Lago de Maracaibo*. Unpublished Master's thesis, Department of Anthropology, Instituto Venezolano de Investigaciones Científicas, Caracas.

Chanlatte Baik, Luis A.
    1981   *La Hueca y Sorcé (Vieques, Puerto Rico): Primeras migraciones agroalfareras Antillanas: Nuevo esquema para los procesos culturales de la arqueología Antillana*. Privately printed, Santo Domingo.

    1983   *Catálogo arqueología de Vieques: Exposición del 13 de Marzo al 22 de Abril de 1983*. Museo de Antropología, Historia y Arte, Universidad de Puerto Rico, Río Piedras.

Chanlatte Baik, Luis A. and Yvonne M. Narganes Storde
    1983   *Vieques-Puerto Rico: Asiento de una nueva cultura aborigen Antillana*. Privately printed, Santo Domingo.

Cruxent, José M. and Irving Rouse
    1958-1959 *An Archeological Chronology of Venezuela*. Pan American Union, Social Science Monographs No. 6. 2 vols. Washington, D.C.

Fewkes, Jesse Walter
    1907   *The Aborigines of Porto Rico and Neighboring Islands*. Bureau of American Ethnology Bulletin No. 25. Smithsonian Institution, 1903-1904, pp.1-220. Government Printing Office, Washington, D.C.

Flannery, Kent V. and Joyce Marcus, editors
    1983   *The Cloud People: Divergent Evolution of the Aztec and Mixtec Civilizations*. Academic Press, New York.

Goodwin, R. Christopher
    1979   *The Prehistoric Cultural Ecology of St. Kitts, West Indies: A Case Study in Island Archeology*. Ph.D. dissertation, Arizona State University. University Microfilms, Ann Arbor.

Haviser, Jay B., Jr.
    1988   *An Archaeological Survey of Sint Maarten/Saint Martin*. Reports of the Archaeological/Anthropological Institute of the Netherlands Antilles No.7. Willemstad, Curaçao.

Howard, George D.
    1947   *Prehistoric Ceramic Styles of Lowland South America, Their Distribution and History*. Yale University Publications in Anthropology No. 37. New Haven.

Lovén, Sven
    1935   *Origins of the Tainan Culture, West Indies.* Elanders Bokfryckeri Äkfiebolag, Göteborg.

Meggers, Betty J. and Clifford Evans
    1983   Lowland South America and the Antilles. In *Ancient South Americans*, edited by Jesse D. Jennings, pp. 287-335. W.H. Freeman, San Francisco.

Morbán Laucer, Fernando
    1979   Cronología del radiocarbono (C-14) para la isla de Santo Domingo. *Boletín del Museo del Hombre Dominicano* 12:l47-159.

Ortiz, Fernando
    1947   *Cuban Counterpart: Tobacco and Sugar.* Translated by Harriet de Onis. Alfred A. Knopf, New York.

Petitjean Roget, Henri
    1987   A propos d'un collier funeraire, Morel Guadeloupe, les Huecoids sont-ils un mythe. Paper presented at the 12th International Congress of Caribbean Archaeology, Cayenne, French Guiana.

Rímoli, Renato O. and Joaquín E. Nadal
    1980   Cerámica temprana de Honduras del Oeste. *Boletín del Museo del Hombre Dominicano* 15:17-81.

Rodríguez, Miguel and Virginia Rivera
    1987   Puerto Rico and the Caribbean Pre-Saladoid "Crosshatch Connection." Paper presented at the 12th International Congress of Caribbean Archaeology, Cayenne, French Guiana.

Rouse, Irving
    1972   *Introduction to Prehistory: A Systematic Approach.* McGraw-Hill, New York. Republished in 1983 as *Introducción a la prehistoria: un enfoque sistemático.* Translated by María José Aubet Semmler. Ediciones Bellaterra, Barcelona.

    1982a Ceramic and Religious Development in the Greater Antilles. *Journal of New World Archaeology* 5:45-55.

    1982b The Olsen Collection from Ile à Vache, Haiti. *The Florida Anthropologist* 35(4):169-185.

    1983   La frontera Taína: Su prehistoria y sus precursores. In *Las culturas de América en la época del descubrimiento: Seminario sobre la investigación de la cultura Taína*, pp.25-36. Comisión Nacional para la Celebración del V Centenario del Descubrimiento de América, Madrid.

    1985   Social, Linguistic, and Stylistic Plurality in the West Indies. Paper presented at the 11th International Congress for Caribbean Archaeology, San Juan, Puerto Rico.

    1986   *Migrations in Prehistory: Inferring Population Movement from Cultural Remains.* Yale University Press, New Haven.

    1987   Origin and Development of the Indians Discovered by Columbus. *Proceedings of the San Salvador Conference on Columbus and His World* 1:293-312. Bahamian Field

Station, San Salvador, Bahamas.

Rouse, Irving, and José M. Cruxent
   1963   *Venezuelan Archaeology*. Yale University Press, New Haven.

Rouse, Irving and Louis Allaire
   1978   Caribbean. In *Chronologies in New World Archaeology*, edited by R. E. Taylor and Clement W. Meighan, pp. 431-481. Academic Press, New York.

Rouse, Irving, Louis Allaire, and Aad Boomert
   1985   Eastern Venezuela, the Guianas, and the West Indies. Ms. prepared for an unpublished volume, *Chronologies in South American Archaeology*, compiled by Clement W. Meighan, Department of Anthropology, University of California, Los Angeles.

Rouse, Irving and Ricardo E. Alegría
   1989   *Excavations at María de la Cruz and Hacienda Grande, Loiza, Puerto Rico*. Yale University Publications in Anthropology, New Haven, in press.

Sanoja Obediente, Mario
   1979   *Las culturas formativas del Oriente de Venezuela: La tradición Barrancas del Bajo Orinoco*. Biblioteca de la Academia Nacional de la Historia No. 6. Caracas.

Schvoerer, Max, P. Guibert, F. Bechtel, Mario Mattioni, and J. Evin
   1985   Des hommes en Martinique vingt siecles avant Christophe Colomb? *Proceedings of the International Congress for the Study of the Pre-Columbian Cultures of the Lesser Antilles* 10:369-397. Montréal.

Veloz Maggiolo, Marcio
   1983   Para una definición de la cultura Taína. In *Las culturas de América en la época del descubrimiento: Seminario sobre la investigación de la cultura Taína*, pp. 15-21. Comisión Nacional para la Celebración del V Centenario del Descubrimiento de América, Madrid.

Veloz Maggiolo, Marcio, Elpidio Ortega, and Plinio Pina P.
   1974   *El Caimito: Un antiguo complejo ceramista de las Antillas Mayores*. Museo del Hombre Dominicano, Serie Monográfica 3. Ediciones Fundación García Arevalo, Santo Domingo.

Willey, Gordon R., Charles C. DiPeso, William A. Ritchie, Irving Rouse, John H. Rowe, and Donald Lathrap
   1956   An Archaeological Classification of Culture Contact Situations. In *Seminars in Archaeology: 1955*, organized and edited by Robert Wauchope, pp.11-30. Memoirs of the Society for American Archaeology, No. 11. Salt Lake City.

Wilson, Samuel
   1987   The Settlement History of Nevis, West Indies. Ms. in possession of author.

Table 1. Radiometric Dates for the Initial Saladoid Styles
from Trinidad to the Virgin Islands.

Island	Style[a]	Sample No.	Site	Years B.P.[b]	Median Date
Trinidad	Cedros	IVIC-642	Cedros	2140±70	190 B.C.
Trinidad	Cedros	IVIC-643	Cedros	1850±80	A.D. 100
Barbados	Chancy. Lane	I-2486	Chancery Lane	1570±95	A.D. 380
Grenadines	Chatham Bay	RL-70	Chatham Bay	1470±100	A.D. 480
St. Vincent	Post Office	RL-28	Kingston P.O.	1790±100	A.D. 160
St. Lucia	Troumassée A	Y-1115	Grande Anse	1460±80	A.D. 490
Martinique	Horizon I	Nancy	Fond Brûlé	2480±40	530 B.C.
Martinique	Horizon I	Nancy	Fond Brûlé	2215±115	265 B.C.
Martinique	Horizon I	Ly-2197	Fond Brûlé	2100±210	150 B.C.
Martinique	Horizon I	BDX-156	Fond Brûlé	2010±300	60 B.C.
Martinique	Horizon I	BDX-161	Fond Brûlé	1865±220	A.D. 85
Martinique	Horizon I	Y-1116	La Salle	1770±100	A.D. 180
Martinique	Horizon I	RL-156	Vivé	1730±110	A.D. 220
Martinique	Horizon I	S-85	Vivé	1655±150	A.D. 295
Martinique	Horizon I	Ny-478	Fond Brûlé	1650±260	A.D. 300
Martinique	Horizon I	Ly-2196	Fond Brûlé	1630±210	A.D. 320
Martinique	Horizon I	?	Vivé	1555±?	A.D. 395
Martinique	Horizon I	UGa-113	Vivé	1530±75	A.D. 420
Guadeloupe	Morel 1	Y-1137	Morel	1730±70	A.D. 220
Guadeloupe	Morel 1	Y-1138	Morel	1710±100	A.D. 240
Marie Galante	?	Ny-500	Taliseronde	1515±85	A.D. 435
Antigua	Ind. Crk. 1	I-7980	Indian Creek	1915±80	A.D. 35
Antigua	Ind. Crk. 1	I-7981	Indian Creek	1855±80	A.D. 95
Montserrat	Trant's	Beta-18491	Radio Antilles	2390±60	440 B.C.
Montserrat	Trant's	Beta-18490	Radio Antilles	2210±70	260 B.C.
Montserrat	Trant's	Beta-18489	Trant's	2140±80	190 B.C.
Montserrat	Trant's	Beta-18581	Radio Antilles	2120±60	170 B.C.
Montserrat	Trant's	Beta-18582	Trant's	1620±90	A.D. 330
St. Martin	Hope Estate	Pitt-0219	Hope Estate	2275±60	325 B.C.
St. Martin	Hope Estate	Pitt-0220	Hope Estate	2250±45	300 B.C.
St. Thomas	Prosperity	Gx-12845	Main Street	1770±235	A.D. 180

[a] All these styles are assignable to the Cedrosan Saladoid subseries because they have both painted and zic wares.

[b] The Martinique dates are from Schvoerer el al. (1985:Table 5), the Montserrat dates from David R. Watters (personal communication 1988), the St. Martin dates from Haviser (1988), the St. Thomas date from Anna C. Roosevelt (personal communication 1987), and the others from Rouse et al. (1985:Tables 2-4). BDX-156 and BDX-161 are thermoluminescence dates; the rest are radiocarbon. They are uncorrected.

Table 2. Radiocarbon Dates for the Initial Saladoid Styles
of Trinidad and the Coast of Venezuela.

Area	Style[a]	Sample No.	Site	Years B.P.[b]	Median Date
Trinidad	Cedros	IVIC-642	Cedros	2140±70	190 B.C.
Trinidad	Cedros	IVIC-643	Cedros	1850±80	A.D. 100
Güiria	Irapa	Y-1113	Punta de Piedras	1680±80	A.D. 270
Güiria	Irapa	Y-290	Irapa	1580±50	A.D. 370
Carúpano	El Mayal	Y-297	El Mayal 2	1795±80	A.D. 155
Carúpano	El Mayal	IVIC-777	El Cuartel	1660±70	A.D. 290
Carúpano	El Mayal	Y-1230	La Cucaracha	1600±100	A.D. 350
Carúpano	El Mayal	I-9729	Puerto Santo	1525±80	A.D. 425
Carúpano	El Mayal	SI-855	El Cuartel	1505±80	A.D. 445
Carúpano	El Mayal	SI-857	El Cuartel	1380±65	A.D. 570
Carúpano	El Mayal	SI-859	El Cuartel	1325±70	A.D. 625
Carúpano	El Mayal	SI-853	El Cuartel	1295±50	A.D. 655

[a] All these styles are assignable to the Cedrosan Saladoid subseries because they have both painted and zic wares.

[b] The dates are from Rouse et al. (1985:Table 2), except that two measurements of Sample Y-290, listed separately there, are averaged here. All are uncorrected.

Table 3. Pertinent Radiocarbon Dates from Central Venezuela.

Area	Style[a]	Sample No.	Site	Years B.P.[b]	Median Date
Río Chico	Río Guapo	Y-1231	Río Guapo	1630±120	A.D. 320
Puerto Cabello	El Palito	Y-579	Aserradero	1640±120	A.D. 310
Puerto Cabello	El Palito	Y-580	Aserradero	1615±120	A.D. 335

[a] The Río Guapo style is assignable to the Huecan Saladoid subseries because it has zic ware but not painted ware. The El Palito style is Barrancoid, but is accompanied by trade sherds of zic ware that appear to be derived from the Río Guapo style.

[b] The dates are from Rouse and Allaire (1978:Table 13.4). They are uncorrected.

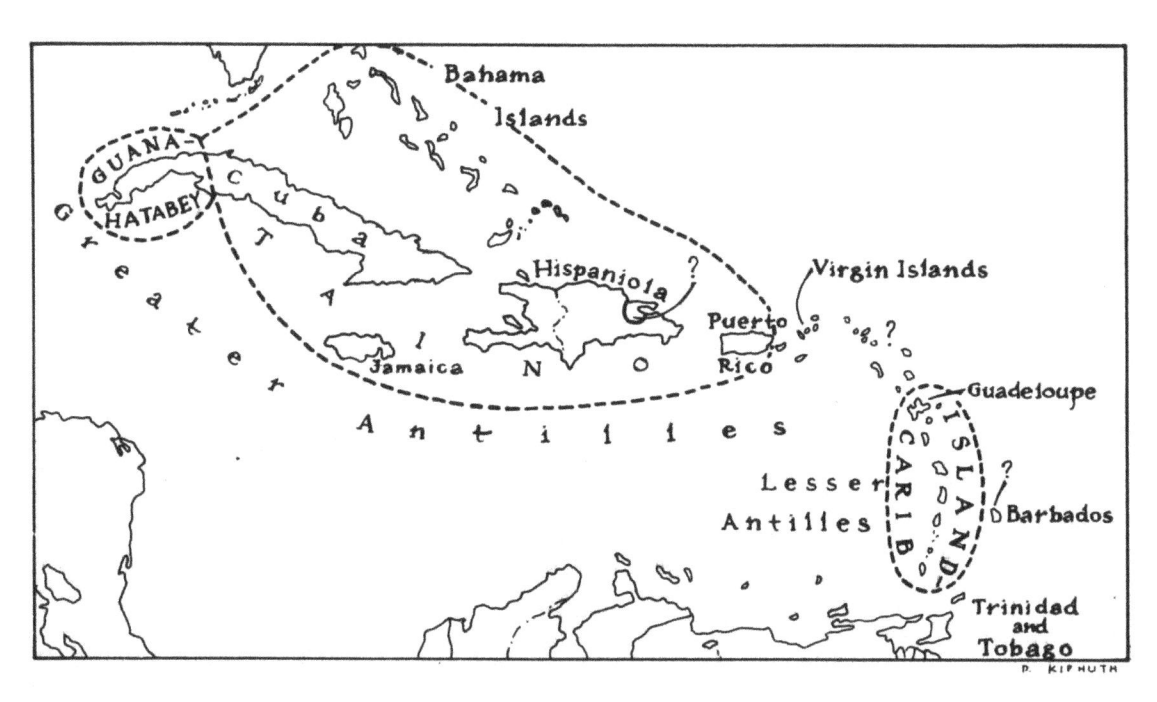

Figure 1. Ethnic groups of the West Indies in the time of Columbus (from Rouse 1987:Figure 2).

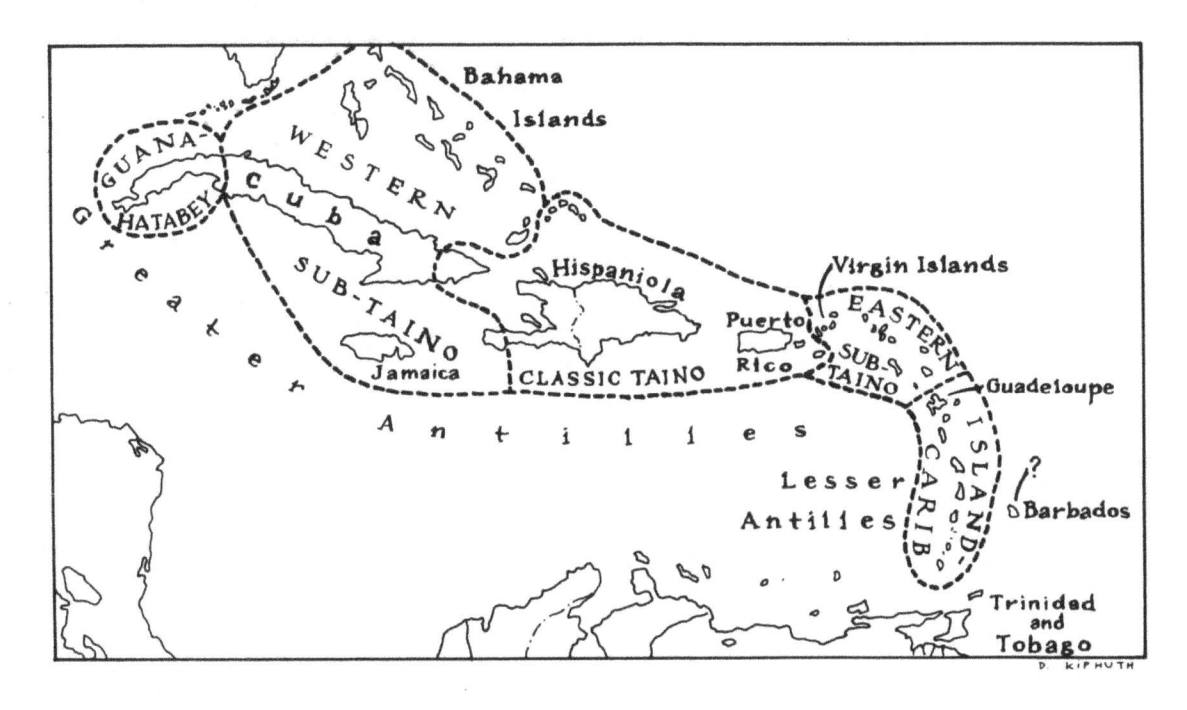

Figure 2. Peoples and cultures of the West Indies in the time of Columbus (from Rouse 1987:Figure 4).

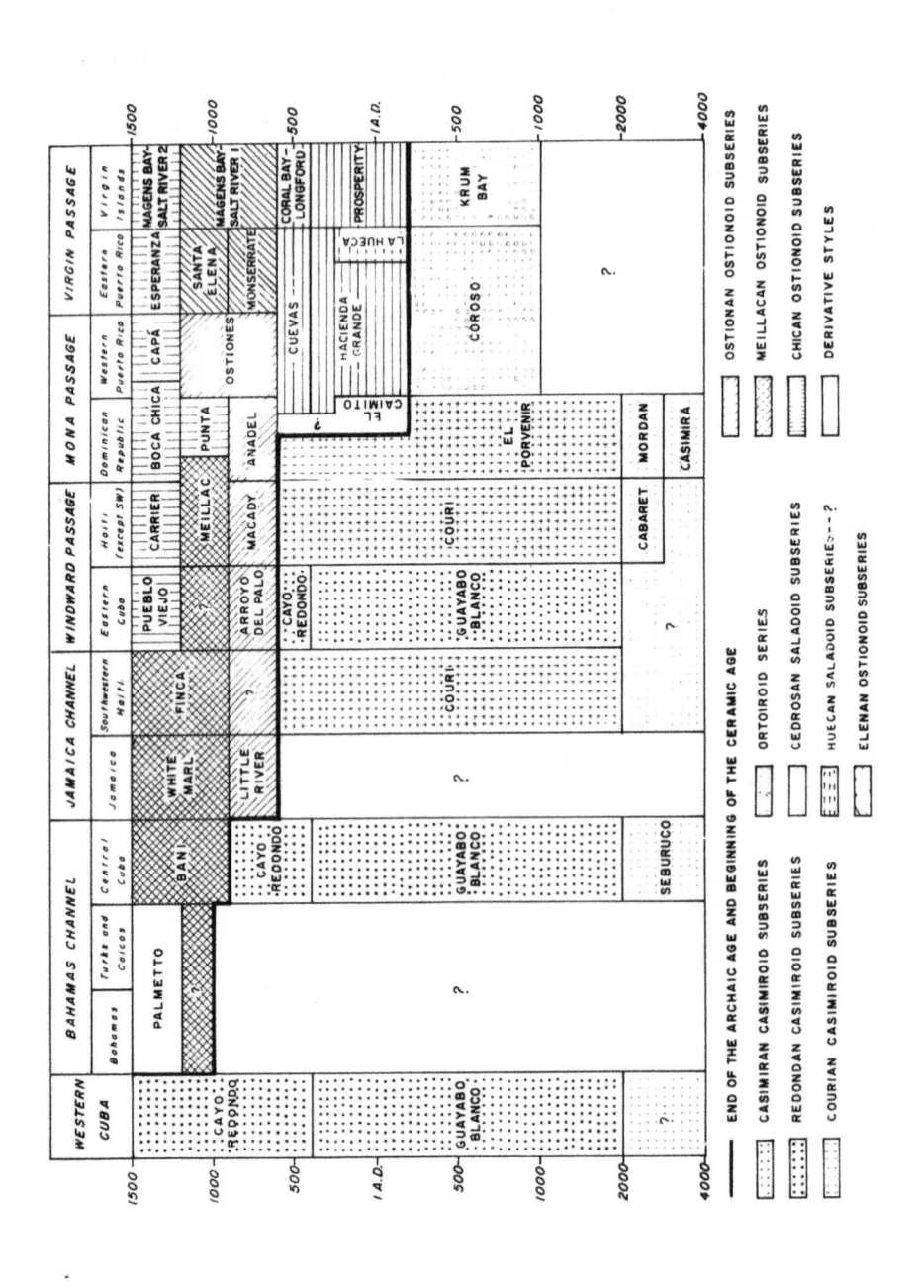

Figure 3. Chronology of the peoples and cultures in the Greater Antilles (from Rouse and Alegría 1989:Figure 15).

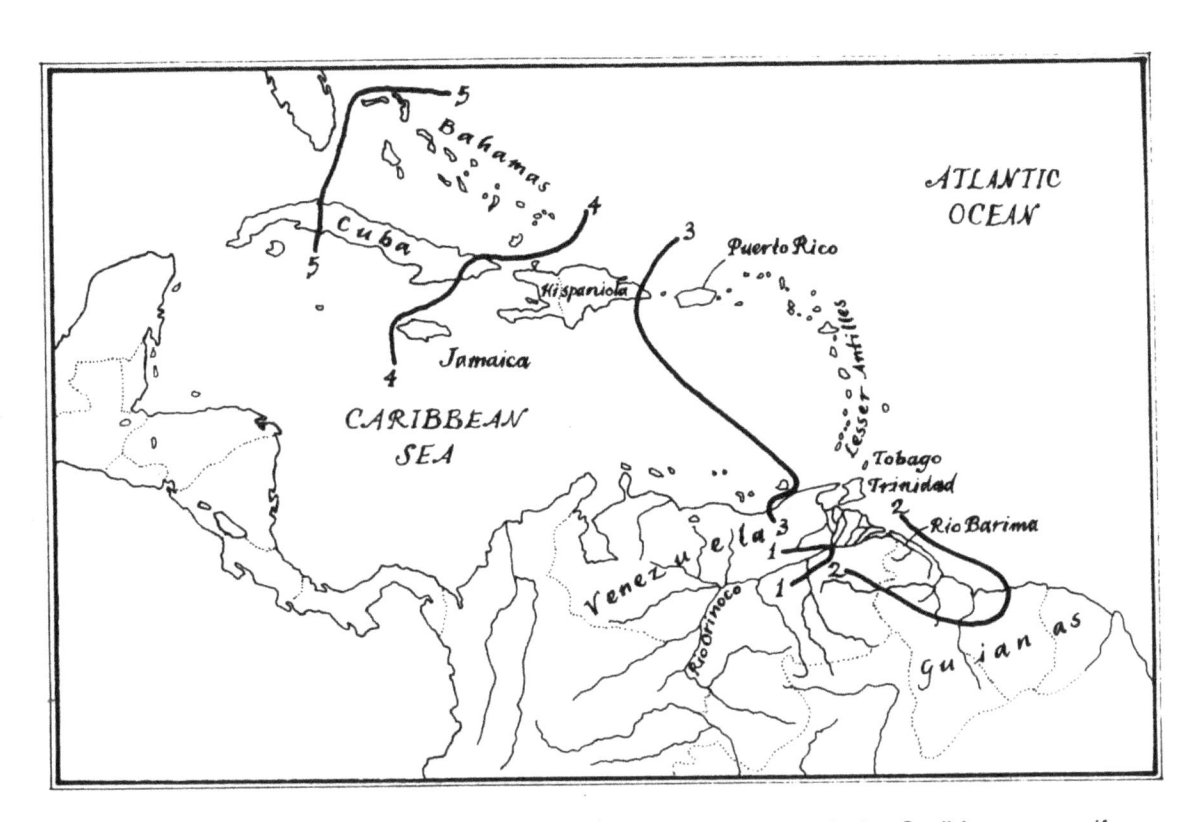

Figure 4. Advance of the Ceramic/Archaic age frontier through the Caribbean area (from Rouse 1986:Figure 24).

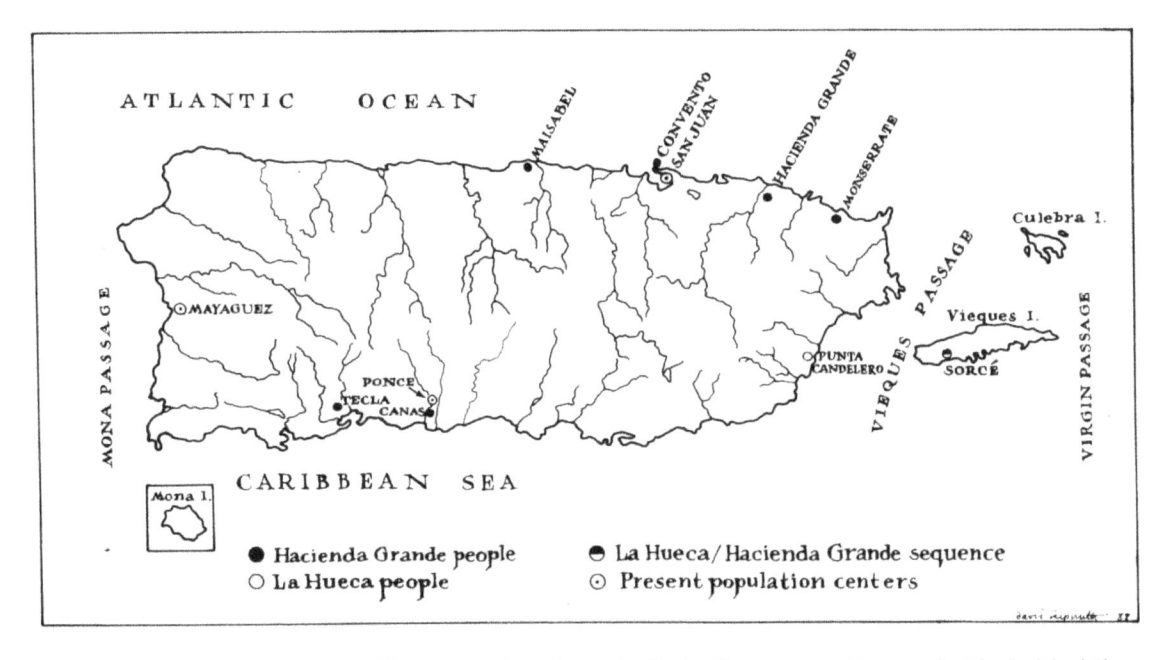

Figure 5. Map of Puerto Rico, showing the principal sites on and immediately behind the Saladoid frontier.

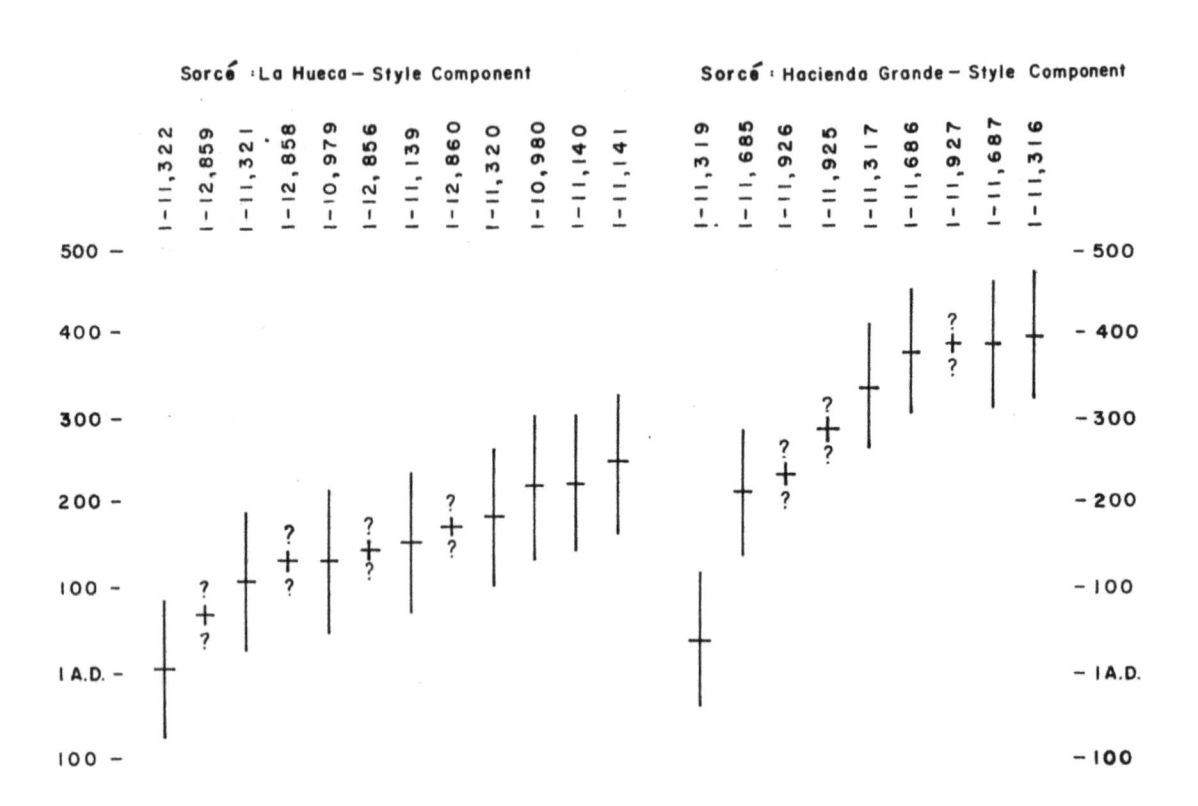

Figure 6. Comparison of the acceptable radiocarbon dates for the first two components of the Sorcé site (from Rouse and Alegría 1989:Figure 14).

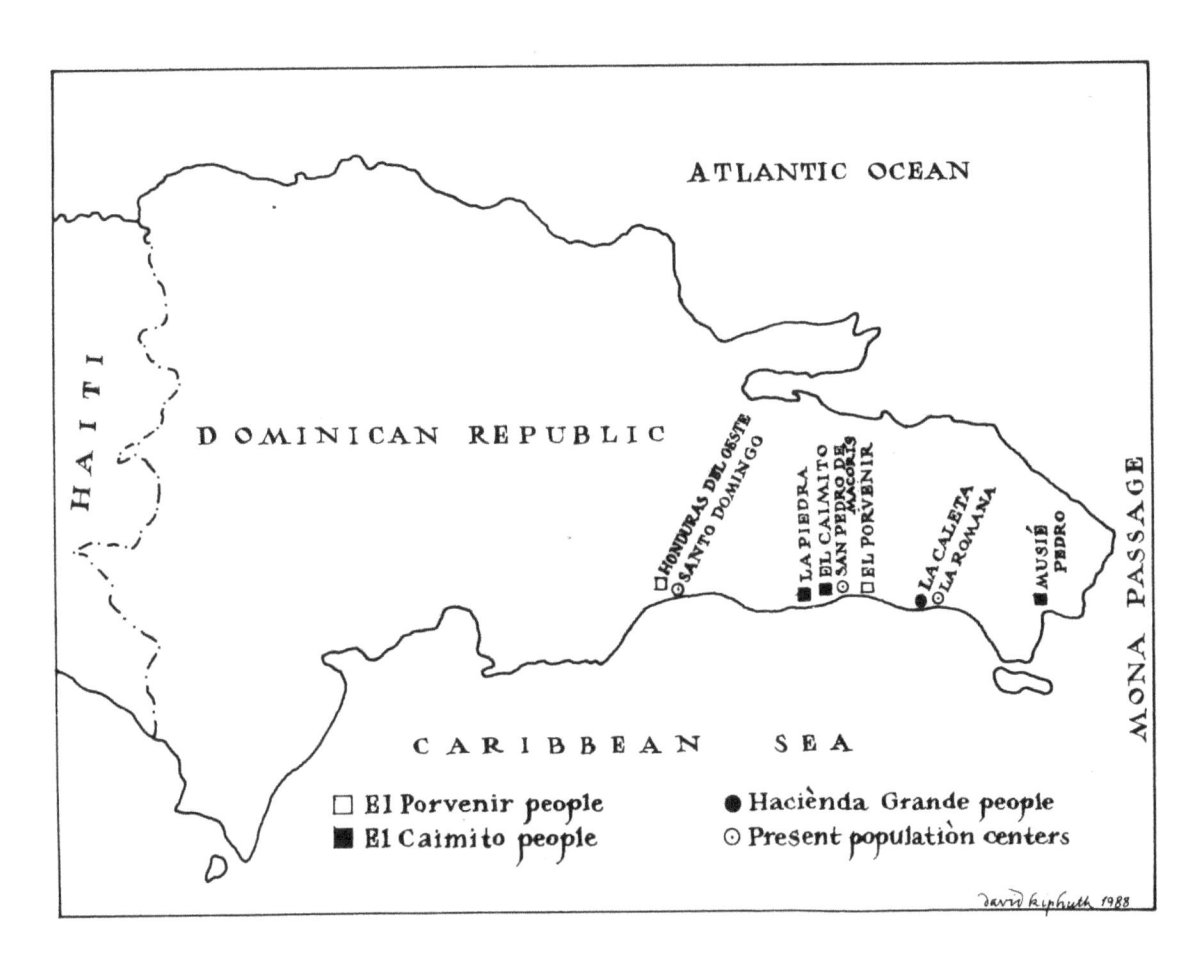

Figure 7. Map of the Dominican Republic, showing the principal sites on and immediately ahead of the Saladoid frontier.

PART 5:

COMMENTARY

DISCUSSION OF

EARLY CERAMIC POPULATION LIFEWAYS

AND ADAPTIVE STRATEGIES IN THE CARIBBEAN

Anna C. Roosevelt

The purpose of this book was to investigate the nature of ecological and social adaptations of the early ceramic stage peoples of the Antilles. My assignment was to evaluate the significance of the volume papers and compare their findings to what we are learning about comparable populations in the lowlands of the South American mainland. My comments on these diverse and interesting papers will be positive and constructive, rather than negative, I hope, but, as I proceed, I will point out contradictions and weaknesses in some of the approaches, as well as their strengths, from the perspective of lowland South America, where I work.

The strengths manifested by the papers are many. There appears to be in Caribbean archaeology a much greater awareness of the utility of middle range theory than is usual in mainland research. The papers by Haviser, Keegan, deFrance, and Jones are good examples of this strength. In response to the critical discussion of theory, application of well-designed empirical research on subsistence has yielded data of a richness and specificity that few mainland projects have achieved. Antillean archaeologists are also much more aware than lowland South American archaeologists of the fruitfulness of studying the patterning within sites for social inference, as the papers by Versteeg and Siegel show. And finally, Caribbean archaeologists are gaining regional chronologies and settlement pattern data that, though not uniform in quality, are most illuminating about prehistoric adaptations and also productive of testable hypotheses to follow up in the future. Rouse, in particular, has always kept chronology at the center of interest in the field, encouraging the excavation and re-excavation of sites exemplifying important segments of the chronological sequences. Many who have come into the field more recently represent the salutary interest in regional settlement patterns and site composition. The papers by Allaire, Morse, Drewett, Haviser, and Rouse summarize some of this valuable chronological data for settlement pattern information. In the mainland, we have nothing like your data yet, though I think we've been working on it for longer. The lack of such data in my area is attributable to the fact that few archaeologists have been interested in exploring intensively the stratigraphic and artifactual variability that exists within and between sites. Although many of us have worked in institutions along with scholars who have been interested in such research, we have preserved the early American archaeological tradition (Willey and Sabloff 1974) of non-systematic site survey and non-stratigraphic excavation methods (Roosevelt 1989c). This rather ineffective research strategy has often been defended as appropriate for tropical lowland sites (Meggers 1985), but, clearly, you have had good results, despite the fact that the Caribbean is a tropical lowland area. In this particular area of research, we have much to learn from your example.

The papers presented some epistemological problems, in addition to the strengths. These arose partly from problems in the quality of methods of data collection. Often it was not clear in a paper what were the sampling methods that produced chronological and settlement information. In particular, methods of excavation and the nature of ground coverage in site surveying were unclear. In some papers, there was no clear sense of a research strategy, a statement of problem and development of methods appropriate to the problem. Work in particular projects was often inadequately integrated with that of other projects, and authors sometimes seemed to oppose other types of work that seemed, to me, to be complementary to theirs, such as within-site studies versus studies of regional settlement systems for demographic information. As another example of operational problems, there was among the authors a curious lack of interest in archaeobotanical evidence, despite the fact that one of your major interests is to understand prehistoric subsistence, which all seem to agree was horticulturally based, among the early sedentary ceramic populations of the Caribbean.[1] The authors also seem unaware of the uses of human osteology as evidence for some of the main processes that you are interested in, such as social and political interaction, conflict, and population pressure on resources.

In some studies there are problems in operationalizing theories at the middle range, resulting in unconvincing test implications and misunderstanding of what would constitute the evidence for a given interpretation. The lack of interest in archaeobotany may be part of that general problem. I also found a lack of awareness of where hypotheses came from, i.e., their theoretical and historical background, and I missed citations to previous studies similar to yours, carried out in other parts of the world. Sometimes you seem to be trying to re-invent the wheel, inheriting methods pioneered in other areas but not benefitting from subsequent refinements in the methods. But most troubling, for me, was the rather passive use of the general theoretical models, such as Chomskian generative grammar and optimal foraging theory. Such theories were used to generate hypotheses that were in some cases tested with data but were not themselves evaluated and then improved by comparison of the predictions of the hypotheses and the results of research. Without this last step, there is no hope for advancing our general theories toward a better understanding of human behavior, human history, and the human condition.

Since the papers were very diverse, I will organize my discussion around the interpretive themes that I discern in the volume, bringing in specifics about the papers as I go through the themes. The topics of interest manifested in the papers include: (a) the chronology or the history of occupation, (b) the ecological adaptation, which includes demography and subsistence, and (c) social, political, and religious adaptations. At the end of the discussion, I will summarize two general interpretive problems of special importance: the nature of our base of general theory and our use of ethnographic analogy in lowland prehistory.

The majority of the papers had something interesting to say about ecological adaptations to island environments, but, though many papers touched on characteristics of local environments, none summarized the range of habitats for the region nor made comprehensive comparison with the mainland areas from which the early ceramic cultures are thought to come. I think such information would be helpful for assessing what the change in environmental context might have meant, in terms of permitting, constraining, or shaping ecological adaptations. In general, what occurred to me upon reading the participants' comments on ecology and the environment, is that there are some general aspects of such environments for preindustrial human adaptation that seem to be going unnoticed.

For example, relevant to the authors' interests in early ceramic adaptations to the Caribbean islands, there are significant differences between island environments and the classic tropical rainforests and floodplains of the mainland that make the latter inappropriate ecological models for the former. My reading and travel in the islands reveals much lower, more seasonal, and more variable rainfall; more xerophytic, low biomass vegetation; much more heterogeneous geology; a greater predominance of nutrient-rich near-neutral to alkaline soils (Alfisols and Mollisols), rather than acid, leached, *terre firme* soils (Oxisols and Ultisols). I suspect that the lower leaching rate and bedrock richer in soil nutrients mean that island terrestrial biomes may have been more propitious for intensive, seasonal agriculture than those in many *terra firme* areas of the Orinoco and Amazon. For this reason, and because of the lower biomass of xerophytic vegetation, I think it's probably a mistake to assume, as many of the authors do, that early ceramic people in the islands were necessarily doing swidden cultivation primarily, the mainstay of many Amazonian Indian groups today.

In many parts of the world with somewhat similar environmental conditions, such as in Oaxaca, Mexico, the Aegean Islands, parts of the Iberian Peninsula, and Mesopotamia, various methods of land-surface alteration were carried out in aid of permanent agriculture. It seems to me that these are the areas whose land-use histories can provide useful models for the study of Caribbean lifeways, rather than the humid tropical lowlands of South America. The tropical forest swidden model is more appropriate for areas with high rain and acid soils than it is for areas with relatively low rain and mafic bedrock. Many areas in the Caribbean seem apt for terracing, to retain soil from erosion and to conserve moisture.[2] I think it is important to mention that in these aspects the island environments contrast with the mainland *terra firme* environments, because of the assumptions that we commonly make about the limiting effect of adaptation to "tropical rain forest" environments on prehistoric development and demography.

Another point about island environments, which was made in an article in *Human Ecology* by Sue Levin in 1983, is that in the tropical zone, freshwaters are usually much more productive per unit area than marine waters. Some of the results of subsistence studies described in the papers make sense in terms of this fact, but the writers do not seem to be aware of the contrast. It could help explain why Archaic subsistence seems to focus on estuarine resources, rather than on purely marine resources. But I make this point mainly to emphasize that Caribbean environments have not yet been comprehensively assessed by archaeologists for their implications for prehistoric human adaptation. Authors interested in the environment tend to adapt from their biological colleagues assessments keyed to patterns of species diversity (as in the paper by Watters and Rouse), but these measures need to be augmented with studies of biomass, turnover, and per hectare productivity, which I would argue are factors of the greatest importance for understanding the environmental constraints on ancient subsistence.

I thought the paper by Allaire showed the potential of catastrophe theory in developing the significance of the effect of abrupt environmental change on histories of prehistoric adaptation. He points out that the ancient inhabitants could not have been unaffected by volcanic eruptions that impacted large areas of Martinique. Consideration of the impact of vulcanism on prehistoric peoples has been a fruitful area of research in the adjacent Cental American mainland. Also, important concrete evidence of ancient lifeways may be available in fields and habitations destroyed by sudden eruptions. For example, at Ceren in El Salvador, the products of a volcanic eruption preserved a sprouting monocrop cornfield and a farmhouse. Martinique and other islands may have some similar features preserved. Also in regard to environmental history, I would have liked hearing more about secular change in climate and sea levels, factors certain to have influenced the biota and their use by humans. In some cases such changes may have influenced the location of settlements. It would also be interesting to know more about the impact of prehistoric humans on their environments, as intensification progressed. One of the facts that island biologists have taught us is the great vulnerability of such habitats to alteration by humans.

In regard to the relationship of settlements to landscape, Haviser's site catchment analysis is interesting, because it shows elegantly how a quantitative analysis of the location of sites vis-à-vis environmental resources can illuminate the subsistence system, even without a scrap of evidence about food remains. His results are very strong evidence for intensive agriculture during the early ceramic stage of occupation. He and others also present interesting evidence on site context, which tends to suggest a heavy horticultural orientation of subsistence during the early ceramic occupation.

The faunal data presented in the papers and the description of sampling procedures and analyses, showed me that Caribbean archaeologists, probably due to the influence of Elizabeth Wing of the Florida Museum of Natural History, are light-years ahead of mainland archaeologists. I was especially impressed by the meticulous analysis exemplified by deFrance's paper, but many of the others had excellent information, and they all showed how much significant information about changing adaptations can be derived from this source. The interesting information about differences between archaic and early ceramic adaptations from the faunal data suggest that the use of horticulture may have influenced the manner of faunal capture.

Nonetheless, Caribbean archaeologists, like mainlanders, have really not yet comprehensively defined prehistoric subsistence either for any point in time or as it changed through time. And they are not benefitting from the discoveries that others are making about methodologies of paleodietary reconstruction in other areas of the tropics. More of this in a moment.

Keegan's paper was for me the most interesting because it was the most self-conscious theoretically but also the most problematical epistemologically. Keegan's explicit use of theory is refreshing and most welcome, though he has inherited some problems from his predecessors in this area. One of the salient characteristics of optimal foraging theory is that it does not, as it stands, predict changing diets correctly through considering such factors as handling time, etc. (Roosevelt 1987a). As an example, in a paper for the Wenner-Gren Conference on Food Preferences and Aversions, Winterhalder (1987) reconstructed Cree diet based on the theory, and came up with a foraging diet that emphasized large game animals and certain plant foods. In fact, actual Cree diet is based on store bought flour supplemented with some wild foods and paid for with money gained from the sale of small animals whose pelts are valued in the world luxury trade. As another example, all over the world, as subsistence has been intensified per unit land and labor through change in wild food sources or through the use of agriculture, there has been a strong trend towards ecological simplification and specialization, regardless of labor costs and instability of harvests, both of which have increased during the process. Diets have rarely been broadened and made more stable through time as the theory predicts.

The tropical lowlands is a very good example of this phenomenon, in that the Archaic was a time of progressive narrowing of a broad spectrum of species towards exploitation of localized, productive, small-package foods. Then the staple-ization of manioc narrowed diets still further, placing the burden of supplying calories on one crop, leaving protein to faunas, and finally maize becomes the staple and major source of both protein and calorie. Optimal foaging theory doesn't predict such sequences because it does not take into consideration many things that humans take into consideration when making decisions about food-getting: such as the competitive advantage of large, dense populations in a context of warfare, though they may be more expensive to feed, or the benefits of linkage to the world economy in the face of habitat destruction and ecological marginalization, in the case of the Cree. In early prehistoric times and at low levels of population density people may act to optimize in the fashion that animals do, but as habitats fill in and neighbors become obstreperous, decision-making becomes more complicated. The standard theory is, in other words, not sufficiently complex to do the job. If we had been truly critical in evaluating results in terms of the predictions of the theory, we would have worked harder on improving the theory. But somehow human ecologists have become fond of the theory and are using it passively rather than actively, working constantly to improve it.

It seems to me that the Caribbean subsistence studies in this volume do not support the predictions of the theory, which were that as populations increased and began to over-use the land crabs, new items would be added to broaden the resource base to try to maintain stability and keep things as much the same as possible. Keegan finds the high late prehistoric carbon isotope ratios evidence that maize was added to the diet to broaden it.

But the problem is complicated and needs to be further explained. Since it was so important in Keegan's argument, I would like to discuss the uses of bone chemistry studies, which have been of great benefit in my own research and which Keegan has introduced to Caribbean studies, to their great benefit. Some of you may know that bone chemistry studies went far in providing independent evidence of hypotheses about the role of maize cultivation in tropical lowland prehistory on the mainland (van der Merwe et al. 1981; Roosevelt 1989a). However, it is important to make clear that the information obtainable from isotopic chemistry of bone is very, very vague indeed, without strong empirical evidence of subsistence from food remains and skeletal pathologies. It is the case, in other words, that bone chemistry simply cannot stand on its own but relies on standard paleodietary data for even the simplest conclusion. Let me explain.

Unless there is evidence of food species, stable carbon isotope results can do little more than tell you how much of the food supply was derived ultimately from the two main photosynthetic plant groups, C-3 or C-4. If C-3 is in emphasis, then, in the tropical lowlands, the diet could have been almost anything, for the environment is often almost completely C-3. All animal and plant foods except maize would give the same pattern. There would be no way from carbon chemistry to tell which species were important. If maize was the only C-4 plant, then a diet high in C-4 plants would presumably have been high in maize, unless you are near the seashore, where seafood could be giving the same pattern. Nitrogen analysis can tell you a little more, because it reflects trophic levels of diets, to some extent. Using the methods together can help distinguish between maize and seafood diets, though conclusions are at present weakened by some poorly understood effects of climatic aridity. But my point is that the chemistry relies on the identification of archaeological food remains for specific conclusions about diet composition. Further, it is important to measure the bone chemistry of the faunal remains, for more background for the interpretation of human bone results (Roosevelt 1989a).

Thus, the faunal studies referred to by the authors are important for interpreting Keegan's results. However, given the horticultural orientation expected for the ancient people, plant remains would have been even more important, so I found it rather a big flaw that no paper refers to any archaeobotanical evidence. This, despite the fact that almost all the papers acknowledge that cultivated plants must have been the major source of calories, with faunal food just a supplement. Why is there no archaeological botany in your studies? All tropical sites that I have ever examined were full of plant remains and these can provide an important test of subsistence hypotheses. If, as you hypothesize, maize became a staple at one point, then there will be large quantities of carbonized maize fragments in the samples. Some lowland sites, such as Valdivia components in Ecuador, hypothesized to have been supported by maize but with little or no carbonized maize in the flotation samples, turned out to have non-maize isotopic signatures (van der Merwe, personal communiation). Even manioc genera can be identified from the wood, and other roots, such as South American Taro, or *Xanthosoma*, can be identified from the remains of tubers. Collecting this kind of plant material will be important for testing your subsistence reconstructions. Except for the Archaic stage, and possibly the earliest Saladoid occupation, what you have been studying so meticulously may have been the least important element in the diet. If maize was a staple, then it, not fauna, supplied the large majority of the protein in the diet, quantitatively. (This means, incidentally, that low nitrogen isotope ratios are not necessarily an indication of consumption of reef fishes, as has been suggested by Keegan, but may reflect the influence of the staple plant on the isotope ratio of bone protein.)

The carbonized plant remains are all-important to arguments such as Keegan's, who hypothesizes that, when the carbon isotope ratio lowers appreciably, the diet has been broadened to include maize. In fact, maize must have been added earlier, for, according to van der Merwe, maize would only begin to affect the isotope ratios after it had become more than 10% of the diet. What is actually happening in the diet, then, is not the increase in breadth predicted by optimal foraging theory, but a narrowing and specialization through staple-ization of maize. The diet has become even more focused on one food source. Collection of the carbonized plant remains from numerous sites in the Orinoco clearly showed that relatively primitive maize had been in the subsistence system for several hundred years before it became a dietary staple ca. A.D. 500, when races with large cobs and kernels appeared (Roosevelt 1980; van der Merwe et al. 1981). Thus, the carbonized plant remains gave the needed empirical background to interpret the bone chemistry. I want to mention that the optimal foraging theory is not the original source of the prediction that maize would become a staple in the context of growing populations in the Antilles. Suzanne Levin (1983) suggested it several years ago for the Antilles in a paper in *Human Ecology* and cites our Orinoco work as the source of the idea. Thus it was intensification theory that the idea came from, so it's not surprising that optimal foraging theory cannot predict this event.

What these considerations mean is that optimal foraging theory was interestingly but somewhat uncritically applied in this case. More critical attention to the test implications as well as to empirical aspects would have forced a reevaluation of the utility of the theory. Such an approach seems necessary unless we are ready to take the theory on faith.

Now, in terms of testing theory, deFrance's paper was most useful, because of her command of the interpretive framework of her study, her awareness of the impact of sampling bias on inference and because of her deft, complex, and interesting interpretation of the results, which gave evidence of shifts in percentages of species emphasized as intensification occurred. It will be interesting to see how direct evidence of population pressure compares to the changes in faunal utilization. Although up to now, "bioarchaeological" studies in the Caribbean have been mostly confined to faunal studies, the field can be much broader, including demography, disease patterns, physiological stress patterns, etc. I know that some scholars, such as L. Budinoff, a colleague of Siegel's, are studying these other aspects, but they are not represented in this book, perhaps as an oversight. Thus, a population's ecological adaptation involves much more than just subsistence, including reproductive strategy, physiological adaptation, etc. These other aspects are going to be of crucial importance, as you begin to test theories about patterns of differential access to resources.

I am not going to spend much time on chronology, which is more a parochial concern, of more interest to regional specialists. But a couple of positive comments, at least. One thing that occurs to me is that the gains you have made in clearing up chronology are in large part due to the continuing interest and commitment of Rouse to the problem. What I have heard from you and have experienced myself is that, no matter what other duties and concerns may be filling his life or piling up on his desk, he is always more than willing to consider a new possibility, to follow up on yet another site, to commission one more set of dates, to include one more complex in the sequence. In any case, those of you working in the Caribbean are way ahead of us mainlanders in solidifying chronological sequences for the study of settlement and subsistence. I thought Morse's paper interesting, for illustrating the value of detective work on collections and archives in this area.

Your papers, almost to a one, have demonstrated how important chronology is to interpretations of broader scope, whether it be to reveal the origins of things and therefore the role of the environment or the specific kinds of social interaction in cultural development. You also show, in the faunal studies, how important chronology can be in understanding the significance of the details of sequences (as in Jones's paper). As to specifics of early ceramic chronology in the Caribbean, you have made great strides, but I am very uneasy with the assumption of Saladoid being the first ceramic complex of the area. It seems unwise, when the state of research is still rather preliminary, to forget that what seems the earliest at first never turns out to be the earliest in archaeology. Though there have been some spectacular reversals in the other direction, the majority of revisions tend to move events and processes earlier as research proceeds. I think it would be safest to assume that there was pottery in the Caribbean before the Saladoid phenomenon. Perhaps the late "Archaic" coastal foragers made pottery, like those on the mainland (Roosevelt 1989a; Simoes 1981). This observation may be of relevance to Rouse's El Caimito situation.

You did not say too much about craft history and its meaning, except for Roe, whose paper I'll discuss shortly. But I wonder if, as you all seem to accept, the fine Saladoid lapidary work really can be taken as evidence for ranking. Do egalitarian people not make labor intensive objects and import fine materials long distances? They do, of course, though no doubt in much lower volume and with different patterns of distribution. But you need to develop the argument about this further, I think.

Several of the papers mentioned hypotheses about the social organization of early ceramic peoples in the Caribbean. The majority seem to like the tribal model derived from studies of present-day tropical lowland Indians, but an alternative, of a more complex, stratified, and centralized societies, is also mentioned. Roe uses contrasts in material culture in an interesting way, to compare Taino and Saladoid communities, concluding that the mass-production and "publification" of art during Taino times indicates a more complex society than that exemplified by the high-quality, personal art of the Saladoid people. I think he's on to a significant process, there. But one thing I worry about for the Saladoid culture, is whether perishable art might not have existed in monumental forms very different in function from the lapidary and ceramic art. Perhaps, in the future, wet site archaeology will provide us some examples of perishable art. But I think, in the main, his points are well-taken and apply very well to Amazonian prehistory, where the later "chiefdoms," like the Taino, have mass-production and monumental architecture and types of funerary art not found in earlier cultures (Roosevelt 1987b).

In terms of empirical studies of community patterns, Siegel and Versteeg are outstanding. Very few of us in the lowland mainland are doing anything comparable. Siegel's work at Maisabel is notable for the creative sampling plan. Versteeg's work is admirable to his meticulous, broad-area excavation, but he is less aware of the utility of selective sampling but just as aware of the meaningfulness of within-site patterning. Both are working in a productive area of research, the study of the distribution of different kinds of material within sites. Our work on Marajo has been very fruitful in this area, too, showing large contrasts in material culture in different kinds of facilities, structures, and use areas. Neither of you, however, seem aware of the utility of nondestructive sampling. For most of the information desired by archaeologists, it's not necessary to dig up the whole site, and remote sensing can be more effective than peppering the site with auger holes. I think Siegel is very likely right about the existence of additional burials at Maisabel, and, because of the site's sandy soil texture, radar could be used for mapping the burial pits. It worked well for David Thomas in similar soils on St. Catherine's Island and should work well in the often porous soils of Caribbean sites. On Marajo, other methods such as conductivity survey and magnetometer survey proved effective at locating earthworks and hearths, respectively. Regardless of the choice of method, I think the site-oriented archaeologists need to think more about research strategy before starting out at a site.

Work such as Haviser's, Allaire's, and Keegan's on regional settlement patterns has given the Caribbean an edge over the mainland in demonstrating the value of this important area of research, for ecological, demographic, and sociological information. Versteeg claims that the total excavation of individual sites is a better source of information about demography than regional studies, but this stand seems indefensible. Individual site studies such as Siegel's and Versteeg's need to be integrated with more comprehensive regional studies, rather than being an alternative method. The slow and destructive process of total excavation of sites could never supply the information about the size and distribution of sites through a region, without which the regional population could not be assessed. Studies of the population of settlements in relation to settlement area and roofed area give very similar results overall (Roosevelt 1980). Because of the wide range of population numbers per unit roofed area, it is only when there are unitary, countable household facilities, such as family hearths, that archaeological house remains give a better idea of site population than general site area (Roosevelt 1989b, 1989c). For this and the aforementioned reasons, the site-oriented and region-oriented studies ought to be considered complementary, rather than alternative.

As mentioned above, you do not make much use of the morphology of human osteological remains as a source of evidence about social organization. It's useful to remember that the practical and theoretical difference between ranked and stratified societies is that the former have significant differences between people in life-sustaining resources. Study of skeletal populations seems to me a type of research that could supply the information needed to determine what kind of ranking system may have been in effect at different times. Not only can osteological studies reveal changes through time in physiological stress levels but they can also reveal differences within populations. Also, osteological information is a basic source of data about the composition of a population, something very relevant to understanding its organization. Though most Caribbean archaeologists seem to be taking the normative view of these societies, assuming a similar adaptation for most people within the societies, it is more likely that there were systematic differences of some kind. In the ancient stratified societies there would have been differential access to resources according to rank and occupation. In Amazonia today, where ranking is rare, gender distinctions in access to food and health are very prominent, especially among Jivaroans and Yanomamo, who have been in a state of war until recently. I don't see any sign that Caribbeanists interested in social organization are aware of such patterning and its archaeological relevance. Further, given the strong cross-cultural association of localized cemeteries and the importance of exogamous unilineal descent groups, which Kingsley (1985) has uncovered and that Siegel refers to, we must consider using the Caribbean cemeteries as sources of information relevant to the investigation of social organization. Especially in the Caribbean, with its heterogeneous geology, strontium isotope ratios could be used to investigate patterns of post-marital residence. In any case, the study of human osteology has much to give to the reconstruction of social organization, demography, and economy if there is more collaboration between archaeologists and physical anthropologists. In Amazonia we are using genetic information from osteology to test theoreis of migration (Roosevelt 1989c), and Rouse (1986) has suggested its application to the Antilles.

In regard to Siegel's conclusions about the organization of Maisabel, I'm not sure that having a central ceremonial area necessarily means a society is ranked. Many Amazonian groups and others that are not ranked have this pattern. As Brown (1971) has shown, egalitarian societies often have differential burial patterns. The problem for the archaeologist is to try to find out what kinds of interpersonal differences are being distinguished and symbolized. Before leaving the subject of social organization, I would also like to caution that no systematic comparisons of prehistoric community patterning have been made between the mainland and island Saladoid. It really is not yet true, as Siegel asserts, that the mainland sites are less structured and elaborate. What do we know of the mainland site structure? Most of the sites were dug before community archaeology was done. Since we do not in fact know what the pattern was at the centers of migration, we cannot say that the frontier had the greater elaboration.

I am going to spend some time on the subject of art and cosmology because this is a very important new research direction, admirably suited, as Roe points out, to the cultures of the area, because of their rich symbolic vision. All of us have in the past focused on the use of ancient art for solving time-space relationships and have missed its utility for understanding prehistoric ideology and organization. There has even been something of a prejudice against studies of art iconography and aesthetics, particularly by some "processual" archaeologists. But many of us have come to be interested in this subject in the last five years, primarily, in my case, through inspiration by Precolumbian art historians (Roosevelt 1989c). Except for Roe, I am not sure that I think Caribbean specialists are exploiting the art as much as it could be for inference on religious, social, and political aspects of life. Saladoid is one of the richest stylistic and iconographic complexes in the world, but I think, as I will discuss further in my conclusions, existing uses of ethnographic analogy to interpret art iconography and aesthetics are hindering our understanding of change in these areas.

In addition, it would be useful to have more quantitative and interpretive analyses of the representational iconography. For example, for the animal art, scholars could work more with zoologists, comparing with faunal remains and paleontology, what animals were there, what did they represent of exclusively mainland taxa they could never have seen, etc. I have found this approach very useful in my work on Amazonian iconography (Roosevelt 1989c), and the brief section in Roe's paper reveals how much can be learned about Caribbean art by study of significance of the taxonomic identity of symbolic representations. He suggests that early Saladoid animal styles show many mainland species not found in the islands, as well as some indigenous ones. I was bothered by the lack of reference in Roe's paper to others on the iconography of prehistoric art (such as Brown's 1975). Again, I think this is an example of trying to re-invent the wheel. In order to be understood in context, your scholarly aparatus needs to acknowledge the background of your studies in prior work. Also, you can do much more in analyzing images in their iconographic, stylistic and archaeological contexts and by comparing systematically both the similarities and differences between ethnographic and prehistoric art, rather than simply projecting recent ethnographic concepts backward. We need to be aware that things have changed as well as stayed the same and the differences are most illuminating. In general, since art is very closely linked to ideology, and ideology to social organization and religion, prehistoric art can be a potent source of information about change in these areas. In addition, many hypotheses generated by art studies are testable by work in other areas. The art as well as site structure can yield theories about what people thought about each other and the universe to be tested with other evidence. For example, if we think an ancient society had a system of gender classes, as the Jivaroans and Yanomamo do, we can look for osteological evidence of the occupational and health differences that arise between men and women in such societies. Or, if the architectural and iconographic evidence suggests the existence of social ranking or stratification, the osteology can be reviewed for occupational and health differences not associated with gender. In these ways the different kinds of data can be integrated to gain interpretive information unavailable in one particular type of data.

In the Lower Amazon, we are finding some interesting similarities and differences between ethnographic and prehistoric symbolic concepts. We find in the prehistoric art images related to ethnographic accoutrements and concepts of shamanism, such as certain kinds of clothing, special seats, hats, images of animals such as scorpions and snakes, which are considered important shamans' helpers, etc. We also see that the social and religious roles of people differ in the prehistoric symbolic systems. Although we are wary of interpreting these as representing the reality of the day, rather than the way in which someone thought to show it, nonetheless there is a distinct contrast through time between different archaeological cultures and ethnographic art, in the symbolic roles of people. For example, Marajo polychrome art has very few male figures and many female, and though both males and females are represented in shamanistic roles, wearing regalia, or with animals of shamanism, women do not usually take shamans' roles today and are not depicted doing so. In later Amazonian art, such as that of Santarem, men are represented as shamans and chiefs but women not, and more animals that Amazonian Indians consider male, such as the jaguar, are shown, wheras the majority of animals shown in Marajoara art are those that Amazonian Indians consider part of the female side of the world (Urton 1985). Thus, the archaeological imagery, interpreted in the light of other information, suggests fundamental changes through time in the nature of societies' organization and their world views. Such changes are testable in many ways, and if verified, are significant new evidence for the relationship of ideological change to changes in other areas of human existence.

Now, I should summarize and make my final comments. I've discussed the empirical aspects of your papers and commend the directions in which you are going. The work on individual sites and settlement systems is admirable, forming a good basis for future comparisons between regions, islands, and with the mainland. It is also exciting to see the fruits of your faunal work, which is revealing thousands of identifiable specimens where previously there were few or none. I urge you to do more with plants, they will be equally informative and will complement your faunal and chemical data significantly.

I would like to suggest that the body of general theory that informs Caribbean archaeology needs to be broadened and enriched, as a guide to the collection and interpretation of empirical data. Both the structural Marxist and the ecological models espoused here seem too narrow and programmatic to comprise adequately the interactions between people, each other, and their environments. I believe that the idealist and materialist paradigms need to be integrated for a better understanding of human history and the human condition (Roosevelt 1989d). There is absolutely no reason to feel that studies of human ecology that many of you are involved in are in any way more admirable than those of ideology or vice versa, as Roe argues. Even if you believe that material conditions "cause" human social organization and ideology, the latter would still be important to study in order to document how the former "caused" it. And no matter what we learn about symbolism and ritual it would be irrelevant without the knowledge of the social, political, economic, and ecological patterns that they were integrated with.

In both areas of theory, I see a need for more rigorous justification for the applicability of theories, the development of better test implications, and design of more exigent tests. We need to ask the questions: Why are we interested in a certain process; why do we think this was the process; what is the evidence that that should be so; and how would we know that was the case? It is helpful to keep in mind that much that happens in the world is counter-intuitive, which is why our hypotheses are usually false, but hypotheses are necessary because they help us realize what we think about the world and narrow the likely possible explanations down to manageable numbers for purposes of research.

My final comments are about ethnographic analogy. Though I find the ethnoarchaeological work of scholars such as Roe and Siegel exciting, I find that Caribbean and Amazonian archaeologists are still using ethnographic data and concepts uncritically, though scholars such as Hutterer and others have pointed out the problem that this causes. People assume that the ethnographic record represents the archaeological, and they expect to find similar patterns, but everything I know of lowland archaeology and ethnology suggests that the ethnographic record is greatly impoverished in types of social and economic organization structures and patterns in comparison with the prehistoric period. In other words, many well-documented archaeological patterns are simply not represented among living Amazonian Indians, and we will never understand the ancient ones if we restrict ourselves to ethnographic models. Some examples of the differences are: The intensive seed cropping economies of the floodplains in late prehistoric times; the existence of urban scale settlements and earthworks where there are now only small villages; intensive prehistoric craft production of lithics and ceramics, where none exist today; etc. Physiological patterns also contrast between the ethnographic and archaeological populations, such as pathological patterns and stature, with the prehistoric Indians being much taller and less subject to bone disease. These contrasts suggest that the present Indians have been marginalized ecologically, geographically, economically and politically by the European conquest. Their habitat has changed greatly. They are concentrated today in areas that held the minority of Indians in ancient times, and in the areas where the majority of Indians lived, the floodplains, there are few or none today.

Thus, ethnographic patterns simply cannot be automatically projected backwards into prehistoric times in order to understand ancient lifeways. I mention these problems because Antillean archaeology, like lowland mainland archaeology, has been heavily influenced by knowledge of living Indians of lowland South America. This knowledge is a potent source of interpretation and could be developed even more in the future, if we keep in mind that one function of archaeology can be to falsify the hypothesis of ethnographic projection. In this way we can learn a great deal about why Indians live today as they do and why the prehistoric ones were so different. Without understanding how life was transformed both by indigenous processes and by the European conquest, it will be difficult to elucidate the nature and causes of prehistoric lifeways.

NOTES

1. Editor's Note: However, as Lee Newsom commented during the symposium discussion, there are people currently attempting to retrieve and analyze the appropriate archaeobotanical data. Newsom is examining flotation samples from the Maisabel site in the hopes of finding carbonized botanical remains. In addition, she is studying the carbon samples from Maisabel for species identification. This latter set of data will be helpful in identifying fuel woods used by the prehistoric inhabitants and for assisting in paleoenvironmental reconstruction.

In the same context, Mary Jane Berman, who was in the symposium audience, commented that they too were doing archaeobotany in their Bahamas late prehistoric site. They brought Richard Ford from the University of Michigan to assist them in their efforts.

2. Siegel's observations are appropriate here:

I've noticed in many areas in the hills and mountains along the north coast of Puerto Rico obviously constructed terraces. Some of them are stone-lined and others seem to be completely earthen. I've always wondered about these terraces, especially as to their antiquity. One project that I would like to do in the future is to systematically sample a set of terraces, in different contexts (perhaps stratified by soil type, slope, drainage, size, construction techniques, or some combination of these variables), to see what the fill of them looks like (are there artifacts? soil types? pollen and/or phytolith types? internal construction methods, etc.) [Peter Siegel, personal communication 1989].

REFERENCES CITED

Brown, J. (editor)
    1971 *Approaches to the Social Dimensions of Mortuary Practices.* Memoirs No. 25. Society for American Archaeology, Washington, D.C.

    1975 Spiro Art and its Mortuary Context. In *Death and the Afterlife in Pre-Columbian America,* edited by E.P. Benson, pp. 1-32. Dumbarton Oaks, Washington, D.C.

Kingsley, R.G.
    1985 *Kin Groups and Mortuary Practices: Ethnographic Implications for Archaeology.* Ph.D. dissertation, Michigan State University. University Microfilms, Ann Arbor.

Levin, S.
    1983 Food Production and Population Size in the Lesser Antilles. *Human Ecology* 11:321-338.

Meggers, B.J.
    1985 Aboriginal Adaptation to Amazonia. In *Key Environments: Amazonia,* edited by G. Prance and T. Lovejoy, pp. 307-327. Pergamon, Oxford.

Roosevelt, A.C.
    1980 *Parmana: Prehistoric Maize and Manioc Subsistence along the Amazon and Orinoco.* Academic Press, New York.

    1987a The Evolution of Human Diets. In *Food and Evolution,* edited by M. Harris and E. Ross, pp. 565-578. Temple University Press, Philadelphia.

    1987b Chiefdoms in the Amazon and Orinoco. In *Chiefdoms in the Americas,* edited by R. Drennan and C. Uribe, pp. 153-185. University Press of America, Lanham, Maryland.

    1989a Natural Resource Management in Amazonia before the Conquest: Beyond Ethnographic Projection. In *Natural Resource Management among Folk and Indigenous Societies in Amazonia,* edited by D. Posey and W. Balee, pp. 30-62. New York Botanical Garden, New York.

    1989b *A cultura Marajoara.* Revista do Museu Paulista No. 33. Sao Paulo.

    1989c *Moundbuilders of the Amazon: Geophysical Archaeology in the Marajoara Chiefdom.* Academic Press, New York.

Roosevelt, A.C. (editor)
    1989d Amazonian Synthesis: An Integration of Paradigms, Disciplines, and Methodologies. Ms. in preparation.

Rouse, I.
    1986 *Migrations in Prehistory: Inferring Population Movement from Cultural Remains.*

Yale University Press, New Haven.

Urton, G. (editor)
1985 *Animal Myths and Metaphors in South America*. University of Utah Press, Salt Lake City.

Simoes, M.
1981 *Coletores-pescadores ceramistas do litoral do Salgado (Para)*. Boletim do Museu Paraense Emilio Goeldi, ns. 78. Belem.

van der Merwe, N., A.C. Roosevelt, and J.C. Vogel
1981 Isotopic Evidence for Prehistoric Subsistence Change at Parmana, Venezuela. *Nature* 292:536-538.

Willey, G.R. and J.A. Sabloff
1974 *History of American Archaeology*. W.H. Freeman, San Francisco.

Winterhalder, B.
1987 The Analysis of Hunter-Gatherer Diets: Stalking and Optimal Foraging Models. In *Food and Evolution*, edited by M. Harris and E. Ross, pp. 311-340. Temple University Press, Philadelphia.

Lightning Source UK Ltd.
Milton Keynes UK
UKHW050833181222
414024UK00008B/132